Cultivated Plants of the WORLD

TREES • SHRUBS • CLIMBERS

DON ELLISON

National Library of Australia Cataloguing-in-Publication

Ellison, Donald Phillip 1934-
Cultivated plants of the world

Includes index.
ISBN 1 876060 00 X (Trees, Shrubs and Climbers)

1. Plants, Cultivated - Dictionaries. 2. Plants, Cultivated - Identification. 3. Botany - Dictionaries.
4. Plant names, Popular - Dictionaries. I. Title.

582

First published 1995

Published by: Flora Publications International Pty Ltd
GPO Box 2927
Brisbane Queensland Australia 4001

Telephone 61 7 3229 6366
Facsimile 61 7 3229 8782

Artwork by: CopyRight Publishing Company Pty Ltd
Film separations by: Graphic Skills Pty Ltd
Printed by: Griffin Press Limited

Every effort has been made to ensure this publication complies with current state-of-the-art plant identification and nomenclature. However this is constantly being revised and no responsibility can be taken for any misidentification or incorrect application arising from reference to this work. In particular the names of many cultivars vary from country to country, and even may vary from region to region within the same country. The author has endeavoured to apply the most common or accepted of these in this edition. Also as the book is intended primarily for the nursery and horticultural trade, in some cases the latest botanical classification has simply been noted, with the name listed and placement of the photograph to suit current trade practice e.g., Azaleas are not grouped with Rhododendrons. Finally, the photographs were taken in field conditions in which the slightest breeze, poor lighting or difficult access, in some cases affected the quality of the image. The publishers have opted to include the occasional less-than-perfect image as this collection is aimed at plant identification, and the odd exception to an overwhelmingly magnificent collection is still valued for the information it conveys.

This book was created on a Power Macintosh 8100/110 and a 9500/132 each carrying 64Mb of RAM and 6Gb of hard drive. The photographs were digitised and enhanced by James Sokoll using a Umax PowerLook flatbed scanner and Adobe Photoshop with Power Calibrator plug-in. The pioneering colour calibration plug-in software was developed by Dale Coulthard of Digital Developments Pty Ltd. The layout was performed by Kim Herringe and Melinda Jackson using Quark Express. Over 30 gigabytes of data were generated and managed in the production, with a database now in place for CD Rom or electronic transmission of any of the images. The text of the book is in Bookman 8pt with the genus headers in Franklin Gothic 18pt.

Front cover art: Background bark —*Eucalyptus sieberi.*
Flower box frame bark —*Eucalyptus grandis.*
Flowers of trees, shrubs and climbers have been selected from cold, temperate and hot climates.
Top row left to right —*Cornus florida* cv. Rubra; *Rhododendron* cv. Blue Diamond; *Clematis* cv. Nelly Moser.
Middle row —*Plumeria rubra* cv. Acutifolia; *Tibouchina lepidota*; *Pyrostegia venusta.*
Bottom row —*Colvillea racemosa*; *Chorisia speciosa*; *Ipomoea horsfalliae.*
Interior art: Background bark —*Eucalyptus grandis.*

ISBN 1 876060 00 X

Contents

This book is dedicated to my wife
Lyn Ellison

Organisations and individuals who have assisted in cross checking or who have provided photographs to complement this collection.

Aspley Nursery
Don Blaxell
Gary Bridge
Alan & Joan Burton-Jones
Cairns Botanical Gardens
Philip Cameron
Malcolm Campbell [12]
Bert Chandlers Nursery [2]
Alan & Susie Carle
Colour My World
Conifer Gardens Nursery
Brian Cooney
Cowells Nursery
Neale Dahl [14]
Dow Flora
Lyn Ellison
Ross Evans Garden Centre
Fairhill Native Plants
Dr A.B. Graf [3]
Joanne Green [10]
Hardy Plant Society [1]
Harlequin Nursery
Harts Nursery
Hawkins Garden Centre
Nev Higgs Nursery
Nicholas Hill [13]
Jan Iredell
E.F. Jenkin & Sons
J.F.T. Nurseries [7]
Kenibreed Plants [4]
Greg Kirby
David & Rhonda Le Brocque
Liddle's Nursery [5]
Peter Luscombe
Ross McKinnon
Elizabeth McRobert
Mossmont Nursery
Carol Newman
Nursery Traders Pty Ltd
Paradise Garden Centre
Parkwood Nursery
Merryon Ryall
Sue Spinks
The Vireya Venue
Sheila Thompson
Lydia Tumbilis
Valley Clematis Nursery [9]
John van der Plank [6]
Barry Vaughan [11]
Ian Walton [8]
Bob Whitten
Jack Wick
Tim Willing

Note [1, 2, 3, 4, 5, 6, 7, 8, 9, 10, 11, 12, 13, 14] Photographs supplied where indicated in the text.

Preface

This first volume of *Cultivated Plants of the World* is designed to present, in the form of a pictorial dictionary, an extremely wide selection of trees, shrubs and climbers, planted and grown, for whatever reason, by the people who inhabit a remarkable diversity of geographic environments around this planet. It offers the reader a simple, quick and accurate method of visual identification by illustrating each variety with a representative, close-up colour photograph of the most distinctive part of the plant, generally the flower, but other unique features such as the leaves, fruit, bark or seed pods in the relevant season, are sometimes shown. Some of the plants included are quite rare, but most are cultivated regularly worldwide, either outdoors, or in conservatories or greenhouses where the climate is unfriendly to the species.

In this presentation, lengthy botanical descriptions have been avoided in favour of a precise and straightforward text. Professionals, students and anyone interested in the cultivation of plants should appreciate the pictorial style as an invaluable identification aid, particularly where large numbers of varieties are encountered such as in nurseries and botanical gardens. A ready application for this collection is apparent in silviculture, revegetation and land reclamation, landscaping, horticultural societies and in the home garden. The book will fill an obvious gap in technical and general libraries.

One of the most valuable uses for this publication will be found in the nursery industry, with the detailed appearance of each species clearly evident from the photographs. The book will become a point-of-sale guide for customers buying unfamiliar or new species, while the corresponding descriptions provide information on propagation along with a brief general guide for the cultivation of the plant and its likely size. In using the book for plant identification, it should be kept in mind that colour variation of flowers may be found with different climates, soil types and age of the flower.

The *Cultivated Plants of the World* series has been devised also for the reader's enjoyment and to familiarise the non-professional with the amazing range of flora in cultivation today. This book includes many photographs of plants not shown in other references but it is not possible to include all possible plants, as the reader will note. While there are omissions of many genera in this collection, those not included may feature in succeeding volumes.

I have travelled extensively around the world, photographing specimens in more than 60 countries throughout North, South and Central America, Europe, the Caribbean, Asia, Africa and Australia. My travels have been timed, where possible, to arrive at the crucial time for plant photography—when the plant is at the peak of flowering, or, in the case of foliage plants, when the leaves are most colourful. The illustrations on which the series *Cultivated Plants of the World* is based, have been selected from approximately 60,000 photographs of plants from a wide variety of environments in those countries visited. Species from all climates including tropical, sub-tropical, temperate, mild, cold, desert and wetland are represented. This book therefore is international in its application, as will be the following volumes in this comprehensive series.

In compiling this book, a considerable amount of cross-checking has been carried out, and many horticulturists, botanists and nurserymen who specialise in certain plant groups throughout the world have assisted in this process to ensure correctness. Some of the organisations and individuals who have been outstandingly helpful with identification, checking, or who have supplied photographs needed to complement my collection for this publication, are listed opposite. In thanking them, I am particularly grateful to Ross McKinnon and his technical staff at the Brisbane Botanic Gardens, principally Philip Cameron, for their professional assistance over the years and in the final proof reading. Finally it was the skill and patience of the editing, artwork and typesetting team, particularly James Sokoll, Elizabeth McRobert, Kim Herringe, Melinda Jackson and John McRobert, who brought it all together.

Don Ellison
Brisbane, 1995

Foreword

***ultivated Plants of the World*** has been compiled with the aim of assisting anyone, from the amateur to the professional, interested in plants and gardening.

The world has an extremely rich flora with approximately 250,000 different species of higher order, or vascular, plants. Of these approximately 50,000 species are currently in cultivation. These really are huge numbers and it is easy to see how there can be difficulty in identifying one particular plant or flower.

Nevertheless there are many enthusiasts, including the author, Don Ellison, who can seemingly just look at a plant and tell you its name, or at least the generic (or first) part of its name. Others who have only recently become interested in plants are quite entitled to ask, *"How on earth do they do it?"*

The answer to this question is simple: *"By the use of short cuts"*.

They say a picture is better than a thousand words. Our own 'brain computer'—linked with an enquiring mind-set—has the ability to store more facts, over the years, than we are ever really aware of having put on memory. Plant details register consciously or subconsciously in our brains and we are able to recognise almost immediately the common garden plants around us. We develop short cuts, some flowers have open-petalled flowers, while others may be tubular or starry. Plant identification becomes a process of elimination and—'hey presto'—illumination and a sense of great achievement when the correct name slots in to place!

There are many parts of a plant used in its identification. Floral structure (the flower) is by far the single most easily identifiable part of a plant. Flowers and sometimes leaves, fruit or bark form the basis of most visual identification hence the photographic focus on these elements in this publication.

Don Ellison has scoured the world's Botanic Gardens in search of the everyday, the rare and the exotic plants for this collection. Being a practical horticulturist he "knows" the kinds of plants that you—the home gardener, nurseryman, professional botanic garden officer and amateur plants enthusiast—want in a handy reference format.

Cultivated Plants of the World will become this Botanic Gardens' first line of defence for the public seeking names for their plants! I recommend its purchase and commend its author, my friend—Mr Don Ellison—on a fine publication.

Ross D McKinnon
CURATOR-IN-CHARGE
BRISBANE BOTANIC GARDENS
AUSTRALIA

This book is designed to help people identify the plants they see in cultivation. Plants are nurtured for many reasons, but trees, shrubs and climbers grown for their ornamental value are the principal subjects of this book. The range of plants encompassed within this group is as extensive as it is diverse.

Plants were first cultivated thousands of years ago as static settlements replaced the hunter-gatherer lifestyle. At that time cultivation was of course, not for aesthetic purposes, but for the basic necessities of life. Those plants which produced valuable nourishment, could relieve pain, or ward off evil spirits, were cultivated to provide a continuous supply.

The cultivation of plants for their ornamental value rather than for food, flavour, fragrance and physic, developed with the increase in living standards. Field expeditions took botanists to remote regions across the world in search of new and rare plants. Tales of epic journeys into the depths of China, climbing steep mountainsides beside raging rivers in search of an elusive species of Rhododendron, are not uncommon.

As world transport developed so did the dispersal of plants, and travelling settlers carried favourite plants 'like a piece of home' with them to the new world. The path of some early Portuguese explorers has been traced by a little wild rose, *Rose da Santa Maria*. To this day, newcomers to a country prefer to grow in their gardens, those plants which are familiar to them.

However, after centuries of plant cultivation throughout the world, the place of origin of our many beautiful plants is often overlooked, and indeed the parental origins of new plants have been dispersed as a result of plant breeding. Yet through this ongoing cultivation, gardeners throughout the world share a magnificent array of plants for their gardens.

How to use this book

Plants are listed in alphabetical order of their genus. Each genus is briefly described giving country of origin, climatic preference, planting use and propagation method. This is followed by relevant species for the genus, their common name or names, and typical characteristics. Reference to the text in combination with the colour plates allows a clear visualisation of the growth habits and special characteristics of each plant.

Generally the conventions and nomenclature of family and genera follow that of Cronquist *"An integrated system of classification of flowering plants"* (1981), whilst species conform to the *"New Royal Horticultural Society Dictionary of Gardening"* (1992). Where there are differences, the latter version is noted in parenthesis thus [...].

What are cultivated plants?

The plant kingdom is divided into groups which conveniently separate simple plants such as algae, from the more complex vascular plants such as pines, ferns and flowering plants. It is these plants which are primarily cultivated worldwide for their usefulness or beauty, and through plant breeding, new and improved forms extend the list continuously.

Plants cultivated for their ornamental value range from the tallest trees of the world to tiny succulents. It was therefore necessary to organise *Cultivated Plants of the World* into volumes, with one volume for each group, or groups, of plants.

This first volume contains cultivated trees, shrubs and climbers of the world. The definition of trees and shrubs is subject to debate, but broadly a tree is a woody plant with a defined main stem or trunk, a shrub has many woody stems. A climber is a plant which is not self-supporting.

The size and shape of the potted plant in the nursery gives little or no indication of its eventual size and shape. To provide a realistic picture of the size of each tree, shrub and climber at maturity, guidelines to their size are detailed below. However it must be remembered that plants perform differently under dissimilar soil and climatic conditions.

Classification of Plants

Scientists have used Latin names for both plants and animals for hundreds of years as it is an international language and names can be understood equally well in any country. Although not in general use today, Latin continues to be the language of scientists worldwide.

In order to study the millions of plants in the world, botanists classified the plant kingdom into groups of species sharing common features—the more characteristics they share, the closer their relationship. There are several major groups. The one relevant to this book is the Angiospermae—the flowering plants. This grouping includes most trees, shrubs and climbers.

This group is further divided, with those plants having several characteristics in common placed together in families—trees known commonly as alders, birches and hazels are members of the Betulaceae family and all are deciduous catkin-bearing trees. Families play an important role and recognition of these is the first step in identifying the plant, e.g., if the flower shape or seed capsule of an unknown plant can be matched to that of a known plant, their family group may be discovered. In the text, family names are printed in small capitals.

Within each family, plants are divided into smaller groups. Each one of these groups is called a genus (genera = plural), thus alders are members of the Alnus genus, birches—Betula, and hazels—Corylus. In *Cultivated Plants of the World*, each genus has a separate section with a bold heading and is listed alphabetically.

Within each genus plants are divided into species. As an example, species in the Alnus genus include *Alnus cordata*, and *A. glutinosa*. This is the full scientific name of each alder. The species name usually describes an aspect of the plant which makes it distinct. Thus *A. cordata* has heart-shaped leaves, and *A. glutinosa* has sticky leaves. Not all plant names describe the plant's appearance and often it commemorates a person or a place. For example, *Camellia japonica* refers to the Japanese camellia and the Banksia genus was named in honour of Sir Joseph Banks. Species normally breed only with plants of the same species.

The botanical names we use for plants were invented by the 18th century Swedish botanist, Carl Linnaeus, and as each plant has two parts to its name, it is called the binomial system. In the text the botanical names are written in italics and while the genus is given a capital letter, the species is not.

Subdivisions of species are often combined under the heading 'variety' (var.) as they carry relatively minor variations, for example, size, or colour of the flower. Natural geographical varieties and subspecies (shown as ssp.) have Latin names written in italics after the species. Many varieties are garden raised and are called cultivars. The names are given a capital letter and are shown with the abbreviation 'cv.' For example, the yellow leaved hazel is named *Corylus avellana* cv. Aurea.

Hybrids are crosses between two varieties or in some cases two species. They look different from either parent and do not generally breed true from seed. Where they belong to no single species, they are given names in cultivar style, without a species name, while true-breeding hybrids are given species-style names with the addition of the x sign. For example *Daphne* x *burkwoodii*.

Common names enjoy popular use amongst gardeners and horticulturists alike, but they can cause confusion as many plants have more than one common name, and that name may not only vary from one country to another, but from one locality to another. To complicate the matter further, some quite different plants share one common name. For instance, the name Dusty Miller is given to many quite different silver-leaved plants, hence the reliance on the botanical name to identify a plant precisely.

Name changes are not restricted to common names and one of the biggest problems for gardeners, authors and the horticultural trade, is the changing of botanical nomenclature. Botanists argue this is a necessary part of the revising process and misidentifications must be corrected. Incorrect naming also occurs because a plant has been grown under the wrong name or is incorrectly labelled. The abbreviation syn. (synonym) indicates other or previous names of various plants.

Trees

There is a tree for all situations. In parks and gardens, trees provide height, and they should be chosen carefully to be in proportion to their surroundings. Single specimens may look magnificent standing alone but trees also combine well with smaller plants in a mixed garden landscape.

Most trees are long-lived and long-term planning is needed before planting to ensure the mature specimen is appropriate for the place. Care must be taken not to plant near buildings, trees which will grow to great heights. Roots of a tree are often as extensive as the branches above, and the effect of roots on surrounding pavements and buildings should be considered.

Trees develop their own characteristic shape, for example some poplars and conifers grow to a columnar form and liquidambars have a pyramidal form. For such types, pruning is only necessary in the first years to develop a strong framework. Later pruning simply involves removing broken or badly placed branches.

Trees can be planted as single specimens or grouped attractively, yet not all trees are suited to both situations and the species should be selected accordingly. Specific requirements of summer shade and winter sun, or shade all year round will determine whether a deciduous or evergreen species is chosen as a shade tree.

While tree height and foliage density are prime considerations, some tree species are chosen purely for their decorative flowers, colourful foliage or beautiful bark.

Tree Sizes

Tall	= over 16 metres (50 ft)
Medium	= 6 - 16 metres (20 - 50 ft)
Small	= 3 - 6 metres (10 - 20 ft)

Recommended Minimum Planting Distance

As there are as many shapes of trees as there are trees, correct spacing varies according to the situation. As a general guideline planting distances for trees (except columnar trees) can be calculated as follows:-

Add the mature height of tree A to the mature height of tree B and divide by two.

Shrubs

Shrub foliage is usually more dense than that of a tree and this quality is most useful in the garden. Shrubs can be planted as background to a flower border, single specimen plants or solid screens of vegetation which may or may not be trimmed as hedges. In addition to forming neat shapes, hedges have a multitude of uses. They can be used to divide one area of the garden from another, to create privacy or windbreaks, mark a boundary or simply to line a pathway.

Diversity in shrub size even within one genus provides great choice for particular situations—some species grow tall and narrow, others spread low and wide. Deciduous shrubs allow sun to penetrate to small plants beneath while evergreens provide year-round foliage cover protecting small plants from hot sun and wind.

Each type of shrub exhibits its own character and while some species are noted for their colourful flowers, berries or decorative foliage, others may form excellent windbreaks. Most require pruning to retain good shape and this is generally carried out after flowering. Foliage reduction is particularly important with hedging shrubs—regular trimming producing a compact shape and dense foliage.

Care must be taken not to plant shrubs too closely as crowded shrubs require constant pruning to contain branch growth.

Shrub sizes

Tall	= 2 - 3 metres (6 - 10 ft) Growing taller than it is wide.
Medium	= 1 - 2 metres (3 - 6 ft) Growing as tall as it is wide.
Small	= less than 1 metre (3 ft) Growing wider than it is tall.

Recommended Minimum Planting Distance

Where more than one shrub is to be planted, the correct spacing which will provide sufficient room for growth is calculated as follows:-

Add the mature height of shrub A to the mature height of shrub B and divide by three.

When planted in a continuous line as a hedge, the planting distance is generally less as follows :-

Tall	= 1000 - 1200 mm (39 - 47 ins)
Medium	= 500 - 800 mm (20 - 30 ins)
Small	= 350 - 450 mm (14 - 18 ins)

Climbers

These plants require support to grow vertically but can very often be grown unsupported as ground covering plants. Different types of climbers have different mechanisms for attaching to a support. Those with tendrils, aerial roots or adhesive pads are self-clinging while other types require tying.

In the garden, climbers are valuable plants to cover ugly fences or bare trunks and clothe pergolas and arches for shade to homes and gardens—but their greatest value in small gardens is in saving space by extending the garden upwards. While evergreen climbers will create permanent cover, deciduous climbers are perfect plants to create shade from the summer sun.

Climbers vary enormously in size and vigour—a large-flowered clematis is suitable for confined spaces, a wild rose or honeysuckle will cover a wide area. Pruning is not usually necessary except to remove unwanted growth.

Climber sizes

Vigorous — This includes climbers which extend over a large area given favourable conditions. Vigorous climbers are suited to growing on fences or large pergolas and caution should be taken not to plant near guttering or formal plantings.

Moderate — This describes climbers which grow in a controlled manner even under favourable conditions. Appropriate situations include garden trellising and verandah pillars.

Climate and Soil Types

Climatic and soil differences within one country are vast, and worldwide the differences are extreme. These factors govern what can and cannot be grown in a given area. Some species are adapted to continental inland areas which experience extremes of heat and cold, whereas other species are adapted to more even temperatures found near the coast.

The degree to which plants tolerate drought, wet winters or hot summers, depends largely on the region from which they come. This is nature's adaptation to the environment and although local conditions vary within a region, plants will generally not survive in situations very different from that of their origin. Fruiting has special requirements and for some plants to flower and set fruit, winter chilling is essential.

The amount of cold that plants can survive is generally referred to as their hardiness and is the greatest restricting factor. Extreme heat is also a limitation although its effect on cultivated plants is reduced in a garden situation where plant cooling and soil moisture is maintained through watering and mulching.

A garden soil which is friable and well-drained, and which contains plenty of organic matter, provides the most ideal habitat for the widest range of plants. However some plants are better adapted to clay or water-logged soils and others to light sands.

The pH of the soil is a limiting factor to growth as most plants prefer a fairly neutral soil with a pH near to 7.0. Exceptions to this are the rhododendrons and camellias which are lime-haters and require an acid soil with a lower pH, and olives and lavenders which prefer chalky soils and a slightly higher pH.

Propagation methods for Trees, Shrubs and Climbers

Seed Propagation

Propagation from seed is not widely used with ornamental trees, shrubs and climbers. This is due to the fact that germination is not always straightforward as some seeds take months to germinate and others need exposure to low temperatures. In addition, seed-grown plants may not breed true as the genetic material contained within seeds is diverse, and it is not uncommon for each plant which grows to show slightly different characteristics. While in nature seed variation is desirable, such diversity is not usually sought after with plants in cultivation. Another disadvantage particularly with decorative varieties, is that a tree may take several years to show its decorative flowers. Despite these problems, many trees, shrubs and climbers are raised from seed.

Cuttings

As a cutting is grown from a piece of a parent plant, it grows as an exact replica of that parent. Most trees, shrubs and climbers are propagated from cuttings, either hardwood cuttings taken in late autumn, or semi-ripe cuttings taken in summer and placed under glass.

Division

Small shrubs which form clumps of stems can be lifted and split into new plants. This method of propagation is more commonly used with perennials.

Layering

Shrubs with low, flexible stems can be layered by bending the stem down to the ground and covering with soil. When roots have formed on the buried stem, it is severed from the parent plant.

Grafting

This involves the union of a shoot or bud with a larger rooted plant. Rootstock plants are generally raised from seed for a year or two before a shoot or scion, or bud from a preferable plant is placed on the stem of the rootstock plant so that their tissues unite and growth results. Through grafting, a plant can be grown on a more vigorous root system. Usually the stock and the scion are of the same or closely related species.

Tissue Culture

Under appropriate laboratory conditions, plant tissue can be made to regenerate new plants. This produces a vast number of new plants with the exact genetic make-up of the parent plant.

Points for the home gardener to consider when selecting a tree, shrub or climber for the garden

Why do you need the plant?

For its usefulness.
You need a plant to screen a fence, cover a pergola, provide a feature in the garden, provide shade, provide colour. You can use its flowers, fruit or seed pods, it will enhance your landscape, it will encourage fauna to your garden.

For its attractiveness.
Features of the plant appeal to you.

You like a challenge.
The plant needs special conditions, it is rare and/or endangered.

Other.
You like to collect plants, you have heard about it, it has been recommended.

Decisions should also be made considering:

Climate and soil type.
While some hardy plants will grow in most conditions, many plants have special needs. Plants that are succeeding in gardens near you are most likely to succeed in your garden. Plants which are native to a particular area should do well in other areas which offer the same characteristics as that area. If your soil is heavy and holds water, plants which require good drainage will not thrive. Plants which require cold to stimulate flowering will not do well in tropical areas, and most tropical plants cannot tolerate heavy frosts. In many cases it is possible to modify gardens—e.g. by providing an acid type soil; creating mounds for drainage; providing windbreaks for wind-susceptible plants; controlling water supply—but there will be some characteristics of soil and climate which cannot be changed.

The space available.
Consider the approximate height of the mature tree or shrub, or vigour of the climber. Will the tree/shrub hang over fences or cut out desired sunlight from an area, will the roots endanger building foundations, drainage or sewerage pipes? (Repairs and removal can be costly exercises). Will the plant "fit" in proportion to the rest of the garden? Will falling leaves block gutters, or could the whole plant fall and endanger life or buildings? Will the climber escape to smother other plants or endanger any structure?

Sunlight and shade.
Be aware of the requirements of the plant for either sunlight, part light or shade, and consider whether your area will meet those requirements. Natural understorey plants will thrive in areas of low light, but if the plant needs full sun to promote flowering, and is planted in shade, then you will be disappointed. If you need a plant that will give shade in summer but allow light through in winter, then you will need a plant that loses its leaves in autumn. The density of the crown of the tree will determine the amount of shade the tree gives—your "shade and sun requirements" need to be taken into consideration.

Resistance to local diseases and insect pests.
Natural predators and other control measures vary from area to area and some plants may be susceptible to pests of some kind when grown away from their area of origin. If these can be controlled, the plant will give pleasure, but occasionally the control takes away from the enjoyment/function of the plant.

Special cultivation needs.
Should the plant be pruned to keep it in shape or under control? Does it have heavy fruit which may need to be "harvested" (e.g. *Kigelia africana*)? Does it have soft fruit that will fall and rot if not collected and removed? Will it grow too large to allow for effective special attention?

Other issues.
Is your selection readily available at a price you want to pay? Is the supplier reputable and able to give you reliable cultivation information? Is the plant likely to become a "weed" in your local area? Will falling leaves create problems with neighbours? Will prickly leaves fall on paths? Will its toxins create a danger for young children? Is the plant "fashionable" now but likely to go out of favour at some stage (e.g. topiary trees)? It may have a beautiful fragrance, but could it become too overpowering?

If you make a selection based on full consideration of the issues, then your gardening experience should be a happy one.

ABELIA

CAPRIFOLIACEAE

Small shrubs from both China and Mexico, Abelias flower from spring to autumn. Flower colours are red, pink, mauve or white. Most have shiny leaves. They prefer a rich well drained soil in an open site. It is beneficial to prune after flowering. Most Abelias are tolerant of some frost and may be grown in climates ranging from mild temperate to sub-tropical. Propagation is best from new growth cuttings under mist conditions.

Abelia chinensis GLOSSY ABELIA
A compact bushy shrub with white, perfumed, small, funnel shaped flowers. The glossy leaves darken in cold weather.

Abelia graebneriana
A compact shrub with clusters of pinkish-mauve tubular shaped flowers in spring.

Abelia* x *grandiflora
A hardy compact shrub with clusters of perfumed white to pale pink flowers. Cold weather gives the leaves a brownish look.

***Abelia* x *grandiflora* cv. Aurea**
This cultivar has shiny golden leaves which darken with age.

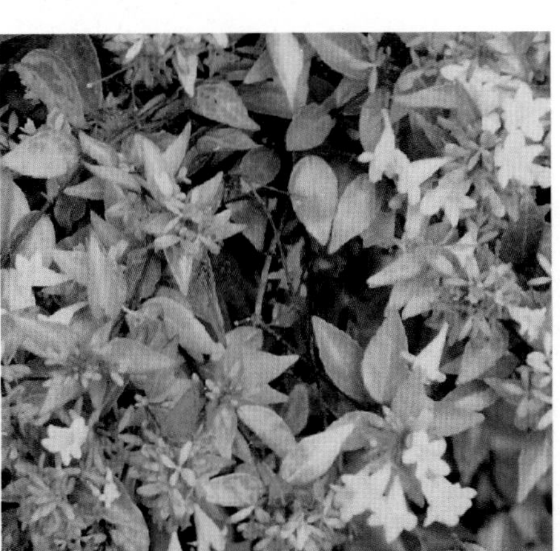

***Abelia* x *grandiflora* cv. Francis Mason**
A very showy cultivar with leaves having a mixture of green, gold and pink colouring.

***Abelia* x *grandiflora* cv. Nana**
Quite a low growing cultivar.

Abelia schumannii
A semi-deciduous open shrub with arching branches. Flowers are tubular and in clusters of mauve-pink.

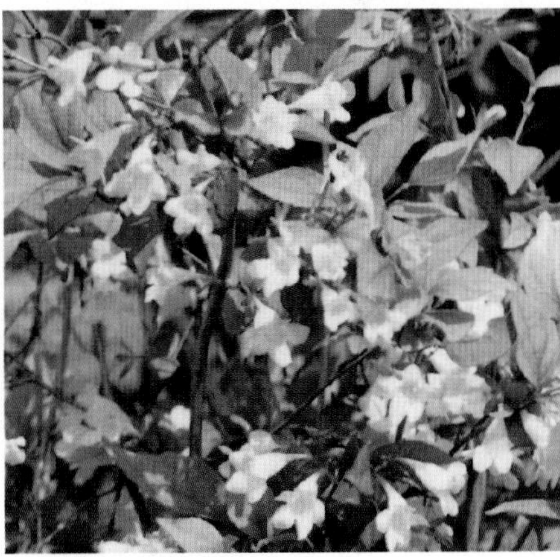

Abelia spathulata
In spring this open shrub has small bunches of white flowers.

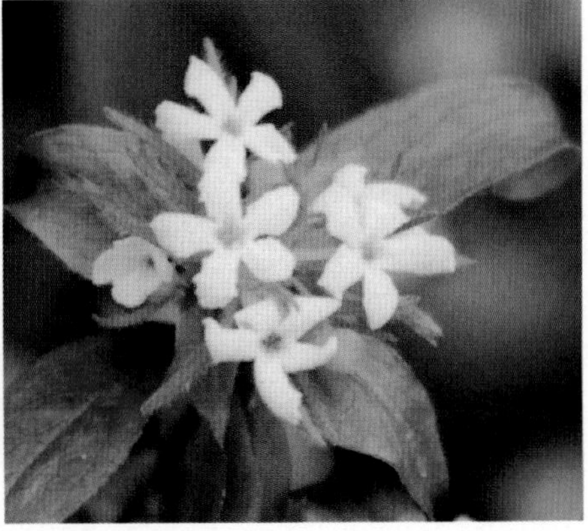

Abelia triflora
A small shrub with long pink buds which open to white star shaped flowers in spring.

ABROMA

Sterculiaceae

Small open crowned trees with arching branches from tropical eastern Australia. They will grow well in temperate climates and prefer sheltered areas among other trees. Propagate from seed.

Abroma fastuosa

A fast growing rain forest tree with unusual maroon flowers and very decorative large seed pods. Prefers a sheltered position and good soil.

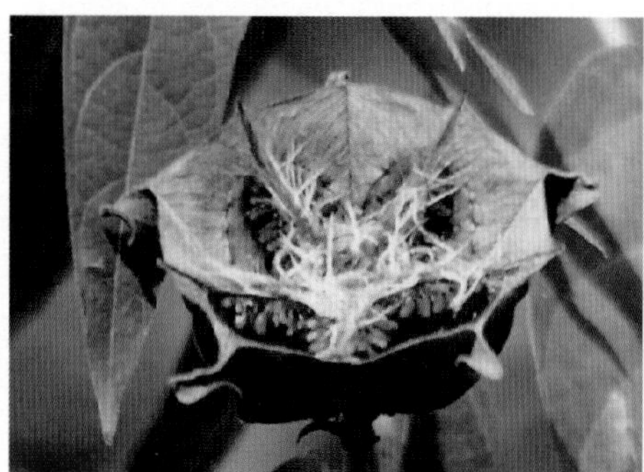

Abroma fastuosa - seed pods

ABRUS

Fabaceae [Leguminosae]

Abrus precatorius CRAB'S-EYE CREEPER

A modest growing forest vine native to tropical and sub-tropical Australia. This vine has very attractive seeds which resemble crabs' eyes—seeds are poisonous. The roots are used in India to produce an edible licorice-like compound. Flowers are small and coloured white to deep pink, in racemes. Seed clusters are retained on the vine for some time. Propagate from seeds which need to be soaked before sowing.

ABUTILON

CHINESE LANTERN; INDIAN MALLOW

Malvaceae

Soft wooded flowering shrubs and perennial plants which are widespread throughout the world's mild to warm-climate countries. The shrub forms are mostly sparse and need pruning after flowering. Propagate from seeds or cuttings. Many hybrids of unknown origin are the most widely grown. Hybrid varieties are listed as 'x' rather than being grouped as 'x hybridum'.

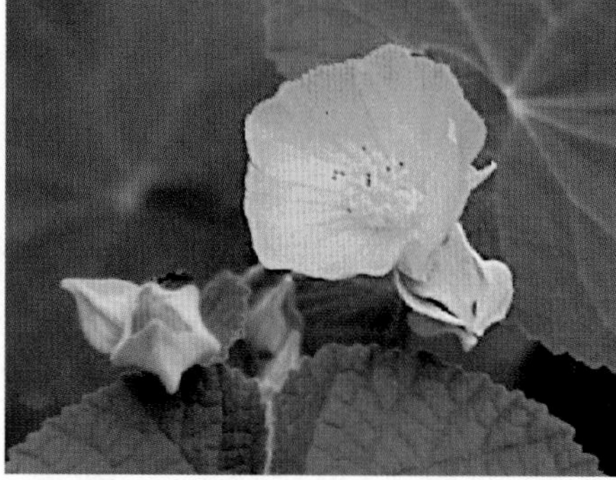

Abutilon arboreum

This medium shrub has golden cup flowers and wheel-like seed pods.

Abutilon x cv. **Ashford Red**

An open free flowering hybrid shrub with pendulous bell shaped flowers coloured dark red.

Abutilon auritum

Free flowering, this shrub has large leaves and masses of yellow bell shaped flowers tinged with brown.

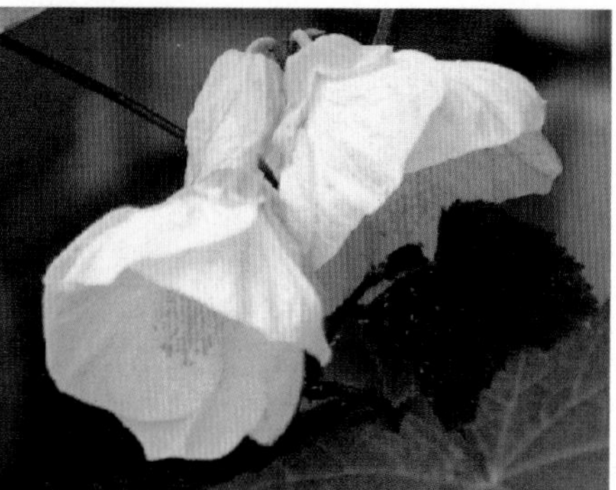

Abutilon x cv. **Canary Bird**

Another free flowering hybrid shrub with large maple shaped leaves and yellow bell shaped flowers.

Abutilon x cv. **Cerise Queen**

A free flowering hybrid with masses of cerise coloured bell shaped flowers over a long period.

ABUTILON (cont)

Abutilon **x cv. Golden Fleece**

Golden bell shaped flowers distinguish this free flowering open shrub.

Abutilon megapotamicum

A low growing spreading shrub with arrowhead shaped leaves. The plant is free flowering over many months with red and yellow tubular flowers.

Abutilon megapotamicum **cv. Variegatum**

Similar to the above, this plant has golden variegated leaves.

Abutilon **x *milleri***

A free flowering hybrid of *A. pictum* and *A. megapotamicum*, with orange, red and brown marked tubular flowers.

Abutilon molle

Hardy, this medium shrub has small yellow flowers.

Abutilon **x cv. Nabob**

A free flowering hybrid shrub with large maple shaped leaves and shiny red flowers.

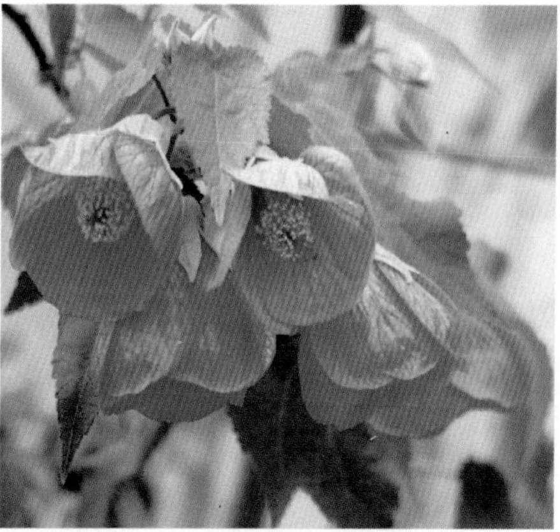

Abutilon **x cv. Orange Cascade**

Orange bell shaped flowers cascade all over this shrub most of the year.

Abutilon **x cv. Orange King**

This plant has very large, bell shaped, orange coloured flowers.

ABUTILON (cont)

Abutilon pictum

An open shrub with small, tight, bell shaped flowers coloured orange-red.

Abutilon* x *suntense

Masses of mauve pendulous flowers cover this hybrid Abutilon in spring. It grows well in cold temperate climates.

***Abutilon* x cv. Ruby Glow**

A popular garden cultivar which bears ruby red flowers in profusion.

***Abutilon* x *suntense* cv.Gorer's White**

A free flowering cultivar with large white flowers.

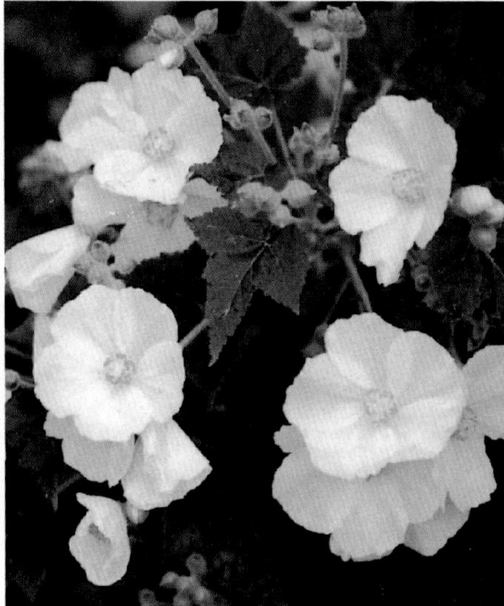

***Abutilon* x *suntense* cv. White Charm**

A tall bushy shrub with masses of white flowers which are smaller than Gorer's White.

***Abutilon* x cv. Souvenir de Bonn**

A compact variegated hybrid with blue-green leaves edged cream. Flowers are orange but not as showy as other hybrids.

***Abutilon* x *suntense* cv. Ralph Gould**

The large flowers on this tall growing cultivar are lilac in colour.

***Abutilon* x cv. Yellow Belle**

This outstanding yellow flowered form has bright yellow flowers over a very long flowering period.

ACACIA

MIMOSACEAE [LEGUMINOSAE]

Acacias, or wattles as they are commonly called, are shrubs or trees. A few have spikes or thorns. There are more than 1150 different Acacias from Africa, Pacific Islands, Central and South America, but predominantly from Australia where more than 700 different Acacias have already been named. Many do not have true leaves, flattened leaf stems, called phyllodes, perform the leaf function. The plants have a wide range of leaf and phyllode shapes. Small flowers form into clusters which are borne singly, or in heads, racemes or spikes. Most flowers are cream, yellow or gold in colour. Some species have relatively short life spans whilst others live a very long time. Uses for Acacias throughout the world include provision of timber for building and fuel, tanning, medicine, perfumery and paper making as well as decoration using either flowers or leaves. They grow in a very wide range of areas in Australia—wet tropics, deserts, pure sand, clay and gravel soils and in alpine areas.
The plants are propagated from seed which needs to be placed in a container of boiling water and then allowed to cool and soak for 10 to 24 hours before sowing.

Acacia brachystachya

An open small, hardy tree with silverish phyllodes and golden short rod-type flowers in spring. Ideal for dry areas.

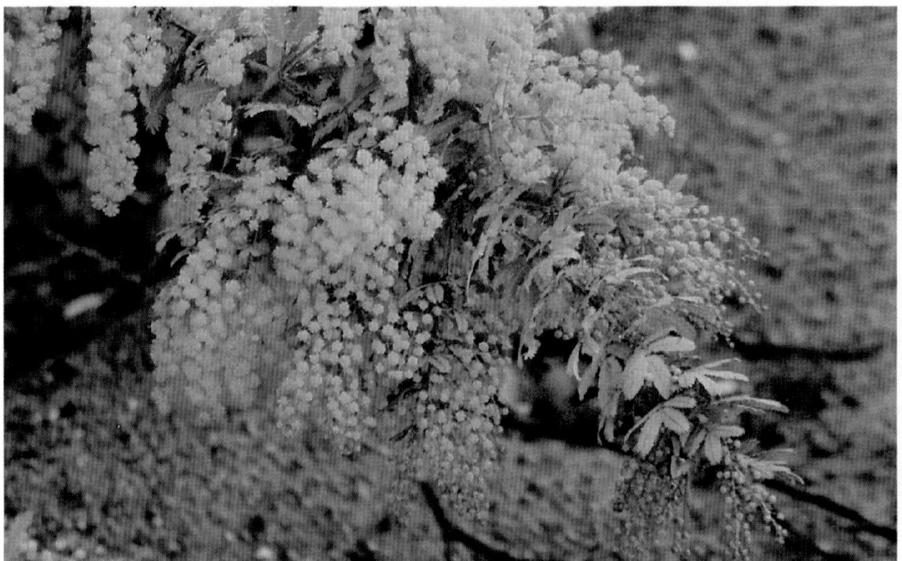

Acacia baileyana COOTAMUNDRA WATTLE

A small tree with silver ferny leaves and covered with deep yellow ball shaped flowers in spring. Prefers well drained soil. Purple and golden tipped foliage forms can be grown.

Acacia concurrens

A tall shrub to small tree with dense foliage and clusters of cream rod-type flowers in spring.

Acacia boliviana

A thicket shrub with ferny green leaves and masses of cream ball flowers in spring.

Acacia cultriformis
cv. **Austraflora Cascade**
CASCADING KNIFE-LEAF WATTLE

A small cascading shrub with globular yellow flowers.

ACACIA (cont)

Acacia dealbata SILVER WATTLE

A small tree with silver ferny leaves and masses of yellow clusters of ball shaped flowers in spring. Widely grown in Europe for the cut foliage trade. The bark is used for tanning, the leaves to produce dye, and gum arabic is produced from the sap.

Acacia elata CEDAR WATTLE

This medium tree is one of the larger and long lived wattles. The round flowers are dark cream.

Acacia decurrens

EARLY BLACK WATTLE; GREEN WATTLE

The true, 'feathery' leaves of this Acacia are dark green, and the bark dark grey to black—hence its common names. The ball flowers are bright yellow and held in heads. Fast growing, it is widely used to provide windbreaks and firewood. Frost tolerant once established, but prefers mild to cooler climates. Subject to borers.

Acacia drummondii ssp. ***affinis***

A dwarf shrub with showy golden rod flowers in spring. More sparse than *A. drummondii.*

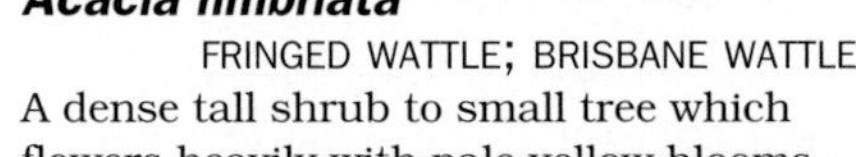

Acacia fimbriata

FRINGED WATTLE; BRISBANE WATTLE

A dense tall shrub to small tree which flowers heavily with pale yellow blooms.

Acacia drummondii

DRUMMOND'S WATTLE

A small shrub with cane-like branches and fine ferny leaves. The rod-type golden flowers make this outstanding as a garden plant.

Acacia dunnii ELEPHANT EAR WATTLE

Very large blue-green phyllodes and golden ball shaped flowers distinguish this tall shrub. For tropical situations.

Acacia floribunda

A dense free flowering shrub with pendulous, cream, rod shaped flowers.

ACACIA (cont)

Acacia giraffae CAMELTHORN

An African thicket wattle with thorns. Free flowering with long rod cream flowers and very attractive pods.

Acacia holosericea

A tall shrub with rod-type golden flowers. Ideal plant for dry, sandy and arid areas.

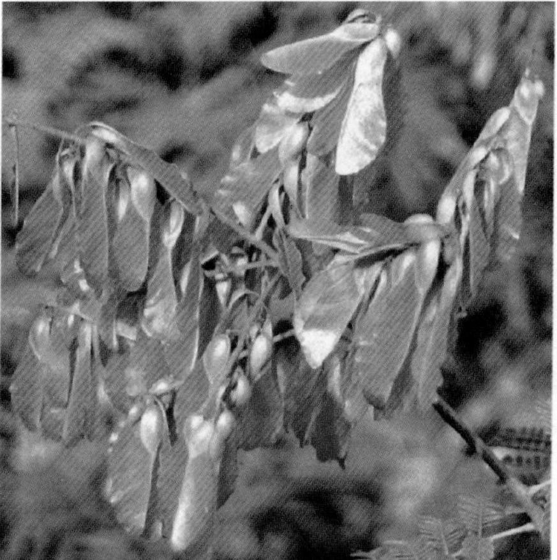

Acacia giraffae - seed pods

Acacia glaucoptera FLAT WATTLE

An unusual small shrub with flat phyllodes and round golden flowers. Suitable for clay soils.

Acacia hubbardiana

A small shrub with unusual triangular phyllodes. This free flowering shrub has cream ball shaped flowers.

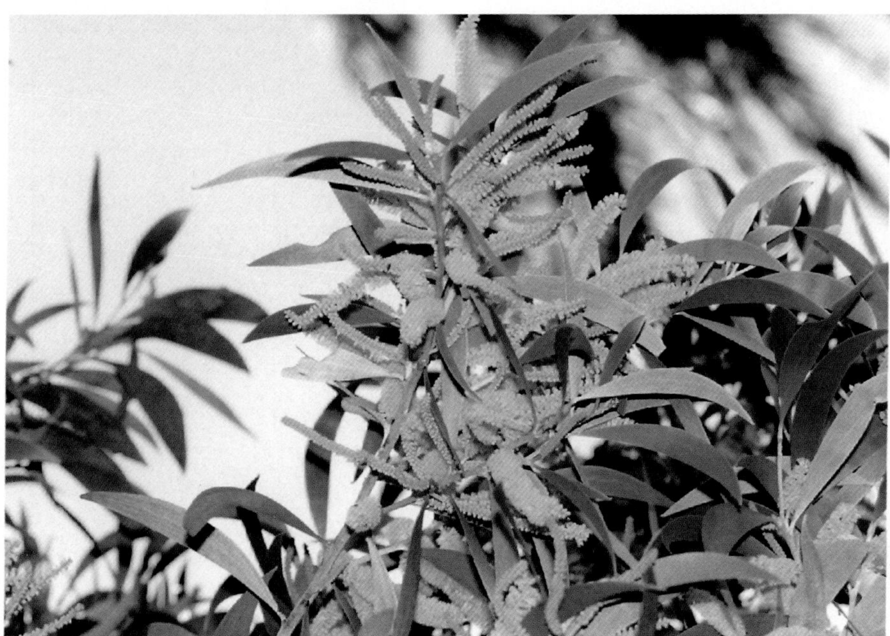

Acacia glaucescens COAST MYALL

A very attractive small tree with blue foliage and yellow rod-type flowers. Tolerates salt spray.

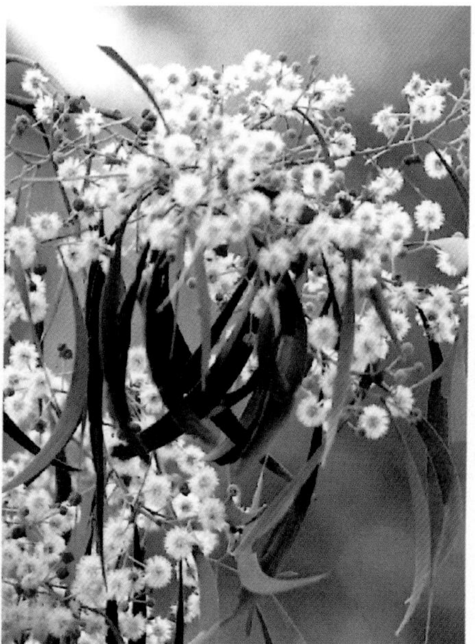

Acacia implexa LIGHTWOOD

A free flowering tall shrub with sickle shaped phyllodes, pale yellow round flowers and twisted seed pods.

ACACIA (cont)

Acacia karroo

A hardy thorny spreading shrub from Africa. Golden yellow round flowers.

Acacia monticola MOUNTAIN WATTLE

This tall shrub is grown as an ornamental plant for its unusual bark formation as illustrated above. It grows best in arid areas with poor soils. Singular flowers are roundish and gold in colour.

Acacia longifolia

SYDNEY GOLDEN WATTLE

A tall shrub with golden rod flowers in spring and long phyllodes. Tolerant of some salt spray.

Acacia melanoxylon BLACKWOOD

This medium size tree is grown in many countries throughout the world. It produces good quality timber. The bark is used for tanning and foliage is used for dyes. Flowers are round and cream in colour.

Acacia myrtifolia

A small growing, hardy shrub which has pale cream, ball shaped flowers in early spring.

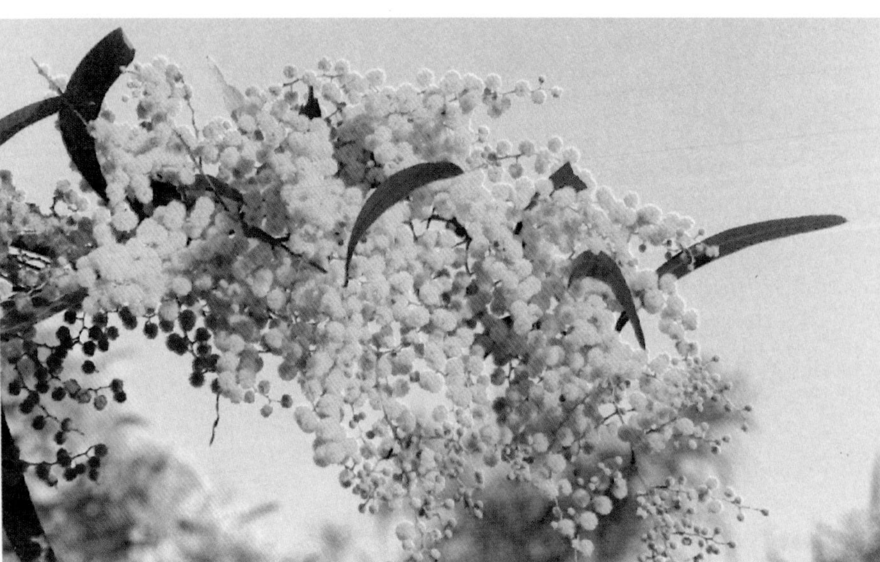

Acacia macradenia ZIG-ZAG WATTLE

A spreading tall shrub with elongated glands on the phyllode formation—the source of its specific name. The globular flowers are bright gold.

Acacia nuperrima

A dwarf shrub with eye catching globular flower heads which cover the plant in spring.

Acacia pendula WEEPING MYALL

A hardy small tree with weeping silverish foliage. Flowers are pale yellow and round. Grown as a feature tree in dry inland gardens and streets.

Acacia polybotrya WESTERN SILVER WATTLE

A small spreading shrub with silver ferny leaves. Flowers are yellow in long racemes. Grows in low rainfall areas.

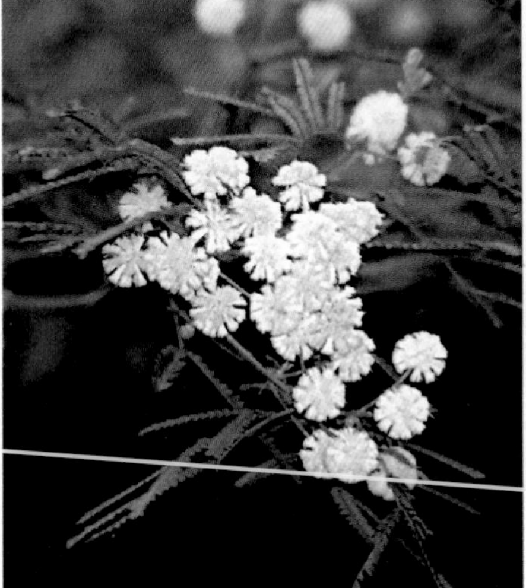

Acacia pentadenia KARRI WATTLE

A medium sized shrub which grows best in dappled shade. It is grown as an ornamental. The pale yellow flowers are round and colourful.

Acacia pilligaensis

This hardy medium shrub is best suited to warm dry climates. The globular flowers are gold in colour.

Acacia pravissima OVEN'S WATTLE

A dense medium shrub with attractive triangular shaped bluish phyllodes. The clusters of golden globular flowers are seen along drooping branches. Widely grown as an outstanding ornamental.

Acacia perangusta

A bushy small tree grown as an ornamental in sub-tropical climates. The round yellow flowers and graceful narrow phyllodes make this a showy plant.

Acacia podalyriifolia QUEENSLAND SILVER WATTLE

A very attractive medium shrub with silver-blue foliage. The plant is covered with masses of gold, ball shaped flowers in spring. An outstanding garden plant.

ACACIA (cont)

Acacia pulchella WESTERN PRICKLY MOSES

A small, spreading, thorny shrub with very colourful round golden flowers.

Acacia pycnantha GOLDEN WATTLE

A very good ornamental small tree with masses of golden ball flowers in clusters. The bark is used for tanning and foliage for dyes. The floral emblem of Australia.

Acacia saligna GOLDEN WREATH WATTLE

syn. ***A. cyanophylla***

A free flowering, medium shrub with masses of ball shaped, golden flowers in spring. This plant is widely cultivated throughout the world for tan bark production and for soil stabilisation in arid countries.

Acacia semilunata HALF MOON WATTLE

This medium shrub derives its name from the half-moon shaped silver phyllodes. The golden round flowers in profusion make this a good ornamental wattle.

Acacia sophorae COASTAL WATTLE

This medium shrub grows on frontal sand dunes near the sea. It is free flowering with yellow rod-type flowers. Used throughout the world for sand dune stabilisation.

Acacia stenophylla RIVER COOBA

A small tree with weeping foliage which grows near rivers on land which is often flooded and sometimes salty. It has racemes of small, ball shaped, yellow flowers.

Acacia subcaerulea - seed pods

An open medium shrub with racemes of round golden flowers. It has attractive blue foliage and reddish seed pods.

Acacia spectabilis MUDGEE WATTLE; GLORY WATTLE

A very showy, tall shrub covered with golden, ball shaped flowers in spring. Its fine fern-like leaves and heavy flowering make this plant a popular ornamental.

Acacia subtilinervis RIDGE WATTLE

A very hardy shrub which withstands prolonged dry and wet spells. Flowers are golden coloured and rod shaped.

Acacia wickhamii

A tropical shrub which has sticky new growth. It has rod-type yellow flowers and is a good ornamental in hot inland tropical areas.

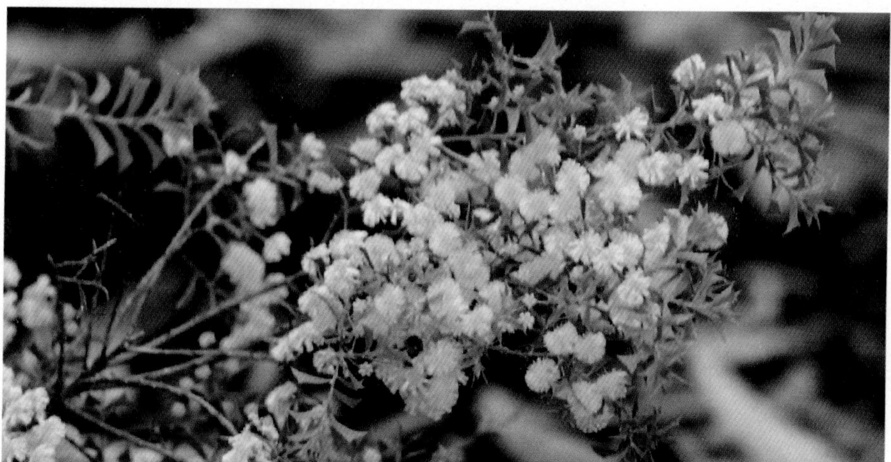

Acacia subulata AWL-LEAF WATTLE

A medium shrub with cascading branches and fine foliage. The small, yellow, ball shaped flowers cover the plant in a showy display.

Acacia truncata

An open shrub with arching branches and unusual semicircle-like phyllodes with points. Flowers are ball shaped and yellow in colour. Makes a good ornamental.

ACALYPHA

EUPHORBIACEAE

Tropical shrubs which are grown outdoors in warm climates and indoors in colder climates. They prefer good quality soils and adequate water. Propagate from cuttings. They benefit from annual pruning and fertilising.

Acalypha hispida CHENILLE PLANT

An eye catching medium shrub from Malaysia, with red chenille-like catkins.

Acalypha reptans RED CAT TAILS

A low growing spreading plant with masses of small red chenille-like catkins. This plant is used as a ground cover in warm climates and as an indoor plant or hanging basket in cooler climates.

ACALYPHA (cont)

Acalypha wilkesiana FIRE DRAGON PLANT

Native to the Pacific Islands, these bushy highly coloured shrubs with large leaves are widely grown throughout the world as decorative ornamentals. There are hundreds of named cultivars, however many are very similar and the same cultivar may have different names from country to country. Those listed are the more popular types.

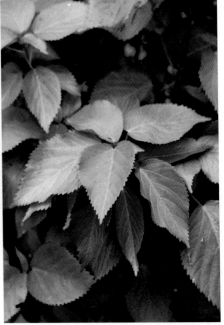

Acalypha wilkesiana cv. **Copper Leaf**

Large copper brown leaves, lightly serrated. A bushy shrub.

Acalypha wilkesiana cv. **Brownie**

A deep-red leaf, dense shrub. Leaves are smaller than most Acalyphas.

Acalypha wilkesiana cv. **Coral Glow**

The leaves of this bushy shrub are mostly pink with a little green and brown.

Acalypha wilkesiana cv. **Canary**

A cultivar which has pale yellow leaves with a few green markings.

Acalypha wilkesiana cv. **Ceylon**

A highly coloured pink, red and brown, twisted, serrated leaf shrub.

Acalypha wilkesiana cv. **Firestorm**

On this small leaf cultivar the leaves are coloured orange, brown and pink.

ACALYPHA (cont)

Acalypha wilkesiana cv. **Godseffiana**

The leaves of this very bushy shrub are green with cream margins, unevenly serrated and partly twisted. The leaves are smaller than most Acalyphas and have a weeping habit.

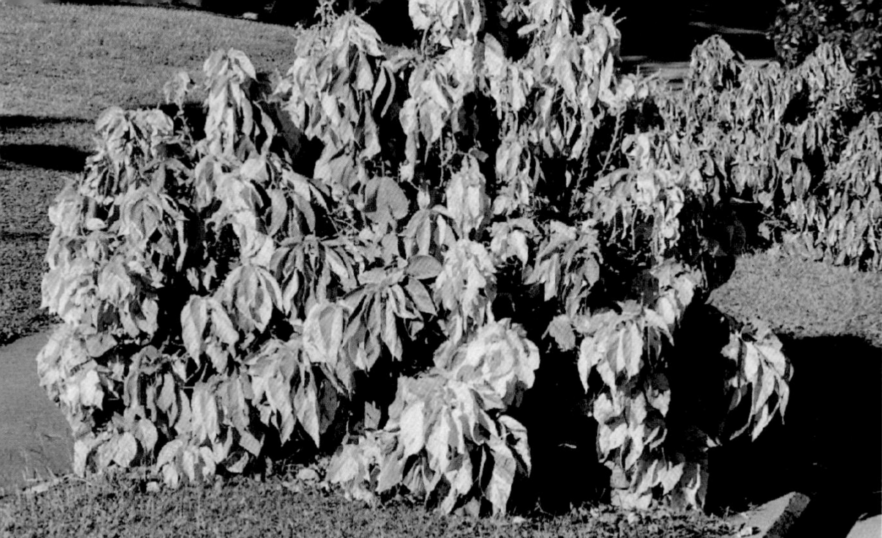

Acalypha wilkesiana cv. **Java White**

A bushy shrub with large, mostly cream, leaves. The leaves are very variable.

Acalypha wilkesiana cv. **Hoffmanna**

A dark leaf cultivar with a narrow cream margin and deep serrations. The leaves are twisted.

Acalypha wilkesiana cv. **London Tan**

A very bushy cultivar with large, oval, brownish tan leaves.

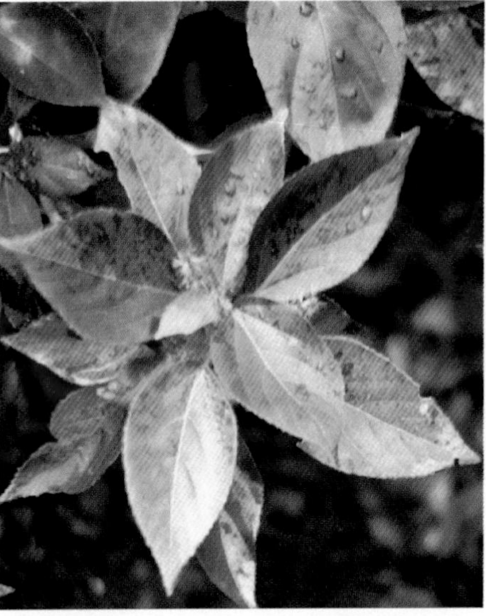

Acalypha wilkesiana cv. **Macafeeana**

A very popular bushy form with pinky red and tan bi-colour leaves—with the tan predominant.

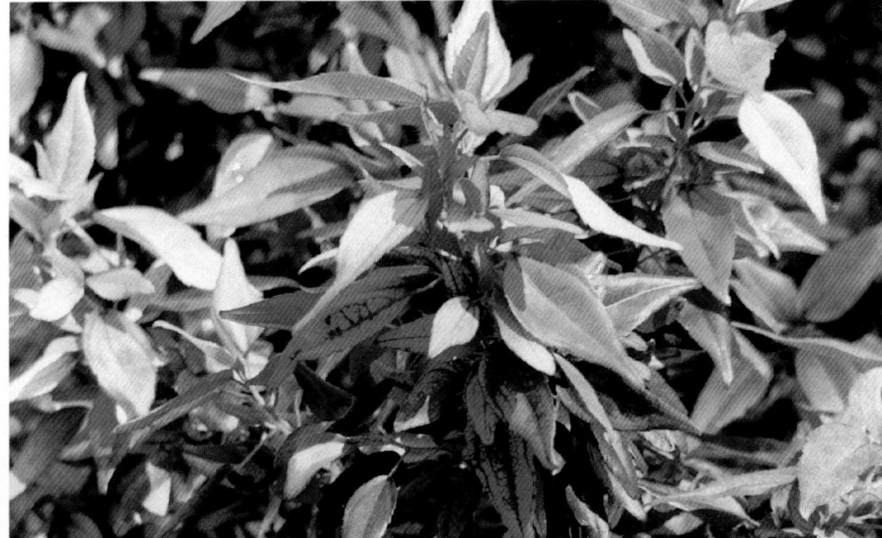

Acalypha wilkesiana cv. **Inferno**

A small leaf cultivar. Leaves vary in colour from yellow to orange to red.

Acalypha wilkesiana cv. **Macrophylla**

A large leaf bushy shrub with red and brown marked leaves. The leaves are more red than brown.

ACALYPHA (cont)

Acalypha wilkesiana **cv. Marginata**
The drooping leaves of this plant are dark green with a pink picotee margin and light serration.

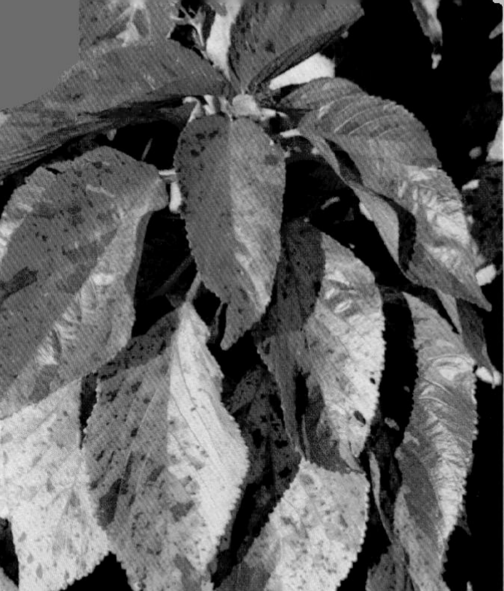

Acalypha wilkesiana **cv. Rose Glow**
This very bushy shrub has large leaves mostly deep rose-pink turning to red. There are a few green marks on some leaves and odd leaves may be cream. Lightly serrated.

Acalypha wilkesiana **cv. Miltoniana**
This bushy plant has large drooping leaves of brown, cream and pink colours.

Acalypha wilkesiana **cv. Moorea**
The leaves of this upright bushy shrub are very deep brown and are serrated.

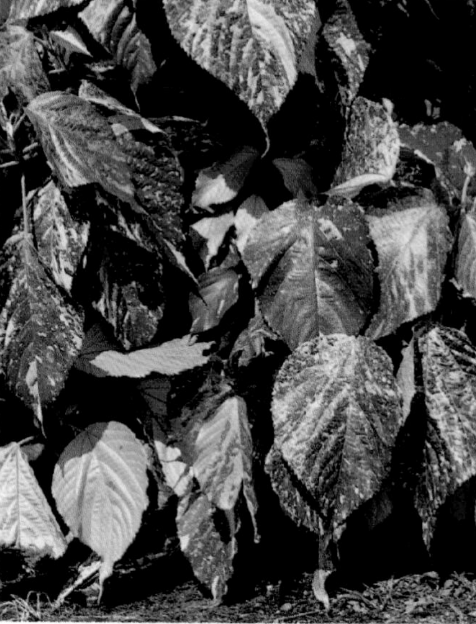

Acalypha wilkesiana **cv. Spotted Dog**
This cultivar has olive, green and copper coloured leaves with cream spots.

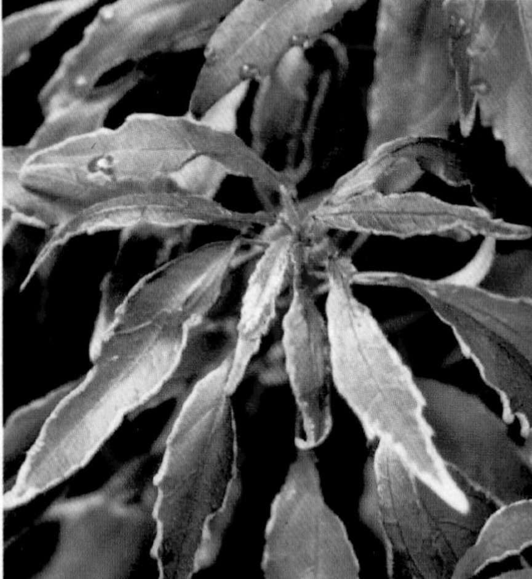

Acalypha wilkesiana **cv. Mini Marginata**
The deep green leaves of this Acalypha are unevenly serrated and have a pink picotee margin. Leaves are smaller than most Acalyphas.

Acalypha wilkesiana **cv. Pink Picotee**
A cultivar with greenish brown, mostly rounded leaves which are delicately edged with pink.

Acalypha wilkesiana cv. **Sunset Hue**

The large leaves of this plant have two shades of green, cream and yellow in their make-up. They are lightly serrated and some have cream margins.

Acalypha wilkesiana cv. **Tahiti**

The twisted large leaves of this plant are mostly deep cream with some green markings. Leaves are serrated.

Acalypha wilkesiana cv. **Tricolor**

The large, slightly serrated leaves of this bushy plant are coloured red, cream and brown. This is the most popular of the *A. wilkesiana* and in some countries it is called 'Rainbow'.

Acalypha wilkesiana cv. **White Picotee**

A vigorous cultivar with green leaves edged cream to white.

ACER

MAPLE

ACERACEAE

Acers are native of North and Central America, Europe, Africa and Asia. They are mostly deciduous but sometimes evergreen shrubs and trees. Propagation is from cuttings, grafts or from seed which, for cold climate types, needs to be stratified. There are at least 150 species of Acer and hundreds of cultivars. Those listed here are some of the most popular species and cultivars. Most of the deciduous maples are cold tolerant.

Acer campestre HEDGE MAPLE

A tall shrub sometimes a small tree, grown often as a hedge plant. This deciduous plant has yellow autumn foliage.

Acer cappadocicum cv. **Aureum**

GOLDEN CAUCASIAN MAPLE

A suckering small to medium deciduous tree which turns bright gold in autumn.

ACER (cont)

Acer carpinifolium HORNBEAM MAPLE

A small to medium tree which has racemes of small green flowers. The leaves turn bright yellowish brown in autumn.

Acer caudatifolium

A small to medium deciduous tree of the mountainous regions of China and Taiwan. Highly coloured autumn leaves. Takes a considerable amount of cold.

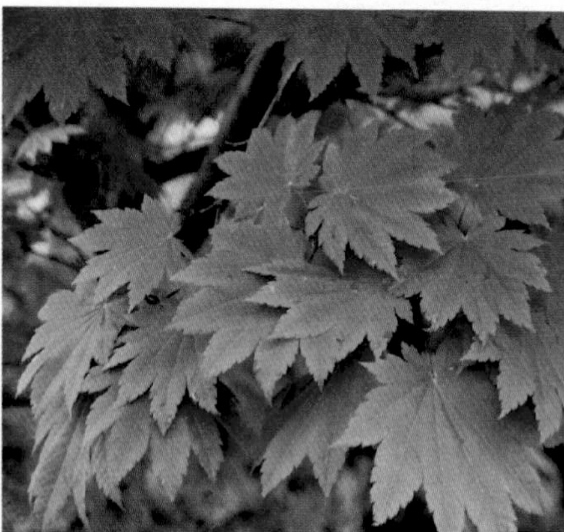

Acer circinatum VINE MAPLE

A thicket type tall shrub to small tree. This deciduous plant has yellow and red autumn foliage.

Acer* x *dieckii

A hybrid maple which is a medium size tree and grown in large gardens.

Acer erianthum

A small to medium tree with upright spikes of cream coloured flowers.

Acer grosseri

A small deciduous tree with bright red autumn foliage.

Acer griseum PAPERBARK MAPLE

A small deciduous tree with thin paper-like reddish brown bark. Autumn foliage is bright red, orange and gold.

Acer japonicum cv. **Aconitifolium**
A small deciduous tree with attractive many lobed leaves which have colourful autumn foliage.

Acer japonicum cv. **Green Cascade**
A small deciduous tree with many lobed green cascading leaves which give good autumn colour.

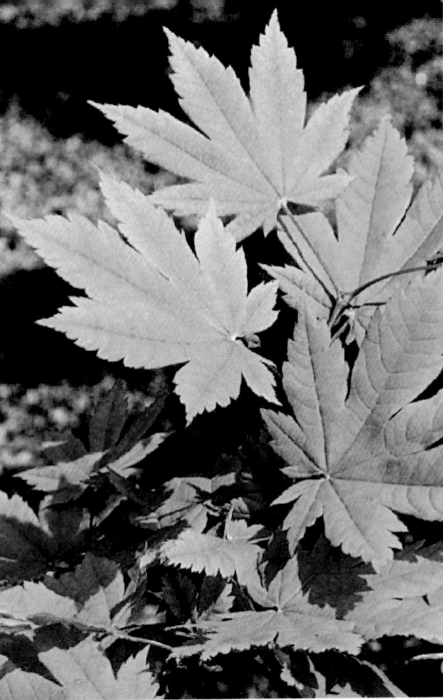

Acer japonicum cv. **Vitifolium**
This small deciduous tree has leaves which are yellowish in spring and red to orange in autumn.

Acer japonicum cv. **Aureum**
A showy cultivar which has attractive golden foliage.

Acer japonicum cv. **Green Cascade**
Showing early autumn foliage.

Acer japonicum cv. **Vitifolium**
Showing autumn foliage.

Acer japonicum cv. **Filicifolium**
A very showy, small, deciduous tree with attractive spring foliage and colourful purple autumn foliage which is shown in the illustration.

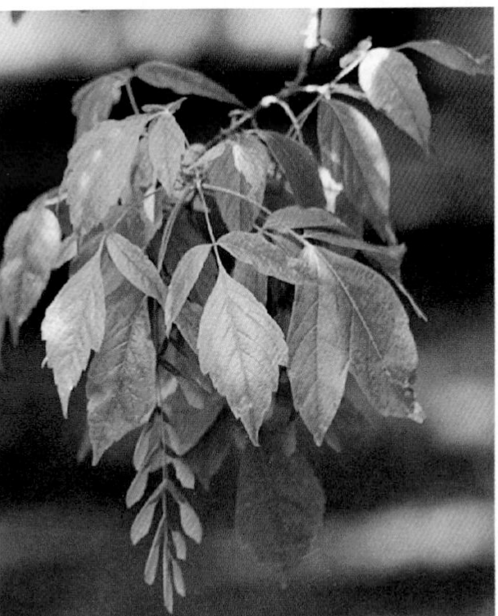

Acer negundo BOX ELDER
syn ***A. fraxinifolium***
A widely cultivated, medium, deciduous tree with green leaves.

ACER (cont)

Acer negundo cv. **Argenteo-variegatum**
A variegated cultivar with white and green leaves.

Acer negundo cv. **Flamingo**
A cultivar with variegated foliage which has bright pink colouring when the leaves are young.

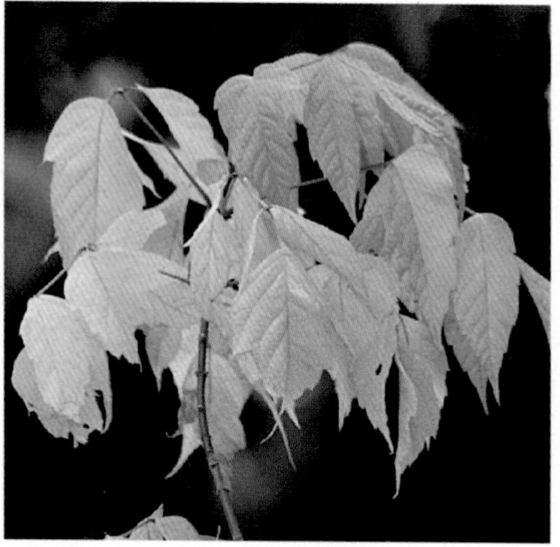

Acer negundo cv. **Auratum**
The leaves of this cultivar are cream in spring, turn pale green in summer and yellow in autumn.

Acer negundo cv. **Kelly's Gold**
An attractive, ornamental, gold leaf form of this tree.

Acer palmatum JAPANESE MAPLE
A popular, highly ornamental small deciduous tree with colourful orange and red autumn foliage. Illustration shows early spring foliage.

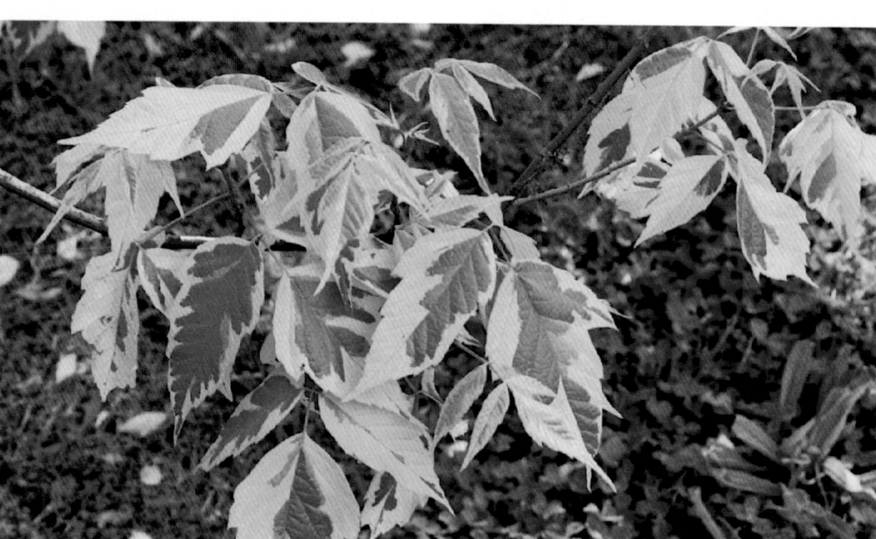

Acer negundo cv. **Aureo-variegatum**
This variegated cultivar has cream and green mottled leaves.

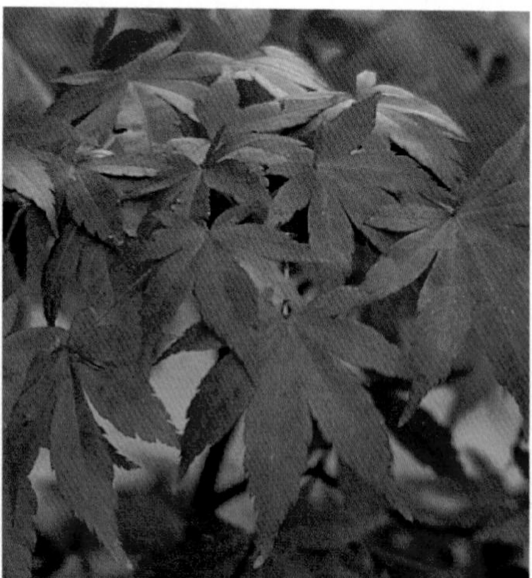

Acer palmatum - autumn foliage
This illustration shows the leaves in autumn. It has deeply lobed palmate leaves and is grown from seed and sometimes from cuttings. This form is used as an understock for grafting most of the cultivars listed below.

Acer palmatum **cv. Asahi Zuru**
A compact shrub with variegated leaves of pink and green.

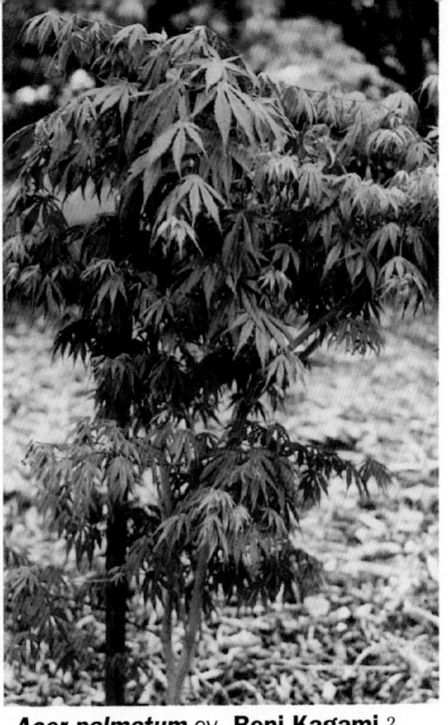

Acer palmatum **cv. Beni Kagami** 2
The very deeply lobed leaves of this form are a very bright shade of reddish brown.

Acer palmatum **cv. Atropurpureum**
The leaves of this very popular cultivar are bronze-brown, from the new foliage onwards. This cultivar is grown from seed or cuttings, or can be grafted.

Acer palmatum **cv. Aureum**
The new growth of this maple is yellowish. Autumn foliage is highly coloured.

Acer palmatum **cv. Beni Schichihenge**
The attractive small leaves of this maple are green with cream markings and a pink picotee edge.

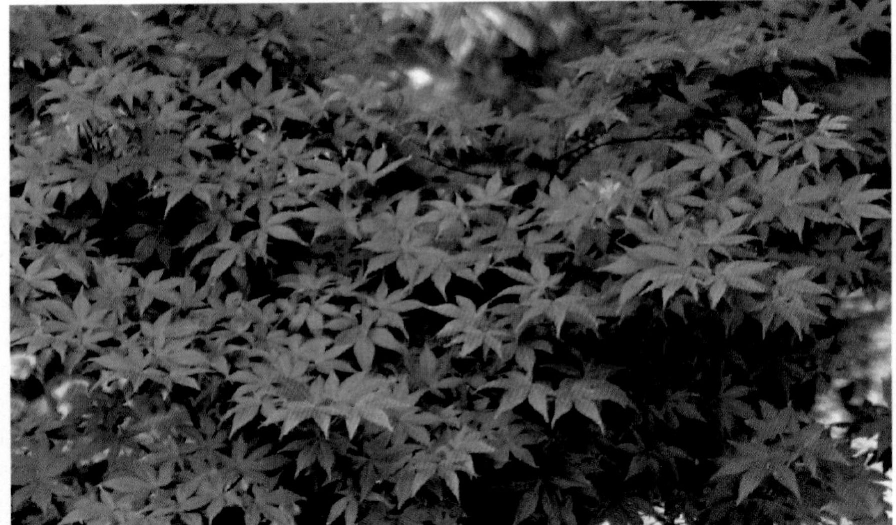

Acer palmatum **cv. Atropurpureum Nigrum**
This select form has very dark, brownish burgundy leaves.

Acer palmatum **cv. Bloodgood**
The dark red, deeply lobed leaves of this form make a very showy maple, being bright crimson in autumn. It is a popular plant in Europe.

ACER (cont)

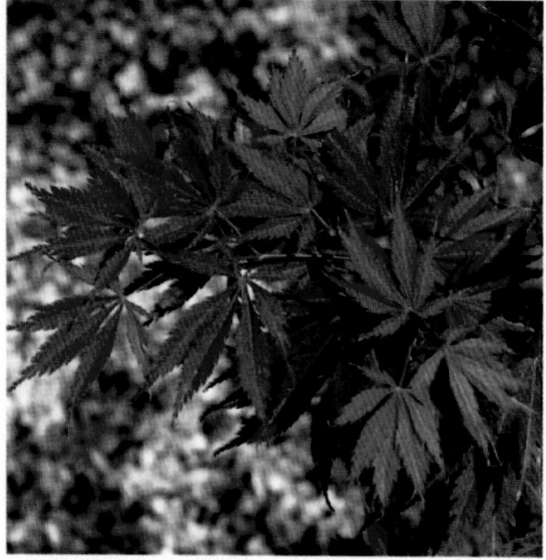

Acer palmatum cv. **Burgundy Lace**
This cultivar has deeply lobed and serrated leaves which are burgundy in colour.

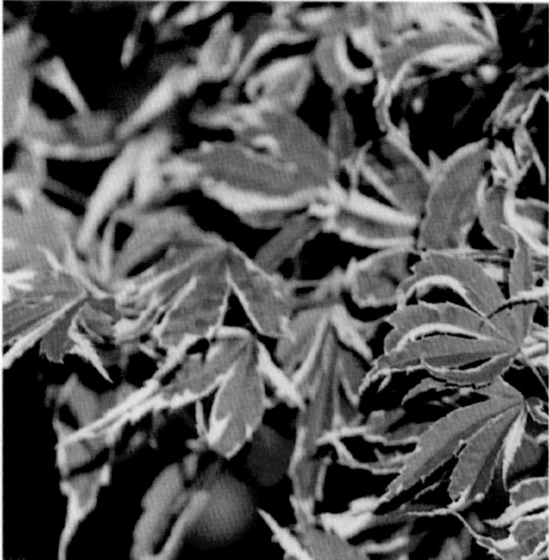

Acer palmatum cv. **Butterfly**
The multi-coloured small leaves of this plant are green and cream with the odd touch of pink on the new foliage.

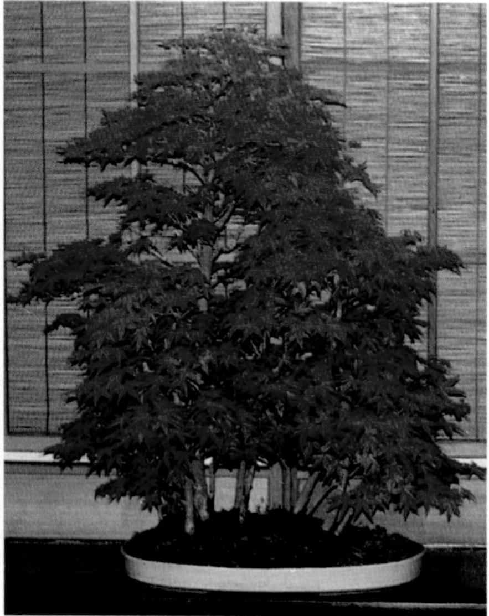

Acer palmatum cv. **Deshojo**
A cultivar, widely used for Bonsai, which has outstanding red coloured autumn leaves.

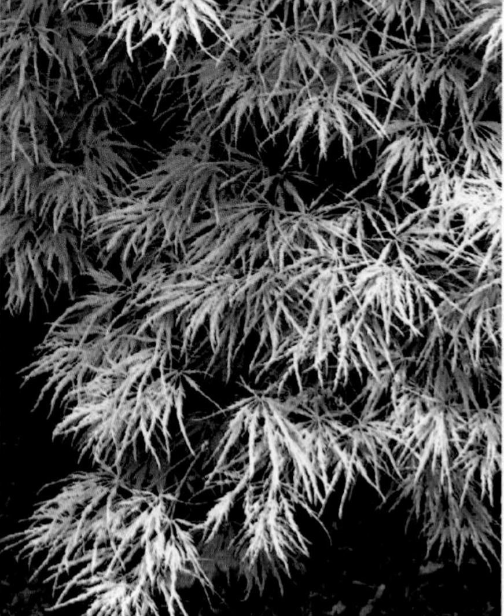

Acer palmatum cv. **Dissectum**
The fine deeply lobed and serrated leaves of this plant are green and displayed on arching branches. Dissectum cultivars are often grafted as standards.

Acer palmatum cv. **Dissectum Ornatum**
The attractive, fine, reddish brown colour of this plant make it one of the most popular of the Acer family. It is mostly grown as a standard.

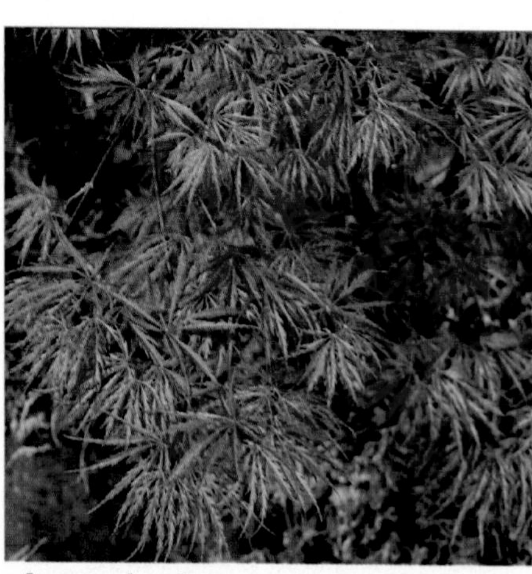

Acer palmatum cv. **Dissectum Ornatum Crimson Queen**
The fine delicate leaves of this maple are deep chocolate-red in colour. Usually grown as a standard. Scarlet in autumn.

Acer palmatum cv. **Dissectum Ornatum Garnet**
The fine attractive leaves of this cultivar are one of the deepest red-browns of these plants. Grown mostly as a standard, it needs full sun for best colour.

Acer palmatum cv. **Dissectum Seiryu**
The leaves of this Acer start as brownish red, and change to green in summer.

Acer palmatum cv. **Dissectum Seiryu**
This illustration shows the autumn foliage.

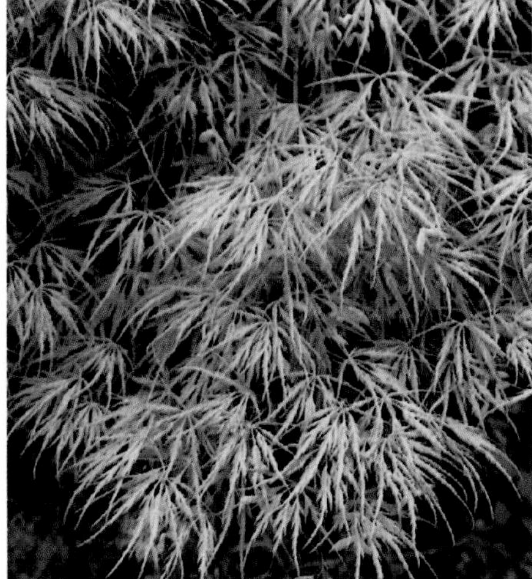

***Acer palmatum* cv. Dissectum Variegatum**
The fine leaves of this plant are green with a white and brown variegation.

***Acer palmatum* cv. Mishki Gasane**
A colourful shrub. New leaves are crinkled and coloured yellow with a red picotee.

***Acer palmatum* cv. Dissectum Viridis**
This is a very pale form of the green *A. palmatum* cv. Dissectum. Leaves are gold in autumn.

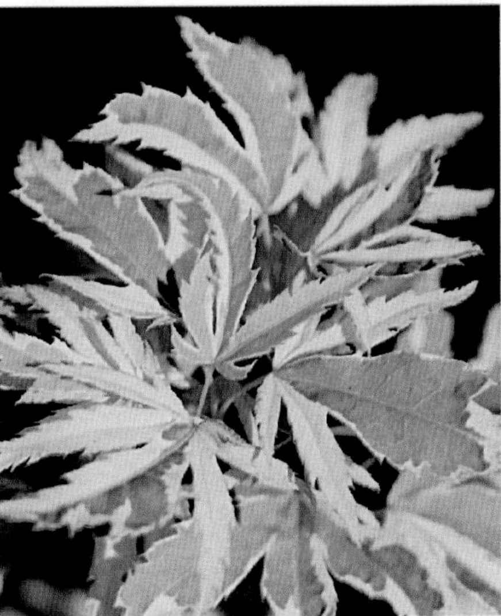

***Acer palmatum* cv. Panache**
Occasional touches of pink occur on the cream and green foliage of this cultivar.

***Acer palmatum* cv. Reticulatum Como**
This is an outstanding form from Como Nursery. The leaves are overlaid with pink in spring.

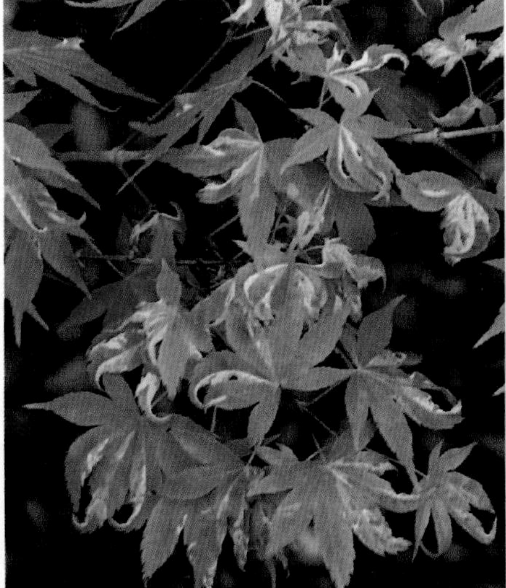

***Acer palmatum* cv. Karasugawa**
The unusual twisted leaves of this plant are variable in colour, mostly green and cream but at times showing pink.

***Acer palmatum* cv. Reticulatum**
The showy leaves of this maple are creamy yellow with prominent green veins. It is outstanding for its spring foliage.

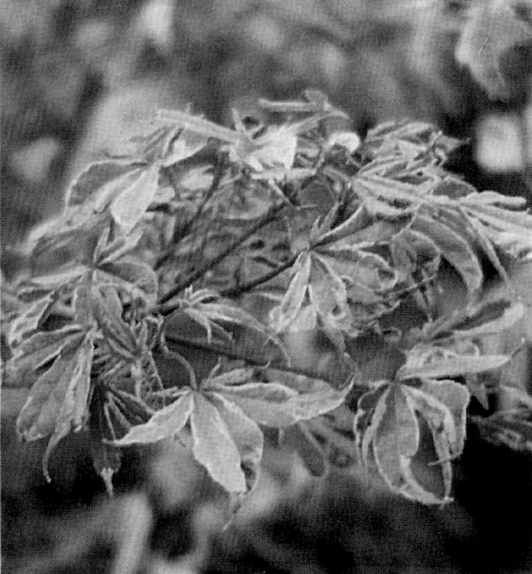

***Acer palmatum* cv. Roseo Marginatum**
This is an attractive and unique maple. Most of the small green leaves which are widely margined with pink, will turn to white in summer.

ACER (cont)

Acer palmatum **cv. Sagara Nishiki**
The multi-colour leaves of this maple are green, cream and pink. It is an open crowned plant.

Acer palmatum **cv. Shikushi Gata**
This is a broad leaf maple with very deep red foliage from spring to autumn.

Acer palmatum **cv. Scolopendrifolium Rubrum**
The deeply lobed leaves of this Acer change from purple-red to fiery red in autumn. One of the smaller growing *A. palmatums.*

Acer palmatum **cv. Senkaki**
This upright small tree has soft green leaves in spring turning to brilliant red in autumn.

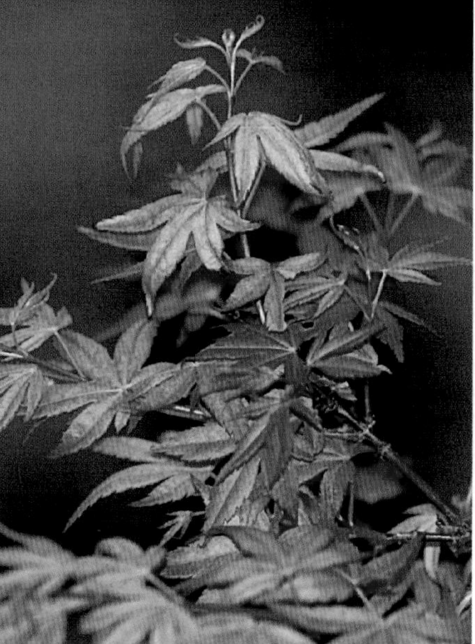

Acer palmatum **cv. Shindeshojo**
A cultivar which has outstanding red autumn foliage.

Acer palmatum **cv. Senijen**
A maple widely grown for Bonsai. The autumn foliage is coloured yellow and orange.

Acer palmatum **cv. Sherwood Flame**
The outstanding deep red foliage is seen through spring to autumn. The leaves are deeply lobed.

Acer palmatum **cv. Ukigumo**
This large leaf cultivar has pale green leaves mottled with white and overlaid with touches of pink.

ACER (cont)

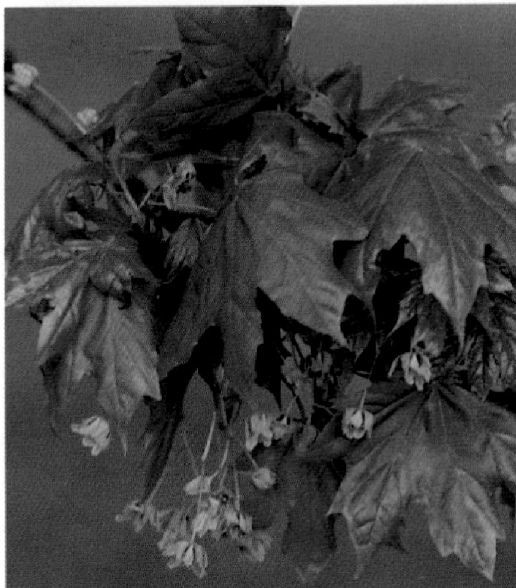

Acer platanoides
A medium spreading tree. The large leaves colour in autumn.

Acer platanoides cv. **Drummondii**
A small to medium tree with green and cream variegated leaves.

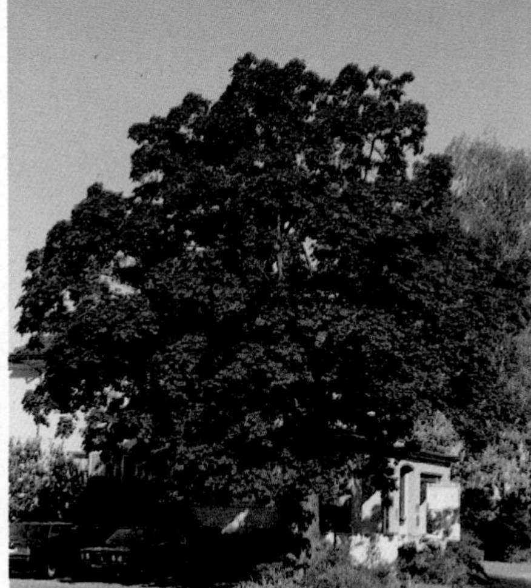

Acer platanoides cv. **Schwedleri**
A dark leaf small to medium tree for cold climates.

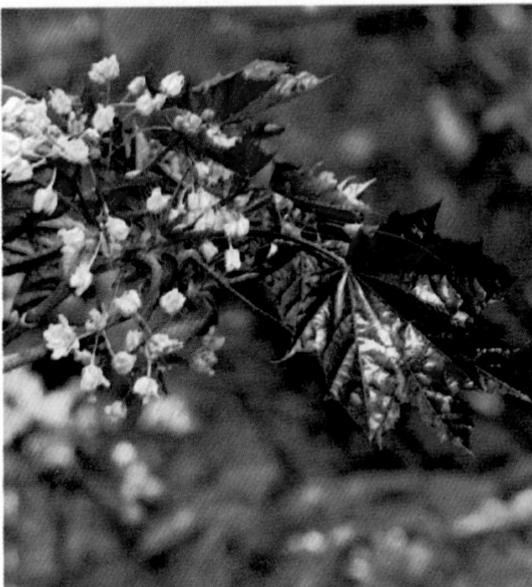

Acer platanoides cv. **Crimson King**
This small to medium tree has outstanding dark crimson foliage and is regarded by many gardeners and nurserymen as the most outstanding dark leaf tree. It is very cold tolerant.

Acer platanoides cv. **Palmatifidum**
A small to medium tree with finely cut green leaves which turn yellow in autumn.

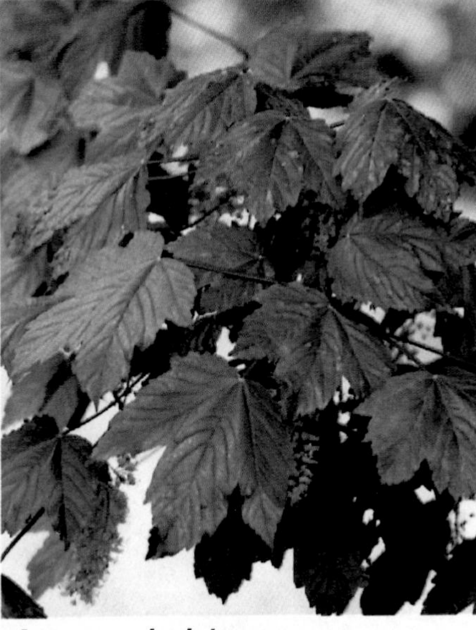

Acer pseudoplatanus cv. **Purpureum**
The maroon coloured new leaves of this cultivar change to dark green as they age.

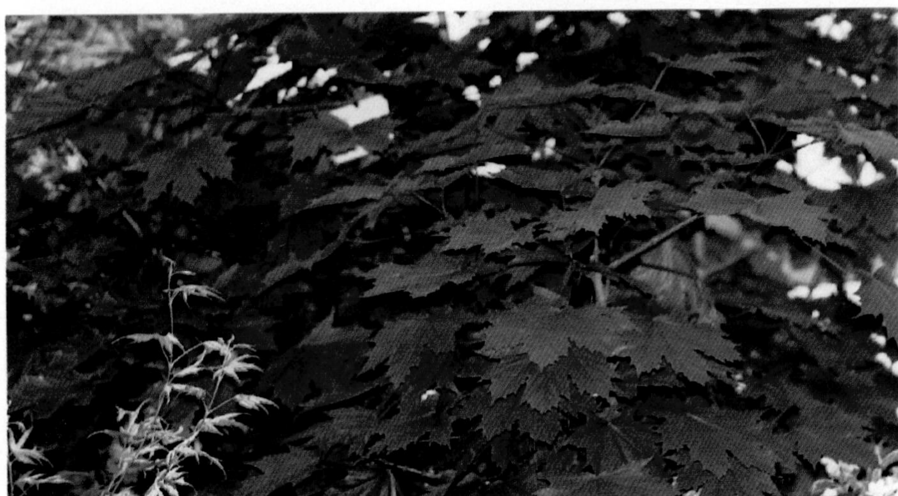

Acer platanoides cv. **Crimson Sentry**
A small to medium tree with crimson to maroon coloured foliage.

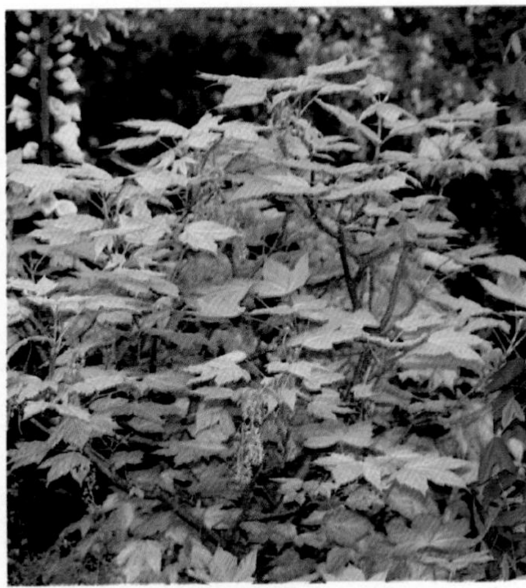

Acer pseudoplatanus cv. **Brilliantissimum**
An outstanding cultivar which has colourful spring foliage, gold overlaid with some red.

ACER (cont)

Acer pseudoplatanus cv. **Leopoldii**
This cultivar has spring foliage coloured gold with some green markings.

Acer rufinerve
A small deciduous tree with white striped bark. Autumn leaves turn from green to yellow to red.

Acer ukurunduense
A medium tree with upright clusters of spikes of cream flowers.

Acer pseudoplatanus cv. **Prinz Handjery**
This cultivar has spring foliage coloured yellow to amber with overtones of red.

Acer shirasawanum cv. **Aureum**
A cold-hardy deciduous small tree with pale yellow leaves which colour brilliantly in autumn.

Acer pseudoplatanus cv. **Variegatum**
A deciduous small tree. New leaves are of yellow, cream and pink.

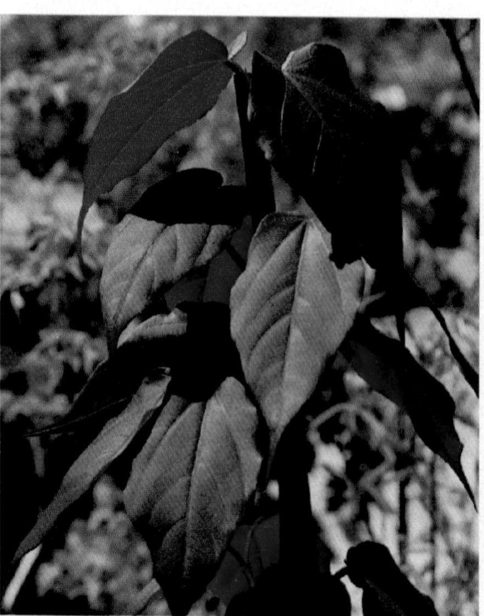

Acer sikkimense ssp. ***hookeri***
A medium deciduous tree from the Himalayan mountains. Brightly coloured autumn foliage. Very cold tolerant with new leaves coloured purple.

Acer wilsonii
A rare small tree from China with three lobed leaves and yellow autumn leaves.

ACMENA

MYRTACEAE

Small to medium evergreen trees which have attractive edible fruit in profusion. They are native to Australia and New Guinea and grow from mild temperate to tropical climates. They prefer good soil with plenty of water. These plants are widely grown throughout the world as ornamental garden specimens or as street trees and grow easily from fresh seed. The fruit was used as food by indigenous people.

Acmena hemilampra ssp. ***hemilampra***

BROAD-LEAVED LILLY PILLY

A dense small tree with shiny leaves and attractive new foliage. Masses of white berries.

Acmena smithii LILLY PILLY

A dense small to medium tree grown for its showy white fruit.

Acmena smithii - purple form

A purple fruited form of this lilly pilly.

ACOKANTHERA

APOCYNACEAE

Tall shrubs which are known both for their toxic poisons and their sweet smelling perfume. They are native to Africa and will grow in quite poor soils. The sap was used to poison arrows and spears. Easily grown from fresh seed.

Acokanthera oblongifolia

WINTERSWEET

syn ***A. spectabilis***

A tall green to bronze leaf evergreen shrub. The clusters of white flowers are highly perfumed.

Acokanthera oblongifolia - fruit

This plant has large attractive red fruit which, together with the sap, are poisonous.

Acokanthera oblongifolia cv. **Variegata**

A cultivar with attractive green and white variegated leaves.

ACROCARPUS CAESALPINIACEAE [LEGUMINOSAE]

Acrocarpus fraxinifolius PINK CEDAR

A tall fast growing deciduous tree which is widely grown in sub-tropical and tropical areas for timber and for its attractive bunches of red flowers. It is native to India and Burma and is propagated from seed.

ACTINIDIA

ACTINIDIACEAE

A group of deciduous shrubs and vines from Asia which are grown for ornamental purposes or for fruit production. They grow freely from seed. The fruit production cultivars are grafted and prefer cool to temperate climates.

Actinidia deliciosa

KIWI FRUIT; CHINESE GOOSEBERRY

syn ***A.chinensis***

A hardy deciduous vine widely grown for the commercial production of a very popular light brown skinned fruit. Both male and female plants are needed for pollination. In commercial plantations five females to one male are planted.

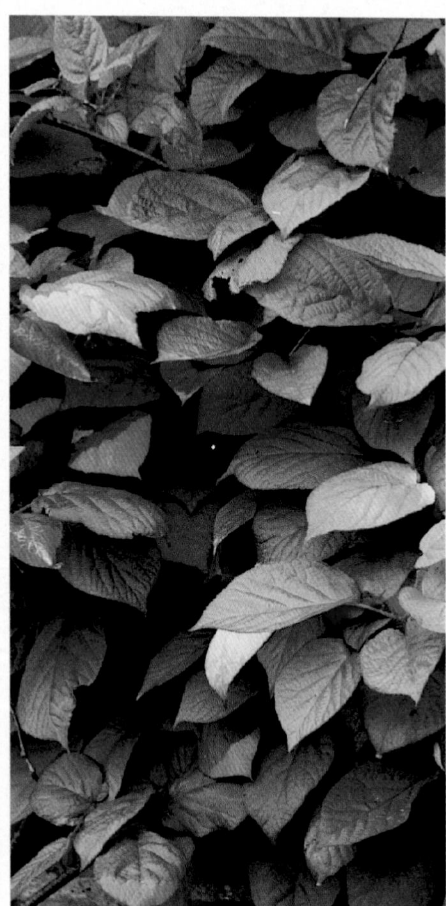

Actinidia kolomikta

A hardy shrubby vine grown for its very decorative foliage. Propagate from seed or cuttings. Grows in mild to sub-tropical climates.

ADANSONIA

BOMBACACEAE

Small to medium deciduous trees from Australia, Madagascar and Africa. They all have very large swollen trunks which are used for storing moisture to help them survive in the long dry spells they endure. Adansonias are all grown from seeds which are found in very large pulpy, hard shelled fruit.

Adansonia digitata BAOBAB

A swollen trunked medium tree with attractive leaves and white flowers, from South Africa. Some specimens of these trees in the wild are estimated to be 2000 years old.

Adansonia gregorii BOTTLE TREE; BOAB

A large trunked deciduous tree with white flowers and seed pods up to grapefruit size, from the Kimberley area in Western Australia. The pods are long lasting and are used for light carving art. The trunks are often much larger in diameter than height. Old tree trunks in Broome and Derby were so large they were hollowed out and used as jails. They are still growing and are tourist attractions as 'Jail trees'. An excellent bonsai plant.

Adansonia gregorii - large trunked group

Adansonia gregorii - decorated seed pod

ADENANDRA

RUTACEAE

Adenandra uniflora

A hardy cold tolerant small shrub native to South Africa. It is spring flowering and is covered with white flowers for a long period. It prefers a well drained site. Propagate from seed or cuttings.

ADENIUM

APOCYNACEAE

Popular ornamental shrubs from tropical Africa. The plants are fleshy with white milky sap. They are seen often in very dry areas and at times may reach small tree size. Adenium plants will benefit from copious supplies of water in summer when grown in a warm climate. Propagation is from seed or cuttings but when grafted onto oleanders they are seen at their best. The author has been involved in raising some of the cultivars shown in this book. Adeniums are grown in cold climates in glass houses and conservatories.

Adenium multiflorum
syn. ***A. obesum*** var. ***multiflorum***
A free flowering Adenium which may be covered with hundreds of flowers at a time, with flowers coming continuously over several months. This species is the most cold tolerant of the Adeniums and may be grown outdoors in warm temperate climates.

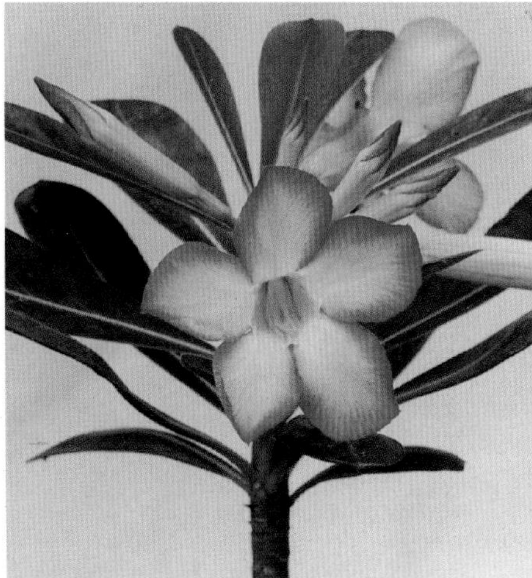

Adenium obesum DESERT ROSE
This plant is mostly found in desert areas, hence its common name. The obesum of the botanical name comes from the trunk which is often very swollen or obese. Flowers are terminal clusters and are pale pink, pink and red.

Adenium obesum cv. **Alba**
A cultivar with white flowers.

Adenium obesum cv. **Bangkok Rose**
This form has a wide red edge and was raised in Bangkok, Thailand.

Adenium obesum cv. **Kenya Rose**
A cultivar with almost pure red colour, very flat flowers which are mostly singular and larger than *A. obesum* cv. Jakarta Rose.

Adenium obesum cv. **Flamingo Giant**
This cultivar was raised by the author and the flowers are twice as large as most of the other *A. obesum* cultivars.

Adenium obesum cv. **Jakarta Rose**
Raised in Jakarta, Indonesia this plant has flowers which are almost totally red. It is one of the smaller flowered varieties.

Adenium obesum cv. **Mini Marginata**
This plant has lots of small white, red-margined flowers in clusters. Free flowering.

ADENIUM (cont)

Adenium obesum **cv. Pastel Princess**
A very pale pink form of this attractive flowered plant.

Adenium obesum **cv. Rhonda**
A new large flowered form raised by the author. It has heads of six to ten flowers at a time. Flowers are bright pinky red with pale pink and are slightly reflexed.

Adenium obesum **cv. Picotee Queen**
Another attractive flowered form having a broad red picotee or margin around a white centre.

Adenium obesum **cv. Variegata**
A free flowering cultivar with rose-pink and white flowers, and cream and green leaves.

Adenium obesum **cv. Sharney**
A vigorous cultivar with large reddish flowers with rounded petals.

AESCHYNANTHUS

GESNERIACEAE

Vines and sub-shrubs from India, China, Asia and the Pacific. These plants are used as small shrubs and ground covers outdoors in temperate to tropical climates. They are also popular as indoor plants in colder areas and are often grown in hanging baskets. They prefer a rich soil and regular fertilising. Propagate from cuttings or seed.

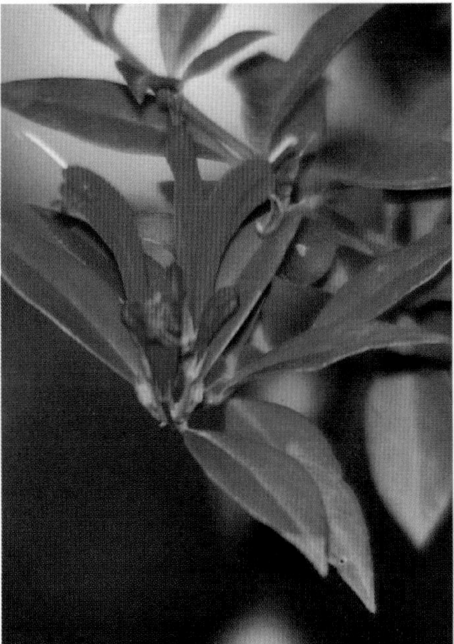

Aeschynanthus evrardii

A spreading semi-climber with shiny leaves and clusters of red and orange tubular flowers.

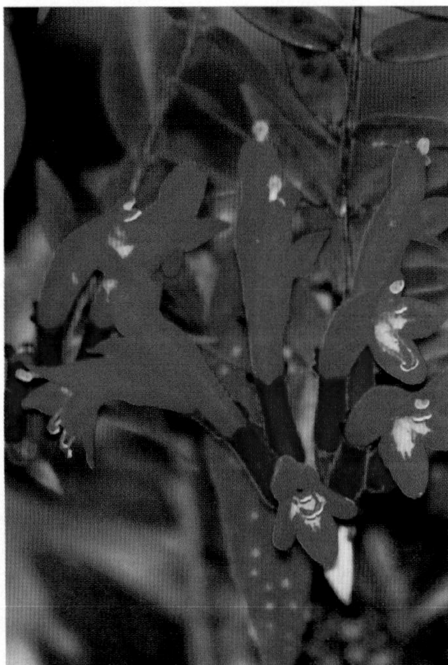

Aeschynanthus lobbianus

A cascading semi-climbing plant with clusters of bright red flowers which have white throats.

Aeschynanthus cv. **Purple Star**

A shiny leaf sub-shrub with clusters of tubular flowers which are deep red to purple in colour.

Aeschynanthus radicans

A semi-climber with shiny leaves and reddish orange clusters of flowers each protruding from a purple calyx.

Aeschynanthus speciosus

A spreading plant with orange-red tubular flowers.

AESCULUS

HIPPOCASTANACEAE

Deciduous small to medium trees from North America, Europe and Asia. These trees are mostly cold hardy. Some are used to produce chemicals for ultra-violet screening. They are very rapid growers. Propagation is from cuttings, seeds or root cuttings or by grafting.

Aesculus x ***carnea***

RED HORSE CHESTNUT

This medium tree has large flower spikes pale pink in colour, flowering in spring. Used as a shade tree.

Aesculus x ***carnea*** cv. **Briotii**

A select cultivar noted for its large flower spikes of cerise-pink.

AESCULUS (cont)

Aesculus flava

A small to medium spreading tree with large upright spikes of flowers coloured cream, with red centres.

Aesculus flava cv. **Alba**

A cultivar which has ivory coloured flowers.

Aesculus indica

A medium spreading tree which has upright flower spikes which are pinkish mauve in bud and ivory when the flowers open.

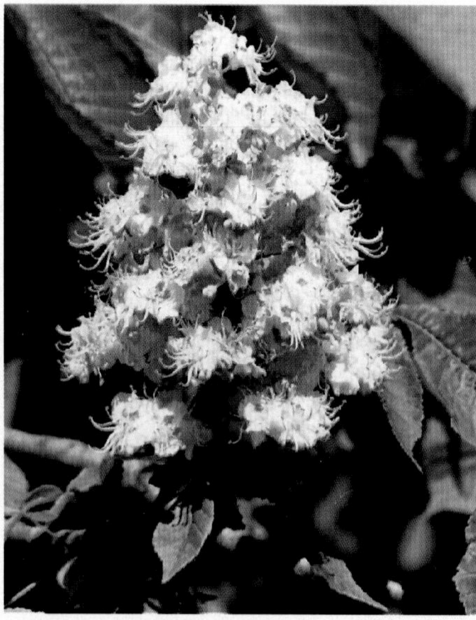

Aesculus hippocastanum

HORSE CHESTNUT

A spreading medium tree used in parks and large gardens. The flowers in large spikes are white with touch of yellow and red.

Aesculus pavia

A tall shrub to small tree with upright spikes of red flowers in spring.

AFGEKIA

FABACEAE [LEGUMINOSAE]

Afgekia sericea

A very showy, rare, warm climate climber. The spikes of bright pink flowers last over many months, starting from the bottom of the spike. As the old flowers drop from the bottom of the spike new buds appear at the top. Propagate from cuttings.

AGAPETES

ERICACEAE

Agapetes serpens

Native to the Himalayas, this semi-climbing shrub is grown as an ornamental for its attractive pendulous benches of red tubular flowers which occur over many months. It is mostly grown in climates from cool temperate to sub-tropical. Propagation is from cuttings.

AGONIS

Myrtaceae

A group of shrubs and small trees with weeping foliage and small white flowers, from Australia. Hardy in sandy areas and will tolerate some salt spray. Propagate from seed or cuttings.

Agonis flexuosa WILLOW MYRTLE
A very attractive small evergreen tree with fine drooping leaves and masses of white starry flowers. Good for seaside planting and streets where a small tree is needed.

***Agonis flexuosa* cv. Variegata**
A gold and green variegated form of this small tree.

AKEBIA

Lardizabalaceae

Vigorous semi-evergreen twining vines, native to Japan, China and Korea. They are grown as fragrant, free flowering ornamentals in cool to temperate climates. Propagate from stratified seed or cuttings under mist with bottom heat.

Akebia* x *pentaphylla
The purple-maroon flowers of this hardy, cold tolerant vine emerge in spring.

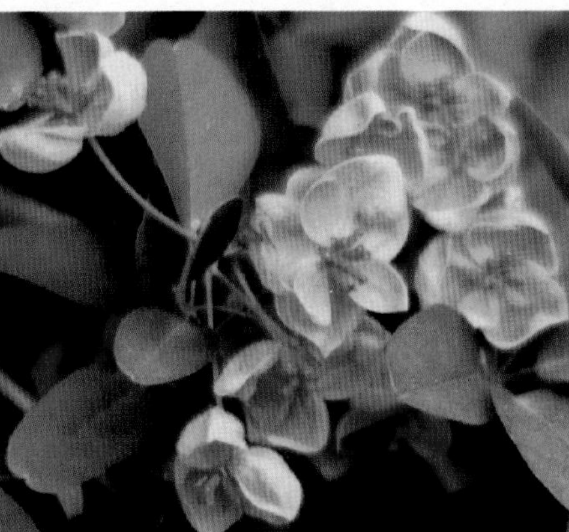

Akebia quinata CHOCOLATE VINE
Has perfumed purple-maroon flowers followed by fleshy edible fruit.

ALBERTA

Rubiaceae

Alberta magna
A showy tall shrub from Africa and Madagascar which is hardy and free flowering. It has red tubular flowers in large terminal clusters. It is propagated from seed and cuttings.

ALBIZIA

Mimosaceae [Leguminosae]

A range of deciduous and evergreen shrubs, trees and sometimes vines native to many tropical and temperate countries. The plants are usually free flowering and fast growing. Some adapt to frost prone areas. Propagate from seed.

Albizia adianthifolia
A medium spreading tree with fern like leaves and clusters of red, white and pink paintbrush like flowers. Suitable for warmer climates.

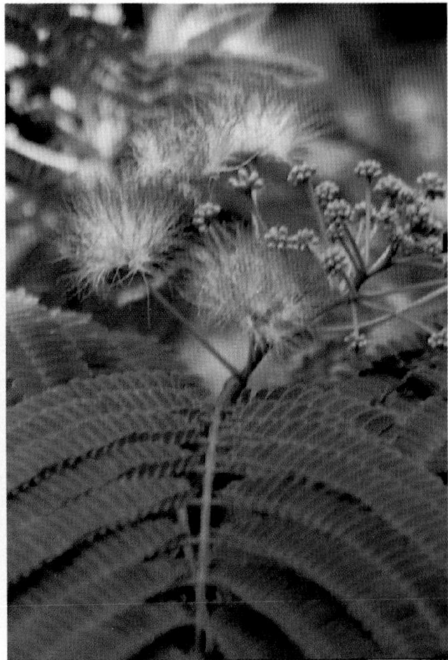

Albizia julibrissin SILK TREE
A medium spreading tree with fine ferny leaves. Flowers are red and white tufted and are displayed in profusion during spring. A cold tolerant Albizia.

ALBIZIA (cont)

Albizia lebbeck WOMAN'S TONGUE TREE

A cream flowered, ferny leaf, medium spreading tree. Seed pods are long, wide and tongue like.

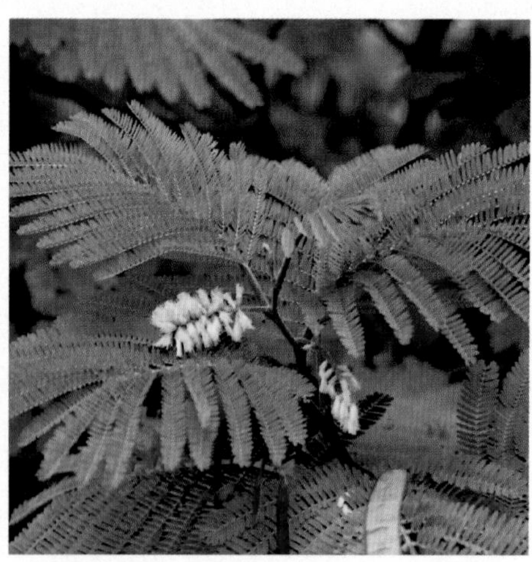

Albizia lophantha

A medium shrub with dark green ferny leaves. Flowers are bottle brush like and coloured creamy yellow. It is hardy near the sea and suitable for mild climates.

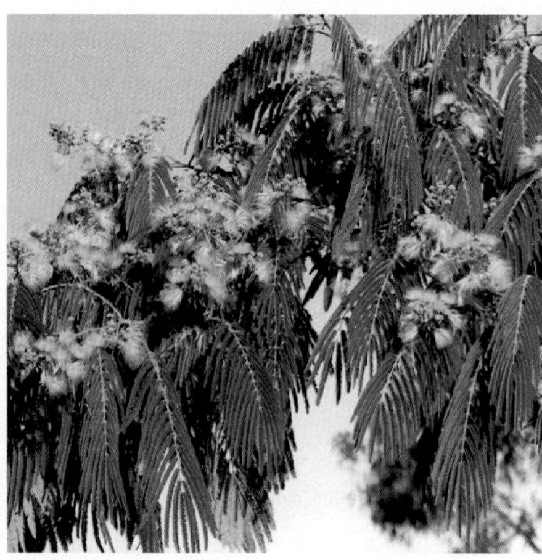

Albizia stipulata

A fine ferny leaf spreading tree with masses of cream flowers in spring. Grow in climates from temperate to tropical.

ALEURITES

EUPHORBIACEAE

Trees of the Aleurites group are medium sized spreading trees for tropical and sub-tropical areas. All have large seed pods which produce high yielding good quality drying oils used in paints and varnishes. These trees are also used as ornamental shade trees in parks and as street trees. Fast growing, they are propagated from seeds and occasionally from cuttings.

Aleurites fordii TUNG OIL TREE

This spreading tree has large off white flowers with red centres. The oil of the large seeds is widely used in paints and quick drying varnishes.

Aleurites moluccana CANDLENUT

This tree derives its common name from its use as a candle. The large seeds are threaded onto a wire and lit. They burn for long periods. The white flowers are seen in large clusters at the ends of the branches.

Aleurites montana MU OIL TREE

This medium spreading tree has large clusters of starry white flowers and large seeds. Used as a park tree and for the production of Mu oil.

ALLAMANDA

APOCYNACEAE

Allamandas are natives of Central America and are compact shrubs or climbers with showy trumpet-like flowers. They prefer a rich soil and plenty of water in hot weather. Grows outdoors in warm temperate to tropical climates. Propagate from seed and cuttings.

***Allamanda cathartica* cv. Golden Butterflies**

This cultivar is more shrub like than the other *A.cathartica* plants. The flowers are more tubular than trumpet type and it is a very heavy flowering cultivar. The petals flap in the wind like butterfly wings.

Allamanda blanchetii

PURPLE TRUMPET FLOWER

syn ***A. violacea; A. purpurea***

A small to medium shrub with masses of violet to purple flowers in warm weather.

Allamanda cathartica

COMMON TRUMPET VINE

A vigorous free flowering vine with lots of bright yellow trumpet flowers in warm weather.

Allamanda cathartica
cv. Halley's Comet

This vigorous vine has both double and semi-double flowers and is free flowering.

Allamanda cathartica
cv. Jamaican Sunset

This plant is a shrub to semi-climber. The flowers are a smoky pink in colour.

Allamanda cathartica
cv. Caribbean Sunrise

syn. ***A. catharctica* cv. Cherry Jubilee**

A pink flowered cultivar which is a shrub to semi-climber. It is a very free flowered ornamental from the Caribbean.

Allamanda cathartica
cv. Hendersonii

A free flowering cultivar with flowers which are a little smaller than the other cultivars. Unopened buds are brown on the outside.

***Allamanda cathartica* cv. Nobilis**

A large open flowered Allamanda. Buds are brown outside and the flower tubes are narrower in diameter than other Allamandas.

ALLAMANDA (cont)

Allamanda cathartica **cv. Schottii**

The most popular of the Allamandas. It flowers over a long period with large blooms which have swollen tubes and brown stripes inside.

Allamanda schottii

syn. ***A. neriifolia***

A shrubby plant which is covered with golden trumpet flowers in warm weather. More cold tolerant than *A. cathartica*.

Allamanda cathartica
cv. Stansill's Double

A free flowering vine with double golden flowers. Flowers are more fully double than the Halley's Comet form.

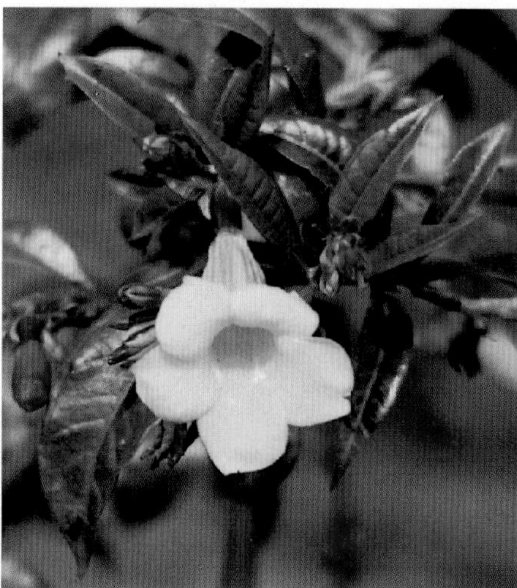

Allamanda schottii **cv. Baby Gold**

syn. ***A. neriifolia*** **cv. Baby Gold**

A cultivar which is an open crowned shrub with small golden yellow flowers.

Allamanda schottii **cv. Variegata**

syn. ***A. neriifolia*** **cv. Variegata**

A shrub with golden trumpet flowers and green and cream variegated leaves.

Allamanda cathartica **cv. Sunnee**

A low spreading Allamanda with flushes of golden medium sized flowers.

Allamanda schottii **cv. Grey Supreme**

syn. ***A. neriifolia*** **cv. Grey Supreme**

A cultivar with variegated leaves of grey and cream. Flowers are more yellowish than gold.

ALLOXYLON

PROTEACEAE

Small bushy free flowering trees from Australian rainforests. They make a very showy feature tree in warm temperate to tropical climates, in rich soils. Any fertiliser should be used sparingly and should not contain phosphorous. Propagation is from seed or cuttings.

Alloxylon flammeum ORANGE TREE WARATAH

A small attractive tree with large clusters of orange flowers in spring. A good cut flower.

Alloxylon pinnatum DORRIGO TREE WARATAH

syn. ***Oreocallis pinnata; Emobothrium pinnatum; E. wickhamii*** var. ***pinnatum***
This small tree has pinnate leaves and showy pinky red flowers in spring. Used as a cut flower.

Alloxylon wickhamii TREE WARATAH

syn ***Oreocallis wickhamii; Embothrium wickhamii***
This small tree has a fiery display of pinky-red flowers in spring, thus they differ from the very orange coloured flowers of *Alloxylon flammeum.*

ALNUS

BETULACEAE

A group of deciduous shrubs and trees which come from the sub-arctic and the Andes in Peru. They are popular trees, often being used as wind breaks or grown as ornamental trees in mild to cold climates. They grow easily from seed, cuttings and suckers. Plants have both male and female catkins.

Alnus tenuifolia MOUNTAIN ALDER

A small to medium tree from North America. The plant has cream catkins.

Alnus viridis GREEN ALDER

A tall shrub with showy red catkins in spring.

a

ALOE

LILIACEAE

These succulent leaf plants from Africa may be trees, shrubs or herbs. They are very arid-hardy and are widely planted as ornamental flowering plants. Much natural hybridisation has occurred in cultivation and variation from the native stands of Aloes appears to be quite common, giving both leaf and colour variation. Propagation is from seeds, or cuttings and by division. Most Aloes have spiny leaves.

Aloe chabaudii

A clumping spreading shrubby plant forming rosettes. The erect multi-branched flower stems have multiple heads of deep salmon pink flowers.

Aloe arborescens TORCH PLANT

A spreading much branched shrub having spikes of scarlet and orange flowers.

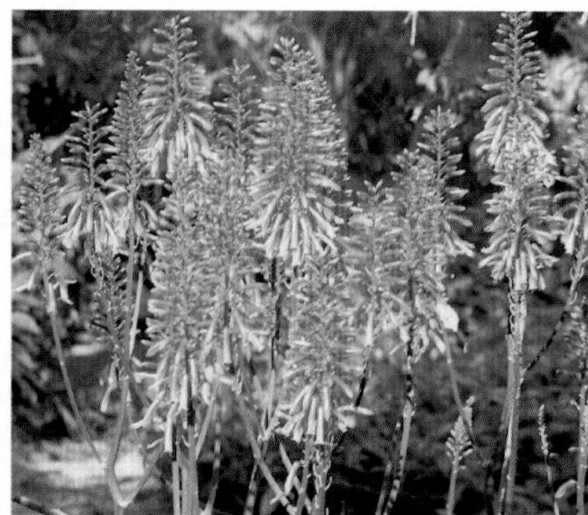

Aloe cameronii

A low spreading fleshy shrub with spikes of orange flowers.

Aloe camperi

A branching fleshy shrub with prominent spiny leaves. The multi-branched flower stems have orange and yellow flowers.

Aloe excelsa

A tall shrub to small tree with large leaves and persistent dead leaves. The much branched flower stem has long spikes of orange coloured flowers.

Aloe ferox CAPE ALOE

A fleshy and spiny leaf shrub with very large spikes of orange flowers.

Aloe marlothii

A clumping tall shrub with large fleshy leaves. The branched stems have spikes of golden orange flowers.

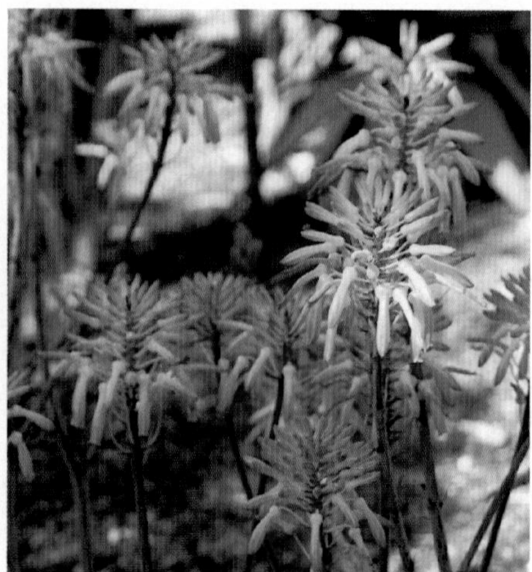

Aloe saponaria SOAP ALOE

A clumping suckering rosette plant with yellow and orange flowers on tall erect stems.

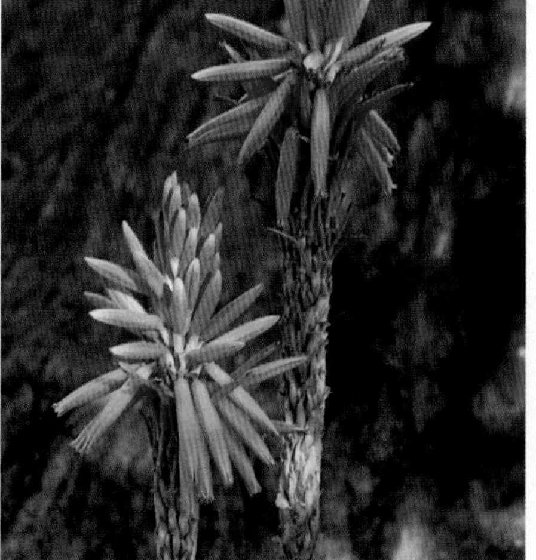

Aloe suprafoliata
A dense rosette clumping plant with tall stems and deep salmon flowers.

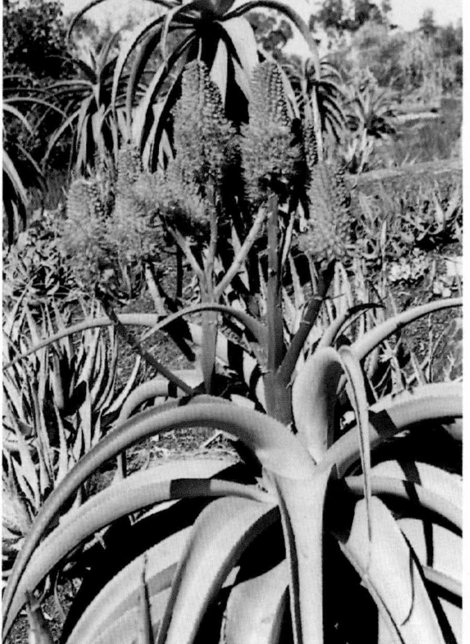

Aloe thraskii
A dense shrubby plant with large curved fleshy leaves, it has a branched flower head and deep gold flowers.

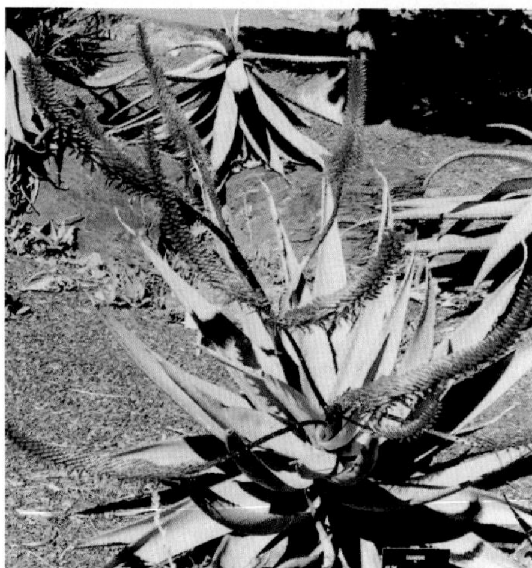

Aloe vryheidensis
A fleshy leaf shrub with an open flower stem. Flower spikes are long and flowers coloured yellow and orange-red.

ALSTONIA

APOCYNACEAE

Evergreen shrubs and trees with milky sap from Africa, Central America, Asia, Pacific and Australia. They prefer a warm climate. Propagation is from seed and cuttings.

Alstonia scholaris DEVIL TREE
A bushy upright small tree which has bunches of cream flowers in profusion.

Alstonia venenata
An ornamental tall shrub grown in warm climates for its attractive clumps of white star-shape flowers.

ALYOGYNE

MALVACEAE

Open shrubs with hibiscus like flowers from Australia. They are hardy plants and grow in semi-arid areas. Alyogynes are very free flowering and flowers may cover the whole plant in spring. Some outstanding specimens are seen in California U.S.A. Grow from seed or cuttings.

Alyogyne huegelii LILAC HIBISCUS
A medium size shrub which is free flowering with lilac coloured flowers.

Alyogyne huegelii CV. **Lavender Lady**
An upright cultivar having lavender coloured flowers.

Alyogyne huegelii CV. **American Beauty**
Very free flowering, this outstanding cultivar has cerise coloured flowers.

Alyogyne huegelii CV. **Sky Blue**
The large flowers on this form are sky blue.

a

ALYXIA

APOCYNACAE

Alyxia ruscifolia CHAIN FRUIT

A compact shrub which has clusters of white star shaped flowers and is native to Australia. As well as having attractive flowers it has chains of orange-red fruit. The plant tolerates sun or shade and grows well in temperate to tropical climates. Propagate from seed and cuttings.

AMHERSTIA

CAESALPINIACEAE [LEGUMINOSAE]

Amherstia nobilis

There is only one species of this tree, from Burma. Medium sized, it is regarded as one of the most outstanding flowering trees of the world. The very attractive red and yellow orchid like flowers hang down in chains. The tree is very tropical and rarely sets seed. Propagate from medium wood cuttings or by layering.

ANACARDIUM

ANACARDIACEAE

Anacardium occidentale CASHEW NUT

A medium size evergreen tree from a spreading crown with large leaves and large seeds which are commercial cashew nuts. Propagate from seed.

ANDERSONIA

EPACRIDACEAE

Andersonia coerulea

A heath land shrub which is native to Australia. It has sharp pointed leaves and small tubular blue flowers. Propagate from seed.

ANDIRA

FABACEAE [LEGUMINOSAE]

Andira inermis

A medium evergreen spreading tree from tropical Africa. It has spikes of bright purple flowers and requires a sub-tropical or tropical climate. It is one of the world's outstanding flowering trees and is propagated from seed.

ANEMOPAEGMA

BIGNONIACEAE

Anemopaegma chamberlaynii

An evergreen climber from tropical South America. It prefers a sub-tropical or tropical climate with rich soil and plenty of water. Propagate from seed or cuttings. This plant has clusters of yellow tubular flowers.

ANGELONIA

SCROPHULARIACEAE

A group of small shrubs from tropical America. They are free flowering on upright flower spikes. Most will grow in temperate to tropical climates. Easily grown from seed or cuttings.

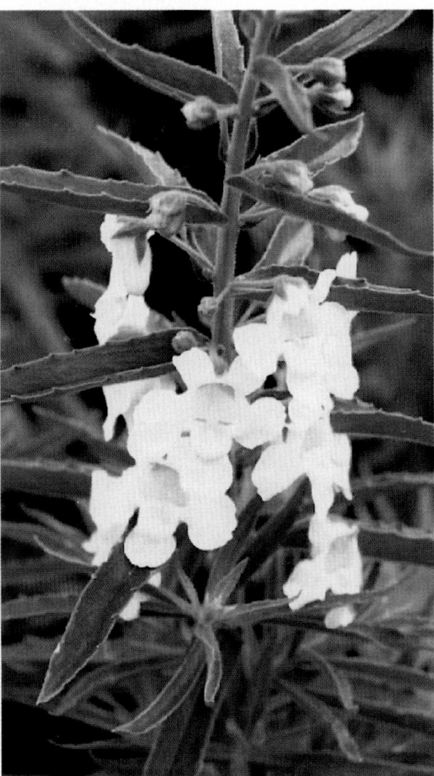

Angelonia angustifolia cv. **Alba**
A cultivar with white flowers.

Angelonia angustifolia cv. **Purple and White**
A purple and white flowered cultivar.

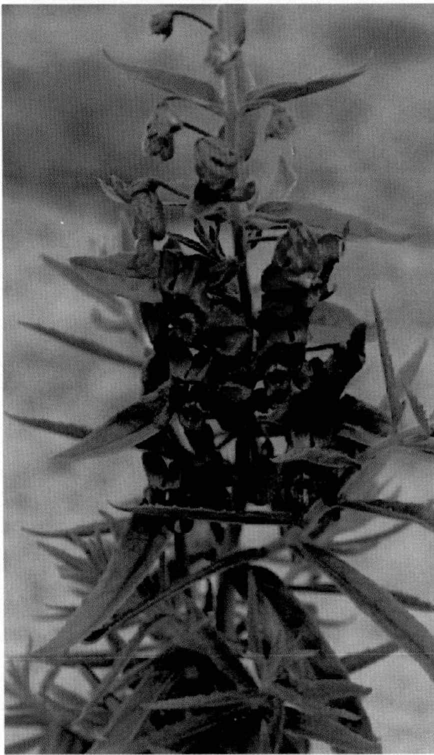

Angelonia angustifolia cv. **Purple**
This sparse small shrub has upright spikes of purple flowers.

Angelonia angustifolia cv. **Rose Pink**
This cultivar has rose-pink flowers.

ANGOPHORA

MYRTACEAE

Shrubs and trees with large heads of cream flowers, from Australia. Used as ornamental and street trees. Propagation is from seed.

Angophora hispida DWARF APPLE
syn. ***A. cordifolia***
A medium shrub with very large showy heads of cream flowers. Prefers mild to sub-tropical climates.

ANTHOCLEISTA

LOGANIACEAE

Anthocleista grandiflora
A very large leaved tall straight tree from Africa. The leaf veins are very prominent. Flowers are white. This tree needs liberal amounts of water and a warm climate. Propagate from seeds.

ANTHOTROCHE

SOLANACEAE

Anthotroche walcottii
A small to medium hardy shrub with attractive purple and white star shaped flowers. It is native to sandy areas of Australia and has some tolerance of salt spray. Grow from seed.

ANTIGONON

POLYGONACEAE

Climbing plants with tendrils, from Mexico and Central America. These vines are quite hardy and will take light frosts. They grow in a wide range of soils from temperate to tropical climates. and are grown from seed.

Antigonon leptopus CORAL VINE

A hardy free flowering vine with clusters of bright pink flowers over many months.

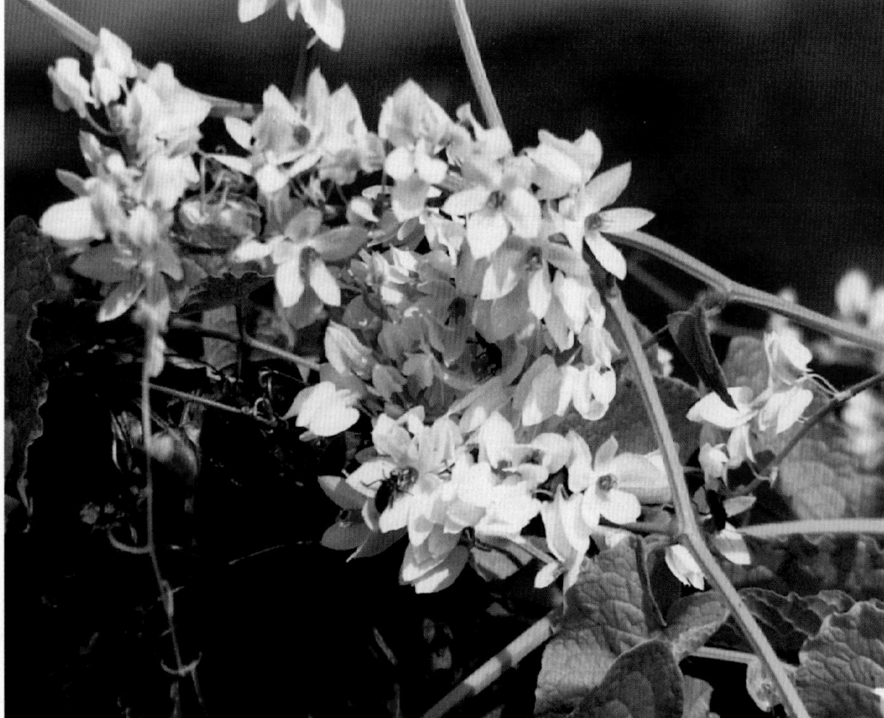

Antigonon leptopus cv. **Album** CHAIN OF LOVE

A free flowering vine which has flowers which are pure white or white with a pink centre.

APHELANDRA

ACANTHACEAE

Evergreen shrubs and sub-shrubs from tropical America. These free flowering plants prefer a rich soil when grown outdoors in sub-tropical and tropical areas. In cooler areas they are widely grown in pots as an indoor plant or in conservatories. Regular applications of fertiliser are needed to keep them flowering. They are mostly grown from cuttings as seed is rare on cultivated plants and in the wild.

Aphelandra aurantiaca

syn. ***A. nitens***

A free flowering small shrub with yellow buds which open to orange flowers. The large leaves have lead coloured distinctive veins.

Aphelandra chamissoniana[3]

YELLOW PAGODA

An erect branching shrub with bright gold flower spikes. The large green leaves have the veins outlined with silver.

Aphelandra deppeana

A free branching shrub with erect heads of flowers coloured yellow, orange and red.

APHELANDRA (cont)

Aphelandra sinclairiana
A very bushy branching small shrub with orange and pink flower spikes. This is a hardy plant and may be grown outdoors in temperate climates.

***Aphelandra squarrosa* cv. Louisae** ZEBRA PLANT
A small plant whose distinctive large leaves have silver markings over the veins. It has a large yellow flower spike. A popular indoor plant.

***Aphelandra squarrosa* cv. Rembrandt**
A cultivar which has the leaves very heavily marked with silver. It has a large yellow flower spike.

***Aphelandra squarrosa* cv. Snow Queen**
A cultivar which has leaves almost completely silver in colour. It has terminal golden flower spikes.

Aphelandra tetragona
A small open branching shrub with red flowers in clusters.

APREVALIA

CAESALPINIACEAE [LEGUMINOSAE]

Aprevalia floribunda
A small evergreen tree which is native to Madagascar. It has very large flat heads of yellow flowers in late spring. The tree prefers a rich soil in a temperate to tropical climate and is grown as a showy ornamental. Propagate from seed.

ARALIA

ARALIACEAE

Shrubs and small trees, many of which are cold tolerant. They are native to America and are used as garden specimens or indoor plants. Some have thorns and all prefer good quality soil. Propagate from seed and cuttings.

***Aralia elata* cv. Variegata**
A cultivar which has cream and grey variegated leaves and is usually grown as an indoor plant.

Aralia spinosa DEVIL'S-WALKING-STICK
A small tree with a thorny trunk and branches. It has large heads of small flowers at the end of the branches.

a

ARBUTUS

Ericaceae

Evergreen shrubs and small trees from Europe, America and Asia. Most are very cold tolerant and are widely used as both ornamental and street trees. Some Arbutus have edible fruit in the winter. They are grown from seed and cuttings. Arbutus prefer acid soils.

Arbutus andrachne

A spreading evergreen tree with clusters of white bell-like flowers, followed by orange fruit.

Arbutus menziesii MADRONA

Red fruit follows the clusters of white, bell shaped flowers on this medium tree which also produces a fine quality timber.

Arbutus* x *andrachnoides

A spreading tree which is a hybrid between *A. andrachne* and *A. unedo.* It has cream flowers and orange fruits and is widely grown in parks and gardens.

Arbutus unedo STRAWBERRY TREE

A tall shrub which is cold tolerant. The trees have white bell-like flowers and orange-red edible fruit.

ARCHIDENDRON

Mimosaceae [Leguminosae]

Small to medium evergreen trees. Flowers are showy clusters of stamens. These tropical to sub-tropical trees are native to Australia and South East Asia. Related to both Abarema and Pithecellobium, they are colourful when covered with seed pods as well as flowers. Often grown in parks and as street trees, the plants grow freely from seeds—it is necessary to nick the hard coating before planting.

Archidendron grandiflorum

FAIRY PAINT BRUSHES

syn. ***Abarema grandiflora; Pithecellobium grandiflorum***

A small to medium tree which has attractive paint brush like flowers of red and white. Seed pods are flat and twisted, red inside and exposing black shiny seeds.

Archidendron hendersonii

WHITE LACE FLOWER

syn. ***Abarema hendersonii; Pithecellobium hendersonii***

A small to medium tree with white paint brush like flowers followed by attractive curling orange seed pods exposing shiny black seeds.

ARDISIA

MYRSINACEAE

A group of tropical and warm temperate climate shrubs to small trees of Australia, Asia and the Americas. They prefer a moist soil and most are prone to frost damage. Ardisias are widely grown for their colourful berries, as an indoor house plant in cooler climates and outdoors in warmer climates. Regular fertiliser is beneficial to their growth. Propagation is from seed or cuttings.

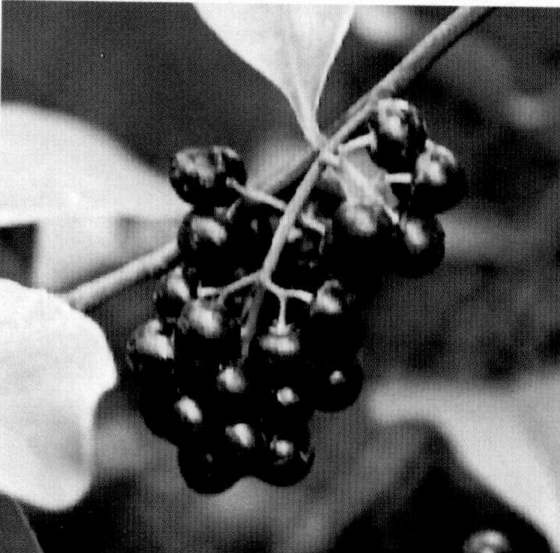

Ardisia compressa

The pink flowers of this open shrub are followed by black fruit, which is illustrated.

Ardisia crenata CORAL BERRY

A small branching shrub with shiny leaves, small white flowers and bright red berries which stay on the plant for many months.

***Ardisia crenata* cv. Alba**

WHITE CORAL BERRY

This shrub is similar to *A.crispa* above but with white berries.

***Ardisia crenata* cv. Pink Pearls**

A select cultivar with shiny bright pink pearl-like berries.

Ardisia guadalupensis

A small bushy shrub with pendulous bright pink flowers. This plant prefers a tropical to sub-tropical climate.

Ardisia humilis

A tall shrub with leathery leaves, pink flowers and black fruit. Used in gardens and parks.

***Ardisia crispa* cv. Variegata**

This variegated form does not always have berries but is grown for its attractive foliage.

ARDISIA (cont)

Ardisia japonica

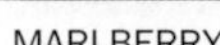

MARLBERRY

A tall shrub with white flowers, red berries and serrated leaves.

Ardisia macrocarpa

A medium shrub with pink flower stalks and flowers which don't fully open, followed by black berries. The leaves are dark green and ribbed.

ARGYREIA

CONVOLVULACEAE

Argyreia nervosa

WOOLLY MORNING GLORY

This woody climber is a native of India and prefers a warm climate. The plant has large heart shaped leaves and violet coloured trumpet flowers. It requires lots of water and a rich soil to perform at its best. Propagate from seed or cuttings.

Ardisia paniculata

A medium tree with small pink open flowers on red stalks, followed by black berries. The green leaves are ribbed.

Ardisia solanacea

A medium shrub with bright rose-pink open flowers and flower stalks. The leaves are ribbed.

ARISTOLOCHIA

ARISTOLOCHIACEAE

Mostly vines but sometimes shrubs or herbs, these plants grow in many countries throughout the world, in varying climates. Most of the flowers have browns as part of their colouring and many have very strong and sometimes overpowering perfume. Some forms have been used for medicinal purposes. The vines are rapid growers in warm climates and are often used as a quick cover. They prefer moist situations outdoors and are widely grown in conservatories and glass houses in cooler climates. Propagate from both seed and cuttings. Many are often called Dutchman's Pipe. Those listed here will take light frosts.

Aristolochia chapmaniana

This vine has hard leathery leaves and small pipe-like flowers of brown and cream.

Aristolochia labiata

syn. ***A. brasiliensis***

A vigorous climber from Brazil with pipe-like flowers of cream and brown. Large soft leaves which are heart shaped.

Aristolochia gigantea

This vigorous vine has heart shaped leaves. In varying shades of brown, the flowers of this plant are among the world's largest being up to two-thirds of a metre in width and more than half a metre long.

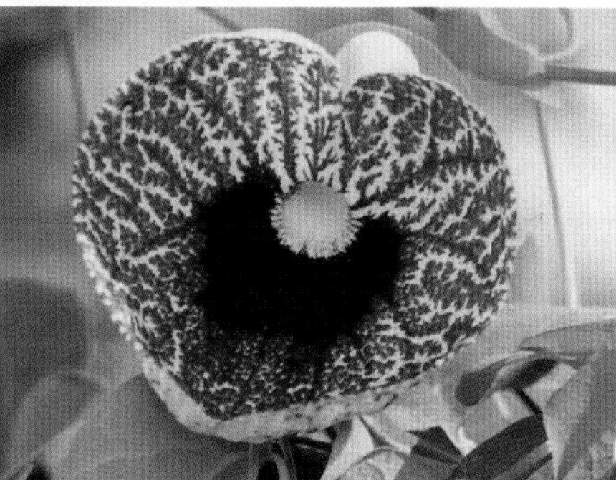

Aristolochia littoralis CALICO FLOWER

syn. ***A. elegans***

A modest vine with heart shaped leaves and flat flowers of brown and cream. In warm climates away from its natural habitat of Brazil it can become a weed as this free seeding plant germinates easily. It can devastate butterflies in some areas as the leaves can be poisonous to these and some other insects.

Aristolochia tagala

A twining plant with small brown flowers. This species as well as *A. praevenosa* is host to the Richmond Birdwing butterfly.

Aristolochia* x *kewensis

Free flowering, this hybrid has cream and brown coloured flowers.

Aristolochia ringens DUTCHMAN'S PIPE

A hardy modest vine with heart shaped leaves and pipe shaped flowers of brown and cream.

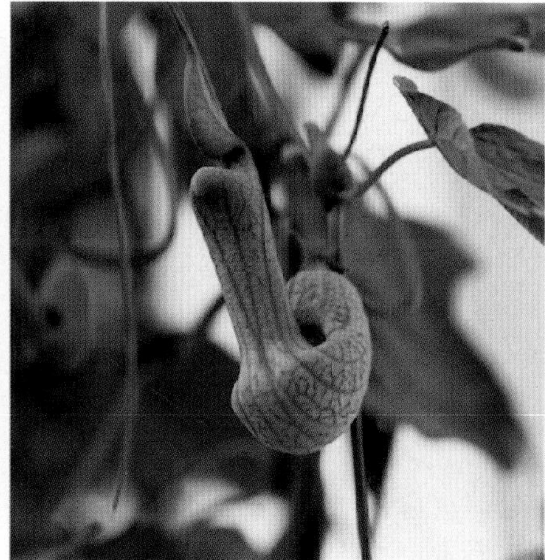

Aristolochia trilobata

An open vine with three-fingered leaves. The flowers are cream, with some brown.

ARONIA

ROSACEAE

Tall shrubs closely related to the pear, Aronias are ornamentals grown for both flowers and bright red fruit. The plants are cold tolerant and may be propagated from cuttings or seed which needs to be stratified at just above freezing for twelve weeks.

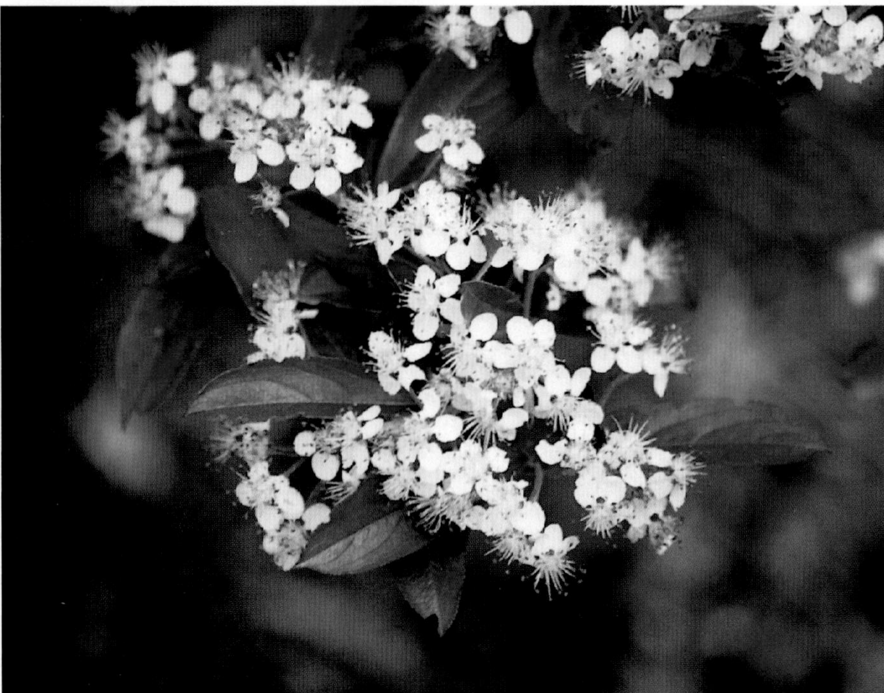

Aronia arbutifolia CHOKEBERRY

A tall shrub with large open clusters of white flowers.

Aronia melanocarpa BLACK CHOKEBERRY

A tall shrub to small tree with clusters of white flowers with red stamens.

ARTANEMA

SCROPHULARIACEAE

Artanema fimbriatum

A small free flowering shrub from the sub-tropical area of Australia. It grows in moist situations and although a perennial shrub, it is grown as an annual in colder climates as it dislikes frosts. This small plant has only recently come into regular cultivation and has proven to be very popular as it flowers freely with blue flowers over many months. Grow from seed or cuttings.

ARTABOTRYS

ANNONACEAE

Artabotrys hexapetalus CLIMBING ILANG-ILANG

A tall semi-climbing shrub from Sri Lanka, with highly perfumed small cream to yellow flowers followed by large yellow colourful fruit. It is grown as an ornamental for both its shape and shiny leaves as well as its perfume. It needs a rich soil, a warm climate and ample water. Grown from seed.

ARTOCARPUS

Moraceae

Evergreen and deciduous trees from Asia and the Pacific. Some are used for timber and others produce edible fruit. They are also ornamental in appearance. Propagate from seed. The trees need a warm climate, rich soil and plenty of water. Seedless cultivars are grafted.

Artocarpus altilis BREADFRUIT

A handsome evergreen tropical medium size tree with deeply lobed leaves. This tree is prized both as an ornamental tree and for the large edible fruit it produces.

Artocarpus hypargyraeus

A shiny leaf evergreen tree with small white flowers.

Artocarpus heterophyllus JACKFRUIT

A medium spreading tree with large shiny leaves. This tree produces a very large, popular, edible, yellow coloured fruit. It grows in tropical and sub-tropical climates.

ASARINA

Scrophulariaceae

Modest twining climbers which are free flowering and have attractive trumpet like flowers. They are grown as annuals in cold climates but are longer lasting in warmer climates. Asarinas prefer to be pruned in winter as they flower more heavily on new growth. They grow best in a good quality soil with regular fertilising and watering in the warmer months. New cultivars of this plant are regularly being released from North America and Europe. Propagate from seed.

Asarina antirrhinifolia

VIOLET TWINING SNAPDRAGON

A small climber which has violet snapdragon-like flowers over many months.

Asarina barclaiana

syn. ***Maurandya barclaiana***

A purple trumpet flowered modest climber. Flowers over a long period.

Asarina erubescens

CREEPING GLOXINIA

syn. ***Maurandya erubescens***

The most vigorous of the Asarinas. This climber has bright rose-pink flowers in abundance over many months.

ASARINA (cont)

Asarina procumbens syn. ***Antirrhinum asarina***
A cold climate modest climber or ground cover with white and cream trumpet flowers over a long period.

Asarina scandens cv. **Bride's White**
syn. ***Maurandya scandens***
A very free flowering modest climber with white flowers in profusion over many months.

Asarina scandens cv. **Violet Glow**
Purple trumpet flowers with white centres are very colourful on this free flowering small climber. Flowers over many months.

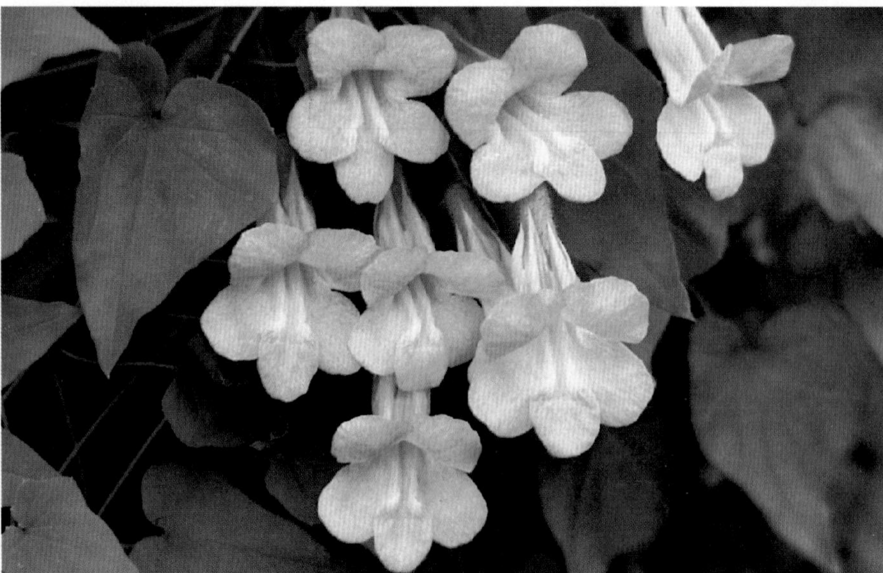

Asarina scandens cv. **Pink Ice**
This modest climber has very showy pale pink trumpet flowers in profusion over a long period. One of the most outstanding Asarinas.

ASCLEPIAS

ASCLEPIADACEAE

A group of shrubby plants with milky sap from Africa and North America. These plants can naturalise and become weeds but in colder climates may be grown as choice plants. Pods are used in dried arrangements. They grow in almost any soil and are grown from seed.

Asclepias curassavica BLOOD FLOWER
A small open shrub with terminal clumps of flowers, blood red with a yellow centre.

ASIMINA

ANNONACEAE

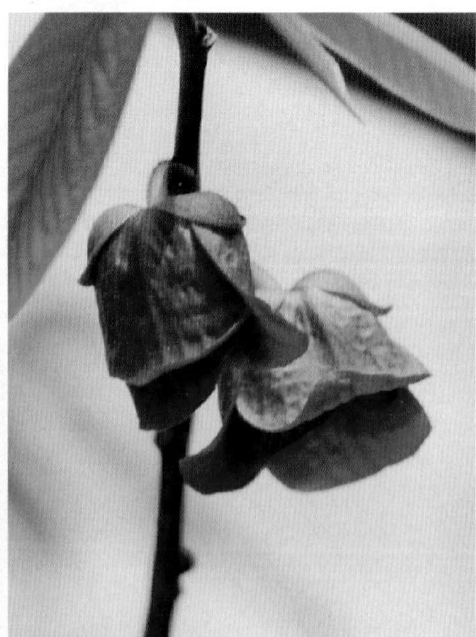

Asimina triloba PAWPAW
A small deciduous tree, native to North America, which grows in mild climates and is tolerant to light salt spray. It has maroon flowers followed by yellow edible fruit. Propagate from seed.

ASPARAGUS

Liliaceae

A group of shrubs, herbs, and climbers from the Mediterranean region, Africa, Canary Islands Asia and Australia. The most well known is *A. officinalis*, the commercial edible Asparagus. Most Asparagus form underground tubers. Some have thorns. Asparagus when grown away from their natural habitat in warm climates may become weeds. Many Asparagus are grown for their very decorative foliage which is used world wide by florists as greenery. They respond well to nitrogen fertiliser applications. They are grown from seed or plant divisions.

Asparagus africanus
syn. ***A. cooperi***
A climbing fine leafed plant used as an ornamental outdoors in mild temperate to tropical areas and indoor in very cold climates. Used for florists' foliage.

Asparagus asparagoides SMILAX
syn. ***A.medeoloides***
Widely grown as a hanging basket plant, this is a spreading climber or ground cover with leaves wider than most Asparagus.

Asparagus densiflorus
syn. ***A. sprengeri***
A shrubby plant which is semi-climbing. The plant has feather duster like frond branches. It has some prickles and is used as cut foliage. This Asparagus is used world wide in mild temperate to tropical areas as sand stabilising plant especially on sea shores.

Asparagus densiflorus cv. **Golden Cascade**
An outstanding cultivar with golden foliage.

Asparagus densiflorus cv. **Myers** PLUME ASPARAGUS
syn. ***A. myersii***
An upright branching asparagus with plume like branches used as a decorative ornamental and for cut foliage.

Asparagus densiflorus cv. **Compacta**
syn. ***A. densiflorus*** cv. **Nana**
Dwarf growing, this form of this Asparagus is suited to pots.

Asparagus densiflorus cv. **Variegata**
A variegated foliage form of this species. It needs full sun to show its variegation properly. When seed grown it usually gives fifty to seventy-five per cent variegated plants.

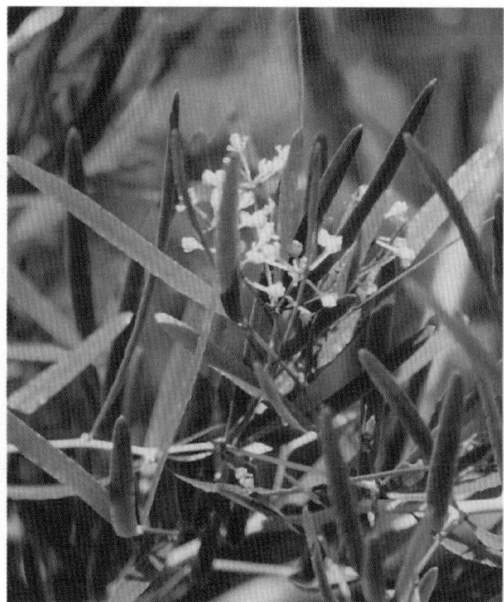

Asparagus falcatus SICKLETHORN
This woody climber with long leaves and thorns is grown as an ornamental. Used as florists' foliage when fronds are young.

ASPARAGUS (cont)

Asparagus fallax

A very rare, modestly climbing or upright plant which makes a good garden specimen. Tolerant of light salt spray.

Asparagus madagascarensis

Bushy and spreading, this semi-climbing plant prefers a warm climate to grow outdoors, or grows indoors in mild climates.

Asparagus pseudoscaber

Used as cut foliage, this multiply-branching shrubby plant has fine foliage.

Asparagus retrofractus

A very dense shrubby plant with masses of creamy white perfumed flowers. Very good cut foliage. Marketed in the nursery trade as *A. myriocladus* and *A. macowanii.*

Asparagus scandens

This drooping semi-climber with fine foliage is used mostly as a hanging basket plant. Prefers some shade.

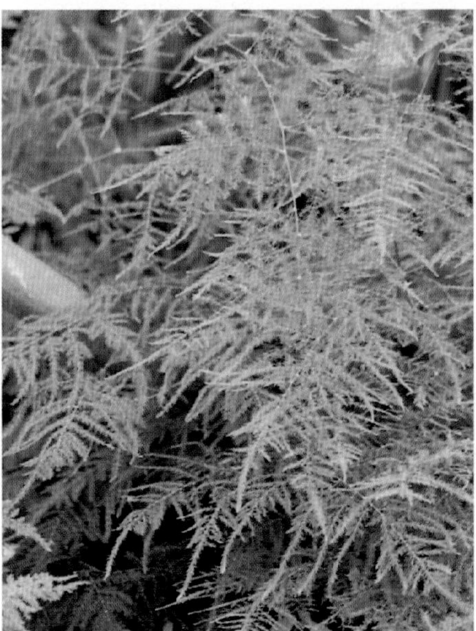

Asparagus setaceus ASPARAGUS FERN

syn. ***A. plumosus***

A fine leaf climbing fern which is a most popular florist greenery. Prefers dappled shade.

Asparagus officinalis COMMON ASPARAGUS

A multi-branched plant with fine ferny foliage. The new shoots are cut as the edible Asparagus. It needs plenty of humus.

Asparagus setaceus cv. **Nanus**

A dwarf form of this very popular Asparagus. Widely grown as a decorative pot plant and for cut foliage.

ASPARAGUS (cont)

Asparagus setaceus cv. **Pyramidalis**
This cultivar is an upright grower with the leaves in tight long sprays.

Asparagus umbellatus
A hardy woody climber not often seen. Grows in very poor clay and gravel soils.

ASYSTASIA

ACANTHACEAE

Shrubs, climbers and herbs from the Asian tropics. Widely grown in warm temperature to tropical climates as ornamentals. They flower over very long periods, some up to ten months of the year, with trumpet like flowers. These plants grow in a wide range of soils and are very hardy. The climbing forms prefer hard pruning after flowering. Grow from seed or cuttings.

Asystasia gangetica
A climbing and spreading plant with a very long flowering period. The trumpet like flowers are mauve with cream inside.

Asystasia gangetica cv. **Alba**
A creamy white free flowering form of this climber.

Asystasia travancorica
A many branched small shrub with white trumpet flowers on erect spikes. Free flowering.

Asystasia travancorica cv. **Violacea**
A violet coloured cultivar of this free flowering shrub.

ATALAYA

SAPINDACEAE

Atalaya hemiglauca
A very hardy small tree from the arid centre of Australia. It is a free flowering tree with clusters of small white flowers when it has ample water. This tree will grow in a wide range of soils. It is propagated from seed.

AUCUBA

CORNACEAE

Evergreen shrubs from Japan to the Himalayas. They are cold tolerant plants, many with colourful leaves. The female plants have very colourful clumps of bright red berries. They prefer a partially shaded situation with good quality moist soil, but will tolerate dry soils and even salty winds. Propagate from cuttings and seed.

Aucuba japonica

A medium shrub with large green leaves which have a hint of yellow. This is a very hardy plant. Pictured is the female plant with ripe red fruit.

***Aucuba japonica* cv. Nana**

A very dwarf form of this plant used as a pot plant. A female plant with berries is pictured.

***Aucuba japonica* cv. Crotonifolia**

A very popular form having leaves heavily dusted with gold. Pictured is the female plant with berries.

***Aucuba japonica* cv. Picturata**

This cultivar has very attractive leaves heavily marked gold. Popular for potting.

AVERRHOA

OXALIDACEAE

Two species of evergreen medium trees, with edible fruit, from tropical Asia. They will grow from warm temperate to tropical climates and prefer a rich open soil with adequate water. These fruit are becoming more popular as a table fruit and are now being grown in plantations for the international western markets. They may fruit up to three times per year in ideal situations. Propagated from seed but commercial selections are budded or grafted.

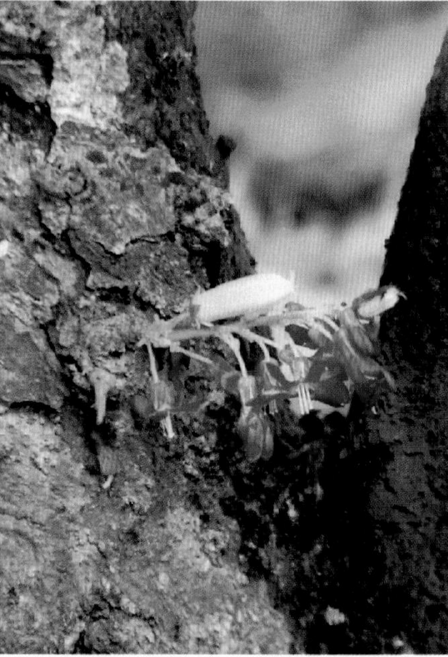

Averrhoa bilimbi CUCUMBER TREE

This unusual medium tree has bunches of red flowers from the trunk, followed by yellow cucumber-like fruit. The fruit are widely used in pickles. The tree also flowers and fruits on the branches.

Averrhoa bilimbi - fruit

AVERRHOA (cont)

Averrhoa carambola STARFRUIT

This small to medium dense tree produces large crops of edible fruit called starfruit. It is now a popular exotic fruit with a hint of apricot in the flavour. It has bunches of violet flowers. This illustration shows the large fruit and some flower.

AZADIRACHTA

MELIACEAE

Azadirachta indica NEEM

A medium tree of the dry tropics, it is a hardy tree which is a rapid grower when it gets lots of water. Neem has become very prominent over the last few years for the environmentally safe pesticide produced from its seed. There are large plantations being grown in South East Asia for pesticide production. It grows easily from seed but selected cultivars are grown from cuttings of high yielding trees. It has white star shaped flowers and yellow bean size fruit.

AZALEA

a

ERICACEAE

Azaleas are recognized by many as Rhododendrons but for the purpose of this book they are being listed as Azalea as this is the most accepted name throughout the horticultural world. Azaleas are free flowering, deciduous or evergreen. Most flower in the late winter and spring but odd flowers may appear at any time especially on the evergreen varieties. They are mostly native of the temperate climates of the northern hemisphere and are plants which have been cultivated and hybridised over hundreds of years. Outstanding cultivars and hybrids have been bred in Belgium, India, France, USA, England, Holland, Australia, New Zealand and to a lesser degree other countries. Cultivars are easily grown from soft wood cuttings under mist. They are also grown from seed where unusual results and colours may be expected. Azaleas prefer an acid soil and peat moss mixed with the soil or potting mix is beneficial. The plants may be attacked by spider mites, leaf miners, aphids and other odd insects. Petal blight is a recent fungus disease of the flowers. Spraying to prevent insects and diseases is recommended. Azaleas are probably the most popular and widely grown flowering shrub. Many of the origins of the cultivars are either unknown or indistinct. Names may also vary from country to country and in a few instances the same name may be used for two totally different Azaleas. Colour variation of the flower is also very noticeable depending on the fertiliser used and if grown in full shade or full sun. The best results and most intense flower colour appear to be when grown in dappled shade. Although many of the illustrations may show a single flower to give clear detail, most Azaleas have large clusters of flowers. Azaleas shown as 'x Exbury cv. Balzac' and 'x Knap Hill cv. Anneke' represent different groupings of hybrids and are shown thus for clarity of presentation.

Azalea x **Back Acres** cv. **Marian Lee**

An evergreen small shrub with single flowers which have a whitish pink centre and are red outside.

Azalea cv. **Dimity**

On this small evergreen shrub the single white flowers have an odd cerise marking. This hybrid is of undetermined origin.

Azalea cv. **Dogwood**

A small evergreen shrub with smallish flowers of salmon-pink marked with white and cerise. A hybrid of undetermined origin.

AZALEA (cont)

Azalea **x Exbury cv. Balzac**
Deciduous and free flowering, this shrub has large heads of orange-red flowers.

Azalea **x Exbury cv. Royal Command**
A deciduous shrub with large heads of orange-red flowers in spring.

Azalea **x Gable cv. Rosebud**
Pink flowers with dark pink centres are held in large heads on this very free flowering shrub.

Azalea **x Exbury cv. Cecile**
A deciduous shrub with large heads of salmon flowers with deep yellow throats.

Azalea **x Exbury cv. Silver Slipper**
On this free flowering deciduous shrub the large heads of flowers are coloured cream with gold markings.

Azalea **x Exbury cv. Klondyke**
This free flowering deciduous shrub has large heads of flowers coloured gold and orange-red.

Azalea **x Exbury cv. Sun Chariot**
A deciduous shrub with single golden coloured flowers in clusters.

Azalea **x Ghent cv. Coccineum Speciosum**
Free flowering, this deciduous shrub has bright red flowers with orange markings. This Azalea has much darker flowers when grown in the shade.

AZALEA (cont)

Azalea **x Ghent** cv. **Corneille**
A hardy deciduous shrub with double pale pink flowers.

Azalea **x Ghent** cv. **Nancy Waterer**
This hardy deciduous shrub has large heads of golden flowers.

Azalea **x Ghent** cv. **Unique**
A free flowering hardy cold-tolerant shrub with heads of golden flowers marked orange.

Azalea **x Glenn Dale** cv. **Kobold**
Heads of large bright red flowers feature on this very free flowering shrub.

Azalea **x Glenn Dale** cv. **Martha Hitchcock**
A showy shrub with heads of large flowers coloured pink with dark mauve edges.

Azalea **x Glenn Dale** cv. **Silver Moon**
A free flowering shrub with large heads of white flowers.

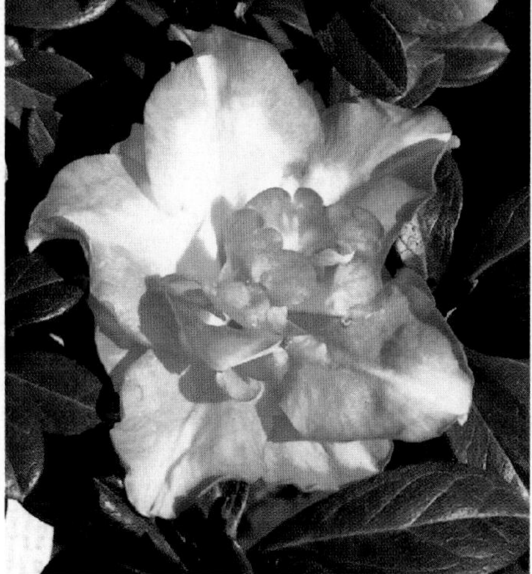

Azalea **x Gold Cup** cv. **Cha Cha**
Held singly or in clusters, the large double flowers of this small evergreen shrub are coloured cerise-pink and white.

Azalea cv. **Honey Bunch**
Of undetermined origin, this hybrid is a small evergreen shrub with pale pink single flowers marked deeper pink.

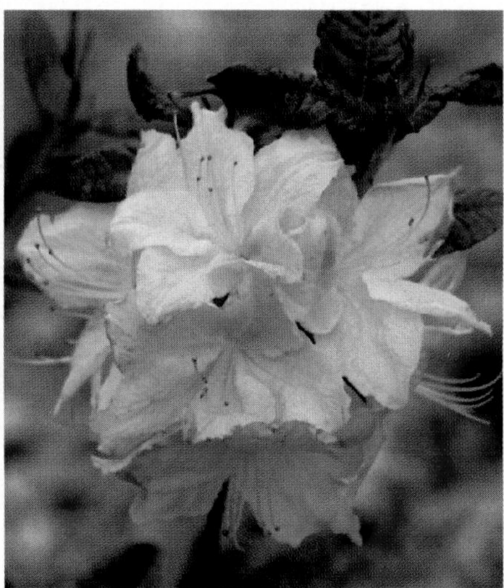

Azalea **x Ilam** cv. **Melford Lemon**
An open shrub with large heads of yellow to gold flowers which are much paler in full sun.

AZALEA (cont)

***Azalea* x Ilam** cv. **Ming**
A free flowering shrub with large heads of orange flowers in spring.

Azalea indica cv. **Ambrosiana**
An evergreen small shrub with deep cerise coloured flowers.

Azalea indica cv. **Beverly Haerens**
The flowers are double white on this small evergreen shrub.

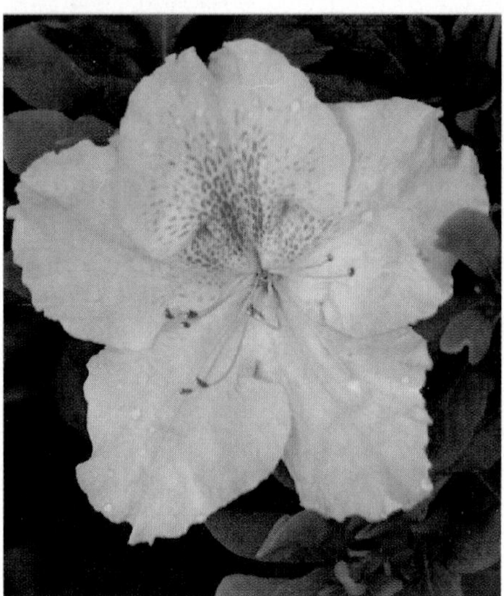

Azalea indica cv. **Agnes Neale**
On this medium evergreen shrub the lavender-violet coloured flowers grow singly or in clusters.

Azalea indica cv. **Aunty Mame**
A medium evergreen shrub. Single flowers are coloured pink with cerise markings.

Azalea indica cv. **Bonnie McKee**
An evergreen shrub with flowers coloured cerise-violet.

Azalea indica cv. **Albert Elizabeth**
An evergreen small shrub with double flowers of white and red. Very popular.

Azalea indica
cv. **Californian Pink Dawn**
This small evergreen shrub is a popular new cultivar. The pale pink flowers are double.

AZALEA (cont)

Azalea indica cv. **Carnival Music**
A small bushy evergreen shrub with single violet-cerise coloured flowers.

Azalea indica cv. **Carnival Time**
The single flowers on this small evergreen shrub are large, and deep cerise-purple in colour.

Azalea indica cv. **Comptesse de Kerchove**
A small evergreen shrub with double ruffled salmon-pink flowers.

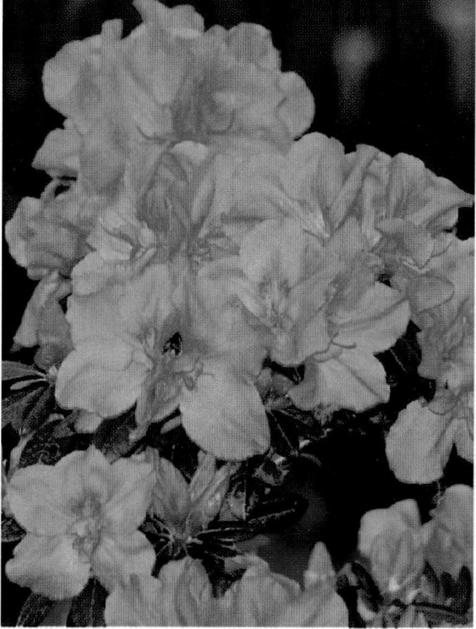

Azalea indica cv. **Concinna**
Large heads of bright pink flowers bloom on this evergreen shrub.

Azalea indica cv. **Dr Arnold Endtz**
An evergreen shrub with single rose-pink flowers.

Azalea indica cv. **Dr Bergman**
The flowers are carmine with shell pink markings on this small evergreen shrub.

Azalea indica cv. **Dr Koster**
A small evergreen shrub with red semi-double flowers.

Azalea indica cv. **Empress of India**
On this small evergreen shrub, the flowers are rose-pink, edged white, with a darker centre.

Azalea indica cv. **Exquisite**
One of the older cultivars, this medium evergreen shrub has shell pink single flowers with a cerise centre.

AZALEA (cont)

Azalea indica cv. **Exquisite Variegata**
A variegated cultivar of this pink flowered Azalea.

Azalea indica cv. **Little Girl**
A small evergreen shrub which has large hose-in-hose pale pink flowers.

Azalea indica cv. **Gretel**
A small evergreen shrub which has double white flowers with cerise markings.

Azalea indica cv. **Lavender Rosina**
The semi-double flowers are coloured lavender-violet on this small evergreen shrub.

Azalea indica cv. **Lucille K.**
The reddish flowers of this small evergreen shrub have a faint white edge.

Azalea indica cv. **Inga Vogel**
A small very free flowering shrub. The flowers are rose-pink edged white.

Azalea indica cv. **Leopold Astrid**
A popular old evergreen Azalea which has white flowers edged red.

AZALEA (cont)

Azalea indica cv. **Madame Auguste Hareans**
This small evergreen shrub has double flowers coloured rose-pink with white markings.

Azalea indica cv. **Magnifica**
A medium to tall evergreen shrub with single purple-violet flowers. An old favourite.

Azalea indica cv. **Mortii**
A strong growing evergreen shrub with large single white flowers.

Azalea indica cv. **Moulin Rouge**
A small evergreen shrub with semi-double orange-red flowers.

Azalea indica cv. **My Fair Lady**
A small evergreen shrub with large double flowers coloured rose-pink and edged white.

Azalea indica cv. **Peter's Pet**
On this small evergreen shrub, the rose-pink double flowers have a pale pink centre.

Azalea indica cv. **Pink Dream**
A small evergreen shrub with large shell-pink single flowers.

Azalea indica cv. **Pink Lace**
The pale pink flowers have rose-pink centres on this small evergreen shrub.

Azalea indica cv. **President Oswald de Kerchove**
A small evergreen shrub which has double salmon-pink flowers with touches of white.

AZALEA (cont)

Azalea indica cv. **Rosa Belton**
On this small evergreen shrub the large single flowers are white in the centre and deep mauve on the outer flower.

Azalea indica cv. **Royal Show**
A small evergreen shrub with double salmon-pink flowers.

Azalea indica cv. **Saidee Kirk**
The flowers on this small evergreen shrub are double, and shell-pink.

Azalea indica cv. **Southern Aurora**
A small evergreen shrub with double flowers which are red with white blotches on the outer part of the petal.

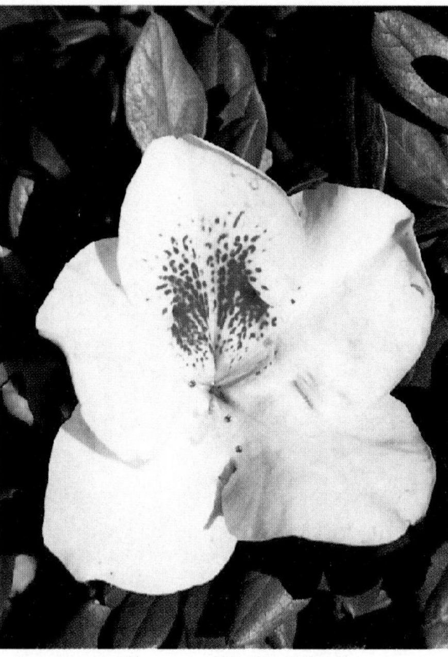

Azalea indica cv. **Stella Maris**
A small to medium evergreen shrub with large white flowers and cerise inner markings.

Azalea indica cv. **Strawberry Blonde**
On this small evergreen shrub the double pink flowers have cerise flecks throughout the petals.

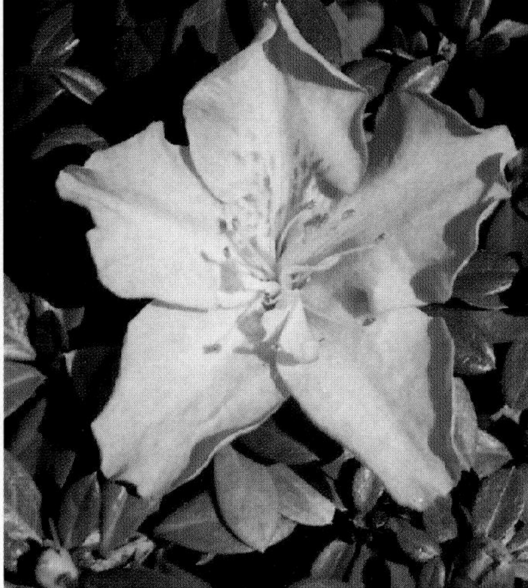

Azalea indica cv. **Thelma Bray**
A small evergreen shrub with single to semi-double flowers which are rosy mauve in colour.

Azalea indica cv. **Thredbo**
This small evergreen shrub has off white semi-double flowers flecked with pink.

Azalea indica cv. **Violacea**
A small open evergreen shrub with double flowers of violet-purple. An old favourite.

AZALEA (cont)

Azalea indica cv. **Wonder Girl**
A small evergreen shrub with silvery pink hose-in-hose flowers.

Azalea x **Kerrigan** cv. **Brides Bouquet**
Small and evergreen, this shrub has formal, white double, gardenia-like flowers.

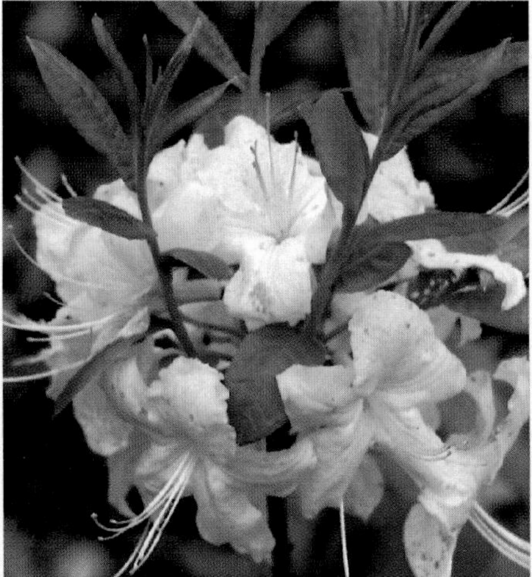

Azalea x **Knap Hill** cv. **Anneke**
A deciduous shrub with heads of golden flowers.

Azalea x **Knap Hill** cv. **Apricot**
A small deciduous shrub with single apricot coloured flowers.

Azalea x **Knap Hill** cv. **Double Damask**
This deciduous shrub has heads of cream flowers with yellow throats.

Azalea x **Knap Hill** cv. **George Reynolds**
Large heads of golden flowers feature on this deciduous shrub.

Azalea x **Knap Hill** cv. **Frilled Apricot**
A small deciduous shrub with deep apricot-pink single flowers.

AZALEA (cont)

***Azalea* x Knap Hill cv. Homebush**
A small deciduous shrub with semi-double pink flowers.

***Azalea* x Knap Hill cv. Honeysuckle**
The white flowers have yellow centres and marks on this medium deciduous shrub.

***Azalea* x Knap Hill cv. Ken's Yellow**
This medium deciduous shrub has pale yellow single flowers.

***Azalea* x Knap Hill cv. Golden Eagle**
Free flowering, this open deciduous shrub has heads of orange and bright red flowers.

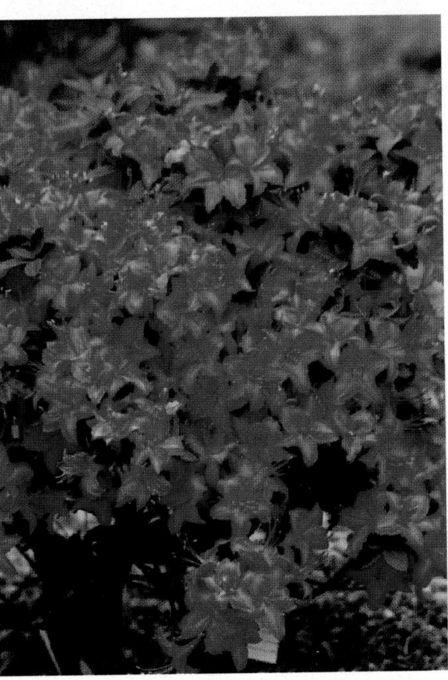

***Azalea* x Knap Hill cv. Lady Rosebery**
A very free flowering deciduous shrub with large heads of orange-red flowers.

***Azalea* x Knap Hill cv. Hiawatha**
A small deciduous shrub with orange-red single flowers.

***Azalea* x Knap Hill cv. O'Dorothy**
A small deciduous shrub with deep salmon-pink single flowers.

Azalea **x Knap Hill** cv. **Persil**
A free flowering deciduous shrub with large heads of white flowers with yellow markings.

Azalea **x Kurume** cv. **Betty Cuthbert**
On this small evergreen shrub the hose-in-hose flowers are pale pink.

Azalea **x Kurume** cv. **Consul of Japan**
A small evergreen shrub with rose-pink hose-in-hose flowers.

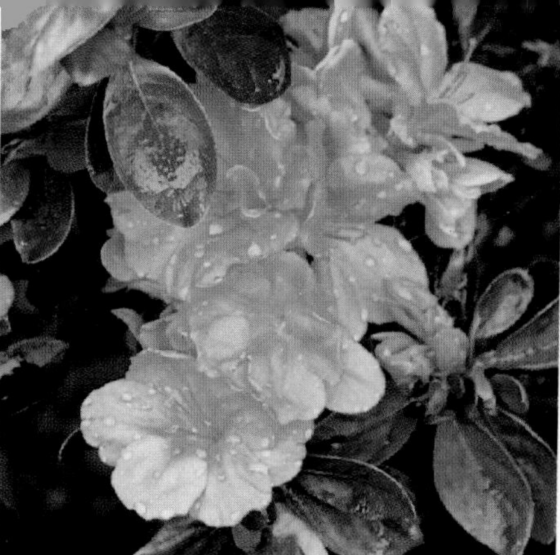

Azalea **x Kurume** cv. **Drummer Boy**
This small evergreen shrub has single lilac-pink flowers.

Azalea **x Kurume** cv. **Elizabeth Belton**
A small evergreen shrub with rose-pink hose-in-hose semi-double flowers with cerise inner markings.

Azalea **x Kurume** cv. **Evening Mist**
The single flowers on this small evergreen shrub are rose-pink and have paler pink centres.

Azalea **x Kurume** cv. **Hatsugiri**
A small evergreen shrub with semi-double hose-in-hose cerise coloured flowers.

Azalea **x Kurume** cv. **Hexe**
A small evergreen shrub with hose-in-hose semi-double dark cerise-red flowers.

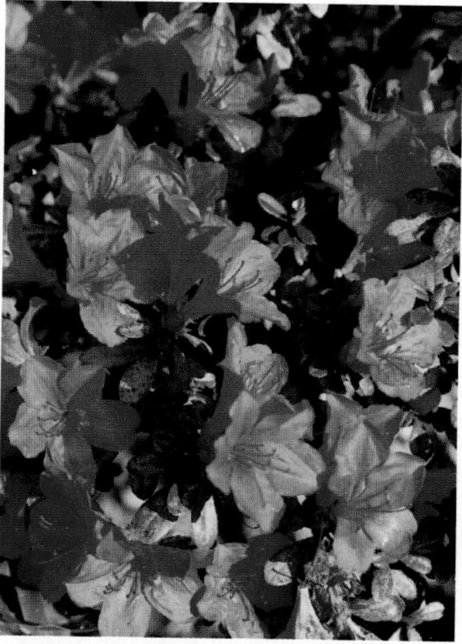

Azalea **x Kurume** cv. **Hinodegiri**
Single reddish coloured flowers bloom on this small evergreen shrub.

AZALEA (cont)

Azalea **x Kurume cv. Kirin**
A small evergreen shrub with small dainty hose-in-hose semi-double pale salmon-pink flowers.

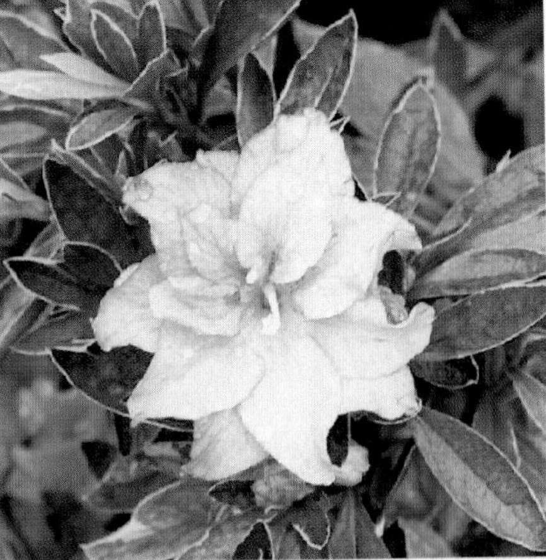

Azalea **x Kurume cv. Rose Queen Variegata**
A variegated foliage form of *A. kurume* x cv. Rose Queen.

Azalea **x Kurume cv. Kuno-no-uye**
A small evergreen shrub with single deep salmon flowers marked inside with deep cerise.

Azalea **x Kurume cv. Mrs Kint**
A small evergreen shrub with rose-pink hose-in-hose flowers.

Azalea **x Mollis cv. Gibralta**
A small deciduous shrub with deep orange coloured flowers in clusters.

Azalea **x Kurume cv. Little Gem**
The flowers on this small evergreen shrub are single and rose-pink.

Azalea **x Kurume cv. Rose Queen**
A small evergreen shrub with rose-pink hose-in-hose flowers.

Azalea **x Mollis cv. Hugo Koster**
In large clusters, the flowers of this small deciduous shrub are pale orange.

AZALEA (cont)

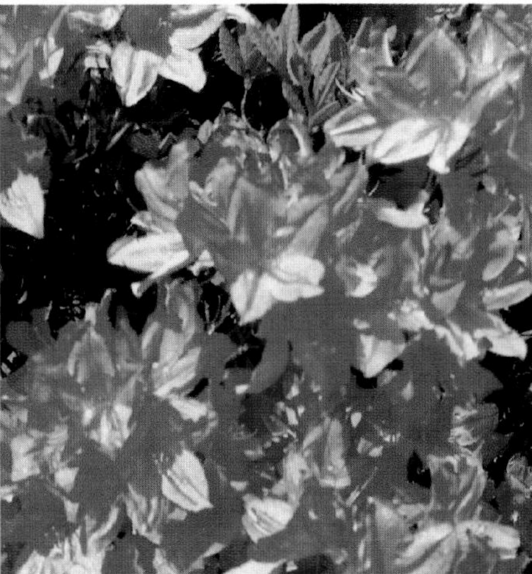

***Azalea* x Mollis cv. Koster's Brilliant Red**
A small deciduous shrub with very large clusters of orange-red flowers.

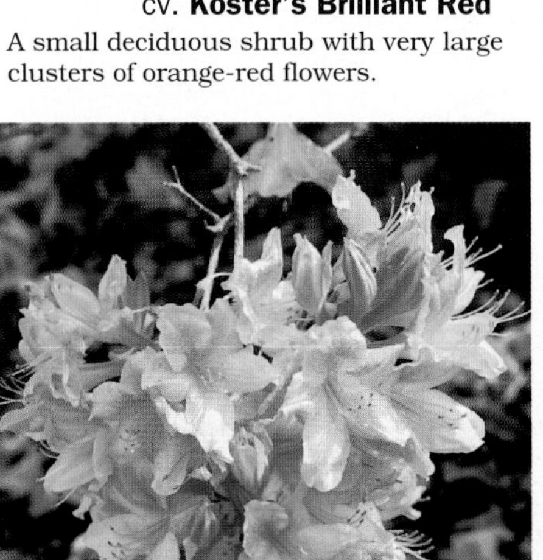

***Azalea* x Mollis cv. Linda Cuthill**
This small deciduous shrub has large clusters of old gold coloured flowers.

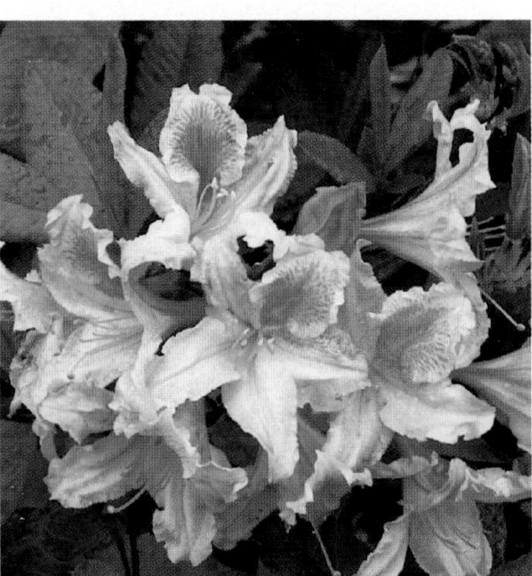

***Azalea* x Occidentale cv. Exquisita**
A small to medium deciduous shrub with large clusters of fragrant pink flowers marked yellow.

***Azalea* x Occidentale cv. Irene Koster**
A small deciduous shrub. The flowers are pale pink with a yellow blotch.

***Azalea* x Occidentale cv. Westminster**
In spring, this deciduous open shrub has large heads of pink flowers.

***Azalea* x Rustica Flore Pleno cv. Phebe**
A small deciduous shrub with clusters of creamy yellow double flowers.

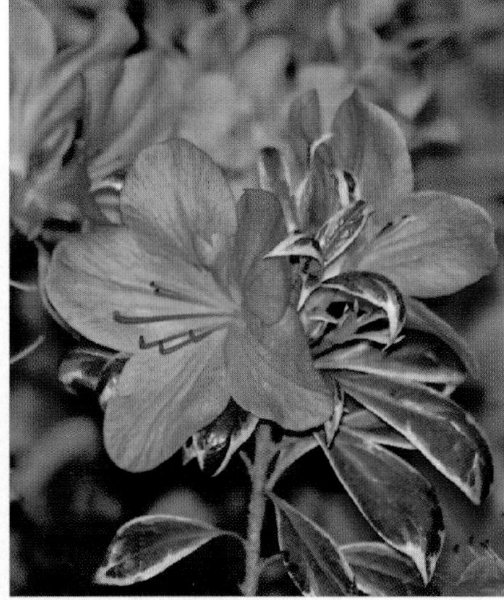

***Azalea* cv. Salmon's Leap**
A bushy shrub with green and cream variegated leaves and large deep pink flowers.

***Azalea* cv. The Teacher**
A small evergreen shrub with large semi-double flowers of bright rose-pink marked with pink. A hybrid of undetermined origin.

***Azalea* cv. Twilight**
This hybrid of undetermined origin is a small evergreen shrub which has orange-red single flowers.

AZALEA (cont)

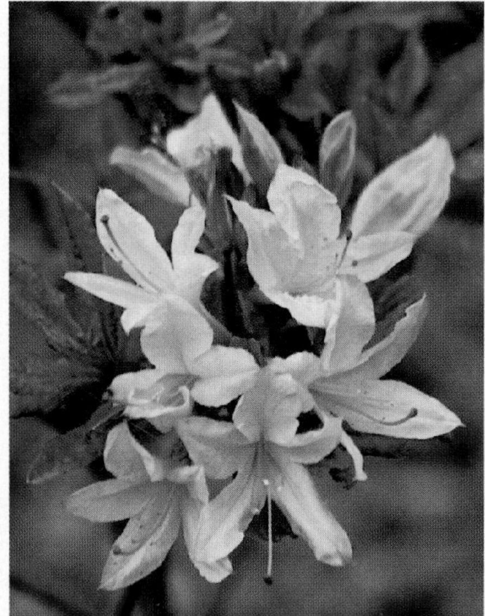

Azalea **x Viscosa** cv. **Arpege**

A deciduous shrub with heads of flowers coloured lemon and yellow.

Azalea x **Viscosa** cv. **Rosata**

In spring this deciduous shrub has heads of bright pink flowers.

Azalea x **Vuykiana** cv. **Rosyred**

VUYK'S ROSYRED

A hardy shrub with large heads of deep rose-pink flowers.

AZARA

FLACOURTIACEAE

Evergreen shrubs and small trees native of Chile. These hardy fragrant plants are grown as ornamentals in cold temperate climates. They grow best as an outer plant to taller trees and need a good soil which is moist for best results. Propagate from seed or cuttings.

Azara dentata

A medium to tall shrub with highly perfumed golden flowers in spring.

Azara lanceolata

A tall shrub with slender arching branches. The yellow flowers in spring are very fragrant.

Azara dentata cv. **Variegata**

This cultivar has cream and green variegated leaves, with touches of pink.

Azara serrata

A tall shrub to small tree with clusters of yellow flowers in spring. Leaves have a serrated edge. The flowers are fragrant.

Azara integrifolia

Flowering in late winter, this tree has golden ball shaped flowers in profusion.

BACKHOUSIA

Myrtaceae

These shrubs and small trees are native to the rainforest areas of Australia and some are widely grown throughout the world as ornamentals and for production of essential oils. They need a well drained humus-rich soil for best results and grow better in some dappled shade. Slow release fertiliser is beneficial as the plants are slow growing early in their life. The plants grow in climates from cool temperate to tropical, but dislike heavy frosts when small. In milder climates some forms are used as small street trees. Propagation is usually from seed. When grown from cuttings they are very slow and difficult to strike.

Backhousia citriodora

LEMON SCENTED MYRTLE

This evergreen upright plant is a tall shrub to small tree and is an outstanding feature tree. A well grown plant may be completely covered with the cream coloured perfumed flowers. The dense shiny leaves produce an aromatic oil with a citrus-like smell.

Backhousia myrtifolia

A tall shrub or small tree with dense shiny foliage. In spring, this attractive plant is covered with creamy white flowers followed by creamy star shaped calyces. It makes an attractive plant in a garden and is quite cold tolerant once established. The foliage is used by florists for decoration.

BAECKEA

Myrtaceae

Small open crowned shrubs to small trees mostly with pendulous branches, usually with small leaves. Many are grown as understorey plants and are generally hardy. Baeckeas are now popular as cultivated plants as most are very hardy and will grow in poor and sandy soils. They benefit from annual pruning and slow release fertiliser. They may be grown from cuttings or seed which is very fine. Baeckeas grow in climates from temperate to tropical—native to Australia.

Baeckea camphorata CAMPHOR BUSH

An open spreading shrub with white star-type flowers. This plant is hardy in a wide range of soils. The leaves when crushed give off a camphor-like smell.

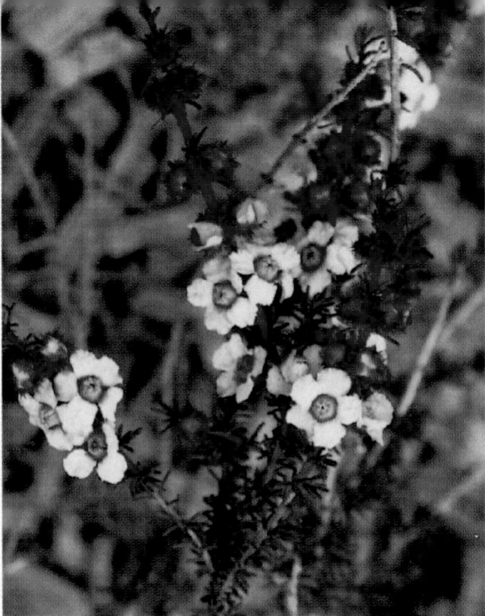

Baeckea muricata

Growing best in open, well drained soils, this open dwarf shrub has pointed small leaves and white flowers.

Baeckea virgata TWIGGY MYRTLE

A tall shrub to small tree which is widely grown as an ornamental. It is an open crowned plant with arching branches and masses of small white flowers in late spring.

Baeckea formosa syn. ***B.*** sp. **Mt Tozer**

A bushy shrub with small clusters of white flowers. This plant from tropical Cape York in Australia is a popular garden plant for warmer climates.

BAIKIAEA

CAESALPINIACEAE [LEGUMINOSAE]

Baikiaea insignis

A medium size spreading tropical tree native to Africa. It is fast growing and is cultivated in the wet tropics as an attractive flowering shade tree in parks or open areas. The flowers which are white and yellow are sometimes seen in long cascades. Propagate from seed.

BANKSIA

PROTEACEAE

These large flowered plants are compact shrubs to small trees. They are native to Australia and are regarded as being among Australia's outstanding horticultural plants. Banksias are grown for their displays of colourful flowers used world wide as cut flowers, both fresh and dried. They grow in a diverse range of soil types and many grow in sandy areas close to the sea. Some are grown from cuttings but the most common method of propagation is from seed. Use only fertilisers containing no phosphorus.

Banksia aemula WALLUM BANKSIA

syn. ***B. serratifolia***

This tall coastal shrub has thick rough bark and serrated leaves. The large flowers are cream to pale yellow and followed by a large woody pod. They flower over many months and are grown in climates from cool temperate to sub-tropical.

Banksia ashbyi ASHBY'S BANKSIA

A tall shrub with long deeply serrated leaves. The large long lasting flowers vary from orange to old gold in colour. A good cut flower.

Banksia baueri POSSUM BANKSIA

A medium compact shrub with large serrated leaves. The large woolly flowers vary from lemon to orange-silver in colour. This is a very hardy plant which grows in a wide range of soils and it makes a good ornamental shrub.

Banksia burdettii BURDETT'S BANKSIA

A compact tall hardy shrub. The large flowers which are acorn shaped are orange and silver in colour. This Banksia is widely cultivated for the production of cut flowers.

Banksia candolleana

The round flowers are old gold to orange in colour on this small shrub, which has long serrated leaves.

***Banksia* cv. Ellisonii**

A medium growing broad leaf shrub which appears to be a natural hybrid between *B. integrifolia* and *B. paludosa*. It grows in sandy soils close to the sea. The flowers are quite long and are yellow and brown in colour. Discovered by and named after the author.

Banksia ericifolia* var. *macrantha

A larger flowered form of this free flowering Banksia.

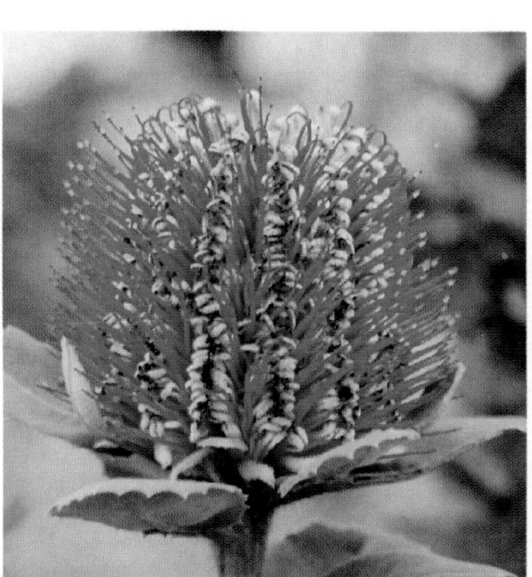

Banksia coccinea SCARLET BANKSIA

A sparse many branched shrub with attractive red and silver flowers. An excellent cut flower plant.

Banksia ericifolia HEATH BANKSIA

A small leaf medium to tall shrub which generally grows in heath lands. It also can be found near the sea. The long orange flowers are borne in profusion over many months.

Banksia elderana

This is a sparse upright shrub with long serrated leaves. The heads are yellow and are often used in cut flower arrangements.

***Banksia ericifolia* cv. Stumpy**

A low compact growing form with much shorter and deeper coloured flowers.

BANKSIA (cont)

Banksia grandis BULL BANKSIA

Large serrated leaves with creamy yellow flower heads grow on this small, corky-barked tree. The seed cones are used by wood turners and for craft work.

Banksia laricina ROSE FRUITED BANKSIA

A small shrub with long thin foliage. The roundish flowers are yellow with brown markings. The seed pods are used in dried arrangements.

Banksia hookerana ACORN BANKSIA

A many branched medium shrub with long serrated leaves. The acorn shaped flowers are orange when fully opened and silver-white in bud. It makes a good cut flower.

Banksia integrifolia COAST BANKSIA

A small open tree with yellow flowers. This tree grows in coastal areas in sandy soils and is salt tolerant. There is also an inland mountain form of this Banksia which will withstand 10 degrees of frost. It also has a tropical form.

Banksia lemanniana

A compact medium shrub with prickles on the rusty looking leaves. The flower heads, which may hang down, are a yellowish green.

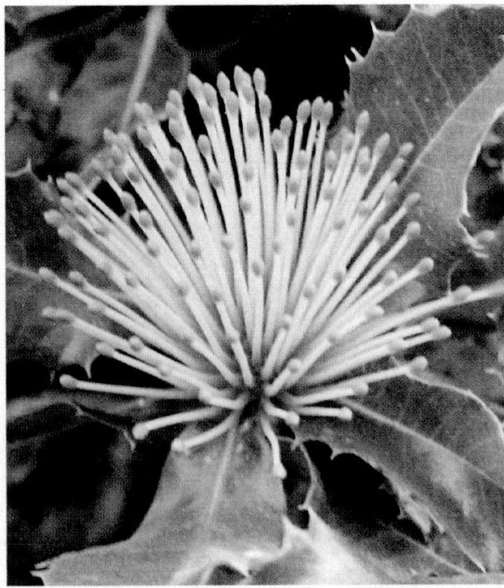

Banksia ilicifolia

HOLLY LEAVED BANKSIA

A tall clumping shrub with large holly-like leaves. The roundish flowers are creamy yellow and green in colour.

Banksia integrifolia* var. *aquilonia

This form grows more densely and has much larger leaves than *B. integrifolia.*

Banksia lindleyana

PORCUPINE BANKSIA

A sparse medium shrub with long narrow leaves. The oblong flower heads are yellow. It grows well in sandy soils.

Banksia littoralis SWAMP BANKSIA

A tall shrub with long narrow leaves. The oblong flower heads are gold in colour.

Banksia oblongifolia

syn. ***B. asplenifolia***

A variable medium shrub with long broad leaves which are rusty grey underneath. The cylindrical flower heads vary from creamish green to yellow in colour. It grows in both sandy and peat-like soils.

Banksia marginata SILVER BANKSIA

A variable tall shrub to small tree. It gets its common name from the silver under the leaves. Flower heads are oblong and yellow in colour. It is tolerant of frosts to at least 6 degrees.

Banksia meisneri MEISNER'S BANKSIA

A small fine leaf shrub with globular flowers which are yellow with an orange-brown centre.

Banksia occidentalis

RED SWAMP BANKSIA

A medium to tall shrub with long leaves which are greyish underneath. The cylindrical flower heads are cream inside and red outside. It grows well in swampy areas with heavy soils.

Banksia media GOLDEN STALK

A medium spreading shrub with serrated leaves. It has cylindrical flowers of old gold to orange in colour and is a hardy plant which will tolerate some salt spray.

Banksia menziesii FIREWOOD BANKSIA

This is a tall shrub with rough bark and large leaves. The acorn shaped flower heads are silver when young then red and gold at maturity.

Banksia oreophila MOUNTAIN BANKSIA

An erect shrub with large leaves. The flowers are silverish when opening, fading to brown. It grows best in a well drained soil.

BANKSIA (cont)

Banksia ornata

A compact shrub which grows in semi-arid sandy situations.

Banksia prionotes [11] ACORN BANKSIA

An open crowned tall shrub with long serrated leaves which grows in sandy soils and is tolerant of light frosts. The very attractive acorn shaped flowers are white when young and open from the bottom to be yellow all over. It is an outstanding commercial cut flower.

Banksia petiolaris

The flowers on this low spreading shrub are of a large cone to cylindrical shape and are cream to yellow in colour.

Banksia quercifolia OAK-LEAVED BANKSIA

An upright medium shrub with large deeply toothed leaves. The cylindrical flower heads are grey when young and orange-brown when mature.

Banksia praemorsa CUT-LEAF BANKSIA

A medium to small dense shrub with blunt prickly leaves. The cylindrical flower heads vary from creamy yellow to old gold, orange and at times red in colour. It is an ideal ornamental in an exposed windy and frost free garden.

Banksia repens CREEPING BANKSIA

Ideal when a prostrate plant is needed, this dwarf horizontal shrub has deeply toothed leaves. The cone shaped flower heads are reddish brown in colour.

Banksia robur SWAMP BANKSIA

An open crowned shrub which has large rough edged leaves. The flowers vary from bright lime-green when young to yellowish brown when mature.

BANKSIA (cont)

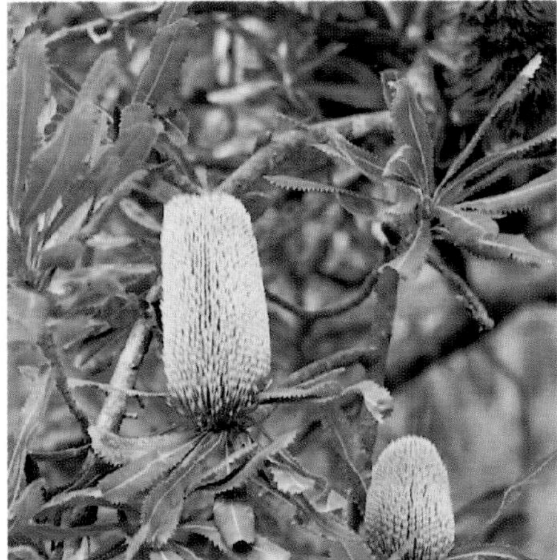

Banksia serrata SAW BANKSIA

A small open tree with grey corky bark and large serrated leaves. The large cylindrical flower heads are silver-grey in colour. It is an ideal tree to grow in sandy seaside situations.

***Banksia spinulosa* cv. Nana**

A dwarf spreading compact shrub. The flowers are shorter and slightly less in diameter than *B. spinulosa* var. *spinulosa*. The flower colour is yellow-orange inside with deep brown outside.

Banksia sphaerocarpa ROUND FRUITED BANKSIA

A small shrub with long thin leaves. It has round flower heads of yellow fading to orange and has decorative seed pods.

Banksia spinulosa* var. *collina

A dense shrub with broader leaves than *B. spinulosa* var. *spinulosa*. The flowers are yellow with golden, or occasionally black, styles. A good garden ornamental which is free flowering.

Banksia spinulosa* var. *spinulosa HAIRPIN BANKSIA

An open shrub with narrow leaves. The orange cylindrical flower heads have styles which are almost black. It makes a good cut flower and is hardy in a wide range of soil types.

BARKLYA

CAESALPINIACEAE [LEGUMINOSAE]

Barklya syringifolia

A shiny leaf small tree with clusters of showy golden flowers. This is an outstanding specimen ornamental tree which grows in climates from mild temperate to tropical. Once established it will withstand some frost. Barklya is native to sub-tropical rainforests of Australia and is one of the outstanding flowering trees of the world. It is propagated from seed which needs hot water treatment as for Acacias.

BARLERIA

ACANTHACEAE

These plants from the old world tropics are mostly shrubs but may also be herbs. They are widely cultivated in climates from tropical to mild temperate and are also grown indoors. Barlerias prefer a slightly moist rich soil. Propagate from seed or softwood cuttings using mist.

Barleria lupulina

A small bushy and hardy shrub with small thorns. The erect flower heads have from 2 to 4 flowers open each morning.

Barleria albostellata

A dense compact shrub with large blue-green coloured leaves. The five petalled white flowers cover the plant in spring.

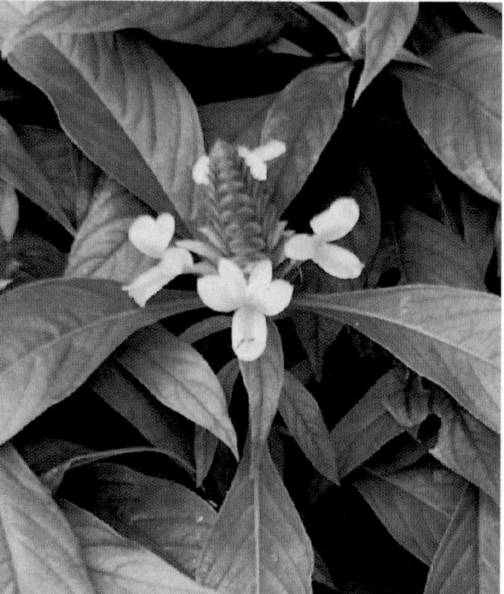

Barleria micans

A very dense multi-branched shrub with erect spikes of golden flowers in spring. It grows best in temperate and sub-tropical gardens.

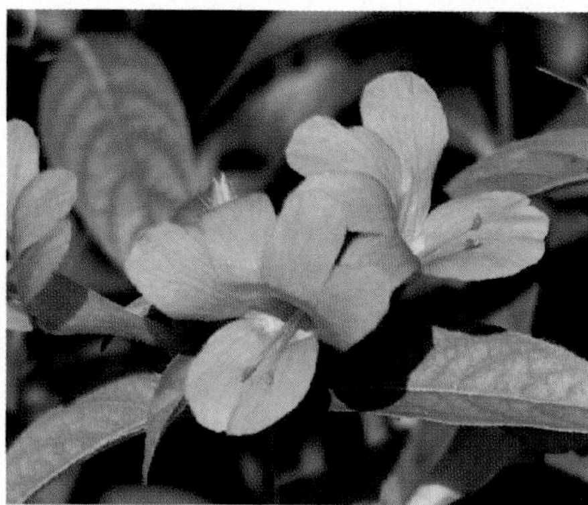

Barleria cristata PHILIPPINE VIOLET

A dense multi-branching and spreading small shrub with masses of dark mauve to violet coloured flowers in spring.

***Barleria cristata* cv. Rosea**

A cultivar with lilac-pink coloured flowers.

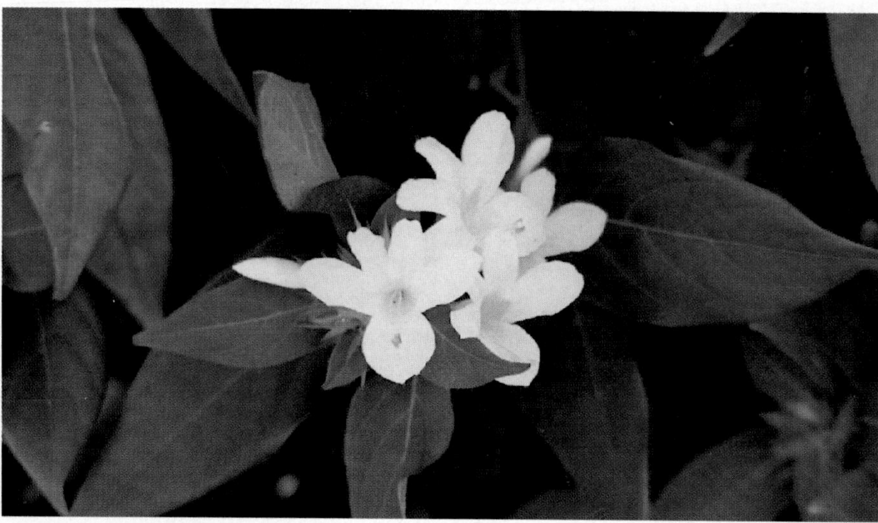

***Barleria cristata* cv. Alba** WHITE PHILIPPINE VIOLET

A multi-branching small shrub with white flowers.

Barleria obtusa PURPLE DAZZLER

A small clumping shrub with masses of purple flowers in spring and summer. It prefers a good rich soil and plenty of water in hot weather. Best suited to warm climates.

BARLERIA (cont)

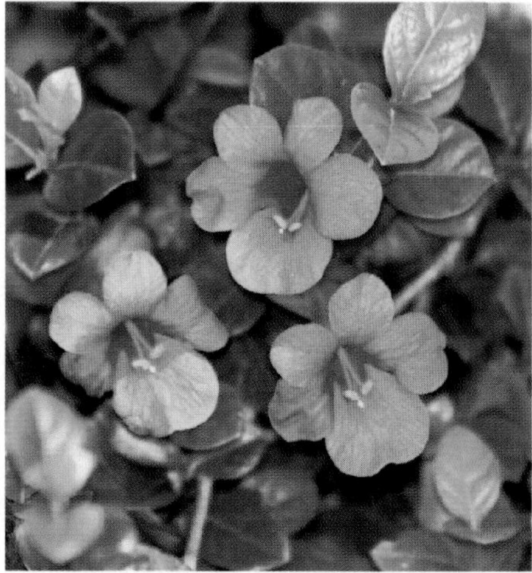

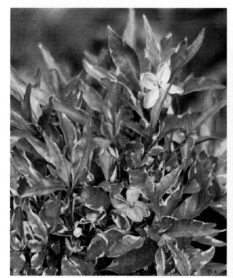

Barleria obtusa cv. **Variegata**

VARIEGATED PURPLE DAZZLER

A variegated form of this colourful plant. The foliage is coloured purple, white and green.

Barleria repens cv. **Orange Bugle**

This dwarf shrub spreads as a ground cover and has orange-red flowers in hot weather. It grows outdoors in sub-tropical to tropical climates.

Barleria strigosa

A free flowering bushy plant with clusters of mauve flowers in spring.

BARNADESIA

ASTERACEAE [COMPOSITAE]

Barnadesia caryophylla

syn. ***B. rosea***

This open branched tall shrub is native to tropical South America. It has masses of bright rose coloured flowers in spring. It is grown outdoors in sub-tropical and tropical gardens. Propagate from seed or cuttings.

BARRINGTONIA

LECYTHIDACEAE [BARRINGTONIACEAE]

Small evergreen bushy trees which grow along fresh water creeks, river banks and around lakes and swamps. They may be used for medicinal purposes and some are used to produce a fish stunning poison. Barringtonia are native to Asia, Australia, Africa and the Pacific. Many are grown as ornamental trees. Propagation is from seed.

Barringtonia acutangula INDIAN OAK

A small bushy tree found along fresh water creeks and rivers. The tree has weeping red flower chains. It is used by Australian Aboriginals to make a fish poison. The tree may lose its leaves in very hot dry weather and prefers a warm climate.

Barringtonia neocaledonica

A small tree which is grown for its highly colourful spring leaves. It will grow in a temperate climate, where it is the most colourful if protected from frosts. It does prefer to grow in sub-tropical and tropical areas.

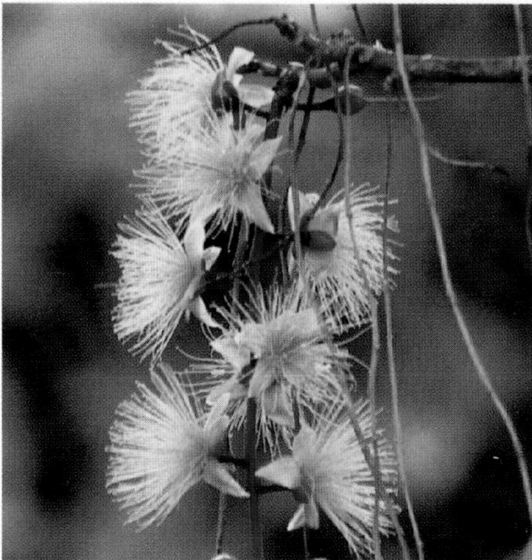

Barringtonia racemosa

A tall shrub with long racemes of flowers which may be white, red or pink.

BARTLETTINA

ASTERACEAE [COMPOSITAE]

Bartlettina sordida MIST FLOWER

syn. ***Eupatorium sordidum***

A multi-branching shrub from Mexico. It is a hardy plant in climates from cool temperate to tropical and has large heads of bluish mauve flowers. Cut back hard after flowering. Grow from seed and cuttings.

b

BAUERA

CUNONIACEAE [BAUERACEAE]

Bauera rubioides

A spreading low shrub from eastern Australia. This free flowering plant is covered with small bright rose-pink flowers in spring. It prefers a mild temperate to sub-tropical climate with plenty of moisture in hot weather. Propagate from seed or cuttings.

BAUHINIA

CAESALPINIACEAE [LEGUMINOSAE]

Evergreen shrubs, trees and vines from tropical and sub-tropical countries. They are generally free flowering and are widely grown as ornamentals in areas from mild temperate to tropical. Bauhinias benefit from annual hard pruning and will grow in a wide range of soils. Many are tolerant of light frosts. Annual fertilising after pruning is beneficial. They are propagated from seed which germinates very easily. The exception to this is *Bauhinia* x *blakeana* which is a sterile hybrid.

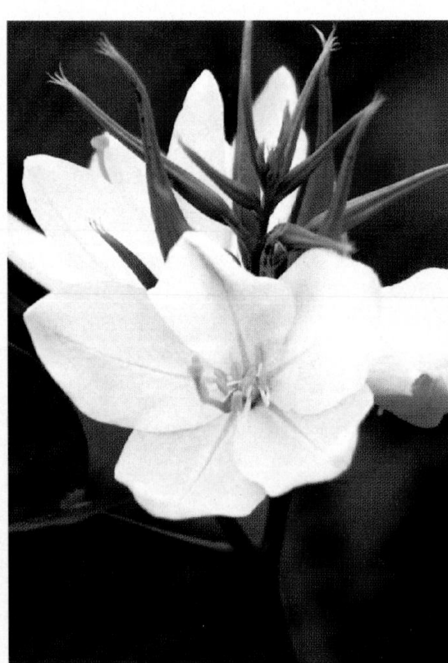

Bauhinia acuminata

DWARF WHITE BAUHINIA

A medium dense, much branched shrub. The pure white flowers open in clusters on the tips of the branches.

Bauhinia alba

Now referred to as *B. variegata*, this small tree has masses of pure white flowers covering the tree in spring. It varies from *B. variegata* cv. Candida which has a distinct green throat.

Bauhinia x ***blakeana***

HONG KONG ORCHID TREE

A small free flowering hybrid tree which is sterile. This very showy tree is covered with masses of purple flowers in spring. Propagation is from cuttings or by grafting.

Bauhinia bowkeri

The white flowers in this medium shrub have cerise stripes in the petals.

Bauhinia corniculata

A small evergreen tree which has masses of delicate white flowers in summer.

BAUHINIA (cont)

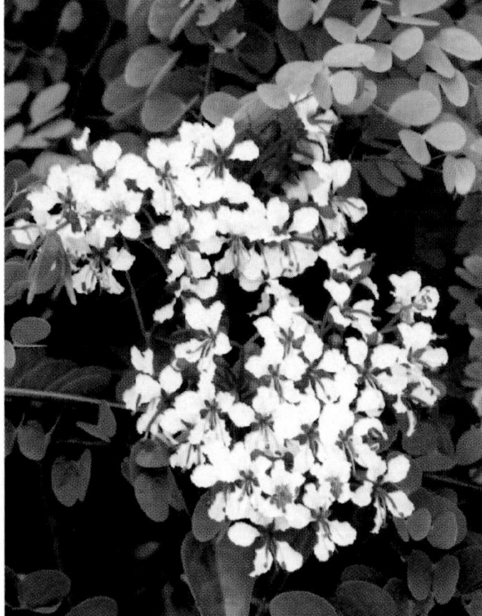

Bauhinia corymbosa

This evergreen semi-climber is widely used as a hedge or fence cover. It prefers sub-tropical to tropical climates. The flowers are pale pink and are borne in large clusters above the foliage. Often sold in the nursery trade as *B. scandens.*

Bauhinia divaricata cv. **Purpurea**

A purple flowered form of this plant. Flowering takes place over many months.

Bauhinia galpinii

syn. ***B. punctata***

A widely spreading tall shrub with large clusters of bright orange flowers in spring and summer. It grows in climates from mild temperate to tropical.

Bauhinia corymbosa cv. **Rosea**

This attractive form has rose-pink flowers.

Bauhinia galpinii cv. **Old Gold**

This cultivar has light amber coloured flowers.

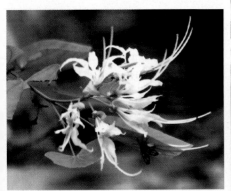

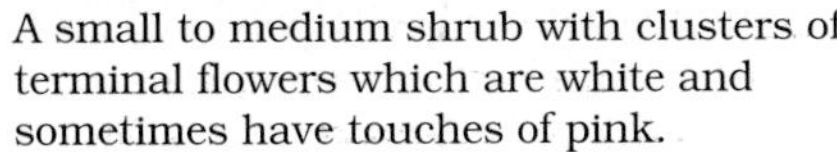

Bauhinia divaricata

A small to medium shrub with clusters of terminal flowers which are white and sometimes have touches of pink.

Bauhinia forficata

Clusters of white flowers bloom in summer on this erect small tree. It flowers at night and flowers are seen at their best in the morning.

BAUHINIA (cont)

Bauhinia galpinii cv. **Red Wings**
An orange-red flowered form of *B. galpinii.*

Bauhinia involucellata
Used as a ground or fence cover, this is an evergreen vine with heads of cream flowers.

Bauhinia glabra
This spreading semi-climber has heads of small flowers coloured pink with cerise markings.

Bauhinia kockiana
A tropical evergreen vine with large heads of bright orange flowers over many months. This plant prefers a rich moist soil.

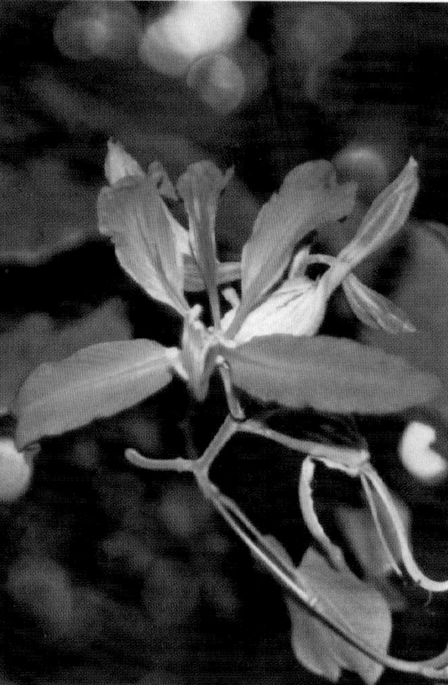

Bauhinia malabarica cv. **Rubra**
A purple-red flowered cultivar of this Bauhinia.

Bauhinia grandidieri
A spreading shrub with small leaves and delicate pale mauve flowers in spring. It has attractive new copper coloured foliage.

Bauhinia malabarica
A small spreading evergreen tree with pale lilac flowers in spring.

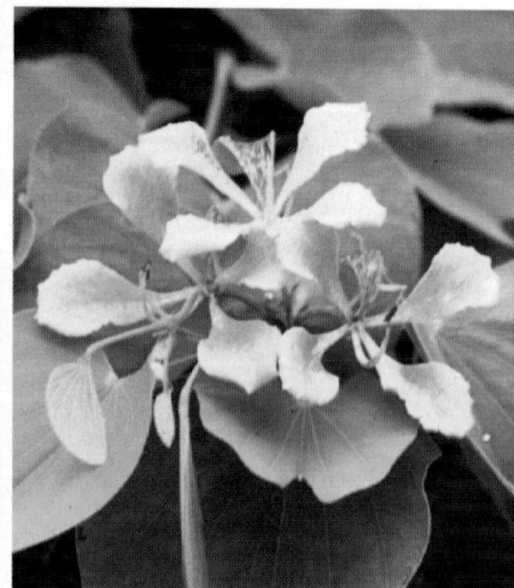

Bauhinia monandra BUTTERFLY FLOWER
Large terminal heads of bright pink flowers feature on this spreading small tree.

BAUHINIA (cont)

Bauhinia multinervia
A tall shrub with terminal heads of white flowers. Unopened buds are velvety brown.

Bauhinia tomentosa YELLOW BELLS
Sometimes grown as a showy hedge, this medium free flowering shrub has clusters of bright yellow bell-like flowers in spring and autumn.

***Bauhinia variegata* cv. Candida**
WHITE ORCHID TREE
This small free flowering tree has two tone white and green throated flowers in spring. The petals overlap. It is often confused with *B. alba* which has almost pure white flowers.

Bauhinia petersiana
A medium spreading shrub with white flowers and red stamens.

Bauhinia purpurea
PURPLE BUTTERFLY TREE
An outstanding small tree, covered with bright purple flowers in spring. Similar to *B. variegata*. Prune hard in autumn.

Bauhinia variegata ORCHID TREE
A small free flowering tree which is covered with two tone purple and mauve flowers in spring. Prune hard in autumn.

BEAUFORTIA

MYRTACEAE

Open spreading shrubs native to Western Australia in cool temperate to temperate climates. They grow in a wide range of soils from sandy to clays. Beaufortias have showy bottlebrush type flowers on their thin branches. Propagate from seed—this is quite fine.

Beaufortia decussata
A much-branched medium hardy shrub with red bottlebrush-like flowers.

BEAUFORTIA (cont)

Beaufortia heterophylla STIRLING RANGE BOTTLEBRUSH

A small spreading fine leaf shrub with dark red flowers which may only open on one side or completely encircle the branch on which they are displayed.

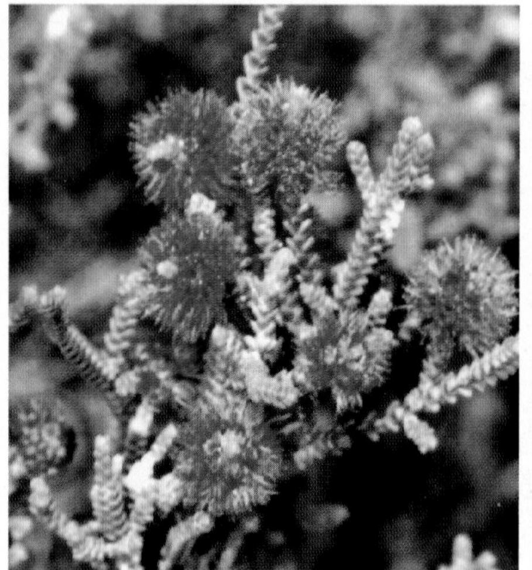

Beaufortia interstans

A small spreading shrub which is free flowering with flowers of cerise-maroon in colour.

Beaufortia sparsa GRAVEL BOTTLEBRUSH

An open upright medium shrub with flowers which are purple-pink to red and have a weeping habit.

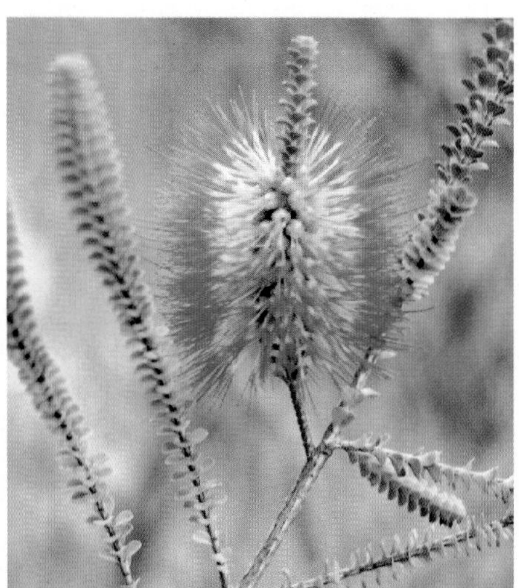

Beaufortia orbifolia

RAVENSTHORPE BOTTLEBRUSH

A medium open upright shrub with cylindrical bottlebrush flowers yellow inside, red outside.

Beaufortia squarrosa

SAND BOTTLEBRUSH

A small much branched shrub. The flowers are bright red. It grows well in sandy soils.

BEAUMONTIA

APOCYNACEAE

From Indonesia and India, these woody vines have large leaves and large white flowers. They are very showy when in full bloom and are regarded as among the most outstanding vines of the world. They prefer good soil, adequate water and a warm climate. Propagate from seed or cuttings.

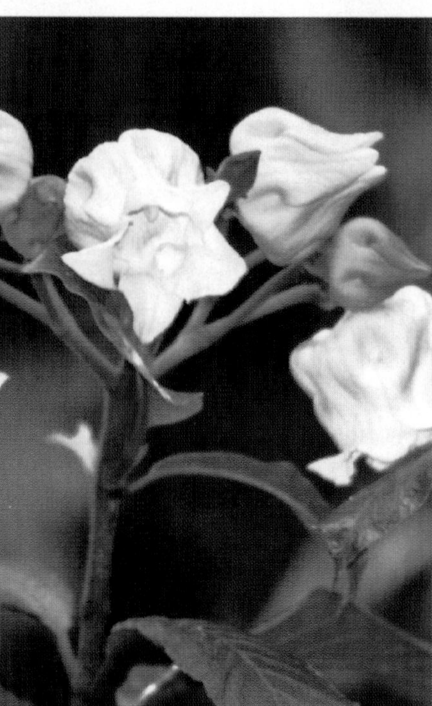

Beaumontia fragrans EASTER LILY VINE

A woody vine with terminal heads of perfumed white cup-like flowers. It requires a warm climate.

Beaumontia grandiflora

HERALD'S TRUMPET

A very large leaf vine which bears big trumpet-like white flowers in profusion in spring. This is an outstanding vine which can be grown in climates from warm temperate to tropical.

BERBERIS BARBERRY

BERBERIDACEAE

There are more than 500 species of Berberis, which are native of North and South America, Africa and Asia. Berberis are usually free flowering, either evergreen or deciduous shrubs with spines, and are grown as specimen shrubs or as hedges both for their clusters of flowers which are mostly yellow and for their colourful foliage. They grow in a wide range of soils and are quite hardy. Many of the deciduous Berberis are tolerant of heavy frosts. Propagate from seed and cuttings.

Berberis coxii
A sparse shrub with arching branches and pendulous yellow flowers.

Berberis edgeworthiana
This open shrub has weeping clusters of bright yellow flowers.

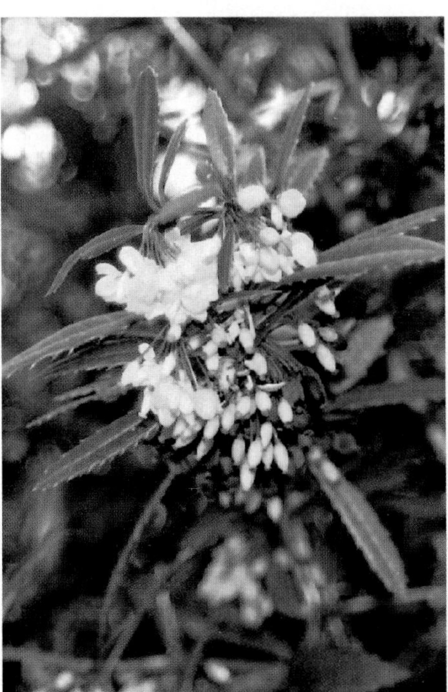

Berberis atrocarpa
An upright evergreen shrub with clusters of pale yellow flowers and long leaves.

Berberis darwinii
Free flowering and evergreen, this bushy shrub has large clusters of golden flowers and stumpy prickly leaves. A popular ornamental.

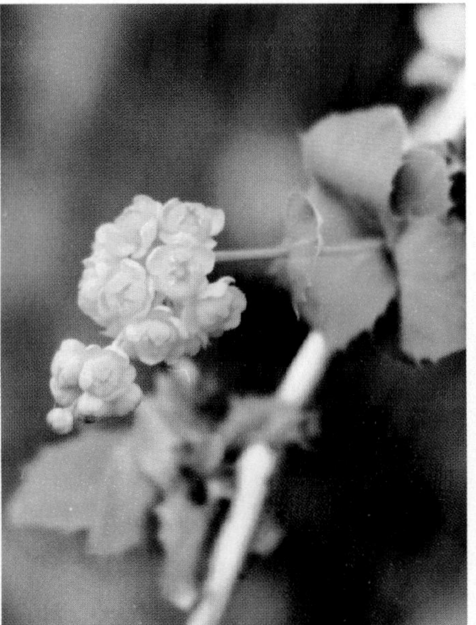

Berberis congestiflora
Round clusters of yellow flowers bloom on this sparse shrub.

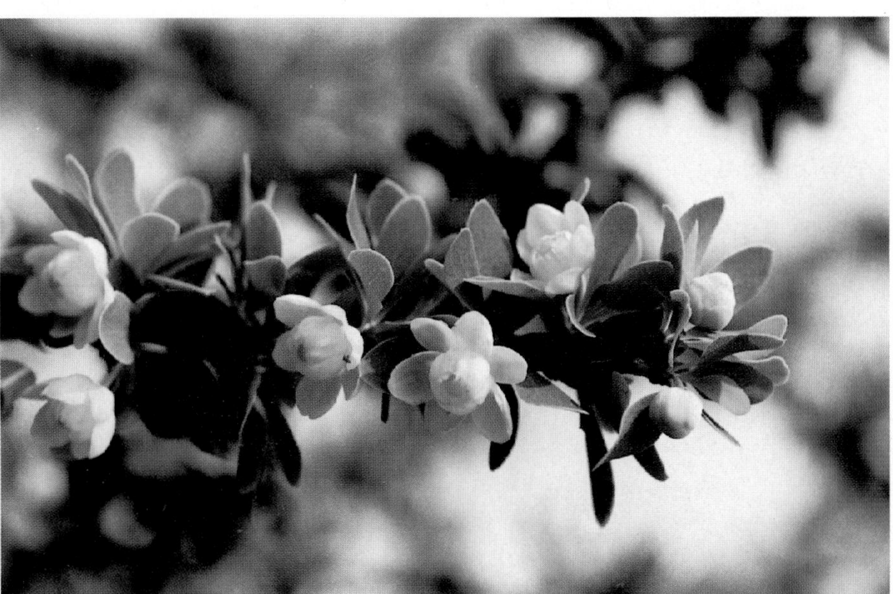

Berberis dictyophylla
Larger flowered, this is an open shrub with yellow flowers.

BERBERIS (cont)

Berberis gagnepainii var. ***lanceifolia***
An open shrub with arching branches. It has pendulous yellow flowers.

Berberis gagnepainii var. ***subovata***
Long thorns, blunt ended leaves and golden flowers feature on this open sparse shrub.

Berberis gracilis
A medium shrub with prickles. It has large clusters of cascading small yellow flowers. Now known as *Mahonia gracilis.*

Berberis hookeri
This is an evergreen shrub with long leaves and terminal clusters of yellow flowers in spring.

Berberis kawakamii
Small clusters of yellow flowers bloom on this sparse thorny shrub.

Berberis x ***hybrido-gagnepainii*** cv. **Chenault**
A sparse open shrub with arching branches which have long thorns and clusters of yellow flowers.

Berberis jamesiana
A sparse shrub with arching branches and pendulous clusters of golden coloured flowers.

Berberis koreana
Native to Korea, this upright shrub has pendulous bunches of yellow flowers.

BERBERIS (cont)

Berberis linearifolia
Free flowering, this open shrub has pendulous clusters of orange coloured flowers.

Berberis oblonga
This open shrub has blunt leaves and pendulous clusters of yellow flowers.

***Berberis* sp.**
This cultivar has small bunches of golden flowers in late winter. Known in the nursery trade as *B.* cv. Stapehill.

Berberis* x *lologensis
Bunches of golden coloured flowers circle the stems of this free flowering hybrid shrub.

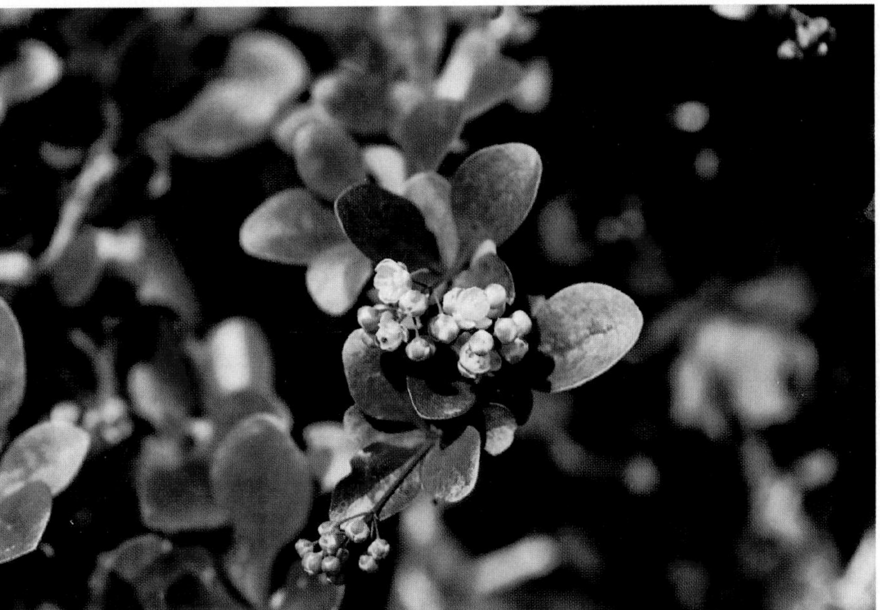

***Berberis* x *ottawensis* cv. Superba**
The arching branches on this sparse shrub have reddish leaves and yellow flowers.

Berberis lycium
An open crowned deciduous shrub with clusters of yellow flowers along the branches.

Berberis pruinosa
A small evergreen shrub with long serrated leaves and terminal clusters of yellow flowers.

BERBERIS (cont)

***Berberis* x *stenophylla* cv. Corallina**
In spring, this open, medium size shrub has masses of golden coloured flowers.

***Berberis thunbergii* cv. Atropurpurea**
A form with purple-brown foliage which is brightly coloured in autumn.

***Berberis thunbergii* cv. Golden Ring**
A cultivar which has golden coloured foliage.

***Berberis* x *stenophylla* cv. Corallina Compacta**
A small spreading evergreen shrub with masses of golden flowers in clusters during spring.

***Berberis thunbergii* cv. Kelleriis**
This cultivar has new leaves coloured silver, white and green.

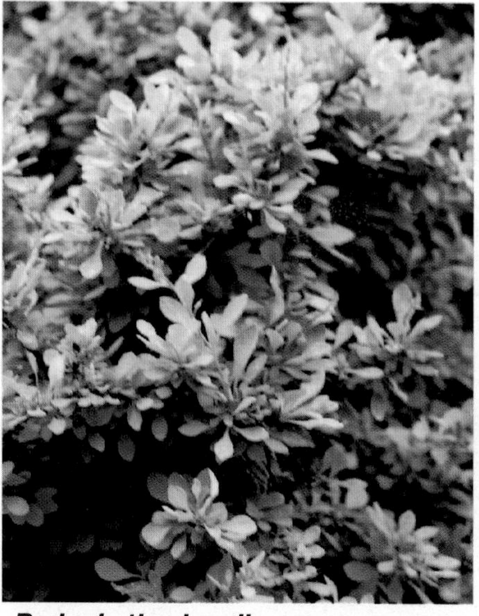

Berberis thunbergii JAPANESE BERBERIS
Dense and deciduous, this is a many branched spiny shrub. The flowers are yellow, and the foliage is highly coloured in autumn.

***Berberis thunbergii* cv. Atropurpurea Nana**
A compact spreading form of this popular shrub.

***Berberis thunbergii* cv. Rose Glow**
A colourful cultivar with new leaves being green, white and pink.

Berberis veitchii
A bushy shrub with thorns and clusters of yellow flowers.

Berberis verruculosa
An open shrub with arching branches and small yellow flowers.

***Berberis vulgaris* cv. Atropurpurea**
An upright thorny shrub with reddish leaves and clusters of yellow flowers.

Berberis vulgaris - fruit
Red fruit follow the yellow flowers which bloom in clusters on this open branched shrub.

BERRYA

TILIACEAE

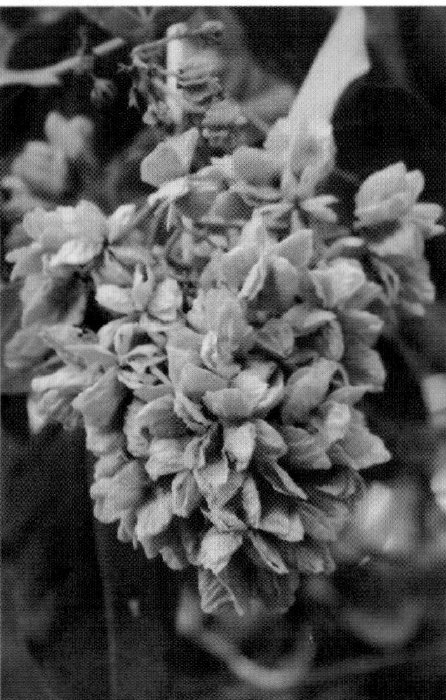

Berrya javanica
An evergreen tree from Java with large tight clusters of green flowers. Propagate from seed and grow in a warm temperate to tropical climates.

BERZELIA

BRUNIACEAE

Berzelia abrotanoides
This small shrub from South Africa has large clusters of white flowers. It is hardy, coming from cold temperate to sub-tropical climates. Grow from seed.

b

BETULA

BIRCH

BETULACEAE

Deciduous cold hardy trees from the northern hemisphere which are grown as ornamental or timber trees. Many are grown for their unusual bark or for their weeping branches. They grow in a wide range of soils. Propagate from seed which needs to be cold stratified. Grafting, layering and cuttings are also means of propagation.

Betula nigra BLACK BIRCH

Medium to tall, this deciduous tree is grown as an ornamental for its paper-like bark, which is illustrated.

Betula pendula SILVER BIRCH

syn. ***B. alba***

An attractive, ornamental, deciduous, medium tree with pendulous branches and silver-white bark.

Betula papyrifera CANOE BIRCH

An open crowned deciduous medium tree which is widely grown for its attractive white paper-like flaky bark.

Betula utilis

Native to the Himalayas, this medium deciduous tree has flaky bark.

BIGNONIA

BIGNONIACEAE

Widely grown, this temperate climate, free flowering, evergreen vine is from North America. Today only one species is recognised of the many different species earlier described as Bignonia, but which have subsequently been renamed.
In mild temperate to sub-tropical climates, the many outstanding cultivars of this plant give an outstanding floral display. Colours are mostly yellows, reds and oranges. The species is propagated from seed, and the cultivars from cuttings.

Bignonia capreolata CROSS VINE

syn. ***Campsis capreolata; Doxantha capreolata***

This evergreen climber has large bunches of trumpet-type flowers which are reddish in bud and open to yellow.

BILLARDIERA

PITTOSPORACEAE

These plants may be twining slender climbers or small shrubs and are free flowering plants native to Australia. They are quite hardy and grow in climates from alpine to tropical but mostly are found in temperate climates. Propagation is from seed and cuttings.

Billardiera erubescens RED BILLARDIERA

This slender evergreen vine is covered with clusters of red tubular flowers in spring. It is widely grown as a fence cover in climates from mild temperate to sub-tropical.

BILLARDIERA (cont)

Billardiera ringens

CHAPMAN RIVER CLIMBER

A slender, free flowering, evergreen climber. The clusters of tubular flowers are pale orange when young turning to orange-red with age.

BIXA

BIXACEAE

Bixa orellana LIPSTICK TREE

A tall shrub to small evergreen tree. It has clusters of bright pink flowers followed by spiky looking seed pods. Seed extracts are used as a dye by indigenous central American tribes. It is also used as a tasteless dye for food colourings especially in margarine. This plant makes an interesting ornamental in sub-tropical to tropical climates and is propagated from seed.

BLIGHIA

SAPINDACEAE

Blighia sapida AKEE

An evergreen small tree of tropical Africa. The tree has small white flowers followed by large orange-red fruit. Part of the fruit is edible when young but as the fruit becomes very ripe it becomes poisonous. It is a tropical to sub-tropical plant which is grown from seed.

BOLUSANTHUS

FABACEAE [LEGUMINOSAE]

Bolusanthus speciosus

TREE WISTERIA

A spectacular flowering, small, evergreen tree from Africa. The dark blue flowers cascade in long bunches like Wisteria flowers. It makes an outstanding feature ornamental tree and an excellent street tree. It is suited to climates from temperate to tropical. It is propagated from seed.

BOMAREA

LILIACEAE [ALSTROEMERIACEAE]

Bomareas are showy flowering climbers from South America. They are grown outdoors in cool temperate to tropical climates. In colder climates they are either grown indoors in conservatories or glass houses or grown outdoors only in spring and summer when frost danger has passed. Bomareas are very spectacular when in flower and are good modest climbers. They like a good mulch and plenty of moisture in summer. Many Bomareas will die off in cold weather and shoot again in spring. Propagate by root division or from seed.

Bomarea caldasii [1]

A slender climber with large showy heads of tubular orange coloured flowers in spring.

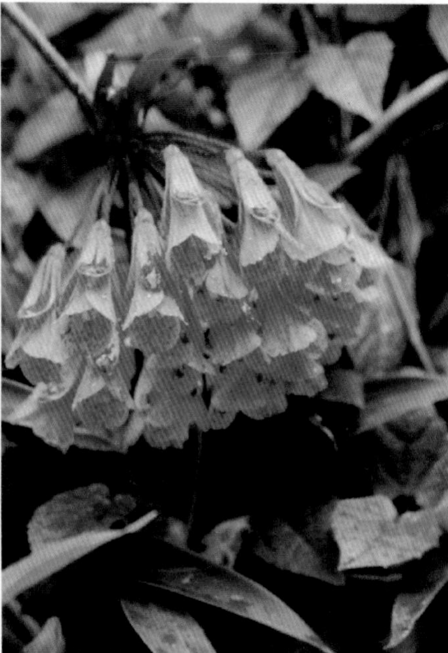

Bomarea multiflora

A very spectacular, free flowering climber with very large heads of tubular flowers which are orange and yellow in colour. Ideal for a trellis or fence.

BOMBAX

BOMBACACEAE

Small to medium palmate leaved deciduous trees from the tropical areas of Australia, Africa and Asia. They are free flowering and have large seed pods which are filled with silky down and seeds. These trees need a sub-tropical to tropical climate and plenty of water in hot weather. Propagate from seed.

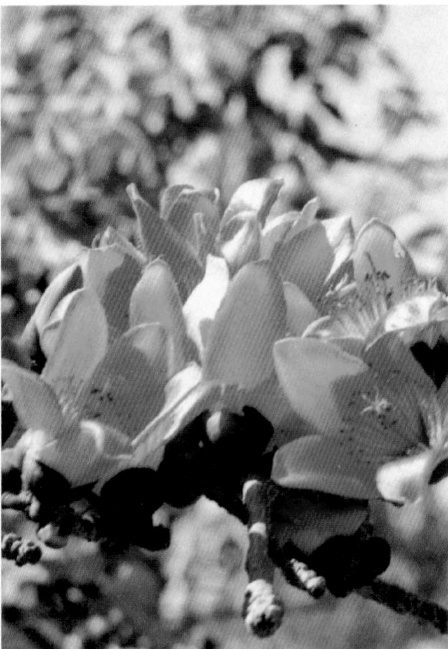

Bombax buonopozense

A medium spreading tree with many clusters of orange coloured cup-like flowers.

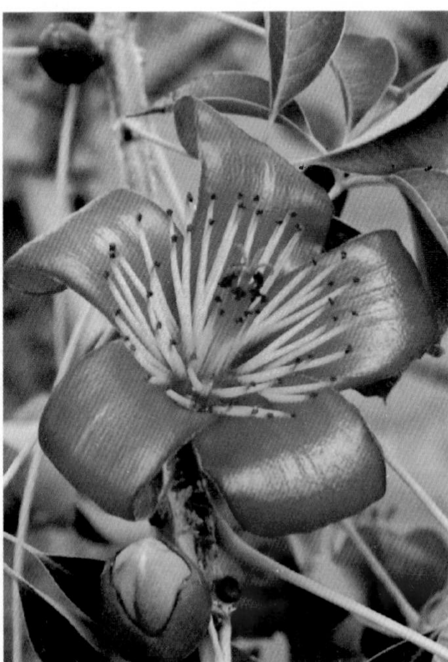

Bombax ceiba RED SILK COTTON TREE

syn. ***B. malabaricum; Salmalia malabarica***

A medium fast growing spreading tree which is covered with large red flowers mostly in bunches during spring.

BORONIA

RUTACEAE

Boronias are mostly small to medium, and occasionally tall, shrubs. They have dainty four petalled flowers and are highly perfumed. Boronias are native to Australia and their growing range is from alpine to tropical. They are widely grown as very showy ornamentals and as cut flowers. Many bloom in winter and bring premium prices as cut flowers. A range of new cultivars has been produced in the last 20 years and more can be expected in the near future. This very popular plant is grown from cuttings or seed which needs nicking or hot water treatment prior to sowing.

***Boronia* cv. Aussie Rose**

A sparse shrub with clusters of highly perfumed rose-pink flowers in spring. It grows in cold temperate to warm temperate climates.

Boronia crenulata

Free flowering and highly perfumed, this small shrub has clusters of rose-pink flowers. It prefers mild temperate to warm temperate climates.

Boronia deanei DEANE'S BORONIA

A sparse upright shrub with masses of rose-pink perfumed flowers in late spring. It is suited to mild temperate to warm temperate climates.

Boronia denticulata

Small and sparse, this shrub has clusters of rose-pink flowers in spring. Suitable for mild temperate to warm temperate climates.

Boronia floribunda PALE PINK BORONIA

A very free flowering, highly perfumed, dense small shrub. The pale pink flowers may totally cover the foliage when in full bloom. This is one of the very popular Boronias, and grows in climates from cool temperate to warm temperate.

Boronia fraseri FRASER'S BORONIA

Growing in cold temperate to warm temperate climates, this sparse, free flowering small shrub has rose-pink flowers.

Boronia heterophylla RED BORONIA

An upright open shrub with bell shaped pinkish red flowers along the stem. This is a widely grown Boronia in climates from cold temperate to warm temperate.

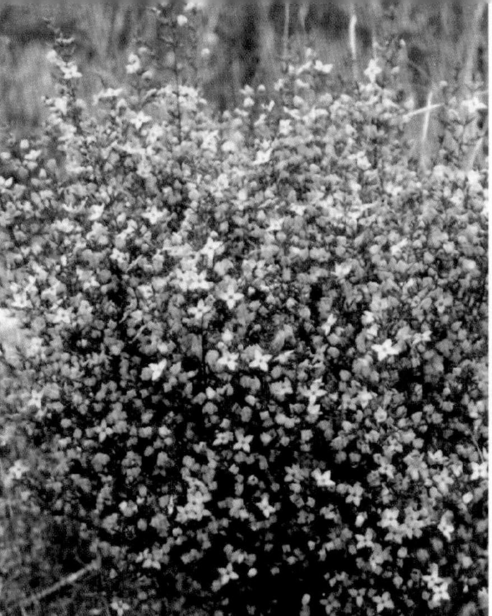

Boronia ledifolia LEDUM BORONIA

The flowers on this small sparse shrub are bright rose-pink. These flowers may totally cover the foliage. It has a very strong perfume and grows in climates from cold temperate to sub-tropical.

Boronia megastigma BROWN BORONIA

This open shrub has unusual cup shaped flowers coloured brown outside and gold inside. It has an excellent perfume and is grown both as an ornamental plant and as a cut flower for its fragrance. This shrub is very widely grown in climates from cold temperate to warm temperate and needs a well drained sandy soil with adequate watering in hot weather. There are many good cultivars of this Boronia.

Boronia megastigma CV. **Lutea**

A yellow flowered cultivar of this fragrant shrub.

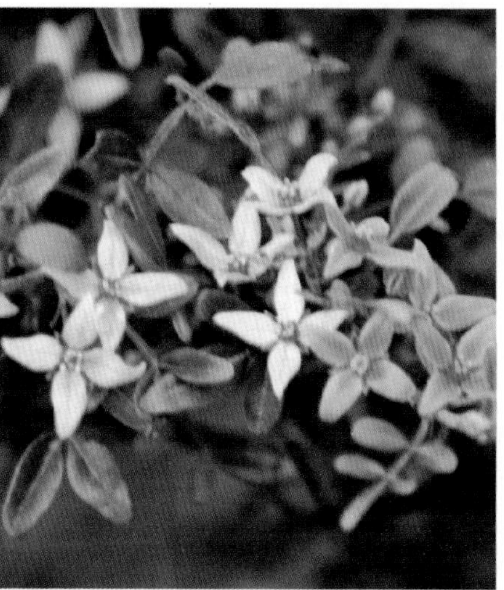

Boronia mollis

This is a small sparse shrub with rose-pink star-like flowers. It grows in climates from cold temperate to warm temperate.

Boronia muelleri FOREST BORONIA

A dense, free flowering, very fragrant shrub. This Boronia is a very popular ornamental shrub which grows in mild temperate to warm temperate climates.

BORONIA (cont)

Boronia muelleri **cv. Sunset Serenade**
A cultivar of this popular Boronia with more flowers which are paler than *B. muelleri.*

Boronia pinnata PINNATE BORONIA
A small to medium shrub with delicate pinnate leaves and highly perfumed bright pink flowers over many months from late winter to mid spring. This popular plant grows in climates from cool temperate to warm temperate.

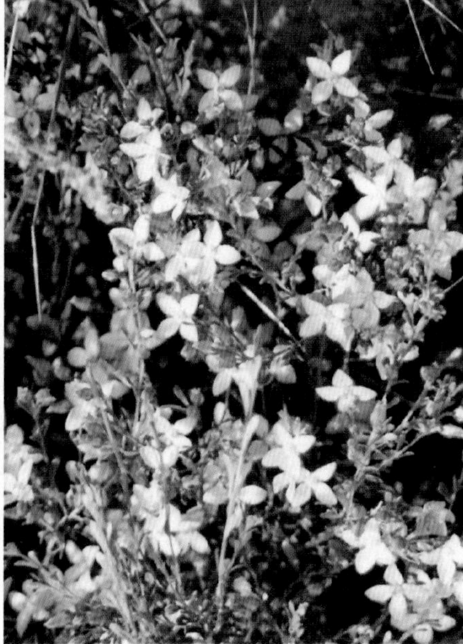

Boronia spathulata
Perfumed, pink flowers bloom on this sparse small shrub. Ornamental, this shrub is adaptable in climates from cold temperate to warm temperate.

Boronia pinnata **cv. Alba**
A rare white flowered cultivar of this shrub.

BOSEA

AMARANTHACEAE

Bosea amherstiana **cv. Variegata**
A medium to tall shrub which has green and cream variegated leaves, the new leaves being pink and cream. It is grown in climates from cool temperate to temperate as a coloured leaf ornamental and is propagated from cuttings.

BOSSIAEA

FABACEAE [LEGUMINOSAE]

Bossiaea ornata
A hardy dwarf shrub from Western Australia. This plant has yellow and orange pea shaped flowers in spring. It prefers a sandy loam in a temperate climate. Propagate from seed.

BOUGAINVILLEA

Nyctaginaceae

Bougainvilleas are mostly vigorous spiny vines but sometimes shrubs from South America. Some have become very popular outdoor ornamentals in climates from mild temperate to tropical with the most outstanding displays being seen in warmer climates. There has been much hybridisation of Bougainvilleas, and whilst most of those listed are of doubtful parentage, nearly all are bred from *B. glabra*, *B. peruviana* and *B. spectabilis*. They grow in a wide range of soils and need ample water in hot weather to promote growth. Those grown in drier and poorer soils seem to have a greater percentage of flower bracts to foliage. Bougainvilleas prefer to be pruned hard after flowering to promote a good display the next season. Flowering time varies depending on the cultivar but six months of flowering may be expected with a careful selection. Some may flower twice a year or more. They are also grown in pots where they flower freely and are restricted in size. Propagate from soft growth cuttings using a mist spray or hard wood cuttings in the winter.

Flower bracts stay on the vine for some months and it should be noted that the colour of each cultivar varies considerably and is influenced by whether it is grown in a poor soil or a soil high in humus and if grown in full sun, partial sun or shade. The colour also varies between new flower bracts and older flower bracts. Because of the wide range of countries producing new cultivars, names of these cultivars may vary from country to country. The colourful parts of the plants are called bracts and the small inner portion is the actual flower.

***Bougainvillea* cv. Apple Blossom**

A compact cultivar with bracts being white overlaid with pink.

***Bougainvillea* cv. Aiskrim**

This showy climber has bi-coloured bracts of pink and pale pink.

***Bougainvillea* cv. Alex Butchart**

A free flowering cultivar with dull red bracts.

***Bougainvillea* cv. Alba**

A cultivar with open bracts coloured white.

***Bougainvillea* cv. Ambience**

Free flowering, this cultivar has bright pink bracts.

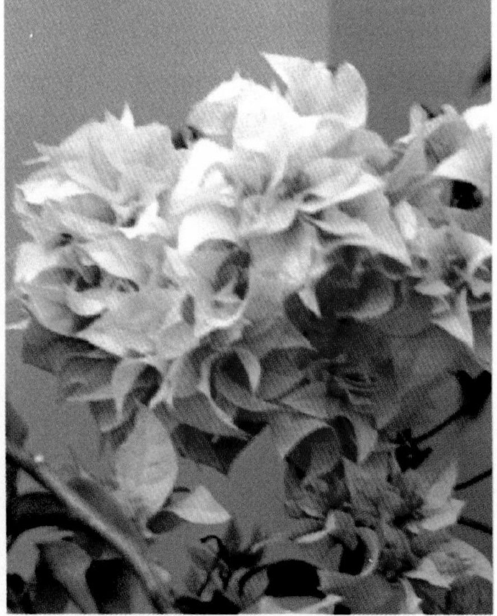

***Bougainvillea* cv. Aussie Gold**

syn. ***B.* cv. Goldie**

A compact form which has double bracts of old gold with touches of mauve.

b BOUGAINVILLEA (cont)

Bougainvillea cv. **Barbara Karst**
This cultivar is bright red in colour.

Bougainvillea cv. **Bois de Rose**
The bracts on this plant are rose-pink.

Bougainvillea cv. **Bua Sawan**
A smaller growing cultivar with rounded bracts coloured orange.

Bougainvillea cv. **Camarillo Fiesta**
A form with very variable colours. This illustration is from a plant grown in shade. The plant would be more old gold in full sun.

Bougainvillea cv. **Champagne**
This new cultivar raised by Russ Higginbotham is suitable for pots or outdoors. Bracts are pink to old gold. Now called *B.* cv. Mischief.

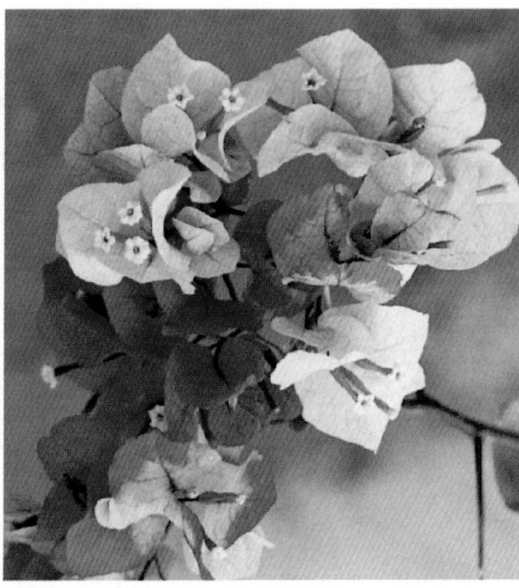

Bougainvillea cv. **Chitra**
A spreading climber with large heads of bracts coloured white, mauve and redish-purple in varying combinations.

Bougainvillea cv. **Brilliance**
A showy cultivar with bracts opening bright orange-pink then turning bright red.

Bougainvillea cv. **Coconut Ice**
A more modest grower having green and white variegated foliage with redish-purple and white bracts. A good pot form.

Bougainvillea cv. **Crimson Jewel**
A cultivar with reddish purple bracts.

Bougainvillea cv. **Elizabeth Angus**
A climber which has large bunches of bracts coloured bright purple-mauve.

Bougainvillea cv. **Donya**
The large bracts on this cultivar are deep pinky-mauve in colour. This plant is often misspelled 'Donyo'.

Bougainvillea cv. **Easter Parade**
A medium grower with large heads of bracts coloured mauve.

Bougainvillea cv. **Excelsior**
Orange-red is the colour of the bracts of this cultivar.

Bougainvillea cv. **Dr H. B. Singh**
This cultivar is very free flowering and long lasting. Bracts are coloured lilac-lavender.

Bougainvillea cv. **Elizabeth**
This cultivar is deep cerise-red in colour.

Bougainvillea cv. **Formosa**
A large bract cultivar coloured pale mauve.

BOUGAINVILLEA (cont)

***Bougainvillea* cv. Gloucester Royal**
A vigorous cultivar with large heads of bracts, deep red in colour. This plant develops a much deeper colour in semi-shade.

***Bougainvillea* cv. Glowing Flame**
This is a variegated leaf cultivar with rosy orange coloured bracts.

***Bougainvillea* cv. Gwyneth Portland**
A compact growing climber with flower bracts being autumn toned varying to salmon-pink.

***Bougainvillea* cv. Harlequin**
This cultivar has variegated foliage of green and yellow with cerise and white bracts.

***Bougainvillea* cv. Harrissi Variegated**
syn. ***B. sanderiana*** var. ***variegata***
A smaller growing Bougainvillea with smaller leaves and bracts. Ideal for a pot plant or hanging basket. The bract colour is purple.

***Bougainvillea* cv. Hawaiian Gold**
syn. ***B.*** cv. **Golden Glow**
A compact grower with bracts coloured old gold. The colour of this cultivar is quite variable.

***Bougainvillea* cv. Golden Summers**
Leaves of this cultivar are yellow and green, bracts are white.

***Bougainvillea* cv. Hawaiian Pink**
Bract colour varies from pink to red on this compact cultivar.

BOUGAINVILLEA (cont)

***Bougainvillea* cv. Jamaica Gold**
A cultivar which has cerise coloured bracts and green leaves heavily dotted with yellow.

***Bougainvillea* cv. Kayata**
The smaller than normal bracts of this heavy flowering cultivar open rosy red then fade to apricot.

***Bougainvillea* cv. Jamaica White**
A pure white cultivar which has very open clusters of bracts.

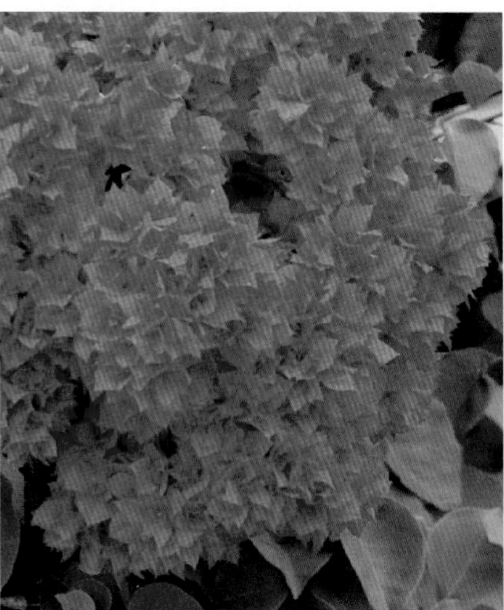

***Bougainvillea* cv. Klong Fire**
syn. ***B.* cv. Mahara**
A cultivar having large bunches of double cerise-red bracts.

***Bougainvillea* cv. Lateritia**
The large bunches of bracts of this cultivar are coloured orange-tangerine.

***Bougainvillea* cv. John Lattin**
A bushy climber with large heads of pale mauve coloured bracts.

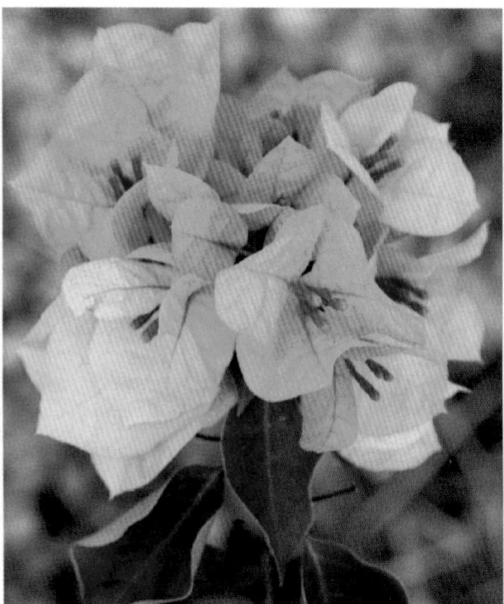

***Bougainvillea* cv. Lady Mary Baring**
Bracts on this cultivar are old gold in colour.

***Bougainvillea* cv. Limberlost Beauty**
syn. ***B.* cv. Cherry Blossoms**
This cultivar has large bunches of bracts which are cerise outside, cream inside and vary in colour with age.

BOUGAINVILLEA (cont)

Bougainvillea **cv. Little Caroline**

A very compact grower used as a ground cover. The bract colour is cerise to red. It is a good pot form.

Bougainvillea **cv. Mary Palmer**

syn. ***B.*** cv. **Snowcap**

A pendulous cultivar with white and mauve bracts.

Bougainvillea **cv. Louis Wathen**

This is an older cultivar with tangerine coloured bracts.

Bougainvillea **cv. Mrs Butt**

One of the early cultivars with showy scarlet bracts.

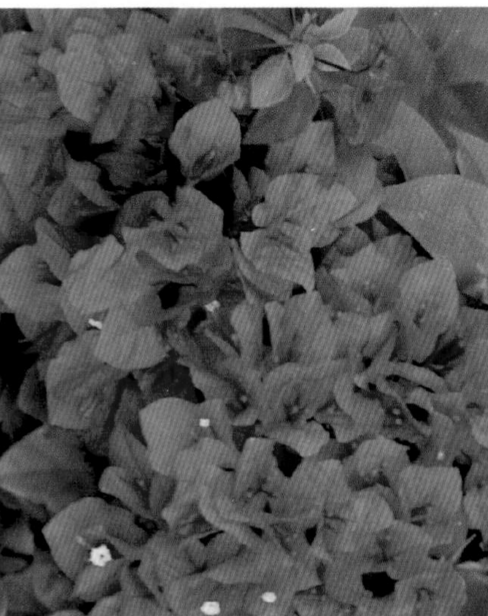

Bougainvillea **cv. Mrs H.C. Buck**

The large bract bunches of this cultivar are cerise-purple in colour.

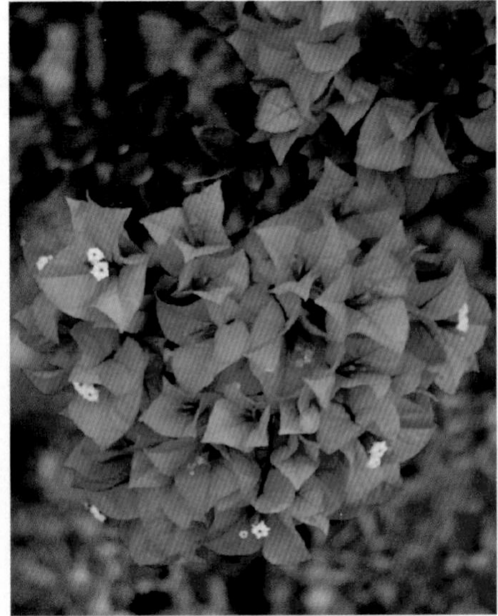

Bougainvillea **cv. Magnifica**

A popular old cultivar which is bright purple in colour.

Bougainvillea
cv. Mrs Eva Mauve Variegata

A compact smaller growing cultivar with mauve flowers and variegated leaves.

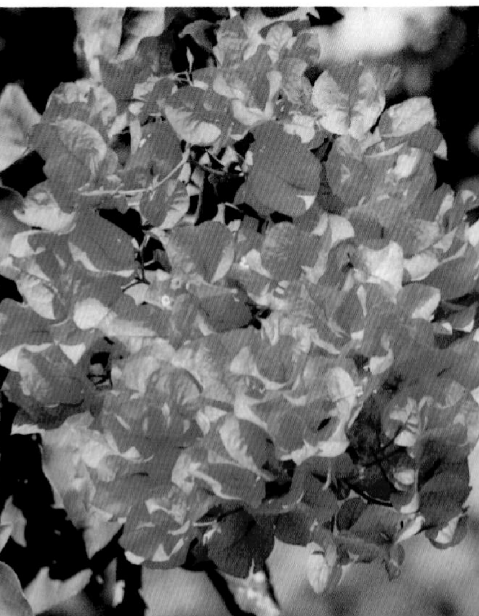

Bougainvillea **cv. Orange King**

This showy cultivar has large heads of bright orange bracts.

BOUGAINVILLEA (cont)

Bougainvillea cv. **Orange Picot**
A cultivar with twisted orange-rose coloured bracts and variegated green and white foliage.

Bougainvillea cv. **Penelope**
This cultivar has bunches of pure white bracts.

Bougainvillea cv. **Poultonii**
Free flowering, this cultivar has deep cerise coloured bracts.

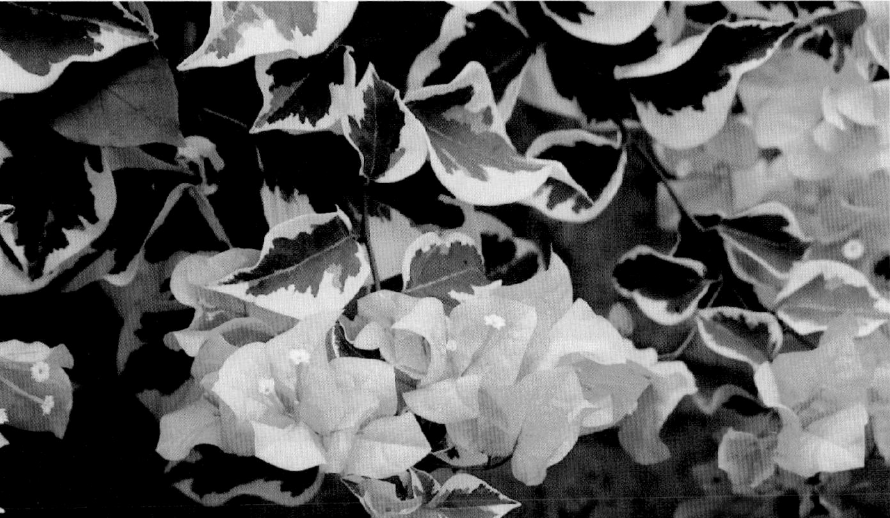

Bougainvillea cv. **Orange Stripe**
The leaves on this cultivar are variegated olive-green and white. The flower bracts are amber-orange in colour.

Bougainvillea cv. **Poulton's Special**
syn. ***B.*** cv. **Carnival**
A bright cerise cultivar which is ideal in tropical climates.

Bougainvillea cv. **Pagoda Pink**
This cultivar has very large bunches of double bracts which are cerise in colour.

Bougainvillea cv. **Picta Aurea**
A variegated leaf cultivar which has purple bracts.

Bougainvillea cv. **Raspberry Ice**
This very popular Bougainvillea has variegated cream and green foliage and cerise-red bracts. A good plant for pot growing.

b

BOUGAINVILLEA (cont)

***Bougainvillea* cv. Ratana Orange**
An unusual cultivar with smallish orange coloured bracts which are partly twisted. The foliage is also partly twisted.

***Bougainvillea* cv. Ratana Red**
A smaller flowered cultivar with cerise-red coloured partly twisted bracts. The leaves are also partly twisted.

***Bougainvillea* cv. Red Fantasy**
This cultivar has green leaves marked with yellow and cerise-red flower bracts.

***Bougainvillea* cv. Red September**
A variegated leaf cultivar with leaves coloured green and yellow. Flower bracts are cerise-red.

***Bougainvillea* cv. Sakura Variegata**
The bracts on this cultivar are white with pinky mauve overtones. The foliage is variegated cream and green.

***Bougainvillea* cv. Rosenka**
A cultivar with bracts which vary in colour from pinky gold to pinky cerise.

***Bougainvillea* cv. Sakura**
A cultivar with bi-coloured bracts, coloured white with pinky mauve overtonings.

***Bougainvillea* cv. Sanderiana**
This compact cultivar has small leaves and purple bracts and is ideal for hanging baskets.

***Bougainvillea* cv. Scarlet Glory**
A large bract cultivar which is scarlet-red all over, including the central flower.

***Bougainvillea* cv. Scarlett O'Hara**
A plant with scarlet coloured bracts. A popular older cultivar.

***Bougainvillea* cv. Scarlet Queen Variegata**
The new leaves of this plant are olive-green, pink and cream. Bracts are scarlet.

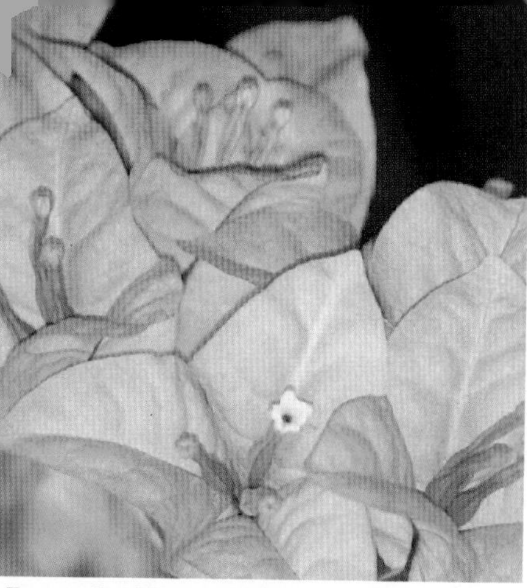

***Bougainvillea* cv. Show Lady**
This cultivar has large lilac-mauve bracts.

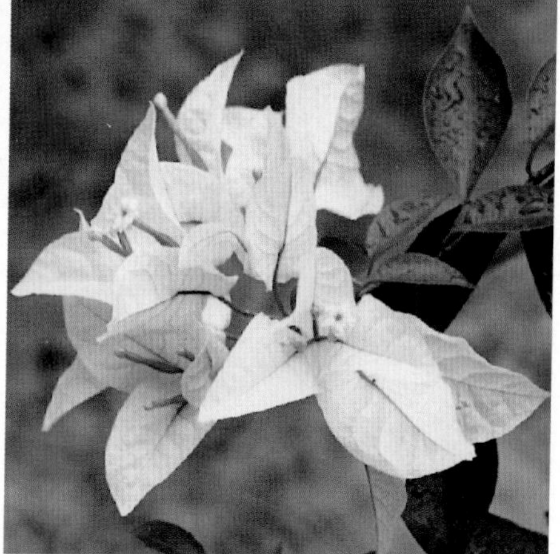

***Bougainvillea* cv. Singapore White**
A new cultivar which is compact and has white flowers.

***Bougainvillea* cv. Singapore Pink**
syn. ***B.*** cv. **Singapore Beauty**
A smaller growing plant which has very large clusters of mauve-pink bracts.

***Bougainvillea* cv. Singapore Pink Variegata**
This cultivar has green and yellow variegated leaves and mauve-pink bracts.

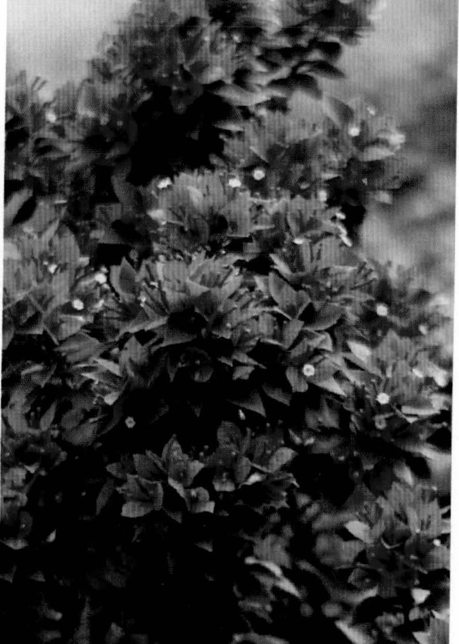

***Bougainvillea* cv. Smartie Pants**
syn. ***B.*** cv. **Pixie Pink**
A very upright grower which is less vigorous than most Bougainvilleas. Bract colour is cerise-purple.

BOUGAINVILLEA (cont)

***Bougainvillea* cv. Sundance**
On this compact cultivar, the bracts are orange.

***Bougainvillea* cv. Temple Fire**
One of the older cultivars with bracts being rosy pink. A good compact form.

***Bougainvillea* cv. Sweet Dreams**
An upright cultivar with lilac-pink bracts.

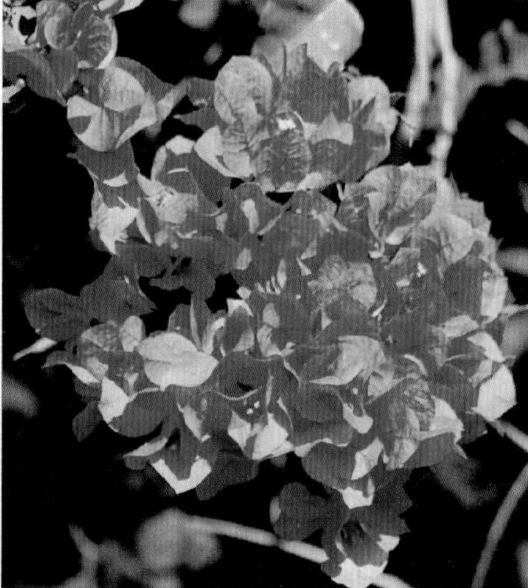

***Bougainvillea* cv. Tango**
syn. ***B.* cv. Miss Manila**
The bract colours vary from old gold to orange on this compact cultivar.

***Bougainvillea* cv. Texas Dawn**
syn. ***B.* cv. Purple King**
A cultivar with rosy cerise bract colour.

***Bougainvillea* cv. Sylvia Delap**
This cultivar has large heads of cerise-pink bracts.

***Bougainvillea* cv. Thai Gold**
This is an outstanding cultivar with large clusters of double bracts which are old gold to tangerine in colour.

BOUGAINVILLEA (cont)

Bougainvillea cv. **Thai Mini**
A small growing cultivar with small rose coloured bracts.

Bougainvillea cv. **Treasure**
An upright cultivar with large heads of cerise-red bracts.

Bougainvillea cv. **Tropical Bouquet**
The bracts of this pendulous growing cultivar are pinky-orange in colour.

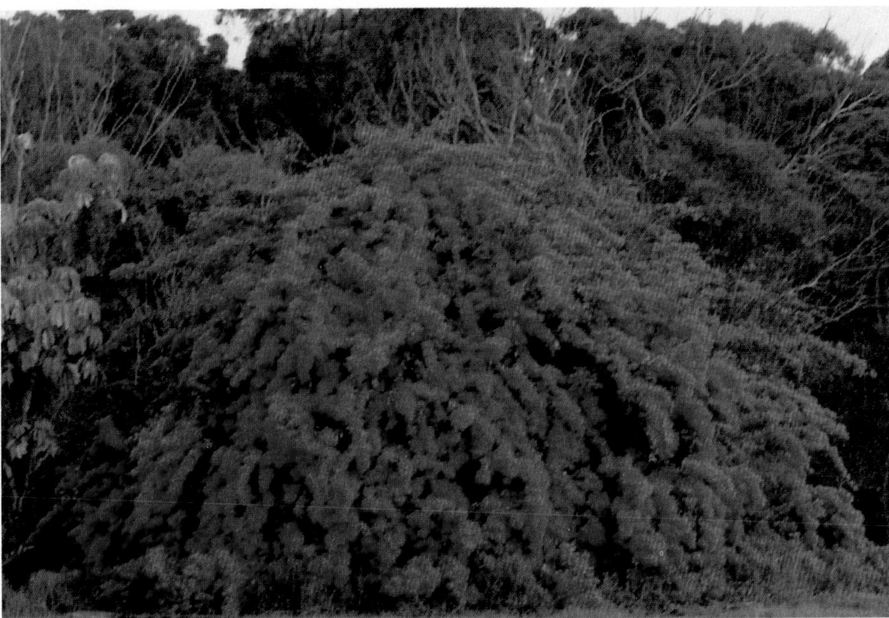

Bougainvillea cv. **Thomasi**
One of the older cultivars with red bracts which may cover the plant.

Bougainvillea cv. **Turley's Special**
This popular cultivar has bracts which are brick red in colour.

Bougainvillea cv. **Tomato Red**
Open clusters of bracts are tomato red in colour on this cultivar.

Bougainvillea cv. **Vera Blakeman**
A cultivar with large clusters of bright red bracts.

b

BOUVARDIA

RUBIACEAE

Evergreen shrubs from Mexico and Central America. They will grow outdoors in mild temperate to tropical climates. These plants flower over a long period. Bouvardias are widely grown in Europe, in heated glass houses, for cut flowers. The bunches of delicate flowers make them popular with florists. They prefer a rich loam and plenty of water in hot dry weather. Propagation is from cuttings.

Bouvardia laevis
A small open shrub with pendulous bunches of long salmon coloured flowers.

Bouvardia longiflora
syn. ***B. humboldtii***
An upright open medium shrub with showy perfumed white flowers in warm weather.

Bouvardia ternifolia cv. **Albert Newner**
A small shrub with heads of double white flowers which are popular for wedding bouquets.

Bouvardia ternifolia cv. **Australia Beauty**
Attractive heads of double pink flowers bloom over many months on this small shrub.

Bouvardia ternifolia cv. **Dutch Miss**
This small shrub has clusters of delicate flowers which are pale pink in colour.

Bouvardia ternifolia cv. **Duchess of York**
This small shrub has clusters of pink flowers in warm weather.

Bouvardia ternifolia cv. **Federal Queen**
A small shrub with heads of bright red single flowers.

Bouvardia ternifolia cv. **Rosea**
The flower heads on this small shrub are bright rose-pink.

BRACHYCHITON

Sterculiaceae

Brachychitons are mostly evergreen tall shrubs to medium trees from Australia. They grow in a wide range of soils and many have swollen trunks. Some varieties are grown for their spectacular floral display, others are grown on farms as shade trees and as reserve fodder in times of drought. Australian Aborigines used the seed as a food. The large seed pods are also used for floral decorations. Brachychitons are grown throughout the world in mild temperate to tropical climates outdoors and are also grown widely in cooler climates as bonsai plants. They are propagated from seed although the hybrid forms are grafted.

Brachychiton acerifolius FLAME TREE

A very showy small tree which is covered with clusters of bright red flowers in late spring. This tree is mostly evergreen but in the years of very intense flowering the tree may lose most of its leaves. It is one of the outstanding flowering trees of the world.

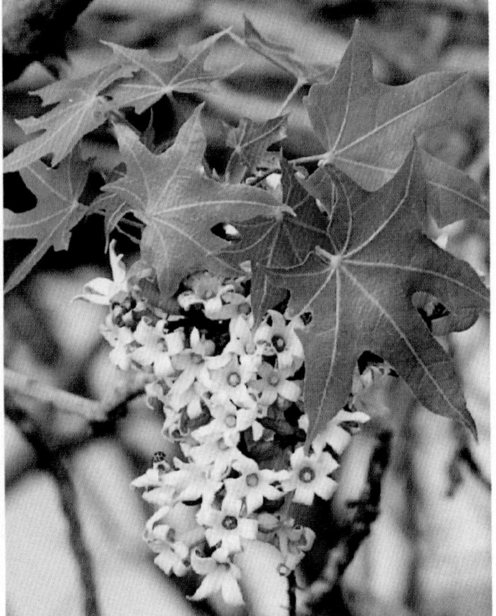

Brachychiton australis BROAD-LEAVED BOTTLE TREE

Preferring a semi-arid climate, this small tree has clusters of white star shaped flowers and a swollen trunk.

Brachychiton bidwillii

A tall shrub which has bunches of rose-pink to red star shaped flowers along its branches. It is an outstanding ornamental plant.

Brachychiton discolor LACEBARK

A small to medium size tree with unusual whitish bark with lace-like patterns. It has large clusters of pink flowers in spring.

Brachychiton gregorii DESERT KURRAJONG

A small tree with a short partly swollen trunk from the semi-desert and desert areas of Australia. The red flowers grow in clusters. It is grown for the shiny unusual shaped leaves which are called turkey foot leaves in U.S.A.

BRACHYCHITON (cont)

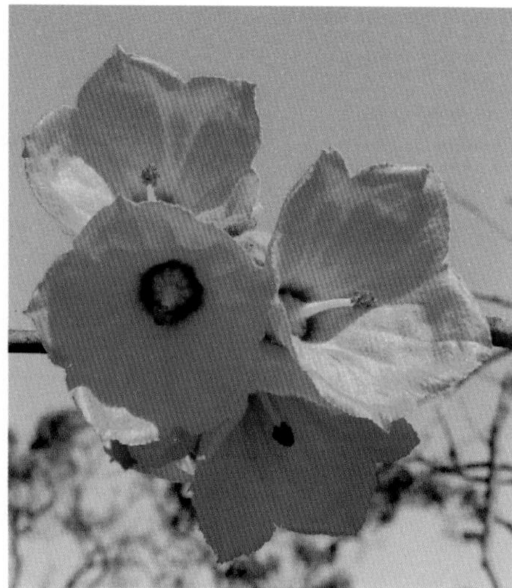

Brachychiton paradoxus

A tall shrub to small tree of tropical Australia. It is semi-deciduous and has clusters of large orange-red flowers.

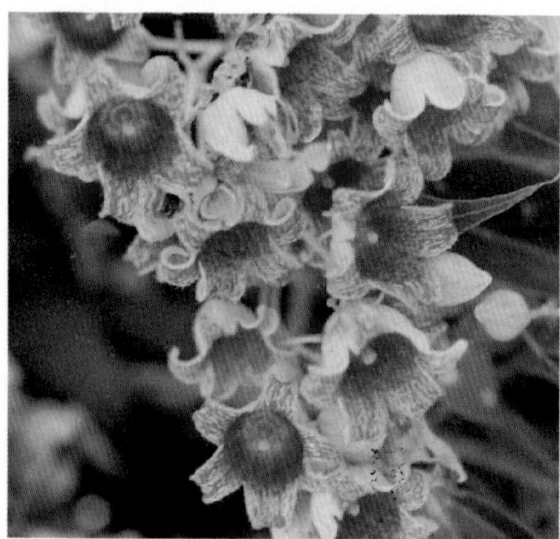

Brachychiton populneus* ssp. *populneus KURRAJONG

Widely grown as a street tree and for drought relief fodder and a shade tree on farms, this dense tall shrub to small tree has bell shaped flowers of cream, pink and red in large clusters.

Brachychiton* x *roseus* n-ssp. *roseus

This hybrid flame tree has large bunches of red flowers in late spring. It is grafted onto rootstock of either *B. acerifolius* or *B. populneus*.

Brachychiton rupestris BOTTLE TREE

A small to medium tree with a very swollen bottle shaped trunk. This tree is prized for its unique shape and is grown on many farms as a shade tree. It is also grown as a spectacular street tree and widely used as a bonsai plant. Bottle Tree has clusters of yellowish flowers and is ideally suited to sub-tropical and tropical areas, but will also tolerate some frost.

Brachychiton* x *vinicolor

A natural hybrid between *B. acerifolius* and *B. discolor* which has large red flowers in cascading bunches.

BRACHYSEMA

FABACEAE [LEGUMINOSAE]

Brachysema lanceolatum SWAN RIVER PEA

This shrub has bright red pea flowers along the stems. Propagate from seed or cuttings. It is native to temperate Australia.

BREYNIA

EUPHORBIACEAE

Breynia nivosa

This colourful shrub has small greenish flowers and is grown for its very showy leaves of green and cream. Propagate from seed or cuttings.

***Breynia nivosa* cv. Rosea-Picta**

A cultivar which has green, cream and pink leaves.

BROUSSONETIA

MORACEAE

Broussonetia papyrifera

PAPER MULBERRY

A small to medium tree which has large leaves. It widely grown as a shade and ornamental tree. It is native to Asia where the bark is used to produce paper. Propagate from seed or cuttings.

BROWNEA

CAESALPINIACEAE [LEGUMINOSAE]

Dense evergreen tall shrubs and small trees from moist areas of tropical America. They have very large heads of showy flowers which have a weeping effect. Browneas, when in flower, are very spectacular in sub-tropical to tropical gardens. The trees often grow to be umbrella shaped and the dense foliage allows them to be good shelter from heavy rain. They are propagated from seed which is rare, from cuttings and by marcot.

Brownea ariza

An evergreen small tree with weeping foliage. The ball shaped very large flowers are orange-red in colour.

Brownea capitella

A small evergreen tree with weeping foliage and large flower heads of pinky red.

Brownea coccinea

SCARLET FLAME BEAN

This is a small weeping tree with large heads of scarlet-red flowers.

BROWALLIA

SOLANACEAE

These small shrubby plants from tropical America are widely grown as outdoor ornamentals or pot plants in temperate to tropical climates and in cold climates are grown in conservatories and glass houses. Browallias prefer a rich soil and are propagated from seeds or cuttings.

Browallia speciosa BUSH VIOLET

A dense small shrubby plant with showy purple flowers. It is grown outdoors in temperate to tropical climates, and is also widely used as a hanging basket plant.

***Browallia viscosa* cv. White Bell**

This small plant has white flowers.

BROWNEA (cont)

Brownea coccinea ssp. ***coccinea***
syn. ***B. latifolia***
A small tree in which the flower stamens are slightly exserted.

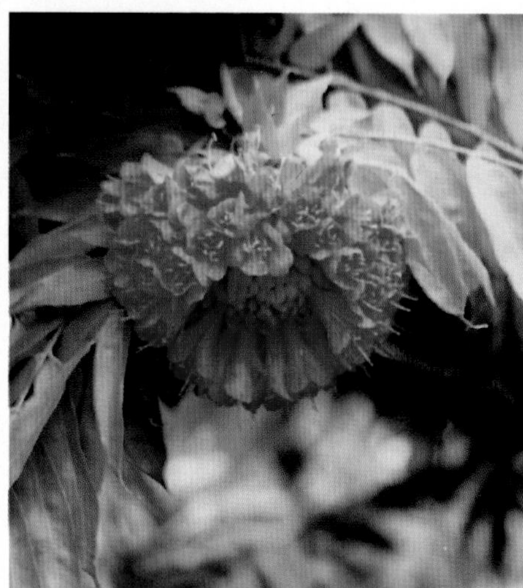

Brownea grandiceps
ROSE OF VENEZUELA
A small tree with very large heads of red flowers which hang beneath the foliage. Ofen confused with *B. ariza.*

Brownea grandiflora
Evergreen, this small tree has large balls of red flowers. This tree has the largest flower clusters of the Browneas.

BRUGMANSIA

ANGEL'S TRUMPET

SOLANACEAE

A group of soft wooded tall shrubs which were previously known as Datura. These shrubs will grow in climates from cold temperate to tropical and are native to South America. Some are said to produce narcotic alkaloids. They have very large trumpet shaped flowers and are widely grown as ornamentals. Brugmansias will grow in a wide range of soils and are propagated from seeds and cuttings.

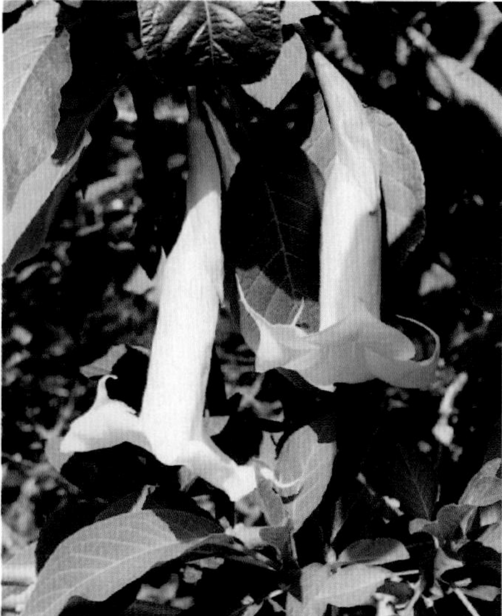

Brugmansia arborea MAIKOA
syn. ***Datura arborea***
An open tall shrub with large, weeping, white, trumpet flowers.

Brugmansia arborea cv. **Flore Pleno**
A double flowered form of Angel's trumpet.

Brugmansia aurea
GOLDEN ANGEL'S TRUMPET
syn. ***Datura aurea***
A bushy tall shrub with masses of golden trumpet flowers.

Brugmansia aurea cv. **Orange Glow**
This cultivar has orange coloured flowers.

Brugmansia x ***candida***
syn. ***Datura candida***
A hybrid of *Brugmansia aurea* and *B. versicolor*. The large trumpet flowers are white overlaid with light touches of yellow and pink.

Brugmansia sanguinea

RED ANGEL'S TRUMPET

A small tree with red flowers. This plant has larger flower tubes than the other Angel's trumpets.

Brugmansia suaveolens

syn. ***Datura gardneri***

This tall shrub has large white weeping trumpet-like flowers.

Brugmansia versicolor

syn. ***Datura mollis***

A very attractive graceful tall shrub to small tree with large weeping trumpet-like flowers, apricot in colour.

BRUNFELSIA

SOLANACEAE

A group of shrubs from Central and South America, some of which are grown as outstanding ornamental shrubs. Brunfelsias tend to flower best when grown hard in poor soils or if pot bound when grown in pots. They are grown in climates from mild temperate to tropical and most forms don't like frosts. Propagate from seeds and cuttings.

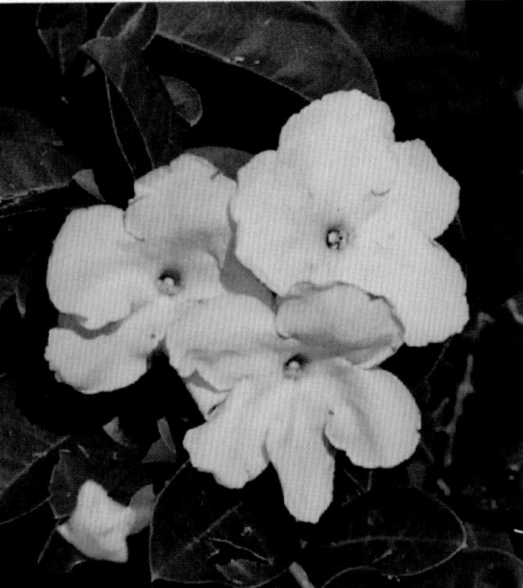

Brunfelsia americana

LADY OF THE NIGHT

syn. ***B. fallax***

This shrub is a highly perfumed plant which releases its fragrance at night. The flowers are cream, yellow and gold and the three colours may all be seen on the shrub at one time as flowers darken as they age over three days.

Brunfelsia australis

PARAGUAYAN JASMINE

syn. ***B. paraguayensis***

A free flowering shrub with masses of flowers which turn from purple to white as they age. Highly perfumed, this is a smaller leaf Brunfelsia.

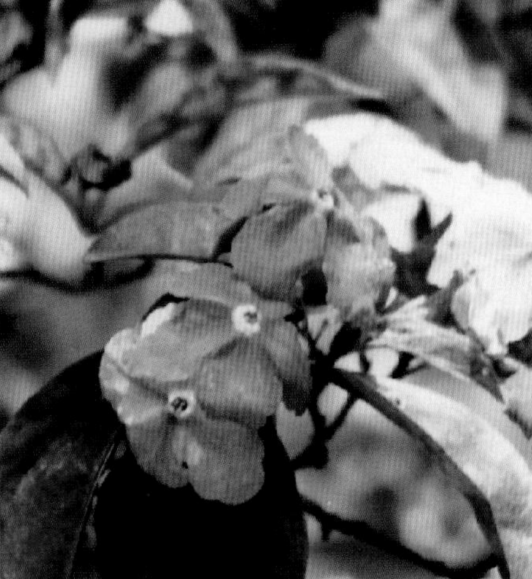

Brunfelsia brasiliensis

This upright shrub has fragrant flowers coloured violet, mauve and white.

Brunfelsia latifolia KISS ME QUICK

A small to medium perfumed shrub with white, mauve and violet coloured flowers which cover the plant in spring.

Brunfelsia pauciflora

YESTERDAY, TODAY AND TOMORROW

A showy medium perfumed shrub with large flowers which open violet, turn mauve the next day and then white on the third day. This shrub has larger leaves than other Brunfelsias.

BRUNFELSIA (cont)

Brunfelsia pauciflora cv. **Floribunda**
This cultivar has many more, but slightly smaller, flowers than *B. pauciflora*. The leaves also are a little smaller.

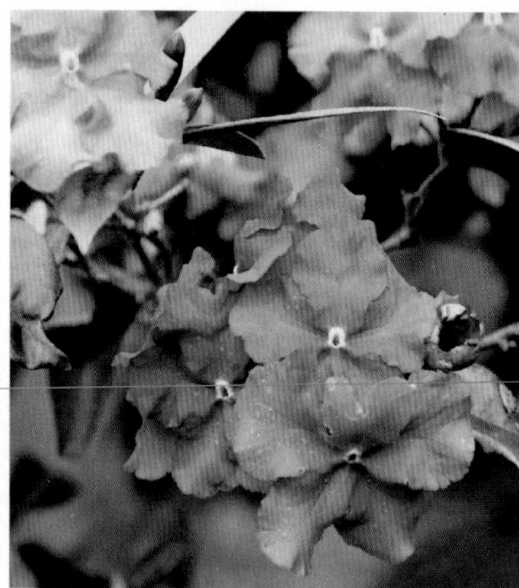

Brunfelsia pauciflora cv. **Macrantha**
A cultivar with large flowers which are mostly violet in colour.

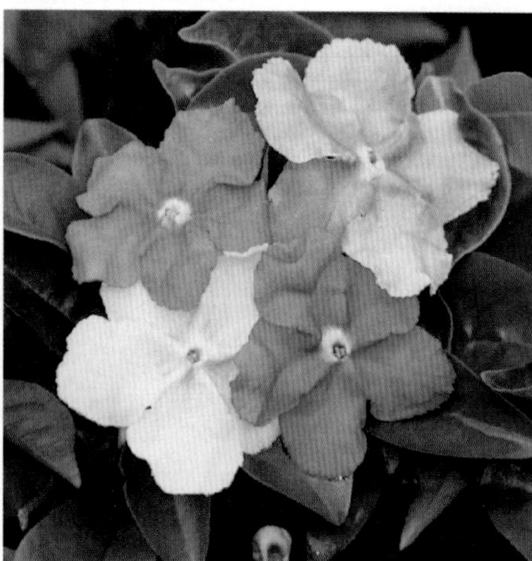

Brunfelsia uniflora MANAC
syn. ***B. hopeana***
A fragrant shrub with large flowers of white, mauve and violet. Leaves are less pointed than other Brunfelsias.

BUCKINGHAMIA

PROTEACEAE

Buckinghamia celsissima IVORY CURL
A small, evergreen, fragrant tree from tropical Australia. The tree is covered with long racemes of cream flowers in summer. It grows in a wide range of soils and makes an ideal ornamental. Buckinghamia is widely grown as a street tree. It will grow in climates from warm temperate to tropical. Propagate from seed.

BUDDLEJA

BUDDLEIA; BUTTERFLY BUSH

LOGANIACEAE

Buddlejas are both evergreen and deciduous spreading tall shrubs. These plants are natives of the Americas, Asia and Africa but many will grow and thrive in cold temperate climates and in a wide range of soils. These shrubs benefit from hard pruning in autumn. They are grown from seed and cuttings.

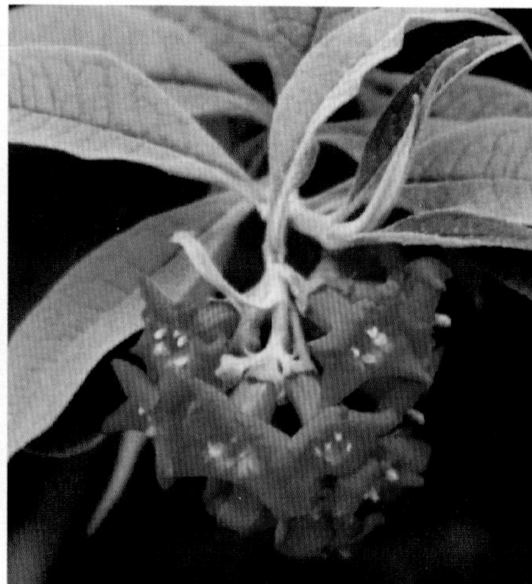

Buddleja colvilei
An open crowned shrub with pendulous heads of flowers coloured crimson-maroon.

Buddleja davidii SUMMER LILAC
This summer flowering tall shrub has lilac coloured yellow-eyed flowers in long racemes. It is a hardy, free flowering evergreen.

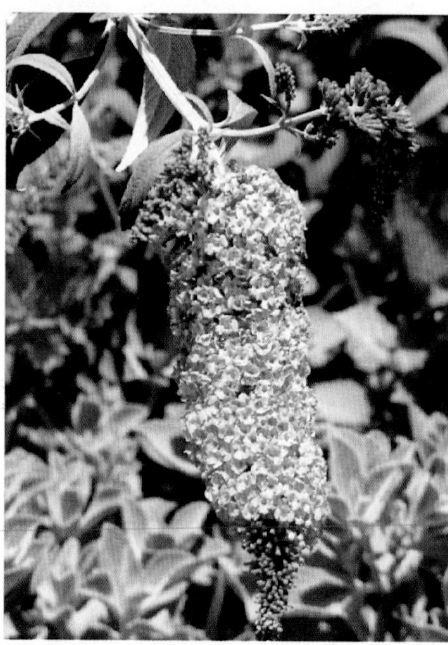

Buddleja davidii cv. **Fascination**
A cultivar with large racemes of deep mauve coloured flowers.

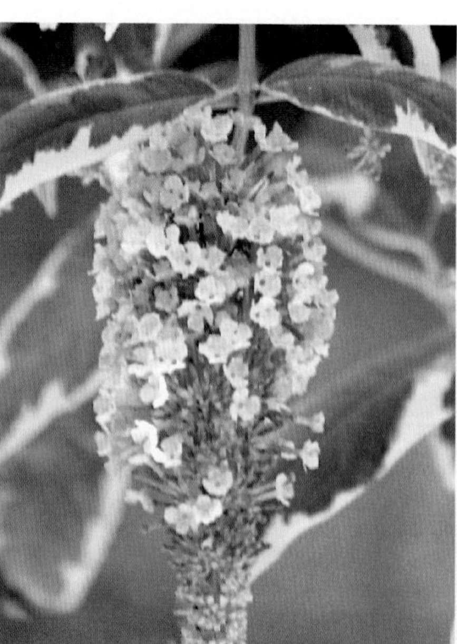

Buddleja davidii cv. **Harlequin**
A cultivar with grey and cream variegated leaves and pale pinky mauve flowers.

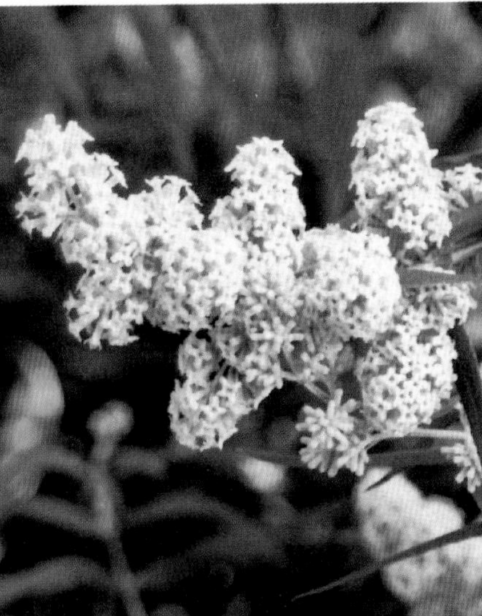

Buddleja davidii cv. **Mauve Magic**
A pale mauve flowered cultivar with lots of smaller racemes of flowers.

Buddleja davidii cv. **Royal Red**
This cultivar has long racemes of magenta coloured flowers.

Buddleja davidii cv. **White Bouquet**
A creamy-white flowered cultivar with large semi-upright racemes of flowers.

Buddleja davidii cv. **White Wings**
A bushy cultivar with long sprays of white flowers.

Buddleja globosa
An open crowned shrub with round heads of yellow flowers.

Buddleja madagascariensis
An open crowned, evergreen, tall shrub with long racemes of old gold coloured flowers.

Buddleja saligna
A compact medium to tall evergreen shrub with clusters of creamy white flowers.

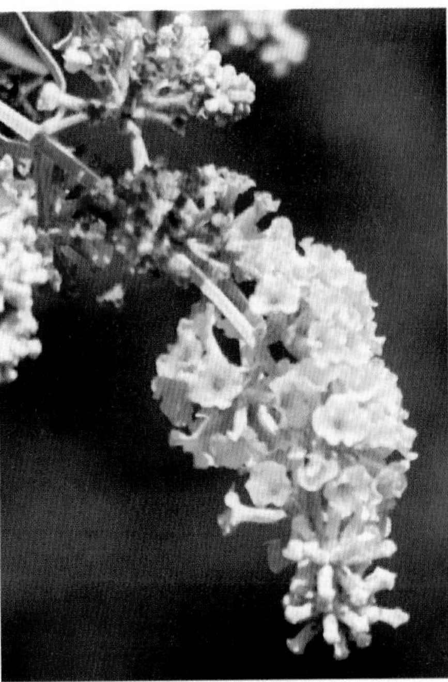

Buddleja x ***weyeriana***
An open evergreen tall shrub with short thick racemes of golden flowers.

Buddleja x ***weyeriana*** cv. **Sungold**
This open branched evergreen shrub has globular heads of golden flowers.

b

BULNESIA

ZYGOPHYLLACEAE

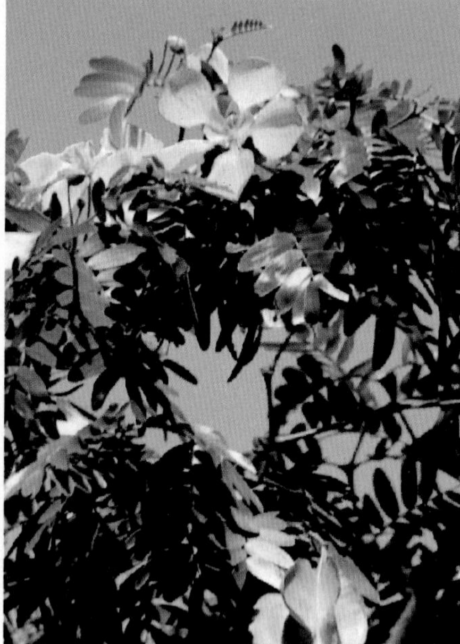

Bulnesia arborea

A medium size evergreen tree which is native to tropical South America. It is highly ornamental and at times is totally covered with golden flowers. This tree is also used for timber. Propagate from seed.

BURCHELLIA

RUBIACEAE

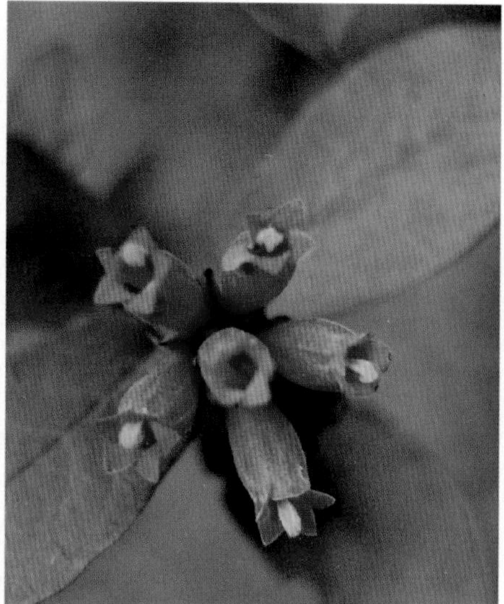

Burchellia bubalina AFRICAN POMEGRANATE

This small to medium evergreen shrub from Africa has bunches of orange-red tubular flowers. This hardy plant has pomegranate-type fruit. It will grow in a wide range of soils and prefers climates from cold temperate to sub-tropical. Propagation is from seeds and cuttings.

BURTONIA

FABACEAE [LEGUMINOSAE]

Burtonia scabra PAINTED LADY

This is a small evergreen shrub with small leaves and rose-pink pea-type flowers in clusters and is native to Western Australia. It is grown as a showy ornamental and prefers sandy, well drained soils. The shrub will grow in climates from cold temperate to sub-tropical. Propagate from seed.

BUNCHOSIA

MALPIGHIACEAE

Bunchosia argentea

A small evergreen tree of tropical America. It is grown as an ornamental and has erect golden flower spikes followed by bright red drupes which encase the seed. The tree will grow in a wide range of soils in climates from temperate to tropical. Propagate from seed.

BURSARIA

PITTOSPORACEAE

Bursaria spinosa SWEET BURSARIA

A highly perfumed, open crowned, evergreen, tall shrub with thorns. This shrub has large clusters of white flowers and grows in very poor soils in climates from cold temperate to sub-tropical. The leaves produce a substance used to shield ultra-violet light. It is grown from seed and is native to Australia.

BUTEA

FABACEAE [LEGUMINOSAE]

Butea monosperma FLAME OF THE FOREST

syn. ***B. frondosa***

This small bright orange flowered tree is deciduous and grows in climates sub-tropical and tropical. It grows in a wide range of soils and is spectacular when in flower. Propagate from seed.

BYRSONIMA

MALPIGHIACEAE

Native to tropical America, these small evergreen trees have terminal spikes, and are grown as ornamentals in sub-tropical and tropical climates. Propagated from seed, they will tolerate a wide range of soils.

Byrsonima coriacea

A small evergreen tree with upright flower spikes coloured yellow.

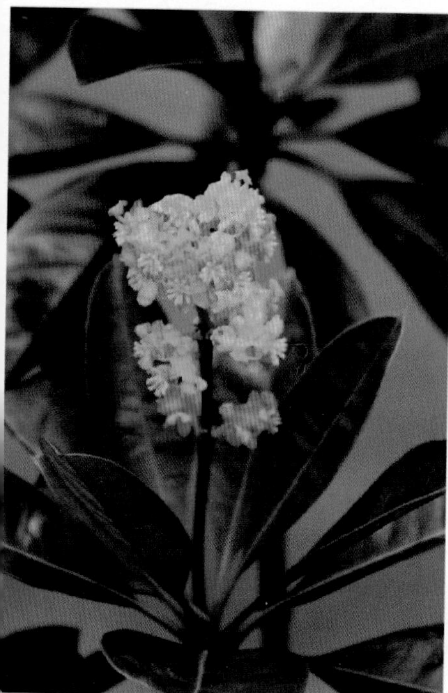

Byrsonima crassifolia

This species has spikes of gold and red flowers.

CADIA

FABACEAE [LEGUMINOSAE]

Cadia purpurea KADI BUSH

A tall evergreen dryland shrub which is native to Africa and the Middle East. It makes a good ornamental. The plant has ferny leaves and bell shaped flowers which are off white as buds then open to a maroon-purple. Propagate from seed.

CAESALPINIA

CAESALPINIACEAE [LEGUMINOSAE]

Shrubs and small trees which are evergreen or deciduous. These mostly tropical plants are from Central and South America and the Caribbean and many are spiny. Some are grown as free flowering ornamentals and are usually confined to warm temperate, sub-tropical and tropical climates. They grow in a wide range of soils but require adequate water to flower at their best. Propagation is from seed.

Caesalpinia conzattii

A tall evergreen shrub with ferny leaves and terminal clusters of red flowers marked yellow.

Caesalpinia decapetala var. ***japonica***

MYSORE THORN

This semi-clumping shrub is tolerant of frosts and has large erect heads of golden yellow flowers in spring.

Caesalpinia ferrea

BRAZILIAN IRONWOOD; LEOPARD TREE

This small tree has attractive mottled bark and clusters of golden flowers in summer.

Caesalpinia gilliesii BIRD-OF-PARADISE

A very hardy shrub which has large clusters of yellow and red flowers in summer.

C

CAESALPINIA (cont)

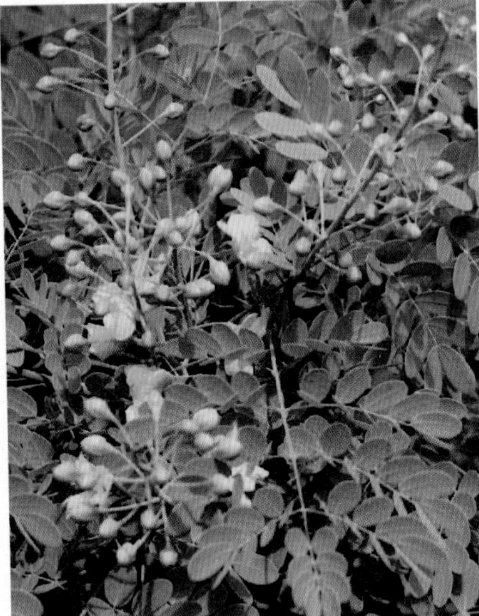

Caesalpinia mexicana
A spreading tall shrub with sprays of golden coloured flowers.

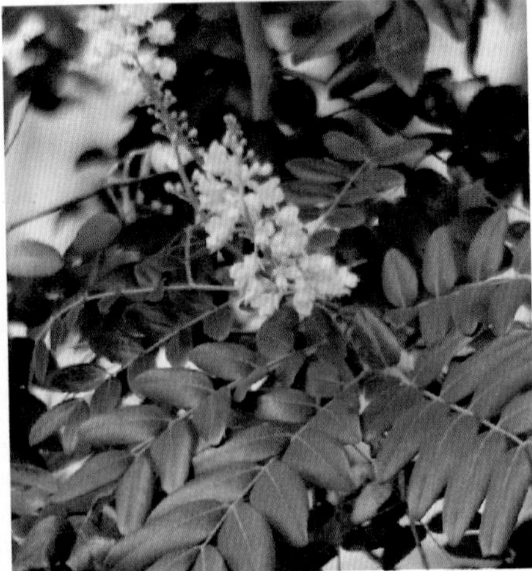

Caesalpinia platyloba
Evergreen, this small tree has terminal spikes of golden yellow flowers.

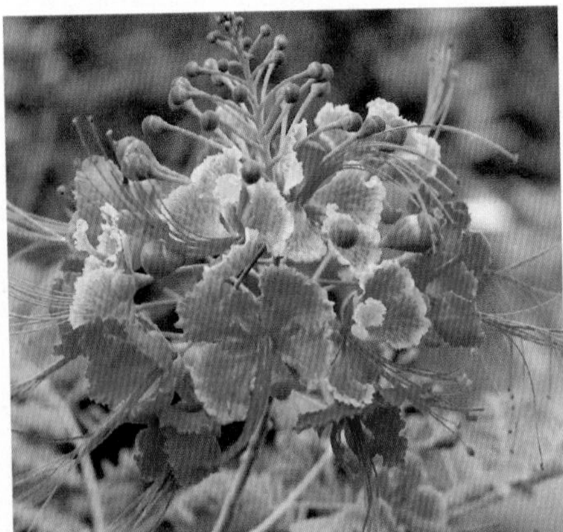

Caesalpinia pulcherrima
BARBADOS-PRIDE
A spiny semi-deciduous shrub which has large clusters of orange-edged yellow flowers during summer months.

***Caesalpinia pulcherrima* cv. Flava**
A golden flowered form of this shrub.

***Caesalpinia pulcherrima* cv. Rosea**
This cultivar has flowers which are coloured bright rose-pink, edged yellow.

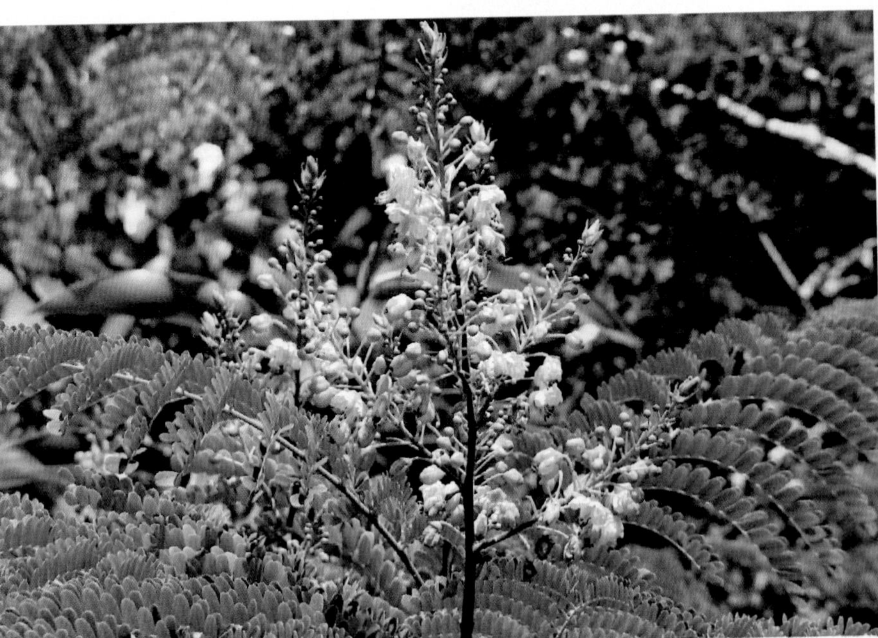

Caesalpinia sappan
BRAZILWOOD
A prickly evergreen small tree. It has yellow coloured terminal flower spikes.

CALLIANDRA

MIMOSACEAE [LEGUMINOSAE]

Tropical evergreen shrubs and small trees native to the Caribbean, North, Central and South America. In warm temperate to tropical climates they are widely grown as ornamentals for their attractive flowers which have a powder-puff appearance. Calliandras grow in a wide range of soils but need adequate water to flower well. Their flowering period can last for many months in summer. They are propagated from seed and cuttings.

Calliandra californica
An open crowned upright shrub with deep red flowers.

CALLIANDRA (cont)

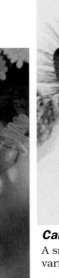

Calliandra conferta
In summer this small shrub may be covered in small white flowers.

Calliandra emarginata
A tall shrub with red flowers in summer.

Calliandra emarginata cv. **Variegata**
A small shrub with cream and green variegated leaves and reddish flowers.

Calliandra haematocephala
RED POWDER PUFF
Open crowned and spreading, this tall shrub has large red flowers.

Calliandra haematocephala cv. **Alba** WHITE POWDER PUFF
A cultivar with large white flowers.

Calliandra houstoniana
An open crowned, spreading, tall shrub with ferny leaves and paintbrush-type flowers of orange-red colour.

Calliandra emarginata cv. **Blushing Pixie**
This small to medium shrub has pinky red flowers.

Calliandra portoricensis
PERFUMED POWDER PUFF
This tall shrub flowers at night. The white flowers are highly perfumed as they open.

CALLIANDRA (cont)

Calliandra cv. **Rosea**
A cultivar which is very free flowering, having rose-pink to light red flowers.

Calliandra tweedii cv. **Horizontalis**
This low spreading form is grown as a ground cover.

Calliandra schultzei
Evergreen, this shrub has fine leaves and white and pink flowers. Often confused with *C. surinamensis*. This plant has larger flowers and smaller leaves.

Calliandra tweedii cv. **Red Flash**
A cultivar which appears to be a more compact grower.

Calliandra surinamensis
An open crowned evergreen free flowering shrub with white and pink paintbrush-type flowers. This plant has broader leaves and smaller flowers than *C. schultzei.*

Calliandra tweedii
A dense rounded medium shrub with bright red flowers.

CALLICARPA

VERBENACEAE

Tropical and sub-tropical evergreen and deciduous shrubs and small trees from Australia, South East Asia and North and South America. They are usually openly branched plants which are grown, in a wide range of soils, for their attractive berries. Mostly summer flowering, they are propagated from seed and cuttings and are suitable to grow in climates from temperate to tropical.

Callicarpa americana BEAUTY BERRY

A very open medium to tall shrub with mauve coloured flowers followed by showy bright cerise coloured berries.

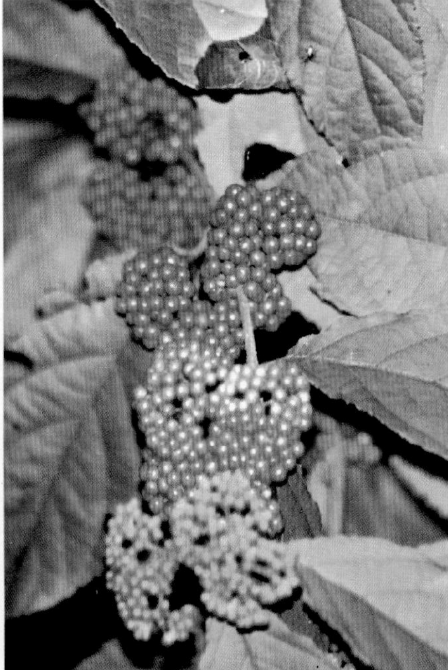

Callicarpa candicans

An open crowned tall shrub with arching branches. Flowers are blue-mauve followed by purplish berries.

Callicarpa dichotoma

A hardy shrub with pinkish flowers followed by showy lilac coloured berries.

Callicarpa japonica

An upright shrub with clusters of pink flowers followed by violet coloured berries.

Callicarpa pedunculata

An open crowned arching shrub with pinkish mauve flowers followed by cerise-purple coloured berries.

CALLICOMA

CUNONIACEAE

Callicoma serratifolia BLACK WATTLE

A tall pendulous shrub from Australia. It grows in sub-tropical to cold temperate areas. It has round ball shaped flowers in spring. Propagate from seed or cuttings.

Callicarpa nudiflora

A small tree with heads of small cerise coloured flowers followed by round blue fruit.

CALLISTEMON

BOTTLEBRUSH

MYRTACEAE

Callistemons are small evergreen shrubs to small trees and are native to Australia. They grow in a wide range of soils and climates from sub-alpine to tropical in their native habitat. Callistemons are usually very free flowering with flowers which resemble a bottlebrush. Some are tolerant of both prolonged dry spells and waterlogging. Many cultivars are grown and this has given a wider range of colours to this group of plants. Propagation is from seed and cuttings. Flowering may be spring, summer or autumn depending on the variety being grown. Some will flower at various times through the year. The origins of many Callistemon cultivars are unknown or indistinct.

***Callistemon citrinus* cv. Alba**

WHITE BOTTLEBRUSH

An outstanding white flowered form of this bottlebrush which grows true to colour from seed.

Callistemon comboynensis

CLIFF BOTTLEBRUSH

A spreading shrub which grows in poor soils and flowers randomly throughout the year. Flower colour is red with yellow anthers.

Callistemon citrinus

LEMON SCENTED BOTTLEBRUSH

This is a widely grown bushy shrub which has lemon scented leaves and bright red flowers. It is the parent of many outstanding cultivars. It is quite cold tolerant and can be seen happily growing in England.

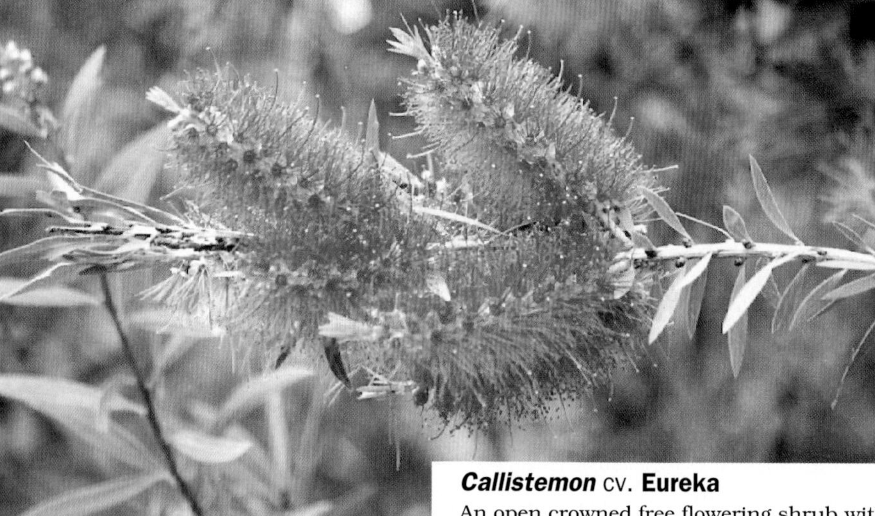

***Callistemon* cv. Eureka**

An open crowned free flowering shrub with red-mauve flowers.

***Callistemon citrinus* cv. Pinkie**

An attractive free flowering cultivar with bright pink flowers.

Callistemon formosus

A tall shrub with fine pointed leaves and clusters of creamy white flowers.

***Callistemon* cv. Harkness**
syn. ***C.* cv. Gawler Hybrid**
A very free flowering small tree which has masses of bright red flowers.

***Callistemon* cv. Mauve Mist**
An open crowned tall shrub with mauve-pink flowers in spring and summer. The colour is much deeper when grown in partial shade.

***Callistemon* cv. Kotara Rose**
A medium open shrub with flowers being very deep rose-pink to red.

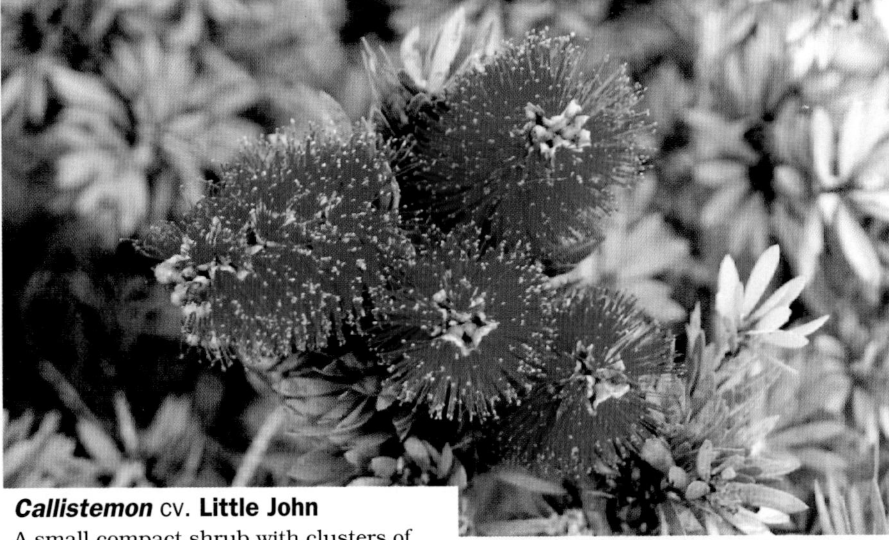

***Callistemon* cv. Little John**
A small compact shrub with clusters of red flowers.

Callistemon linearis
NARROW LEAF BOTTLEBRUSH
A very open crowned medium hardy shrub with thin leaves and bright red flowers.

Callistemon macropunctatus
SCARLET BOTTLEBRUSH
A medium open crowned shrub with scarlet flowers with yellow anthers.

***Callistemon* cv. Mister Foster**
This sparse shrub has bright red flowers.

CALLISTEMON (cont)

Callistemon pachyphyllus

WALLUM BOTTLEBRUSH

An upright open shrub with bright red flowers lightly overlaid with yellow anthers.

***Callistemon pachyphyllus* cv. Smoked Salmon**

An outstanding cultivar with salmon pink flowers.

***Callistemon* cv. Peach Glow**

This open upright rigid shrub has peach coloured medium sized flowers.

Callistemon pearsonii

A fine leaf shrub with red flowers and yellow anthers.

***Callistemon* cv. Perth Pink**

An upright shrub with flowers dark pink to red.

Callistemon phoeniceus

In spring this hardy upright shrub has bright red flowers.

***Callistemon* cv. Pink Champagne**

An outstanding pink flowered bottlebrush. The plant is an upright medium shrub.

Callistemon polandii

An open crowned medium shrub with red flowers and yellow anthers.

***Callistemon* cv. Prolific Pink**
A medium upright shrub with clusters of medium sized bright pink to light red flowers.

***Callistemon* cv. Reeves Pink**
A seedling of *C. citrinus* with long pinky red flowers.

Callistemon rigidus STIFF BOTTLEBRUSH
Very hardy, this narrow leaf open shrub has red flowers.

Callistemon salignus
A small tree which has large quantities of cream flowers and pinky red new growth.

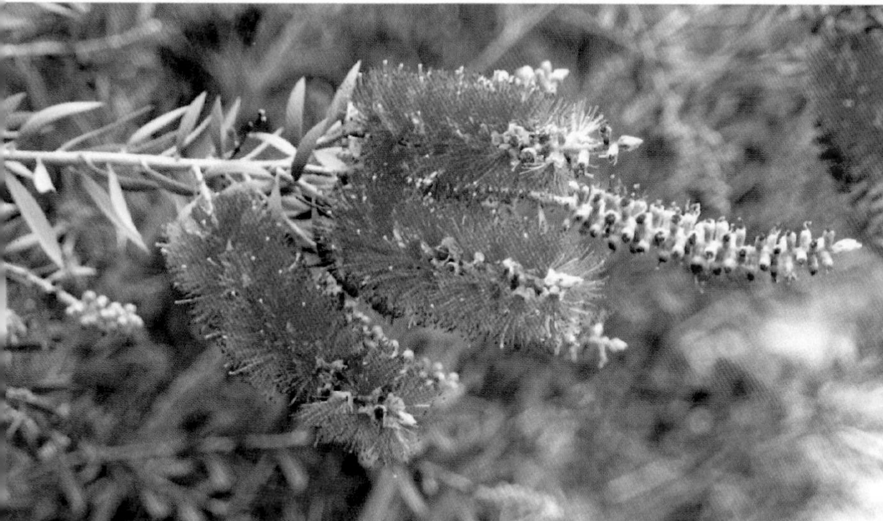

***Callistemon* cv. Purple Splendour**
Large clusters of medium sized flowers coloured cerise to purple bloom on this medium shrub.

***Callistemon* cv. Red Devil**
This spreading open crowned shrub has red flowers overlaid with gold anthers.

***Callistemon* cv. Rocky Rambler**
A small leaf open shrub with short flowers of red with yellow anthers.

***Callistemon salignus* cv. Pink Pearl**
An outstanding free flowering cultivar with clusters of pink flowers.

CALLISTEMON (cont)

Callistemon salignus cv. **Rubra**
This cultivar has masses of bright red flowers.

Callistemon cv. **Taree Pink**
An upright open shrub with long bottlebrush flowers of pinky red.

Callistemon subulatus
A hardy fine leaf shrub with heads of bright red flowers.

Callistemon viminalis
WEEPING BOTTLEBRUSH
C. viminalis is a very popular ornamental small tree which is widely grown throughout the world. It has weeping branches with large clusters of red flowers. There are many excellent cultivars of this small tree.

Callistemon viminalis cv. **Dawson River**
A more upright cultivar with long red bottlebrush flowers.

Callistemon cv. **The Bluff**
A small leaf shrub with cream to pale pink flowers.

Callistemon viminalis cv. **Captain Cook**
A very dwarf form with a less weeping habit. It has bright red flowers.

CALLISTEMON (cont)

Callistemon viminalis
cv. **Hannah Ray**
This upright cultivar has bright red flowers.

Callistemon viminalis cv. **Pindi Pindi**
A cultivar with deeper red flowers.

Callistemon viminalis cv. **Rose Opal**
Free flowering, this cultivar has cerise-purple flowers.

Callistemon viminalis cv. **Wilderness White**
A weeping cultivar with white flowers.

Callistemon cv. **Violaceus**
A medium upright shrub with violet-red flowers.

Callistemon cv. **Wildfire**
A narrow leaf form with bright red flowers.

CALODENDRUM

RUTACEAE

Calodendrum capense

CAPE CHESTNUT

A medium size evergreen spreading tree which is native to Africa. It will grow in climates from mild temperate to tropical and is very spectacular in summer with very large heads of pinky lilac coloured flowers. Propagation is from seed. Outstanding flowering forms are also grafted.

CALOMERIA

ASTERACEAE [COMPOSITAE]

Calomeria amaranthoides INCENSE BUSH

An open tall shrubby plant from Australia with weeping pinky red flowers in catkins. It lives only for a few years and gives off an incense-like odour. This plant grows in temperate climates and is propagated from seed.

CALOPHACA

FABACEAE [LEGUMINOSAE]

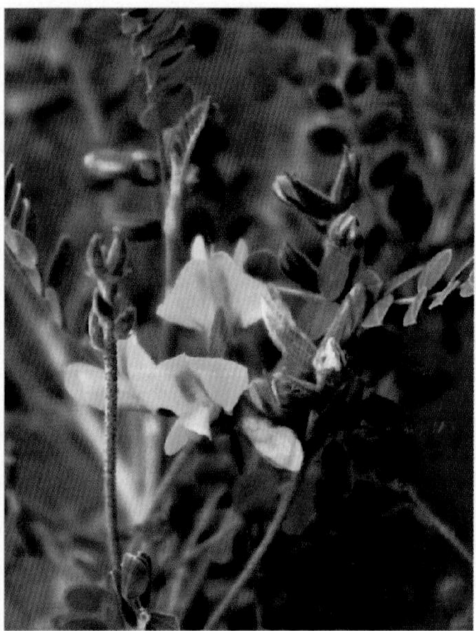

Calophaca wolgarica

A small deciduous shrub which is native to Ukraine. It is cold tolerant and has masses of yellow pea-type flowers in spring. Propagate from seed.

CALOPHYLLUM

CLUSIACEAE [GUTTIFERAE]

Calophyllum inophyllum LAUREL WOOD

An evergreen medium tree from Australia and South East Asia. It is grown as an ornamental street or park tree in sub-tropical and tropical climates. Flowers are large and attractive clusters of white and yellow. Propagate from fresh seed.

CALOPYXIS

COMBRETACEAE

Calopyxis grandidieri

An evergreen climber native to Madagascar. It is free flowering and has clusters of red and cream pendulous flowers most of the year. It prefers a temperate to tropical climate and is propagated from seed or cuttings.

CALOTHAMNUS

MYRTACEAE

Evergreen open crowned shrubs from Australia with tufted, mostly red, flowers along the branches. They are hardy shrubs which grow in a wide range of soils. They grow best in climates from mild temperate to sub-tropical. Propagation is from seed.

Calothamnus blepharospermus

A small spreading shrub with tufted one sided flowers along the branches.

CALOTHAMNUS (cont)

Calothamnus gilesii

Hardy, this upright, open crowned medium shrub has long thin leaves and clusters of pendulous red feathery flowers.

Calothamnus graniticus

A small open shrub with long thin round leaves and red tufted flowers.

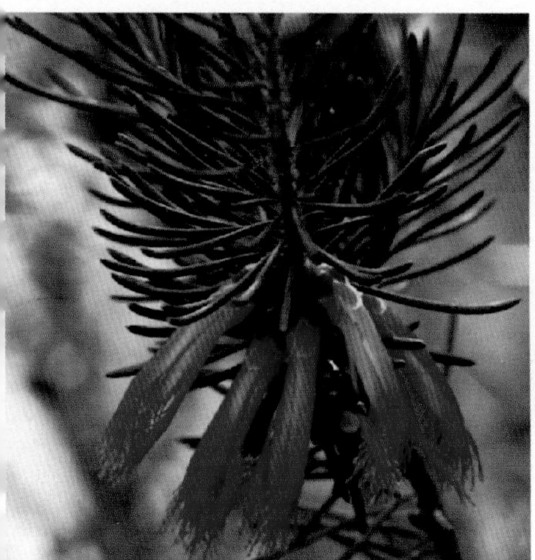

Calothamnus macrocarpus

This open shrub has small round leaves and small clumps of red flowers.

Calothamnus quadrifidus

COMMON NET-BUSH

An open upright shrub with short round leaves and large red flower tufts.

Calothamnus validus

BARRENS CLAW-FLOWER

Small clusters of red, claw-like flowers bloom on this small open shrub.

CALOTROPIS

ASCLEPIADACEAE

Calotropis procera MADAR

A small evergreen shrub native to Africa and the Middle East. It is grown as an ornamental in tropical and sub-tropical areas and it tolerates dry areas. The attractive bunches of flowers are white and purple. Propagate from seed.

CALYCANTHUS

CALYCANTHACEAE

Deciduous tall shrubs from North America. These shrubs have reddish brown, fragrant flowers in spring. Calycanthus grow in mild climates but also have good cold tolerance. They are grown from seed, cuttings and layers.

Calycanthus fertilis

A bushy shrub which has sweet smelling bark and reddish brown flowers in spring.

Calycanthus floridus

CAROLINA ALLSPICE

A bushy shrub with aromatic bark and wood. It has reddish brown flowers in spring.

CAMELLIA

THEACEAE

Camellias are evergreen shrubs and small trees from Asia. They are grown as outstanding winter and spring flowering ornamentals. Some are also grown for oil production from their seed and the leaves of one variety are used to produce tea. Camellias grow best in slightly acid soil and benefit from applications of fertiliser at the end of the flowering season. They are popular garden shrubs in many countries throughout the world and many thousands of cultivars are grown. A few are grown from seed but the vast majority are cutting grown or grafted.

Camellia cv. **Baby Bear**
A small plant with clusters of small pale pink single flowers.

Camellia cv. **Cinnamon Cindy**
A small plant with clusters of small white to pink flowers.

Camellia cv. **Fragrant Pink**
A small spreading plant with clusters of small bright lolly pink coloured flowers.

Camellia japonica

These are the most widely grown and popular Camellias, and prefer to grow in climates from cold temperate to sub-tropical. They flower from winter to spring and are evergreen tall shrubs to small trees which have a long life span.

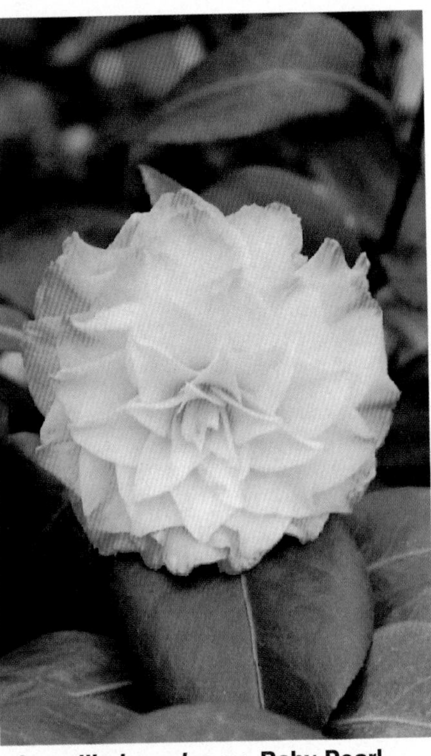

Camellia japonica cv. **Baby Pearl**
A small reflexed flower form. The flower colour is light pink overlaid with carmine.

Camellia japonica cv. **Benten**
A cultivar with variegated foliage and a single pinky red flower with a central cluster of gold stamens.

Camellia japonica **cv. Betty Sheffield Pink**
A very large, loose petalled, double flower, bright pink in colour.

Camellia japonica **cv. Cherries Jubilee**
On this medium upright grower the double flowers have a petaloid centre and are burgundy red in colour.

Camellia japonica **cv. Donckelarii**
The large semi-double flowers of this bushy grower are marbled red and white.

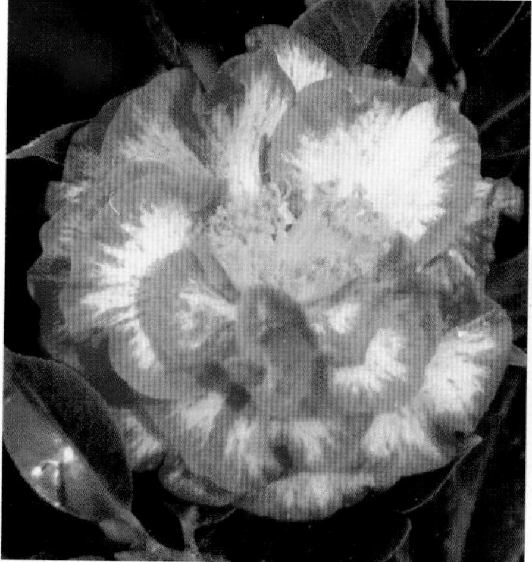

Camellia japonica **cv. Betty Sheffield Supreme**
This outstanding and popular cultivar has very large, loose petalled, double flowers, dark pink, edged red.

Camellia japonica **cv. Commander Mulroy**
This compact grower has formal double flowers of very pale pink edged with pink.

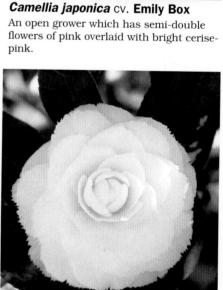

Camellia japonica **cv. Emily Box**
An open grower which has semi-double flowers of pink overlaid with bright cerise-pink.

Camellia japonica **cv. Bob's Tinsie**
An upright grower with small anemone-type red flowers with gold stamens.

Camellia japonica **cv. David Surina**
A compact grower with formal, double, light red flowers.

Camellia japonica **cv. Fimbriata**
On this upright grower the formal double white flowers have a serrated edge to the petals.

CAMELLIA (cont)

Camellia japonica cv. **Geoff Hamilton**
A compact grower which has formal double flowers of pink edged white, and showy variegated foliage.

Camellia japonica cv. **Governor Earl Warren**
An upright grower with peony form, loose, double flowers of pink with odd touches of white.

Camellia japonica cv. **Grace Albritton**
Small double formal flowers of white, edged with pink, feature on this upright bushy growing plant.

Camellia japonica cv. **Grand Prix**
A compact and upright grower. The very large semi-double red flowers have prominent golden stamens.

Camellia japonica cv. **Great Eastern**
A popular old Camellia having a tall bushy growth and loose petalled semi-double flowers of deep rose-pink, toned with white.

Camellia japonica cv. **Helenor**
This popular old form has double flowers of pink flecked with carmine.

Camellia japonica cv. **Hikaru-Genji**
syn. ***C.*** cv. **Herme**
A free flowering bushy grower with semi-double flowers of carmine edged with white.

Camellia japonica cv. **Jean Lyne**
On this compact grower the semi-double off white flowers are marked with carmine. It has yellow stamens.

Camellia japonica cv. **Lady Loch**
A bushy grower with double flowers of pink with white edges and occasional deeper pink marks.

CAMELLIA (cont)

Camellia japonica cv. **Little Slam**
The rich red flowers on this medium bushy grower are of a small peony form.

Camellia japonica cv. **Marie Bracey**
This upright grower has semi-double to loose peony form flowers of deep coral pink.

Camellia japonica cv. **Red Red Rose**
Bright red formal double flowers bloom on this compact grower.

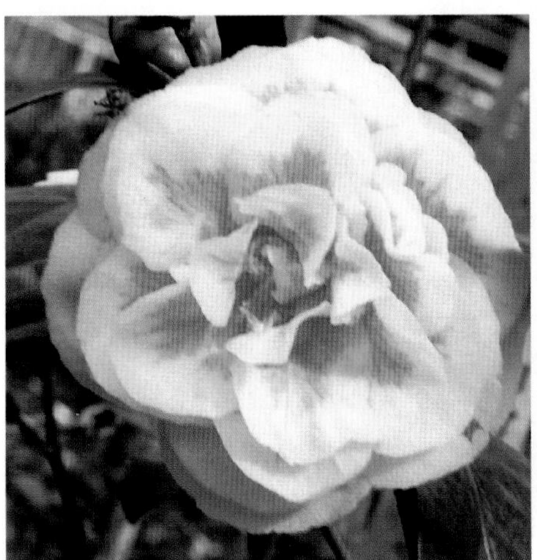

Camellia japonica cv. **Look Away**
An upright grower with semi-double flowers of deep rosy pink inside and white edges.

Camellia japonica cv. **Prince Frederick William**
An old favourite which is an upright grower with formal double, pink flowers.

Camellia japonica cv. **Spring Sonnet**
A bushy grower with double flowers coloured bright and pale pink.

Camellia japonica cv. **Margaret Davis**
An upright grower with peony form flowers, off white, edged with vermilion.

Camellia japonica cv. **Quercifolia**
A compact grower with unusual oak-like leaves. The single flowers are rosy pink with yellow stamens.

Camellia japonica cv. **Tama-No-Ura**
This upright growing plant has showy single flowers of red with a broad white edge.

CAMELLIA (cont)

Camellia japonica cv. **Tiffany**

Tall and upright, this cultivar has double, loose petalled, anemone-form orchid pink flowers.

Camellia japonica cv. **Tinsie**

An open grower with small single red flowers with white peony centres.

Camellia japonica cv. **Tom Knudsen**

A compact grower with loose petalled double flowers of blood red.

Camellia cv. **Kujaku-Tsubaki**

THE PEACOCK CAMELLIA

This plant has weeping foliage with pendulous flowers of red and white. Some authorities list this as a cultivar of *C. japonica*.

Camellia cv. **Night Rider**

A medium upright growing plant with small semi-double flowers of dark orange-red.

Camellia pitardii

An open branched species with small, very pale pink flowers.

Camellia reticulata

The following *C. reticulatas* are predominantly hybrid. The flowers are mostly very large and they tend to prefer a colder climate than *C. japonica*. In cold climates they may be seen flowering in frosts.

Camellia reticulata cv. **Arch of Triumph**

A tall shrub with very large semi-double flowers of deep rosy pink.

Camellia reticulata cv. **Confucius**

A compact upright grower with very large semi-double flowers of deep orchid pink.

Camellia reticulata cv. **Debut**

This compact plant has large, loose petalled, semi-double flowers of deep rose-pink.

Camellia reticulata cv. **Francie L.**

The large rose-pink flowers on this upright shrub are semi-double, with many petals.

Camellia reticulata cv. **Harold L. Paige**

An upright open grower with large, loose, many petalled flowers of blood red.

Camellia reticulata cv. **Jean Pursel**

The very large double flowers of this upright grower are coral pink.

Camellia reticulata cv. **La Petite**

A spreading plant with small, shell pink flowers in profusion.

Camellia reticulata cv. **Miss Tulare**

An upright grower with large formal double red flowers. The flowers at times may be loose petalled double.

Camellia reticulata cv. **Samantha**

This upright grower has very large semi-double flowers coloured china pink with light pink overtones.

Camellia reticulata cv. **Shot Silk**

A vigorous plant with semi-double, many petalled flowers coloured cyclamen pink.

Camellia sasanqua cv. **Beatrice Emily**

A fast growing upright plant with double white flowers with outer guard petals of violet.

CAMELLIA (cont)

***Camellia sasanqua* cv. Chansonette**
An upright vigorous grower which has bright pink double flowers which open as formal flowers then revert to loose petalled.

***Camellia sasanqua* cv. Gay**
The single white flowers on this upright grower have golden stamens.

Camellia tsaii
This is a tall growing species. It has masses of small white flowers with yellow stamens.

***Camellia* x *vernalis* cv. Shibori-Egao**
An upright grower with semi-double flowers coloured rosy pink with white blotches.

***Camellia* cv. Waterlily**
An upright open grower with formal double flowers coloured rose-pink. As the flowers age they get a darker pink edge to the petals.

***Camellia* x *williamsii* cv. Lady Gowrie**
The semi-double flowers on this compact upright grower are coloured pink.

Camellia yunnanensis
This is an upright open shrub which has single white flowers with yellow and brown clusters of stamens.

CAMOENSIA

FABACEAE [LEGUMINOSAE]

Camoensia maxima
A vigorous evergreen climber from tropical Africa which is very showy when covered with its white fragrant flowers. It requires a sub-tropical to tropical climate with good quality moist soil and a sunny situation. Propagate from seed and cuttings under mist.

CAMPSIS

BIGNONIACEAE

Hardy, vigorous, deciduous or evergreen climbers from China and North America, they prefer a rich soil and a sunny aspect. Tolerant of frosts, they give an outstanding floral display in spring and summer. Propagation is from seed or cuttings.

Campsis grandiflora

CHINESE TRUMPET CREEPER

syn. ***Bignonia chinensis***
A robust climber with large heads of scarlet coloured trumpet shaped flowers.

Campsis* x *tagliabuana

A hybrid between *C. grandiflora* and *C. radicans*, it has large heads of scarlet coloured trumpet shaped flowers.

Campsis radicans TRUMPET CREEPER

syn. ***Bignonia radicans***
A vigorous climber with large heads of orange coloured trumpet shaped flowers.

CANARINA

CAMPANULACEAE

Canarina canariensis

CANARY BELLFLOWER

A spreading and climbing plant from the Canary Islands. The orange coloured flowers are bell shaped and occur profusely in spring. They grow in climates from cool temperate to sub-tropical and prefer a rich soil. Propagation is from seed and cuttings.

CANTUA

POLEMONIACEAE

Small to tall pendulous shrubs from the Andes Mountains of South America. They prefer to grow in climates from cold temperate to warm temperate, and also favour a good fertile soil. These shrubs are spring flowering and widely grown as ornamentals. Propagate from seed and cuttings.

Cantua buxifolia

SACRED-FLOWER-OF-THE-INCAS

A medium shrub with small leaves and arching branches. The flowers which grow in weeping clusters are very bright pink.

CAPPARIS

CAPPARACEAE [CAPPARIDACEAE]

From tropical to temperate climates, these evergreen plants are climbers, shrubs and small trees. Capparis are grown as ornamentals and some are grown for their edible parts, known as capers. They grow in a wide range of soils and are propagated from seed.

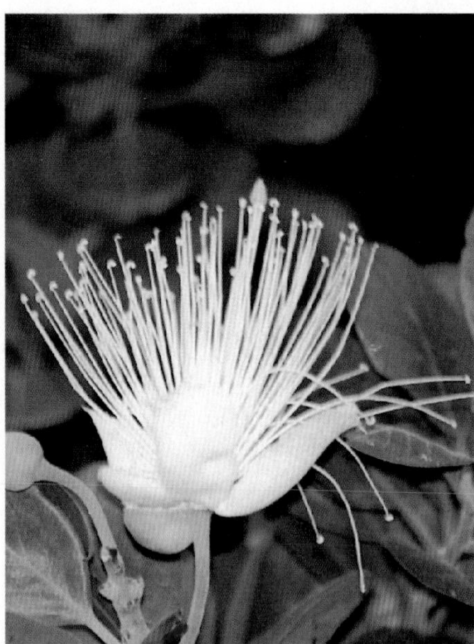

Capparis jacobsii
A tall shrub from the monsoon tropics, it has large white perfumed flowers.

Capparis ornans
A thorny climber with showy perfumed white to pale pink large flowers.

Capparis micrantha
syn. ***C. odorata***
A small evergreen tree with very delicate perfumed cream flowers. Buds are at times used as capers.

CARDWELLIA

PROTEACEAE

Cardwellia sublimis
NORTHERN SILKY OAK
A medium to large evergreen tree which has large clusters of creamy white flower spikes followed by large decorative seed pods. It is grown as an ornamental plant and as a street tree in climates from warm temperate to tropical. Propagate from seed.

CARISSA

APOCYNACEAE

Spreading evergreen spiny shrubs which are often grown as hedges, Carissas have white star shaped flowers and edible fruits. The plants are very hardy and are widely grown as ornamentals in dry situations. They grow in climates from cool temperate to tropical. Propagation is from seed and cuttings.

Carissa carandas NARANDA
An upright thorny shrub with masses of white flowers followed by red fruit which turn black.

Carissa macrocarpa
syn ***C. grandiflora*** NATAL PLUM
A dense thorny tall shrub with large white flowers followed by red edible fruit.

CARPENTERIA

HYDRANGEACEAE [SAXIFRAGACEAE]

Carpenteria californica 3
An evergreen medium shrub from North America. It is arid hardy and cold hardy, and has large white flowers in spring. Propagate from cuttings, suckers and seeds.

CARPHALEA

RUBIACEAE

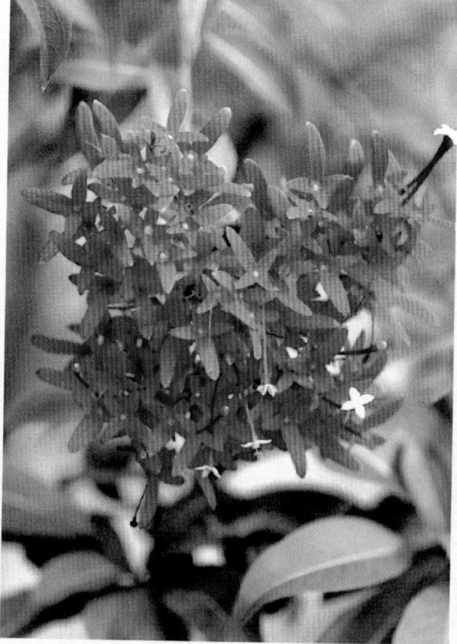

Carphalea kirondron FLAMING BEAUTY
From Madagascar, this is a very attractive evergreen shrub with red flowers which stay on the plant for many months. Carphalea prefers a climate from warm temperate to tropical and is an outstanding ornamental garden shrub. This shrub grows best in a good fertile well drained soil. Propagation is from seed and cuttings.

CASSIA

CAESALPINIACEAE [LEGUMINOSAE]

Cassias are mostly evergreen shrubs and trees and are from many countries. They grow in climates from cool temperate to tropical depending on the variety but most prefer to grow in sub-tropical and tropical climates. A recent revision has seen many Cassias taken from this classification and re-classified as Senna. These plants are popular ornamental trees and are showy when in flower. Propagation is from seed.

Cassia brewsteri LEICHHARDT BEAN
A very showy small tree with attractive flower heads which may cascade. Flowers are a mixture of creams, yellows, browns and pinks. An excellent street tree.

Cassia fistula GOLDEN SHOWER
This is a small tree with long cascading racemes of golden flowers.

Cassia grandis PINK SHOWER
A medium spreading tree with large heads of pink flowers which fade to white.

Cassia javanica
On this spreading, medium tree, the clusters of rose-pink to pale pink flowers fade as they age.

Cassia marksiana
A small tree with pendulous clusters of yellow flowers.

CASSIA (cont)

Cassia nodosa PINK AND WHITE SHOWER
A medium spreading tree with cascading clusters of rose-pink to pale pink flowers which fade as they age.

***Cassia* x Rainbow Shower**
A hybrid cassia which is a medium tree with cascading clusters of flowers which are cream and pink. Flowers vary from tree to tree.

CASSIPOUREA

RHIZOPHORACEAE

Cassipourea verticillata
A small evergreen tree with tufts of pale pink flowers which grow around the branches.

Cassia roxburghii ROSE SHOWER
syn. ***C. marginata***
This medium spreading tree has weeping clusters of bright rose-pink flowers.

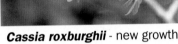

Cassia roxburghii - new growth

CASTANEA

FAGACEAE

Castanea sativa SPANISH CHESTNUT
A hardy deciduous small tree of medium size which has catkins of flowers followed by large prickly looking seed pods which enclose popular edible nuts. These trees prefer cooler climates to set seed but will grow in sub-tropical climates. The tree has been cultivated for thousands of years and exact country of origin cannot be identified but it is thought to have originated in the Balkans or Iraq. It prefers a slightly alkaline soil. Propagation is from seed and by grafting.

CASTANOSPERMUM

FABACEAE [LEGUMINOSAE]

Castanospermum australe BLACK BEAN

From sub-tropical and tropical Australia, and prized for the timber they produce, Castanospermums are grown as ornamental and street trees. The showy clusters of orange and yellow flowers in spring are followed by huge bean-type pods. They prefer lots of water in hot weather and good soil. Castanospermums will grow in climates from cool temperate to tropical and are grown widely in Europe as indoor plants. They grow freely from golf ball size seeds. Seeds and sawdust from timber are toxic. Research is being carried out on the seed of this tree as a possible AIDS or cancer cure.

CATALPA

BIGNONIACEAE

Medium to small deciduous trees from North America and Asia which are grown for their showy heads of flowers. They are used in parks and as street trees and make a good avenue tree. Catalpas are quite tolerant of cold and grow best in cool climates. They are spring flowering and are easily grown from seed.

Catalpa bignonioides INDIAN BEAN

A small to medium tree with terminal clusters of whitish mauve flowers with inner yellow markings.

Catalpa bungei cv. **Variegata**

A small tree which has attractive leaves coloured pink, cream and green.

Catalpa fargesii

This is a medium spreading tree which is covered with showy heads of flowers coloured pink, with pale purple throats.

Catalpa longissima

A bushy conical shaped tree with open clusters of white flowers which have yellow centres. Summer flowering.

Catalpa ovata CHINESE CATALPA

An upright small tree with terminal clusters of cream flowers.

Catalpa speciosa CATAWBA

A medium sized conical shaped tree with terminal heads of white flowers marked with brown.

CAVENDISHIA

ERICACEAE

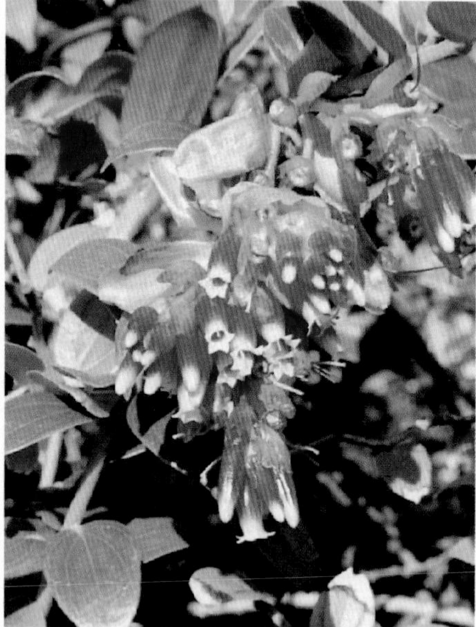

Cavendishia acuminata

This small South American evergreen shrub has weeping clusters of red and white tubular flowers. It is a colourful, small, spring flowering ornamental. Propagate from seed or cuttings.

CEANOTHUS

RHAMNACEAE

Deciduous or evergreen shrubs from North America, they are grown as free flowering ornamentals. There are many hybrids and cultivars. They grow in a wide range of soils and some are quite cold tolerant. Most are spring flowering and are propagated from seed and cuttings.

Ceanothus arboreus

CATALINA MOUNTAIN LILAC

A tall shrub with clusters of lilac-blue flowers.

***Ceanothus* cv. Blue Mould**

A cultivar which has ball shaped clusters of pale blue flowers.

Ceanothus cyaneus

SAN DIEGO CEANOTHUS

A medium evergreen shrub with lilac-blue flowers.

***Ceanothus* cv. Blue Pacific**

An outstanding, free flowering evergreen cultivar with clusters of bright blue flowers. A medium shrub.

***Ceanothus* cv. Delight**

In spring this upright bushy shrub has heads of deep blue flowers.

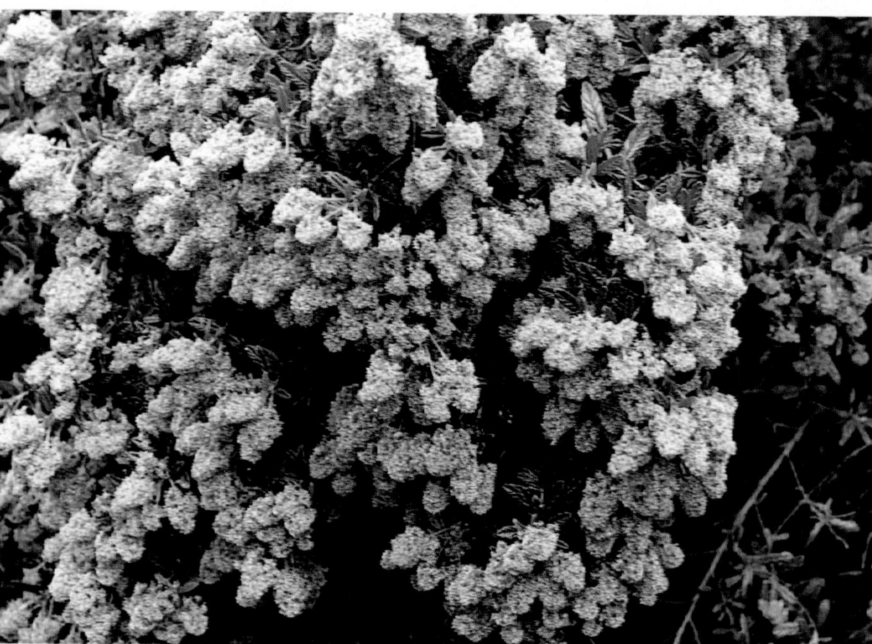

***Ceanothus* cv. Concha**

Free flowering, this cultivar has large heads of blue flowers.

***Ceanothus* cv. Filden Park**
A free flowering cultivar with long pendulous heads of blue flowers.

Ceanothus griseus* var. *horizontalis
A low growing spreading form of this shrub.

***Ceanothus impressus* cv. Puget Blue**
In spring this bushy cultivar has heads of dark blue flowers.

Ceanothus foliosus
This is a small shrub with pendulous clusters of dark blue flowers.

Ceanothus parryi
A semi-open shrub with oval heads of blue flowers.

Ceanothus griseus
This free flowering bushy shrub has showy heads of blue flowers in spring.

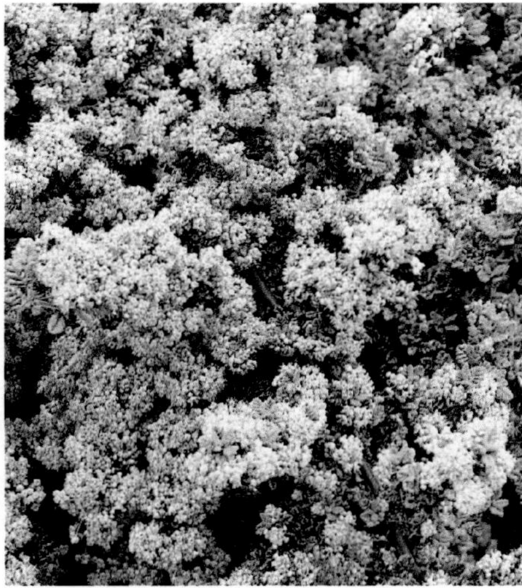

Ceanothus impressus
SANTA BARBARA CEANOTHUS
A free flowering shrub with blue flowers in small, ball shaped clusters.

Ceanothus thyrsiflorus
This bushy, tall shrub has large heads of blue to pale blue flowers.

CEIBA

Bombacaceae

Ceiba pentandra KAPOK TREE

This medium deciduous tree has cream coloured flowers followed by large seed pods which encase the seeds in a silky down. This down is used to make commercial kapok for bedding. The tree grows best in climates from warm temperate to tropical. Grown from seed.

CELTIS

Ulmaceae

Celtis sinensis

This is an evergreen, medium, spreading tree although many Celtis are deciduous. This tree is grown from seed in temperate and sub-tropical climates as a shade or street tree.

CERATOPETALUM

Cunoniaceae

Ceratopetalum gummiferum

NEW SOUTH WALES CHRISTMAS BUSH

This small, upright, evergreen tree is native to Australia, where it flowers at Christmas time. It prefers a cool temperate to sub-tropical climate and when in flower in mid-summer the white flowers are followed by bright red calyces which will completely cover the bush. It grows best in a sandy loam and makes an excellent cut flower. It is propagated from seed and cuttings.

CERATOSTIGMA

Plumbaginaceae

Ceratostigma willmottianum

CHINESE PLUMBAGO

syn. ***Plumbago willmottianum***

In spring, this clumping plant holds its royal blue flowers over a long period. It is hardy to dry spells but prefers a cool to sub-tropical climate. Propagation is from seed, cutting or by division.

CERBERA

Apocynaceae

Small trees or shrubs, native to Australia and Asia and tolerant of salt.

Cerbera manghas

A small evergreen tree. It is grown in warm climates for its attractive flowers followed by large mango-looking fruit. These and other parts of the tree are poisonous. It is grown from seed.

Cerbera odollam

A tall shrub with highly perfumed white flowers. The plant grows well near the sea. Often referred to as *C. manghas*.

CERCIS

Caesalpiniaceae [Leguminosae]

Cercis trees were once common in the Judean Hills. They are deciduous shrubs and small trees which are widely grown as ornamentals in mild to moderately cold climates. Cercis flower freely in the spring and in some conditions the flowers may open before the leaves appear. They are quite rapid growers in good soil and are propagated from seed. The plants are native to Europe, North America and Asia.

Cercis canadensis REDBUD

A spreading tall shrub to small tree with clusters of pinky lilac coloured flowers which are used for flavouring condiments.

Cercis chinensis CHINESE REDBUD

A tall shrub to small tree which has rose-pink to magenta coloured flowers which mostly appear before the leaves.

Cercis griffithii

A dense, free flowering small tree with rose-pink flowers in spring.

Cercis occidentalis WESTERN REDBUD

A tall shrub with large clumps of rose-pink flowers which mostly appear before the new leaves.

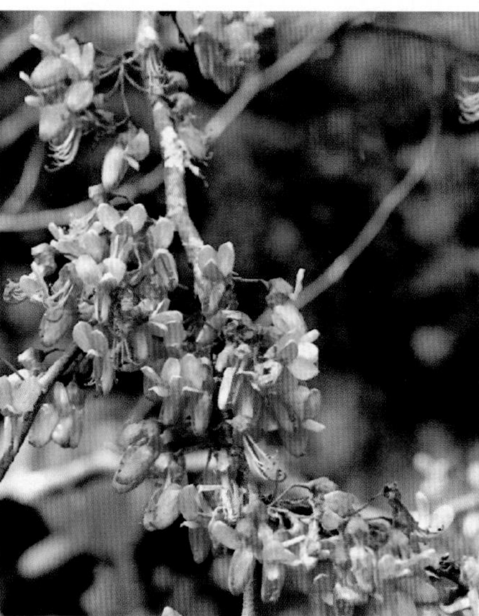

Cercis siliquastrum JUDAS TREE

A tall shrub to small tree with clusters of magenta to violet coloured flowers.

CESTRUM

Solanaceae

Evergreen or deciduous shrubs and small trees, many of which are grown as flowering ornamentals. They are native to tropical and sub-tropical South America and in cultivation many have adapted to cool temperate climates. The plants usually have dense foliage and some have exotic perfumes. Some Cestrums are poisonous. They grow in a wide range of soils and flower in spring and summer. Propagation is from seed and cuttings.

Cestrum aurantiacum GOLDEN JESSAMINE

A dense shrub to semi-climber with old gold coloured flowers in clusters. The leaves have a pungent odour when crushed.

Cestrum elegans

A dense shrub with cascading clusters of rose-pink to reddish flowers.

CESTRUM (cont)

Cestrum elegans cv. **Purpurea**
A purple flowered cultivar of this shrub.

Cestrum fasciculatum
In spring this medium shrub has clusters of red tubular flowers.

Cestrum nocturnum LADY OF THE NIGHT
The cream flowers of this tall shrub open at night and give off a strong sweet smelling perfume.

Cestrum elegans cv. **Rosea**
This cultivar has pink flowers.

Cestrum parqui WILLOW LEAF JESSAMINE
This evergreen shrub has arching branches and clusters of perfumed yellow flowers.

Cestrum endlicheri SCARLET JESSAMINE
A dense evergreen shrub with showy clusters of scarlet coloured flowers.

Cestrum fasciculatum cv. **Newellii**
A dense shrub which resembles *C. elegans*, the difference being that the pinky red flowers on this shrub are larger and the flower heads much larger also.

Cestrum psittacinum
A sparse medium shrub with clusters of tubular flowers coloured old gold to orange.

CHADSIA

FABACEAE [LEGUMINOSAE]

Chadsia grevei
An open branched shrub native to Madagascar, it has heads of long orange-red flowers in spring. The plant requires a well drained soil in a warm climate. Propagate from seed.

CHAENOMELES

FLOWERING QUINCE; JAPONICA

ROSACEAE

These plants are widely grown in cold climates where they flower at their best but they may be grown in climates as warm as sub-tropical. These shrubs produce an edible quince-like fruit. They prefer a good quality soil to get a good show of flowers in early spring. Propagation is from cuttings or by division.

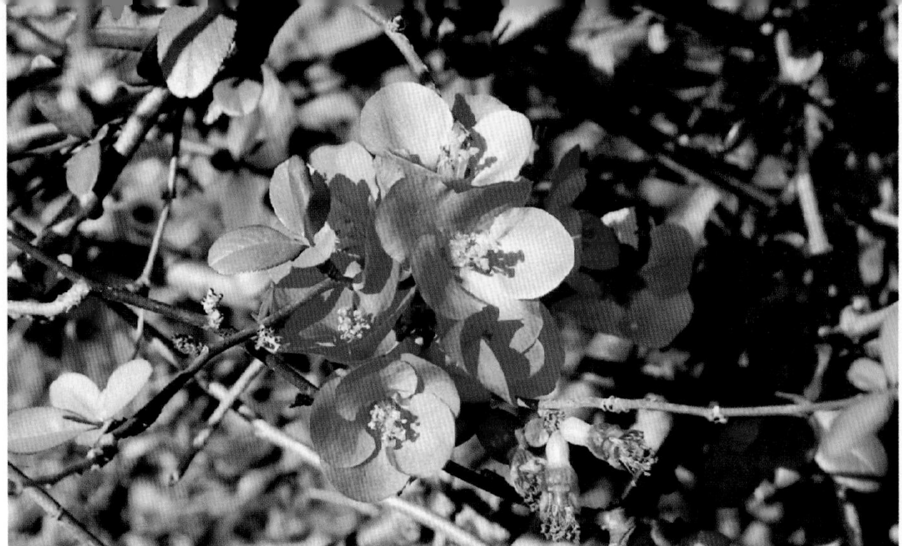

Chaenomeles speciosa JAPANESE QUINCE
A much branched shrub with cup shaped flowers of red with yellow stamens.

Chaenomeles speciosa cv. **Alba**
A cultivar with white flowers.

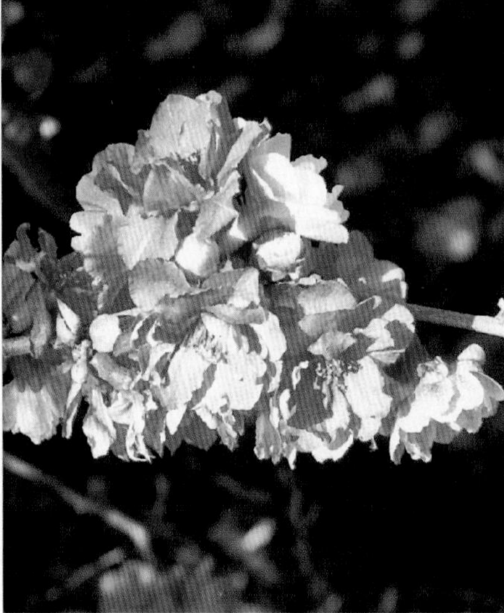

Chaenomeles speciosa cv. **Falconnet Charlet**
On this cultivar the flowers are double, and pinky red.

Chaenomeles japonica cv. **Chosan**
In late winter this sparse shrub has large, pale pink to salmon pink flowers.

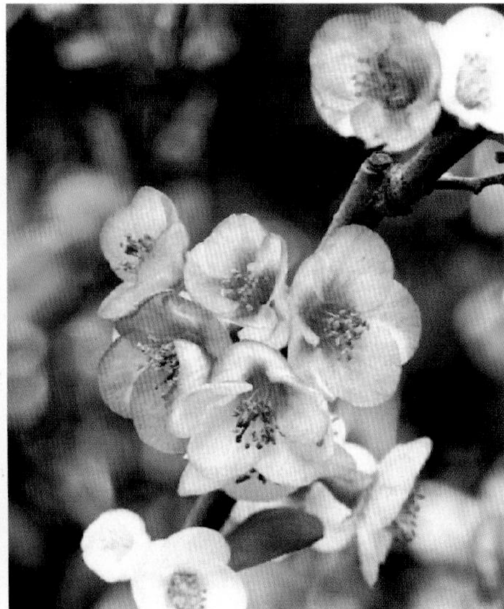

Chaenomeles speciosa cv. **Alba Rosea**
Both pink and white flowers bloom on this cultivar.

Chaenomeles speciosa cv. **Moerloosii**
syn. *C.* cv. **Apple Blossom**
A cultivar with flowers of pale pink marked with darker pink.

CHAENOMELES (cont)

***Chaenomeles speciosa* cv. Nivalis**
A vigorous cultivar with white flowers.

***Chaenomeles speciosa* cv. Phyllis Moore**
This cultivar has bright pink coloured flowers.

***Chaenomeles speciosa* cv. Rowallane**
Free flowering, this cultivar has dark red flowers.

***Chaenomeles speciosa* cv. Sanguinea Plena**
A cultivar which has double scarlet-red flowers.

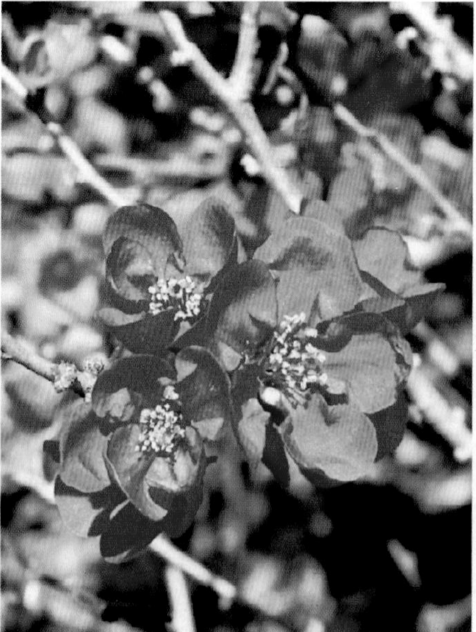

***Chaenomeles* x superba**
A hybrid between *C. speciosa* and *C. japonica* which has clusters of red flowers with slightly ruffled petals.

CHAMAECYTISUS

FABACEAE [LEGUMINOSAE]

Chamaecytisus palmensis

TAGASASTE

This tall evergreen shrub with arching foliage is from Europe. It is widely grown in semi-arid areas as a stock food, especially for goats. The plant is also used in soil stabilisation. It grows rapidly, takes some frost and is grown from seed. It may become a weed in some conditions.

Chamaecytisus purpureus
A low growing shrub with arching branches which are covered with rosy violet coloured flowers in spring.

CHAMELAUCIUM

WAX FLOWERS

MYRTACEAE

These plants are native to Western Australia and have flowers which look and feel like wax. They are widely grown throughout the world as a long flowering ornamental or a long lasting cut flower. Chamelaucium grow well in sandy soils and semi-arid areas and flower in winter and spring. These shrubs are evergreen and have small round needle-like leaves. They are propagated from seed and tip cuttings.

Chamelaucium drummondii

This small upright shrub has terminal clusters of small white flowers with touches of pink.

Chamelaucium floriferum

A medium shrub with large heads of pink flowers with purple centres.

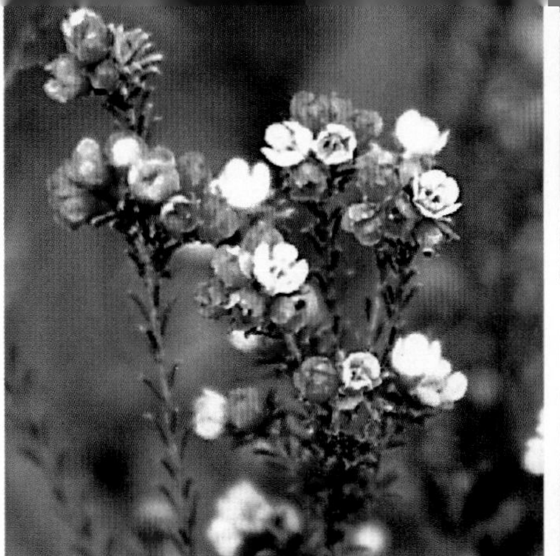

Chamelaucium hallii

This species has deep pink to purple and white flowers.

Chamelaucium uncinatum

GERALDTON WAX

A widely grown spreading medium to tall shrub. It has pink flowers with purple centres as the flowers age. It is an excellent ornamental shrub and a popular cut flower. Some of the popular cultivars follow.

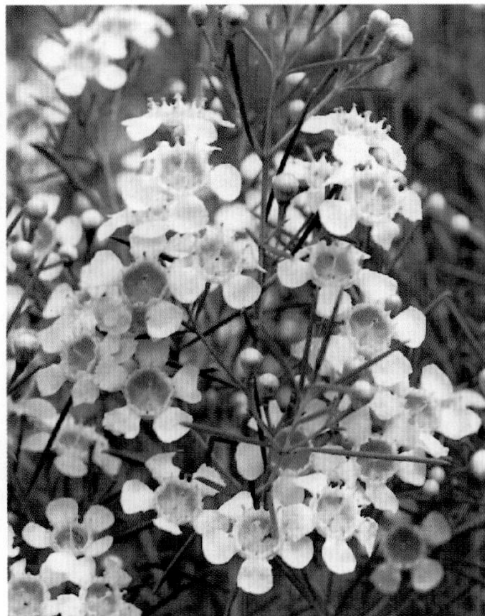

***Chamelaucium uncinatum* cv. Alba**

A white flowered cultivar.

***Chamelaucium uncinatum* cv. Mini White**

This cultivar has smaller white flowers than *C. uncinatum* cv. Alba.

***Chamelaucium uncinatum* cv. Pink Flamingo**

A popular cultivar with flamingo pink flowers.

***Chamelaucium uncinatum* cv. Purple Pride**

A compact grower with masses of purple flowers.

CHAMELAUCIUM (cont)

***Chamelaucium uncinatum* cv. Red Eyes**

The flowers of this cultivar are rose-pink in colour with purple-red centres.

***Chamelaucium uncinatum* cv. Rubra**

A cultivar with cerise coloured flowers.

***Chamelaucium* x cv. Wanneroo beauty**

A hybrid with dainty white and purple flowers.

CHILOPSIS

BIGNONIACEAE

Chilopsis linearis* var. *linearis 3

DESERT WILLOW

An evergreen tall shrub native to southern U.S.A. and Mexico. It is a hardy plant which grows in arid areas and has clusters of pink to cerise coloured flowers. It prefers a dry soil, is grown from seed and takes moderate frosts.

CHIMONANTHUS

CALYCANTHACEAE

Chimonanthus praecox

Native to China, this deciduous shrub is grown in cool to mild climates as a fragrant flowering ornamental. The pendulous, sweet smelling yellow cup shaped flowers appear in late winter before the new foliage appears. These shrubs prefer a well drained soil with ample water in summer and benefit from mulching. Propagate from seed and cuttings or by layering.

CHIONANTHUS

OLEACEAE

Chionanthus retusus FRINGE TRE

A small deciduous spreading tree. It takes considerable cold and prefers cold climates to flower at its best. The delicate spring flowers grow in loose clusters and are white in colour. This tree prefers an alkaline soil and is grown from seed.

CHOISYA

RUTACEAE

Choisya ternata

MEXICAN ORANGE BLOSSOM

A highly perfumed evergreen shrub from Mexico and southern U.S.A. The star shaped white flowers are displayed in large clusters in spring and summer. It grows in climates from cold temperate to sub-tropical but is seen at its best in the cooler climates. Propagation is from seed and soft wood cuttings.

***Choisya ternata* cv. Aztec Pearl**

This cultivar has finer leaves and pale pink flowers.

***Choisya ternata* cv. Sundance**

A cultivar which has golden leaves.

CHONEMORPHA

FRANGIPANI VINE

APOCYNACEAE

Evergreen vigorous vines from India and South East Asia. Growing in sub-tropical and tropical climates, they prefer a rich slightly acid soil and benefit from regular watering in summer. The large cream flowers have a delicate perfume and the plant is widely used as a fence cover. Propagation is from cuttings.

Chonemorpha fragrans

CLIMBING FRANGIPANI

A hardy tropical climber with heads of large perfumed cream flowers.

Chonemorpha penangensis

From Penang, this free flowering perfumed evergreen climber has dark cream flowers with yellow centres.

CHORICARPIA

MYRTACEAE

Choricarpia leptopetala

BRUSH TURPENTINE

An evergreen semi-parasitic tall shrub from eastern Australia. The plant has sparse bunches of round cream flowers. It grows well in climates from cool temperate to sub-tropical and prefers a semi-shaded situation. Propagate from seed.

CHORISIA

BOMBACACEAE

Semi-deciduous small to medium trees with swollen thorny trunks, native to South America. They are free flowering with large flowers in summer to autumn and are very spectacular ornamental trees when in full flower. An outstanding display may be seen outside Disneyland in California U.S.A. and in the main street of Buenos Aires. The large seed pods have a silky substance covering the seed. They are propagated from seed and grow in climates from mild temperate to tropical and will withstand light frosts.

Chorisia insignis

A swollen trunked medium tree with white to cream flowers which at times have a brown centre.

CHORISIA (cont)

Chorisia insignis cv. **Golden Wonder**
An outstanding cultivar with golden coloured flowers.

Chorisia speciosa
A small to medium tree with a very thorny trunk and large heads of flowers coloured cerise and white with brownish markings.

Chorisia speciosa cv. **Majestic Beauty**
An outstanding cultivar with large flowers which are a darker cerise in the colour.

CHORIZEMA

FABACEAE [LEGUMINOSAE]

Chorizema ilicifolia HOLLY FLAME PEA
A spreading shrub native to Australia. The pea shaped orange and red flowers are very colourful. It is grown as an ornamental plant especially in sandy loam soils. Propagate from seed and cuttings.

CHRYSANTHEMOIDES

ASTERACEAE [COMPOSITAE]

Chrysanthemoides monilifera BITOU BUSH; BONESEED
syn. ***Osteospermum moniliferum***
This spreading shrub is a native of South Africa. It is widely grown throughout the world as a sand stabilisation plant but in some places such as coastal Australia it has naturalised and become a noxious weed. It has yellow flowers most of the year and is grown from seed and cuttings.

CHRYSOBALANUS

CHRYSOBALANACEAE

Chrysobalanus icaco COCO PLUM
A tropical, evergreen, tall shrub to small tree which has edible red pulpy fruit. It has small white flowers and is grown in sub-tropical and tropical climates. It is propagated from seed.

CHRYSOTHEMIS

GESNERIACEAE

Chrysothemis pulchella
This small shrubby plant is grown as an indoor plant. It has fleshy bronze-green leaves and showy terminal clusters of orange and yellow flowers. The plant is native to tropical America and is grown outdoors in tropical climates and as an indoor plant in milder climates. Propagation is from cuttings.

CHUKRASIA

MELIACEAE

Chukrasia tabularis INDIAN REDWOOD

A small to medium tree native to India and Malaysia. It is grown as a spectacular ornamental for its brightly coloured pink, red and orange coloured leaves in spring and is also used for timber. This tree will grow in climates from warm temperate to tropical and is propagated from seed.

CINNAMOMUM

LAURACEAE

Cinnamomum verum CINNAMON
syn. ***C. zeylanicum***

This small evergreen tree is native to India and Sri Lanka. It has small creamy yellow flowers and bright red new growth. The tree is used to make commercial Cinnamon and is grown in frost free climates. Grown from seed.

CISSUS

VITACEAE

Cissus are vines and shrubs from many countries throughout the world, growing in climates from cool temperate to tropical. They are widely grown in horticulture as ground covers, indoor plants or feature shrubs. Cissus prefer a rich, slightly acid soil. Some have edible grape-like fruit. Propagate from seed and cuttings.

Cissus adnata

A deciduous woody vine from tropical Australia. The leaves are used for medicine. It has insignificant flowers and black grape-like fruit.

Cissus hypoglauca WATER VINE

An evergreen climber with palmate leaves from Australia. Grown as an indoor foliage plant, it has black grape-like fruit.

Cissus antarctica KANGAROO VINE

From Australia, this shiny leaved vigorous vine is grown throughout the world as an indoor plant and grown in warm climates as a ground cover. It has black grape-like fruit and takes some frost.

Cissus juttae

A tall succulent leaf shrub which has insignificant flowers and showy red berries.

Cissus discolor

A colourful climber which has leaves coloured dark green to purple, overlaid with silver.

Cissus quadrangularis VELDT GRAPE

A leafless climber with fleshy branches. The clusters of white flowers are followed by red berries.

CISSUS (cont)

Cissus rhombifolia

VENEZUELA TREEBINE

A vigorous vine with attractive leaves grown as an indoor plant.

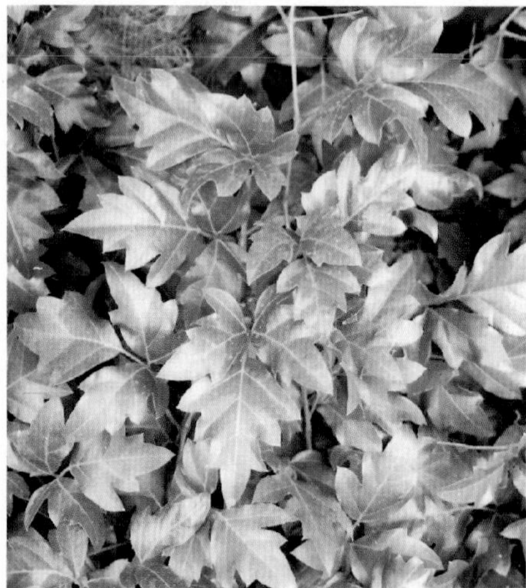

Cissus rhombifolia cv. **Ellen Danica**

An attractive cultivar with multiple pointed leaves.

Cissus striata

syn. ***Ampelopsis sempervirens; Vitis striata***

This is a modest growing evergreen climber which is used to cover fences or as a ground cover, or grown in hanging baskets.

CISTUS

ROCK ROSE

CISTACEAE

Hardy evergreen shrubs from the Mediterranean region. They have fragrant foliage and prefer to grow in alkaline soil. Cistus are widely grown in climates from cold temperate to sub-tropical and are grown from seed or cuttings. They flower freely in spring and summer.

Cistus x ***canescens*** cv. **Albus**

A free flowering shrub with white flowers and prominent yellow stamens.

Cistus cv. **Grayswood Pink**

A free flowering spreading small shrub with large flowers coloured pale pink to rose-pink.

Cistus incanus

A small free flowering shrub with cerise flowers and yellow stamens.

Cistus incanus ssp. ***creticus***

The leaves on this plant are more pointed than on *C. incanus*.

Cistus ladanifer cv. **Albiflorus**

A thin leaf bushy shrub with large white flowers which have prominent yellow stamens.

Cistus laurifolius cv. **Elma**

This popular shrub has white flowers with yellow stamens.

CISTUS (cont)

Cistus libanotis
A small shrub with thin leaves and white flowers which have yellow central stamens.

Cistus parviflorus
A free flowering spreading shrub with large white to pink flowers with yellow stamens.

Cistus populifolius
A small shrub which has large white flowers with overlapping petals and prominent golden stamens.

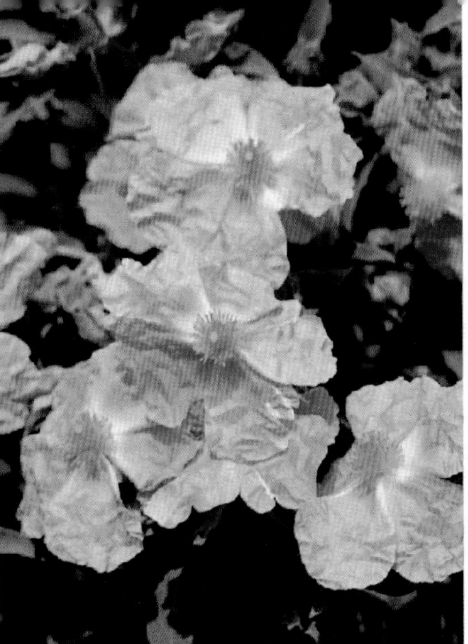

Cistus* x *pulverulentus
A free flowering shrub with large cerise coloured flowers and golden central stamens.

***Cistus* x *purpureus* cv. Brilliancy**
A very popular small shrub. The bright rose-pink flowers have maroon inner markings.

Cistus salviifolius
A very free flowering dwarf shrub having masses of white flowers with yellow stamens.

CITHAREXYLUM

VERBENACEAE

Citharexylum fruticosum FIDDLEWOOD
syn. ***C. subserratum***
A graceful evergreen from the West Indies. It has pendulous racemes of perfumed cream flowers and is grown as an ornamental timber. The timber is highly prized for making musical instruments. It prefers a frost free climate. The leaves turn reddish gold in winter. It is propagated from seed and cuttings.

CLAUSENA

RUTACEAE

Clausena lansium WAMPI
A small evergreen tropical tree, it is grown both as an ornamental and for its edible fruit which are grape size and texture and are orange coloured when ripe. They form in quite large bunches after showy bunches of white flowers. Propagate from seed.

Clausena lansium - fruit

C

CLEMATIS

RANUNCULACEAE

Clematis are mostly woody climbers and native to many countries, growing in climates ranging from very cold, through temperate to tropical. Those from the colder climates are mostly deciduous and are the most popular. Many are prized as ornamentals for their outstanding flowers and at least one is believed to have a medicinal use. They are winter, spring and summer flowering and many new large flowered hybrids and cultivars have been developed. The cultivation of Clematis is recorded as far back as the sixteenth century, making it one of the oldest plants known in cultivation. They grow in a wide range of soils but a soil with a neutral pH is ideal for most varieties. Propagation is from seed and cuttings. Many of the following cultivars are of unidentified origin.

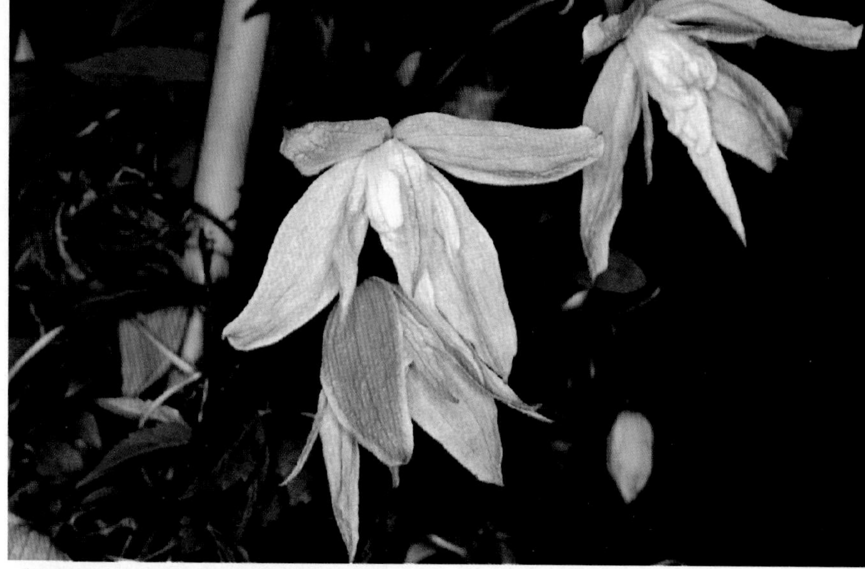

Clematis alpina cv. **Pink Flamingo**

A free flowering cultivar with weeping, pink flowers.

Clematis alpina 6

A deciduous climber which is very popular in colder climates. It has pendulous bell shaped blue flowers with white stamens. There are many cultivars of *C. alpina*.

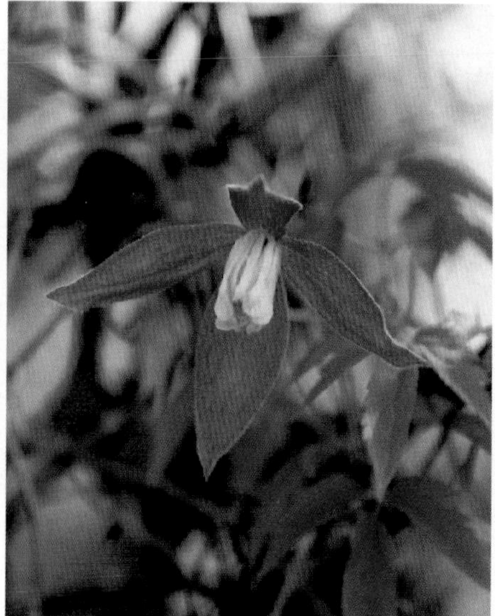

Clematis alpina cv. **Ruby**

An open flowered cultivar with wine coloured flowers.

Clematis alpina cv. **Tage Lundell**

The pendulous flowers of this cultivar are old rose in colour.

Clematis alpina cv. **Frances Rivis**

This cultivar has violet coloured flowers with white stamens.

Clematis alpina cv. **Willy**

A cultivar with pale pink flowers.

Clematis aristata
An evergreen vine from Australia which grows from sub-tropical to cold temperate climates. It has masses of white flowers with cream centres.

Clematis armandii
An evergreen climber with masses of creamy white flowers.

***Clematis* cv. Aumunn**
A cultivar with large violet-blue flowers.

***Clematis* cv. Barbara Dibley**
A free flowering cultivar with large cerise coloured flowers.

Clematis barbellata
From the Himalayas, this climber has mahogany flowers.

***Clematis* cv. Belle of Woking**
This climber has large double flowers coloured pinky mauve.

***Clematis* cv. Blue Boy**
This large flowered cultivar has blue-violet flowers.

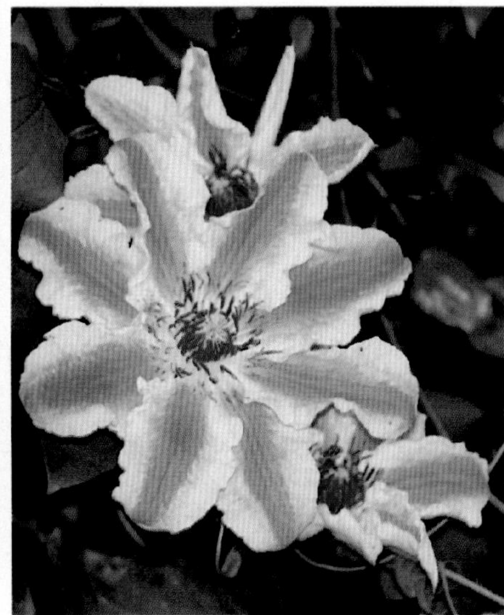

***Clematis* cv. Captain Thuilleaux**
A large flowered cultivar with flowers coloured pink and cerise.

CLEMATIS (cont)

Clematis chrysocoma

Free flowering, this vine has small flowers of pale pink.

Clematis cv. **Constance**

A large flowered plant with mauve flowers.

Clematis cirrhosa

An evergreen climber which has pendulous flowers coloured cream and dusted with cerise markings inside the flower. It flowers in late winter.

Clematis cv. **Corona**

This plant has large flowers of pink with cerise markings.

Clematis cv. **Crimson King** 6

The large flowers of this plant are deep maroon-crimson.

Clematis cv. **Comtesse de Bouchard**

This cultivar has large flowers which are pinkish, with sometimes a touch of mauve.

Clematis cv. **Countess of Lovelace**

A cultivar with large double flowers coloured lavender.

Clematis cv. **C. W. Downman**

A large flowered climber. The flowers are pink with rose-pink markings.

CLEMATIS (cont)

***Clematis* cv. Daniel Deronda**
Bluish violet is the colour of the large semi-double flowers of this cultivar.

***Clematis* cv. Duchess of Edinburgh**
This Clematis has large, double flowers of white.

***Clematis* cv. Dawn**
This cultivar has large, pale pink flowers.

Clematis* x *durandii
The four-petal flowers of this hybrid are violet-blue in colour.

***Clematis* cv. Elsa Spath**
This large flowered climber has violet coloured flowers.

***Clematis* cv. Doctor Ruppell**
The large flowers of this cultivar are coloured bright pink with carmine markings.

***Clematis* cv. Edith**
A large flowered cultivar with flowers of white to very pale pink.

***Clematis* cv. Fireworks**
The large flowers of this cultivar are rose-pink, with cerise markings.

CLEMATIS (cont)

Clematis florida **cv. Alba Plena** 9
The double flowers of this cultivar are coloured green and white.

Clematis florida **cv. Sieboldii**
This climber has white flowers with a purple centre.

Clematis forsteri
A spreading climber which is covered with small cream flowers in spring.

Clematis glycinoides [glycioides]
A very free flowering, evergreen, white flowered climber from Australia. The fragrance of the crushed leaves is said to alleviate headaches if inhaled.

Clematis **cv. Guernsey Cream**
This large flowered cultivar has cream coloured flowers with touches of green.

Clematis **cv. Hagley Hybrid**
A hybrid cultivar with large bright pink flowers.

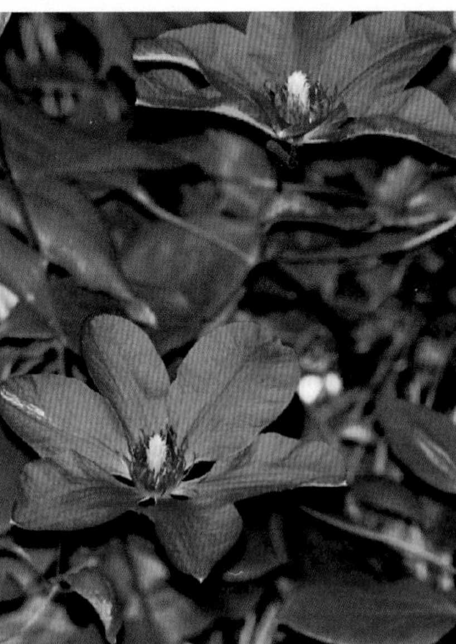

Clematis **cv. Hainton Ruby**
Very showy, this cultivar has large plum-red coloured flowers.

Clematis heracleifolia cv. **Wyevale**
A bushy upright plant with perfumed, small blue flowers.

Clematis cv. **H. F. Young**
The flowers are large and violet coloured on this free flowering climber.

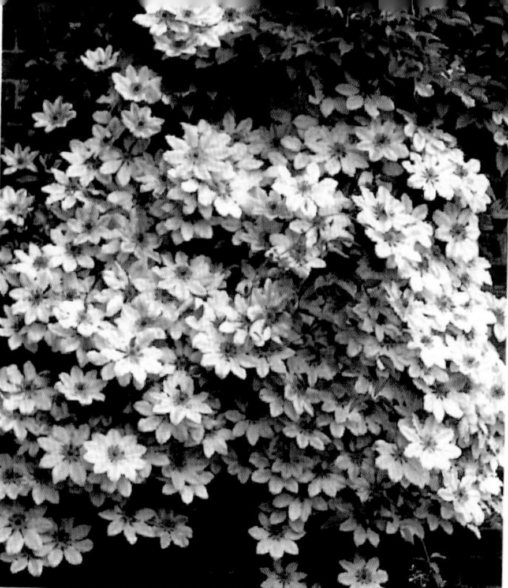

Clematis cv. **Jean Wilcox**
A large very free flowering cultivar. Flowers are mauve-lilac with a darker centre.

Clematis cv. **John Warren**
The large flowers of this cultivar have greyish white petals overlaid with pink.

Clematis cv. **Ken Donson**
Flowers of this cultivar are very large, and blue.

Clematis koreana
A sparse climber with pendulous pinkish violet flowers.

Clematis cv. **Lady in Red**
A large flowered cultivar. Flowers are wine red in colour.

Clematis cv. **Lilacina**
This large flowered form has purple flowers.

CLEMATIS (cont)

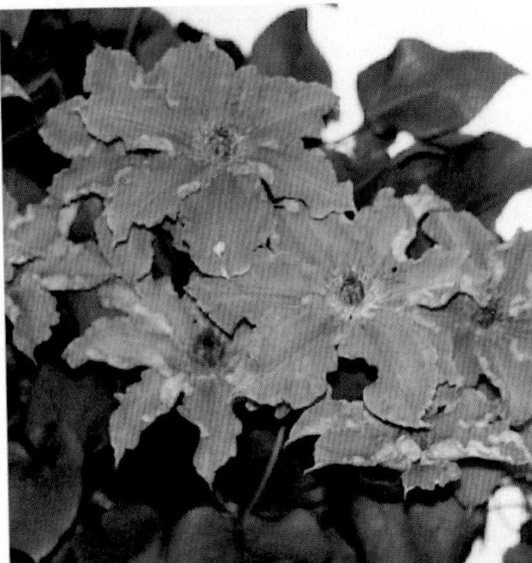

Clematis cv. **Lord Nevill**
A free flowering cultivar which has crinkled edges to the petals of the bluish violet coloured flowers.

Clematis cv. **Lunar Lass**
Masses of cream flowers bloom on this free flowering, modest, sparse climber.

Clematis macropetala 6
Free flowering, this climber has pendulous double blue flowers.

Clematis macropetala cv. **Lincolnshire Lady** 9
Purple-blue is the colour of the double flowers on this free flowering cultivar.

Clematis macropetala 6 cv. **Markham's Pink**
A cultivar with double pink flowers.

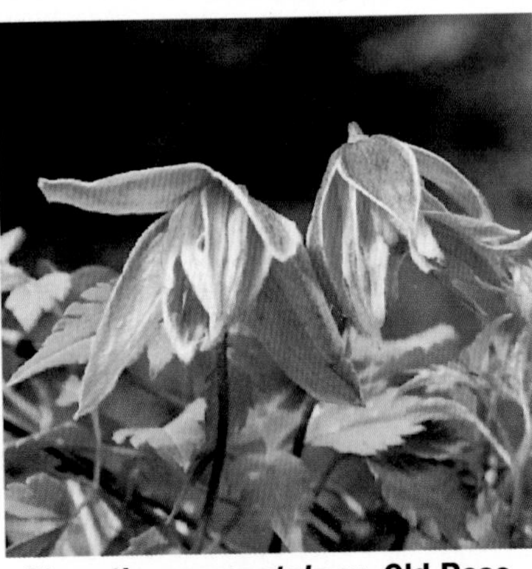

Clematis macropetala cv. **Old Rose**
Double flowers of old-rose pink bloom on this cultivar.

Clematis cv. **Madame Le Coultre**
A large flowered Clematis with white flowers.

Clematis cv. **Marcel Mosser**
The pink petals of this cultivar have a darker pink bar.

Clematis cv. **Margaret Gordon**
This hybrid has large flowers of pink with darker pink markings.

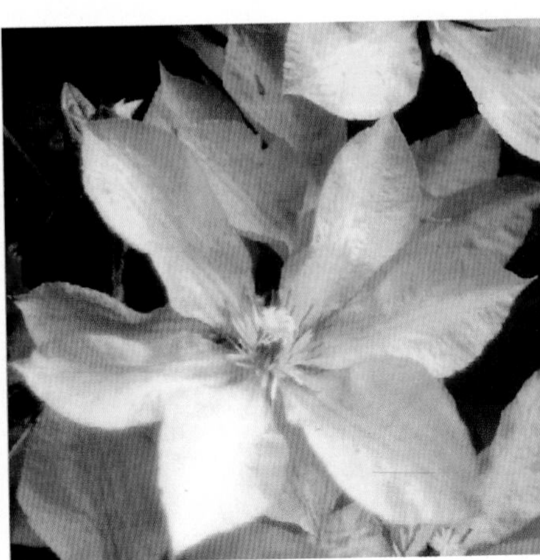

Clematis cv. **Margaret Hunt** 9
A free flowering cultivar with old-rose pink coloured flowers.

CLEMATIS (cont)

Clematis **cv. Mauve Beauty**
This climber has large pale mauve flowers.

Clematis montana
Vigorous and free flowering, this climber has cream coloured flowers often tinged pink.

Clematis microphylla
An evergreen climber with masses of small cream flowers.

Clematis montana **cv. Alba**
A clear white flowered cultivar of this free flowering climber.

Clematis montana **f. *grandiflora***
A form with larger white flowers.

Clematis **cv. Miss Bateman**
On this cultivar, the large flowers are white with occasional purple centre markings.

Clematis montana **cv. Elizabeth**
This cultivar has pale pink flowers.

CLEMATIS (cont)

Clematis montana **cv. Marjorie** 9
The semi-double flowers of this free flowering cultivar are cream with pinky red tints.

Clematis montana **cv. Mayleen**
Very free flowering, this cultivar has pale pink flowers.

Clematis montana **var. *rubens***
This variety has new leaves tinged with purple and mid-pink flowers.

Clematis montana **cv. Tetrarose**
A pink cultivar with ruby-red stems.

Clematis montana **var. *wilsonii***
The white flowers of this variety have partly twisted petals.

Clematis **cv. Mrs Cholmondeley**
This cultivar has very large lavender coloured flowers.

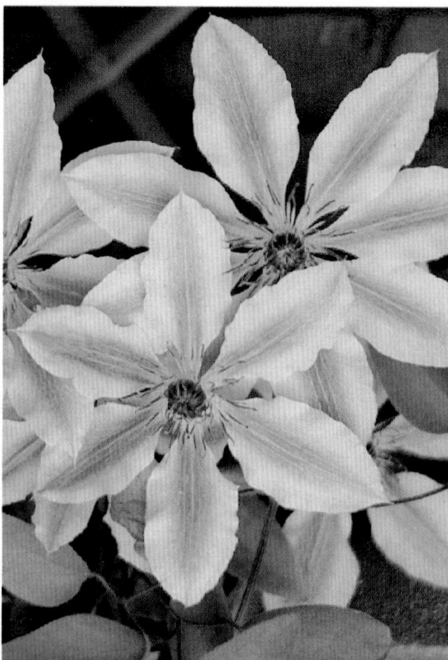

Clematis **cv. Nelly Moser**
A popular old cultivar having pink-mauve flowers with rose-pink bars.

Clematis **cv. Niobe**
The large flowers of this compact cultivar are deep ruby-red.

CLEMATIS (cont)

Clematis orientalis 6

A scrambling vine with singular pendulous yellowish flowers on long stems.

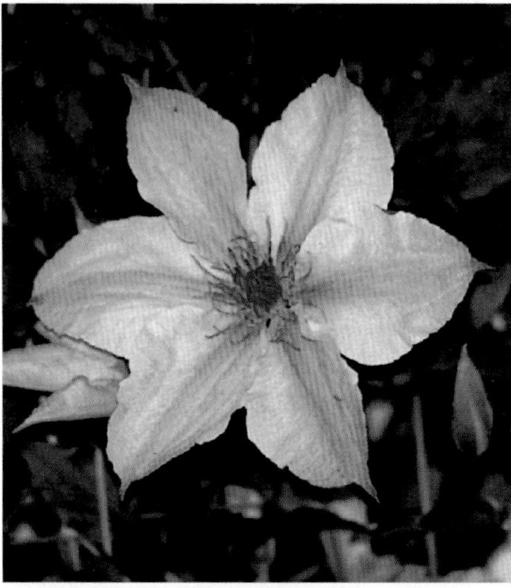

***Clematis* cv. Pink Fantasy**

Free flowering, this cultivar has pink flowers with rose-pink markings.

***Clematis* cv. Prince Charles**

A free flowering cultivar which has moderate sized bluish mauve coloured flowers.

Clematis pubescens

This illustration shows the attractive clusters of silky seed heads which follow the small white flowers of this evergreen climber.

***Clematis* cv. Red Cavalier**

A large flowered cultivar with more than normal numbers of petals. Flower colour is deep rose-pink edged lighter pink.

***Clematis* cv. Royal Velvet**

This is a new cultivar with reddish velvety flowers.

***Clematis* cv. Silver Moon**

A cultivar with large, silver-pink flowers.

***Clematis* cv. Sir Garnet Wolseley**

On this climber the large flowers are bluish mauve.

***Clematis* cv. Snow Queen**

A cultivar with large flowers, off white in colour.

C

CLEMATIS (cont)

Clematis spooneri 9
This is a vigorous vine with masses of small white flowers in spring.

Clematis **cv. Sugar Candy**
The large flowers of this cultivar have pink petals with a darker pink central bar.

Clematis tangutica
This is a pendulous climber with erect stems and yellow flowers.

Clematis texensis **cv. Etoile Rose**
A climber with pendulous flowers coloured deep rose-pink.

Clematis texensis **cv. Pagoda**
Free flowering, this climber has pendulous pink flowers.

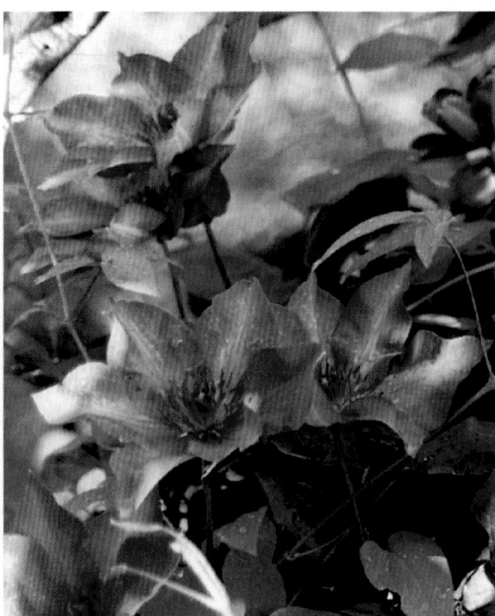

Clematis **cv. The President**
A large flowered cultivar with purple-violet flowers.

Clematis x ***vedrariensis***
The new foliage is reddish brown on this free flowering climber which has pale pink flowers.

Clematis **cv. Veronica's Choice**
The flowers of this cultivar are semi-double, and very pale, lavender-pink in colour.

Clematis viticella **cv. Alba Luxurians**
The white flowers of this cultivar are marked with mauve at times.

CLEMATIS (cont)

C

Clematis viticella cv. **Etoile Violette** [1]

A very free flowering French hybrid. Flowers are purple-violet with a white centre.

Clematis cv. **Vyvyan Pennell**

Violet-mauve is the colour of the large semi-double flowers of this vine.

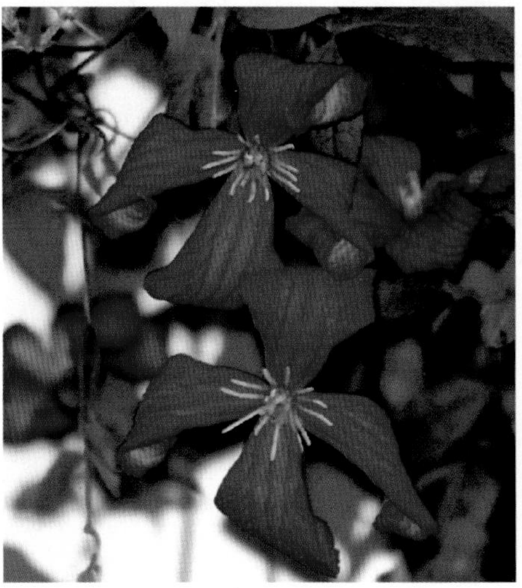

Clematis viticella cv. **Madame Julia Correvon**

A cultivar with wine red flowers which have reflexed petals.

Clematis viticella cv. **Venosa Violacea**

A cultivar with purple-red flowers which have some white markings.

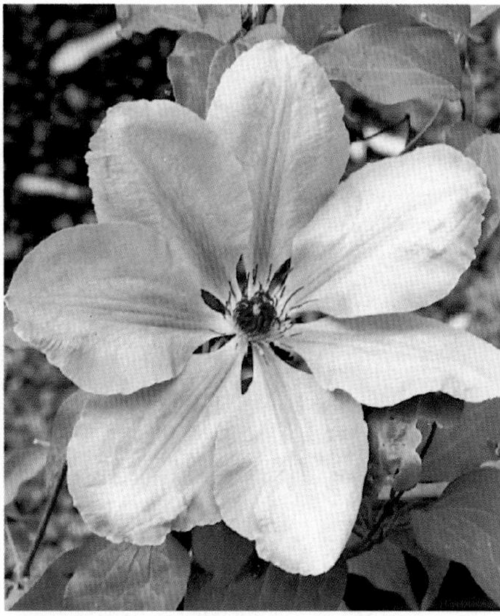

Clematis cv. **W.E.Gladstone**

This climber has large flowers, dark lavender in colour.

Clematis viticella cv. **Royal Velours**

A free flowering cultivar with velvety maroon coloured flowers.

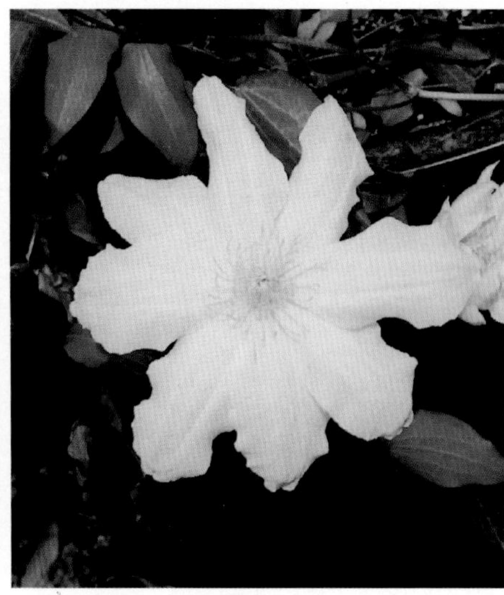

Clematis cv. **Xerxes**

A cultivar with large white flowers.

C

CLERODENDRUM

VERBENACEAE

These plants are deciduous or evergreen shrubs, trees and climbers from many countries in climates from temperate to tropical. They come in a wide range of colours and many make outstanding free flowering ornamental plants for both outdoors and indoors or conservatories in cold climates. Most prefer a soil rich in humus but others are very tolerant of sandy soils and some salt sprays near the sea. Clerodendrums mostly prefer a slightly acid soil and shade for part of the day. Some Clerodendrums have been used for medicinal purposes. Propagation is from seeds and cuttings.

***Clerodendrum heterophyllum* cv. Variegata**

A variegated leaf form of this dense tall shrub.

Clerodendrum cunninghamii

A tall shrub with showy clusters of long tubed white flowers.

Clerodendrum incisum

This is a dense tropical shrub with terminal clusters of bud-like flowers.

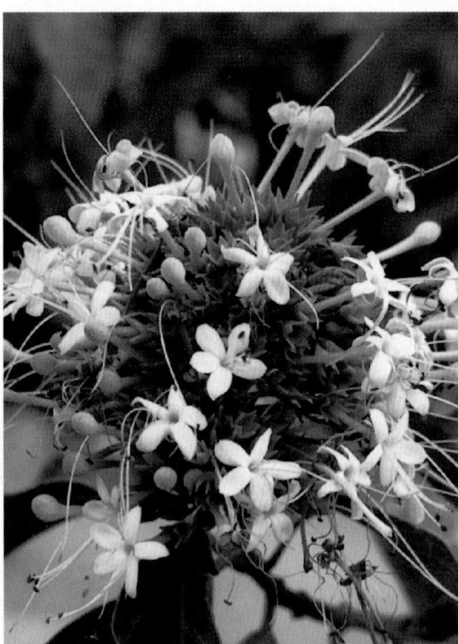

Clerodendrum floribundum THURKOO

This tall slender shrub has large heads of white long tubed flowers. Used by Australian aborigines for medicinal purposes, this shrub has attractive black seeds above a bright red calyx.

Clerodendrum heterophyllum

On this dense branching, tall shrub the perfumed white flowers bloom in clusters.

Clerodendrum paniculatum

PAGODA FLOWER

A medium to tall shrub with large terminal heads of scarlet buds which open to pink flowers.

Clerodendrum philippinum

Mauve flowers form in large heads on this branching shrub.

Clerodendrum* x *speciosum

This climbing hybrid between *C. splendens* and *C. thomsoniae* has clusters of red and sometimes whitish flowers.

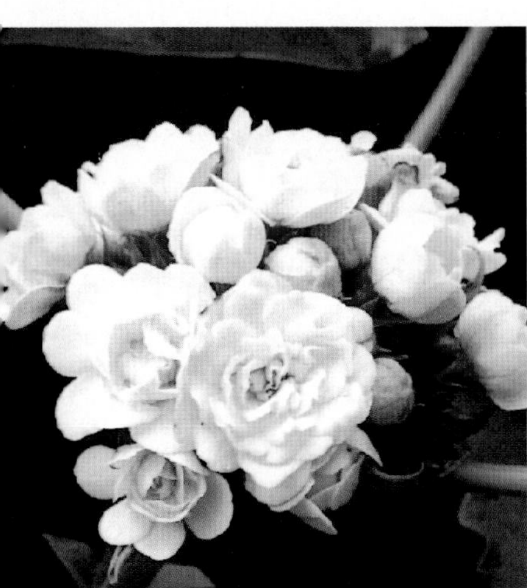

Clerodendrum philippinum* var. *pleniflorum

syn. ***C. fragans*** var. ***pleniflorum***

A multi-stemmed suckering shrub with clusters of double white fragrant flowers which have touches of pink.

Clerodendrum splendens

This twining semi-shrub has large bright showy heads coloured scarlet.

***Clerodendrum thomsoniae* cv. Variegata**

This cultivar has green and cream variegated leaves.

Clerodendrum speciosissimum

A medium to tall shrub with terminal heads of scarlet flowers.

Clerodendrum thomsoniae

BLEEDING HEART

A very showy climber with white heart shaped flowers which have red centres.

Clerodendrum tomentosum

LOLLY BUSH

A tall upright shrub with heads of white tubular flowers followed by dark blue to black fruit.

CLERODENDRUM (cont)

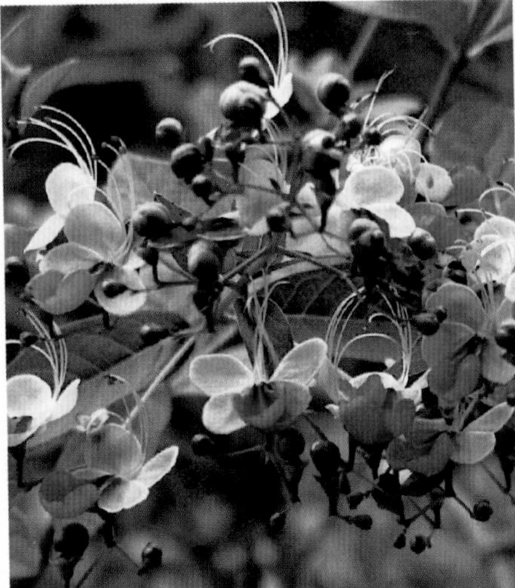

Clerodendrum ugandense
BUTTERFLY BUSH

Open and upright, this shrub has large heads of flowers coloured light blue and dark blue.

Clerodendrum vinosum

An upright shrub with large terminal heads of white flowers.

Clerodendrum wallichii
syn. ***C. nutans***

White flowers follow the pendulous heads of red buds on this dense, erect shrub.

Clerodendrum zambesiacum

A medium dense shrub with large heads of long tubular white flowers.

CLETHRA

CLETHRACEAE

Clethra arborea LILY OF THE VALLEY TREE

A tall evergreen shrub native to Madeira Island. In mild to cold climates, it is grown as an ornamental for its highly perfumed flowers. Clethra prefers a slightly acid soil with plenty of humus. Propagate from seed and cuttings.

CLIANTHUS

FABACEAE [LEGUMINOSAE]

Clianthus puniceus PARROT'S BEAK

An erect evergreen shrub which has ferny leaves and bright red flowers, resembling a parrot's beak, in racemes. It is native to New Zealand and prefers to grow in mild cool climates. Clianthus are widely grown as showy ornamentals. There are colour variations of white and pinks. They grow easily from seed or soft wood cuttings under mist.

Clianthus puniceus CV. **Albus**

A cultivar which has creamy white flowers.

CLIANTHUS (cont)

Clianthus puniceus cv. **Flamingo**
This cultivar has rosy pink flowers.

CLITORIA

FABACEAE [LEGUMINOSAE]

Clitorias are evergreen tropical climbers and semi-climbers. They prefer a tropical or sub-tropical climate. In colder climates they need to be grown in a conservatory or glass house. Propagate from seed.

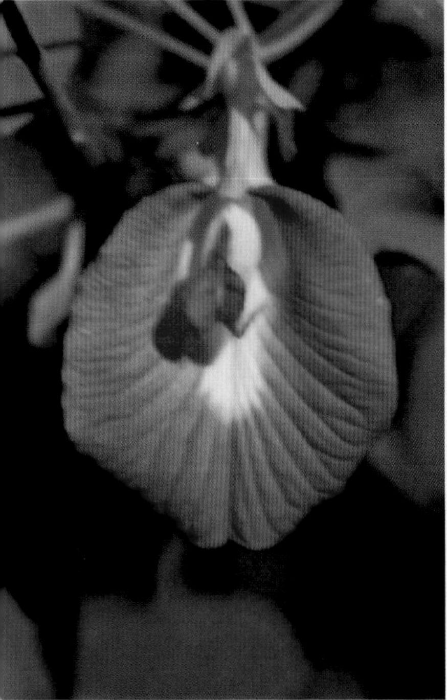

Clitoria ternatea BUTTERFLY PEA
A twining vine with colourful royal blue flowers with a white centre.

Clitoria ternatea cv. **Flore Pleno**
A very attractive double flowered cultivar which is a more compact grower.

CLUSIA

CLUSIACEAE [GUTTIFERAE]

Clusia major cv. **Variegata**
syn ***C. rosea***
A fleshy tall shrub with attractive variegated leaves and pink and white flowers. This plant from tropical America likes a hot to warm climate and is propagated from seed or cuttings.

CLYTOSTOMA

BIGNONIACEAE

Clytostoma callistegioides
ARGENTINE TRUMPET VINE
syn. ***Bignonia callistegioides***
An evergreen vine from tropical America, it is a free flowering vine with attractive clusters of mauve coloured trumpet flowers. It will grow in climates from temperate to tropical and prefers a rich soil and plenty of water in hot weather. Propagate from seed, cuttings or suckers.

C

COBAEA

POLEMONIACEAE

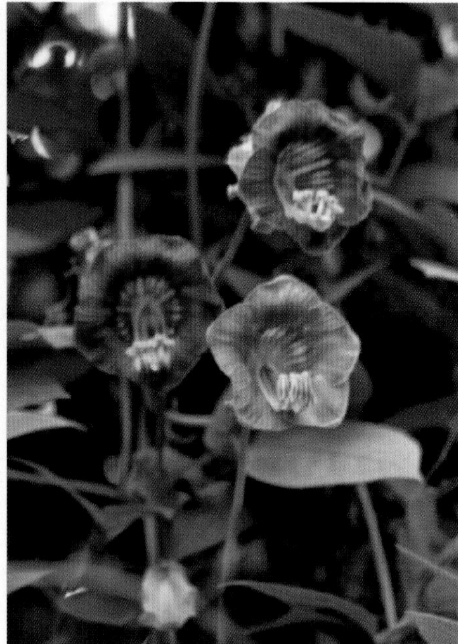

Cobaea scandens MONASTERY BELLS

A hardy evergreen vine from Central America. It has large violet or green, bell shaped pendulous flowers and will grow in climates from mild temperate to tropical. It flowers during spring and summer and is propagated from seed.

COCCOLOBA

POLYGONACEAE

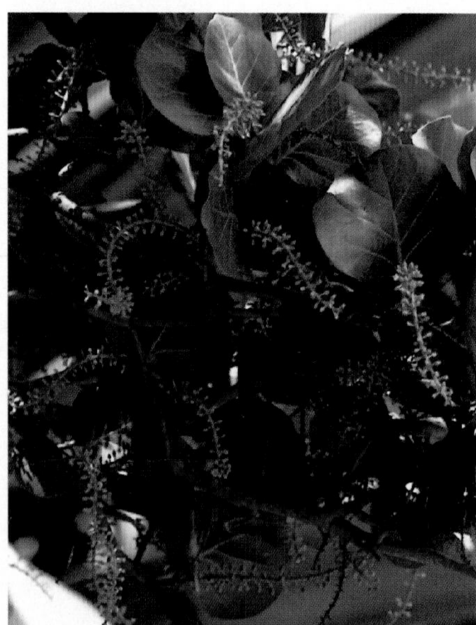

Coccoloba uvifera SEA GRAPE

From sub-tropical and tropical America, this small tree is found close to the sea and is tolerant of salt spray and sandy soils. This tree has attractive copper coloured new growth. The small white flowers are displayed on long spikes and are followed by grape-like fruit. Propagate from seed.

COCHLOSPERMUM

COCHLOSPERMACEAE [BIXACEAE]

Semi-deciduous small trees from the tropics. They have yellow flowers and large seed pods which have the seeds encased in a substance like cotton wool. They are native to monsoon areas and prefer dry winters. Propagate from seed which may be difficult to germinate.

Cochlospermum fraseri WESTERN KAPOK BUSH

A small tree or tall shrub with terminal clusters of large golden flowers from north western Australia.

Cochlospermum gillivraei KAPOK BUSH

A small tree with large heads of large yellow flowers, native to eastern and central north Australia.

Cochlospermum vitifolium

A small tree from South America, with attractive heads of large double yellow flowers.

CODIAEUM

CROTON

EUPHORBIACEAE

From the Pacific Islands, Malaysia and Australia, these small trees and shrubs are widely cultivated throughout the world for their highly coloured leaves especially *C. variegatum* var. *pictum* (syn. *C. pictum.*). All of the cultivars illustrated are synonymous with *C. variegatum* var. *pictum*. They are grown as indoor plants in cool climates and outdoor shrubs in sub-tropical and tropical climates. The leaves are prized by florists for decoration. These leaves colour more intensely with fertiliser and plenty of water. Propagation is from cuttings. Those in the following list are some of the cultivars. It should be noted that a cultivar may have many different names depending on the country in which it is grown. Also two entirely different cultivars may have the same name. The colours shown may vary as the colour does get deeper in warmer weather and at different stages of growth.

***Codiaeum variegatum* cv. Burgundy Queen**

The leaves of this plant are pinky red with dark burgundy markings.

***Codiaeum variegatum* cv. America**

This popular croton has leaves of green, yellow, red and orange.

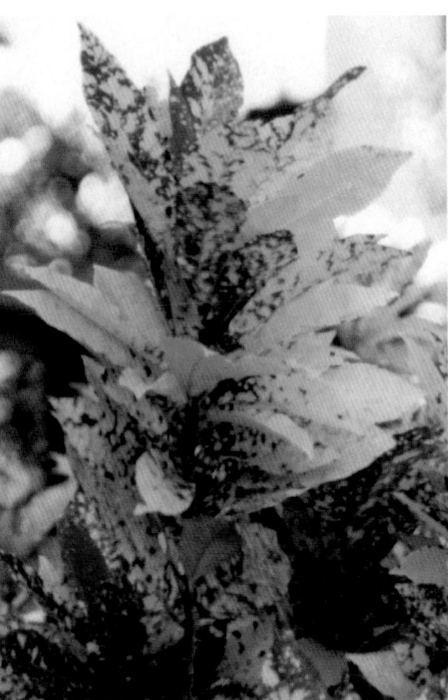

***Codiaeum variegatum* cv. Aucubifolium**

This cultivar gets its name from Aucuba-like leaves which are yellow and green.

***Codiaeum variegatum* cv. Captain Kidd**

A long time favourite, this croton has leaves of red, dark burgundy and some yellow.

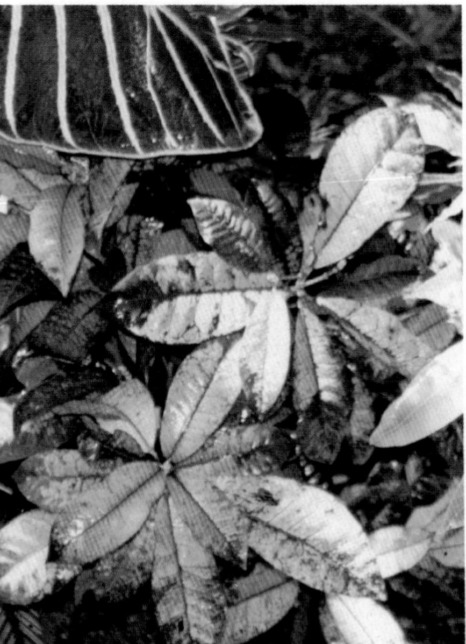

***Codiaeum variegatum* cv. Appleleaf**

An old favourite with new leaves being pinky magenta in colour.

***Codiaeum variegatum* cv. Baronne de Rothschild**

This upright croton has new leaves mostly yellow with red and green markings as they age.

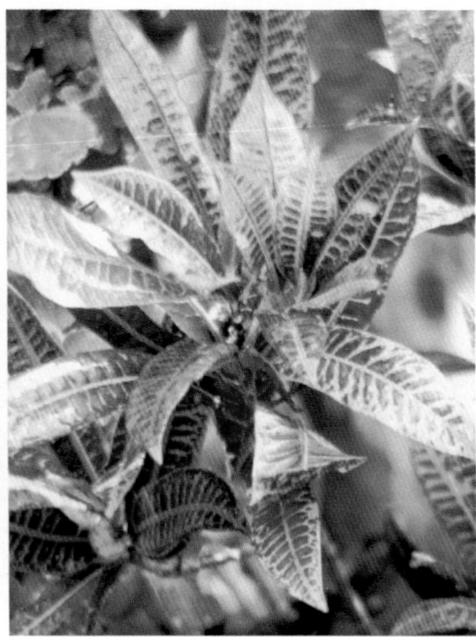

***Codiaeum variegatum* cv. Clipper**

The leaves of this croton are red, yellow, green and burgundy with distinct yellow leaf veins.

CODIAEUM (cont)

Codiaeum variegatum cv. **Crispum**

This croton has twisted leaves of reds, greens and yellows with a distinct central vein of burgundy.

Codiaeum variegatum cv. **Delaware**

The large leaves of this plant are mostly yellow with green markings.

Codiaeum variegatum cv. **Elegantissima**

This croton has large leaves which open yellow and then turn green with yellow markings.

Codiaeum variegatum cv. **Flame Dance**

The multi-coloured leaves of this cultivar are pink, rose-pink, red and yellow.

Codiaeum variegatum cv. **Flaming Fire**

This croton has brightly coloured new leaves of orange, red and yellow intermingling.

Codiaeum variegatum cv. **Gloriosa**

The strong arching leaves of this plant are yellow and green turning to burgundy, red and yellow.

Codiaeum variegatum cv. **Gloriosum Superbum**

This upright grower has leaves coloured gold with touches of green and faint pink colouring.

Codiaeum variegatum cv. **Gold Show**

A very compact rounded shrub having leaves which are almost entirely golden in colour.

CODIAEUM (cont)

Codiaeum variegatum
cv. **Golden Shower**
This is a compact bushy shrub with drooping narrow leaves of mostly gold with green markings.

Codiaeum variegatum
cv. **Golden Torch**
The oak shaped leaves of this croton are mostly golden yellow with green markings.

Codiaeum variegatum
cv. **Interruptum**
A compact bushy shrub with narrow leaves mostly coloured gold with red, burgundy and green colourings.

Codiaeum variegatum
cv. **Joseph's Coat**
A croton with multi-coloured leaves of red, orange, yellow, gold and burgundy.

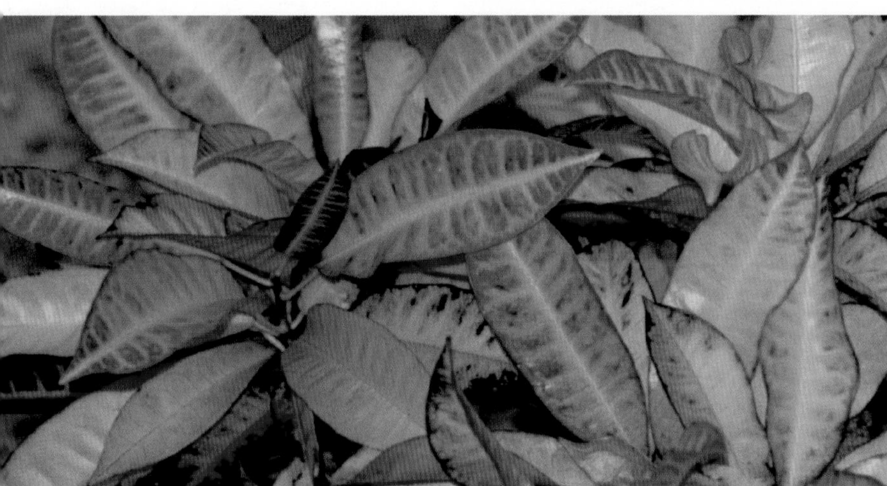

Codiaeum variegatum cv. **Iceton**
An upright cultivar with mostly golden leaves which turn red with age.

Codiaeum variegatum cv. **Katonii**
This cutivar has oak shaped leaves of green overlaid with lemon.

Codiaeum variegatum
cv. **Madam Blanc**
This croton has clumping heads of long leaves yellow in the centre and green on the outer end.

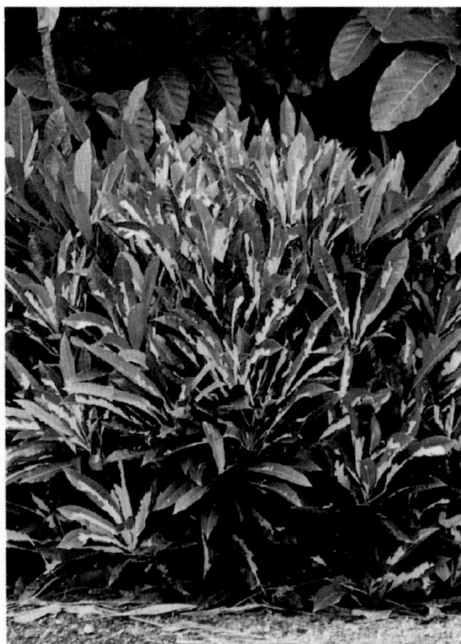

Codiaeum variegatum cv. **Magnifica**
A compact grower with green and gold leaves.

C

CODIAEUM (cont)

Codiaeum variegatum cv. **Mamay**
A showy cultivar with partly twisted upright strap leaves coloured red, orange, yellow and green.

Codiaeum variegatum cv. **Mons Florin**
A large leaf croton. The green leaves are heavily marked with yellow.

Codiaeum variegatum cv. **Norma**
An upright large leaf croton. Leaves are coloured green, yellow, red, orange and burgundy.

Codiaeum variegatum cv. **Norwood Beauty**
The oak-like leaves of this cultivar are gold, yellow, orange and red, with some green.

Codiaeum variegatum cv. **Petra**
This oakleaf cultivar has leaves of green, yellow, red and burgundy.

Codiaeum variegatum cv. **Pink Beauty**
A large leaf croton with new leaves mostly coloured bright pink and some orange.

Codiaeum variegatum cv. **Tamara**
A bushy cultivar which has slightly wavy leaves mostly cream with some green.

Codiaeum variegatum cv. **Thai Gold**
The twisted leaves of this cultivar are coloured green and gold.

Codiaeum variegatum cv. **Zigzag Gold**
The long rippled leaves of this cultivar are green on the edges and yellow along the centre.

CODONANTHE

GESNERIACEAE

***Codonanthe* cv. Aurora**

A compact climber with delicate pink flowers which is native to Brazil. In mild climates it is grown as an indoor plant in hanging baskets or on totems, and it is grown outdoors in warm climates. The plant prefers a slightly acid soil with plenty of humus. Propagate from cuttings.

COFFEA

RUBIACEAE

These bushy evergreen shrubs and small trees produce commercial coffee and are also grown as ornamentals. They grow outdoors in sub-tropical and tropical climates but need a glass house or conservatory in cooler climates. Coffeas are slow growing in their early years and need dappled light to perform at their best. They are propagated from seed and are native to the old world tropics.

Coffea arabica ARABIAN COFFEE

A bushy small tree which produces fragrant small white flowers in clusters followed by bright red fruit which enclose the coffee beans.

Coffea arabica

This illustration shows the bright red fruit.

***Coffea arabica* cv. Golden Delight**

A cultivar which has golden fruit and is grown as an ornamental. The fruit is usually larger than the red form.

Coffea canephora ROBUSTA COFFEE

This tall shrub needs a hot climate to produce coffee beans. It is more open and grows faster than *C. arabica* and has larger white flowers and much larger fruit.

COLEONEMA

RUTACEAE

These small leaf heath like shrubs are native to South Africa. Free flowering, the plants may be covered with small star shaped flowers in spring. They grow in climates from cold temperate to sub-tropical in a wide range of soils. Coleonemas benefit from pruning after flowering to keep the plants compact and to give a better flowering the next year. Propagate from tip cuttings. It is still widely known as Diosma.

Coleonema pulchrum

A small open shrub with pinky mauve star shaped flowers.

***Coleonema pulchrum* cv. Aureum**

This compact grower has golden foliage and pinky mauve flowers.

COLEONEMA (cont)

Coleonema pulchrum cv. **Compactum**
A very dwarf form of this shrub.

Coleonema pulchrum cv. **Rubrum**
On this taller cultivar the flowers are cerise, but some stems may also have mauve flowers.

COLUMNEA

Gesneriaceae

These evergreen plants are either shrubs or vines native to tropical America. There are many hybrids and cultivars in cultivation. Plants are grown outdoors in climates from temperate to tropical and in glass houses and conservatories in cooler climates. Columneas have a long flowering period and prefer a rich soil with regular applications of fertiliser. They are propagated from seeds and cuttings.

Columnea cv. **Aladdin's Lamp**
A free flowering cultivar which has orange-red flowers over many months.

Columnea arguta
Widely grown as a basket plant, this pendulous vine has clusters of scarlet coloured bugle-like flowers.

Columnea* x *banksii
A pendulous plant with orange-red bugle like flowers. Mostly grown in hanging baskets.

Columnea* x *banksii cv. **Variegata**
This variegated leaf plant with orange-red bugle-like flowers is an ideal plant for a hanging basket.

Columnea cv. **Calibri**
A bushy upright plant with bright red tubular flowers.

Columnea cv. **Hostag**
A spreading plant which is grown for its yellow and green variegated foliage.

Columnea cv. **Inferno**
On this cultivar, the long yellow flowers are tipped with orange.

Columnea cv. **Mercur**
A cultivar with golden yellow flowers.

Columnea cv. **Midnight Lantern**
The flowers of this cultivar are coloured orange and yellow.

Columnea cv. **Rising Sun**
This cultivar is very bushy and has red flowers with odd touches of yellow.

Columnea cv. **Saturn**
Free flowering, this cultivar has orange-red flowers.

Columnea scandens cv. **Fendleri**
A cultivar with long orange coloured flowers.

Columnea schiedeana
A sparse, spreading, semi-climbing plant with brownish orange flowers which are marked with yellow.

Columnea x ***vedrariensis***
A hybrid plant with flowers coloured orange-red with yellow markings.

C

COLVILLEA

CAESALPINIACEAE [LEGUMINOSAE]

Colvillea racemosa

A deciduous ferny leaf small to medium tree from Madagascar. It is very spectacular when covered with its drooping large racemes of bright orange flowers in summer to autumn. Colvilleas need to be grown in a frost free area in climates from warm temperate to tropical. This tree is one of the outstanding flowering trees of the world and is propagated from seed.

COMESPERMA

POLYGALACEAE

Comesperma ericinum

A very sparse small shrub which is nativ to Australia and flowers in spring with terminal spikes of bright pink flowers. Mostly grown from seed.

COMBRETUM

COMBRETACEAE

Trees, shrubs and vines from many tropical and sub-tropical countries. Many have spines and some are grown as outstanding flowering ornamentals. They grow in a wide range of soils and can be evergreen or deciduous, and are propagated from seeds and cuttings.

Combretum fruticosum

An arching tall shrub with brush-like flowers coloured orange and old gold.

Combretum constrictum

A bushy tall shrub with powder puff heads coloured red.

Combretum microphyllum

An open arching tall shrub with red bushy flower heads.

:ONGEA

'ERBENACEAE

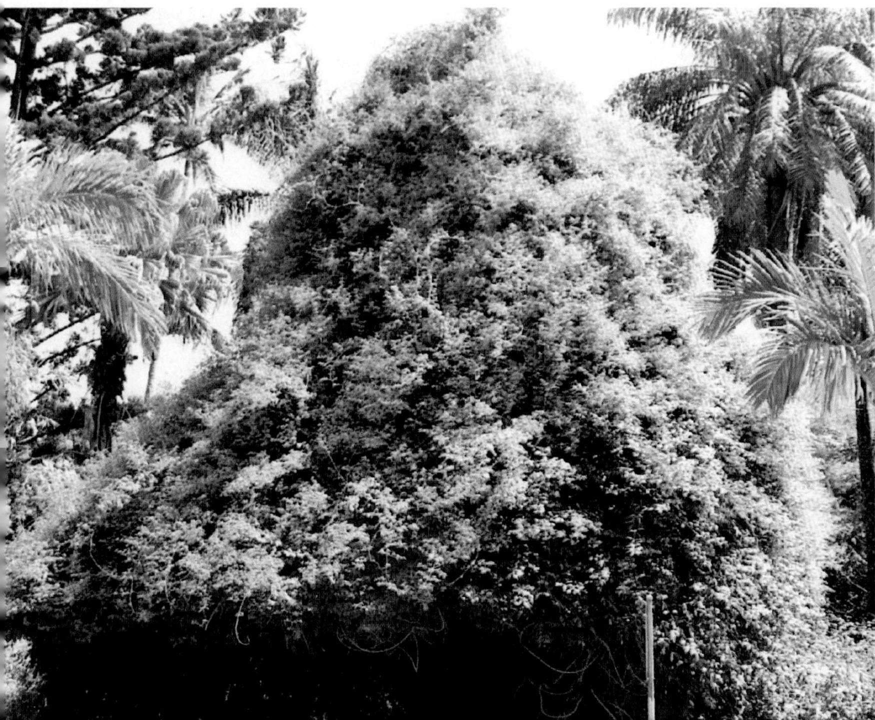

:ongea tomentosa SHOWER ORCHID

. vigorous climbing plant. Native to South East Asia, it needs a hot climate to perform 'ell. Congea is a free flowering climber and is covered with dark pink to mauve flowers ›r long periods of time. Propagate from seed or cuttings.

:ONOSPERMUM

'ROTEACEAE

)pen crowned evergreen shrubs from ustralia. In spring, they have white owny spikes of flowers which are long ısting and popular with florists. They row in a wide range of soils and prefer ool to temperate climates. Conospermums re propagated from seed.

:onospermun stoechadis SMOKEBUSH

A multi-branched rounded shrub which has ›moky white woolly flowers on tall spikes.

Conospermum triplinervium TREE SMOKEBUSH

A medium erect shrub with heads of smoky white flowers in spring.

CONVOLVULUS

CONVOLVULACEAE

Twining plants and occasionally shrubs, native to many countries. They are grown as ornamentals and as soil stabilising plants. Many of these plants, when grown away from their natural habitat, can become weeds. They are grown from seed and cuttings.

Convolvulus cneorum SILVERBUSH

A bushy semi-climber with silver foliage and cream flowers with yellow centres.

Convolvulus floridus

Woody and upright, this sparse shrub has terminal heads of white flowers.

Convolvulus sabatius

syn ***C. mauritanicus***

A climbing plant with clusters of large mauve flowers.

C

COPROSMA

Rubiaceae

These evergreen small trees and shrubs are native to Australia and New Zealand and are widely grown for their attractive shiny leaves which are tolerant of salt spray. They are propagated from seed and cuttings.

Coprosma baueri

An evergreen salt tolerant tall shrub with shiny green leaves, sometimes edged with maroon. Generally regarded as a synonym of *C. repens.*

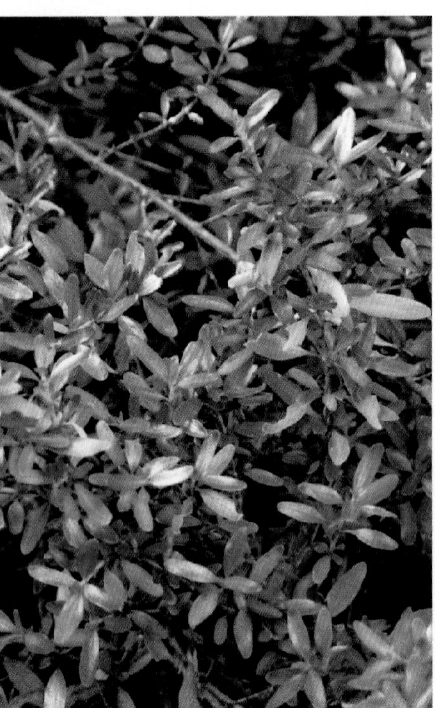

Coprosma* x *kirkii

This spreading groundcover shrub has shiny green leaves.

***Coprosma* x *kirkii* cv. Variegata**

A variegated cultivar, having leaves of grey and cream.

***Coprosma repens* - fruit**

LOOKING GLASS PLANT

syn. ***C. baueri***

This tall shrub has very shiny green leaves and is very tolerant of salt spray. Leaves may be rounded or pointed.

***Coprosma repens* cv. Argentea**

A cultivar which has shiny leaves green inside and cream outside.

***Coprosma repens* cv. Marble Queen**

This cultivar has green and cream leaves which have a marble effect.

***Coprosma repens* cv. Marginata**

A cultivar which has green leaves with a dark cream margin around the edges.

***Coprosma repens* cv. Painter's Palette**

A cultivar which has leaves which are multi-coloured with colours of red, yellow orange and green.

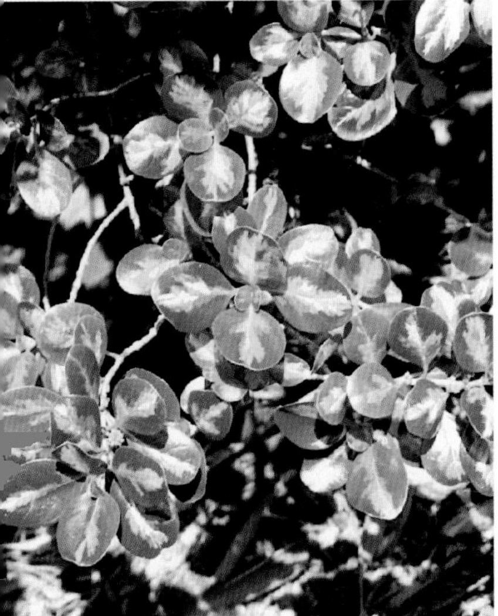

Coprosma repens cv. **Picturata**
This cultivar has shiny green leaves with a little yellow inside.

Coprosma repens cv. **Pink Splendor**
A cultivar which has leaves of pink, cream and green.

Coprosma repens cv. **Pride**
The leaves of this cultivar are coloured green, yellow and cream.

CORDIA

BORAGINACEAE

Deciduous and evergreen trees and shrubs of the tropics and sub-tropics, they are grown as ornamentals and also some for their edible fruit. These plants grow in a wide range of soils in climates from temperate to tropical. Cordias benefit from fertiliser applications and are grown from seed.

Cordia africana
syn. ***C. abyssinica***
A small to medium tree with large heads of white flowers.

Cordia boissieri ANCAHUITA
From North America, this tall evergreen shrub has attractive clusters of flowers which are cream with an old gold centre.

Cordia dichotoma
A small evergreen tree which has masses of small white flowers followed by lots of orange grape-like fruit, which are shown.

Cordia dodecandra
This small tree has large heads of orange-red flowers with multiple toothed petals.

Cordia sebestena GEIGER TREE
A small evergreen tree which has large heads of bright orange flowers.

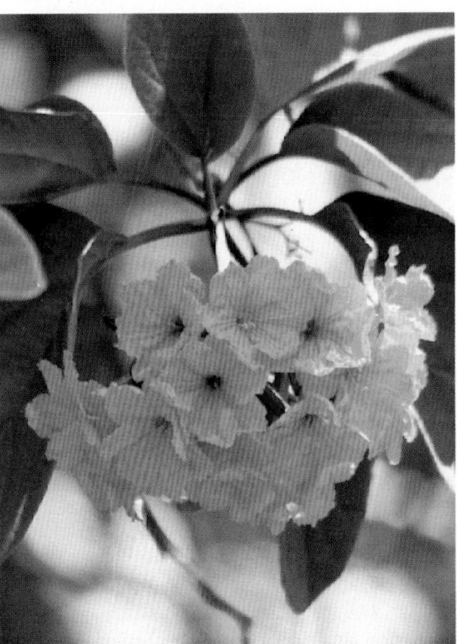

Cordia sebestena cv. **Harvest Gold**
Large heads of old gold to amber coloured flowers bloom on this cultivar.

CORDIA (cont)

Cordia subcordata
A small evergreen tree with roundish heads of orange crepe-like flowers.

Cordia superba
Tall and evergreen, this shrub has large, trumpet-like, white crepe flowers.

Cordia wallichii
A small to medium evergreen tree with small cream flowers followed by orange plum-like fruit.

CORDYLINE

AGAVACEAE

Bushy shrubby plants which are grown for their attractive foliage. They are native to Australia, India and tropical America and the Pacific. There are many cultivars throughout the world. Their climate range is from tropical to cold temperate and many are grown outdoors in Europe. The most widely grown are the cultivars of *C.terminalis* which are warm climate types. They are easily grown from seed but cultivars are grown from cuttings. Cordylines prefer a rich, slightly acid soil and benefit from applications of fertiliser.

Cordyline australis CABBAGE TREE
A hardy, branching, long leaf shrub which is quite cold tolerant in Europe. It has large terminal heads of small white flowers.

***Cordyline australis* cv. Bobby Dazzler**
This cultivar has multiple coloured leaves of green, cream, brown and touches of pink.

***Cordyline australis* cv. Purpurea**
A cultivar which has purple-brown leave It is grown from seed and about 40% grc true to colour.

***Cordyline australis* cv. Rubra**
The wider leaves of this cultivar are reddish-brown. It grows about 40% true to colour from seed.

Cordyline indivisa
A tall shrub with green strap-like leaves and clusters of flowers, white with purple markings. Cold tolerant.

Cordyline manners-suttoniae
Red berries follow the clusters of white flowers on this upright branching shrub with broad pale green leaves.

Cordyline petiolaris
A tall rainforest shrubby plant with whitish lilac flowers followed by dark wine-red berries.

Cordyline rubra
This is an upright plant with few branches and broad green leaves. The white and lilac flowers are followed by large bunches of bright red berries.

Cordyline stricta
The deep mauve flowers are followed by black berries on this upright branching plant with narrow leaves.

Cordyline terminalis
An upright plant with green leaves, purple flowers and red berries. There are many outstanding coloured leaf cultivars of this plant following.

***Cordyline terminalis* cv. Amabilis**
A cultivar with leaves coloured cream, pink and green.

***Cordyline terminalis* cv. Angusta**
A narrow leaf cultivar with leaves coloured green with a red edge and cream markings.

***Cordyline terminalis* cv. Angusta Bicolor**
This cultivar has red and cream leaves.

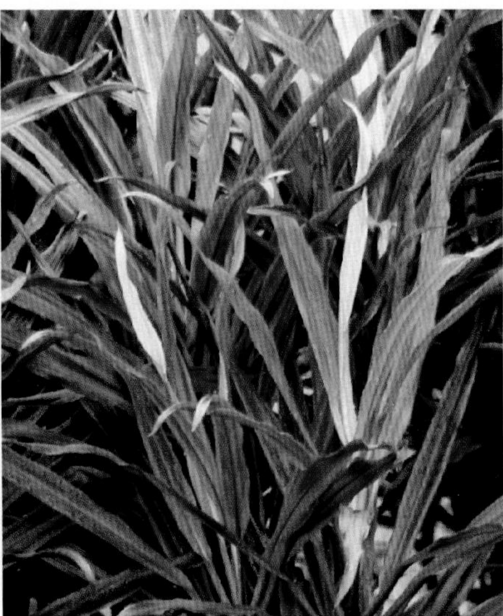

***Cordyline terminalis* cv. Angusta Rubra**
The leaves of this cultivar are mostly dark pink and red.

CORDYLINE (cont)

Cordyline terminalis cv. **Baby Ti**
A small growing cultivar with green and red leaves.

Cordyline terminalis cv. **Bicolor**
This cultivar has leaves of cream and green with odd touches of pink.

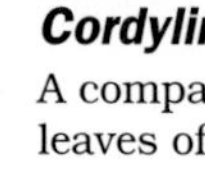

Cordyline terminalis cv. **Black Heart**
A compact cultivar with shorter broader leaves of deep maroon-brown.

Cordyline terminalis cv. **Cardinal Stripe**
As the new leaves of this cultivar age, their pinky red stripes change to reddish green.

Cordyline terminalis cv. **Colour Carnival**
A multi-coloured cultivar with leaf colour being green, white, cream, pink and red.

Cordyline terminalis cv. **Firebrand**
The leaves of this showy cultivar are bright carmine-red.

Cordyline terminalis cv. **Flamenco Dancer**
A broad leaf cultivar with leaves coloured maroon and old gold.

Cordyline terminalis cv. **Hawaiian Rose**
The new leaves of this broad leaf cultivar are cream with pink and yellow markings, turning to greeny brown as they get older.

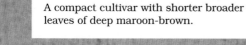

Cordyline terminalis cv. **Hawaiian Sunset**
A compact broad leaf form with old leaves being deep burgundy and red with new leaves being green, edged pink.

CORDYLINE (cont)

Cordyline terminalis cv. **Inscripta**
A narrow leaf cultivar with leaves being burgundy and red.

Cordyline terminalis cv. **Rosea**
This cultivar has pink new leaves. Older leaves are pinky green.

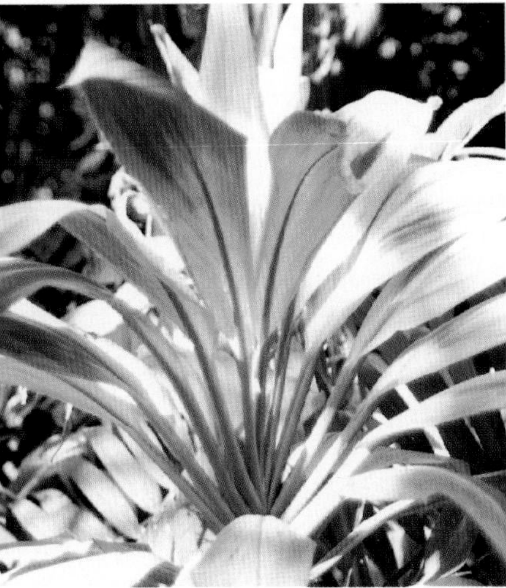

Cordyline terminalis cv. **Ivory Tower**
This cultivar has cream leaves with pink and green markings.

Cordyline terminalis cv. **Margaret Storey**
Compact and bushy, this cultivar has leaves coloured dark burgundy.

Cordyline terminalis cv. **Rose Queen**
On this cultivar, the leaves are deep rose-pink in colour.

Cordyline terminalis cv. **Kiwi**
A compact cultivar with broad leaves coloured red, pink, yellow and green.

Cordyline terminalis cv. **Red Picotee**
An outstanding cultivar with the new leaves coloured cream and edged bright red. The older leaves are green, edged red.

CORDYLINE (cont)

***Cordyline terminalis* cv. Tricolor Supreme**

An attractive cultivar with leaves being rose-pink, green and cream in colour.

***Cordyline terminalis* cv. Volcano**

The narrow leaves of this cultivar are coloured red, cream and burgundy.

***Cordyline terminalis* cv. Wenisgold**

A compact very broad leaf cultivar with leaf colouring of red, gold and green.

CORNUS

DOGWOOD

CORNACEAE

Cornus grow in many cold climates throughout the world. They are shrubs and tall trees and most are deciduous and are noted for their outstanding flowers which mostly open before the foliage appears. They need to be grown in a cold climate to have a good flower display. Some are noted also for their colourful autumn foliage. Propagation is from stratified seed or softwood cuttings under mist in spring.

Cornus bretschneideri

A deciduous shrub which has large heads of creamy white flowers in spring.

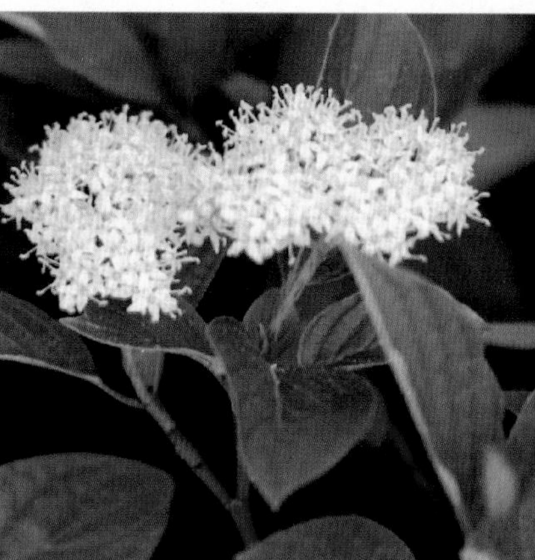

Cornus controversa GIANT DOGWOOD

A deciduous small to medium tree with large heads of creamy white flowers in spring.

Cornus canadensis BUNCHBERRY

This deciduous, low, spreading shrub has white flowers in spring.

***Cornus controversa* cv. Variegata**

A cultivar with green and cream variegated leaves.

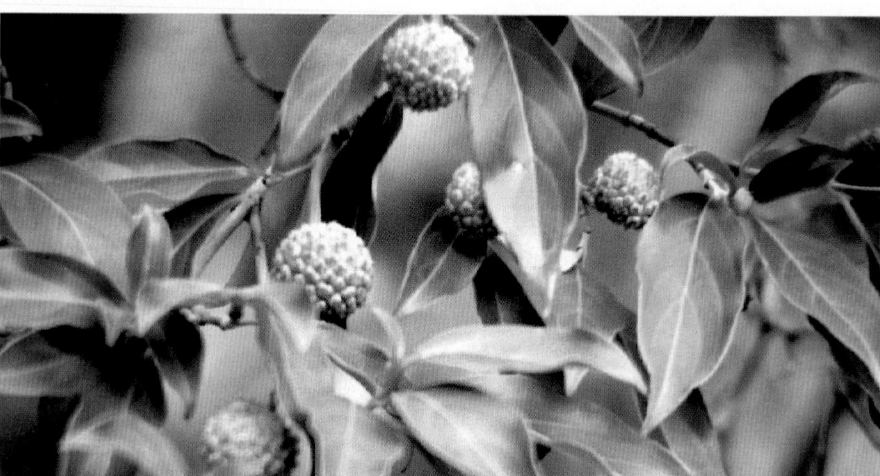

Cornus capitata - Fruit

Mostly evergreen, this small to medium tree has creamy flower bracts and large strawberry-like fruit.

Cornus florida FLOWERING DOGWOOD
This is a small to medium, cold loving, deciduous tree with showy large white flowers. The following cultivars are some of the outstanding forms.

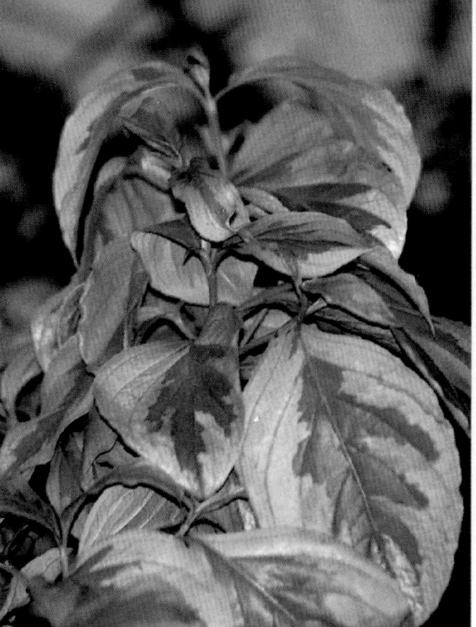

Cornus florida cv. **Rainbow**
The green and yellow leaves of this cultivar turn to purple-red and bright pink in autumn.

Cornus kousa
A tall shrub to small tree with creamy white flowers.

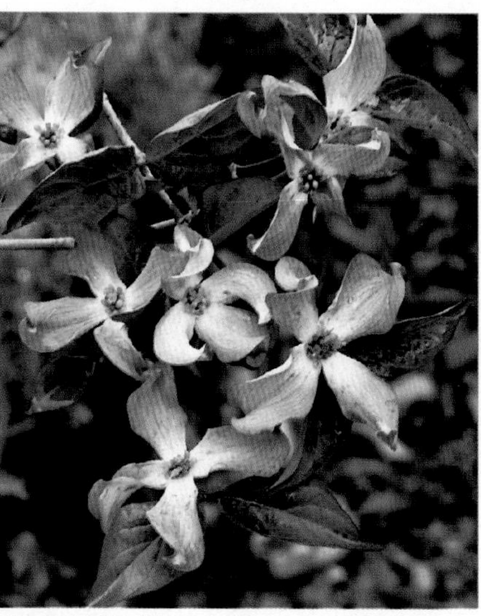

Cornus florida cv. **Cherokee Chief**
This cultivar has rose-pink flower bracts which are white in the centre.

Cornus florida cv. **Rubra**
A very showy Cornus with large pale pink flowers.

Cornus kousa var. ***chinensis***
A variety with large flowers, with their deeper cream colour changing to pink as they age.

Cornus florida cv. **Pluribracteata**
A cultivar with double white flowers.

Cornus florida cv. **Springtime**
Free flowering, this cultivar has white flowers with odd touches of pink.

C

CORNUS (cont)

Cornus mas SORBET
In spring, this tall shrub has masses of small yellow flowers. The red fruit is edible.

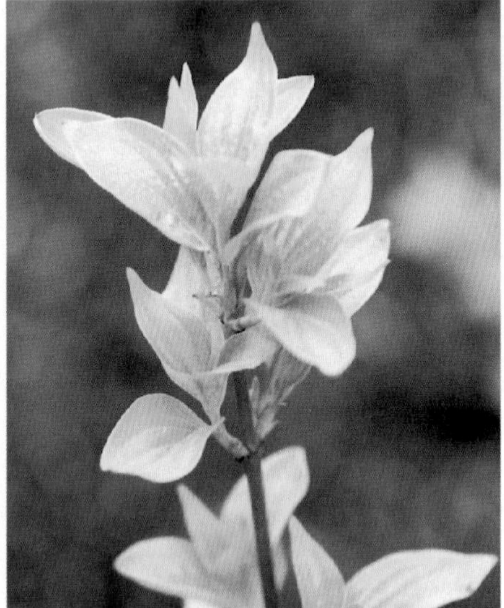

Cornus mas cv. **Aurea**
This cultivar has yellow foliage.

Cornus nuttallii MOUNTAIN DOGWOOD
A medium tree with large white flowers.

Cornus cv. **Ormonde**
This is a free flowering hybrid between *C. florida* and *C. nuttallii.*

Cornus porlock
A tall shrub with showy white flowers.

COROKIA

CORNACEAE

Corokia cotoneaster
A sparse and open, medium to tall shrub, native to New Zealand. Covered with star shaped yellow flowers in spring, this hardy plant is widely grown as an ornamental. It is tolerant of cool climates and also grows in warm temperate climates. Propagate from seed or cuttings.

CORONILLA

FABACEAE [LEGUMINOSAE]

Small evergreen shrubs native to Europe, Asia and Africa. Many are cold tolerant. There are also annual and perennial plants in this genus. They are propagated from seed and tip cuttings and are grown as ornamentals.

Coronilla emerus SCORPION SENNA
A small shrub which is covered with golden coloured pea-type flowers in spring.

Coronilla valentina

In late winter this small shrub has yellow pea-type flowers.

Coronilla valentina **ssp.** ***glauca***

Low and spreading, this shrub has masses of small golden pea-type flowers in spring.

Coronilla valentina **ssp.** ***glauca*** **cv. Variegata**

A variegated leaf cultivar which has fewer flowers.

CORREA

RUTACEAE

Correas are shrubs and occasionally small trees generally from the temperate areas of Australia. They are grown as ornamental shrubs for their unusual flowers. These plants grow best in cool to temperate climates. Correas like well drained soils and ample water in summer. Propagate from seed and cuttings. They are evergreen plants.

Correa alba WHITE CORREA

A dwarf shrub which grows near the sea. It has rounded leaves and white waxy flowers.

Correa pulchella BEAUTIFUL CORREA

A small spreading shrub with tubular red flowers.

Correa backhousiana

This medium shrub has pendulous cream coloured tubular flowers.

Correa reflexa **var.** ***reflexa*** COMMON CORREA

This small shrub has tube flowers coloured red with green and yellow tips.

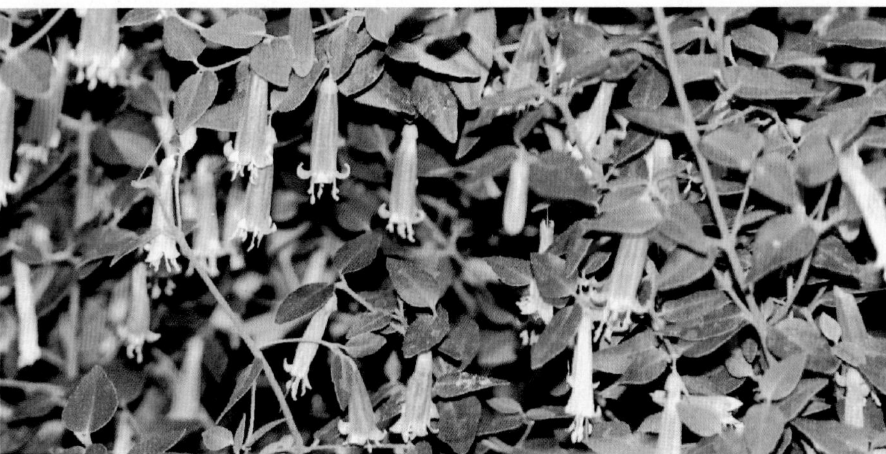

Correa **x** ***harrisii***

A hybrid between *C. pulchella* and *C. reflexa*, which is very free flowering with tubular rose-pink flowers tipped with cream.

CORYLOPSIS

HAMAMELIDACEAE

Cold loving deciduous shrubs and small trees from Asia and the Himalayas. These plants are widely grown as ornamentals. The attractive clusters of pendulous flowers appear before the foliage. They are propagated from seed or softwood cuttings under mist.

Corylopsis pauciflora BUTTERCUP WITCH-HAZEL

A deciduous shrub which has attractive new foliage coloured yellow and pink. The downy flower bracts are cream in colour, and fragrant.

Corylopsis sinensis WINTER HAZEL

This medium shrub has cascading clusters of lemon coloured, small, bell shaped flowers.

Corylopsis spicata SPIKE WITCH-HAZEL

A small shrub with pendulous spikes of small, yellow, bell shaped flowers.

CORYLUS

BETULACEAE

Corylus avellana HAZELNUT

A widely grown in cool climates, this small to medium deciduous tree produces commercial Hazelnuts. The tree also produces an interesting timber.

Corylus avellana cv. **Contorta** TWISTED HAZELNUT

A tall shrub with contorted branches. This deciduous shrub has attractive yellowish cascading catkins in spring. It is grown both as an ornamental and for the edible nuts it produces. It prefers a cold climate and it is propagated from cuttings.

COTINUS SMOKE BUSH

ANACARDIACEAE

These deciduous shrubs to small trees are native to North America and Asia. They are widely grown as ornamentals for their very attractive leaves both in the spring and summer and when they change colour in the autumn. The best colouring occurs in a cold climate. Propagation is from seed and cuttings.

Cotinus coggygria SMOKE BUSH

A bushy shrub with purplish leaves. The small insignificant flowers are formed in large spreading bunches. The autumn leaves are highly coloured red, orange and yellow.

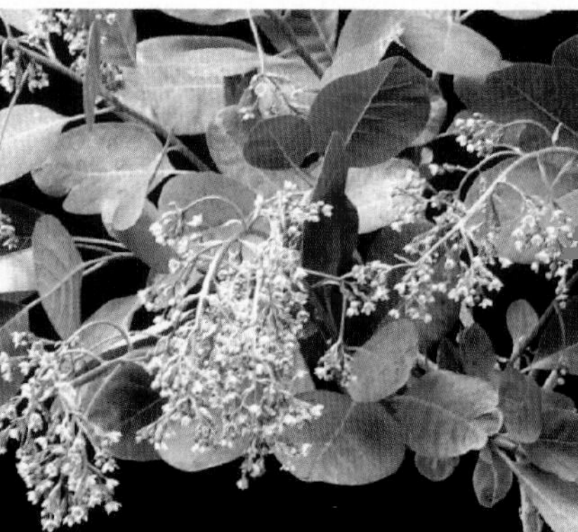

Cotinus coggygria cv. **Purpureus** 2

The leaves of this cultivar are more purple in colour.

Cotinus coggygria cv. **Royal Purple**

This cultivar has very purple-red leaves which are very bright red in autumn.

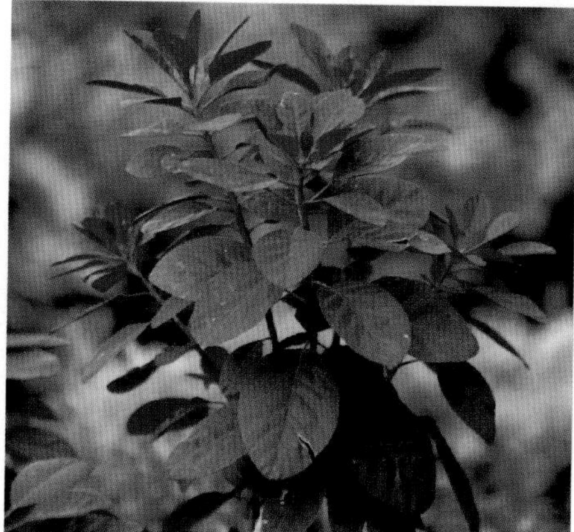

Cotinus coggygria cv. **Ruby Red**
An outstanding cultivar having leaves of deep purple-red.

Cotoneaster dammeri
The white flowers of this low spreading shrub are followed by bright red berries.

Cotoneaster lacteus
syn. ***C. parneyi***
Evergreen and tall, this shrub has clusters of red fruit.

COTONEASTER

ROSACEAE

Shrubs and small trees both evergreen and deciduous from a wide range of northern hemisphere countries. They are widely grown for their prolific displays of spring flowers followed by showy displays of brightly coloured berries which are retained for months. Many take a considerable degree of cold while others are quite hardy in sub-tropical climates. They are propagated from seed and cuttings.

Cotoneaster glaucophyllus
Dense clusters of white flowers followed by pendulous clusters of orange-red fruit form on this tall evergreen shrub.

Cotoneaster microphyllus
A spreading, low growing, evergreen shrub with white flowers followed by reddish carmine berries.

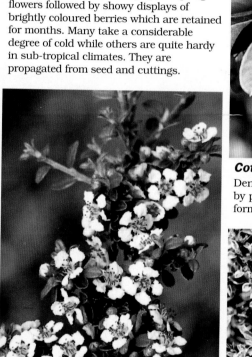

Cotoneaster conspicuus
A spreading semi-evergreen shrub with white flowers followed by scarlet berries.

Cotoneaster horizontalis cv. **Variegatus**
A cultivar of a low growing deciduous shrub, with variegated foliage.

Cotoneaster x ***watereri***
A hybrid, evergreen, tall shrub with small whitish flowers followed by clusters of red fruit.

C

COUROUPITA

Lecythidaceae

Couroupita guianensis

CANNONBALL TREE

This is a medium, upright, tropical, evergreen tree with clusters of large flowers of red and rose-pink, with white centres. The flowers form on branchlets along the trunk of the tree, followed by large, hard, round seed pods the size of coconuts or cannonballs. The tree needs a tropical climate and lots of water. It is propagated from seeds.

+CRATAEGOMESPILUS

Rosaceae

***+Crataegomespilus dardarii* cv. Jules d'Asnières**

This deciduous small tree is a graft hybrid between *Crataegus monogyna* and *Mespilus germanica*. The cultivar came from the hybrid and has bunches of showy white flowers in spring. The tree also has spines on the branches.

CRATAEGUS HAWTHORN

Rosaceae

These mostly deciduous, thorny shrubs and trees are grown in cool climates for their attractive spring flowers and showy fruit and are propagated from seed and cuttings. They are widely grown for hedges. Many hawthorns are highly perfumed.

Crataegus atrosanguinea

A small tree with bunches of creamy white flowers in spring.

Crataegus brainerdi

This small tree has large bunches of white flowers in spring.

Crataegus* x *durobrivensis

A small hybrid tree with large clusters of showy white spring blossoms.

***Crataegus* cv. Giant Red**

Large red fruit follow the white flowers of this cultivar.

Crataegus* x *grignonensis

A hybrid with clusters of small white flowers followed by red fruit.

***Crataegus* cv. Horizontalis**

This hawthorn has limbs which grow horizontally. It has large clusters of white blossom in spring.

CRATAEGUS (cont)

Crataegus laevigata cv. **Coccinea Plena**

RED ENGLISH HAWTHORN

This tall bushy shrub has showy clusters of double pinky red spring flowers followed by red fruit. Known to the nursery trade as ***C. oxyacantha*** cv. **Coccinea Plena** and ***C. laevigata*** cv. **Paulii.**

Crataegus x ***lavallei***

A hybrid hawthorn which is a tall shrub to small tree and, in spring, has large bunches of pale pink flowers followed by orange-red fruit.

Crataegus pubescens f. ***stipulacea***

MEXICAN HAWTHORN

syn. ***C. mexicana***
This is a small tree with white spring flowers followed by edible yellow-orange fruit.

Crataegus laevigata cv. **Paul's Scarlet**

A tall shrub to small tree with showy bunches of small double red flowers in spring.

Crataegus monogyna

ENGLISH HAWTHORN

A tall thorny shrub with clusters of white flowers in spring.

Crataegus laevigata cv. **Rubra Plena**

In spring, this cultivar has large bunches of double pink flowers.

Crataegus x ***ruscinonensis*** var. ***aronioides***

A vigorous hybrid which has clusters of white flowers in spring.

X CRATAEMESPILUS

ROSACEAE

X *Crataemespilus grandiflora*
A naturally occuring hybrid between Crataegus and Mespilus which has white flowers in spring.

CRINODENDRON

ELAEOCARPACEAE

Crinodendron hookerianum
CHILE LANTERN TREE
Native to Chile and Argentina, this small evergreen tree is grown, in mild to moderately cold climates, as an ornamental for its showy pendulous red flowers. It prefers semi-shade and ample water with a humus rich soil. Propagate from seed or cuttings.

CROSSANDRA

FIRE CRACKER FLOWERS

ACANTHACEAE

Small clumping shrubs which are popular as garden plants in tropical and sub-tropical climates outdoors and as indoor or conservatory plants in milder climates. They have a long flowering period in warm weather. These plants prefer a slightly acid soil and regular applications of fertiliser. They are native to Madagascar and the Arabian Peninsula. Propagation is from seed, cutting and by division.

Crossandra infundibuliformis
FIRE CRACKER FLOWER
syn. ***C. undulifolia***
A small spreading shrub with shiny leaves and bright orange flowers.

***Crossandra infundibuliformis* cv. Lutea**
The paler flowers of this cultivar are yellow to light orange.

Crossandra pungens
This plant has dull leaves which have a strong smell when crushed. The flowers are coloured old gold.

CROTALARIA

RATTLE PODS

FABACEAE [LEGUMINOSAE]

Shrubs from a wide range of tropical and sub-tropical countries. Some are grown as ornamentals and others are grown for various commercial uses including the production of a fibre called hemp. Having pea-type flowers, they are fast growing in climates from temperate to tropical and are grown from seed.

Crotalaria capensis
A spreading shrub with bunches of old gold coloured flowers.

CROTALARIA (cont)

Crotalaria cunninghamii
This sparse upright shrub has terminal bunches of green flowers marked with yellow.

Crotalaria grahamiana
A compact bushy shrub with terminal bunches of golden flowers.

Crotalaria laburnifolia
A medium spreading shrub with large flowers coloured lime-green and yellow along the branches.

Crotalaria lanata
Open and upright, this shrub has heads of golden flowers.

Crotalaria novae-hollandiae
A dwarf shrub with flowers of gold along erect flower spikes.

Crotalaria semperflorens
An open branching tall shrub with terminal spikes of yellow flowers.

CROWEA

RUTACEAE

Small evergreen perfumed shrubs from Australia. These free flowering shrubs are grown as ornamentals in climates from cool temperate to tropical. They are propagated from seed and cuttings.

Crowea exalata
An upright branching open shrub with bright pink star shaped flowers.

CRYPTOCARYA

LAURACEAE

Cryptocarya laevigata* var. *bowiei
Native to Australia, this small evergreen rainforest tree is grown as an indoor plant in Europe, for its shiny leaves. It is also an attractive garden specimen, with showy red berries. The plant prefers semi-shade and a rich moist soil. Propagate from seed.

CRYPTOSTEGIA

Asclepiadaceae

Cryptostegia grandiflora

RUBBER VINE

A robust vine which produces attractive rose-pink flowers and a milky sap. This vine is native to Africa and Madagascar and prefers a hot climate. In some countries of the world, especially northern Australia, the plant has become naturalised and is a noxious weed which is hard to eradicate. It is propagated from cuttings and seed.

Cryptostegia grandiflora cv. **Alba**
A white flowered cultivar.

CUPHEA

Lythraceae

Small mostly dense evergreen shrubs which are grown as ornamentals. They have small tubular flowers and grow best in climates from cool temperate to sub-tropical. Cupheas are propagated from seed and tip cuttings.

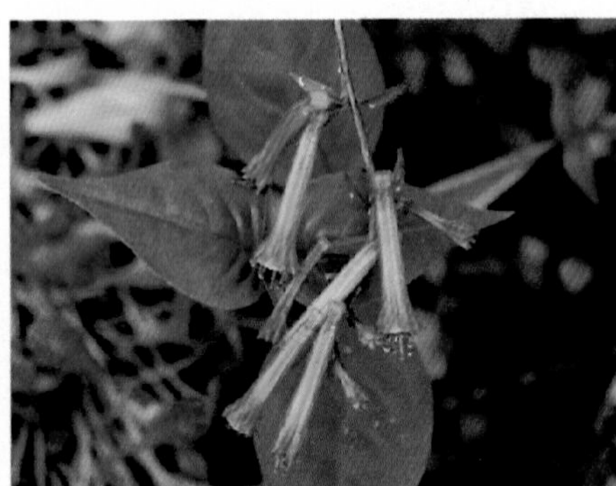

Cuphea caeciliae
The long tubular flowers are orange-red on this small, sparse shrub.

Cuphea hyssopifolia FALSE HEATHER
A dense small shrub with masses of cerise coloured flowers.

Cuphea hyssopifolia cv. **Aurea**
This cultivar has golden leaves.

Cuphea hyssopifolia cv. **Cocktail**
A cultivar which has cerise coloured flowers and multi-coloured leaves of green and yellow.

Cuphea hyssopifolia cv. **Mad Hatter**
A compact cultivar.

Cuphea hyssopifolia cv. **Star White**
The flowers of this cultivar are white.

Cuphea ignea MEXICAN CIGAR FLOWER
A small shrub with orange and red tubular flowers.

CUPHEA (cont)

Cuphea ignea cv. **Crackers**
This free flowering cultivar has white tubular flowers.

Cuphea ignea cv. **Variegata**
An open shrub with green and gold variegated foliage and orange-red tubular flowers.

Cuphea micropetala
This is a compact small shrub which has tubular flowers coloured red and yellow.

Cuphea llavea
A small open shrub with cerise coloured flowers.

Cuphea llavea cv. **Mauve Marvel**
Showy, this cultivar has mauve flowers.

CUSSONIA

ARALIACEAE

Cussonia spicata
An evergreen small tree which is widely grown as a foliage plant. Native to South Africa, it has large heads of small white flowers and is propagated from seed.

CYDISTA

BIGNONIACEAE

Evergreen shrubs and climbers native to tropical America, grown in warm temperate to tropical climates for their showy flowers. They prefer a rich soil and adequate water in hot weather. Propagate from seed, cuttings and by layering.

Cydista aequinoctialis
A free flowering vine with clusters of trumpet-type flowers coloured from cerise to lavender.

CYTISUS

BROOM

FABACEAE [LEGUMINOSAE]

Almost leafless shrubs native to the Canary Islands and countries in the Mediterranean region. Spring flowering, they have pea-type flowers along the branches. Cytisus seem to grow best in cool temperate climates and some can easily naturalise and become weeds. There are many hybrids and cultivars grown. They are propagated from seed and cuttings.

Cytisus cv. **Boskoop Ruby**
This Dutch cultivar has ruby-red flowers in spring.

CYTISUS (cont)

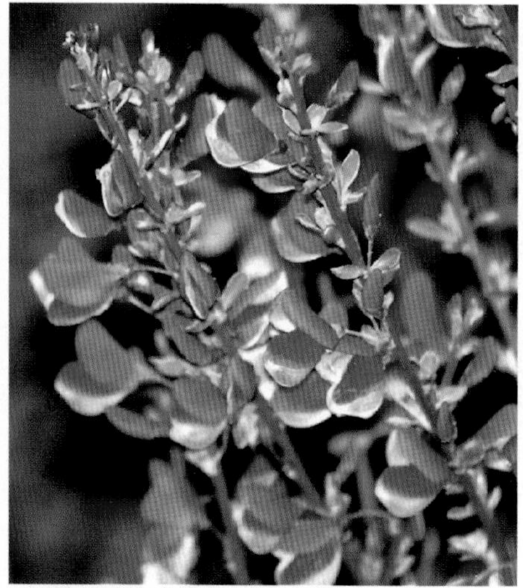

***Cytisus* cv. Burkwoodii**
The flowers of this cultivar are reddish brown in colour.

***Cytisus* cv. C.E.Pearson**
A cultivar with multi-coloured flowers of yellow, orange and brown.

***Cytisus* cv. Cornish Cream**
This cultivar has yellow and cream coloured flowers.

***Cytisus* cv. Dukaat**
A Dutch cultivar with cream and yellow coloured flowers.

***Cytisus* cv. Garden Magic**
This cultivar has flowers of yellow and brownish red.

***Cytisus* cv. Lady Moore**
A cultivar with flowers coloured yellow, orange and brown.

***Cytisus* cv. Lilac Time**
Lilac coloured flowers are a feature of this cultivar.

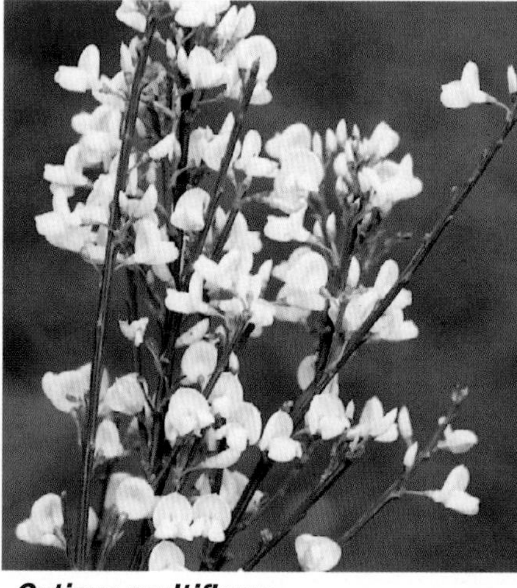

Cytisus multiflorus
WHITE SPANISH BROOM
A medium to tall, open shrub with white pea-type flowers in spring.

***Cytisus* cv. Peach Glow**
This cultivar has peach coloured flowers.

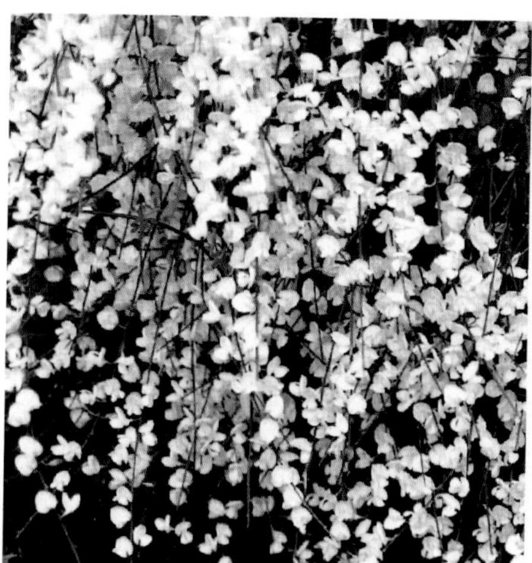

***Cytisus* x *praecox* cv. Albus**
A hybrid having white flowers.

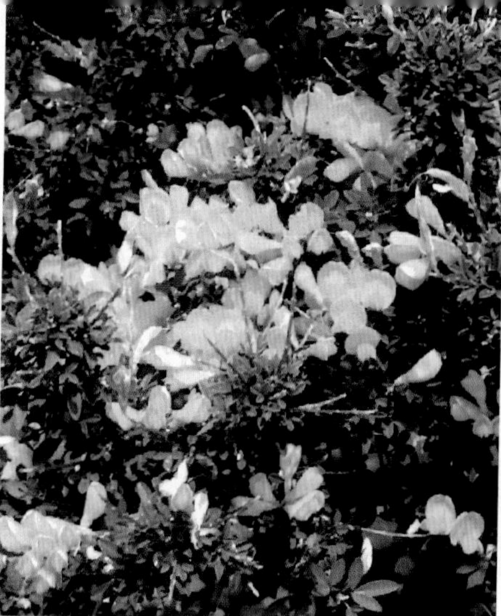

***Cytisus racemosus* cv. Nana**
A dwarf cultivar of this shrub.

Cytisus sessilifolius
A compact pendulous shrub with yellow flowers in spring.

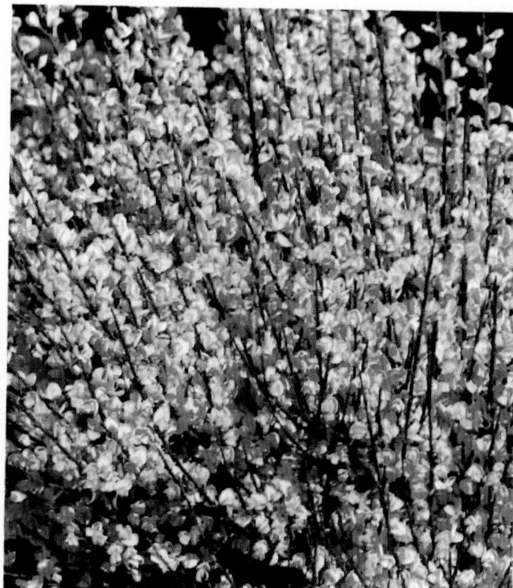

***Cytisus* x *praecox* cv. Allgold**
A cultivar with flowers coloured cream and yellow.

***Cytisus scoparius* cv. Andreanus**
A cultivar with yellow and orange flowers.

***Cytisus* cv. Snow Queen**
White flowers hang on the pendulous branches of this cultivar.

Cytisus racemosus
This leafy plant has spikes of golden coloured flowers.

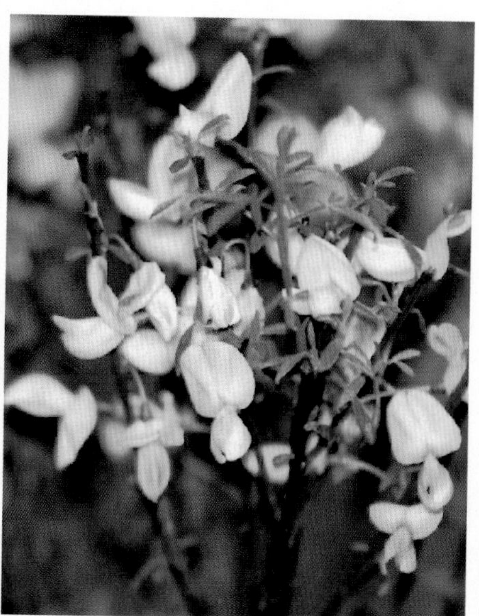

***Cytisus* cv. Zeelandia**
A Dutch cultivar with pale mauve flowers.

DABOECIA

ERICACEAE

Low growing and spreading evergreen shrubs native to mainland Europe. These plants are relatively cold hardy and prefer a peaty soil and plenty of moisture. Propagate from seed and cuttings.

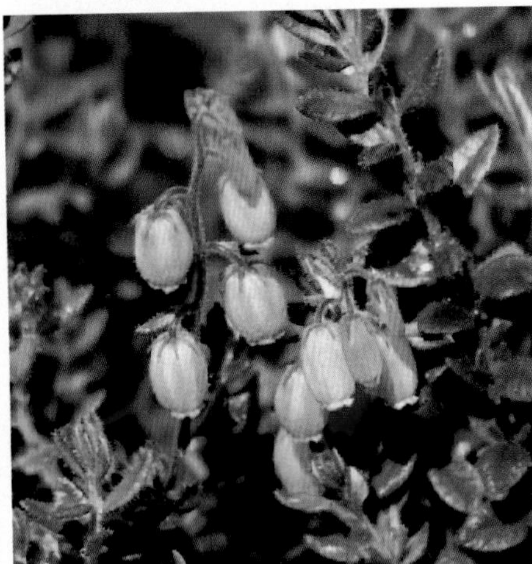

Daboecia cantabrica

CONNEMARA HEATH

A low spreading shrub with upright small spikes of pendulous bright pink flowers in spring.

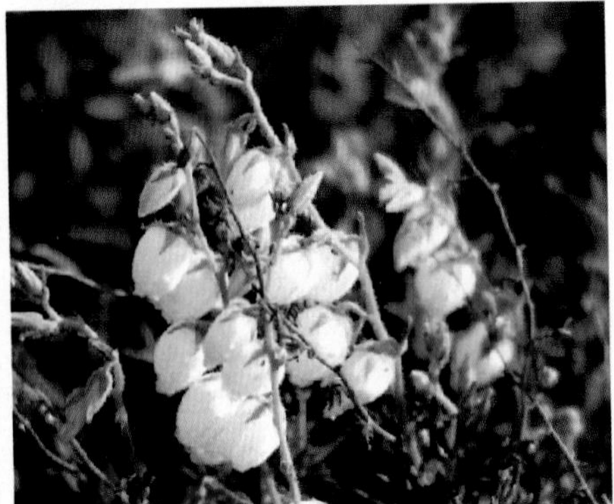

***Daboecia cantabrica* cv. Alba**

A white flowered cultivar of this plant.

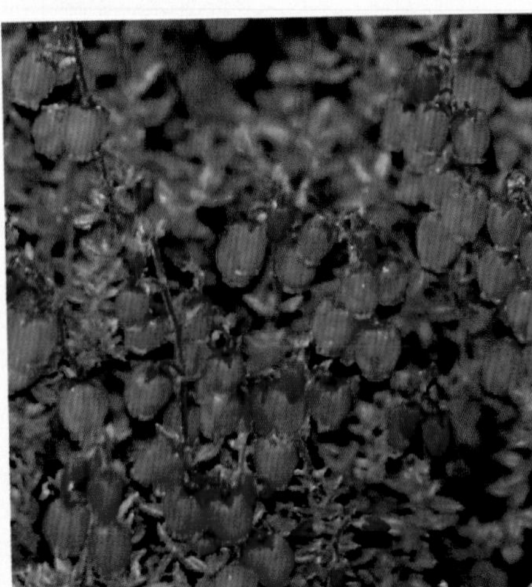

***Daboecia* cv. William Buchanan**

In spring this spreading low growing shrub has spikes of crimson flowers.

DAHLIA

ASTERACEAE [COMPOSITAE]

Dahlia imperialis

BELL TREE; TREE DAHLIA

A tall shrub to small tree, from Central America. It is a tuberous rooted plant which is fast growing and has very large showy heads of pendulous bright pink flowers in summer. This plant grows in a wide range of soils and prefers a warm climate. Propagation is from tuber division and soft tip cuttings under mist.

DAIS

THYMELAEACEAE

Dais cotinifolia

This semi-evergreen shrub is native to South Africa. It is widely grown as an ornamental plant in climates from cool temperate to sub-tropical. The round bright pink flowers are very colourful during spring. Propagation is from seed and cuttings.

DALBERGIA

FABACEAE [LEGUMINOSAE]

Dalbergias are deciduous or evergreen tropical trees and shrubs native to many countries. They prefer a warm temperate to tropical climate and many like a slightly alkaline soil. Propagation is from seed and cuttings.

Dalbergia obovata

This is a dense, spreading, small tree with clusters of cream coloured flowers.

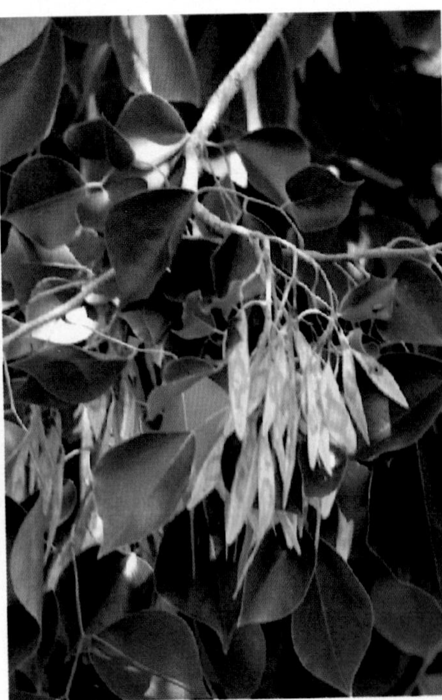

Dalbergia sissoo

A small to medium tree with pendulous foliage and large heads of cream flowers.

DALECHAMPIA

EUPHORBIACEAE

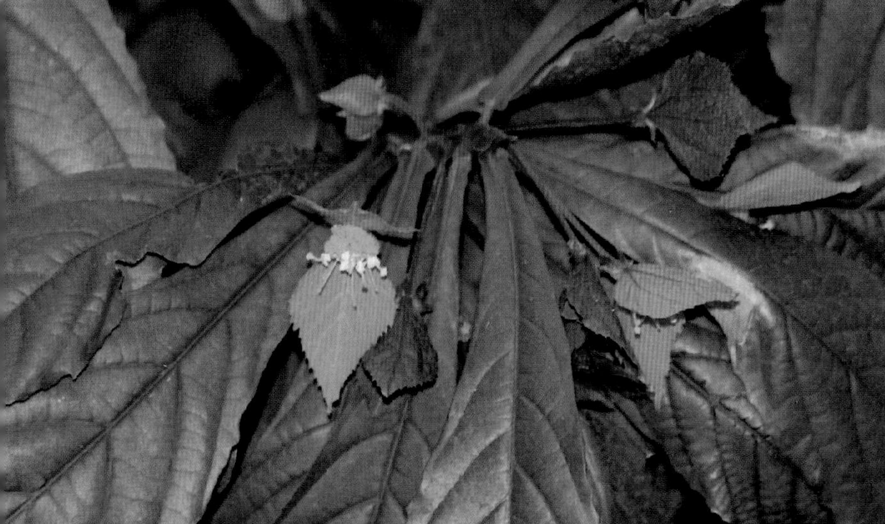

Dalechampia roezliana

A freely branching small shrub native to tropical Mexico. It has highly fragrant small white flowers with bright pink flower bracts. It prefers a rich moist soil and is propagated from seed or tip cuttings under mist. The plant benefits from regular fertilizer applications.

DAPHNE

THYMELAEACEAE

From Europe and Asia, Daphnes are small to medium shrubs which are evergreen or deciduous. They are grown as ornamentals for both their attractive flowers and their perfume. Most of these shrubs are very cold tolerant and are rarely grown in climates warmer than temperate. Propagation is from seed which has been cold stratified and from cuttings.

Daphne alpina

A deciduous small shrub with highly perfumed bunches of cream flowers in spring.

Daphne arbuscula

In spring this low, spreading shrub has masses of bright rose-pink flowers.

Daphne bholua

Highly perfumed, this evergreen winter flowering shrub has white and mauve star shaped flowers.

Daphne blagayana

A small shrub with highly perfumed white flowers in spring.

Daphne* x *burkwoodii

This hybrid is a bushy, erect, semi-evergreen small shrub. The clusters of pale pink flowers are very fragrant.

***Daphne* x *burkwoodii* cv. Lavenirii**

A French cultivar with bright pink flowers.

d DAPHNE (cont)

***Daphne* x *burkwoodii* cv. Nana**

Low growing and spreading, this cultivar has smaller pale pink flowers, coloured rose-pink outside.

Daphne cneorum GARLAND FLOWER

This small, evergreen shrub has fragrant rose-pink flowers in spring.

Daphne collina

Spring flowering, this evergreen shrub has fragrant rose-pink coloured flowers.

***Daphne* x *burkwoodii* cv. Variegata**

This cultivar has green and cream variegated leaves.

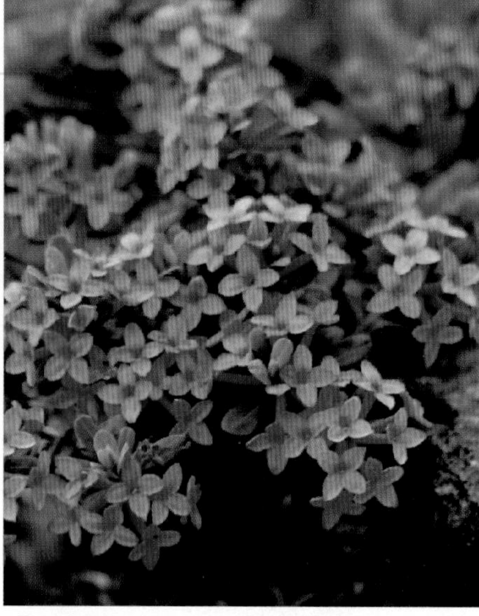

***Daphne cneorum* cv. Eximia**

GARLAND FLOWER

A free branching evergreen small shrub with red buds followed by pink flowers.

Daphne genkwa

Deciduous, this small erect shrub has clusters of lilac flowers which are delicately fragrant.

Daphne caucasica

A deciduous shrub with terminal heads of white flowers.

***Daphne cneorum* cv. Ruby Glow**

Very free flowering, in spring this cultivar has rose to deep rose-pink flowers.

DAPHNE (cont)

Daphne* x *hendersonii
In spring this small, spreading hybrid shrub has perfumed pink flowers.

Daphne kosaninii
Pinky red buds opening to perfumed white flowers feature on this low growing shrub.

Daphne mezereum
This is an upright deciduous shrub which has fragrant white and violet coloured flowers in winter, before the new foliage appears.

Daphne jasminea
A dwarf, spreading, evergreen shrub with masses of perfumed flowers which are white inside and rose outside.

Daphne mezereum* f. *Alba
A fragrant form with creamy white flowers.

***Daphne* cv. Kilmeston**
A low growing cultivar with highly perfumed pink flowers.

Daphne longifolia
A small shrub with long leathery leaves and white highly perfumed flowers.

Daphne* x *napolitana
Perfumed pink flowers bloom in spring on this small, sparse, spreading shrub.

d

DAPHNE (cont)

Daphne odora WINTER DAPHNE
On this small evergreen shrub carmine coloured buds are followed by pink, highly perfumed flowers.

Daphne oleoides
A small evergreen shrub with clusters of fragrant white flowers in spring.

Daphne retusa
Small and sparse, this evergreen shrub has pink, perfumed flowers in spring.

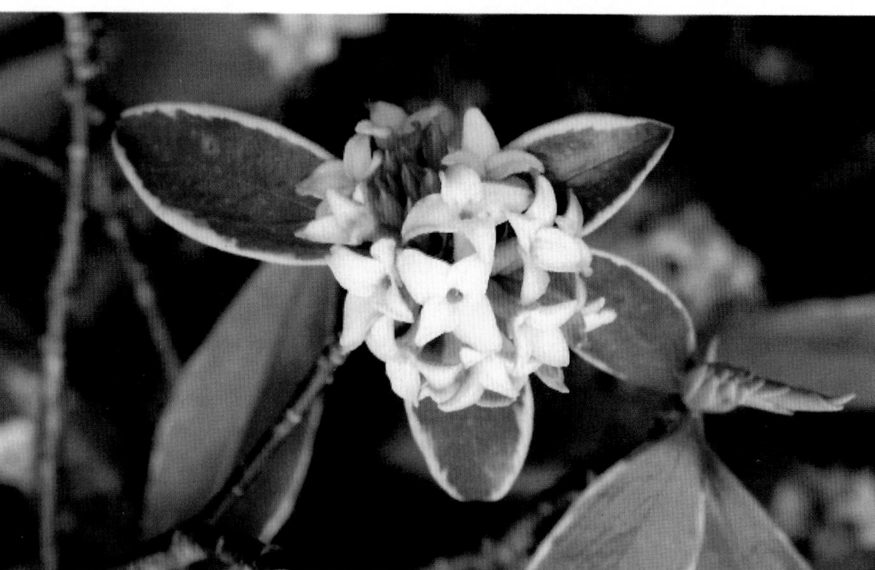

Daphne odora cv. **Variegata**
A cultivar with cream edged leaves.

Daphne sericea
This small, spreading evergreen shrub, in spring, has fragrant heads of rose-pink flowers.

Daphne odora cv. **Walberton**
This cultivar has leaves with thin cream edges.

Daphne pontica
In spring this evergreen shrub has clusters of fragrant yellowish flowers.

Daphne tangutica
This open crowned shrub has highly perfumed pink and white coloured flowers in spring.

DARLINGIA

PROTEACEAE

Darlingia ferruginea ROSE SILKY OAK

This evergreen small to medium tree is native to the rainforests of tropical eastern Australia. It has very attractive clusters of fragrant cream flowers on erect spikes. The dark green leaves have a rusty appearance underneath. These trees prefer rich soils and warm temperate to tropical climates. Propagate from seed.

DARWINIA

MYRTACEAE

Darwinias are small evergreen shrubs from Australia which are grown for their pendulous bell shaped flowers. They grow in a wide range of soils and are mostly cultivated in climates from cool temperate to sub-tropical. Propagation is from seed and cuttings.

Darwinia carnea MOGUMBER BELL

A spreading multi-branched small shrub with brownish pink flowers.

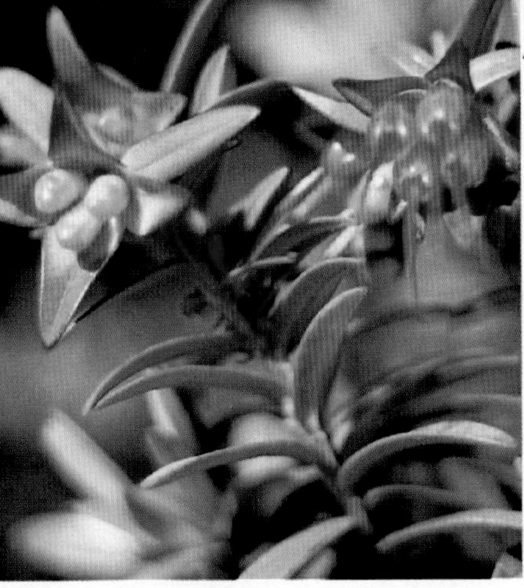

Darwinia citriodora

LEMON-SCENTED MYRTLE

This small shrub has nodding flowers coloured orange-red.

Darwinia macrostegia MONDURUP BELL

A small spreading shrub with bell shaped flowers coloured white and red.

Darwinia meeboldii CRANBROOK BELL

This is a small upright shrub with pendulous branches and nodding flowers of white, tipped red.

Darwinia oldfieldii

An open dwarf shrub with flower heads coloured deep red.

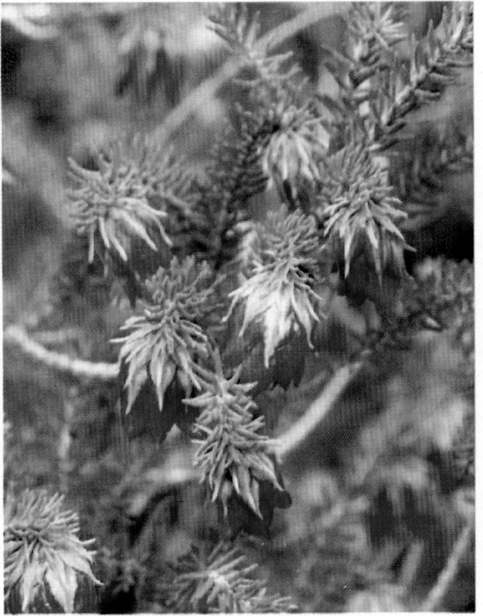

Darwinia oxylepis

Upright and small, this shrub has pendulous foliage and nodding red flower heads.

Darwinia taxifolia ssp. ***macrolaena***

A small open shrub with conifer-like leaves. The upright red flowers are displayed along the branches.

d

DAVIDIA

DAVIDIACEAE [NYSSACEAE]

Davidia involucrata DOVE TREE

A small deciduous tree native to China. In cold climates it is a very ornamental tree, having large pendulous white bracts in spring. Propagate from seed or cuttings.

DAVIDSONIA

DAVIDSONIACEAE

Davidsonia pruriens DAVIDSON'S PLUM

A small evergreen tree native to the rain forests of eastern Australia. It is grown as an ornamental and for its edible, though acidic, plum-like fruit. The tree has clusters of red flowers on the trunk, followed by the large fruit. It will grow in climates from cool temperate (if protected in winter when young) to tropical. Propagate from seed.

Davidsonia pruriens - fruit

DAVIESIA

FABACEAE [LEGUMINOSAE]

These plants are upright, open, hardy, evergreen shrubs native to Australia. They have heads of yellow-orange pea type flowers and grow in poor quality soils in cold temperate to sub-tropical climates. Propagate from seed which requires nicking or hot water treatment.

Daviesia corymbosa

An upright medium shrub with clusters of old gold and orange flowers.

Daviesia horrida

This is an open upright shrub which has yellow and brick-red coloured flowers.

DELAIREA

ASTERACEAE [COMPOSITAE]

Delairea odorata GERMAN IVY

syn. ***Senecio mikanioides***

A bushy climber which is almost totally covered with large heads of golden coloured flowers in spring.

DELONIX

CAESALPINIACEAE (LEGUMINOSAE)

Semi-deciduous spreading trees from Africa, Madagascar and India which are grown as ornamentals for their flamboyant flower display. These trees are widely grown in the tropical countries of the world, needing a frost free sub-tropical to tropical climate and plenty of water in hot weather. Propagate from seed.

Delonix regia ROYAL POINCIANA

A fern-leaf spreading tree which has very large heads of orange flowers with white markings in summer.

DELONIX (cont)

Delonix regia var. ***flavida*** cv. **Gold Cascade**

A cultivar of this variety which is golden flowered.

Delonix regia cv. **Orange Fire**

A cultivar with bright orange flowers.

Delonix regia cv. **Red Fire**

This cultivar has showy red flowers in large heads.

DENDROMECON

PAPAVERACEAE

Dendromecon rigida TREE POPPY

A tall evergreen shrub, this plant has golden poppy-like flowers and is native to North America and Mexico. It prefers a temperate to sub-tropical climate. Propagate from seeds.

DERRIS

FABACEAE [LEGUMINOSAE]

Derris koolgibberah

A tropical to sub-tropical robust woody vine with rusty coloured new leaves. The rose-pink flowers hang in long bunches. Propagate from seed or cuttings.

DEUTZIA

HYDRANGEACEAE

Medium shrubs from the mountains of Central America and Asia. They have clusters of small flowers in spring and grow well in mild climates. Propagate from seed and cuttings.

Deutzia x ***candelabrum***

A hybrid which is a spreading shrub with panicles of white flowers in spring.

Deutzia x ***elegantissima***

In spring this small hybrid shrub has clusters of small pink flowers.

Deutzia (cont)

Deutzia* x *elegantissima
cv. Fasciculata
A cultivar which has slightly darker flowers.

Deutzia gracilis
This medium shrub has racemes of white flowers.

Deutzia* x *kalmiiflora
A small hybrid shrub with heads of pale pink flowers in spring.

Deutzia purpurascens
In spring this freely branching shrub has heads of off white flowers.

***Deutzia scabra* cv. Variegata**
A cultivar with variegated cream and green leaves.

Deutzia* x *rosea
A hybrid bushy shrub with large heads of small flowers which are pink when in bud and open to pinkish white.

Deutzia scabra
cv. Candidissima
A medium shrub with panicles of double white flowers in summer.

DICHROA

SAXIFRAGACEAE [HYDRANGEACEAE]

Dichroa versicolor
Native to China, this hardy shrub has large heads of small pink flowers in spring. It is grown as an ornamental in climates from cool temperate to sub-tropical. Propagate from cuttings.

DILLENIA

DILLENIACEAE

Evergreen trees and shrubs native to Asia, Australia and Madagascar. They are warm climate plants and grow only in sub-tropical and tropical climates. They are grown as ornamentals and some for their fruit which are used in curries and chutneys. Propagate from seed.

Dillenia alata - seed pod RED BEECH

A small to medium tree which tolerates some salt spray. It has showy yellow flowers followed by bright red seed pods.

Dillenia indica

A medium sized spreading tree with clusters of yellow flowers followed by large fruit.

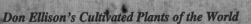

Dillenia indica - fruit

This illustration shows the large apple sized fruit which are called elephant apples.

Dillenia ovata

A medium spreading tree having pale yellow flowers with white centres.

Dillenia suffruticosa

This is a small spreading tree with large leaves and large yellow flowers with a white eye.

DIPELTA

CAPRIFOLIACEAE

Dipelta ventricosa

This deciduous shrub has spring flowers coloured pink, white and yellow.

Dipelta floribunda

A tall deciduous shrub which is grown as a colourful spring flowering ornamental in cool climates. The flowers are pale pink with old gold coloured centres. Propagate from seed or cuttings.

DIPLOGLOTTIS

SAPINDACEAE

Diploglottis cunninghamii NATIVE TAMARIND

A small attractive evergreen tree native to Australia. This tree prefers climates from temperate to sub-tropical and is grown for its unique foliage. It has clusters of brownish yellow flowers and prefers a rich soil and lots of water in hot weather. Propagate from seed.

d

DIPLOLAENA

RUTACEAE

Evergreen shrubs native to Australia. They have pendulous flower heads and grow in well drained sandy soils mostly in cool temperate to warm temperate climates. These plants make good compact ornamentals and are propagated from seed and cuttings.

Diplolaena grandiflora

A small shrub with red nodding flower heads in spring.

Diplolaena microcephala

A small shrub with pendulous flower heads coloured red and yellow.

DIPTERYX

FABACEAE [LEGUMINOSAE]

Dipteryx odorata TONKA BEAN

A small to medium tree native to tropical America. It is grown in warm temperate and sub-tropical climates as an ornamental for its showy upright heads of pink and cerise coloured flowers and also, in tropical climates, for the production of commercial Tonka beans. Propagate from seed which should be planted where the tree is to grow.

DISSOTIS

MELASTOMATACEAE

Small evergreen shrubs and climbers from Africa. They are widely grown in climates from cool temperate to tropical as free flowering ornamentals which flower over a long period. Propagate from seed and cuttings.

***Dissotis* cv. Mauve Blanket**

A vigorous ground cover or semi-climber with masses of mauve flowers.

Dissotis plumosa

The flowers are coloured cerise on this spreading semi-climbing plant widely grown as a ground cover or hanging basket.

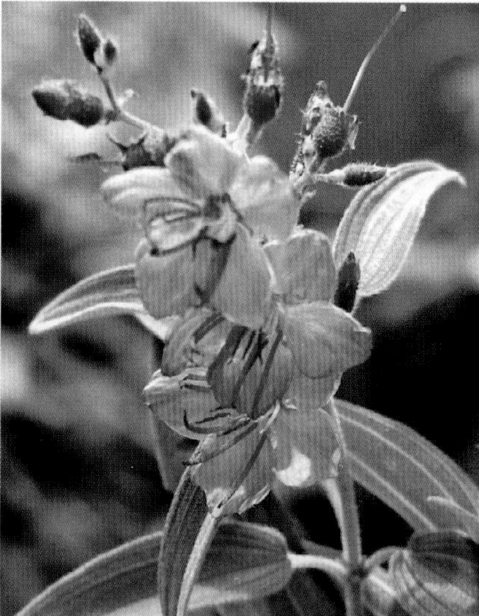

Dissotis princeps

An erect open shrub with terminal heads of dark mauve flowers.

Dissotis rotundifolia

Semi-climbing and spreading, this plant at times is covered with mauve-lilac coloured flowers in spring to summer.

ɔISTICTIS

ƷIGNONIACEAE

ːvergreen climbers native to Mexico and he Caribbean. They are tolerant of light ·osts and prefer a rich soil and plenty of ʋater in the summer. Propagate from eed, cuttings under mist, or by layering.

Ɔistictis buccinatoria
ɹn evergreen climber with bunches of arge orange trumpet flowers.

ƆIZYGOTHECA

ⱯRALIACEAE

Ɔizygotheca elegantissima
ɹyn. ***Aralia elegantissima***
ɹ small evergreen tree which is native to ɹome Pacific Islands. The plant has ɔronze-green leaves and is widely grown ɹs an indoor plant. It may be grown ɔutdoors in climates from temperate to ropical. Propagation is from seed and ·uttings. This genus is now regarded as ɔelonging to the genus Schefflera.

Dizygotheca elegantissima cv. **Variegata**
A cultivar with variegated leaves.

DODONAEA — HOP BUSH

SAPINDACEAE

These evergreen shrubs and small trees are native to tropical to temperate climates of many countries. They are mostly grown for ornamental or soil stabilisation purposes but some have been used in medicine. Propagation is from seed and cuttings.

Dodonaea adenophora
An open shrub grown for its copper coloured hop-like seed pods.

Dodonaea boroniifolia FERN-LEAF-HOP-BUSH
This bushy upright shrub has attractive ferny leaves and highly colourful red seed pods.

Dodonaea oxyptera
A small shrub with greyish green leaves and brown coloured seed pods.

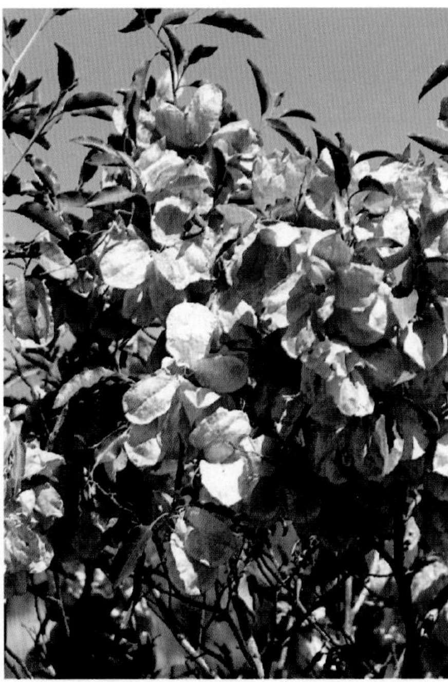

Dodonaea petiolaris GIANT LANTERNS
An upright bushy shrub with large whitish brown seed pods.

Dodonaea ptarmicaefolia
A medium shrub with serrated leaves and brownish red seed pods.

DODONAEA (cont)

Dodonaea triquetra
Widely used for soil stabilization, this open shrub has three sided seed pods.

Dodonaea viscosa
syn. ***D. cuneata***
An open shrub with pendulous clusters of copper coloured seed pods.

DOLICHANDRONE

BIGNONIACEAE

Evergreen shrubs and small trees of the tropics. They are grown as ornamental plants for their flowers and delicate perfume. These plants are grown from seed, in tropical and sub-tropical climates.

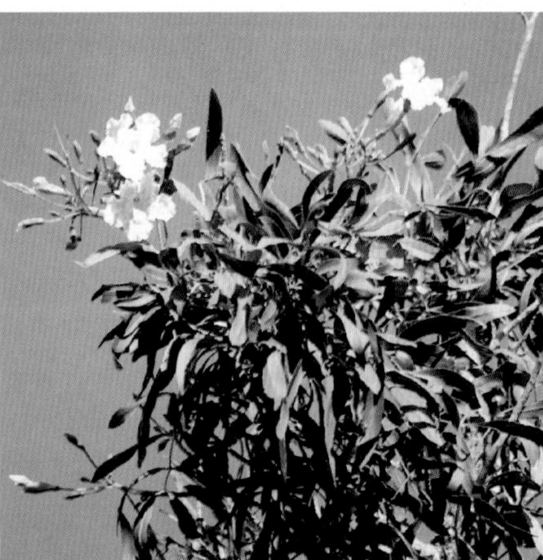

Dolichandrone heterophylla
LEMONWOOD
A small tree with white trumpet shaped flowers.

Dolichandrone spathacea
syn. ***Bignonia spathacea***
A small tree with trumpet shaped flowers coloured white with a yellow centre.

DOMBEYA

STERCULIACEAE

Mostly evergreen free flowering shrubs and small trees native to Africa and Madagascar. They are outstanding as flowering ornamentals and are grown in climates from cool temperate to tropical. These plants are mostly fast growing and benefit from pruning after flowering. They are usually propagated from seed.

Dombeya burgessiae
syn. ***D. mastersii***
Spring flowering, this tall bushy shrub has large heads of white flowers.

Dombeya cacuminum
A very spectacular small tree regarded as one of the most outstanding flowering trees of the world. It has large heads of bright pinky red flowers which cover the tree in late spring.

Dombeya calantha
A dense tall shrub with large heads of rose-pink flowers in spring.

DOMBEYA (CONT)

Dombeya x ***cayeuxii***
This hybrid has pendulous round heads of pink flowers.

Dombeya macrantha
A tall, upright, sparse shrub with large flowers coloured orange-red with a white centre.

Dombeya spectabilis
ssp. ***spectabilis*** cv. **Rosea**
A pale pink flowered cultivar.

Dombeya ianthotricha
A bushy tall shrub with large heads of red bell shaped flowers in spring.

Dombeya pulchra
A tall bushy shrub with large bunches of white flowers with red centres.

Dombeya kirkii
In spring this dense tall shrub has large heads of small white flowers.

Dombeya spectabilis
ssp. ***spectabilis***
Flowering in spring, the white flowers of this dense tall shrub are tightly packed in large heads.

Dombeya tiliacea
A bushy tall shrub with loose bunches of pendulous white flowers in spring.

DORYANTHES

Agavaceae

Native to Australia, these large leaf evergreen clumping plants have very tall flower stalks. They are grown both as ornamentals and for the cut flower trade. They prefer a well drained soil and a climate from cool temperate to sub-tropical. Propagate from seed.

Doryanthes excelsa GYMEA LILY
The very long lasting heads of red flowers grow on stalks up to 4 metres tall on this bushy plant.

Doryanthes palmeri SPEAR LILY
A clumping plant with long flower stalks and long heads of red flowers.

DOVYALIS

Flacourtiaceae

Dovyalis caffra KEI APPLE
A spiny, evergreen, tall shrub which is native to Africa. It is widely grown as a hardy hedge and also for its large yellow fruit which are used in jams and pickles. Propagate from seed and cuttings.

DRACAENA

Agavaceae

Evergreen shrubby plants of the old world tropics. The plants are grown as coloured leaf ornamentals or for their resin which is used in photography and also in varnishes. They prefer temperate to tropical climates and are propagated from seed and cuttings.

Dracaena angustifolia cv. **Honoriae**
syn. ***Pleomele angustifolia*** cv. **Honoriae**
A showy ornamental with strap-like leaves coloured olive-green with a cream outer stripe.

Dracaena deremensis cv. **Lemon and Lime**
This cultivar has leaves that are coloured green, lemon and white.

Dracaena deremensis cv. **Longii**
A cultivar with olive-green strap leaves with a white stripe down the centre.

Dracaena deremensis cv. **Surprise**
The leaves of this cultivar are coloured green, gold and white.

***Dracaena deremensis* cv. Souvenir de Schriever**
A widely cultivated plant with grey leaves striped white.

***Dracaena fragrans* cv. Massangeana** LUCKY PLANT
This cultivar has green and yellow leaves.

***Dracaena marginata* cv. Bicolor**
A cultivar with leaves of green, edged yellow.

Dracaena draco
A tall shrub with bare trunks and bushy tops.

Dracaena goldieana
A large leaf plant with silver and green coloured leaves.

***Dracaena marginata* cv. Colorama**
The leaves of this cultivar are red, green and pink.

Dracaena fragrans
Upright plants with large green pendulous leaves.

Dracaena marginata
Branching and tall, this shrub has bushy heads of leaves green edged red, and large heads of cream flowers.

***Dracaena marginata* cv. Carmine Tricolor**
This cultivar has leaves coloured carmine, red and pink.

DRACAENA (cont)

Dracaena marginata cv. **Tricolor**
A cultivar with green, cream and pink leaves.

Dracaena reflexa
cv. **Variegata Marginata**
syn. ***Pleomele reflexa***
cv. **Variegata Marginata**
This popular bushy indoor plant has strap-type leaves, coloured grey inside and cream outside.

Dracaena surculosa
cv. **Florida Beauty**
A cultivar with coloured leaves of cream with green markings.

Dracaena reflexa
syn. ***Pleomele reflexa***
Widely grown indoors, this multi-stemmed plant has recurved green strap leaves.

Dracaena sanderana cv. **Gold**
A bushy upright plant having yellow leaves with a green central stripe.

Dracaena surculosa cv. **Milky Way**
This cultivar has a broad cream stripe along the middle of each leaf.

Dracaena reflexa
cv. **Aurea Variegata**
syn. ***Pleomele reflexa***
cv. **Aurea Variegata**
A popular cultivar with reflexed strap leaves coloured olive-green, with golden central stripes.

Dracaena surculosa
syn. ***D. godseffiana***
Cane-like branches and leaves of green with cream markings feature on this compact plant.

Dracaena surculosa cv. **Punctulata**
A cultivar with green leaves and a few yellow markings.

DRIMYS

WINTERACEAE

Drimys winteri WINTER'S BARK

A medium sized tree, native to South America. It is a cool climate tree which has pendulous clusters of white highly perfumed flowers in spring. The bark is used for medicinal purposes. There are both male and female forms. Propagate from seed or cuttings.

DRYANDRA

PROTEACEAE

Evergreen shrubs to small trees with prickly leaves, native to Australia. They are hardy, free flowering plants and the long lasting flowers are widely used by florists. This plant grows in a wide range of soil types and prefers to grow in climates from cool temperate to sub-tropical. Propagate from seed. Many Dryandras produce large amounts of honey.

Dryandra carduacea PINGLE

An upright open shrub with cream to lemon coloured flowers.

Dryandra formosa SHOWY DRYANDRA

A widely grown tall shrub with old gold and orange coloured terminal flowers.

Dryandra hewardiana

This is an erect shrub with prickly leaves and creamy yellow flower heads all the way along the branches.

Dryandra nivea COUCH HONEYPOT

A very dwarf spreading shrub with browny yellow flowers.

Dryandra nobilis GOLDEN DRYANDRA

There are long prickly leaves and large flower heads coloured old gold on this bushy shrub.

Dryandra obtusa SHINING HONEYPOT

A very dwarf spreading shrub with long serrated leaves and large brick-red coloured flowers.

Dryandra polycephala

MANY HEADED DRYANDRA

A prickly leaf shrub with large clusters of cream flowers.

DRYANDRA (cont)

Dryandra praemorsa

CUT-LEAF DRYANDRA

This is an upright branching shrub with wide prickly leaves and large golden coloured flower heads.

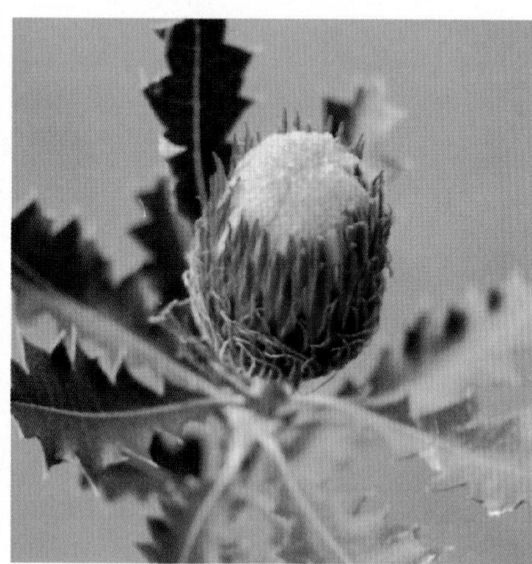

Dryandra quercifolia

OAK-LEAVED DRYANDRA

A much branched shrub with oak shaped leaves and large flower heads of brown outside and yellow inside. A popular cut flower.

Dryandra sessilis PARROT BUSH

Flowers are coloured light cream on this spreading shrub.

DUABANGA

SONNERATIACEAE

Duabanga grandiflora

A tall, evergreen, fast growing tropical tree, native to South East Asia, which is used for timber. It has big leaves and showy bunches of large cream flowers. Propagate from seed.

DURANTA

VERBENACEAE

From Central America and the West Indies, these bushy shrubs are grown as ornamentals or hedge plants. They can become weeds in some instances. These shrubs grow in climates from cool temperate to tropical, and flower over many months. Propagate from seed or cuttings.

Duranta lorentzii

A bushy shrub with pendulous bunches of white flowers.

Duranta repens SKYFLOWER

The sky blue flowers are followed by orange berries on this dense, spiny, shrub.

Duranta repens cv. **Alba**

This cultivar is white flowered.

Duranta repens cv. **Variegata**

The foliage of this cultivar is variegated cream and green.

DURANTA (cont)

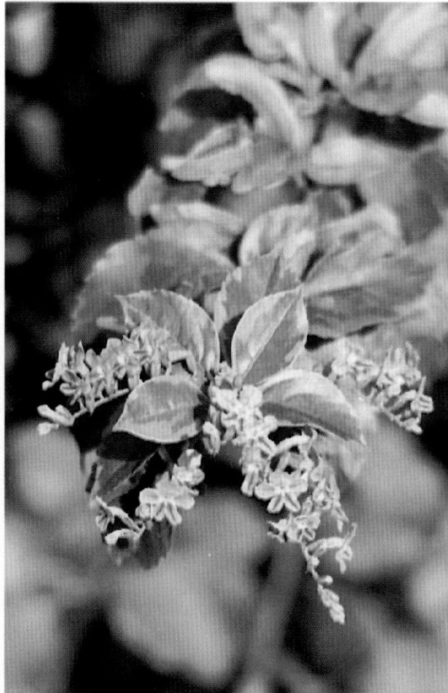

Duranta repens CV. **Variegata Aurea**
This cultivar has variegated foliage, coloured green and yellow.

ECCREMOCARPUS

BIGNONIACEAE

Evergreen vines which are native to South America. They are cool climate plants and are free flowering in the spring and summer, preferring a soil which is moist and high in humus. Propagate from seed or tip cuttings under mist.

Eccremocarpus CV. **Anglia Hybrid**
Free flowering, this vine has tubular flowers which may be red, orange or yellow in colour.

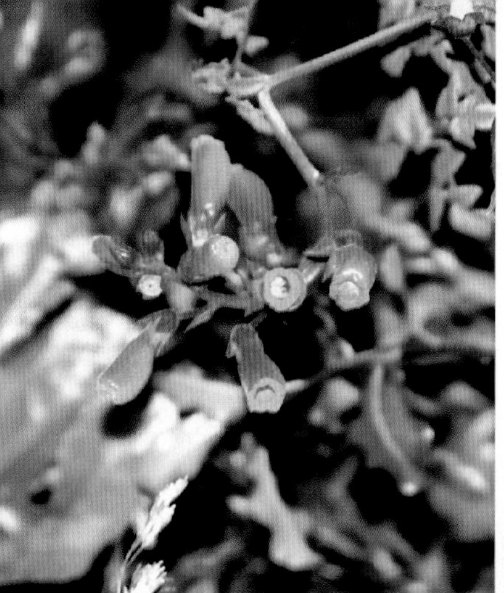

Eccremocarpus scaber
A twining vine with tubular flowers which are mostly gold and red in colour.

Eccremocarpus scaber CV. **Carmineus**
A cultivar with red flowers.

Eccremocarpus scaber CV. **Tresco Hybrid**
Free flowering, this hybrid has tubular flowers coloured orange and yellow.

ECHIUM

BORAGINACEAE

Freely branching shrubs native to Europe and the Canary Islands. They are hardy plants which grow in sunny positions and tolerate poor soils. These plants are widely grown throughout the world in cool temperate to sub-tropical climates. Propagate from seed and cuttings, or by layering.

Echium candicans
syn. ***E. fastuosum***
A freely branching, spreading shrub with blue-white flowers growing in tall spikes.

Echium decaisnei
Multi-branching, this spreading shrub has tall spikes of flowers coloured white, with purple inside.

Echium thyrsiflorum
Mauve flowers on tall spikes bloom on this much branched, spreading shrub.

EDGEWORTHIA

Thymelaeaceae

Fragrant mostly deciduous shrubs from China and the Himalayas. These attractive cold loving shrubs are widely grown as spring flowering ornamentals. Grow from seed or cuttings. These plants are used to produce high quality paper.

Edgeworthia papyrifera PAPERBUSH

A medium deciduous shrub with clusters of tube shaped flowers coloured white and red.

Edgeworthia papyrifera cv. **Grandiflora**

A cultivar with larger flowers coloured white and gold.

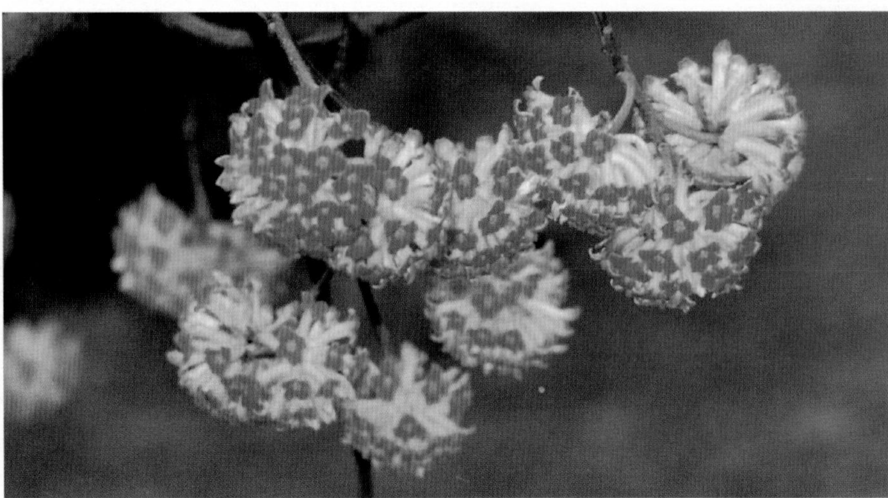

Edgeworthia papyrifera cv. **Red Robin**

This is a showy cultivar with orange-red flowers.

EHRETIA

Boraginaceae

Mostly evergreen shrubs and small trees from the tropics. They are grown throughout the world as ornamentals in climates from temperate to tropical. Propagate from seed or cuttings.

Ehretia acuminata var. ***acuminata*** KODO WOOD

This small Australian tree has clusters of perfumed flowers in spring.

Ehretia rigida

A tall shrub to small tree grown for its clusters of perfumed, small, pale blue flowers.

ELAEAGNUS

Elaeagnaceae

Hardy, cold tolerant shrubs with stiff leaves. These plants are propagated from seed and cuttings. They are native to Asia, Europe and North America and northern Australia and many have small edible fruit.

Elaeagnus x ***ebbingei*** cv. **Gilt Edge**

This cultivar has leaves coloured green inside and golden yellow outside.

Elaeagnus x ***ebbingei*** cv. **Limelight**

Squat and spreading, this shrub has colourful variegated foliage of green and yellow.

Elaeagnus pungens cv. **Aurea**

A hardy bushy shrub with leaves green inside and creamish yellow outside.

Elaeagnus pungens cv. **Maculata**
The variegated leaves of this cultivar are coloured yellow inside and green outside.

ELAEOCARPUS

ELAEOCARPACEAE

Small to medium evergreen trees from the warm climates of the world. They are grown as ornamentals and some as timber trees. The plants grow in climates from cool temperate to tropical and tolerate a wide range of soils. Propagation is from cuttings or seed. When growing from seed the outer skin needs to be removed when harvested and the seed soaked in water for up to 2 months to remove from the seed the chemical which prevents germination. This water must be changed regularly to stop stagnation.

Elaeocarpus grandis
A medium size tree which is grown as a tree and an ornamental. It has clusters of white flowers followed by marble size bright blue fruit. At times the tree may have single branches of bright red leaves.

Elaeocarpus reticulatus
BLUEBERRY ASH
A tall shrub to small tree which is covered with white, pendulous, small, bell shaped flowers in spring followed by showy clusters of bright blue, hard berries which remain for up to 6 months.

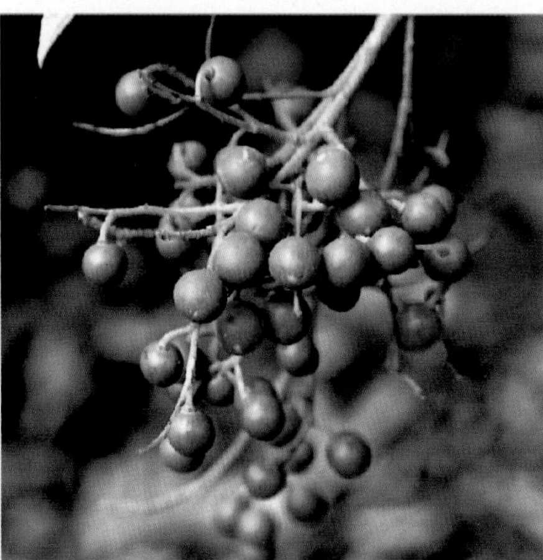

Elaeocarpus reticulatus
This illustration shows the bright blue berries (or fruit).

Elaeocarpus reticulatus cv. **Flamingo**
A pink flowered cultivar. There are other named pink cultivars but all appear to be similar to this old favourite.

EMBOTHRIUM

PROTEACEAE

Embothrium coccineum
CHILEAN FIREBUSH
An evergreen tall shrub to small tree native to the Andes of South America, it is grown in cool to temperate climates as a free flowering ornamental with bright red flowers in spring. The plant prefers a rich, moist, slightly acid soil. Propagate from cuttings and seed.

Embothrium coccineum var. ***lanceolatum***
A variety with narrower leaves.

EMMENOSPERMA

RHAMNACEAE

Emmenosperma alphitonioides

YELLOW ASH

A small to medium evergreen rainforest tree from Australia, which is grown for timber and as an ornamental. When cultivated it rarely gets larger than a small tree size and it has very attractive bright orange berries for many months. The tree prefers a rich soil and regular applications of fertiliser. It is propagated from seed.

ENKIANTHUS

ERICACEAE

Deciduous shrubs from Asia which are widely grown as ornamentals in cool climates. They prefer a well drained, rich soil and regular fertilising. Propagate from seed, or cuttings and by layering.

Enkianthus campanulatus

A tall shrub with large cascading bunches of small, bell shaped flowers coloured pink and white.

***Enkianthus campanulatus* cv. Albiflorus**

On this cultivar the flowers are white.

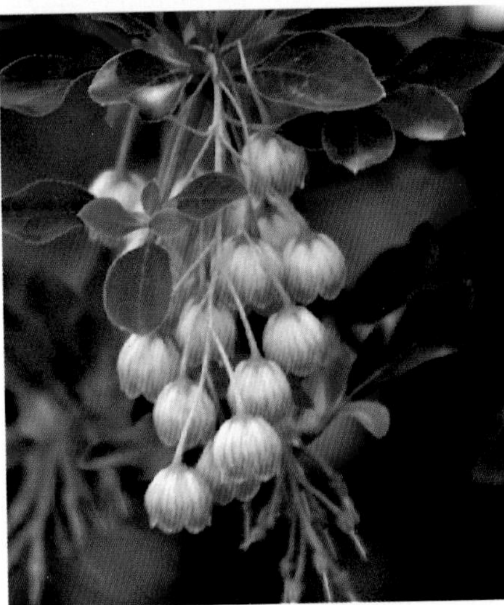

***Enkianthus campanulatus* cv. Pink Bells**

A showy cultivar with pink, bell shaped flowers.

***Enkianthus campanulatus* cv. Red Bells**

This cultivar has pale red, bell shaped flowers.

ENTADA

MIMOSACEAE [LEGUMINOSAE]

Entada abyssinica

A small deciduous African tree which is grown in warm climates as an ornamental flowering tree. It is covered with long spikes of yellow flowers in spring. Propagate from seed.

EPACRIS

EPACRIDACEAE

Small, spiked leaf, evergreen shrubs from the Australian heath land. They are free flowering in climates from cold temperate to sub-tropical and prefer a peaty soil. Propagate from seed or cuttings.

Epacris impressa COMMON HEATH

A showy small shrub with masses of pendulous, red, tubular flowers. The floral emblem of Victoria, Australia.

EPACRIS (cont)

Epacris longiflora FUCHSIA HEATH
This small shrub has masses of red and white pendulous tubular flowers.

EPIPREMNUM

ARACEAE

This plant is tropical and native of South East Asia. It is widely grown both as an indoor plant and outdoors in tropical and sub-tropical climates. Propagation is from cuttings.

Epipremnum aureum GOLDEN POTHOS
syn. ***Scindapsus aureus; Raphidophora aurea; Pothos aureus***
A climbing plant with large variegated leaves of green and gold. This climber has had many name changes.

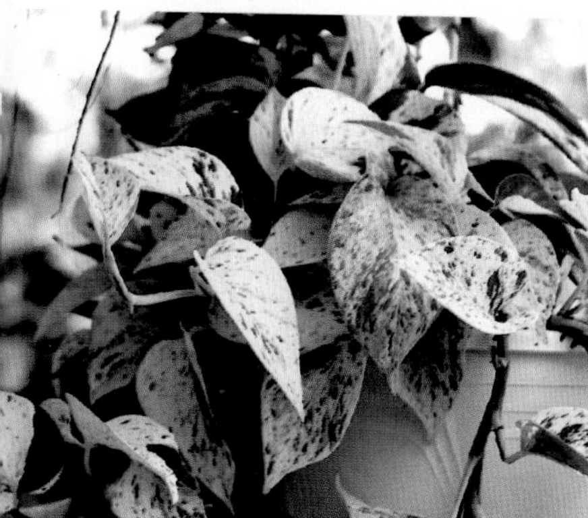

Epipremnum aureum cv. **Marble Queen**
A cultivar with white and green variegated foliage.

ERANTHEMUM

ACANTHACEAE

Clumping evergreen shrubby plants from India. In warm temperate to tropical climates, they are grown outdoors for their very colourful flowers. These plants prefer a rich soil and a semi-shaded situation. Propagation is from seed and cuttings or by division.

Eranthemum pulchellum BLUE SAGE
A clumping plant with large heads of mid-blue flowers.

Eranthemum wattii
This clumping plant has clusters of violet coloured flowers.

EREMAEA

MYRTACEAE

Eremaea fimbriata
A small evergreen shrub from Western Australia. This plant prefers a well drained sandy soil and a climate from cool temperate to sub-tropical. In spring, it has paintbrush-type flowers of bright orange with yellow tips. Propagate from seed and cuttings.

EREMOPHILA

MYOPORACEAE

From Australia, these dry climate shrubs are mostly evergreen. They are cultivated, in a wide range of soil types, for their attractive flowers. Many of the arid area types grow for very long periods of time without rain. Propagation is from seed, which needs acid treatment, and cuttings.

Eremophila cuneifolia PINYURU
A small spreading shrub with bluish mauve coloured flowers.

EREMOPHILA (cont)

Eremophila gilesii

DESERT FUCHSIA; TURKEY BUSH

This small evergreen shrub has blue to mauve coloured flowers.

Eremophila longifolia EMU BUSH

An upright shrub with long leaves and orange flowers.

Eremophila nivea

A small open shrub with silver leaves and violet coloured flowers.

Eremophila hygrophana

A spreading shrub with clusters of mauve flowers.

Eremophila maculata NATIVE FUCHSIA

A dense shrub with varying coloured flowers which may be red, yellow, orange or pink.

Eremophila laanii - mauve form

There are violet-mauve coloured flowers on this small spreading shrub.

Eremophila maculata cv. **Aurea**

This cultivar has golden coloured flowers.

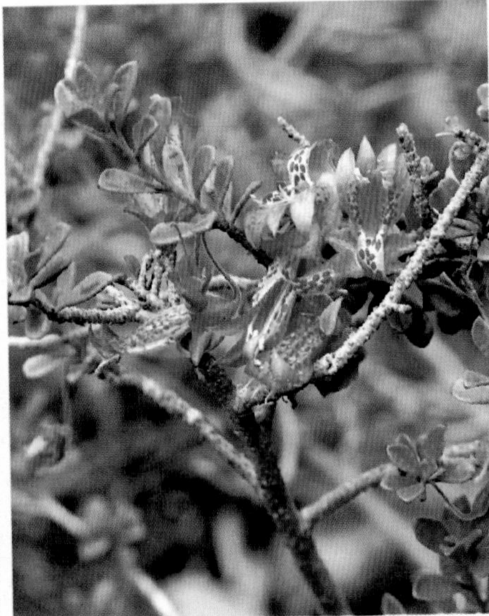

Eremophila purpurascens

The flowers on this open shrub bloom in clusters and are coloured pinky red to purple.

EREMOPHILA (cont)

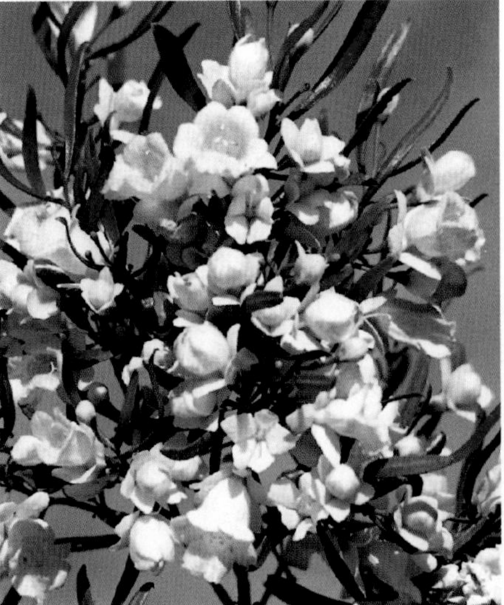

Eremophila sturtii
This dense tall shrub has masses of mauve flowers in spring.

Eremophila viscida VARNISH BUSH
The flowers of this free flowering medium shrub are mauve to purple in colour.

***Eremophila viscida* cv. Alba**
A white flowered cultivar of this plant.

ERICA

ERICACEAE

From Africa and Europe, these fine leaf evergreen shrubs are widely grown for their floral display. They are hardy in a wide range of soils in climates from cold temperate to sub-tropical. Plants benefit from regular applications of fertiliser. Propagate from cuttings or seed which is very fine.

Erica arborea TREE HEATH
In spring this medium to tall spreading shrub has masses of small white flowers.

***Erica arborea* cv. Albert's Gold**
A cultivar with yellow foliage.

Erica baccans
This is a small upright shrub with pendulous heads of pale pink, bell shaped flowers.

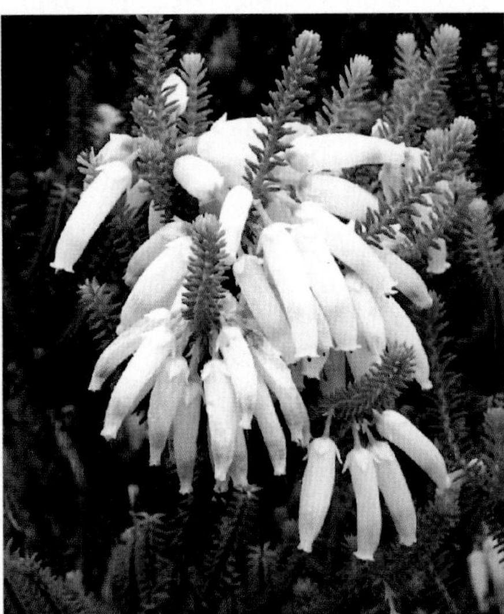

Erica bauera BRIDAL HEATH
An open shrub with clusters of white, sometimes pink, tubular flowers.

Erica canaliculata
Hardy and free branching, this small shrub has mauve-pink flowers.

ERICA (cont)

Erica canaliculata **cv. Rosea**
A freely branching shrub with masses of small, bright pink flowers.

Erica carnea
In spring this small spreading shrub has heads of pendulous, small, bell shaped flowers.

Erica cerinthoides
A sparse erect shrub with clusters of orange tubular flowers.

Erica colorans
An upright, erect, small shrub with tubular flowers along the branches. The flowers open white and change to pinky red with age.

Erica colorans **cv. White Delight**
An erect and sparsely branching shrub with white tubular flowers all along the branches.

Erica glandulosa
A sparse erect shrub with terminal clusters of flowers rose-pink, tipped white.

Erica hebecalyx
The tubular flowers of this fine leaf, sparse shrub are coloured red and pale yellow.

Erica **cv. Linton's Red**
A cultivar with dense clusters of orange-red tubular flowers.

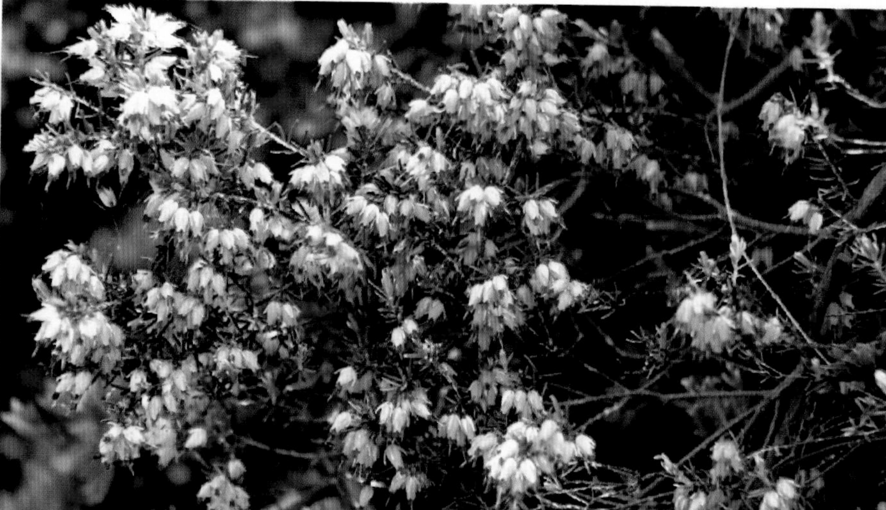

Erica melanthera
A compact free flowering shrub with small rose-pink flowers.

Erica versicolor
A sparse erectly branching shrub with clusters of red tubular flowers tipped with yellow.

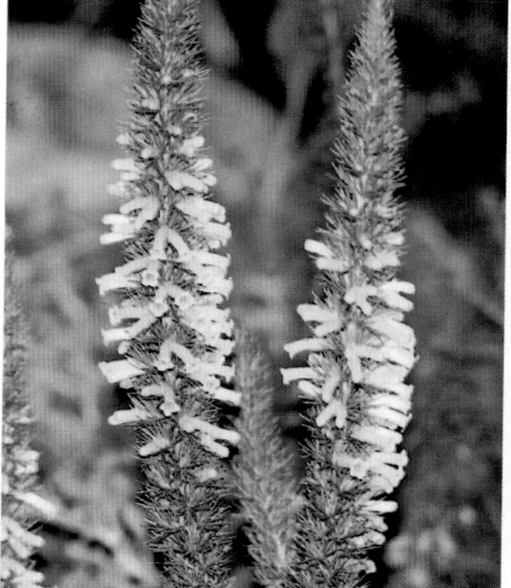

Erica patersonia
Tubular yellow flowers bloom along the spike-like branches of this upright, small shrub.

***Erica* cv. Ruby Glow**
This cultivar has clusters of tubular flowers coloured ruby red, tipped with white.

Erica* x *wilmorei PINK BELLS
An open erect shrub. The tubular red flowers along the branches are tipped with white.

***Erica* cv. Pink Hybrid**
A hybrid cultivar with pale pink tubular flowers.

Erica sicula
The mauve, bell shaped flowers form in pendulous heads on this sparse shrub.

***Erica* cv. Wittunga Satin**
This small bushy shrub has masses of pale pink flowers in spring.

ERIOPE

Lamiaceae [Labiatae]

Eriope macrostachya

A large leaf, open, tall shrub native to Central America. The plant has long spikes of pink flowers over many months and is grown as an ornamental in temperate to tropical climates. Propagate from seed or cuttings.

ERIOSTEMON

Rutaceae

Evergreen shrubs and occasionally small trees with waxy flowers, from Australia. They are highly perfumed and are widely grown as spring flowering ornamentals. These plants prefer a well drained soil and care should be taken not to over fertilise. The most suitable climates are from cool temperate to sub-tropical. Propagate from cuttings or seed which needs hot water treatment.

Eriostemon australasius

PINK WAX FLOWER

An open erect shrub with showy pink star shaped flowers in spring.

Eriostemon myoporoides

LONG LEAF WAX FLOWER

Spring flowering, this sparse small shrub is covered with waxy, white, star shaped flowers.

Eriostemon spicatus

An open upright sparse shrub which is covered with pale mauve flowers in spring.

Eriostemon verrucosus

cv. Semmen's Double Wax Flower

This sparse shrub has very pale pink double flowers.

ERYTHRINA

Fabaceae [Leguminosae]

Deciduous thorny shrubs and trees from Africa, Australia, South and Central America, which are widely grown as hardy showy ornamentals. They prefer climates which are temperate to tropical and grow in a wide range of soil types. The flowers are very attractive to birds. Propagation is from seed and cuttings. The timber of this tree is very light in weight.

Erythrina abyssinica

RED HOT POKER TREE

A small spreading tree with large upright clusters of bright scarlet flowers.

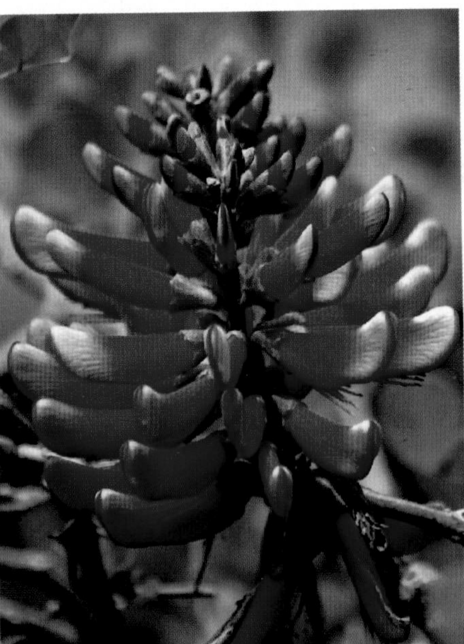

Erythrina acanthocarpa

A thorny spreading shrub with very large clusters of flowers coloured red with yellow and green markings.

ERYTHRINA (cont)

Erythrina acanthocarpa - seed pods
This illustration shows the thorny seed pods.

Erythrina* x *bidwillii
A hybrid between *E. crista-galli* and *E. herbacea*, this shrub has red to crimson flowers in long racemes.

Erythrina atitlanensis
An open, spreading, small tree with conical clusters of bright red flowers.

Erythrina burttii
This spreading small tree has clusters of orange-red flowers.

Erythrina chiapasana
An open crowned small tree with clusters of scarlet flowers.

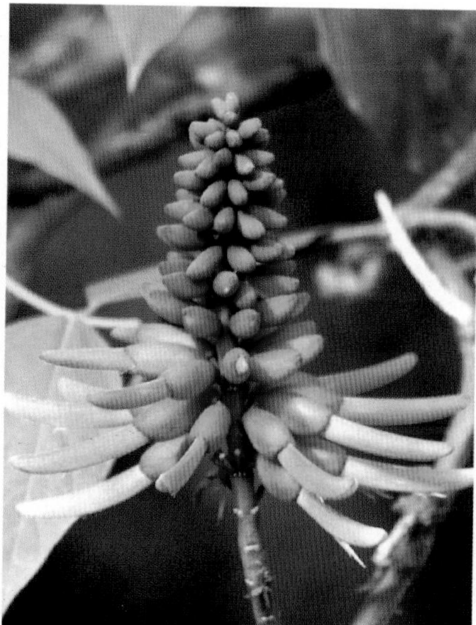

Erythrina berenices
Open crowned, this small tree has conical shaped heads of flowers, coloured rose-pink.

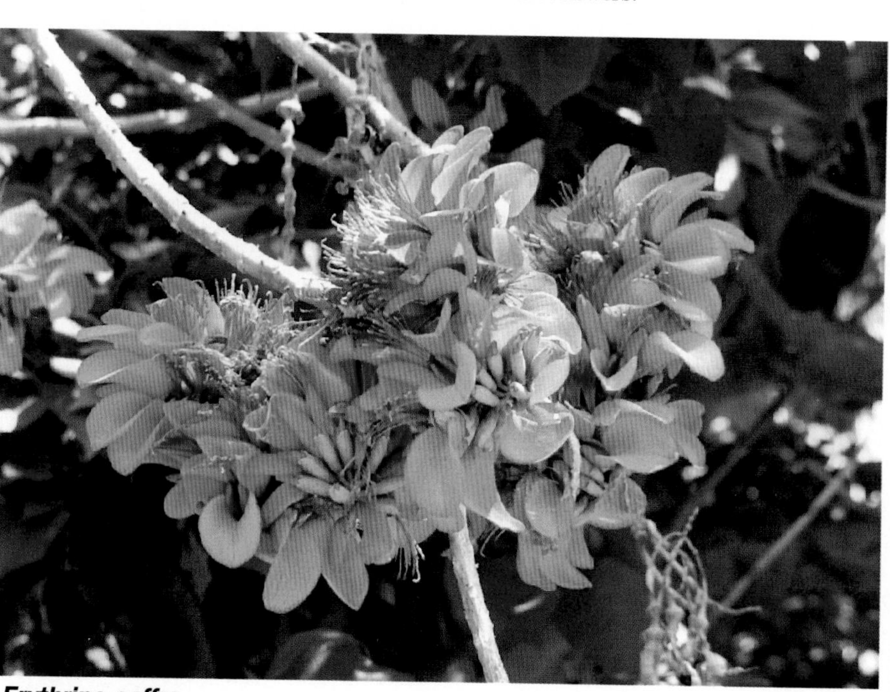

Erythrina caffra KAFFERBOOM
A broad crowned small tree with large clusters of orange-red flowers.

ERYTHRINA (cont)

Erythrina costaricensis
This is a spreading small tree with very showy conical clusters of orange-scarlet flowers.

Erythrina fusca SWAMP IMMORTELLE
This small tree has a crooked trunk and limbs with racemes of crimson flowers.

Erythrina crista-galli COCKSPUR CORAL
A dense small tree with long racemes of dark red flowers.

Erythrina dominguezii
Long clusters of flowers coloured pale pink and red bloom on this small tree.

Erythrina haerdii
With dense foliage, this small tree has red flowers and unusual seed pods.

Erythrina crista-galli cv. **Crimson Princess**
Long pendulous racemes of crimson-red flowers bloom on this cultivar.

Erythrina falcata
A small tree with cascading racemes of bright red flowers.

Erythrina cv. **Harold Caulfield**
A small tree with cone shaped heads of orange-red flowers.

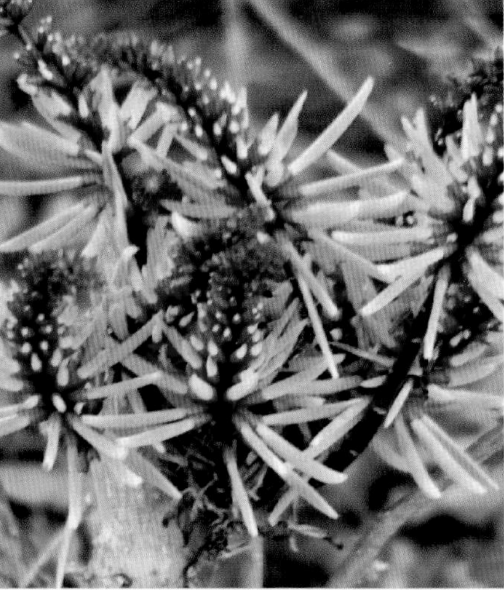

Erythrina herbacea ssp. ***herbacea***
CHEROKEE BEAN
A tall open shrub with large clusters of pink flowers.

Erythrina huehuetenangensis
This small, open crowned tree has long conical clusters of red flowers.

Erythrina latissima
In late spring this small open crowned tree has bright red flowers, in round bunches.

Erythrina livingstonia
An open crowned small tree with long conical shaped spikes of red flowers.

Erythrina lysistemon CORAL TREE
A full crowned, spreading, small tree with red to crimson flowers in conical heads.

Erythrina rubrinervia
This is a small tree with crimson to red flowers in upright conical clusters.

Erythrina salviiflora
A small tree with bright red flowers in clusters and unusual twisted seed pods—illustrated.

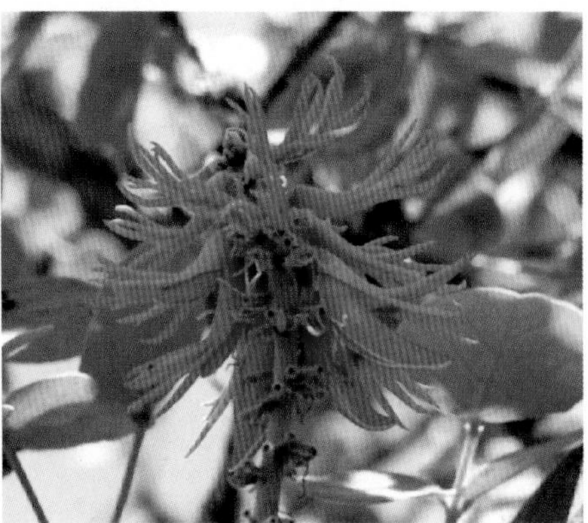

Erythrina sigmoidea
Leathery leaves and corky bark feature on this small spreading tree. The flowers in large upright heads are coloured bright red.

ERYTHRINA (cont)

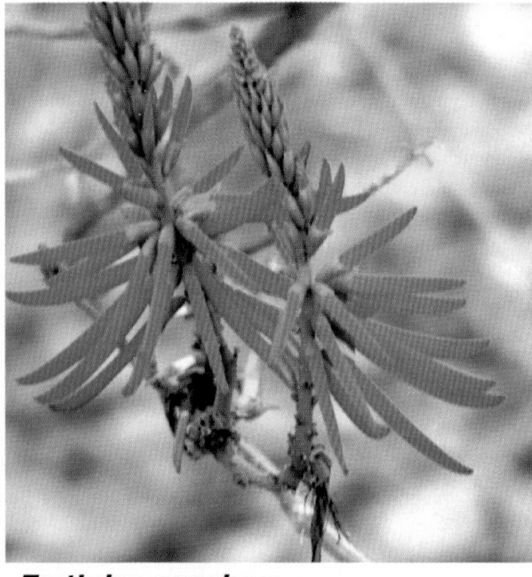

Erythrina speciosa
A small open crowned tree with conical clusters of red flowers.

Erythrina speciosa cv. **Alba**
This cultivar has white flowers.

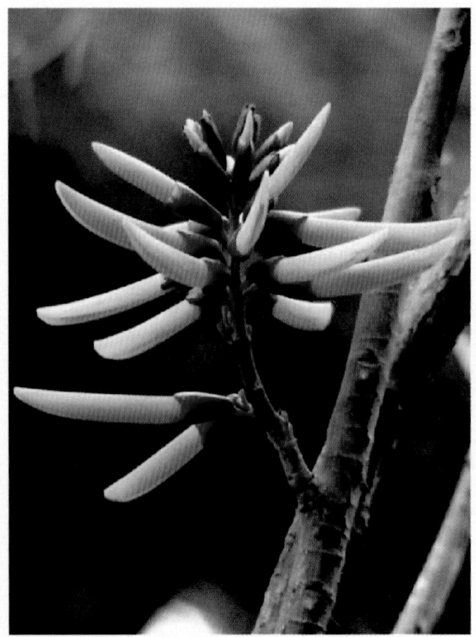

Erythrina speciosa cv. **Rosea**
A cultivar with pink flowers.

Erythrina variegata syn. ***E. indica; E. variegata*** var. ***orientalis***
This is a densely crowned small tree with green and gold variegated leaves and red flowers.

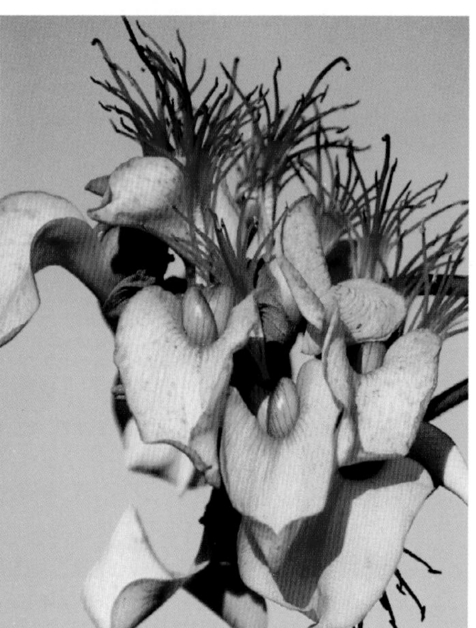

Erythrina velutina
A small spreading tree with showy heads of orange coloured flowers in spring.

Erythrina vespertilio BATSWING CORAL
The unusual leaves on this upright small tree are shaped like bats' wings. The flowers are in long racemes and red in colour.

Erythrina vespertilio cv. **Pine Mountain**
A natural variation with flowers of cream, yellow and light red.

ERYTHROPHYSA

SAPINDACEAE

Erythrophysa transvaalensis
RED BALLOON
A tall fine leaf shrub from Africa. It is widely grown for its crimson coloured flowers and attractive balloon-like red seed pods. The plant will grow in poor soils. Propagate from seed.

ESCALLONIA

GROSSULARIACEAE [ESCALLONIACEAE]

Evergreen shrubs and small trees from the Andes region of South America. These hardy plants are cultivated worldwide, irom cold temperate climates to sub-tropical, as ornamentals for their attractive terminal clusters of flowers. Many cultivars are grown. They respond to regular applications of fertiliser. Propagation is from seed and cuttings.

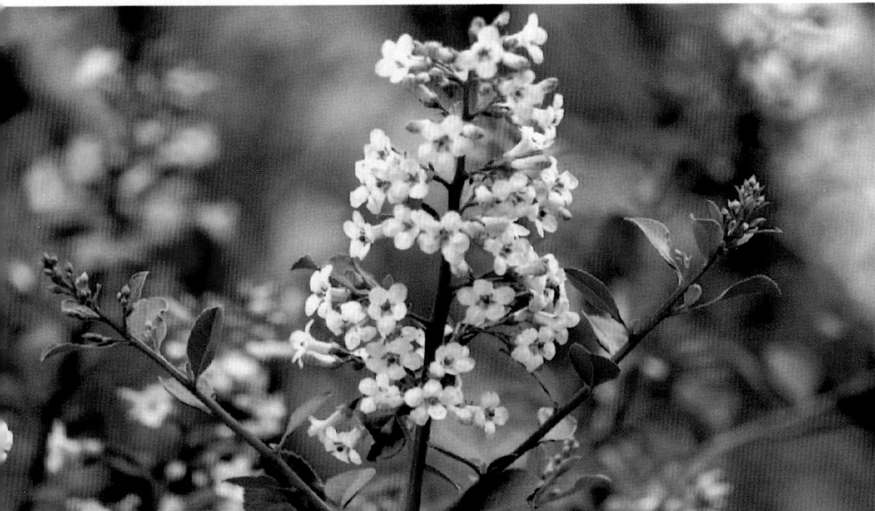

Escallonia **cv. Apple Blossom**
A free flowering hardy shrub with pale pink flowers.

Escallonia rosea
This is a hardy shrub with rose-pink flowers.

Escallonia bifida
syn. ***E. floribunda***
This tall shrub has white flowers.

Escallonia* x *rockii **cv. Alba**
The flowers of this tall open shrub are white.

Escallonia rubra **var.** ***macrantha***
A free flowering shrub with red flowers.

Escallonia **cv. Prix Flash**
A French cultivar which is a compact grower and has rose-red flowers.

EUADENIA

CAPPARACEAE [CAPPARIDACEAE]

Euadenia eminens
A warm climate evergreen shrub from South East Asia with clusters of cream coloured terminal flowers.

e

EUCALYPTUS

MYRTACEAE

Evergreen shrubs to large trees which are native mostly to Australia, with some in South East Asia. They are grown for a wide range of purposes, including timber and honey production, medicinal and industrial uses, musical instruments, weapons, perfumes, food, dyes, cut foliage, cut flowers, ornamental and arts and crafts. These plants are among the most widely grown in the world. Their habitat ranges from tropical to alpine and desert. Many horticulturalists and gardeners throughout the world mistakenly think that all Eucalypts are large trees, not realising that many of the outstanding ornamental forms are shrubs to small trees. Eucalyptus grow in a wide range of soils. Propagate from seed, which benefits from cold stratification for alpine varieties. The term mallee is used to describe multi-stemmed small Eucalypts which have underground lignotubers. When planting Eucalyptus, small plants which are not root bound in their containers will grow much more quickly than larger potted plants.

Eucalyptus beardiana

A medium mallee shrub with pendulous clusters of cream flowers. Suited to semi-arid temperate areas.

Eucalyptus burdettiana

BURDETT MALLEE

A medium spreading shrub with yellow-green flowers followed by decorative seed pods. Suited to temperate climates. Used in honey production.

Eucalyptus burracoppinensis

BURRACOPPIN MALLEE

A medium spreading shrub. The flowers are cream and the seed pods are used for ornaments. Suitable for semi-arid temperate areas.

Eucalyptus caesia GUNGURRU

A very decorative tall shrub to small tree with large red flowers and silver on the pods and branches. Widely grown in climates from cool temperate to warm temperate.

Eucalyptus caesia - pods

This illustration shows the decorative silver seed pods.

Eucalyptus caesia ssp.***magna*** - pods

SILVER PRINCESS

A select cultivar which has more flowers which are darker in colour and very showy silver seed pods.

Eucalyptus calophylla MARRI

A small to medium spreading tree with very large heads of cream flowers. Suited to cool temperate to sub-tropical climates

EUCALYPTUS (cont)

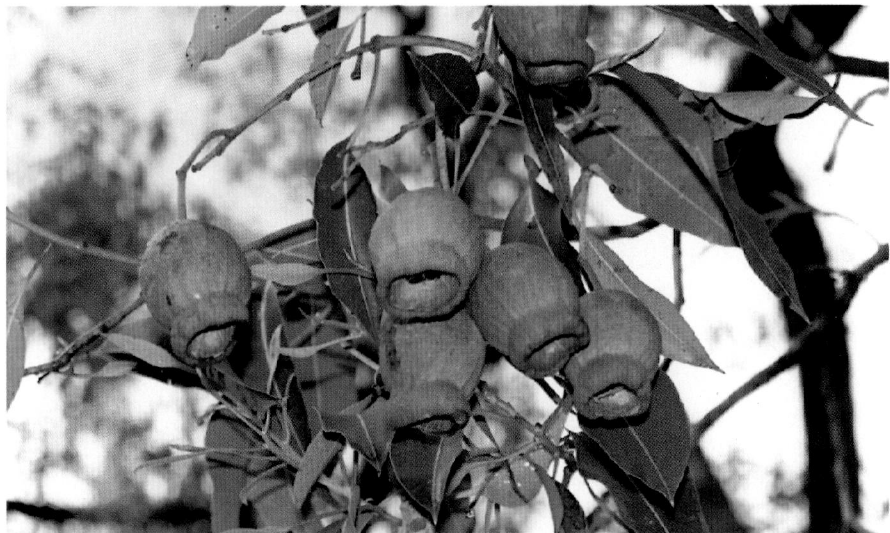

Eucalyptus calophylla - pods

This illustration shows the very large seed pods which are widely used as ornamentals.

Eucalyptus calophylla cv. **Rosea**

A very showy pink flowered cultivar.

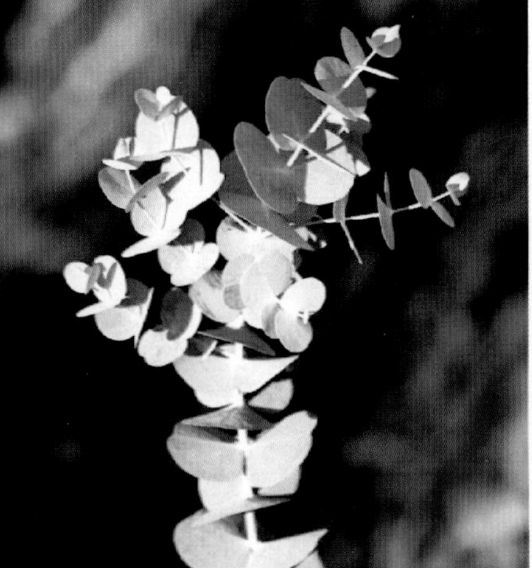

Eucalyptus cinerea ARGYLE APPLE

A small sometimes medium tree widely grown for its blue foliage which is prized by florists. It has white flowers and grows best in sub-alpine to warm temperate climates. Seed germination will benefit from cold stratification.

Eucalyptus conferruminata BUSHY YATE

A medium mallee shrub which has yellow flowers and is best grown in semi-arid temperate climates.

Eucalyptus cooperiana MANY FLOWERED MALLEE

A tall dense mallee shrub with large clusters of cream flowers. Alkaline and sandy soils in temperate climates suit this shrub. Suitable for honey production.

Eucalyptus crucis SILVER MALLEE

A tall mallee shrub with attractive silver foliage and yellow flowers. Grows in semi-arid conditions in cold temperate to warm temperate climates. Used by florists for flowers and foliage.

Eucalyptus curtisii PLUNKETT MALLEE

A tall shrub grown in climates from mild temperate to sub-tropical as an ornamental, for its display of white flowers.

Eucalyptus deglupta

A vigorous tropical tree which has very attractive striped bark and large clusters of cream flowers. Grown for timber and as an ornamental in the tropics.

EUCALYPTUS (cont)

Eucalptus elata RIVER PEPPERMINT

A straight growing medium tree with pendulous foliage. It needs a temperate climate and is used for timber and the leaves in oil production.

Eucalyptus erythrocorys - seed pods

This illustration shows the decorative seed pods.

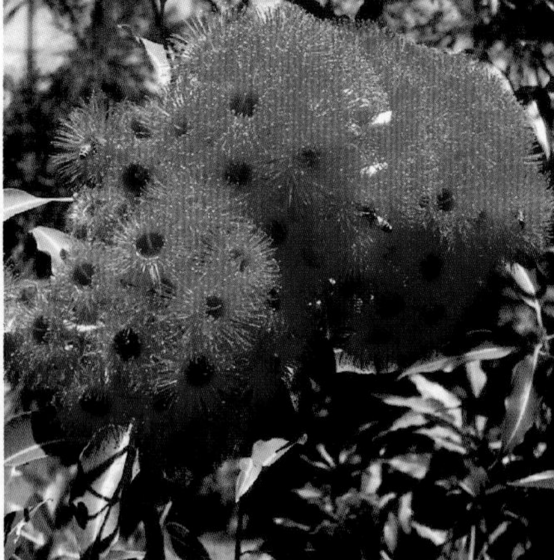

Eucalyptus ficifolia

RED FLOWERING GUM

A small to medium tree with very large heads of pink, red or orange flowers. This tree is an outstanding ornamental in climates from mild temperate to sub-tropical. It has very decorative large seed pods.

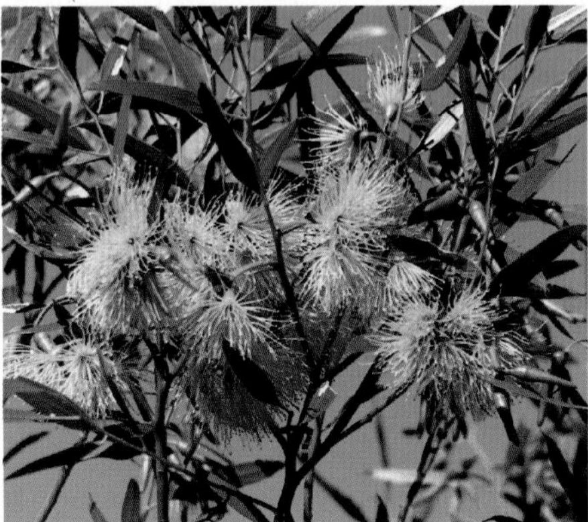

Eucalyptus eremophila

TALL SAND MALLEE

A tall mallee shrub which has very attractive golden flowers. It prefers a semi-arid climate and a sandy soil. Widely grown as an ornamental and for honey production.

Eucalyptus eximia YELLOW BLOODWOOD

A small densely crowned tree with large clusters of pale yellow flowers. Grown as an ornamental in temperate to sub-tropical climates.

Eucalyptus erythrocorys

RED CAP GUM; ILLYARRIE

A small tree with very large yellow flowers which follow the bright red buds. It is widely grown as an ornamental in climates from cool temperate to sub-tropical in a well drained soil. The large seed pods are very ornamental.

Eucalyptus eximia cv. **Nana**

A smaller growing cultivar of this plant.

Eucalyptus ficifolia - pink form

A cultivar with bright pink flowers.

Eucalyptus forrestiana FUCHSIA GUM

A tall spreading shrub with bright red seed capsules and yellow flowers. This shrub is grown as an ornamental in semi-arid temperate climates.

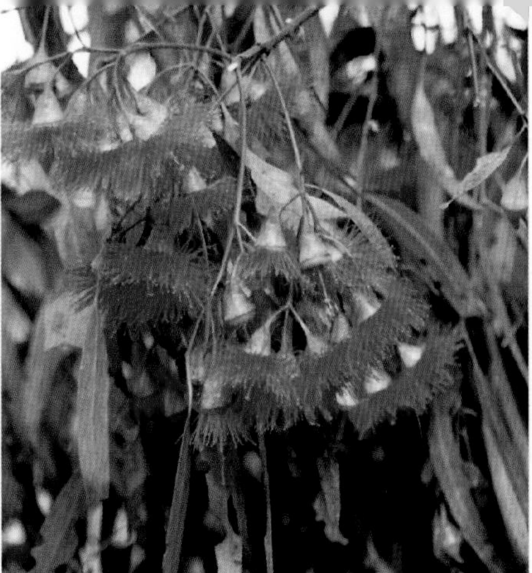

***Eucalyptus leucoxylon* cv. Rosea**

LARGE FRUITED YELLOW GUM

syn. ***E. leucoxylon*** ssp. ***megalocarpa***
An open crowned small tree with pendulous clusters of reddish flowers. Grows in a wide range of soils in climates from cool temperate to sub-tropical.

Eucalyptus gunnii CIDER GUM

A cold loving small tree with roundish blue leaves. The foliage of this tree is widely used by florists. It has white flowers.

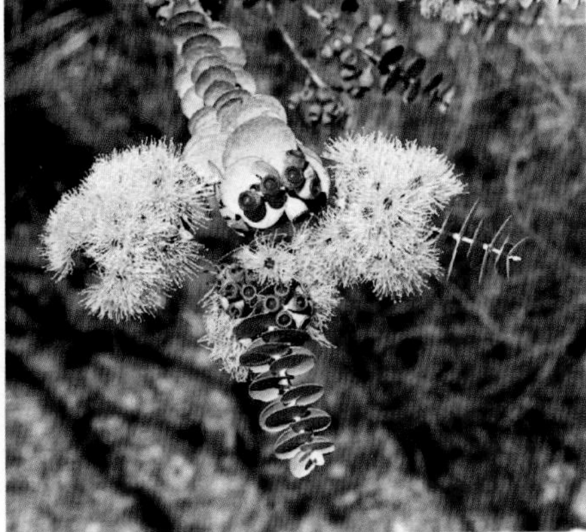

Eucalyptus kruseana

BOOK LEAF MALLEE

A spreading tall mallee shrub which has attractive silver leaves and yellow flowers. The foliage is widely used by florists. It prefers well drained soils in cool temperate to temperate climates.

Eucalyptus macrocarpa

MOTTLECAH; ROSE OF THE WEST

A sprawling mallee shrub with blue-grey leaves and showy large pinkish red flowers followed by very large ornamental seed pods which are prized for decoration. This plant grows in well drained soils in cool temperate to warm temperate climates—an excellent ornamental.

Eucalyptus intermedia

PINK BLOODWOOD

A medium tree with large clusters of cream flowers. Suits temperate to sub-tropical climates. It extrudes pinkish sap.

Eucalyptus lansdowneana

PURPLE MALLEE

A tall mallee or small tree with attractive clusters of crimson-purple flowers. It is grown as an ornamental in well drained soils in temperate climates.

***Eucalyptus macrocarpa* -**

salmon form

A cultivar with salmon-pink flowers.

EUCALYPTUS (cont)

Eucalyptus macrocarpa* x *pyriformis MACRO-FORMIS

A hybrid between *E. macrocarpa* and *E. pyriformis*, which has large yellow flowers followed by attractive seed pods. Suitable for climates from cool temperate to sub-tropical.

Eucalyptus pachyphylla RED BUDDED MALLEE

A dense medium mallee shrub with clusters of large pale yellow flowers followed by very attractive seed pods which are highly ornamental. This plant prefers a well drained soil in climates from cool temperate to tropical.

Eucalyptus megacornuta WARTY YATE

A tall shrub to small tree with a dense crown. Having a warty appearance, the buds are followed by showy yellow flowers and decorative seed pods. Needs a well drained situation in a temperate climate.

Eucalyptus occidentalis SWAMP YATE

An open crowned small tree with yellow flowers. This tree grows in swampy areas in climates from cool temperate to sub-tropical. It is good for honey production and produces a long lasting timber.

Eucalyptus papuana GHOST GUM

A small to medium tree which has an outstanding white trunk which can appear ghostly on a moonlight night. It has small white flowers, needs a well drained site in a sub-tropical to tropical climate and is very tolerant of arid conditions.

Eucalyptus miniata 13

DARWIN WOOLLYBUTT

A straight trunked medium tree with a dense crown. The attractive clusters of flowers are orange and yellow. This tree needs a tropical climate. It is honey producing and the seeds are edible.

Eucalyptus orbifolia ROUND-LEAVED MALLEE

A spreading, medium mallee shrub with very attractive round leaves greyish in colour and edged red. The gold flowers are produced in clusters. It prefers a well drained situation in a semi-arid climate from temperate to sub-tropical.

Eucalyptus polycarpa - pink form
LONG FRUITED BLOODWOOD

A small to medium tree with an open crown. The flowers are normally white but this form has showy pink flowers. It prefers a well drained soil and grows in climates from temperate to tropical. It is a good ornamental and produces large quantities of nectar.

Eucalyptus preissiana
BELL FRUITED MALLEE

A tall spreading mallee shrub with greyish leaves. The yellow flowers grow in clusters and are followed by very ornamental bell shaped seed pods. It prefers a well drained soil in climates from cool temperate to sub-tropical.

Eucalyptus pruinosa SILVER BOX

A small tropical tree with attractive blue foliage which appears as if it has been covered with silver dust. It has clusters of cream flowers and needs a well drained soil in sub-tropical to tropical climates. It is good as cut foliage.

Eucalyptus ptychocarpa
SWAMP BLOODWOOD

An open crowned small tree which has very big heads of large showy cream flowers, followed by decorative seed pods. It is widely grown as an ornamental in climates from warm temperate to tropical and it will tolerate poorly drained soils and light frosts.

Eucalyptus ptychocarpa cv. **Rosea**
A pink flowered cultivar.

Eucalyptus ptychocarpa cv. **Rubra**
This cultivar is red flowered.

Eucalyptus pulverulenta
A tall shrub to small tree which has roundish blue leaves and is cold tolerant. It is grown widely for florists' cut foliage and has white flowers.

Eucalyptus pyriformis
PEAR FRUITED MALLEE

A tall mallee shrub which may have large red or cream coloured flowers followed by big decorative seed pods. These plants need a well drained situation and grow in climates from cool temperate to warm temperate. It is a good nectar producer.

EUCALYPTUS (cont)

Eucalyptus redunca

An open crowned tall mallee shrub with showy yellow flowers followed by decorative seed pods. It prefers a well drained soil in a temperate climate.

Eucalyptus rhodantha ROSE MALLEE

A sprawling mallee shrub. The very large flowers consist of red stamens which are heavily tipped with gold pollen and are followed by large decorative seed pods. It has attractive silver foliage widely used by florists. This shrub requires a well drained soil in a dry temperate climate.

Eucalyptus robusta SWAMP MAHOGANY

A fast growing small tree which has clusters of white flowers. It grows well in swampy or poorly drained soils and produces good quantities of nectar. The tree will grow in climates from cool temperate to tropical.

Eucalyptus sepulcralis WEEPING GUM

A thinly trunked tall mallee shrub with pendulous foliage. This plant is grown as an ornamental. It has showy clusters of yellow flowers. The shrub prefers a well drained soil in climates from cool temperate to warm temperate.

Eucalyptus sideroxylon MUGGA

A straight trunked medium tree with hard furrowed bark and pendulous clusters of white flowers. This tree produces an outstanding hard timber and is recognised as a top honey producer. It will grow in a wide range of soils and climates from cold temperate to sub-tropical.

Eucalyptus sideroxylon cv. **Rosea**

A cultivar with pinky red flowers, grown as an ornamental.

Eucalyptus tetragona WHITE MARLOCK

A tall mallee shrub with attractive blue foliage which appears to have been dusted with silver. This foliage is very popular with florists. It has clusters of white flowers followed by seed pods overlaid with silver. The shrub needs a well drained or sandy soil in a cool temperate to warm temperate climate.

Eucalyptus tetraptera

FOUR WINGED MALLEE

An open crowned tall mallee shrub with showy, red, square buds and pinky red flowers. It is widely grown as an ornamental in climates from cool temperate to warm temperate and prefers a well drained soil.

Eucalyptus CV. **Torwood**

A hybrid between *E. torquata* and *E. woodwardii* which is a small tree with large clusters of yellow to golden coloured flowers. An ideal ornamental for gardens, street trees and parks in temperate to sub-tropical climates in low rainfall areas.

Eucalyptus woodwardii

LEMON FLOWERED GUM

An open crowned small tree with large heads of lemon-yellow flowers. It needs to be grown in low rainfall areas in warm temperate to sub-tropical climates.

Eucalyptus torelliana CADAGHI; CADAGI

A fast growing densely crowned medium tree which has large clusters of cream flowers. It is grown as a landscape tree, produces a good quality timber and is a good source of honey. The tree needs ample water for good growth and grows in temperate to tropical climates.

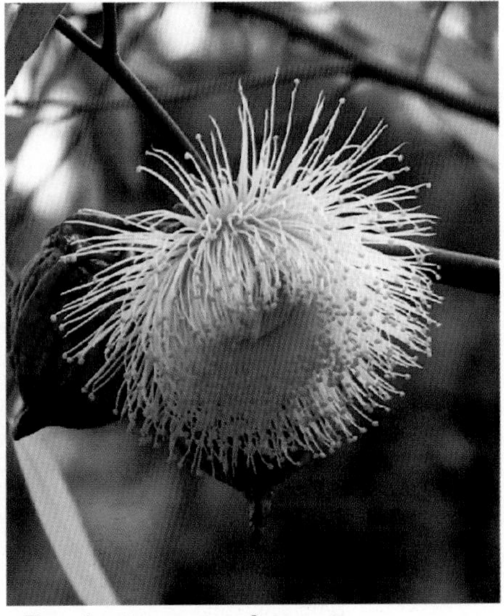

Eucalyptus youngiana

LARGE-FRUITED MALLEE

A tall mallee shrub with large lemon coloured flowers followed by large decorative seed pods. It is an outstanding ornamental in semi-arid areas in temperate to sub-tropical climates.

Eucalyptus torquata CORAL GUM

An open crowned small tree which has large heads of attractive salmon-pink flowers. It is a very decorative ornamental and widely grown as a garden, street or park tree in semi-arid areas. The tree prefers a temperate to sub-tropical climate. It is tolerant of some salinity and light frosts.

Eucalyptus youngiana - red form

A red flowered form of this outstanding ornamental shrub.

EUGENIA

MYRTACEAE

Evergreen shrubs and trees from many countries of the world in climates from temperate to tropical. There has been a revision of this group and many former Eugenias are now renamed Syzygiums. Many of these plants are grown for their edible fruit and ornamental foliage. They are propagated from seed and cuttings.

Eugenia brasiliensis BRAZIL CHERRY

A small evergreen tree with perfumed white flowers followed by sweet cherry-like black fruit.

Eugenia uniflora

SURINAM CHERRY; RED BRAZIL CHERRY

An evergreen tall shrub to small tree with cream flowers followed by edible red fruit.

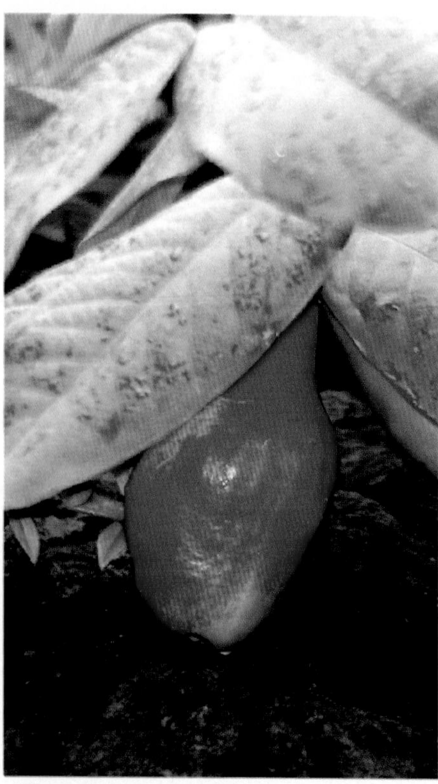

Eugenia megacarpa

A large leaf, small tree with white flowers and large bright red fruit.

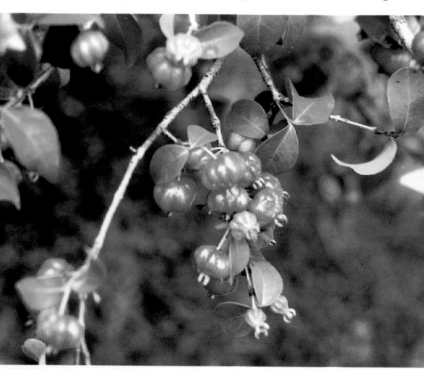

Eugenia uniflora - fruit

This illustration shows the edible red fruit.

EUODIA

RUTACEAE

Evergreen tropical and sub-tropical shrubs and small trees from many countries. They are grown for their flowers and foliage and prefer a rich soil in warm temperate to tropical climates. Propagation is from seed and cuttings.

Euodia hortensis

A small tree with dense golden foliage whi is grown as an ornamental foliage tree.

EUONYMUS

CELASTRACEAE

eciduous or evergreen shrubs and small ees from many countries throughout the orld. Grown for their attractive foliage, ıost have small white flowers. They are rown from seed and cuttings.

uonymus fortunei cv. **Emerald Gaiety**
. bushy spreading shrub with variegated eaves of green and white.

uonymus fortunei cv. **Emerald 'N' Gold**
. cultivar with green and gold variegated eaves.

Euonymus fortunei cv. **Silver Pillar**
An upright, evergreen, hardy hedge or feature shrub grown for its attractive leaves of green edged with cream.

Euonymus fortunei cv. **Silver Queen**
A cultivar with cream and green leaves.

Euonymus fortunei cv. **Sunshine**
The leaves of this cultivar are coloured gold and marked with green.

Euonymus japonicus cv. **Argenteovariegatus**
With showy leaves of green and white, this erect evergreen shrub is grown as an ornamental or a hedge.

Euonymus japonicus cv. **Aureomarginatus**
An erect evergreen shrub with showy leaves of greyish green, edged with cream. Used as a hedge or ornamental.

Euonymus japonicus cv. **Aureopictus**
A cultivar with gold and green variegated leaves.

EUONYMUS (cont)

Euonymus japonicus
cv. **Ovatus Aureus**
This cultivar has oval leaves of green and yellow.

Euonymus myrianthus
A tall evergreen shrub with clusters of cream to yellow flowers.

EUPHORBIA

EUPHORBIACEAE

A large range of shrubs, trees and herbs with milky sap, mostly from the African continent. They are grown as ornamentals for their colourful flower bracts, outdoors and indoors world wide. They grow in most soils and benefit from applications of fertiliser. Propagate from seed and cuttings.

Euphorbia ceratocarpa
This is a bushy plant with olive-green foliage and golden coloured flower bracts.

Euphorbia characias
A bushy upright plant with blue-green foliage and large flower heads with greenish bracts.

Euphorbia characias
cv. **Burrow Silver**
The flower heads of this cultivar have whitish bracts. The leaves are greenish silver and white.

Euphorbia characias ssp. ***wulfenii***
Multi-stemmed, this shrubby plant has large heads of greenish yellow flower bracts

Euphorbia characias ssp. ***wulfenii***
cv. **Lambrook Gold**
A showy cultivar with large heads of golden coloured bracts.

Euphorbia cotinifolia
A tall shrub to small tree grown for its glowing copper-red leaves.

Euphorbia fulgens SCARLET PLUME
This is a small, branching shrub with bright red flower bracts along the branches.

Euphorbia griffithii [1]
A shrubby plant with heads of orange flower bracts.

Euphorbia griffithii cv. **Dixter**
The bracts of this cultivar are reddish.

Euphorbia griffithii cv. **Fireglow**
The flower bracts are orange-red on this showy cultivar.

Euphorbia heterophylla
JAPANESE POINSETTIA
Small and branching, this shrub has red flower bracts.

Euphorbia lactea HATRACK CACTUS
A succulent tall shrub grown for its unusual foliage.

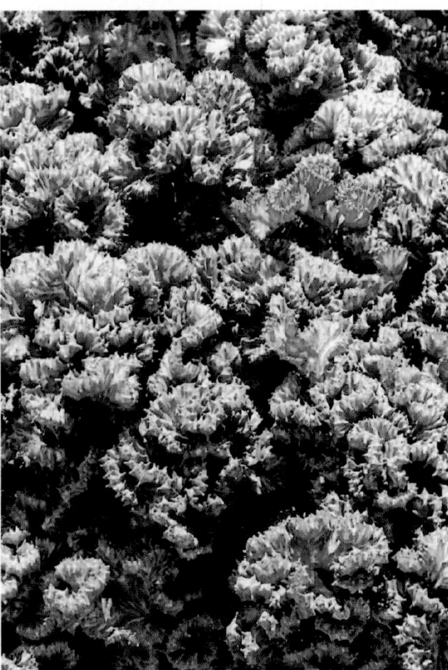

Euphorbia lactea cv. **Cristata**
CRESTED EUPHORBIA
This cultivar is grown for its unique fan-like foliage.

Euphorbia leucocephala SNOWFLAKE
A showy small shrub with white flower bracts.

EUPHORBIA (cont)

Euphorbia* x *martinii [1]
Greenish yellow flower bracts form in large heads on this hybrid plant.

Euphorbia milii CROWN OF THORNS
A spreading small shrub with long thorns and erect heads of red flower bracts.

***Euphorbia milii* cv. Lutea**
Cream flower bracts feature on this cultivar.

***Euphorbia milii* cv. Lutea Rosea**
This cultivar has cream flower bracts, edged rose-pink.

Euphorbia polychroma [1]
A clumping plant with large heads of golden flower bracts.

Euphorbia pulcherrima POINSETTIA
A widely grown tall shrub which has large red showy bracts mostly in winter. Many popular cultivars of the poinsettia are grown and used as indoor plants.

***Euphorbia pulcherrima* cv. Alba**
The bracts on this cultivar are creamy white, but it shows a red mutation on some branches and if cuttings are taken from those branches the subsequent plants will flower red.

***Euphorbia pulcherrima* cv. Annette Hegg**
This cultivar is a very compact grower with red bracts.

***Euphorbia pulcherrima* cv. Antirrhinum**
A compact cultivar with pale pink bracts.

Euphorbia pulcherrima cv. **Bicolor**
A showy dwarf cultivar with pink and cream flower bracts.

Euphorbia pulcherrmia cv. **Dorothy**
On this showy cultivar, the large bracts are coloured pink, with some cream markings.

Euphorbia pulcherrima cv. **Femina**
A cultivar with many bracts coloured bright pink.

Euphorbia pulcherrima cv. **Freedom**
The bracts on this cultivar are bright red.

Euphorbia pulcherrima cv. **Green Vein**
A dwarf cultivar having whitish bracts with a green vein.

Euphorbia pulcherrima cv. **Henrietta Ecke**
This cultivar has double red bracts.

Euphorbia pulcherrima cv. **Lemon Drop**
A dwarf cultivar with lemon coloured bracts.

Euphorbia pulcherrima cv. **Marbella**
Compact and free flowering, this cultivar has bracts of cream with pink markings.

Euphorbia pulcherrima cv. **Maren**
This bushy cultivar has upright bracts coloured rose-pink.

EUPHORBIA (cont)

Euphorbia pulcherrima cv. **Menorca**
Free flowering, this cultivar has bright red bracts which, at times, are semi-double.

Euphorbia pulcherrima cv. **Pink Peppermint**
The bracts on this spreading cultivar are coloured bright pink, pale pink and cream.

Euphorbia pulcherrima cv. **Regina**
On this cultivar the large bracts are coloured cream.

Euphorbia pulcherrima cv. **Peter Star**
This very widely grown cultivar has large red bracts.

Euphorbia pulcherrima cv. **Pink Perfection**
A dwarf cultivar with pink bracts.

Euphorbia pulcherrima cv. **Ria**
This very free flowering cultivar has bright red bracts.

Euphorbia pulcherrima cv. **Pink Marble**
A dwarf cultivar with large bracts coloured pink and pale cream.

Euphorbia pulcherrima cv. **Praecox**
A medium sized cultivar with red bracts.

Euphorbia pulcherrima cv. **Rosea**
A tall grower with rose-pink bracts.

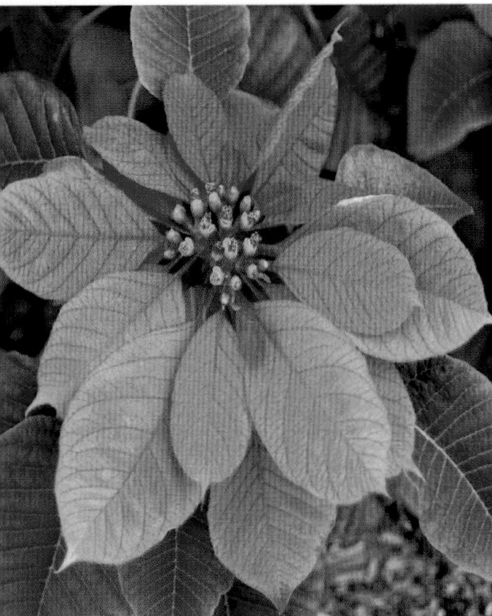

***Euphorbia pulcherrima* cv. Rosea Compacta**

There are rose-pink bracts on this dwarf cultivar.

***Euphorbia pulcherrima* cv. Top White**

The bracts on this cultivar are pendulous, and pale cream in colour.

Euphorbia schillingii [1]

A small spreading plant with heads of yellow flower bracts.

Euphorbia sikkimensis [1]

A compact plant with bright yellow flower bracts.

Euphorbia rigida [1]

A compact spreading plant with bluish leaves and large clusters of greenish yellow flower bracts.

EUPOMATIA

EUPOMATIACEAE

Eupomatia laurina COPPER LAUREL

An evergreen tall shrub or small tree of Australia and New Guinea, which has cream and green perfumed flowers followed by large edible fruit. Propagate from seed and cuttings. Suited to climates from cool temperate to tropical.

EUSTREPHUS

SMILACACEAE [PHILESIACEAE]

Eustrephus latifolius WOMBAT BERRY

From Australia, this slender evergreen climber has small pink flowers and round yellow fruit. The leaves are similar to bamboo leaves. It grows well in semi-shade in a wide range of climates from cool temperate to tropical. Propagate from seed and cuttings.

EVODIELLA

RUTACEAE

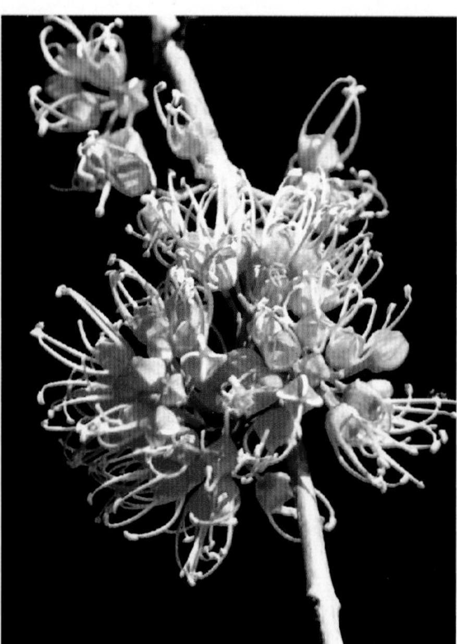

Evodiella muelleri
This small evergreen tree from Australia and New Guinea prefers a rich soil and filtered shade. It will grow in climates from warm temperate to tropical. Propagate from seed.

EVOLVULUS

CONVOLVULACEAE

Evolvulus pilosus **cv. Blue Daze**
A shrubby evergreen plant native to North America. It is a popular landscape plant in climates from temperate to tropical. It has showy blue flowers with white eyes. Propagate from seed and cuttings.

EXOCHORDA

ROSACEAE

Deciduous shrubs from Asia which are grown as ornamentals in cool climates. They prefer a sunny well drained situation sheltered from winds. Propagate from cuttings.

Exochorda giraldii
White flowers bloom in terminal heads on this tall shrub.

Exochorda korolkowii
Spring flowering, this tall shrub has white flowers along the branches.

Exochorda* x *macrantha
cv. The Bride
This hybrid cultivar is a free flowering, tall shrub which may be totally covered with white flowers in spring.

Exochorda racemosa PEARL BUSH
A tall shrub with masses of white flowers along the branches in spring.

FABIANA

SOLANACEAE

Fabiana imbricata
An evergreen heath type shrub which is native to Chile. It prefers a temperate climate and tolerates light frosts. The plant benefits from regular pruning and fertilizing. Propagate from seed and tip cuttings.

FAGRAEA

LOGANIACEAE

Evergreen shrubs and trees from tropical Australia and South East Asia which are grown as ornamentals for their showy flowers and fruit. They need a subtropical or tropical climate. Propagate from seeds.

Fagraea auriculata
A medium, large leaf shrub with yellow flowers followed by yellow five-cornered fruit.

Fagraea fragrans
A small tree with clusters of perfumed white flowers.

FAGUS

BEECH

FAGACEAE

Deciduous ornamental trees widely grown in the cooler climates of the world for their foliage. They prefer an alkaline soil. Propagate from seed or graft selected cultivars.

Fagus sylvatica EUROPEAN BEECH
A medium tree with showy green foliage.

Fagus sylvatica cv. **Rohanii**
This outstanding cultivar has reddish copper coloured leaves.

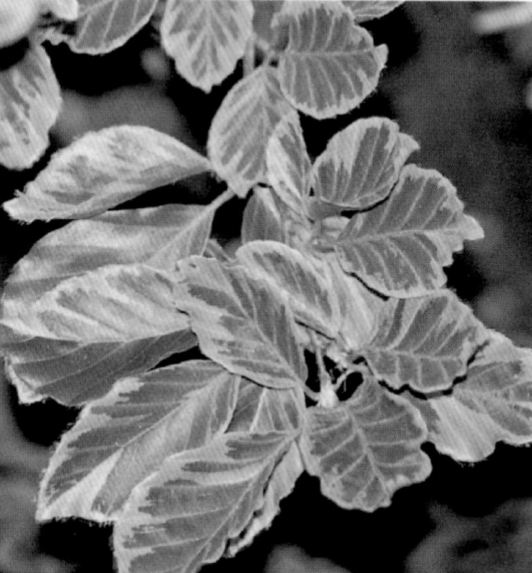

Fagus sylvatica cv. **Luteo-Variegata**
The variegated leaves of this cultivar are coloured green and yellow.

Fagus sylvatica cv. **Roseo-Marginata**
This showy cultivar has reddish brown leaves, edged with pink.

Fagus sylvatica f. ***purpurea***
Copper coloured leaves feature on this tree.

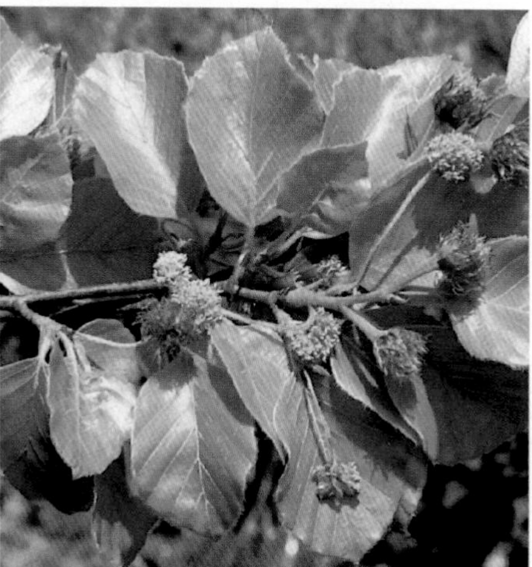

Fagus sylvatica cv. **Zlatia**
The new leaves of this cultivar are shiny yellow.

f

FARADAYA

Verbenaceae

Faradaya splendida

In tropical and sub-tropical climates this vigorous evergreen climber from Australia is grown for its large showy heads of white flowers. Propagate from seed or cuttings.

FEIJOA

Myrtaceae

Feijoa sellowiana PINEAPPLE GUAVA

This evergreen shrub from South America is grown for its attractive flowers and edible fruit. It grows in climates from cold temperate to sub-tropical. Propagate from seed and cuttings.

FELICIA

Asteraceae [Compositae]

Shrubs with daisy flowers from Africa. They are widely grown as ornamentals throughout the world in climates from cold temperate to sub-tropical. Propagate from seed and cuttings.

Felicia amelloides BLUE MARGUERITE

A small spreading shrub with blue flowers which have yellow centres.

Felicia petiolata

In spring this small spreading shrub has mauve-pink daisy flowers.

Felicia amelloides cv. **Variegata**

The foliage of this cultivar is green and cream in colour.

Felicia fruticosa

This small spreading shrub has bluish mauve daisy flowers with yellow centres. These are carried along the branches.

FERNANDOA

Bignoniaceae

Fernandoa madagascariensis

Native to Madagascar, this small tree has bright red trumpet flowers. It is an outstanding flowering tree in warm to hot climates and is propagated from seed.

FICUS FIG

MORACEAE

Mostly evergreen shrubs, trees and vines with milky sap. From many countries of the world, some are grown for their edible fruit and others are grown as ornamentals either outdoors or as indoor plants. They come from a wide range of climates from cool temperate to tropical. Propagation is from seeds, cuttings and by marcotting.

Ficus altissima COUNCIL TREE

A large leaf medium tree with long orange fruit.

Ficus aspera cv. **Canonii**

syn. ***Ficus canonii***

A small tree with reddish brown coloured leaves, which is grown as an ornamental.

Ficus aspera cv. **Parcellii** CLOWN FIG

This tall shrub has large leaves coloured white and green.

Ficus auriculata ROXBURGH FIG

A large leaf, small tree with large pear shaped fruit.

Ficus auriculata

This illustration shows the pear shaped fruit.

Ficus benghalensis BANYAN

A large spreading tree with large leaves and round orange fruit.

Ficus benjamina WEEPING FIG

Highly ornamental, this medium to tall tree has weeping foliage and small reddish brown fruit.

Ficus benjamina cv. **Baby Ben**

A cultivar with small leaves.

f

FICUS (cont)

***Ficus benjamina* cv. Bushy King**
A very bushy cultivar with variegated leaves of green, edged cream.

***Ficus benjamina* cv. Bushy Prince**
On this bushy cultivar the new leaves are greenish cream.

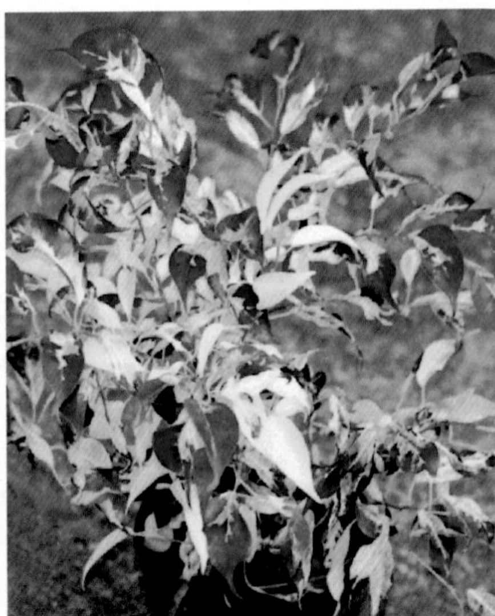

***Ficus benjamina* cv. Curly**
A cultivar which has green, white, or green and white leaves.

***Ficus benjamina* cv. Monique**
This cultivar has rippled leaves.

***Ficus benjamina* cv. Natasia**
A cultivar with small curved leaves.

***Ficus benjamina* cv. Reginold**
There are greenish yellow leaves on this cultivar.

***Ficus benjamina* cv. Shorty**
Compact growing, this cultivar has small leaves.

***Ficus benjamina* cv. Starlight**
A cultivar with green and pale cream leaves

***Ficus benjamina* cv. Variegata**
On this cultivar the leaves are grey, edge with cream.

Ficus celebensis
A medium tree with long leaves and a weeping habit.

Ficus dammaropsis DINNER-PLATE FIG
A small tree with very large leaves and round fruit.

***Ficus elastica* cv. Burgundy**
Widely grown, this ornamental fig has large shiny leaves which turn plum to burgundy in colour.

Ficus coronulata PEACH LEAF FIG
This is an ornamental fig with a drooping habit and long leaves.

Ficus deltoidea MISTLETOE FIG
This ornamental tall shrub has small roundish leaves.

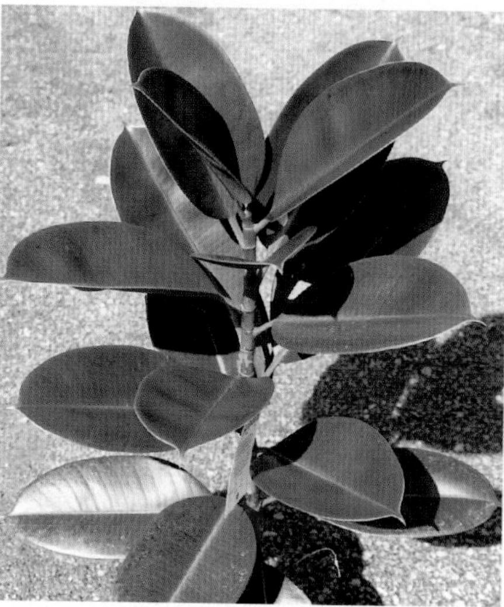

***Ficus elastica* cv. Decora**
A very popular ornamental Ficus with large shiny green leaves.

Ficus crassipes ROUND LEAF BANANA FIG
The long fruits of this large leaf, medium tree are yellow to orange in colour.

Ficus destruens STRANGLER FIG
A large spreading tree with long wide leaves. This fig may strangle other trees.

***Ficus elastica* cv. Schrijveriana**
This popular cultivar has green and yellow leaves.

FICUS (cont)

Ficus elastica cv. **Variegata**

The leaves are green and cream on this cultivar.

Ficus kurzii

This is a spreading tree with small leaves and clusters of brown fruit.

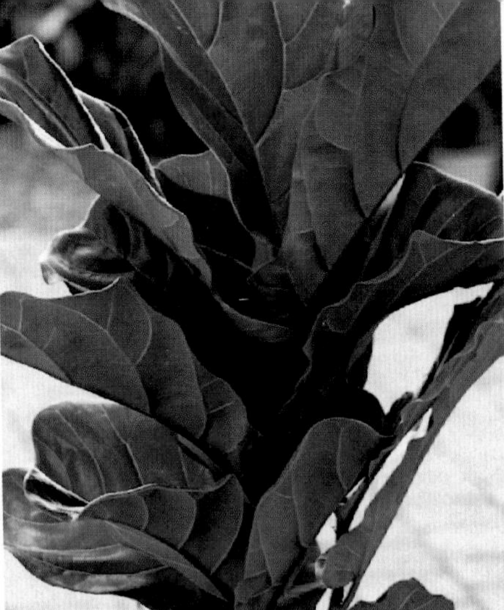

Ficus lyrata FIDDLE LEAF FIG

This Ficus has large coarse leaves with distinct veins.

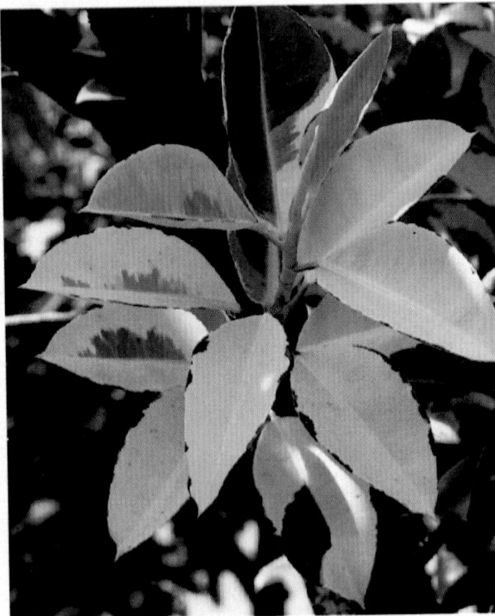

Ficus elastica cv. **White Wonder**

A cultivar with pale cream leaves.

Ficus leucotricha

A small growing semi-deciduous Ficus which is ideal for dry climates and bonsai.

Ficus macrophylla MORETON BAY FIG

A large spreading tree with big shiny leaves.

Ficus eucalyptoides

A medium evergreen tree with long leaves resembling Eucalyptus leaves.

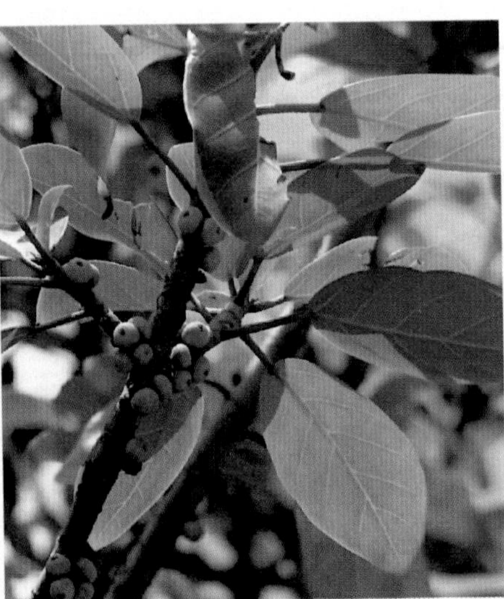

Ficus lutea ZULU FIG

syn. ***F. nekbudu***

A small to medium tree which has large leaves. The yellow fruit turn red when ripe.

Ficus microcarpa INDIAN LAUREL

Masses of small purple fruit form on this medium size spreading tree which has medium leaves.

FICUS (cont)

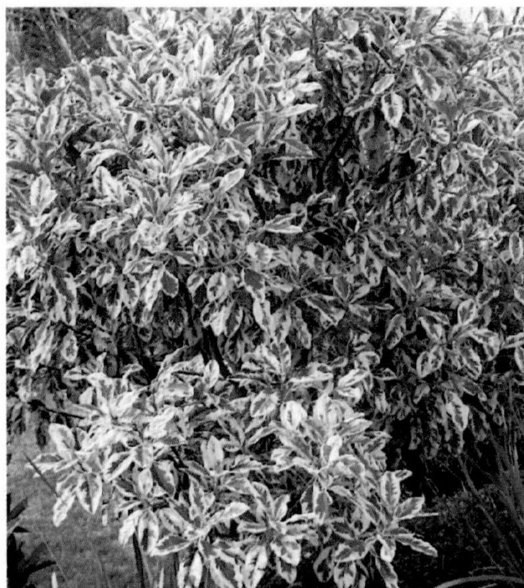

Ficus microcarpa cv. **Hawaii**

An ornamental cultivar with green and cream leaves.

Ficus microcarpa cv. **Milky Stripe**

This cultivar has leaves of greyish green with wide bands of white.

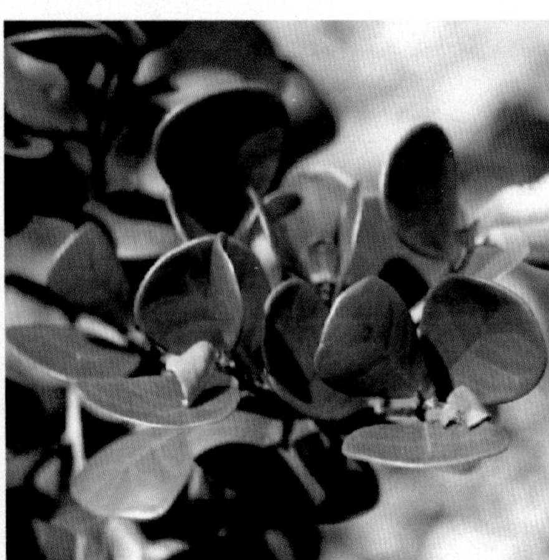

Ficus natalensis ssp. ***leprieurii***

syn. ***F. triangularis*** NATAL FIG

A medium size tree with unusual triangular shaped leaves.

Ficus natalensis ssp. ***leprieurii*** cv. **Variegata**

This cultivar has variegated leaves coloured cream and greyish green.

Ficus obliqua

A medium sized tree which has small leaves and oval orange fruit.

Ficus obliqua var. ***petiolaris***

This form has pointed leaves and bears more fruit than *F. obliqua*.

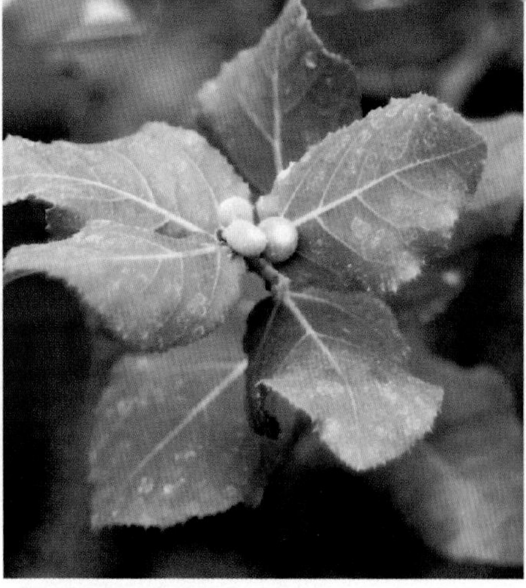

Ficus opposita

A small tree with large slightly serrated leaves and green fruit.

Ficus platypoda var. ***platypoda***

ROCK FIG

Small round orange fruit form on this tall shrub which is found in dry areas.

Ficus pleurocarpa BANANA FIG

A large leaf spreading tree which has orange fruit shaped like bananas.

FICUS (cont)

Ficus pumila CREEPING FIG
The small young leaves of this climbing Ficus will become quite large if it is grown in the ground in warmer climates.

***Ficus pumila* cv. Dorte**
A cultivar which has twisted leaves coloured dark green with yellow markings.

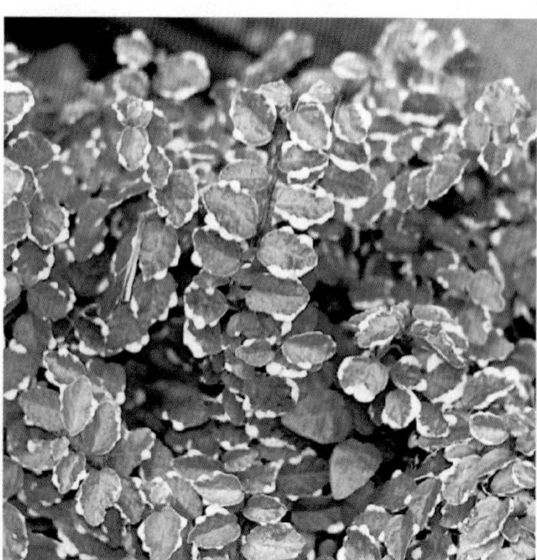

***Ficus pumila* cv. Frosty**
Widely grown as a ground cover, this cultivar has white edges to the leaves.

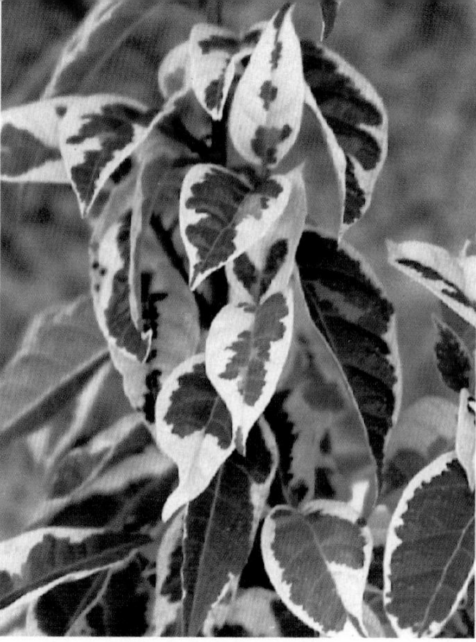

***Ficus pumila* cv. Marginata**
A cultivar which has cream and green variegated leaves.

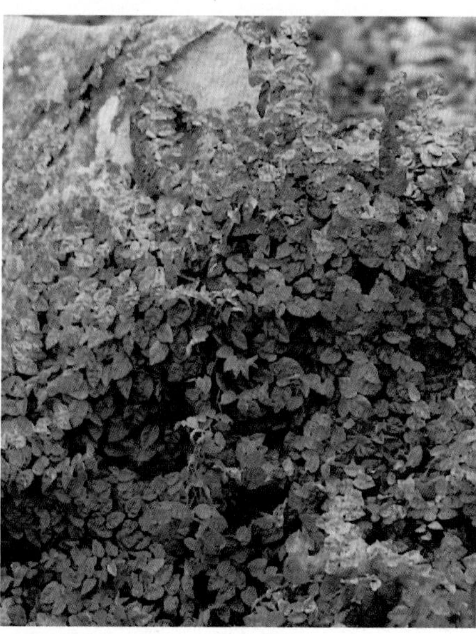

***Ficus pumila* cv. Minima**
This cultivar has very small leaves.

***Ficus pumila* cv. White Sunny**
A cultivar which has variegated leaves coloured green with a wide white band around the edges.

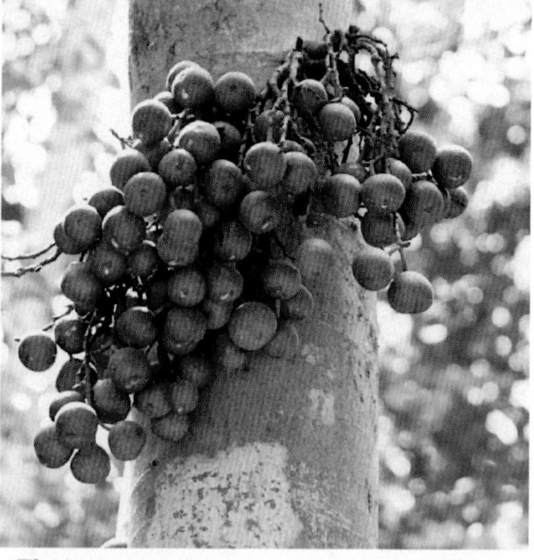

Ficus racemosa CLUSTER FIG
This is a deciduous small spreading tree. The fruit forms in clusters on the trunk.

***Ficus rubiginosa* cv. Variegata**
VARIEGATED RUSTY FIG
A medium spreading tree with variegated cream and green leaves which have a rusty appearance on the underside.

Ficus sagittata
This climbing plant has occasional white markings on its leaves

FICUS (cont)

Ficus sagittata cv. **Variegata**
A wiry climber which has greyish coloured leaves edged with cream. Known to the nursery trade as ***F. radicans.***

Ficus sycomorus SYCAMORE FIG
Clusters of round fruit form on the trunk of this large buttressed medium tree.

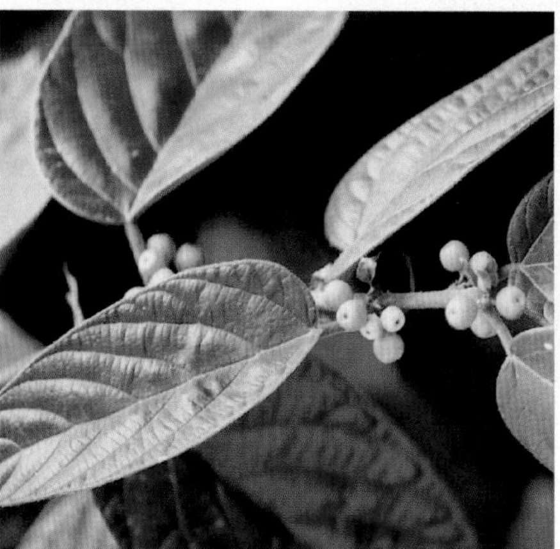

Ficus villosa
A large leaf tree with small bright orange fruit.

Ficus vogeliana
On this medium spreading tree, large clusters of yellow fruit form at the ends of the branches.

FIRMIANA

STERCULIACEAE

Firmiana simplex
CHINESE PARASOL TREE
A small to medium tree native to Asia. It is grown as an ornamental in climates from cold temperate to sub-tropical and has insignificant cream flowers followed by very attractive red seed pods. Propagate from seed.

FLINDERSIA

RUTACEAE

Evergreen small to large trees native to Australia and the Pacific. They are grown both as ornamental trees and for their timber. These trees also have very decorative seed pods which are sought after by florists. They grow in climates from temperate to tropical and are propagated from seed.

Flindersia australis CROW'S ASH
A medium size tree with a dense crown. It has showy heads of cream flowers and very attractive seed pods.

Flindersia brayleyana
QUEENSLAND MAPLE
A tall timber tree which has large heads of cream flowers and attractive seed pods.

Flindersia oppositifolia
MOUNTAIN SILKWOOD
This is a small tree with large bunches of small red flowers and decorative seed pods.

FORSYTHIA

Oleaceae

Deciduous shrubs grown for their ornamental yellow spring flowers. They are quite cold tolerant and produce flowers all along their branches. Propagate from cuttings.

Forsythia* x *intermedia
A hybrid between *F. suspensa* and *F. viridissima* which has bright yellow flowers in profusion during spring.

***Forsythia* x *intermedia* cv. Spring Glory**
This shrub has very large terminal clusters of bright yellow flowers.

Forsythia suspensa
The yellow flowers of this tall, sparse shrub have reflexed petals.

***Forsythia viridissima* cv. Bronxensis**
A cultivar with delicate yellow flowers.

FOTHERGILLA

Hamamelidaceae

Deciduous shrubs, native to North America, which are grown in cold climates as ornamentals. They are propagated from seeds, layers and suckers.

Fothergilla gardenii WITCH ALDER
A small spreading shrub with cream flowers before the new leaves.

Fothergilla major
This small shrub has flowers of white with odd touches of pink.

Fothergilla major 2 - cream form
syn. ***F. monticola***
A spreading medium shrub with cream terminal flowers.

FRANKLINIA

Theaceae

Franklinia axillaris
syn. ***Gordonia axillaris***
A tall shrub to small tree from South East Asia. It is free flowering in climates from cool temperate to sub-tropical and has large white flowers with clusters of yellow stamens. Propagate from cuttings or seeds.

FRAXINUS

OLEACEAE

Deciduous or sometimes evergreen trees native to many Northern Hemisphere countries. They are grown both as ornamental street or park trees and for their timber. Found in a wide range of climates from very cold temperate to tropical, most are from temperate regions. They are propagated from seed. Cultivars are grafted or budded.

Fraxinus excelsior

In spring this small deciduous tree has large heads of white flowers. Seed pods are illustrated.

Fraxinus ornus

A small deciduous tree with large heads of fluffy white flowers.

Fraxinus griffithii syn. ***F. formosana***

This small to medium tree is widely grown as a street tree in warm climates. It has very decorative clusters of seeds.

Fraxinus insularis

Showy seed heads form on this small to medium size tree which will grow in warm climates.

Fraxinus pennsylvanica RED ASH

This is a deciduous small to medium tree which has highly coloured autumn foliage.

FREMONTODENDRON

STERCULIACEAE

These tall, free flowering, evergreen shrubs, native to the cool arid deserts of North America, are widely grown in mild to temperate climates for their large, showy, golden yellow flowers in spring. They benefit from annual applications of complete fertilizer and are propagated from seed or cuttings.

Fremontodendron californicum

A tall, open shrub with large, golden yellow flowers in spring.

Fremontodendron californicum
cv. **Pacific Sunset**

This cultivar has yellow flowers.

FREMONTODENDRON (cont)

Fremontodendron decumbens
A free flowering, tall, bushy shrub with golden flowers.

Fremontodendron mexicanum
The flowers of this tall shrub open over a period of several months rather than all at once as does *F. californicum*.

FREYCINETIA

PANDANACEAE

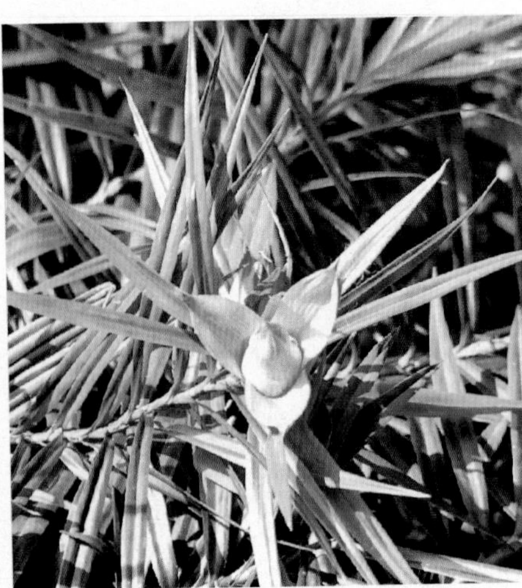

Freycinetia multiflora
An evergreen semi-climbing plant. It has showy red terminal flower bracts and white flowers. Propagate from seed.

FREYLINIA

SCROPHULARIACEAE

Freylinia lanceolata HONEY BELLS
A tall evergreen shrub with long lance-like leaves and clusters of cream and yellow flowers. Propagate from seed or cuttings.

FUCHSIA

ONAGRACEAE

Showy shrubs from Mexico, South America and the Pacific. They are generally free flowering and many colourful cultivars are grown. They are grown in climates from cold temperate to tropical but seem to flower best in cool temperate climates. These shrubs are hardy in most soils and prefer to be pruned after flowering. Propagate from cuttings.

***Fuchsia* cv. Applause**
A cultivar with pendulous double flowers coloured pinkish white outside and bright rose-pink inside.

Fuchsia arborescens
An open shrub with showy clusters of small bright pink flowers.

Fuchsia boliviana
An erect shrub with pendulous clusters of red tubular flowers.

***Fuchsia* cv. Cardinal Farges**
A cultivar which has double pendulous flowers coloured red outside and pinkish white inside.

Fuchsia cinnabarina
syn. ***F. reflexa***
An open crowned shrub with bright red tubular flowers along the branches.

***Fuchsia* cv. Devonshire Dumpling**
A cultivar which has pale pink coloured double pendulous flowers.

***Fuchsia* cv. Hobson's Choice**
On this cultivar the double pendulous flowers are coloured pink inside and red outside.

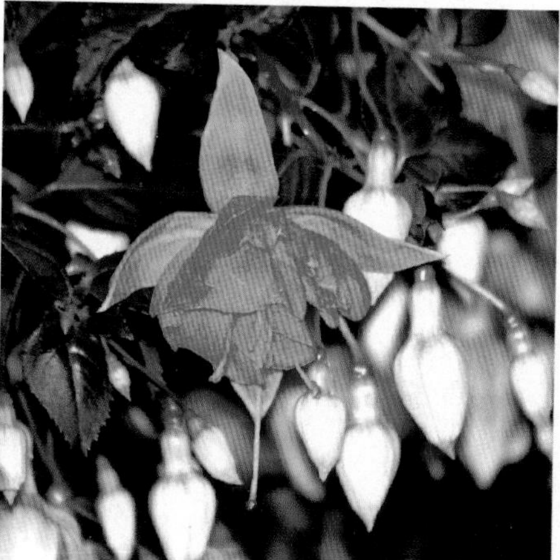

***Fuchsia* cv. Dancing Flame**
A cultivar which has double rosy pink coloured pendulous flowers.

***Fuchsia* cv. Dr Olson**
The large double flowers of this cultivar are pink and red.

***Fuchsia* cv. Ice Maiden**
A cultivar with large double white flowers.

***Fuchsia* cv. Dark Eyes**
On this cultivar the pendulous double flowers are coloured deep rose-pink outside and purple inside.

***Fuchsia* cv. Fine Cloud**
This cultivar has ivory coloured double pendulous flowers.

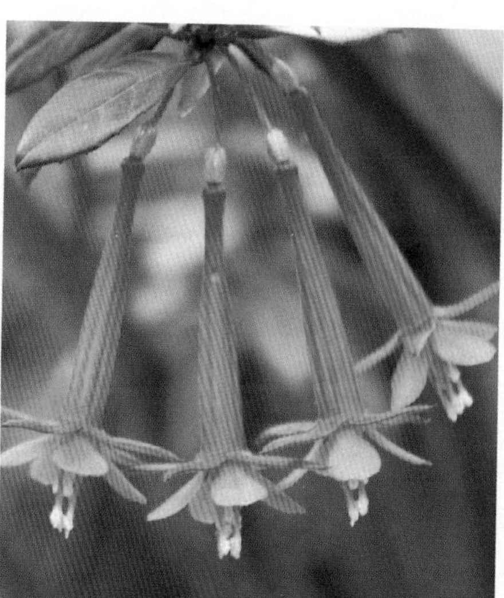

***Fuchsia loxensis* cv. Rio Mazon**
This shrub has long pendulous flowers coloured rosy pink outside, with salmon florets.

FUCHSIA (cont)

Fuchsia lycioides
An open shrub which has large clusters of pendulous small cerise-red flowers.

***Fuchsia* cv. Lye's Unique**
A cultivar with pendulous flowers coloured cream outside and carmine-red inside.

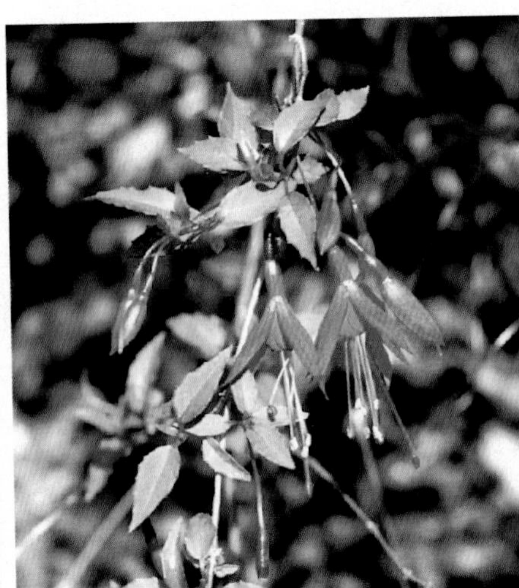

Fuchsia magellanica
syn. ***F. magellanica*** var. ***discolor***
Clusters of pendulous red flowers bloom on this medium shrub.

Fuchsia microphylla* ssp. *helmsleyana
A medium shrub with masses of small pendulous tubular flowers.

***Fuchsia* cv. Mrs Lovell Swisher**
Pendulous flowers coloured pale pink outside and cerise inside feature on this cultivar.

***Fuchsia* cv. Orange Mirage**
A cultivar with pendulous rose-pink coloured flowers.

***Fuchsia* cv. Pink Fantasia**
This cultivar has masses of open bright pink coloured flowers.

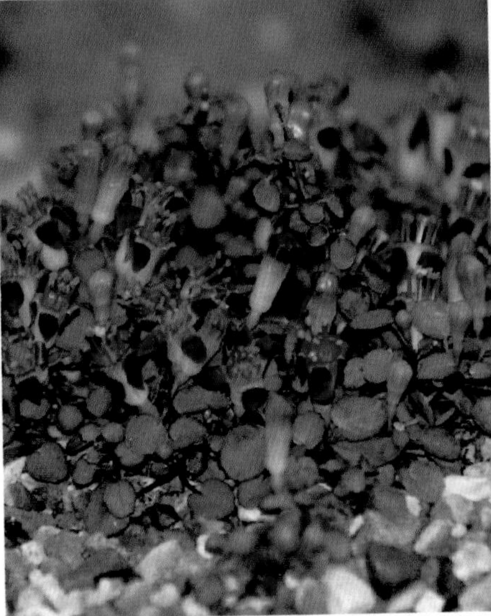

Fuchsia procumbens
Spreading and low growing, this shrub has upright small blue flowers.

***Fuchsia* cv. Royal Velvet**
This cultivar has double pendulous flowers coloured red outside and inside purple, varying to crimson.

***Fuchsia* cv. Snow Burner**
A cultivar with large double flowers of red and white.

Fuchsia splendens
syn. ***F. cordifolia***
This open shrub has pendulous tubular flowers coloured crimson with green tips.

***Fuchsia* cv. Tennessee Waltz**
A cultivar with double pendulous flowers coloured lilac-pink inside and bright rosy-pink outside.

***Fuchsia* cv. Therese Dupuis**
The delicate pendulous flowers of this cultivar are salmon coloured.

***Fuchsia* cv. Torchlight**
A cultivar with broad pendulous flowers coloured very pale pink inside and pinkish red outside.

Fuchsia triphylla
This is a dense shrub with pendulous clusters of bright red flowers.

***Fuchsia* cv. Wedding Bells**
A cultivar with double white pendulous flowers which has touches of bright pink.

G

GALPHIMIA

MALPIGHIACEAE

Galphimia glauca

An evergreen shrub from Central America. This plant has terminal clusters of golden coloured star shaped flowers. It grows in climates from warm temperate to tropical. Propagate from seed and cuttings.

GARCINIA

CLUSIACEAE [GUTTIFERAE]

Tropical and sub-tropical evergreen shrubs and small trees native to Africa, Asia and the Pacific. Some are grown for their edible fruit and others as ornamentals. Propagate from seed or cuttings.

Garcinia xanthochymus GAMBOGE

A small tree grown as an ornamental for its conical shape and colourful new leaves. It has white flowers.

GARDENIA

RUBIACEAE

Evergreen shrubs and trees from tropical and sub-tropical areas. They are widely grown as ornamentals for their showy perfumed flowers. In cultivation they grow in climates from cool temperate to tropical. Propagate from seed and cuttings.

Gardenia augusta CAPE JESSAMINE

This medium shrub has perfumed, mostly double, white flowers.

***Gardenia augusta* cv. Aimee Yoshiba**

A cultivar with larger white flowers.

***Gardenia augusta* cv. Glacier**

The foliage of this cultivar is cream and green.

***Gardenia augusta* cv. Golden Magic**

This cultivar has cream flowers which turn to old gold as they age.

GARDENIA (cont)

Gardenia augusta cv. **Florida**
A popular cultivar with masses of white perfumed double flowers.

Gardenia augusta cv. **Radicans**
Low growing, this spreading shrub has masses of white flowers.

Gardenia augusta cv. **Magnifica**
This cultivar has larger double white flowers.

Gardenia augusta cv. **Radicans Variegata**
This cultivar is low growing with grey and cream variegated leaves.

Gardenia coronaria
On this small tree the masses of perfumed flowers are old gold in colour.

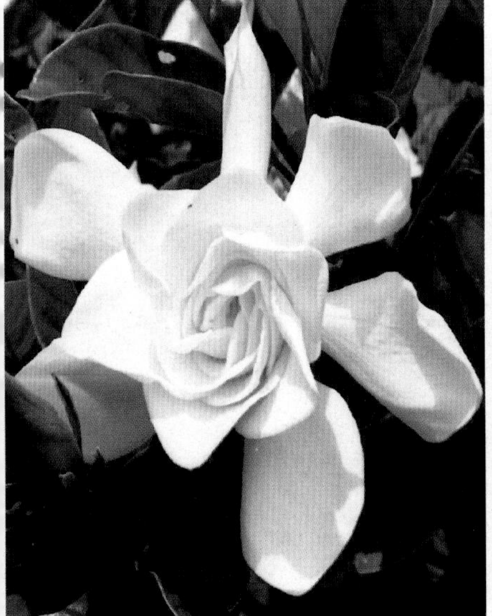

Gardenia augusta cv. **Professor Pucci**
A larger flowered cultivar with white flowers.

Gardenia carinata
An evergreen small tree with large, single, highly perfumed, white to cream flowers.

Gardenia jardinei
A hardy tropical shrub with single white perfumed flowers.

GARDENIA (cont)

Gardenia kershawii
Large white star shaped flowers form on this bushy shrub.

Gardenia sootepensis
As they age, the large, white, perfumed flowers of this small tree change colour to cream then to old gold.

Gardenia spatulifolia
A small tree with masses of large, perfumed, white flowers.

Gardenia taitensis 3
This is a tall shrub with large white perfumed flowers.

Gardenia thunbergia
A tall shrub with masses of large, perfumed, white flowers.

Gardenia thunbergia - seed pod
This illustration shows a seed pod which may be as large as a tennis ball.

GARRYA

GARRYACEAE

Cold hardy shrubs and small trees grown as ornamentals for their showy tassels. They are native to North America and are propagated from seed, cuttings and layers.

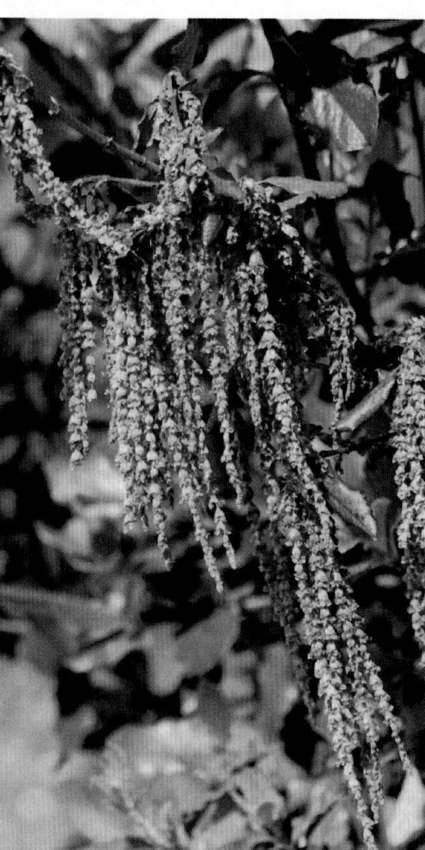

Garrya elliptica SILK TASSEL
A small tree with cascading tassels in spring.

Garrya laurifolia var. **_macrophylla_**
In spring this tall shrub forms clumping short tassels.

GAULTHERIA

Ericaceae

Dwarf evergreen shrubs which are native to many countries, mostly with cool to cold climates, throughout the world. These plants have waxy looking perfumed flowers in spring and are widely grown as ornamentals. They prefer sunny moist situations with slightly acid soils. Propagate from seed or tip cuttings.

Gaultheria crassifolia

A compact bushy small shrub with bunches of pendulous white waxy flowers in spring.

Gaultheria mucronata

In spring this hardy, spreading, many branched shrub has sprays of white waxy flowers.

Gaultheria* x *wisleyensis

This hardy hybrid is very free flowering, with dense sprays of white flowers.

Gaultheria forrestii

On this bushy shrub, the racemes of white flowers are followed by blue berries.

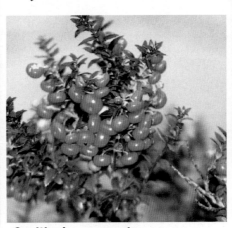

***Gaultheria mucronata* cv. Bell's Seedling**

This showy cultivar has shiny red berries in winter.

***Gaultheria* x *wisleyensis* cv. Wisley Pearl**

A free flowering cultivar which has white flowers tinged with pink.

Gaultheria hirtiflora

Hardy, this spreading shrub has pendulous pink flowers in spring. The stems, leaves and flowers are covered with small hairs.

Gaultheria shallon

A dense spreading shrub with large sprays of pendulous pink flowers in spring.

g

GEIJERA

Rutaceae

Geijera parviflora WILGA

A small tree which grows in the low rainfall areas of Australia in climates from cool temperate to sub-tropical. It has pendulous foliage and clusters of small white flowers. Propagate from seed.

GELSEMIUM

Loganiaceae

Gelsemium sempervirens CAROLINE JASMINE

An evergreen climber from North and Central America, it is grown as an ornamental for its showy yellow trumpet flowers, in climates from cool temperate to tropical. It is propagated from seed and cuttings.

GENISTA

Fabaceae [Leguminosae]

Genista hispanica SPANISH GORSE

A hardy spiny shrub which is native to Spain. It is covered with golden yellow flowers in spring and prefers a mild climate. Propagate from seed or cuttings.

GESNERIA

Gesneriaceae

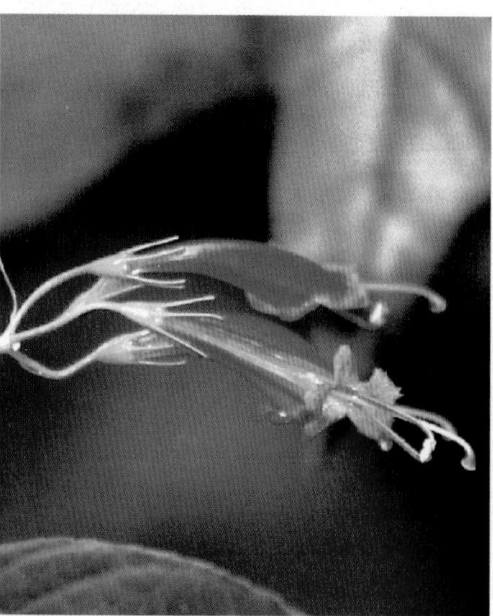

Gesneria ventricosa

This is a tall shrub native to the Antilles. In warm climates it is grown as an ornamental for its red tubular flowers. The shrub prefers a rich, moist, slightly acid soil and is propagated from seed and tip cuttings under mist.

GINKGO

Ginkgoaceae

Ginkgo biloba MAIDENHAIR TREE

A deciduous ornamental tree from China. Though they are larger, the attractive leaves resemble those of a maidenhair fern. The seed is eaten and parts of the tree are used medicinally. It prefers a cold climate and is propagated from seed which needs to be stratified, from layers or cuttings or by grafting.

GLIRICIDIA

Fabaceae [Leguminosae]

Gliricidia sepium MADRE DE CACAO

A small to medium deciduous tree from Central America. It is grown as an ornamental and as a shade tree for coffee plantations. This tree needs a warm climate and is propagated from cuttings and seeds which are poisonous.

GLORIOSA

LILIACEAE

Climbing plants from Africa with lily-like flowers in spring and summer. They are grown as ornamentals outdoors in climates from cool temperate to sub-tropical where they will do well in sandy soils and will tolerate some salt spray. Propagate from seed or by tuber division.

Gloriosa superba CLIMBING LILY
This is an upright climber. The red and yellow flowers have crinkled petals.

Gloriosa superba cv. **Rothschildiana**
An upright climber with red flowers having touches of yellow.

Gloriosa superba cv. **Carsonii** [3]
syn. ***G. carsonii***
A climbing plant with flowers of orange and yellow.

Gloriosa superba cv. **Simplex** [3]
syn. ***G. plantii; G. simplex***
A sparse climber with the flowers coloured old gold.

GMELINA

VERBENACEAE

Shrubs and trees from South East Asia and Australia, grown as ornamentals or as timber trees. Most require a tropical or sub-tropical climate and a rich soil with good rainfall. Propagate from seed or cuttings.

Gmelina arborea
A medium to large deciduous tree which has attractive spikes of yellow and brown coloured flowers. It is widely grown in timber plantations.

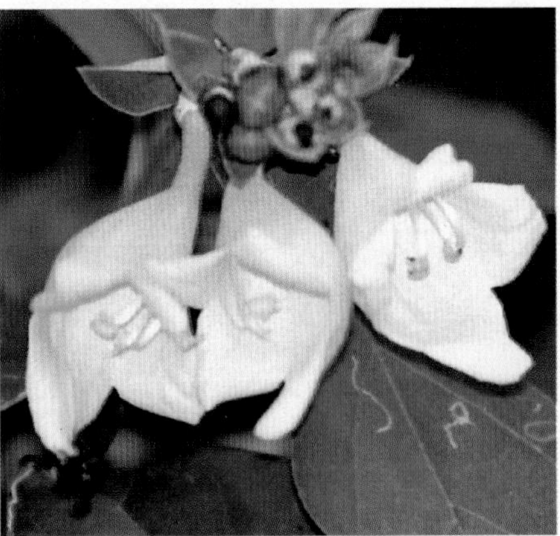

Gmelina asiatica
This is a tall sometimes spiny shrub with terminal clusters of yellow flowers.

Gmelina hystrix
This medium shrub has long catkins of yellow flowers. Now referred to as a synonym of *G. philippensis*.

GMELINA (cont)

Gmelina leichhardtii WHITE BEECH

A medium to tall tree with white and violet coloured flowers and large purple fruit. This tree will grow in a temperate climate and produces a very high quality timber.

Gmelina leichhardtii - fruit

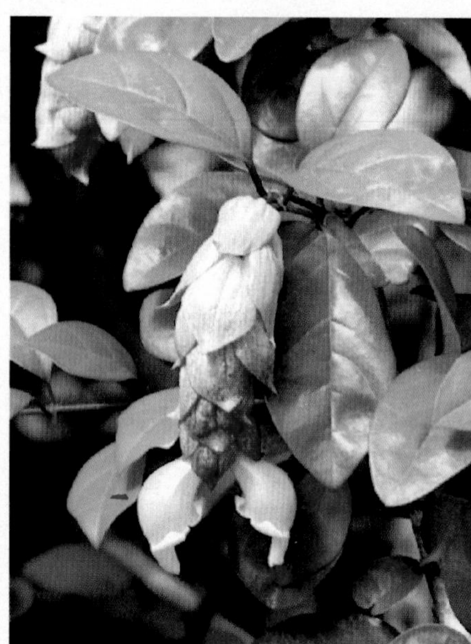

Gmelina philippensis

A medium shrub with racemes of yellow flowers.

GOETHEA

MALVACEAE

Goethea strictiflora

An evergreen medium shrub from South America. It requires a hot climate and good soil. Propagate from seed and cuttings.

GOODIA

FABACEAE [LEGUMINOSAE]

Goodia lotifolia

CLOVER TREE; GOLDEN TIP

From Australia, this is a tall evergreen shrub. It has attractive foliage which looks like clover leaves, with pea type flowers of yellow with an orange centre. This shrub is grown as a landscape plant in cool temperate to sub-tropical climates. Propagate from seed which needs hot water treatment.

GOSSYPIUM

MALVACEAE

Shrubs and trees from tropical and sub-tropical climates and native to many countries. Some are used to produce commercial cotton and others are grown as ornamentals. They grow best in climates from temperate to tropical and many prefer arid climates. Most are grown from seed and those with hard shells need hot water treatment.

Gossypium australe

An erect open crowned shrub with Hibiscus-like flowers coloured pink with a maroon centre. Suited to a semi-arid climate.

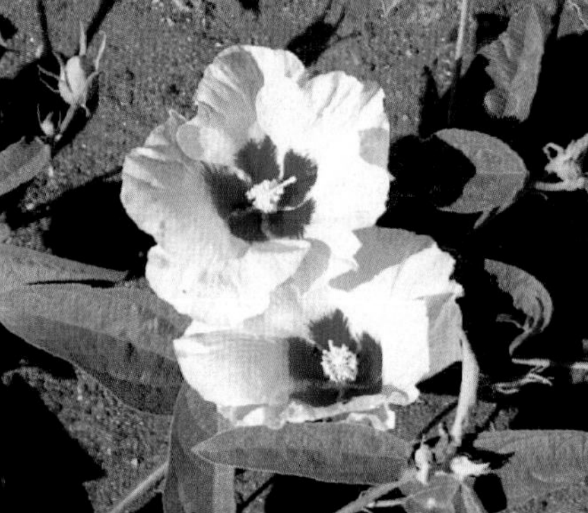

Gossypium bickii

From a semi-arid climate, this low growing spreading shrub has pink flowers with a maroon centre.

Gossypium sturtianum

STURT'S DESERT ROSE

This medium shrub is from a semi-arid climate. It has large Hibiscus-like flowers of pink through to mauve, with a maroon centre. This is the floral emblem of the Northern Territory, Australia.

ɜRAPTOPHYLLUM

ɪCANTHACEAE

vergreen shrubs and small trees from Australia and the Pacific, they are grown for ıeir attractive foliage or for their showy flowers. They are mostly grown in tropical to ɜmperate climates outdoors. *G. pictum* and its cultivars are grown as indoor plants in ɔoler climates. Propagation is from seed and cuttings.

ɪraptophyllum excelsum SCARLET FUCHSIA

tall shrub which has showy heads of red fuchsia-like flowers.

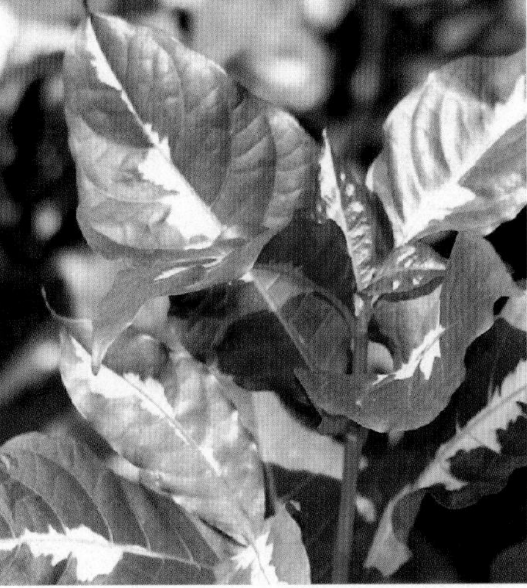

***ɪraptophyllum pictum* cv. Alba Variegata**

'his much branching shrub is grown for :s colourful foliage of green and white. It ıas purple flowers.

***Graptophyllum pictum* cv. Bronze Variegata**

The showy leaves of this cultivar are bronze and pink and the flowers are purple.

***ɪraptophyllum pictum* cv. Aurea Variegata**

'he variegated leaves of this colourful shrub are green and yellow. It has purple flowers.

***Graptophyllum pictum* cv. Purpurium Variegatum**

This cultivar has highly coloured leaves of purple, bronze and red and it has purple flowers.

***Graptophyllum pictum* cv. Rosea Variegata**

An outstanding cultivar which has pink and green variegated leaves and reddish-purple tubular flowers.

***Graptophyllum pictum* cv. Tricolor**

This cultivar has leaves coloured green and pink with some yellow markings. The flower colour is crimson.

g

GREVILLEA

PROTEACEAE

Evergreen shrubs and trees which are native mostly to Australia with a few in New Guinea and the Pacific. They grow all over Australia in all climatic conditions from alpine to tropical and desert. These plants are very free flowering and attract many birds and animals which feed on the nectar produced. Some are used medicinally whilst others are used by florists for their decorative leaves, flowers or seed pods. They are very popular garden ornamentals and some are grown as indoor plants in Europe. There are many cultivars and hybrids being raised and these plants are now very popular as ornamentals. When fertilising, a fertiliser without phosphate or very low in phosphate should be used. Propagation is from seed and cuttings and by grafting, mostly using *G. robusta* rootstock. Most Grevilleas prefer a well drained soil. Many Grevilleas will withstand frost to -6 degrees Celsius. The flowers may be upright, pendulous or grow sideways on branches.

Grevillea alpina cv. **Gold Rush**
MOUNTAIN GREVILLEA
A small spreading shrub with golden flowers which is suited to climates from temperate to alpine.

Grevillea banksii RED SILKY OAK
A tall free flowering shrub with nectar laden heads of light and dark red flowers.

Grevillea banksii cv. **Ruby Red**
The flowers of this cultivar are dark red.

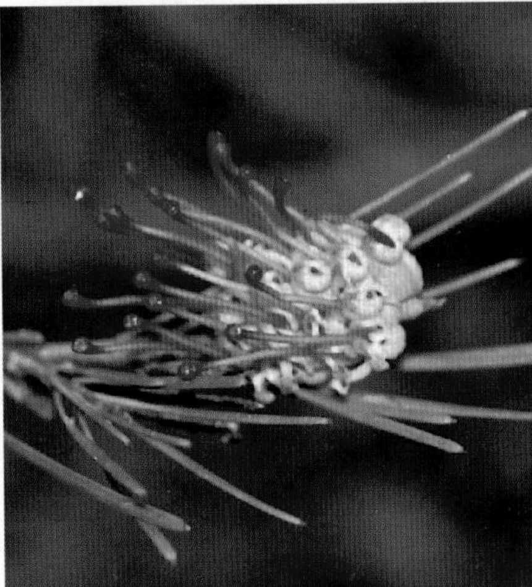

Grevillea baxteri
A needle leaf shrub with toothbrush-like heads of flowers coloured red, orange and yellow.

Grevillea asparagoides
An open crowned prickly leaf shrub with pinkish red flowers.

Grevillea banksii
syn. ***G. banksii*** f. ***albiflora***
A white flowered form of this shrub.

Grevillea beadleana
This is a small spreading shrub with dark red flowers.

Grevillea bipinnatifida

FUCHSIA GREVILLEA

A dense spreading shrub with flowers coloured gold, orange or red.

***Grevillea* cv. Bronze Rambler**

A spreading cultivar with an abundance of red toothbrush-like flower heads.

Grevillea caleyi

The flower heads on this medium spreading shrub are dark red.

Grevillea calliantha

A spreading shrub with fine leaves and brownish red flowers.

***Grevillea* cv. Coastal Glow**

This open spreading shrub has red flowers.

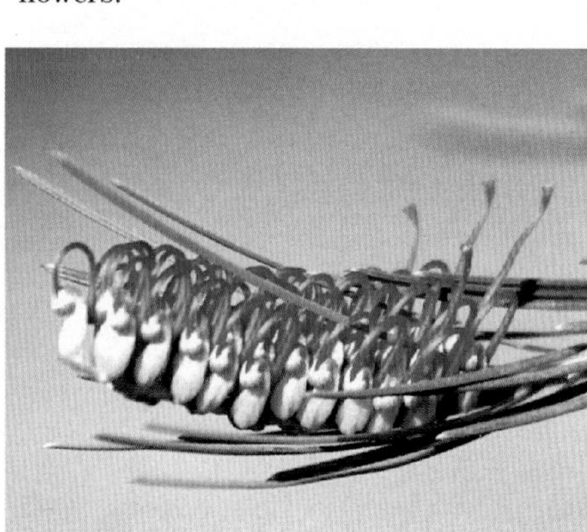

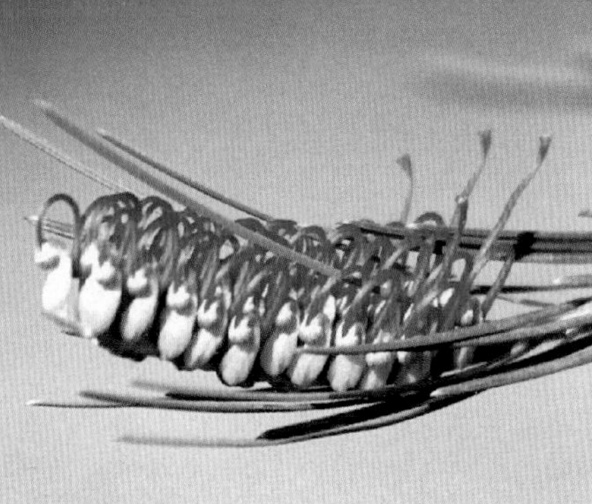

Grevillea coccinea

An open shrub with red toothbrush-like flower heads.

***Grevillea* cv. Coconut Ice**

Flowers coloured pink and red bloom on this bushy shrub.

Grevillea crithmifolia

An open crowned shrub with terminal heads of pale pink flowers.

Grevillea curviloba

A dwarf spreading shrub with terminal heads of white flowers.

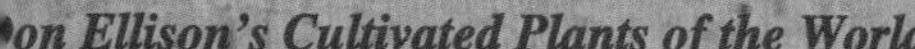

g

GREVILLEA (cont)

Grevillea dielsiana
Very open, this shrub has fine prickly foliage and orange-red flowers.

***Grevillea* cv. Elegance**
This hybrid of *G. johnsonii* and *G. longistyla* is an open crowned tall shrub with large heads of pearly pink and red coloured flowers. Also known as *G.* cv. Long John.

***Grevillea* cv. Evelyn's Coronet**
A fine leaf open shrub with pinky red flowers.

***Grevillea* cv. Fanfare**
This large leaf cultivar has heads of red flowers.

Grevillea flexuosa
This spreading shrub has spiky leaves and long heads of creamy yellow flowers.

Grevillea formosa
A spreading dwarf shrub with fine grey-green foliage and large flower heads of green, opening to yellow.

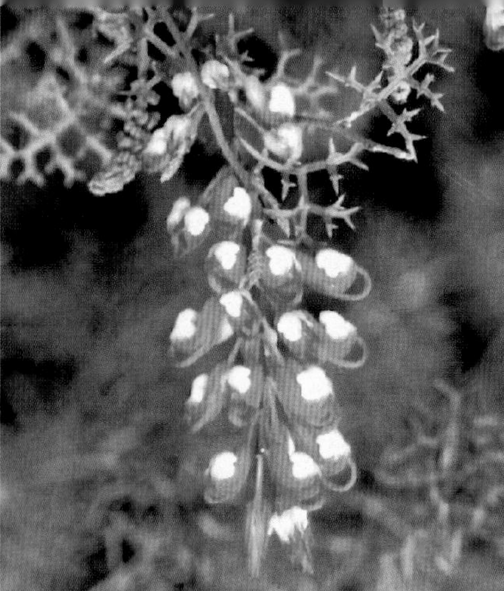

Grevillea georgeana
With prickly leaves, this spreading shrub has flowers coloured red and off white.

Grevillea goodii* ssp. *decora
A medium open crowned shrub with heads of pinky red flowers.

Grevillea heliosperma ROCK GREVILLEA
Large heads of pinky red flowers bloom on this tall, open crowned shrub.

Grevillea hodgei
Hardy and free flowering, this open crowned tall shrub has short flower heads of cream and tan. This was known as *G.whiteana* sp. Coochin Hills before being renamed.

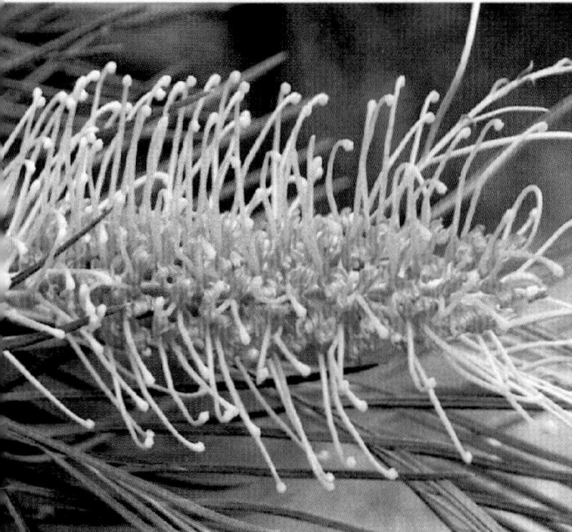

***Grevillea* cv. Honey Gem**
A popular tall shrub with heads of old gold coloured flowers. Produces good quantities of nectar.

***Grevillea* cv. Honey Wonder**
This is a variegated leaf cultivar with heads of old gold coloured flowers.

***Grevillea* cv. Jolly Swagman**
A spreading shrub with toothbrush-like heads of red flowers.

Grevillea juniperina
A spreading shrub with fine prickly leaves and apricot flowers. Flower colour may also be cream, red, yellow or pink.

***Grevillea* cv. Kay Williams**
This bushy shrub has large heads of pinky apricot coloured flowers.

***Grevillea* cv. Landcare**
A showy Grevillea which has long spikes of salmon-red flowers.

***Grevillea lanigera* cv. Mt. Tamboritha**
A small shrub with heads of pink flowers.

***Grevillea lanigera* cv. Prostrata**
Small leaves and reddish pink flowers feature on this spreading shrub.

***Grevillea* cv. Mason's Hybrid**
syn. ***G.* cv. *Ned Kelly***
On this very bushy shrub the large heads of flowers are red and apricot in colour.

GREVILLEA (cont)

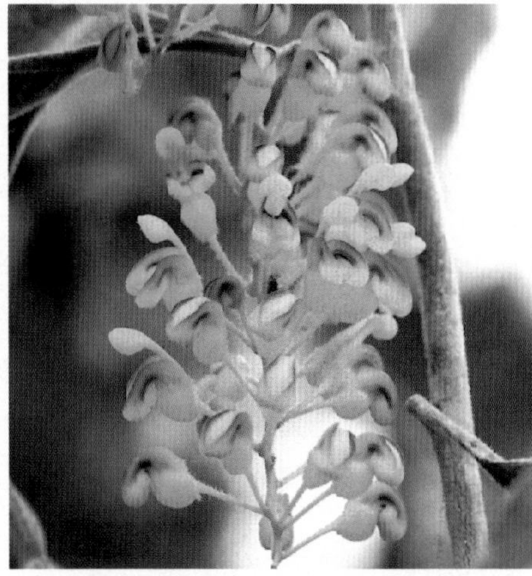

Grevillea miniata cv. **Golden Glory**
A tall shrub with prickles on the leaves and clusters of golden coloured flowers. Suited to a warm dry climate.

Grevillea cv. **Misty Pink**
Tall and bushy, this shrub has large heads of pink flowers. Good for nectar production.

Grevillea cv. **Moonlight**
A tall bushy shrub with large heads of cream flowers. Produces lots of nectar.

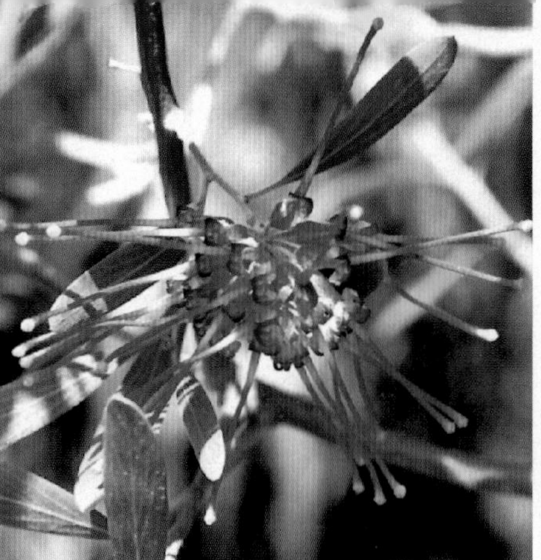

Grevillea olivacea
An open crowned shrub with a tinge of blue in the leaves. The flowers are red.

Grevillea petrophiloides PINK POKERS
A tall open shrub with long thin leaves. The flower heads are long and in colour are reddish pink.

Grevillea cv. **Pink Surprise**
A bushy shrub with large flower heads of pink nectar filled flowers.

Grevillea cv. **Poorinda Blondie**
This cultivar has a bushy growth and flowers coloured pink and old gold.

Grevillea cv. **Poorinda Peter**
An open growing shrub with pinky red toothbrush-like flower heads in spring.

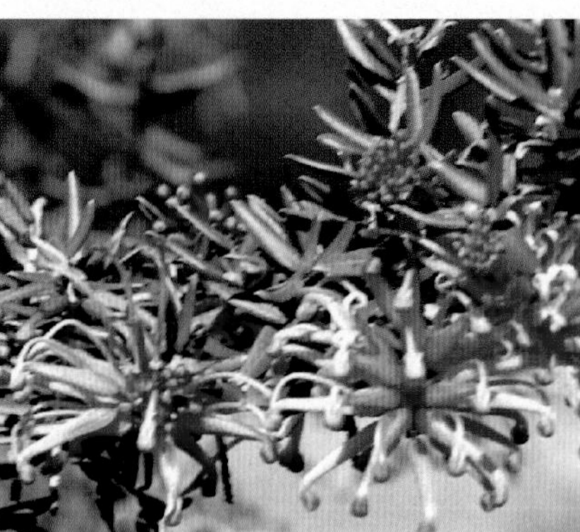

Grevillea cv. **Poorinda Queen**
A cultivar which has cascading branches and orange coloured flowers.

Grevillea cv. **Poorinda Royal Mantle**
This is a spreading large leaf shrub with pinky red flowers—an excellent ground cover.

GREVILLEA (cont)

Grevillea cv. **Poorinda Stephen**
An open shrub with terminal heads of red flowers.

Grevillea pteridifolia GOLDEN GREVILLEA
A medium shrub to small tree with an open crown and long heads of golden flowers. Suitable for hot and dry conditions.

Grevillea pterosperma DESERT GREVILLEA
A medium size open shrub with long thin leaves. White coloured flowers bloom in long heads. Suited to a hot and dry climate.

Grevillea sp. nov. **purnululu**
Recently discovered in the Bungle Bungles, this tall shrub has very large heads of golden flowers.

Grevillea refracta
A tall erect shrub with heads of red and yellow flowers.

Grevillea robusta SILKY OAK
A medium to tall tree which is used for timber production and as an ornamental. It has large heads of nectar laden golden flowers. This plant is grown as an indoor plant in Europe and used as a rootstock for grafting many other Grevilleas.

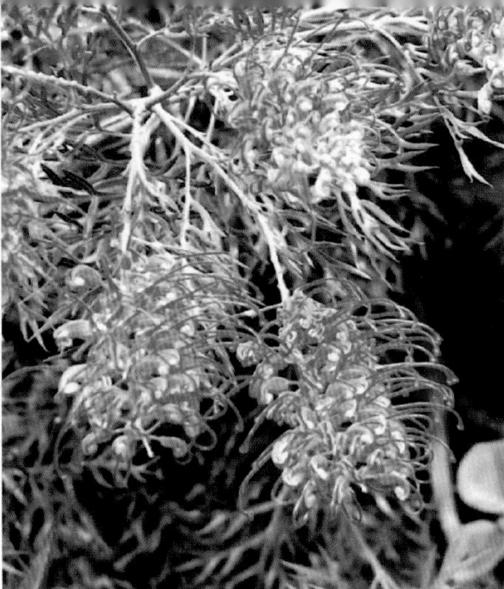

Grevillea cv. **Robyn Gordon**
A very popular ornamental bushy shrub with large heads of pinkish red flowers over a long period.

Grevillea rosmarinifolia cv. **Alba**
A very open shrub with thin pointed leaves and creamish white flowers.

Grevillea rosmarinifolia cv. **Pink Pearl**
An open shrub with pointed thin leaves and bright pink flowers.

GREVILLEA (cont)

Grevillea cv. **Red Hooks**
Toothbrush-like heads of red flowers bloom on this tall bushy shrub.

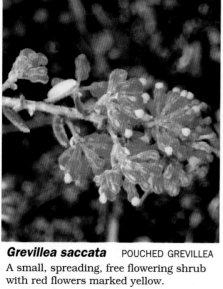

Grevillea saccata POUCHED GREVILLEA
A small, spreading, free flowering shrub with red flowers marked yellow.

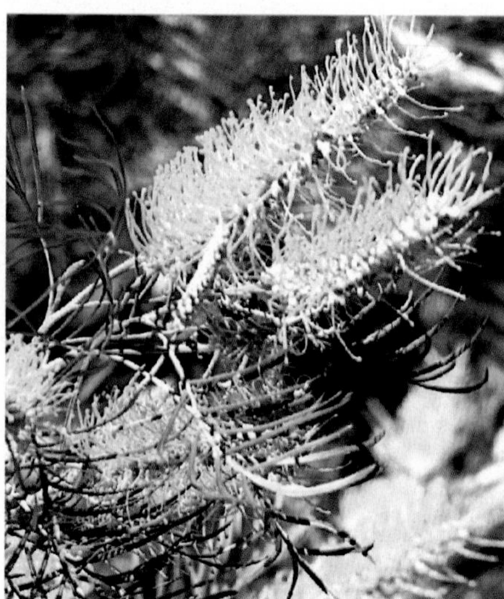

Grevillea cv. **Sandra Gordon**
A spreading tall shrub or small tree with large heads of yellow-gold coloured flowers over a long period. Very popular.

Grevillea sericea
This bushy much branched shrub has terminal heads of bright pink flowers.

Grevillea speciosa ssp. ***oleoides***
A sparse shrub with heads of red flowers.

Grevillea cv. **Star Fire**
Tall and open, this shrub has long thin leaves and large heads of red flowers.

Grevillea stenobotrya
SANDHILL SPIDER FLOWER
Very large heads of cream flowers bloom on this tall shrub of the dry country.

Grevillea stenomera cv. **Kalbarri**
A medium size shrub with greyish coloured leaves and flower heads with orange and yellow coloured flowers.

Grevillea cv. **Strawberry Blonde**
A bushy shrub with toothbrush-like flower heads of red and creamy white.

GREVILLEA (cont)

Grevillea cv. **Superb**
Over many months in spring and summer, this bushy shrub has pinky apricot coloured flowers.

Grevillea cv. **Sylvia**
A bushy shrub with nectar filled flower heads of red coloured flowers.

Grevillea synapheae
Small and spreading, this shrub has prickly leaves and heads of cream flowers in clusters.

Grevillea tenuiloba
A slender, open crowned small shrub with heads of delicate orange coloured flowers.

Grevillea tetragonoloba
On this small spreading shrub the toothbrush-like heads of flowers are red and perfumed.

Grevillea thelemanniana
A medium spreading shrub with thin pointed leaves and orange-red flowers.

Grevillea thelemanniana cv. **Ellendale Pool**
A cultivar with heads of pinkish red flowers.

Grevillea thelemanniana cv. **Magic Lantern**
Crimson-red flowers form on this cultivar.

Grevillea trachytheca
A spreading shrub with spikes of cream flowers.

g

GREVILLEA (cont)

Grevillea venusta

BYFIELD SPIDER FLOWER

This tall bushy shrub has flowers coloured orange, yellow, grey and black.

Grevillea victoriae ROYAL GREVILLEA

A medium shrub with cascading racemes of orange-red flowers.

Grevillea whiteana

Hardy and free flowering, this opened crowned tall shrub has large cream flower heads. A good nectar producer.

***Grevillea whiteana* cv. Honeycomb**

A cultivar with a varied flower form and colour.

Grevillea wickhamii

Cascading heads of gold and red coloured flowers feature on this open crowned shrub which has spiky, greyish leaves.

***Grevillea* cv. Winpara Gem**

A medium spreading shrub with red flowers.

***Grevillea* cv. Winpara Gold**

This medium spreading shrub has gold and red coloured flowers.

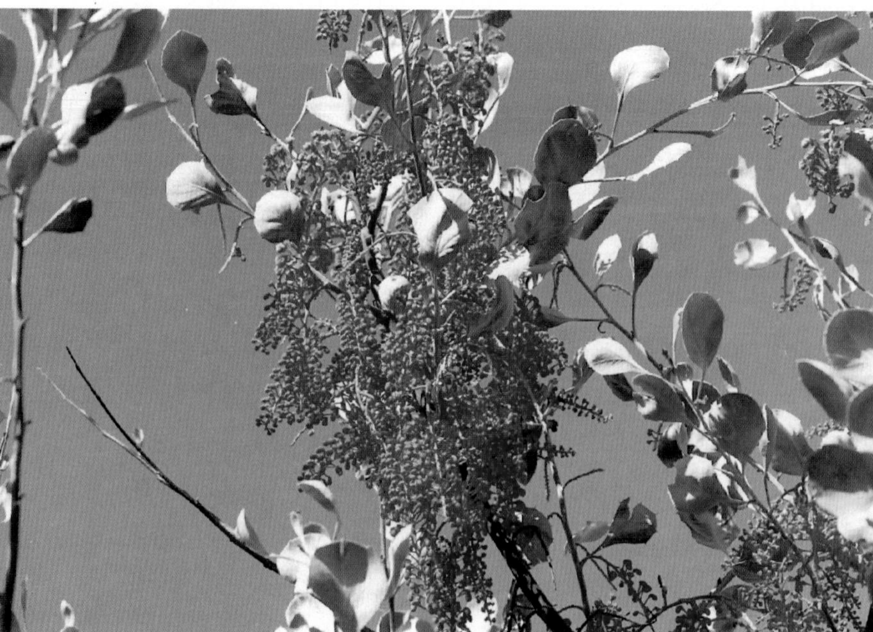

Grevillea wickhamii* ssp. *aprica

An outstanding form of this Grevillea with very large cascading heads of bright red flowers.

GREWIA

TILIACEAE

Evergreen shrubs, trees and climbers from South East Asia, Africa and Australia, some of which are grown as ornamentals. They are grown in temperate to tropical climates and are propagated from seed and cuttings.

Grewia caffra

A spreading evergreen shrub with masses of starry pinky lilac coloured flowers.

Grewia flavescens

This is a dense, arching branched, evergreen shrub with clusters of golden coloured flowers.

GREYIA

GREYIACEAE

From South Africa, these colourful shrubs are grown in climates from cool temperate to sub-tropical as ornamentals for their colourful flowers. Propagate from seed, cuttings or suckers.

Greyia radlkoferi

A medium to tall shrub with large red bottlebrush-like flowers.

Greyia sutherlandii NATAL BOTTLEBRUSH

A medium to tall shrub with red bottlebrush-like flowers which are smaller than *G. radlkoferi.*

GRISELINIA

CORNACEAE

***Griselinia littoralis* cv. Dixon's Cream**

This evergreen shrub with shiny leaves is native to New Zealand. It is tolerant of some frosts and prefers a slightly alkaline soil. Its variegated leaves are coloured cream inside and green outside. Propagate from cuttings.

***Griselinia littoralis* cv. Variegata**

This cultivar has variegated leaves, yellow to cream outside and greyish green inside.

GUAIACUM

ZYGOPHYLLACEAE

Guaiacum officinale

A tropical evergreen small tree with showy heads of mauve flowers. Propagate from seed.

g - H

GUETTARDA

RUBIACEAE

Guettarda uruguensis

A tall evergreen shrub from tropical America. This shrub prefers a rich soil and a tropical or sub-tropical climate. Propagate from seed and cuttings.

GUICHENOTIA

STERCULIACEAE

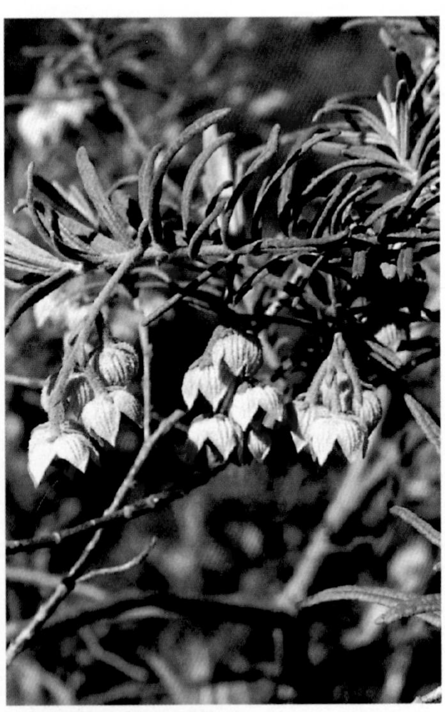

Guichenotia ledifolia

A small Australian shrub with greyish leaves. It is an ornamental plant with mauve coloured bell-like flowers. This shrub prefers a well drained soil in a cool temperate to sub-tropical climate. Propagate from seeds and cuttings.

GUSTAVIA

LECYTHIDACEAE

Small evergreen trees from tropical Central and South America. They have large attractive fragrant waxy flowers and are grown as ornamentals in tropical climates. They need a rich soil. Propagate from seed and cuttings.

Gustavia marcgraaviana

A dense small tree with large highly perfumed flowers coloured white with pink centres.

Gustavia superba

This small densely crowned tree has large perfumed waxy flowers of white and pale pink.

GYNURA

ASTERACEAE [COMPOSITAE]

Gynura procumbens
syn. ***G. sarmentosa***

From the tropics, this is an evergreen climbing plant with velvety purplish leaves. It is grown outdoors in tropical and sub-tropical climates and indoor in cooler climates. Propagate from cuttings.

HAEMATOXYLUM

CAESALPINIACEAE [LEGUMINOSAE]

Haematoxylum campechianum
CAMPEACHY

This tall shrub from tropical America is grown as an ornamental feature or hedge tree in sub-tropical and tropical climates. The tree has attractive clusters of creamy yellow flowers and is tolerant of swampy soils. Propagate from seed.

HAKEA

PROTEACEAE

Evergreen shrubs and small trees which are native to Australia. They are grown as ornamentals and also for their flowers and pods which are used by florists. Hakeas grow in a variety of soil types and a wide range of climates. Propagate from seed.

Hakea bakeriana

A rounded medium shrub with long thin pointed leaves and clusters of bright pink or white flowers.

Hakea bucculenta RED POKERS
This tall open shrub has needle-type leaves and long heads of red flowers.

Hakea cinerea ASHY HAKEA
A dense rigid shrub with round heads of yellow flowers.

Hakea corymbosa CAULIFLOWER HAKEA
Large heads of white flowers which resemble a cauliflower bloom on this stiff spreading shrub.

Hakea cucullata SCALLOPS
A medium upright open shrub with bright pink flowers.

Hakea francisiana NARUKALJA
The long flower heads of this tall shrub are coloured deep pink and sometimes orange-pink.

Hakea laurina PIN CUSHION HAKEA
A dense tall shrub or small tree with red and cream coloured round flowers.

Hakea lissocarpha HONEY BUSH
This is a small shrub with prickly leaves and clusters of white and pink coloured flowers.

Hakea lissosperma MOUNTAIN HAKEA
Cold tolerant, this tall shrub has upright, long, needle-like leaves and masses of white flowers in spring.

Hakea multilineata GRASS LEAVED HAKEA
A tall shrub with long flower heads of bright pink flowers. The flower size and shape of this Hakea are variable.

HAKEA (cont)

Hakea nitida FROG HAKEA

On this small to medium size shrub the clusters of white flowers form along the branches.

Hakea purpurea

This medium shrub has prickly leaves and heads of red flowers.

***Hakea salicifolia* cv. Gold Medal**

An outstanding cultivar which has multi-coloured leaves of green, cream and pink. It is grown for its foliage.

***Hakea sericea* cv. Rosea**

PINK SILKY HAKEA

A hardy tall shrub with needle-like leaves and clusters of pink flowers.

Hakea suberea CORKBARK

This tall shrub to small tree has very corky bark. The pendulous yellow flower heads sprout along the trunk as well as on the branches.

Hakea victoria ROYAL HAKEA

Grown for its multi-coloured foliage of green, cream, yellow and red, this is a medium, erect shrub.

HALESIA

STYRACACEAE

Halesia monticola SILVERBELL TREE

A deciduous small tree native to North America, it is best grown in moderately cold climates and has showy pendulous white flowers in spring. It is grown from seed which needs long cold stratification of at least 3 to 4 months.

Halesia tetraptera

A tall deciduous shrub with pendulous off-white bell-shaped flowers in spring.

X HALIMIOCISTUS

CISTACEAE

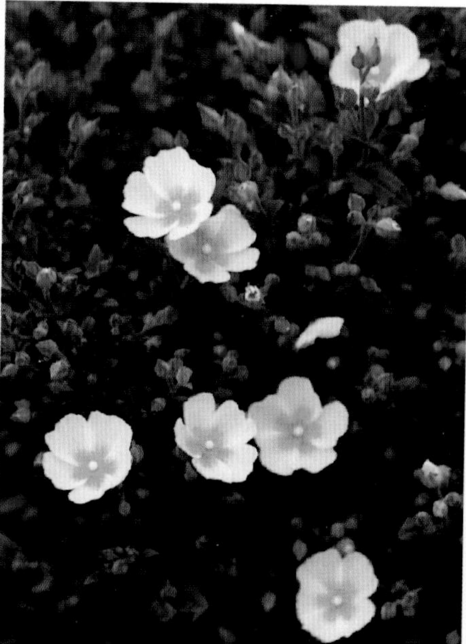

X *Halimiocistus revolii*
A small spreading evergreen shrub which is a hybrid between *Halimium alyssoides* and *Cistus salviifolius*. In spring, it has masses of open white flowers with yellow centres. Propagate from cuttings.

HALLERIA

SCROPHULARIACEAE

Halleria lucida AFRICAN HONEYSUCKLE
A tall evergreen African shrub which has bunches of orange coloured honeysuckle-like flowers. It grows in climates from cool temperate to tropical and is propagated from seed and softwood cuttings.

HAMAMELIS

WITCH HAZEL

HAMAMELIDACEAE

From North America, Asia and Europe, these deciduous shrubs and small trees grow in cool to cold climates. These plants are propagated from seed which needs cold stratification, by grafting and from cuttings. Many Hamamelis are highly perfumed and flower in winter or early spring.

Hamamelis* x *intermedia
This tall shrub is widely grown. A hybrid between *H. japonica* and *H. mollis*, it has yellow flowers with orange centres.

Hamamelis* x *intermedia
cv. **Arnold's Promise**
This medium size shrub has clusters of twisted yellow flowers along the branches.

Hamamelis japonica
cv. **Zuccariniana**
A tall shrub with clusters of twisted cream to yellow coloured flowers

Hamamelis mollis CHINESE WITCH HAZEL
Yellow flowers with orange centres bloom along the bare branches of this tall shrub.

Hamamelis mollis cv. **Brevipetala**
A tall shrub with clusters of golden coloured flowers along the branches.

HAMELIA

RUBIACEAE

Hamelia patens
A small evergreen tree from tropical America. It has upright clusters of orange coloured tubular flowers and needs to be grown in a tropical or sub-tropical climate. Propagate from seed and cuttings.

HARDENBERGIA

FABACEAE [LEGUMINOSAE]

Evergreen climbing plants which flower very densely in spring and are native to Australia, these are ideal plants to cover banks and roadside cuttings as well as fence covers. Tolerant of quite poor soils, they are mostly propagated from seed which needs hot water treatment, or from cuttings of the colour variants. Hardenbergias grow in climates from cool temperate to sub-tropical.

Hardenbergia comptoniana
A showy spreading vine which has dense racemes of bluish purple flowers in early spring.

***Hardenbergia comptoniana* cv. Alba**
A white flowered cultivar of this climber.

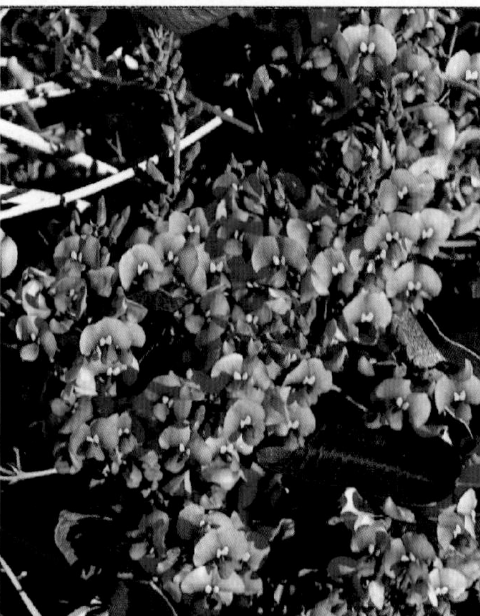

Hardenbergia violacea PURPLE CORAL PEA
syn. ***Hardenbergia monophylla***
This climber flowers in early spring and is covered with showy racemes of purple-violet flowers.

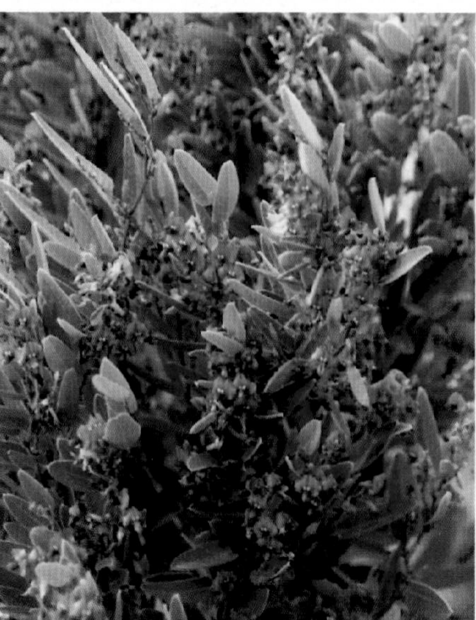

***Hardenbergia violacea* cv. Mini Ha Ha**
This cultivar has an upright growth.

HARPEPHYLLUM

ANACARDIACEAE

Harpephyllum caffrum KAFFIR PLUM
A spreading evergreen medium tree from Africa, it is grown as a street or park tree and has showy red plum-like fruit. This tree grows well in climates from cool temperate to tropical. Propagate from seed.

HARPULLIA

SAPINDACEAE

Evergreen shrubs and small trees from Australia which grow in climates from temperate to tropical. They are used as ornamentals and street trees, for their colourful orange fruit. Propagate from seed.

Harpullia hillii TULIPWOOD
A densely crowned small tree which has small white flowers and erect bunches of orange fruit.

Harpullia pendula BLACK TULIPWOOD
This is a spreading small tree with fragrant greenish white flowers and pendulous orange fruit.

HEBE

SCROPHULARIACEAE

Evergreen shrubs, mostly native to New Zealand, which are widely grown in climates from cold temperate to sub-tropical. They are free flowering and grow in a wide range of soils. Propagate from seed and cuttings. Many were previously named Veronica.

Hebe buxifolia

A compact spreading shrub with clusters of white flowers.

Hebe carnosula

Small white flowers bloom in clusters on this low growing spreading shrub.

***Hebe* x *franciscana* cv. Blue Gem**

A hybrid compact shrub with erect spikes of bluish violet coloured flowers.

***Hebe* x *franciscana* cv. Variegata**

The foliage on this cultivar is cream and green.

***Hebe* cv. Lavender Lace**

A bushy evergreen shrub with clusters of small lavender-blue flowers.

***Hebe salicifolia* cv. Bouquet of Flowers**

A compact free branching shrub with erect spikes of pale pink and cerise coloured flowers.

***Hebe salicifolia* cv. Variegata**

A cultivar with variegated leaves coloured grey and cream.

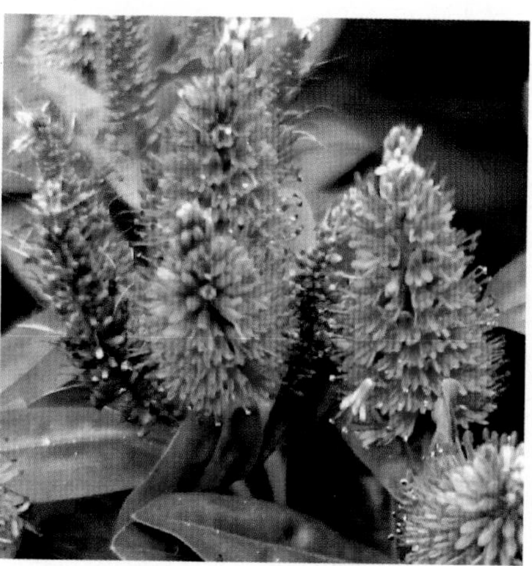

***Hebe speciosa* cv. La Seduisante**

This compact, free branching shrub has erect spikes of cerise coloured flowers.

HEBE (cont)

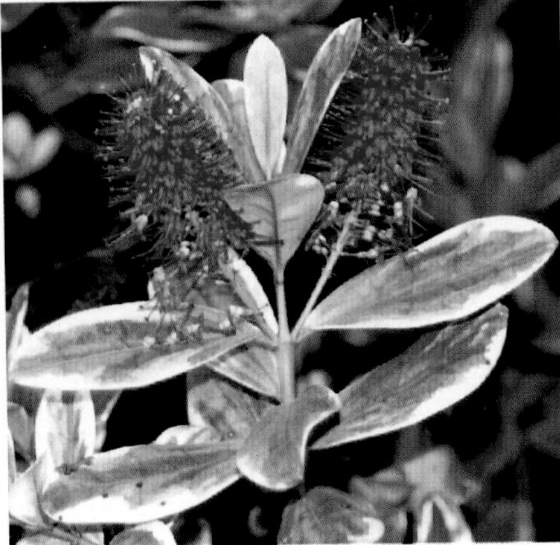

***Hebe speciosa* cv. La Seduisante Variegata**

A cultivar with grey and white variegated foliage.

***Hebe speciosa* cv. Tricolor**

A cultivated form of *H. speciosa*. It is an upright growing shrub with mauve flower spikes and multi-coloured leaves of pink, cream and green.

***Hebe* cv. Wiri Charm**

Small cerise coloured flowers form in erect heads on this bushy evergreen shrub.

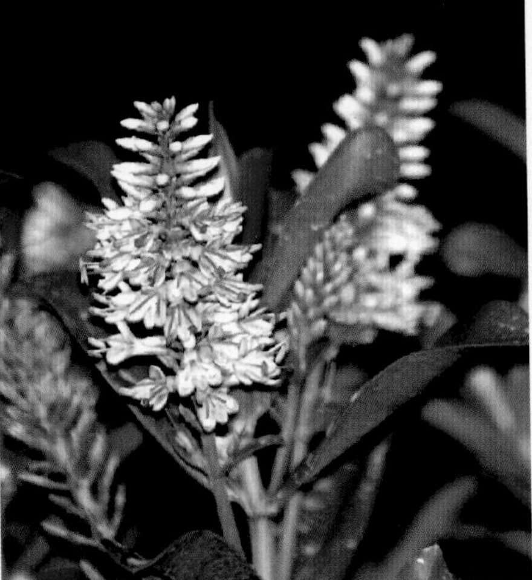

***Hebe* cv. Wiri Image**

A bushy evergreen shrub with upright spikes of lavender-blue flowers.

HEDERA — IVY

ARALIACEAE

A range of evergreen climbing plants from Europe, Africa and Asia, they are widely grown as ornamentals to cover walls and fences and also as ground covers. Ivys are quite cold tolerant but will also grow in climates as warm as sub-tropical. There are hundreds of different cultivars grown throughout the world. Propagation is from cuttings.

***Hedera* cv. Beau Geste**

syn. ***H.* cv. Souvenir de Marengo**

An outstanding bushy cultivar having leaves which are white inside and green outside.

***Hedera canariensis* cv. Variegata**

syn. ***H. canariensis* cv. Gloire de Marengo**

Large partially reflexed leaves coloured cream and green feature on this climber.

***Hedera colchica* cv. Dentata**

A hardy evergreen climber with large green leaves.

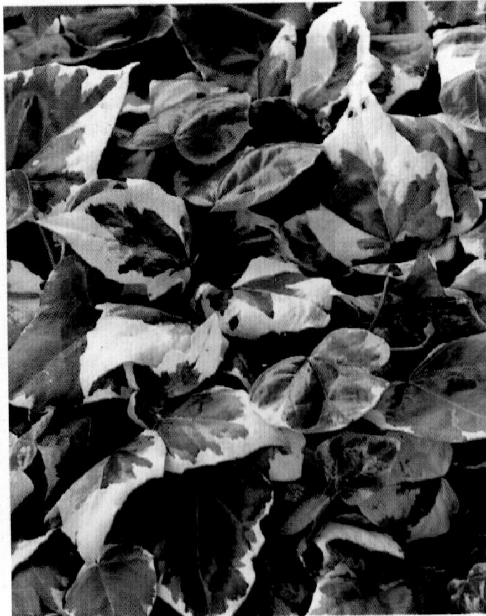

***Hedera colchica* cv. Dentata Variegata**

This cultivar has cream and green leaves.

***Hedera colchica* cv. Sulphur Heart**
A cultivar with variegated leaves coloured yellow inside and green outside.

***Hedera helix* cv. Buttercup**
The golden coloured new growth on this cultivar changes to green with age.

***Hedera helix* cv. Deltoidea**
Unusual clover looking leaves feature on this cultivar.

Hedera helix
Widely grown, this climber has green leaves which are five pointed.

***Hedera helix* cv. Chicago Variegated**
A cultivar having green and white variegated leaves.

***Hedera helix* cv. Flavescens**
When young, the rhomboid shaped leaves of this cultivar are yellow.

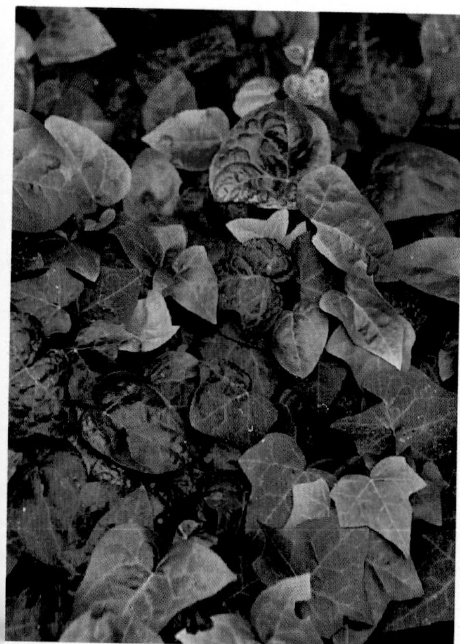

***Hedera helix* cv. Brokamp**
A cultivar which has variable shaped leaves and touches of yellow on new leaves.

***Hedera helix* cv. Chrysophylla**
This cultivar has teardrop shaped leaves.

***Hedera helix* cv. Glacier**
The small leaves of this cultivar are variegated green and white.

HEDERA (cont)

Hedera helix **cv. Goldchild**
A cultivar which has variegated leaves coloured green inside and yellow outside.

Hedera helix **cv. Golden Kolibri**
This cultivar has variegated leaves coloured green and yellow.

Hedera helix **cv. Harold**
This cultivar has variegated leaves coloured green inside and cream outside.

Hedera helix **cv. Goldheart**
This very showy cultivar has leaves coloured yellow in the centre and green on the edges.

Hedera helix **cv. Gracilis**
Unusual partly twisted leaves are the feature of this cultivar.

Hedera helix **cv. Marmorata Minor**
The green leaves are marked with yellow on this cultivar.

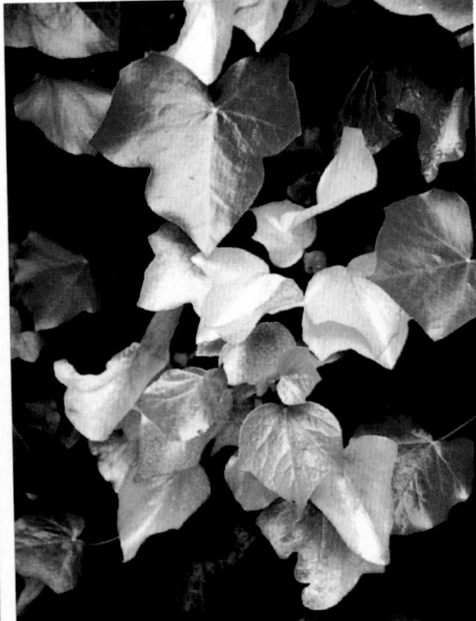

Hedera helix **cv. Golden Emblem**
A large leaf cultivar which has yellow new growth.

Hedera helix **cv. Hahn's Variegated**
A cultivar which has greyish green leaves with ivory markings near the edges.

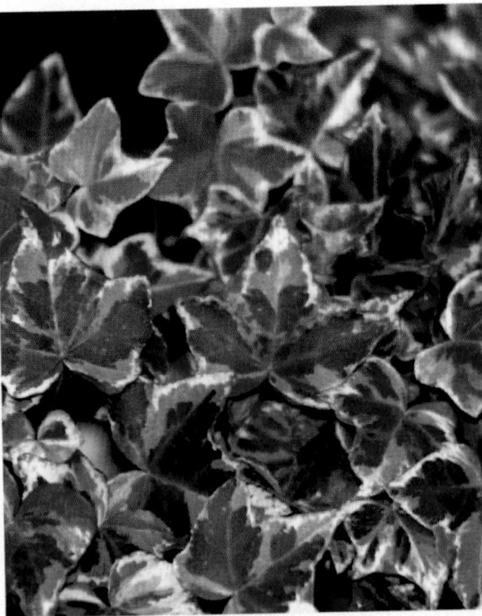

Hedera helix **cv. Mint Kolibri**
A multi-coloured cultivar with leaves coloured dark green, lime-green, grey and cream.

HEDERA (cont)

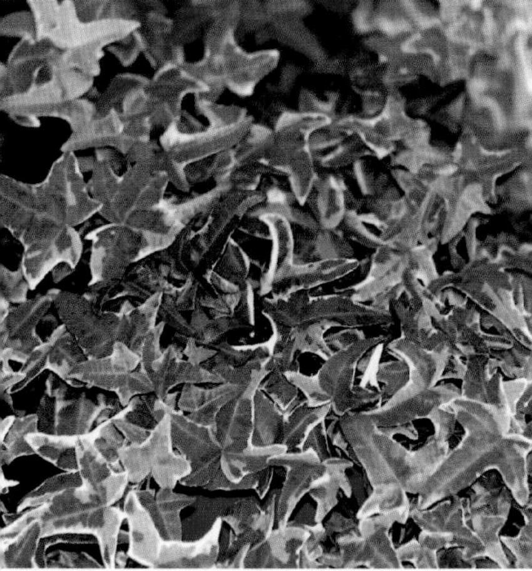

Hedera helix cv. **Mona Lisa**
Arrowhead shaped leaves are coloured green, grey and cream on this small leaf cultivar.

Hedera helix cv. **Sagittifolia Variegata**
A cultivar with small leaves coloured greyish green and cream.

Hedera helix cv. **Pedata**
A cultivar with 'turkeys foot' shaped leaves.

Hedera helix cv. **Triloba**
This cultivar has triangular shaped leaves.

Hedera rhombea
syn. ***H. helix*** var. ***rhombea***
A hardy climber with large leaves which are yellow when young.

Hedera helix cv. **Pittsburg Gold**
The new leaves of this cultivar are green and gold in colour.

Hedera nepalensis
A hardy climber with longish leaves and yellow coloured new growth.

HEIMIA

LYTHRACEAE

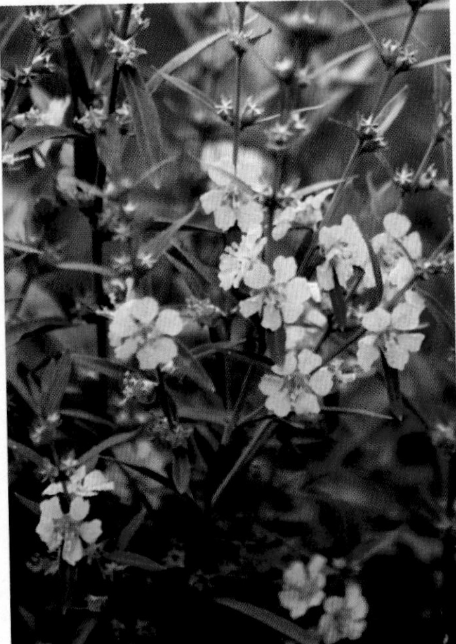

Heimia myrtifolia
A small evergreen shrub from South America. It has small leaves and masses of yellow flowers along the branches. This plant is tolerant of poor soils and grows in climates from temperate to tropical. Propagate from seed and cuttings.

HELIOTROPIUM

BORAGINACEAE

Small branching shrubs from Europe and the Americas. They are widely grown as free flowering ornamentals and many are fragrant. The climate range is from cold temperate to tropical and propagation is from seed and cuttings.

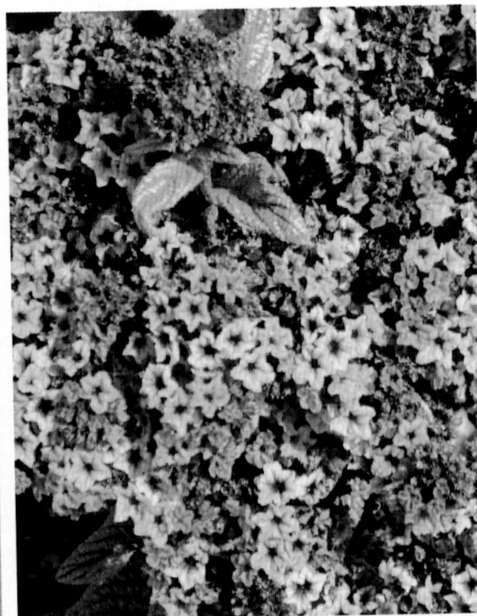

Heliotropium arborescens HELIOTROPE
A small spreading shrub which has large heads of small purple flowers.

***Heliotropium arborescens* cv. Aurea**
A cultivar with yellow leaves and flowers of mauvish purple.

HELICTERES

STERCULIACEAE

Helicteres isora SPIRAL BUSH
Native to Australia, this medium spreading shrub has brownish red flowers and unusual spirally twisted seed pods. It grows in climates from temperate to tropical and is propagated from seed and cuttings.

HERITIERA

STERCULIACEAE

Heritiera macrophylla
LOOKING GLASS TREE
A medium sized tropical tree from India and Burma, it has a buttress trunk, bunches of small pink flowers and large seed pods. It needs a sub-tropical or tropical climate and is propagated from seed.

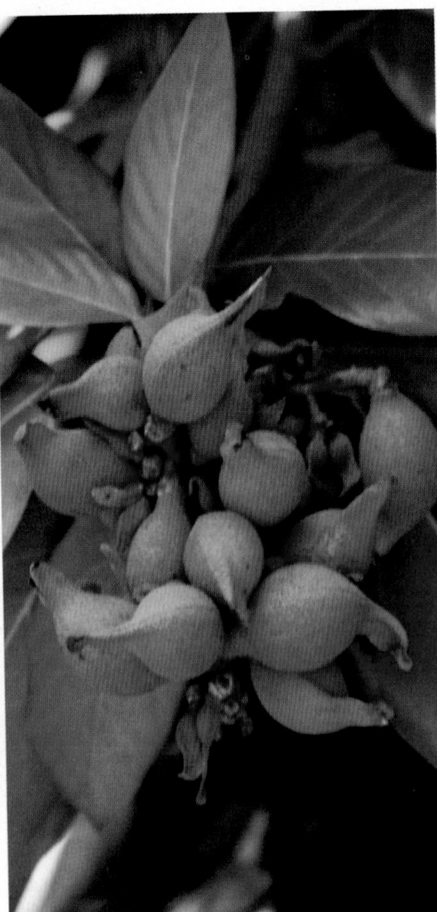

Heritiera macrophylla
This illustration shows the clusters of large seed pods.

HERNANDIA

Hernandiaceae

Evergreen shrubs and trees from Australia, India, Central America, Africa and the Pacific. They are grown for their showy flowers and eye catching seed pods. These plants prefer a warm temperate to tropical climate and are propagated from seed.

Hernandia bivalvis GREASE NUT

A dense ornamental tall shrub to small tree with shiny leaves. It has clusters of cream flowers followed by large bright orange-red seed pods, which are illustrated.

Hernandia cordigera

A small to medium ornamental tree which is covered for up to 3 months with large heads of showy cream flowers. It has colourful marble size seed pods coloured white and pink.

Hernandia cordigera - fruit

HETEROCENTRON

Melastomataceae

Evergreen shrubs and ground covers, native to Central America. These plants are grown for their colourful flowers in climates from cool temperate to tropical. They grow in a wide range of soils and are propagated from seed and cuttings.

Heterocentron elegans SPANISH SHAWL

syn. ***Heeria elegans***

A very colourful ground cover which is covered with rosy violet coloured flowers in late spring.

Heterocentron macrostachyum

A sparse shrub with heads of rosy mauve flowers.

Heterocentron macrostachyum - pink form

syn. ***H. roseum***

HETEROPTERYS

Malpighiaceae

Semi-climbing shrubs which are grown as ornamental plants in temperate to tropical climates.

Heteropterys chrysophylla

A semi-climbing evergreen plant which has heads of cream flowers followed by yellow fruit.

Heteropterys sp.

Clusters of yellow flowers followed by attractive red winged seed pods occur on this semi-climbing plant. Marketed in the nursery industry as *H. salicifolia.*

h

HIBBERTIA

DILLENIACEAE

Small spreading shrubs and climbers which are mostly native to Australia, with others from Madagascar, South East Asia and the Pacific. They are widely grown as ornamental plants. Propagation is mostly from seed but cuttings are also used.

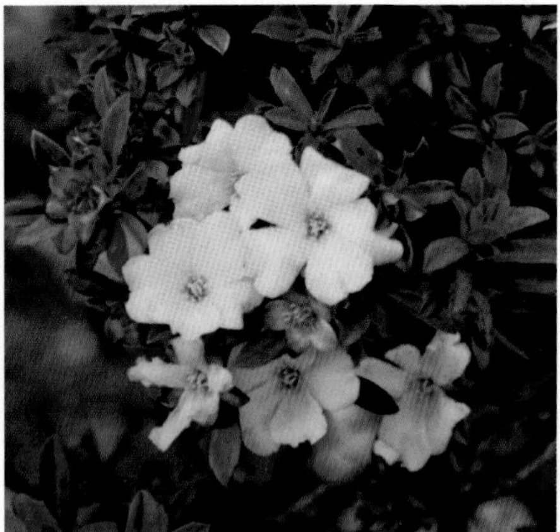

Hibbertia cuneiformis

CUT LEAF GUINEA FLOWER

A spreading shrub with clusters of golden coloured flowers.

Hibbertia hypericoides

YELLOW BUTTERCUPS

This spreading shrub has small leaves and golden coloured flowers.

Hibbertia racemosa

STALKED GUINEA FLOWER

A small shrub with erect branches and greyish leaves. It has yellow flowers along the branches.

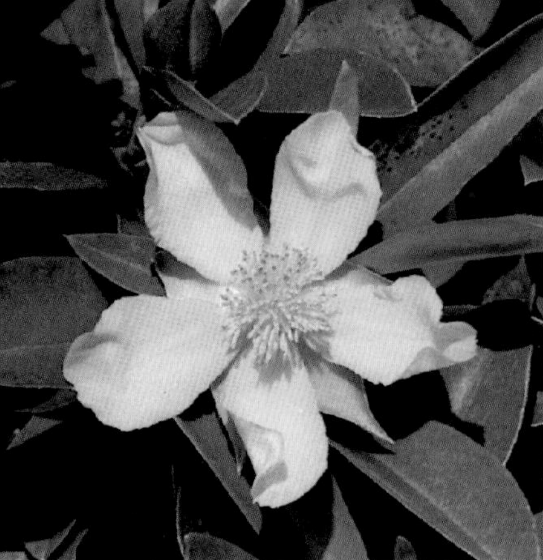

Hibbertia scandens

CLIMBING GUINEA FLOWER

Tolerant of some salt spray, this is a twining climber with large yellow flowers.

Hibbertia serpyllifolia

A prostrate shrub with small leaves and golden yellow coloured flowers.

Hibbertia tetrandra

This bushy shrub has bright yellow flowers. It is now regarded as a synonym of *H. cuneiformis*.

Hibbertia vestita HAIRY GUINEA FLOWER

A small spreading shrub with thin leaves and yellow flowers. A variable species.

HIBISCUS

MALVACEAE

Shrubs and trees which are native to many countries throughout the world, Hibiscus are grown widely as ornamentals but some are used to produce food, fibre, dyes and medicine. They grow in a wide range of soils and are grown outdoors in climates from temperate to tropical. Hibiscus require regular applications of fertiliser to give top quality blooms over a long period. Most of the cultivars are grown from *H. rosa sinensis*. Pruning benefits flowering. Propagation is from seed and cuttings and by grafting.

Hibiscus calyphyllus

syn. ***H. calycinus***

The large yellow flowers of this tall shrub have a brownish maroon coloured centre.

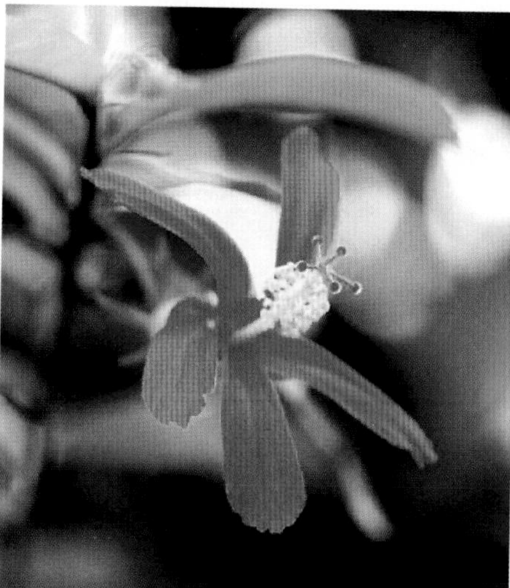

Hibiscus clayii
This bushy shrub has open petalled, red flowers.

Hibiscus coccineus
A deciduous herb-type Hibiscus which has tall branches and large red flowers.

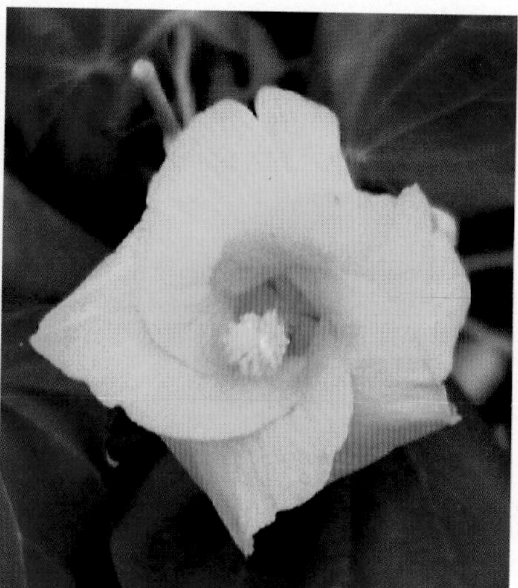

Hibiscus elatus MAHOE
Small and spreading, this Hibiscus has large clear yellow bell-like flowers.

Hibiscus ferrugineus
During warm weather, this tall shrub has small bright pink flowers.

Hibiscus geranioides
A shrubby plant with pink bell shaped flowers.

Hibiscus hamabo
The yellow flowers have a small chocolate coloured centre on this dense, evergreen, tall shrub.

Hibiscus heterophyllus - yellow form
An open crowned tall shrub with prickles and large yellow, pink or apricot coloured flowers.

Hibiscus insularis
NORFOLK ISLAND HIBISCUS
This is a dense medium to tall shrub which is very free flowering, with large flowers coloured cream with a red centre. These flowers change to pink as they age.

Hibiscus ludwigii
This dense, tall, evergreen shrub has large yellow flowers with chocolate coloured centres.

HIBISCUS (cont)

Hibiscus macrophyllus
A small tree with hairy branchlets and foliage. The small bell shaped flowers are yellow. It has very large leaves.

Hibiscus panduriformis
A sparse perennial shrub which has golden coloured bell shaped flowers.

Hibiscus rosa-sinensis cv. **Aloha**
A large flowered cultivar with rosy red flowers, edged old gold.

Hibiscus moscheutos cv. **Southern Bell**
Plate sized pink flowers occur on this woody perennial shrub.

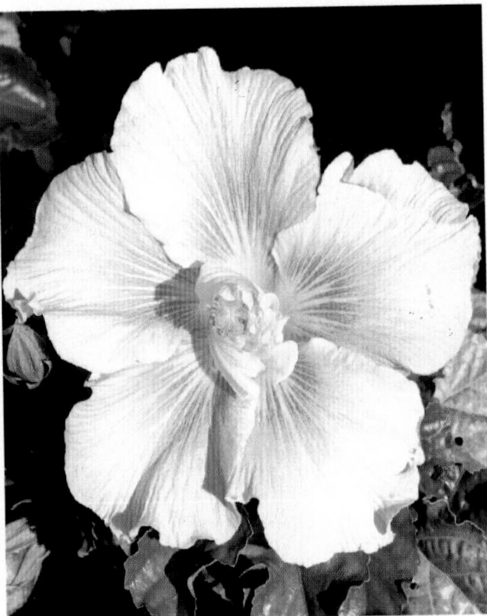

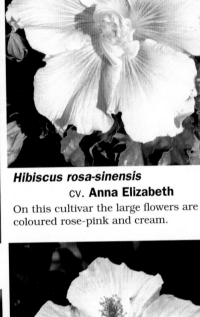

Hibiscus rosa-sinensis cv. **Anna Elizabeth**
On this cultivar the large flowers are coloured rose-pink and cream.

Hibiscus mutabilis COTTON ROSE
A tall free flowering shrub which has pink or pink and white double flowers.

Hibiscus rosa-sinensis
The flowers of this tall shrub are bright red. This Hibiscus is the form from which the following cultivars have evolved.

Hibiscus rosa-sinensis cv. **Annie Wood**
An upright cultivar having large creamy gold flowers with a magenta coloured centre.

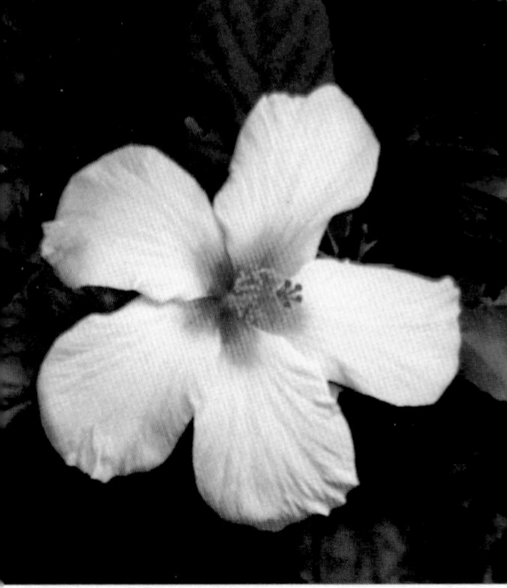

Hibiscus rosa-sinensis cv. **Apple Blossom**
Free flowering, this tall grower has pale pink flowers.

Hibiscus rosa-sinensis cv. **Bookies Brolly**
A medium shrub with large tomato red coloured flowers with pink centres.

Hibiscus rosa-sinensis cv. **Calypso Dancer**
This cultivar has semi-double flowers coloured light orange with pink centres.

Hibiscus rosa-sinensis cv. **Cane Fire**
A large flowered cultivar with bright orange flowers with pinkish red centres.

Hibiscus rosa-sinensis cv. **Catavki**
A medium shrub with large crimson coloured flowers.

Hibiscus rosa-sinensis cv. **Chantai**
A large single flowered cultivar coloured salmon-orange to rose-pink.

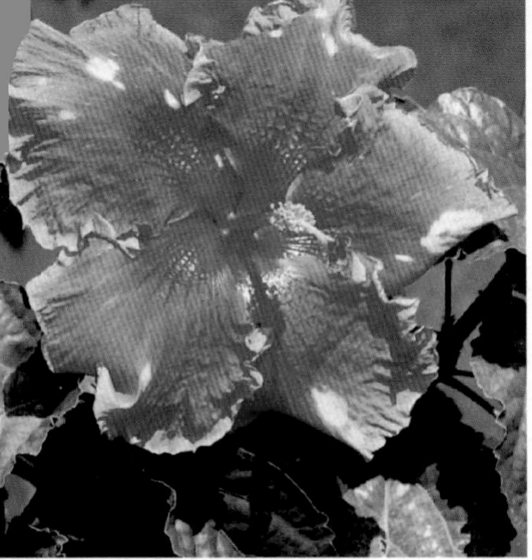

Hibiscus rosa-sinensis cv. **Charles Schmidt**
The large single flowers on this cultivar are coloured orange outside and rosy red inside.

Hibiscus rosa-sinensis cv. **Charles September**
This medium sized shrub has double flowers of bright rose-pink with pale pink edges.

Hibiscus rosa-sinensis cv. **Cooperi Alba**
The variegated leaves are green and white on this tall shrub with medium red flowers.

HIBISCUS (cont)

Hibiscus rosa-sinensis
cv. Cooperi Rose Flake
A showy cultivar grown for its colourful new foliage, coloured pink, red and cream. It has open red flowers.

Hibiscus rosa-sinensis
cv. Copenhagen
This large flowered cultivar has rosy red flowers.

Hibiscus rosa-sinensis
cv. Crimson Ray
A large flowered cultivar which is a compact grower. Flower colour is golden yellow, with a crimson eye.

Hibiscus rosa-sinensis
cv. Crown of Bohemia
A bushy, upright, free branching shrub with double, golden yellow flowers which are overlaid with orange in colder weather.

Hibiscus rosa-sinensis
cv. Crown of Warringah
This is an open crowned shrub with semi-double flowers, coloured apricot.

Hibiscus rosa-sinensis
cv. D.J.O'Brien
The double flowers on this popular old cultivar are coloured orange.

***Hibiscus rosa-sinensis* cv. Erma K.**
A medium growing shrub with double, dark cream flowers.

***Hibiscus rosa-sinensis* cv. Fierylight**
Medium growing, this cultivar has large flowers coloured bright orange with rosy pink centres.

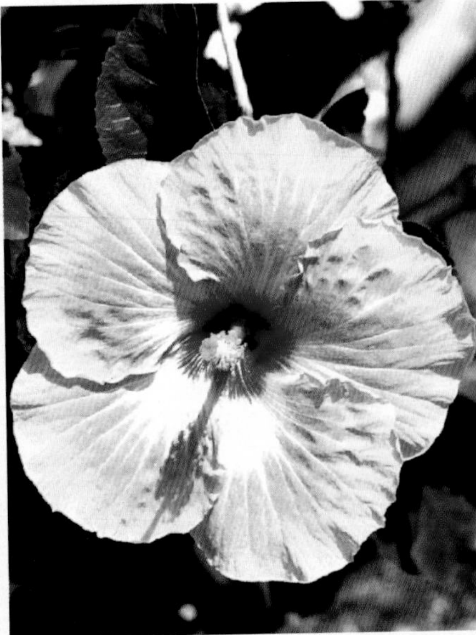

Hibiscus rosa-sinensis
cv. Fifth Dimension
This cultivar has large tri-coloured flowers of dark cream and pale mauve with a red centre. The flower colours are much brighter in hot weather.

Hibiscus rosa-sinensis cv. **Fire Truck**

Free flowering, this medium growing cultivar has large flowers which are bright red.

Hibiscus rosa-sinensis
cv. **Frank's Lady**

A medium sized cultivar with large ruffled flowers coloured bright rose-pink, edged with amber.

Hibiscus rosa-sinensis
cv. **Herm Geller**

An upright growing cultivar with large amber coloured flowers, which have a dark red eye.

Hibiscus rosa-sinensis
cv. **Florida Sunset**

A small growing cultivar with a pale red flower edged with creamish pink to amber.

Hibiscus rosa-sinensis
cv. **Harvest Gold**

The large flowers of this cultivar have crinkled, gold coloured petals and a red eye.

Hibiscus rosa-sinensis
cv. **Herma Garrett**

This large flowered cultivar has semi-double to double flowers coloured yellow, with a red eye.

Hibiscus rosa-sinensis cv. **Frank Green**

This is a low bushy cultivar with double bright orange coloured flowers.

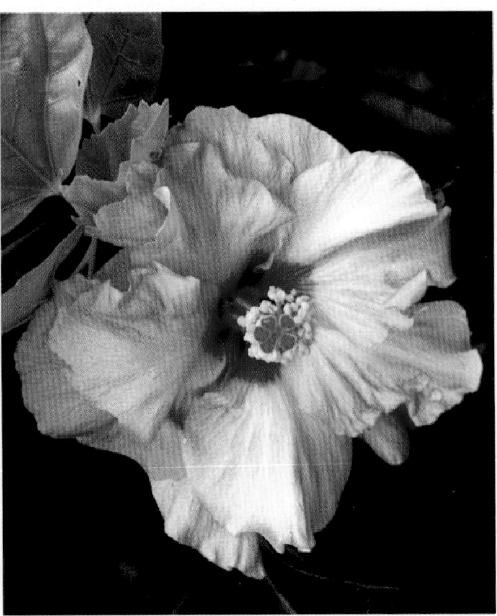

Hibiscus rosa-sinensis
cv. **Isobel Beard**

A medium sized shrub with semi-double flowers of dark lavender with maroon eyes.

HIBISCUS (cont)

***Hibiscus rosa-sinensis* cv. Jay's Orange**
Free flowering, this cultivar has large deep-orange flowers.

***Hibiscus rosa-sinensis* cv. Jol Wright**
A free flowering cultivar with large orange flowers which have cerise centres.

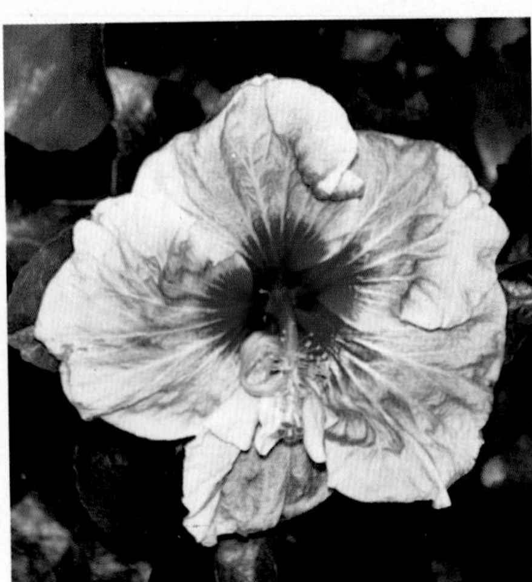

***Hibiscus rosa-sinensis* cv. Lady Adele**
A large flowered cultivar with flowers coloured mauve-grey with crimson centres.

***Hibiscus rosa-sinensis* cv. Lemon Chiffon**
A cultivar with large flowers coloured yellow on the outside and ivory inside.

***Hibiscus rosa-sinensis* cv. Lily Torbert**
A large flowered cultivar with flowers coloured red, overlaid with white.

***Hibiscus rosa-sinensis* cv. Marjorie Beard**
A cultivar with double flowers coloured bright red.

***Hibiscus rosa-sinensis* cv. Marjorie Dollisson**
A cultivar with mauve coloured flowers and deep red centres.

***Hibiscus rosa-sinensis* cv. Mary Wallace**
A small shrub with large flowers coloured orange-red with light orange edges.

***Hibiscus rosa-sinensis* cv. Midnight Frolic**
This cultivar has semi-double flowers of mauve, overlaid with red.

HIBISCUS (cont)

***Hibiscus rosa-sinensis* cv. Mini Mystic**
Flowers are bright pink with a very pale pink edge on this smaller flowered cultiver.

***Hibiscus rosa-sinensis* cv. Miss Kitty**
A free flowering shrub with single lemon-yellow flowers.

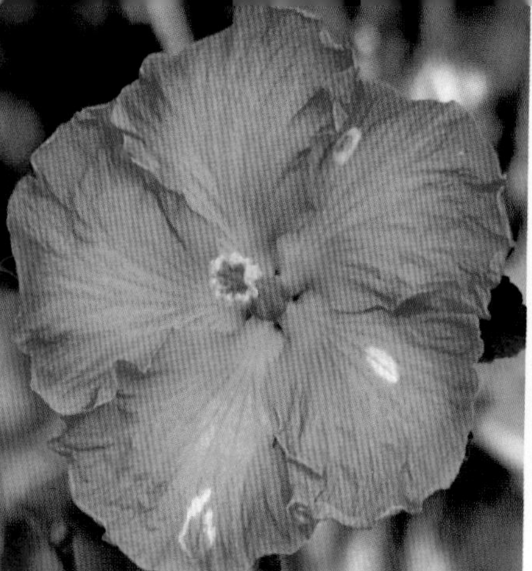

***Hibiscus rosa-sinensis* cv. Monique Maria**
A free flowering cultivar with large pink flowers edged orange.

***Hibiscus rosa-sinensis* cv. Morning Star**
An upright free flowering shrub with large lavender-pink flowers.

***Hibiscus rosa-sinensis* cv. Mrs George Davis**
A tall growing shrub with rose-pink double flowers.

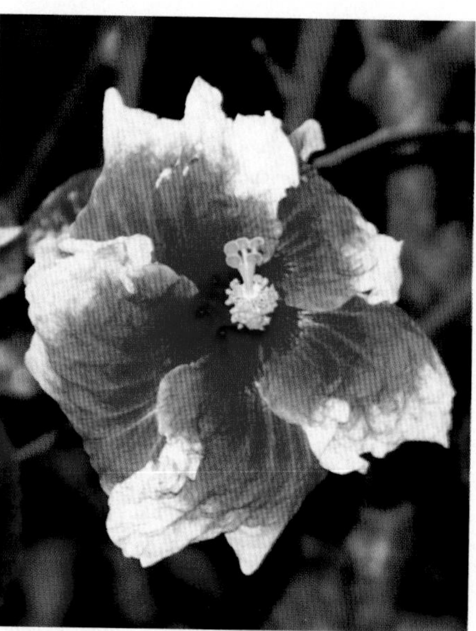

***Hibiscus rosa-sinensis* cv. Mystic Charm**
A tall growing shrub with cerise coloured flowers edged with pale pink.

***Hibiscus rosa-sinensis* cv. Mollie Cummings**
An upright growing cultivar with large bright red flowers.

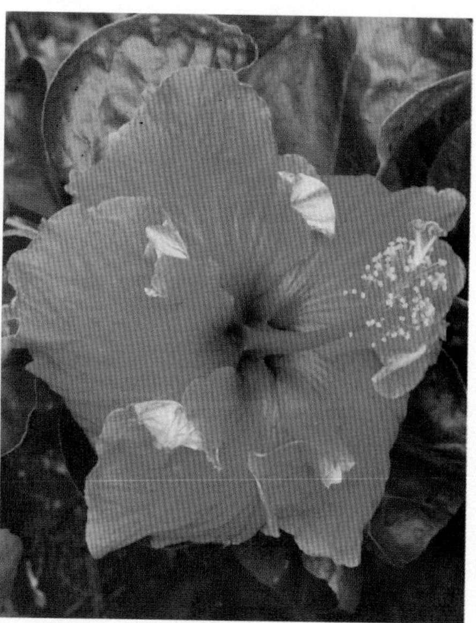

***Hibiscus rosa-sinensis* cv. Nathan Charles**
A cultivar with large ruffled flowers coloured crimson with a darker edge.

HIBISCUS (cont)

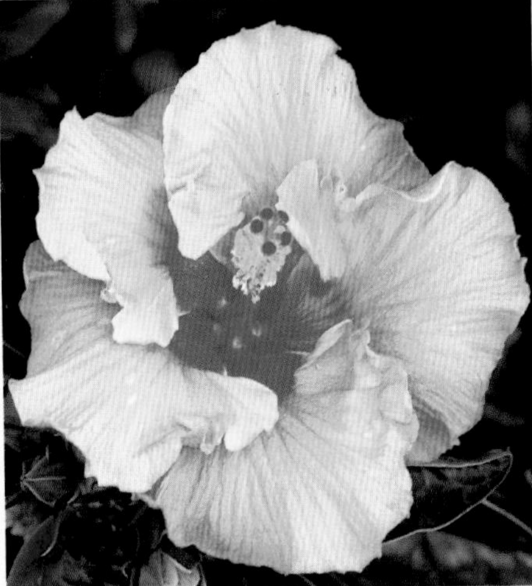

Hibiscus rosa-sinensis cv. **Norma**
A medium growing cultivar with large flowers coloured amber with a deep rose-pink centre.

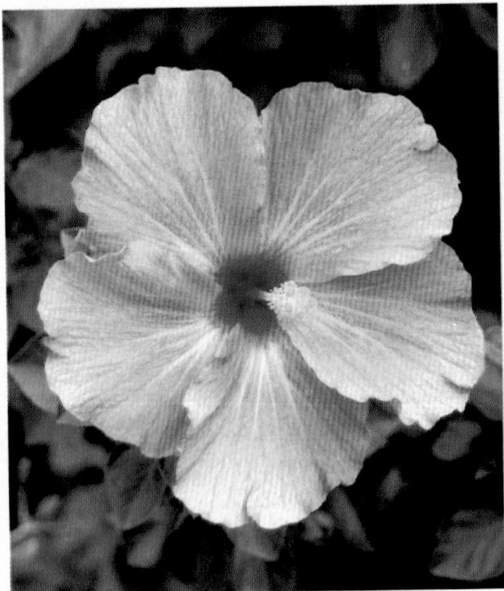

Hibiscus rosa-sinensis cv. **Orange Pride**
A cultivar with large flowers coloured light orange with a magenta eye.

Hibiscus rosa-sinensis cv. **Oyster Pearl**
A large flowered cultivar with flowers coloured rosy purple.

Hibiscus rosa-sinensis cv. **Scarlet Giant**
This upright bushy cultivar has large scarlet coloured flowers.

Hibiscus rosa-sinensis cv. **Silver Rose**
A large flowered cultivar with flower colour being pale pink and bright pink.

Hibiscus rosa-sinensis cv. **Sleeping Single**
A cultivar with large flowers coloured orange-red with an amber edge.

Hibiscus rosa-sinensis cv. **Sun Frolic**
An upright bushy cultivar with flowers coloured apricot-pink to cream, with a cerise eye.

Hibiscus rosa-sinensis cv. **Thelma Bennell**
Flowers are coloured pink to cerise on this large flowered cultivar.

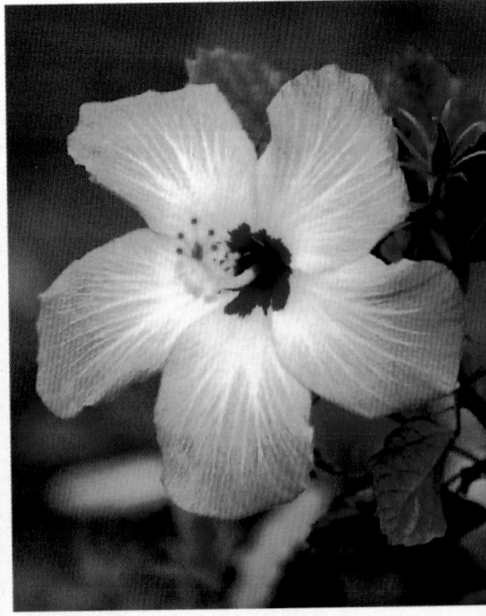

Hibiscus rosa-sinensis cv. **Thumbelina**
A smaller flowered cultivar with single flowers coloured bright pink outside and white inside.

***Hibiscus rosa-sinensis* cv. Tomato Lani**

The large flowers of this cultivar have overlapped petals. Flower colour is deep orange with an apricot edge.

***Hibiscus rosa-sinensis* cv. Topsy**

A large flowered cultivar which is coloured golden orange with a pinky red centre.

***Hibiscus rosa-sinensis* cv. Vasco**

A very spectacular cultivar with large flowers coloured bright yellow with a white centre.

***Hibiscus rosa-sinensis* cv. White Picardy**

A low growing cultivar with large white flowers.

***Hibiscus rosa-sinensis* cv. Wilder's White**

A free flowering tall shrub with large white flowers.

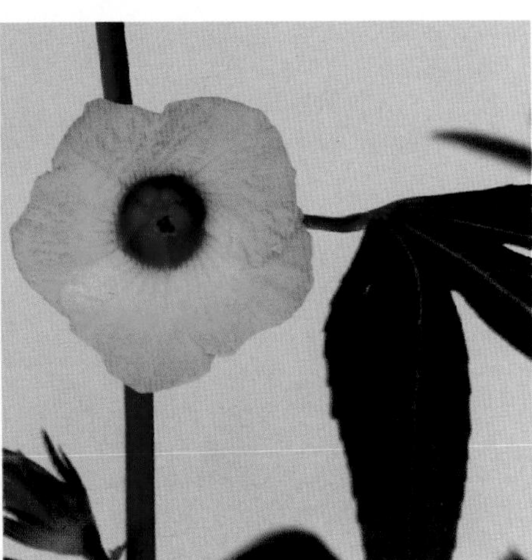

Hibiscus sabdariffa ROSELLA

A sparse growing perennial or annual shrub with creamy pink flowers and maroon seed pods, parts of which are edible and are popular for making jams.

Hibiscus sabdariffa - seed pod

Hibiscus schizopetalus JAPANESE HIBISCUS

A bushy shrub with unusual red flowers which have lace-like petals.

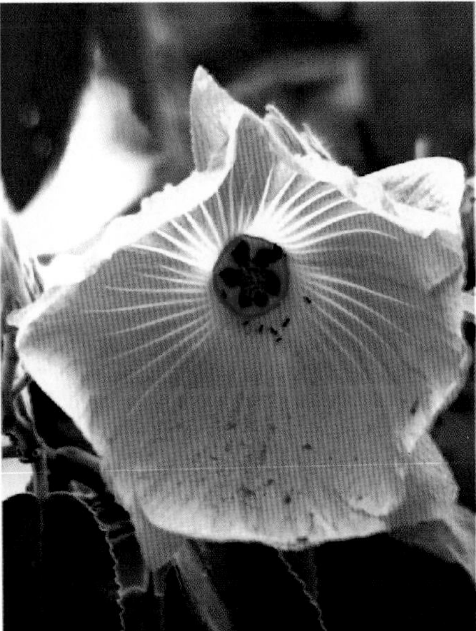

Hibiscus splendens HOLLYHOCK TREE

A sparse tall shrub with greyish leaves and large bright pink flowers.

h

HIBISCUS (cont)

Hibiscus syriacus ROSE OF SHARON
An upright shrub with long flowers coloured mauve with a crimson eye.

Hibiscus syriacus cv. **Double Red**
This bushy cultivar has double flowers coloured deep rose-pink to cerise.

Hibiscus taiwanensis
A tall free flowering bushy shrub with whi flowers which turn to pink as they age.

Hibiscus syriacus cv. **Alba**
A bushy shrub with semi-double white flowers.

Hibiscus tiliaceus COTTON TREE
A small to medium tree which is tolerant of some salt spray. Flowers are coloured bright yellow with a chocolate eye, and turn to deep apricot as they age.

Hibiscus syriacus cv. **Alba Plena**
A cultivar with double white flowers.

Hibiscus syriacus cv. **Woodbridge**
A free flowering cultivar with pink flowers which have a magenta centre.

Hibiscus trionum
A bushy shrub which has cream flowers with a large maroon eye. Better to treat as an annual or biennial shrub.

·IIPTAGE

▪ALPIGHIACEAE

·liptage benghalensis

. tall semi-climbing shrub from South ·ast Asia. It is a highly perfumed ·rnamental with clusters of flowers ·oloured white and yellow. This plant ·refers a climate from warm temperate to ·ropical and will grow in a wide range of ·oils. Propagate from seed and cuttings.

·IOLBOELLIA

.ARDIZABALACEAE

·Iolboellia coriacea

. shiny leaf vine native to China and the ·Iimalayas. Highly perfumed, in cold to ·nild climates it is grown as a cover plant ·or its attractive leaves and mauve and ·vhite flowers. Propagate from seed or ·uttings.

HOLMSKIOLDIA

VERBENACEAE

Sprawling shrubs from Africa and Asia which have long lasting flowers and will grow well in poor and sandy soils. They are widely grown as showy ornamentals in temperate to tropical climates. These plants benefit from pruning after flowering. Propagate from seed and cuttings.

Holmskioldia sanguinea

CHINESE HAT PLANT

An open crowned tall shrub with large clusters of dark orange, long lasting flowers.

Holmskioldia sanguinea

cv. **Mandarin Blue**

A cultivar with bluish mauve flowers.

Holmskioldia sanguinea

cv. **Mandarin Rouge**

This cultivar has red coloured flowers.

Holmskioldia sanguinea

cv. **Mandarin Sunrise**

A popular cultivar with greenish yellow flowers.

Holmskioldia tettensis

A sparse shrub which has pink coloured flowers with violet centres.

HOMORANTHUS

MYRTACEAE

Homoranthus flavescens

A small flattish shrub which is native to Australia. It is grown as a ground cover landscape plant in climates from cool temperate to sub-tropical. The flowers which are coloured greenish yellow may entirely cover the plant. Propagate from seed and cuttings.

HOVEA

FABACEAE [LEGUMINOSAE]

Evergreen shrubs from Australia which are grown for their showy purple to mauve pea shape flowers. They are quite hardy and grow in climates from cool temperate to sub-tropical. Propagate from seed which needs hot water treatment before sowing.

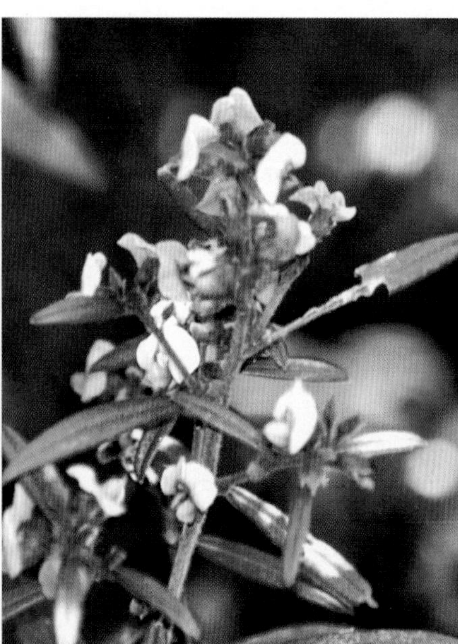

Hovea acutifolia

An upright shrub which has mauve to purple flowers in spring.

Hovea elliptica

An erect shrub with purple pea shaped flowers in spring.

HOYA

ASCLEPIADACEAE

Climbing and twining plants and shrubs which are native to Australia, India, China and the Pacific Islands. They are widely grown indoors as hanging basket plants. When grown outdoors as climbers they need a climate from temperate to tropical. These plants are very hardy and flower at their best when they become pot bound. They will benefit from applications of fertiliser. Propagation for most Hoyas is from cuttings as seed is rare.

Hoya anulata

This plant is grown for its very colourful foliage. Flowers are white and pink.

***Hoya archboldiana* cv. Cream**

A tropical climber with large, cup shaped cream flowers.

***Hoya archboldiana* cv. Pink**

This tropical climber has large bunches of cup shaped pink flowers.

***Hoya archboldiana* cv. Y.M. Excellent**

A red flowered form of this tropical climber.

Hoya australis* ssp. *australis
syn. ***H. keysii***
A twining plant with clusters of white star shaped flowers with cerise inner markings.

Hoya australis* ssp. *sanae
An unusual variation of this popular climber with white flowers.

Hoya australis* spp. *tenuipes
This variation of *H. australis* has white flowers with a red eye.

Hoya bilobata
This is a sparse climber with heads of small red flowers.

Hoya bordenii
A red leaf climber with heads of crimson coloured flowers.

Hoya carnosa
Widely grown, this Hoya does well in temperate climates. It has heads of pink flowers with reddish eyes.

***Hoya carnosa* cv. Little Leaf**
A free flowering cultivar with small leaves and rose-pink flowers with dark eyes.

Hoya calycina* ssp. *calycina 5
This large flowered Hoya has bunches of white flowers with cerise markings in the centre.

HOYA (cont)

Hoya carnosa **cv. Variegata**
The leaves of this cultivar are green and yellow and the flowers are pink with crimson eyes.

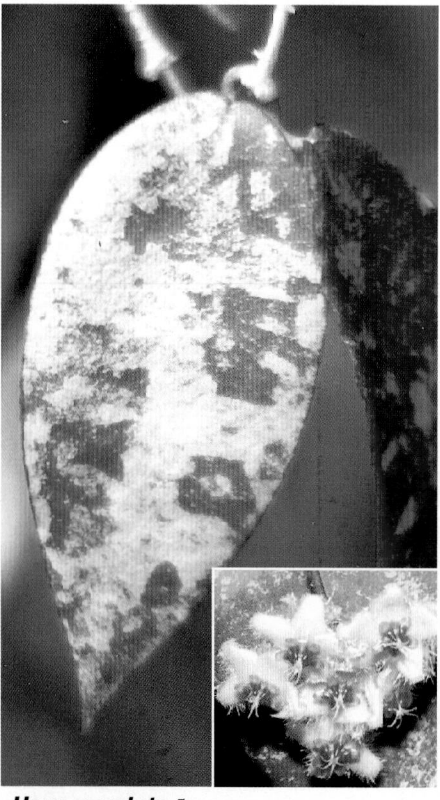

Hoya caudata 5
A Hoya which has showy leaves of reddish purple overlaid with a silvery sheen. Flowers white with red centres.

Hoya cinnamomifolia
This woody vine has yellow flowers with cinnamon coloured eyes.

Hoya compacta **cv. Indian Rope**
A cultivar with twisted leaves. Flowers are pale pinky white with cerise coloured centres.

Hoya compacta **cv. Mauna Loa**
An unusual cultivar with twisted leaves. It has heads of pink flowers.

Hoya compacta **cv. Krinkle 8** 5
This cultivar has large heads of pale pink flowers with a red eye.

Hoya compacta **cv. Regalis**
The leaves of this cultivar are twisted and coloured green, cream and pink. Flowers are pale pink with a cerise centre.

Hoya dischorensis 5
A sparse climber with large heads of cream to pale yellow coloured flowers.

***Hoya* sp. HSI PNG-1** 5
This plant is a sparse climber with heads of small red flowers and does not yet have an official name.

Hoya kentiana 5
Sparse and wiry, this vine has small red flowers in open bunches.

***Hoya* cv. Krimson Princess**
The variegated leaves of this cultivar are green outside, with pale green and cream markings inside. Flowers are dark mauve.

***Hoya* cv. Krimson Queen**
This cultivar has variegated leaves coloured greyish green inside and cream outside. Flowers are dark mauve.

***Hoya lacunosa* cv. Pallidiflora** 5
An open vine with clusters of round white flowers with serrated edges.

Hoya lanceolata* ssp. *bella
syn. ***H. bella***
A small growing Hoya which will grow in mild climates. It has heads of very pale pink flowers with a red eye.

Hoya limoniaca 5
On this wiry vine the roundish bunches of cream coloured flowers have cerise centres.

Hoya macgillivrayi
A twining tropical climber with large red star shaped flowers. This is a very variable Hoya with many different flower colours.

HOYA (cont)

Hoya macgillivrayi 5
cv. **Lankelly Creek**
This variation is from Lankelly Creek near Coen in Queensland and has whitish flowers with a red edge.

Hoya macgillivrayi cv. **Massey River**
A variation from the Massey River area in Queensland which has large red flowers with a white centre.

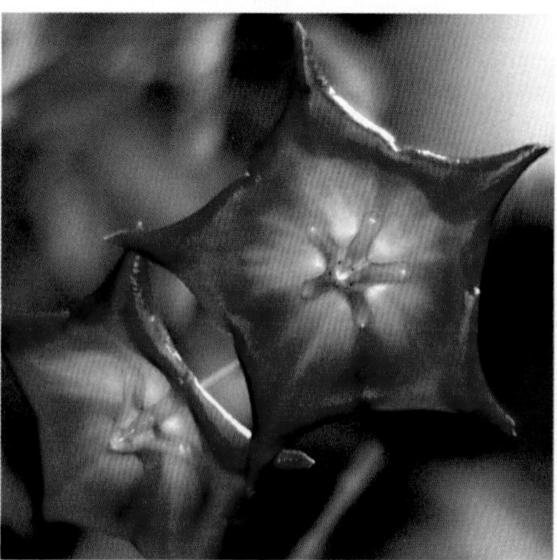

Hoya macgillivrayi
cv. **Nesbit River Valley**
A large flowered variation from the Nesbit River Valley. The flower colour is crimson with a pink centre.

Hoya macrophylla
Grown for its colourful leaves of reddish copper to brown, this is a twining plant.

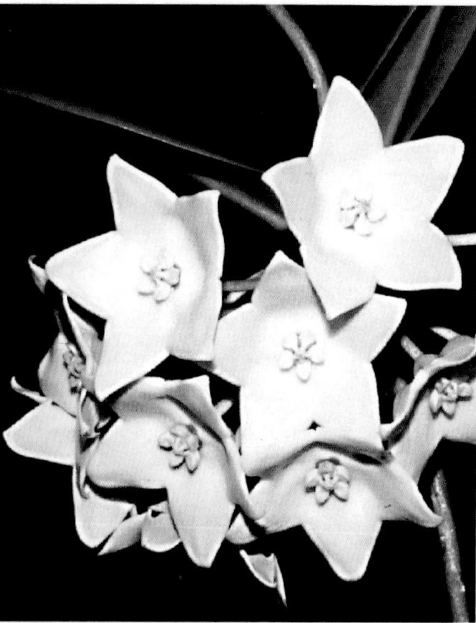

Hoya magnifica 5
A sparse vine with large white flowers.

Hoya membranifolia
This woody climber has clusters of small white flowers.

Hoya motoskei cv. **Thailand White** 5
The flowers of this tropical grower are white with a red centre.

Hoya multiflora cv. **Shooting Star**
A shrubby grower with white and cream coloured flowers.

Hoya pachyclada
With succulent leaves, this slow growing plant has large heads of white waxy flowers.

Hoya padangensis 5
A wiry vine with sparse heads of creamy flowers.

Hoya parasitica cv. **Acuta** 5
syn. ***Hoya acuta***
Clusters of soft apricot-pink coloured flowers bloom on this wiry vine.

Hoya pottsii
syn. ***H. nicholsonii***
A very hardy dense climber which has heads of cream coloured flowers. It is tolerant of light salt spray.

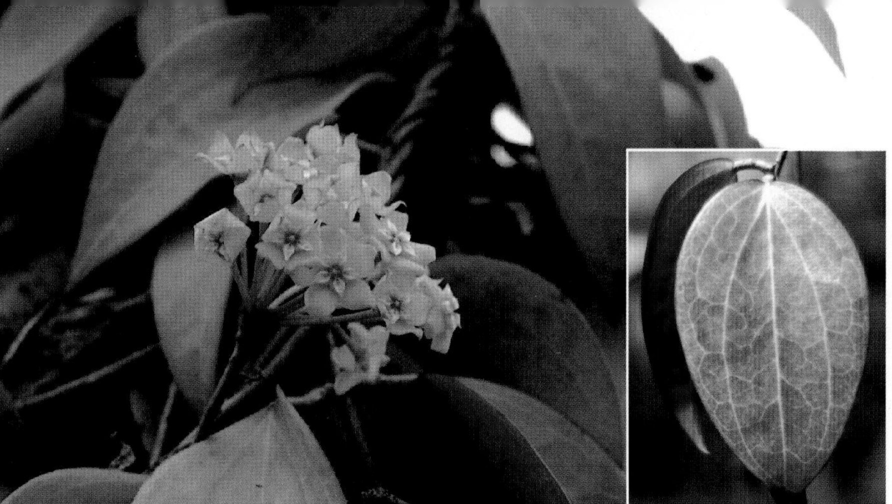

Hoya pottsii cv. **Kuranda**
A cultivar which has varying colour leaves—a typical example is illustrated in insert.

Hoya pottsii cv. **Pascoe River**
This cultivar has reddish maroon coloured leaves and heads of cream flowers.

Hoya pubicalyx cv. **Hawaiian Royal Purple**
A cultivar with large heads of purple coloured flowers which darken with age.

Hoya pubicalyx cv. **Pink Silver**
This free flowering cultivar has pale pink flowers with crimson eyes.

Hoya sussuela
A large flowered Hoya with bright red flowers.

HOYA (cont)

***Hoya* cv. Tricolour**
Vigorous, this Hoya has flowers coloured deep rose-pink with a red centre.

Hoya tsangii
A climber with pale green leaves. It is a heavy flowering plant with clusters of reddish flowers.

Hoya vitiensis 5
An open climber with large dusty pink star shaped flowers.

HYDRANGEA

HYDRANGEACEAE

Deciduous or evergreen shrubs or climbers from Asia and the Americas. They have showy flowers and are widely grown as ornamentals in climates from cold temperate to sub-tropical. These plants prefer a semi-shaded situation and some will have different flower colour if grown in acid or alkaline soil, as this determines the amount of aluminium available to the plants. They are propagated from seed, cuttings or suckers.

Hydrangea aspera
A medium spreading shrub with large heads of flowers coloured white, mauve or pink.

Hydrangea heteromalla
This deciduous shrub has heads of white flowers of which some are sterile and some fertile.

Hydrangea macrophylla
The wide range of *H. macrophylla* cultivars is characterised by a predominance of infertile large flowers. The effect of lime can turn a blue flowered form to pink, and the application of iron sulphate can change a pink cultivar to blue. A neutral soil pH allows the cultivar to retain its normal colour.

***Hydrangea macrophylla* cv. Blue Bonnet**
One of the popular cultivars.

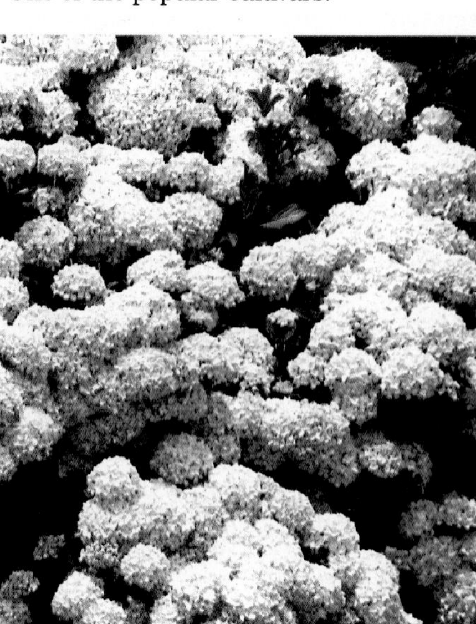

***Hydrangea macrophylla* cv. Blue Ice**
A free flowering cultivar with large heads of pale blue flowers.

Hydrangea macrophylla cv. **Blue Sky**
On this large flowered cultivar only some of the petals are fully formed.

Hydrangea macrophylla cv. **Blue Wave**
A cultivar with blue or bluish violet coloured flowers with only portion of the flowers in the head being fully formed.

Hydrangea macrophylla cv. **Brunegg**
This is a compact growing cultivar with large heads of bright rose-pink coloured flowers.

Hydrangea macrophylla cv. **Freudenstein**
Very large heads of bright pink flowers are carried on this cultivar.

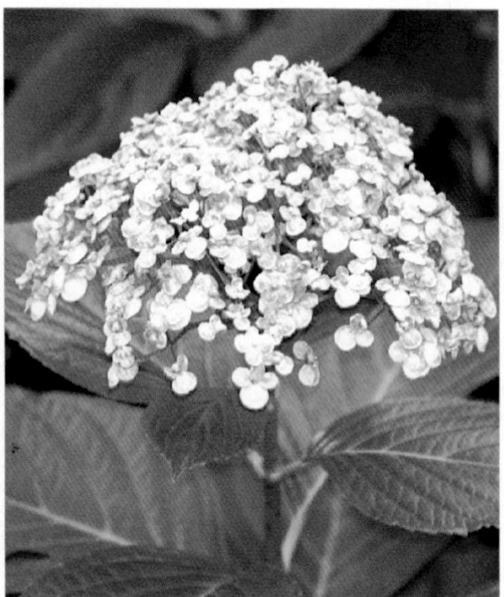

Hydrangea macrophylla cv. **Geisha Girl**
A cultivar with large heads of pink flowers.

Hydrangea macrophylla cv. **Geoffrey Chadbund**
Pinky red flowers bloom in heads on this bushy shrub.

Hydrangea macrophylla cv. **Grant's Choice**
A bushy shrub with large heads of pale pink flowers which are semi-double and partly incurved.

Hydrangea macrophylla cv. **Hamburg**
This bushy shrub has very large heads of flowers coloured pinky red.

HYDRANGEA (cont)

Hydrangea macrophylla cv. **Old Rose**
Hardy, this shrub has large heads of flowers coloured old rose.

Hydrangea macrophylla cv. **Parzival**
An attractive cultivar with large heads of pink flowers which have serrated edges to the petals.

Hydrangea macrophylla cv. **Pink**
This is a popular pink flowered cultivar.

Hydrangea macrophylla cv. **Pink Lady**
A dwarf growing cultivar with pale pink flowers.

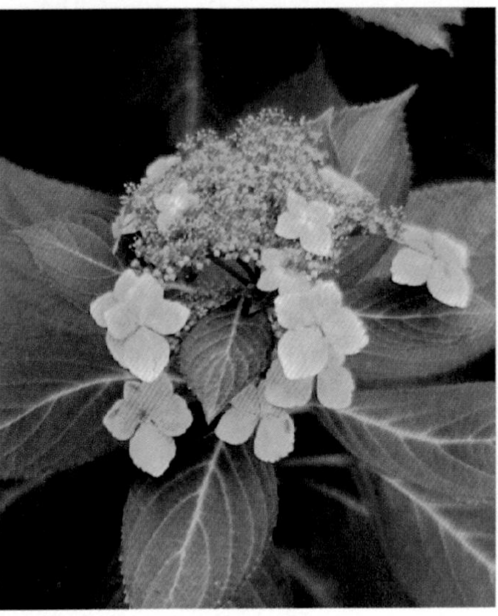

Hydrangea macrophylla cv. **Pink Wave**
On this cultivar the pink flowers are both small and large.

Hydrangea macrophylla cv. **Purple Wave**
Purple-violet flowers bloom in heads on this cultivar.

Hydrangea macrophylla cv. **Purple Rose**
A large flowered cultivar with lavender-violet coloured flowers.

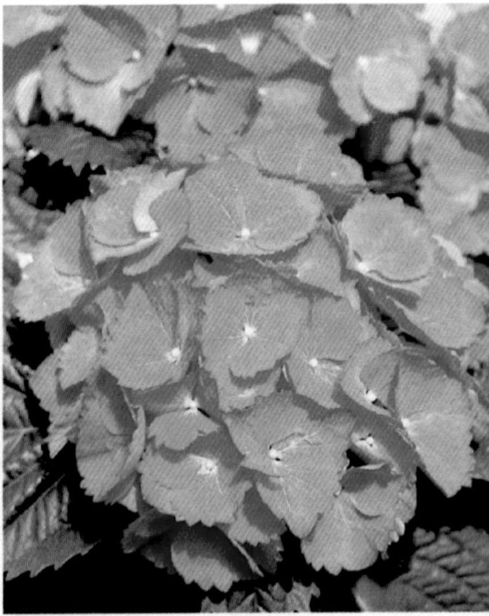

Hydrangea macrophylla cv. **Red Baron**
The deep rose-pink flowers of this free flowering cultivar have serrated petals.

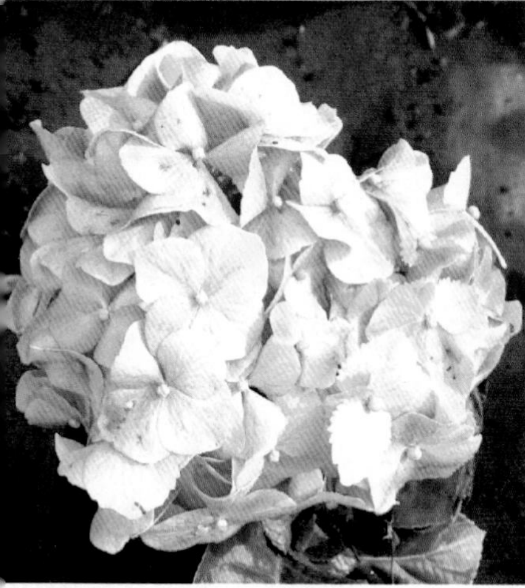

Hydrangea macrophylla cv. **Rose Supreme**
A tall cultivar with large heads of pink flowers.

Hydrangea macrophylla cv. **Sensation**
Very showy, this cultivar has large heads of flowers coloured bright pink, edged with white.

Hydrangea macrophylla cv. **Shower Etaminee**
Only the outer flowers of this cultivar are fully formed. They are coloured bright pink.

Hydrangea macrophylla cv. **Snow Etaminee**
This cultivar has large heads of white flowers.

Hydrangea macrophylla cv. **Tell Rose**
A cultivar with heads of pink flowers which are partly incurved and have small serrations on the petal edges.

Hydrangea macrophylla cv. **(Gèneràle) Vicomtesse De Vibraye**
A free flowering cultivar with large heads of blue flowers.

Hydrangea macrophylla cv. **Variegata**
This cultivar has showy green and white variegated foliage.

Hydrangea macrophylla cv. **Westfalen**
A very heavily flowering plant, the large flowers of this cultivar are red.

HYDRANGEA (cont)

Hydrangea macrophylla cv. **White**
This cultivar has large flower heads of white flowers.

Hydrangea petiolaris
This clumping plant bears heads of white flowers which are both sterile and fertile.

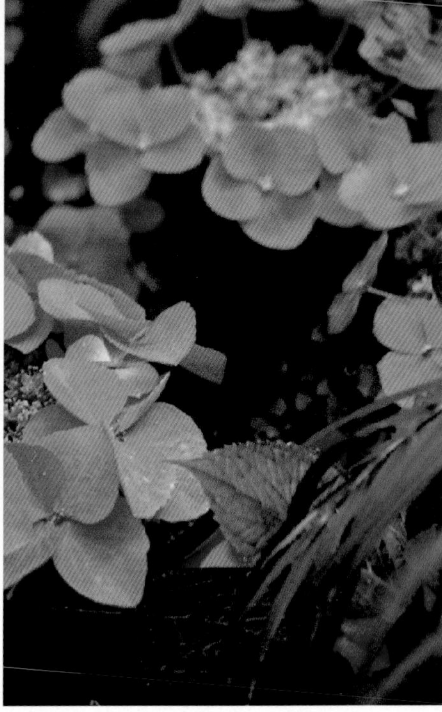

Hydrangea serrata cv. **Preziosa**
A bushy shrub with large heads of cerise-red coloured flowers.

Hydrangea quercifolia
This free flowering shrub has oak-leaf type foliage and white to pale pink flowers.

Hydrangea macrophylla cv. **White**
This illustration shows how the flowers turn to green as they age.

Hydrangea paniculata
A tall deciduous shrub with long flower heads of white flowers which turn pinkish as they age.

HYMENOSPORUM

PITTOSPORACEAE

Hymenosporum flavum

NATIVE FRANGIPANI

A small evergreen tree from Australia which is grown as a showy ornamental for its attractive perfumed cream and yellow flowers. This tree prefers a moist situation and if fertilised, a fertiliser low in phosphorus should be used. It is propagated from seed.

HYPERICUM

Clusiaceae [Guttiferae]

Evergreen or deciduous shrubs and occasionally small trees, native to many countries. Most Hypericums prefer to grow in climates from cool to sub-tropical. They respond well to regular applications of fertiliser and annual pruning. Propagate from seed and cuttings.

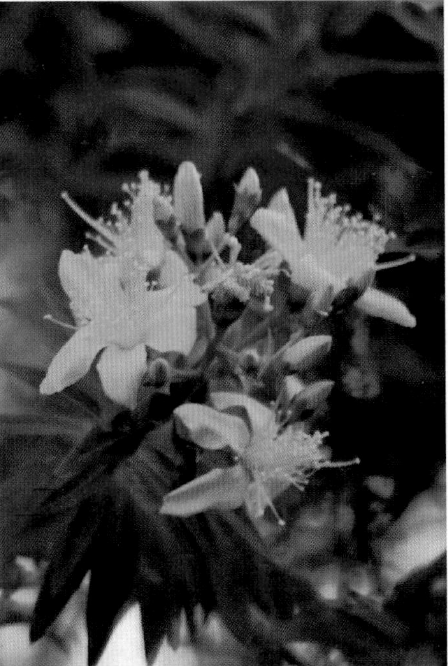

Hypericum canariense
An erect tall shrub with terminal clusters of golden yellow flowers.

Hypericum cerastoides
Very free-flowering, this small shrub has reflexed golden coloured flowers in spring.

Hypericum henryi
Arching branches and large heads of yellow flowers feature on this bushy shrub.

Hypericum kalmianum
A bushy shrub with large heads of yellow flowers.

Hypericum monogynum
This bushy shrub has spreading branches and terminal clusters of yellow flowers.

***Hypericum* x *moserianum* cv. Tricolor**
Low growing and spreading, this shrub has leaves of green, cream and pink. The flowers are yellow.

Hypericum oblongifolium
A medium shrub with arching branches and clusters of yellow flowers.

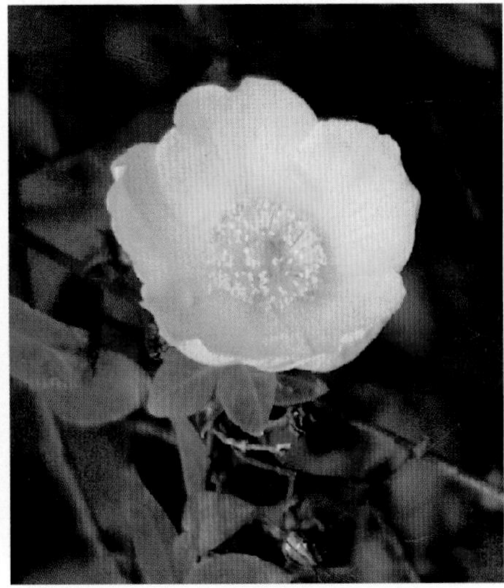

***Hypericum* cv. Rowallane**
On this sparse upright shrub, the cup-type flowers are golden yellow.

HYPOCALYMMA

MYRTACEAE

Small free branching shrubs with evergreen foliage from Western Australia. They are grown as flowering ornamentals and most prefer sandy well drained soils. Propagate from seed or softwood cuttings.

Hypocalymma angustifolium

WHITE MYRTLE

A small shrub with colourful red buds all along the small branches. These buds open to white fluffy flowers.

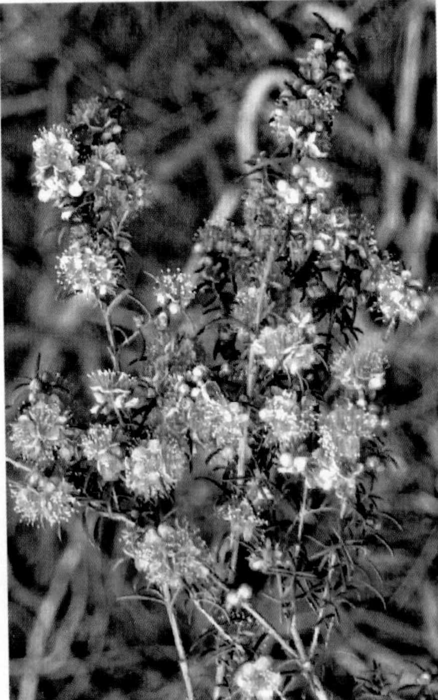

Hypocalymma robustum

SWAN RIVER MYRTLE

This small shrub has small leaves and attractive bright pink flowers.

HYPOESTES

ACANTHACEAE

Small shrubs from South East Asia, Africa, Madagascar and Australia. They grow in climates from temperate to tropical and are grown as outdoor and indoor plants. They prefer a rich soil and benefit from pruning if they become lanky. Propagate from seed and cuttings.

Hypoestes aristata RIBBON BUSH

A compact free flowering bushy plant with violet-cerise coloured flowers.

Hypoestes phyllostachya cv. **Persuasion Pink**

A cultivar which has leaves coloured olive-green with pink markings.

Hypoestes phyllostachya cv. **Persuasion Red**

This cultivar has leaves coloured rosy red with olive-green markings.

Hypoestes phyllostachya POLKA DOT PLANT; FRECKLE FACE

A small shrub which is grown for its showy leaves which are marked with pink dots.

HYPOESTES (cont)

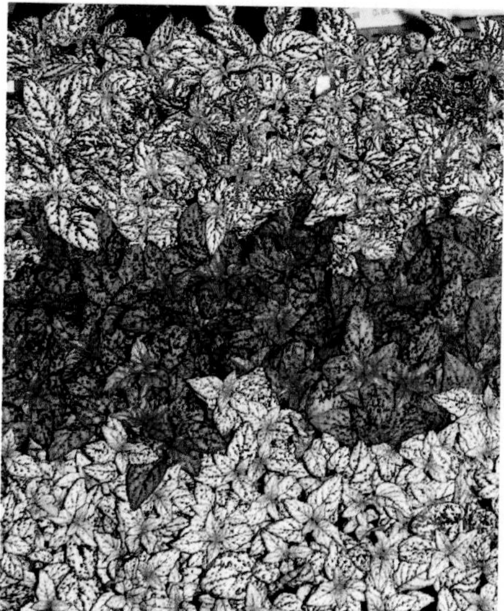

***Hypoestes phyllostachya* CV. Persuasion Series**
A range of new cultivars with various coloured leaves.

***Hypoestes phyllostachya* CV. Persuasion White**
A cultivar which has green leaves with white markings.

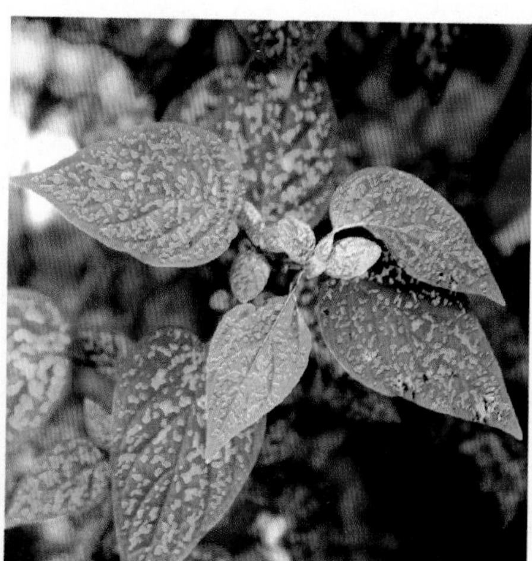

***Hypoestes phyllostachya* CV. Ruby Red**
A cultivar with red markings on the green leaves.

ILEX

HOLLY

AQUIFOLIACEAE

Mostly evergreen shrubs and trees which are native to Asia and North and South America. They are grown as ornamentals for their showy leaves or berries and are widely used by florists. A tea-like drink is also made from one of the Ilex. These plants are mostly grown in cool and cold climates. Propagate from seed and cuttings.

***Ilex* x *altaclerensis* CV. Golden King**
An award winning cultivar which is grown for its leaves which are coloured dark green, light green and yellow.

***Ilex* x *altaclerensis* CV. Lawsoniana**
On this cultivar the variegated leaves are coloured green, yellow and cream.

Ilex aquifolium ENGLISH HOLLY
A small tree which has prickly leaves and small white flowers followed by red berries.

***Ilex aquifolium* CV. Argentea Marginata**
The prickly variegated leaves of this cultivar are coloured green and cream.

***Ilex aquifolium* CV. Ferox Argentea**
A variegated leaf cultivar with prickly green leaves edged pale cream to white.

ILEX (cont)

Ilex aquifolium **cv. Flavescens**
This cultivar has golden yellow leaves.

Ilex aquifolium **cv. Silver Queen**
A cultivar with variegated leaves coloured green and cream.

Ilex **x *koehneana***
A small hybrid evergreen tree with spiny leaves. It has small white flowers followed by bright red berries.

Ilex aquifolium **cv. Golden Milkboy**
A cultivar with leaves mostly gold in colour, with some green.

Ilex cornuta
This is a small tree, with prickly green leaves, grown for its showy red berries.

Ilex aquifolium **cv. Handsworth New Silver**
Variegated leaves of this cultivar are coloured green and cream.

Ilex crenata **cv. Golden Gem** GOLDEN BOX-LEAVED HOLLY
The leaves of this tall bushy shrub are green and yellow in colour.

ILLICIUM

ILLICIACEAE

Evergreen small trees and shrubs native to Asia and North America. They are grown as ornamentals, in climates from very cold temperate to sub-tropical. Propagation is mostly from cuttings.

Illicium anisatum JAPANESE ANISE
A small evergreen tree with highly perfumed cream flowers. This tree is used for religious purposes.

ILLICIUM (cont)

Illicium floridanum 2 PURPLE ANISE
A tall shrub with reddish brown flowers in spring.

INDIGOFERA

FABACEAE [LEGUMINOSAE]

Shrubs and small trees from many countries of the world in climates from cool temperate to tropical. They are grown as ornamentals, as small shade trees for tropical crops and for the production of indigo dye. Propagate from seed.

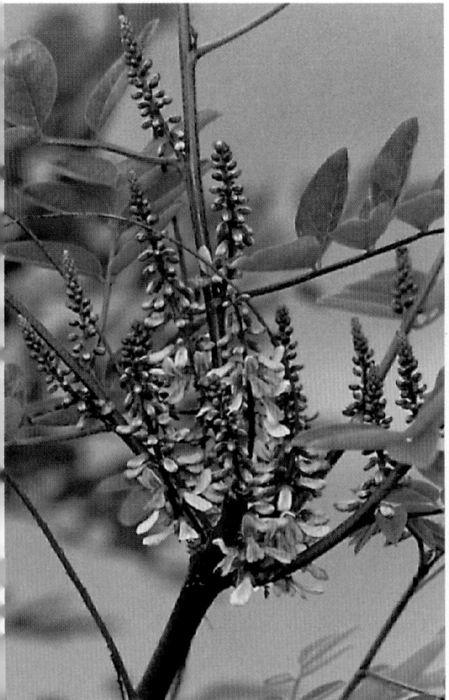

Indigofera amblyantha
A sparse small tree with spike-type bunches of cerise-violet coloured flowers.

Indigofera australis AUSTRAL INDIGO
An evergreen shrub with racemes of flowers from pink to pinky cerise in colour.

Indigofera balfouriana
A sparse tall shrub with erect flower spikes of purple-cerise coloured flowers.

Indigofera decora
syn. ***I. incarnata***
A small spreading shrub with pendulous racemes of deep rose-pink flowers.

Indigofera tinctoria
A bushy spreading tall shrub which has upright spikes of rosy pink flowers.

INGA

MIMOSACEAE [LEGUMINOSAE]

Evergreen shrubs and trees from tropical America which are grown as ornamentals or as food in warm temperate to tropical climates. Propagate from seed which must be planted within a month of maturity.

Inga edulis ICE CREAM BEAN
A small broad crowned tree which has large clusters of white flowers followed by large bean shape seed pods.

Inga edulis - seed pods
The pulp around the seeds in these pods is soft, looks like ice cream and is edible.

INGA (cont)

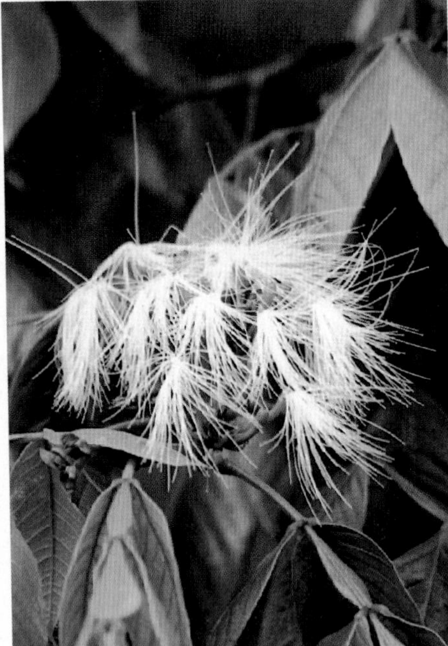

Inga spectablis
A small spreading tree with large heads of white flowers which may at times cover the whole tree.

IOCHROMA

Solanaceae

Shrubs and small trees from tropical South America. They are grown in climates from temperate to tropical as ornamental plants. Propagate from seed and cuttings.

Iochroma coccinea
An upright, medium to tall shrub with heads of orange-red tubular flowers.

Iochroma cyaneum
syn. ***I. tubulosum***
This tall shrub has pendulous heads of violet coloured tubular flowers.

Iochroma cyaneum cv. **Alba**
A cultivar which has white tubular flowers.

Iochroma cyaneum cv. **Apricot Belle**
On this cultivar the pendulous heads of bell-type flowers are apricot in colour.

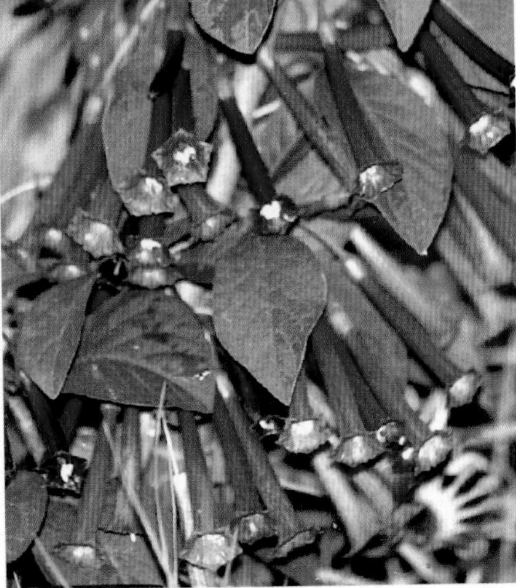

Iochroma grandiflora
A tropical shrub with pendulous bunches of purple tubular flowers.

Iochroma grandiflora cv. **Woodcote White**
This cultivar has pinky white flowers.

Iochroma warscewiczii
A tall shrub with large pendulous heads of violet-blue flowers.

IPOMOEA

CONVOLVULACEAE

Climbing and twining plants or shrubs which are native to many countries world wide and grow in a wide range of climates. Some Ipomoea species may become weeds in ideal conditions away from their native habitat while others are showy ornamentals. Propagation is from seeds and cuttings.

Ipomoea alba MOONFLOWER
syn. ***Calonyction aculeatum***
A large leaf climber with perfumed white flowers which open at night.

***Ipomoea alba* cv. Giant White**
GIANT MOONFLOWER
syn. ***I. alba* cv. Grandiflora**
This cultivar has very large flowers.

Ipomoea cairica RAILWAY CREEPER
syn. ***I. palmata***
A sparse twining plant with masses of large bluish lavender flowers. It can become a weed in some instances.

***Ipomoea cairica* cv. Alba**
The white flowers of this cultivar are large.

***Ipomoea cairica* cv. Red Eye**
A cultivar which has white flowers with a red eye.

Ipomoea carnea* ssp. *fistulosa
Over a long period, this upright shrub to semi-climber has large heads of showy pink flowers.

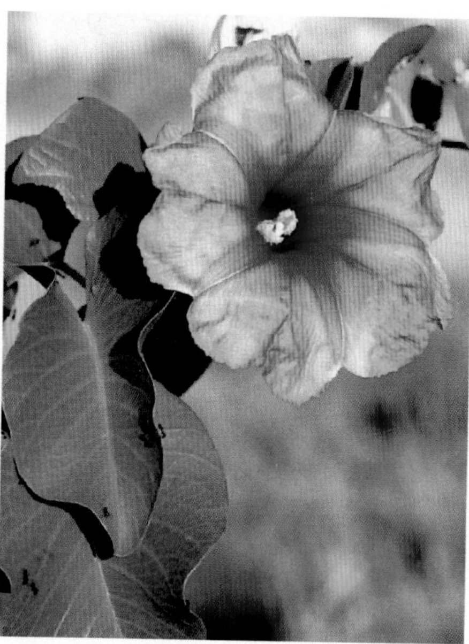

Ipomoea costata
A spreading tropical vine with large flowers coloured rose-pink to cerise.

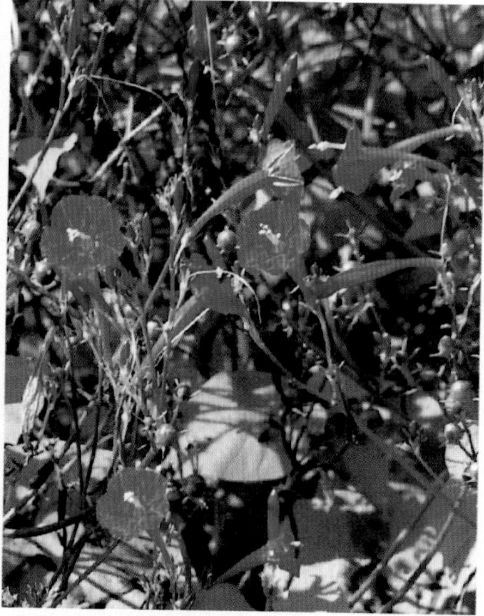

Ipomoea hederifolia
Bright red trumpet-like flowers bloom on this delicate climber.

IPOMOEA (cont)

Ipomoea horsfalliae CARDINAL CREEPER
A twining evergreen which needs a warm climate. It has large clusters of dark-red flowers.

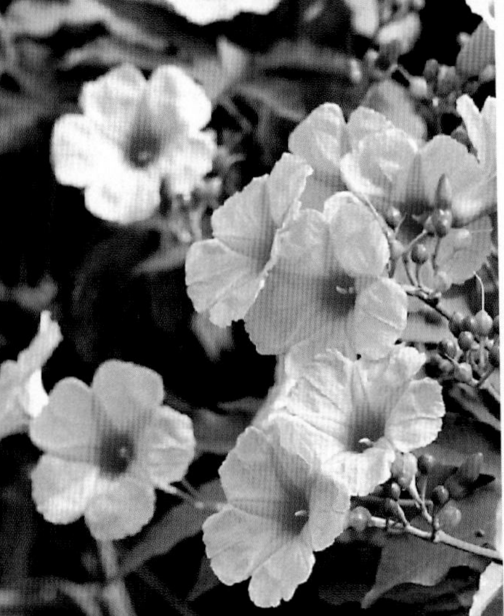

Ipomoea mauritiana
syn. ***I. digitata***
Dense and upright, this shrubby climber has large clusters of deep rose-pink flowers.

Ipomoea purpurea cv. **Caerulea**
This cultivar has blue coloured flowers.

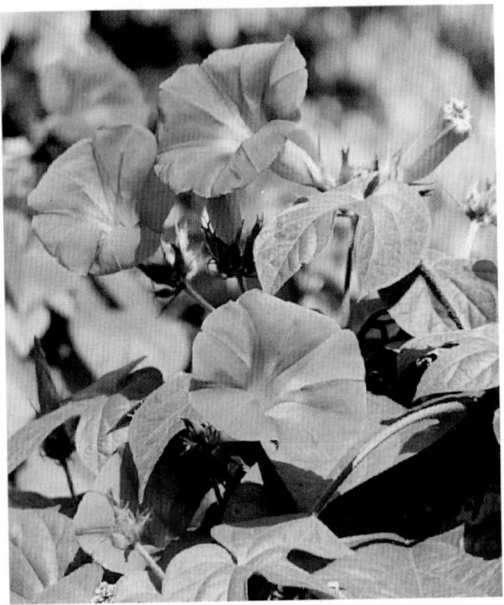

Ipomoea indica BLUE DAWN FLOWER
syn. ***I. acuminata***
This is a spreading climber with large blue flowers.

Ipomoea pes-caprae
BEACH MORNING GLORY
Showy heads of large rose-pink and cerise coloured flowers bloom on this spreading climber which grows along beaches.

Ipomoea quamoclit
syn. ***Quamoclit pennata***
Often grown as an annual, this small fine leaf vine has large quantities of bright red flowers.

Ipomoea indica cv. **Purple Fancy**
A cultivar with rosy purple flowers.

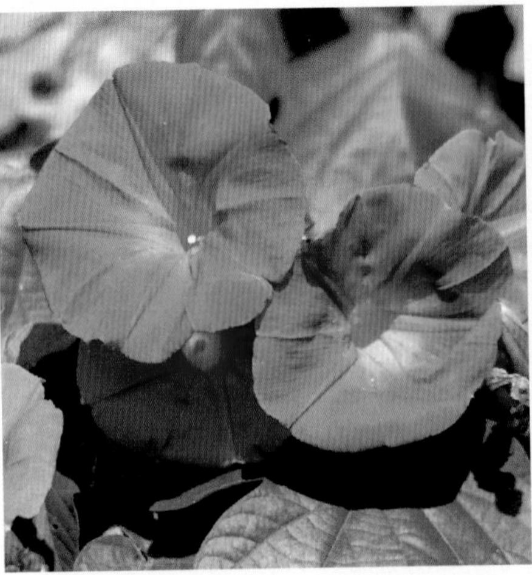

Ipomoea purpurea MORNING GLORY
A climbing spreading plant with clusters of large purple coloured flowers.

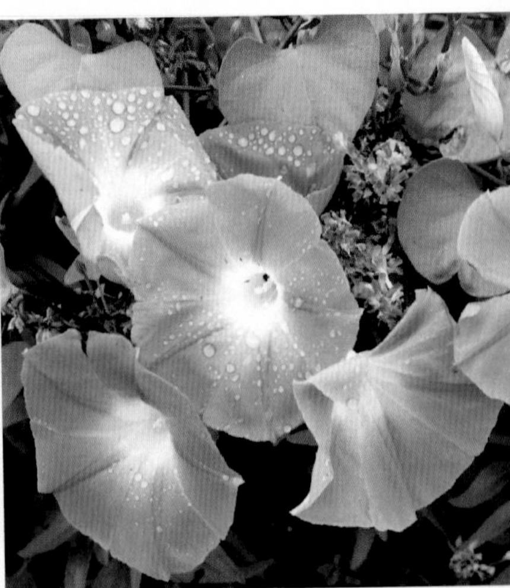

Ipomoea tricolor cv. **Heavenly Blue**
A sparse twining vine which has large sky blue flowers.

ISOPLEXIS

SCROPHULARIACEAE

Free flowering evergreen shrubs which are grown in warm to mild climates as ornamentals. Native to the Canary Islands, they prefer well drained soils with adequate water in hot weather, and regular fertilizing. Propagate from seed and tip cuttings under mist.

Isoplexis canariensis

A showy evergreen shrub with tall spikes of golden coloured flowers.

Isoplexis sceptrum

This is a very colourful evergreen shrub with tall spikes of orange coloured flowers.

ISOPOGON

PROTEACEAE

Evergreen ornamental shrubs native to Australia, they are grown as landscape ornamentals in climates from cold temperate to sub-tropical, in well drained soils. Isopogons are also widely used by florists. Propagate from seed and cuttings.

Isopogon anemonifolius

BROAD LEAF DRUMSTICKS

Seed pods which resemble drumsticks follow the terminal yellow flowers on this small shrub.

Isopogon axillaris

This small shrub has delicate heads of pale pink flowers.

Isopogon baxteri

The large flower heads of this small shrub are composed of pink silky flowers.

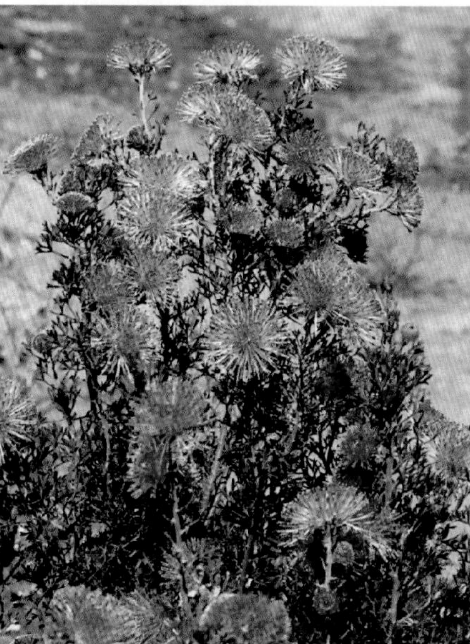

Isopogon dubius

PIN CUSHION CONEFLOWER

A fine leaf shrub with large terminal rose-pink flowers.

Isopogon dubius - flower

ISOPOGON (cont)

Isopogon formosus ROSE CONEFLOWER
Small and open, this shrub has showy rose-pink coloured flowers.

Isopogon latifolius
BROAD LEAF CONEFLOWER
A broad leaf small shrub with bright rose-pink coloured flowers.

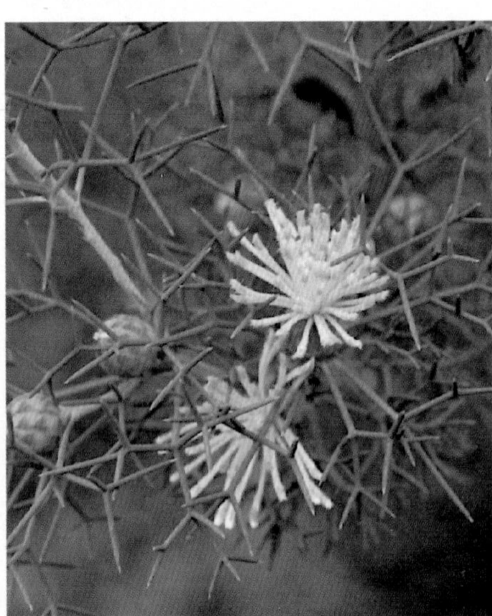

Isopogon teretifolius
NODDING CONEFLOWER
With prickly leaves, this shrub has yellow or pink coloured flowers.

IXORA

RUBIACEAE

Evergreen tropical shrubs which are grown as showy flowering ornamentals. They prefer a rich soil, plenty of water and a sub-tropical or tropical climate. Propagate from cuttings.

Ixora casei
syn. ***I. duffii***
A medium shrub with very large heads of orange-red flowers.

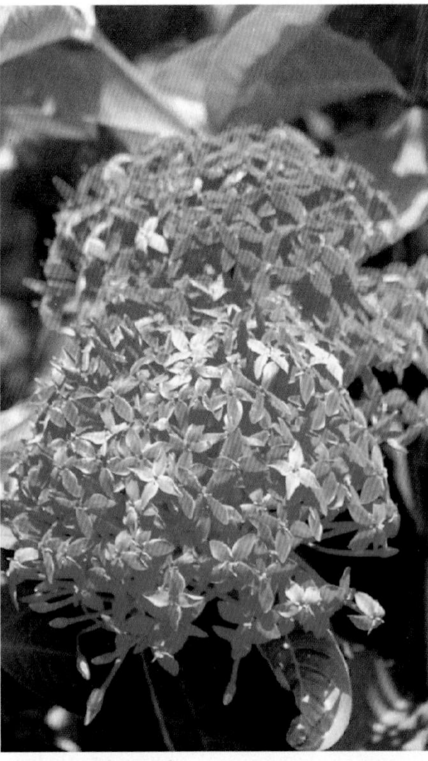

Ixora chinensis PRINCE OF ORANGE
On this medium shrub the very large showy flower heads are orange.

Ixora chinensis cv. **Alba**
A cultivar which has white flowers.

Ixora chinensis cv. **Apricot Queen**
Large heads of apricot coloured flowers bloom on this cultivar.

Ixora chinensis cv. **Lutea**
A cultivar with large heads of amber-yellow coloured flowers.

IXORA (cont)

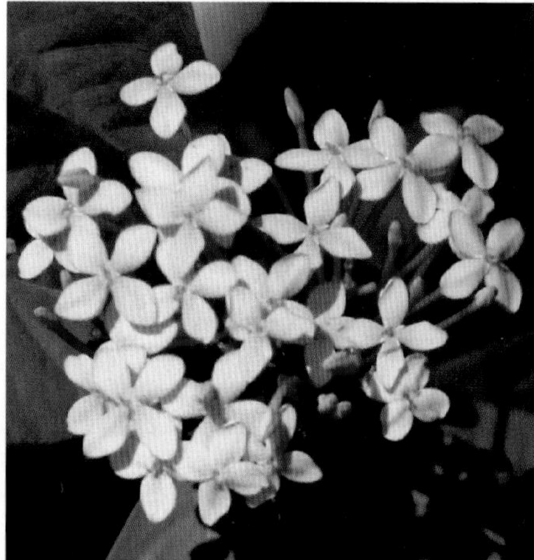

***Ixora chinensis* cv. Sunset**

This cultivar has heads of light orange coloured flowers.

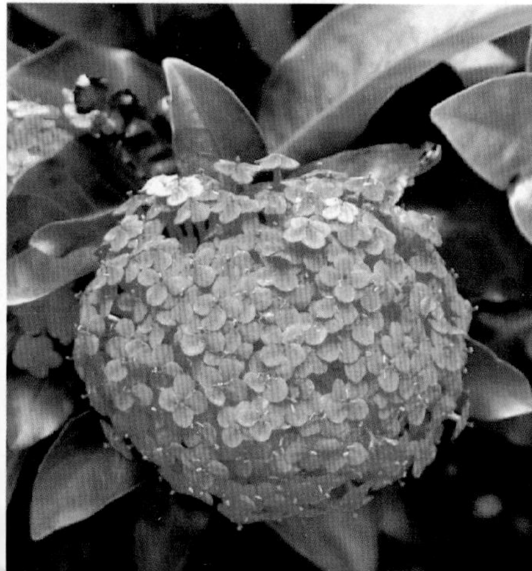

Ixora coccinea FLAME OF THE WOODS

Very showy, this shrub has very large heads of bright orange flowers.

Ixora coccinea* var. *rosea

syn. ***I. coccinea*** cv. **Rosea**

The large heads of this showy variety are coloured rose-pink.

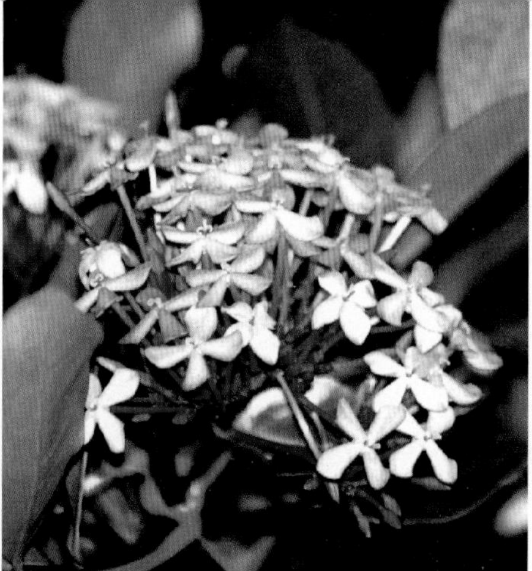

***Ixora* cv. Candy Pink**

A bushy upright cultivar which has large heads of bright rose-pink coloured flowers.

***Ixora* cv. Coral**

Compact and dense, this shrub has flattish heads of orange coloured flowers.

***Ixora* cv. Coral Fire**

A medium shrub with heads of deep rose-pink coloured flowers.

***Ixora finlaysoniana* cv. Rosea**

SIAMESE IXORA

A pink flowered cultivar of this medium sized shrub which normally has white flowers.

***Ixora* cv. Golden Ball**

This upright shrub has semi-round heads of amber-yellow coloured flowers.

Ixora hookeri

syn. ***I. odorata***

A free flowering shrub with heads of rose-pink flowers.

IXORA (cont)

Ixora malabarica

A medium shrub with heads of white flowers.

***Ixora* cv. Orange Glow**

On this free flowering shrub the flowers are bright orange.

***Ixora* cv. Pink Delight**

A cultivar which has heads of deep rose-pink flowers.

***Ixora* cv. Pink Malay**

Upright and evergreen, this shrub has large heads of pink flowers.

***Ixora* cv. Raywoods White**

Heads of white flowers bloom on this open crowned shrub.

***Ixora* cv. Sunkist**

A dwarf growing plant with large heads of pink flowers.

***Ixora* cv. Sunkist Pink**

This dwarf Ixora has large heads of pale pink flowers.

***Ixora* cv. Sunny Gold**

A dwarf compact shrub with round heads of orange-amber coloured flowers.

***Ixora* cv. Thai King**

This is a medium shrub with heads of large orange-red flowers.

JACARANDA

Bignoniaceae

Free flowering shrubs and trees from the Caribbean and South America. Jacarandas are widely grown as showy ornamental features or street trees in climates from mild temperate to tropical. These plants prefer a good quality soil and plenty of water in hot weather. They are mostly propagated from seed, with grafting being the method of growing cultivars. *J. mimosifolia* is the variety used for the grafting rootstock.

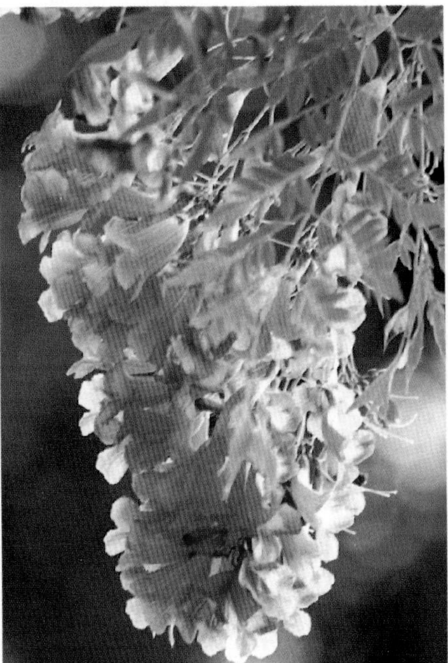

Jacaranda atrolilacina

This showy flowering tree has pendulous heads of pale lilac-mauve flowers in spring.

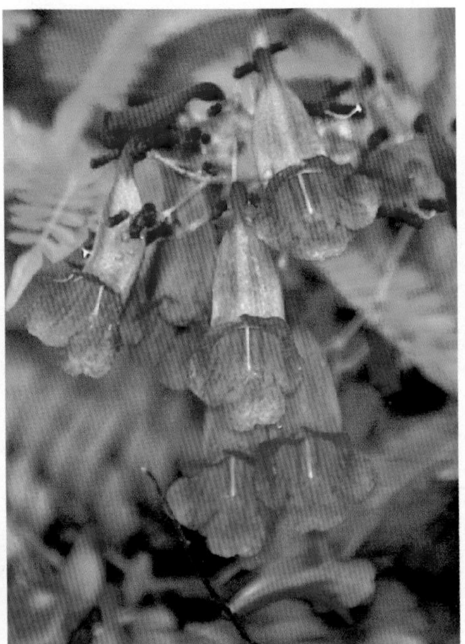

Jacaranda caerulea

An evergreen small upright tree with very large clusters of purplish blue flowers in late spring.

Jacaranda caroba

This evergreen tall shrub to small tree has large heads of maroon flowers in summer.

Jacaranda chelonia

In spring this medium spreading tree has showy heads of pinkish violet coloured flowers. Some authorities list this as synonymous with *J. mimosifolia.*

Jacaranda decurrens

An upright semi-evergreen small tree with large heads of blue flowers in late spring.

Jacaranda mimosifolia

This small to medium semi-evergreen tree has very large heads of bluish mauve flowers in late spring.

***Jacaranda mimosifolia* cv. Rosea**

Mauvish pink flowers occur in late spring on this showy cultivar.

***Jacaranda mimosifolia* cv. Variegata**

This cultivar has green and yellow variegated leaves with bluish mauve flowers.

JACARANDA (cont)

***Jacaranda mimosifolia* cv. Violet Candles**

A cultivar with long upright flower spikes of violet coloured flowers.

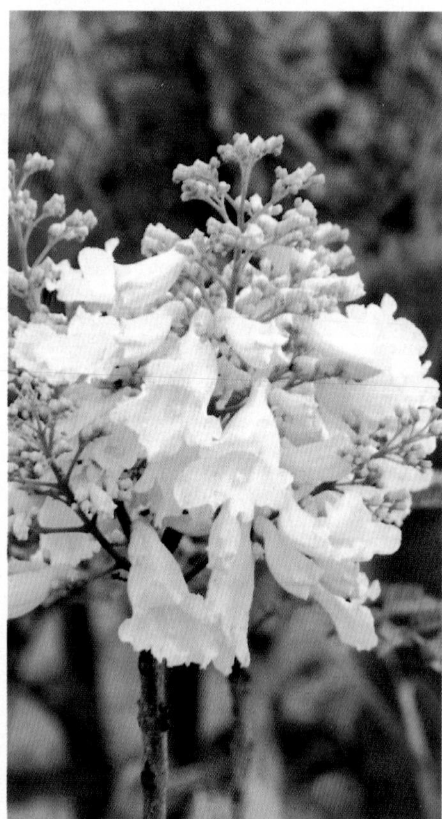

***Jacaranda mimosifolia* cv. White Christmas**

In early summer, this cultivar has large heads of white flowers.

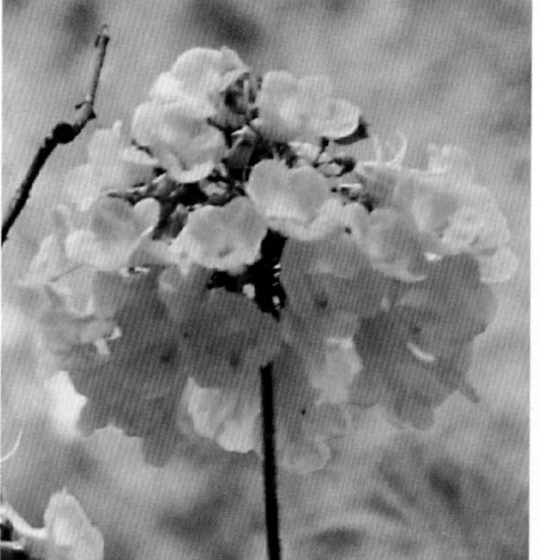

Jacaranda obtusifolia

Small and spreading, this tree has large heads of lavender-blue flowers in late spring.

Jacaranda semiserrata

A tall to medium tree with large heads of magenta coloured flowers in summer.

JACKSONIA

FABACEAE [LEGUMINOSAE]

Jacksonia scoparia AUSTRALIAN DOGWOOD

A tall, thin leaf shrub from Australia, it has large clusters of gold coloured flowers in spring. This plant tolerates poor soils and is propagated from seed which needs hot water treatment.

JAGERA

SAPINDACEAE

Jagera pseudorhus FOAM BARK

A small evergreen Australian tree which is grown as an ornamental for its showy orange coloured fruit. The bark of the tree foams in heavy rain. Propagate from seed.

JAMESIA

HYDRANGEACEAE

Jamesia americana CLIFFBUSH

A deciduous shrub which is native to North America. It has white flowers in small bunches and prefers a moderately rich well drained soil. Propagate from seed and tip cuttings under mist.

JASMINUM

JASMINE

OLEACEAE

Evergreen or semi-evergreen shrubs and climbers which are native to Africa, Australia, South and East Asia. Jasmine are widely grown for their distinct perfume and their showy flowers. They grow in a wide range of soils in climates from cool temperate to tropical. Propagation is from seed and cuttings.

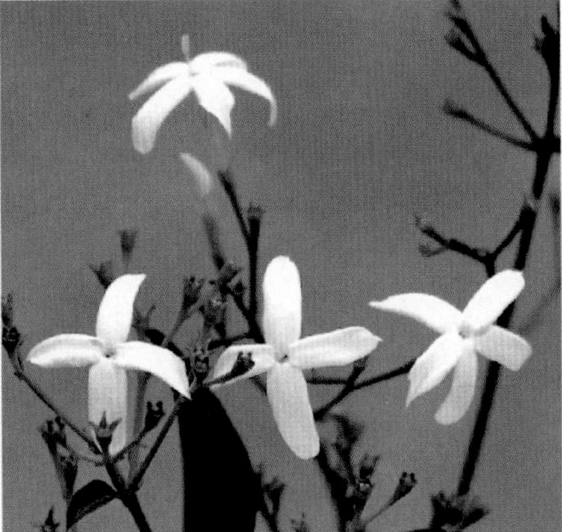

Jasminum azoricum

A semi-climber which has sparse heads of fragrant white flowers.

Jasminum humile YELLOW JASMINE

In spring this bushy shrub has clusters of bright yellow perfumed flowers.

***Jasminum officinale* cv. Aureo-variegatum**

Vigorous, this climber has gold and green variegated foliage.

Jasminum dispermum

On this evergreen climber the open bunches of pendulous perfumed flowers are coloured white, with a yellow eye.

Jasminum mesnyi JAPANESE JASMINE

A bushy shrub with arching branches. The showy flowers are primrose to yellow in colour.

Jasminum parkeri

Small and spreading, this semi-climbing plant has upright golden coloured flowers.

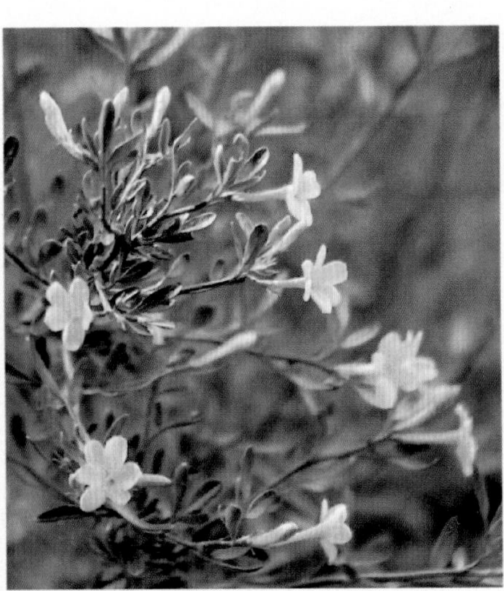

Jasminum fruticans

A semi-climber with sparse foliage and perfumed yellow flowers in spring.

Jasminum nitidum WINDMILL JASMINE

This bushy semi-climbing plant has perfumed white flowers.

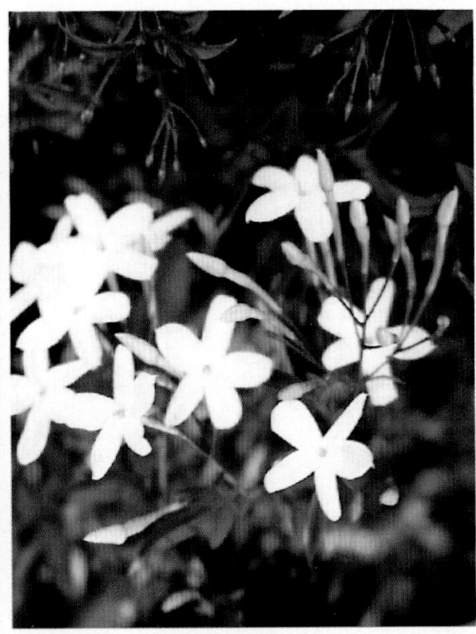

Jasminum polyanthum

A free flowering climber with large flower heads of highly perfumed white flowers which follow the pink buds.

JASMINUM (cont)

***Jasminum polyanthum* cv. Perfumed Princess**
This cultivar has attractive variegated foliage coloured grey and cream.

Jasminum rex ROYAL JASMINE
The perfumed white flowers bloom in large heads on this sparse climber.

Jasminum sambac ARABIAN JASMINE
An evergreen semi-climber which has small heads of white flowers.

***Jasminum sambac* cv. Flore Pleno**
syn. ***Jasminum sambac*** cv. **Grand Duke of Tuscany**
This cultivar has double white flowers.

Jasminum* x *stephanense
A hybrid jasmine which is a vigorous vine with masses of rose-pink flowers.

JATROPHA

EUPHORBIACEAE

Shrubs and small trees with milky sap, which are native to tropical America. They are grown as ornamental plants either for their leaves, flowers or unusual shaped trunks. Propagation is from seed and cuttings.

Jatropha curcas BARBADOS NUT
A dense tall shrub which has greenish cream flowers and large yellow fruit. Most parts of this plant are poisonous.

Jatropha gossypiifolia
A small shrub which has attractive palmate foliage and red buds.

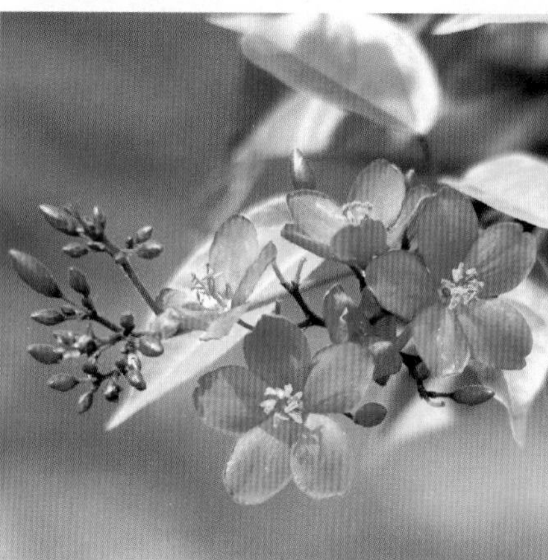

Jatropha integerrima SPICY JATROPHA
This dense tall shrub has showy heads of pinkish red flowers.

Jatropha podagrica GOUT PLANT
A deciduous shrub with a grotesque shaped ornamental trunk. It has heads of bright red small flowers.

JOVELLANA

Scrophulariaceae

A showy medium semi-evergreen shrub native to Chile. It is mostly grown in climates from cold temperate to warm temperate. Propagate from seed and cuttings.

Jovellana violacea

In spring this plant has large heads of pale lilac, bell shaped flowers with yellow centres.

JUANULLOA

Solanaceae

Native to Central America, these open crowned, evergreen shrubs are grown in warm to hot climates as ornamentals for their showy heads of golden flowers protruding from golden, waxy calyces. Best suited to warm sunny situations, they benefit from plenty of water and an application of fertilizer in summer. Propagate from seed and cuttings.

Juanulloa mexicana

An open shrub with clusters of orange-yellow flowers, each protruding from a golden coloured calyx.

JUSTICIA

Acanthaceae

Evergreen shrubs which are native to tropical and sub-tropical North, South and Central America. They are grown outdoors in climates from temperate to tropical and indoors or in glasshouses in cooler climates. The flowers are enclosed in colourful bracts. These plants benefit from pruning and fertilising. Propagate from seed and cuttings.

Justicia adhatoda

syn. ***Adhatoda vasica; Duvernoia adhatodoides***

An open evergreen shrub with clusters of white bracts which have violet markings.

Justicia aurea

syn. ***Jacobinia aurea***

This is a medium shrub with large terminal heads of golden yellow bracts.

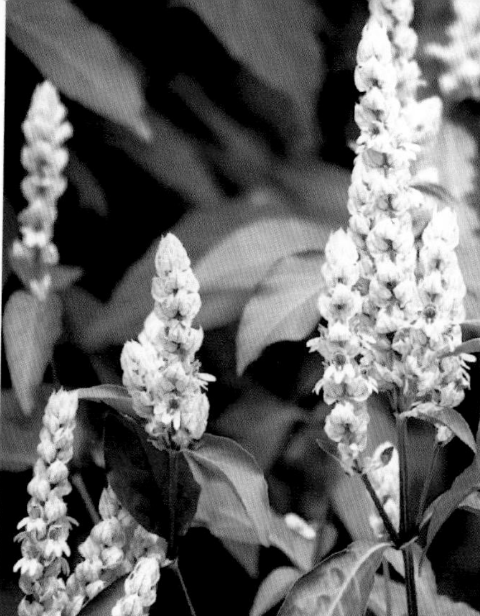

Justicia betonica

A bushy shrub with upright spikes of white bracts which turn pink as they age.

Justicia brandegeana SHRIMP PLANT

syn. ***Beloperone guttata***

A small shrub with upright and cascading heads of orange-red bracts.

***Justicia brandegeana* cv. Yellow Queen** YELLOW SHRIMP PLANT

syn. ***Beloperone lutea***

Heads of flowers encased in yellow bracts can be either upright or cascading on this small shrub.

JUSTICIA (cont)

Justicia carnea
syn. ***Jacobinia carnea***
A dense evergreen shrub with large terminal heads of pink bracts.

Justicia carnea cv. **Alba**
Free flowering, this cultivar has large heads of flowers encased in white bracts.

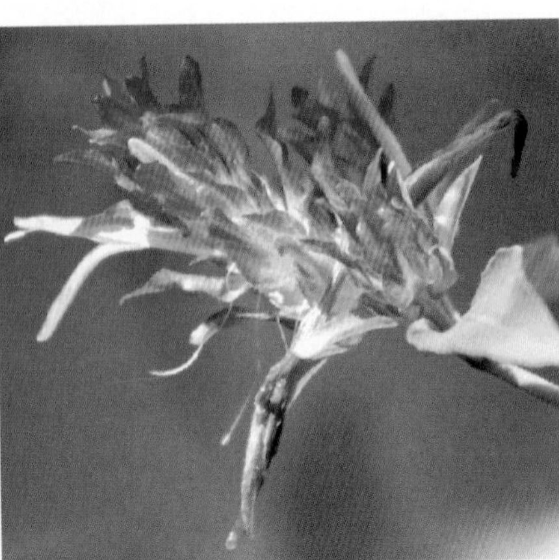

Justicia comosa
A sparse shrub with erect heads of orange-red bracts.

Justicia ghiesbreghtiana
Terminal clusters of orange bracts form on this shrub which has large leaves.

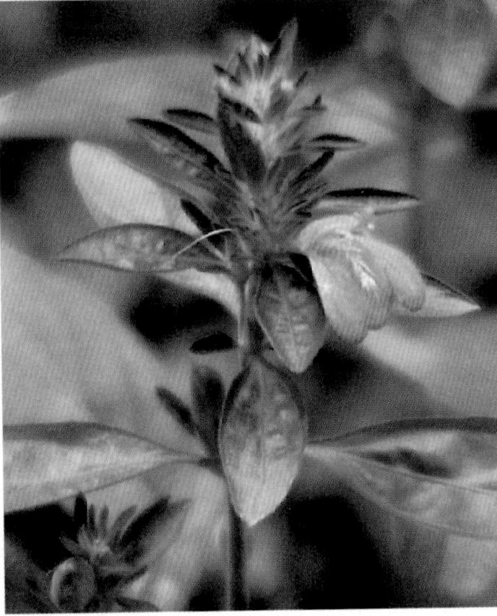

Justicia insularis
A dense shrub with small terminal heads of lilac coloured bracts.

Justicia nodosa
An evergreen sparse shrub with upright bracts coloured bright rose-pink.

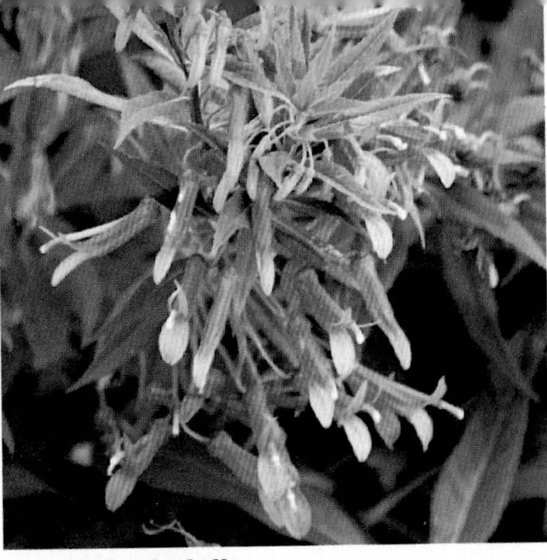

Justicia rizzinii
syn. ***J. pauciflora***
A small bushy shrub with masses of flowers in yellow and orange bracts.

Justicia spicigera
A bushy shrub with sparse heads of orange coloured bracts.

Justicia velutina
A compact bushy shrub with large terminal heads of bright rose-pink bracts.

KALANCHOE

Crassulaceae

Widely grown as ornamentals, these are succulent leaf shrubs and climbers of the tropics. They will grow in a wide range of soils and in climates from temperate to tropical. Kalanchoes are propagated from seed and cuttings.

Kalanchoe beharensis FELTBUSH
A dense crowned tall shrub with very large olive-green leaves.

KALMIA

Ericaceae

Native to North America, these evergreen shrubs are widely grown as showy spring flowering ornamentals in cold climates. They are propagated from cuttings and seed which needs to be cold stratified.

Kalmia angustifolia SHEEP LAUREL
An upright shrub with heads of rose-pink cup-like flowers in spring.

Kalmia latifolia 2 CALICO BUSH
A very showy ornamental shrub which has large heads of pink cup shaped flowers in spring.

***Kalmia latifolia* cv. Pink Charm**
A free flowering cultivar with bright pink buds followed by pink flowers.

KENNEDIA

Fabaceae [Leguminosae]

Climbing and twining plants native to Australia which are grown as ground or fence covers. They grow in sandy and well drained soils in cold temperate to sub-tropical climates. Propagate from seed which requires hot water treatment.

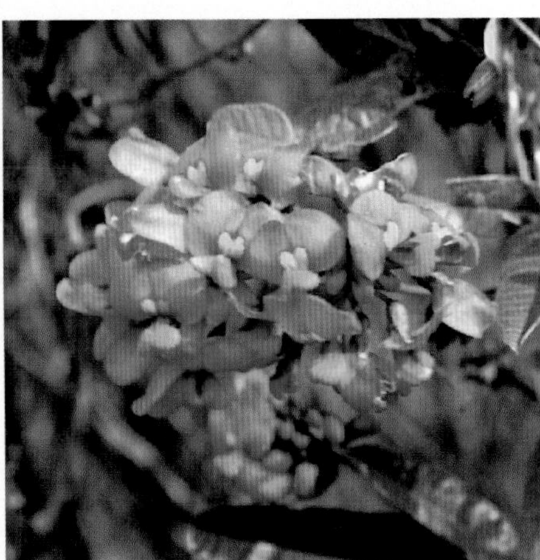

Kennedia coccinea CORAL VINE
Robust, this climber has large heads of orange-red pea-type flowers in spring.

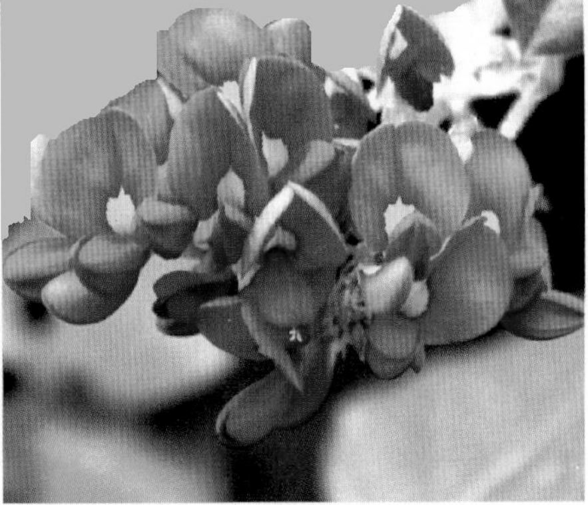

Kennedia macrophylla
A hardy vine with large heads of orange coloured pea-type flowers which have yellow centres.

Kennedia nigricans BLACK CORAL PEA
This is a vigorous climber with heads of yellow and black flowers in spring.

Kennedia prostrata RUNNING POSTMAN
A prostrate spreading plant which has showy red and yellow flowers in spring.

KENNEDIA (cont)

Kennedia retrorsa

This spring flowered vigorous climber has heads of small violet coloured flowers.

Kennedia rubicunda DUSKY CORAL PEA

A vigorous climber with clusters of crimson pea-type flowers in spring.

Kennedia rubicunda cv. **Sharney**

This is a white flowered cultivar which is very hardy and grows true to colour from seed.

KERRIA

ROSACEAE

Kerria japonica

This deciduous shrub from China and Japan has golden yellow flowers and is widely grown as an ornamental in cold temperate to sub-tropical climates. Propagate from cuttings.

Kerria japonica cv. **Gold Cup**

A cultivar which has larger flowers and petals which overlap.

Kerria japonica cv. **Pleniflora**

This cultivar has double yellow flowers.

Kerria japonica cv. **Variegata**

The foliage of this cultivar is variegated cream and green.

KIGELIA

BIGNONIACEAE

Kigelia africana SAUSAGE TREE

syn. ***K. pinnata***

A medium spreading tree from tropical Africa. The tree has pendulous chains of large claret red coloured flowers followed by large sausage looking seed pods as shown below. They need a warm climate and good quality soil. Propagate from seed.

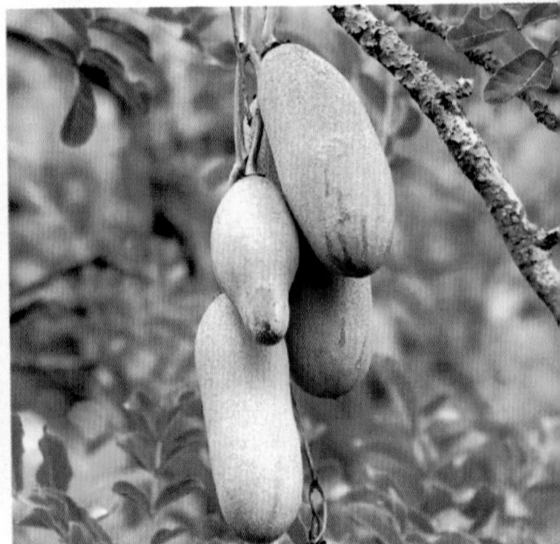

Kigelia africana - seed pods

KOELREUTERIA

SAPINDACEAE

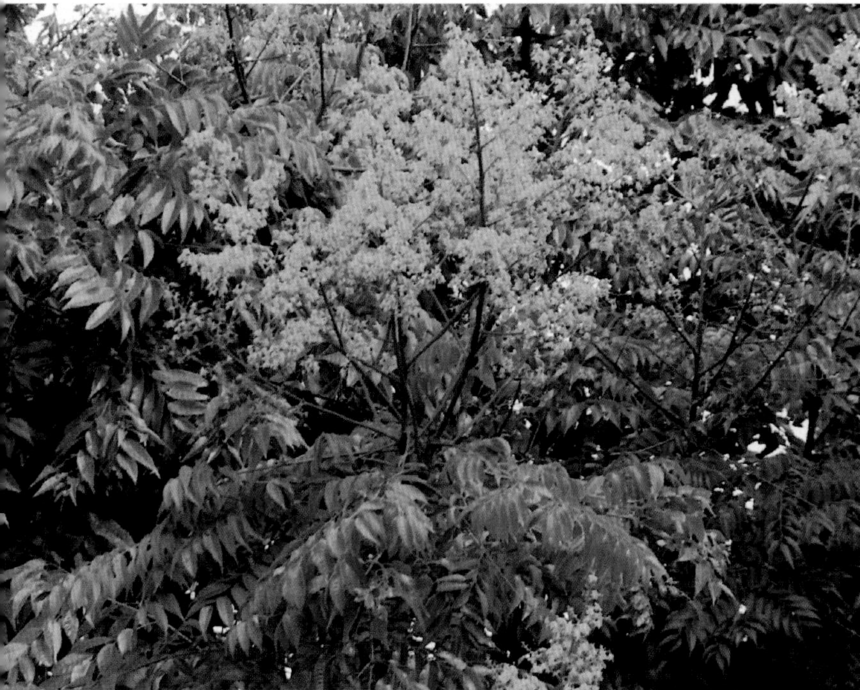

Koelreuteria elegans* ssp. *formosana GOLDEN RAIN TREE

This small deciduous tree from China has large erect heads of small yellow flowers followed by pink to red seed pods. The plant is cold tolerant and grows in a wide range of soils. Propagate from seed. Often referred to as *K. paniculata*, but the name has been changed as a result of recent studies.

KOHLERIA

GESNERIACEAE

Kohleria hirsuta

A small evergreen shrubby plant, native to South America. It has tubular red flowers and is grown widely as an indoor plant. Propagate from cuttings.

KOLKWITZIA

CAPRIFOLIACEAE

Kolkwitzia amabilis BEAUTY BUSH

Widely grown in cool climates as a showy spring flowering ornamental, having heads of pale pink flowers with yellow centres, this upright deciduous shrub is native to China. It is propagated from cuttings.

KOPSIA

APOCYNACEAE

From South East Asia, these evergreen shrubs need a tropical climate. They are grown as ornamentals in rich soil and are propagated from seed and cuttings.

Kopsia fruticosa SHRUB VINCA

A medium shrub which has showy pale pink flowers over many months.

Kopsia singapurensis

This medium shrub has small heads of white flowers.

k

KUNZEA

MYRTACEAE

Small to tall evergreen shrubs from Australia which are grown as ornamentals. They need well drained soils and are propagated from seed and cuttings.

Kunzea ambigua

A medium shrub with arching branches of small white flowers.

Kunzea baxteri

This is a tall shrub with bottlebrush-like heads of red flowers.

Kunzea graniticola

Fluffy white flowers bloom on arching branches on this medium shrub.

Kunzea capitata

Frost tolerant, this is a small shrub with arching branches and clusters of pink flowers along the branches.

***Kunzea* cv. Mauve Mist**

A natural hybrid between *K. ambigua* an *K. capitata*. It has clusters of pale mauve flowers in spring.

Kunzea pauciflora

In spring this open small shrub is covere with cerise coloured flowers. Frost tolerant.

Kunzea pulchella

A tall upright shrub with red bottlebrush type flowers.

+LABURNOCYTISUS

[F]ABACEAE [LEGUMINOSAE]

+Laburnocytisus adamii

[A]n unusual plant which is produced [b]y grafting *Cytisus purpureus* onto a [r]ootstock of *Laburnum anagyroides*. [I]t has cascading racemes of mauve and [y]ellow flowers in separate bunches on [t]he one tree.

LABURNUM

FABACEAE [LEGUMINOSAE]

[O]rnamental shrubs and trees with [c]ascading racemes of golden coloured [f]lowers which are tolerant of cold climates. [T]hey are propagated from seed which [b]enefits from cold stratification, or by [l]ayering, grafting and budding.

[L]aburnum anagyroides

GOLDEN CHAIN TREE

A medium size tree with cascading [r]acemes of golden coloured flowers.

***Laburnum anagyroides* cv. Aureum**

The leaves of this cultivar are coloured yellow and lime-green.

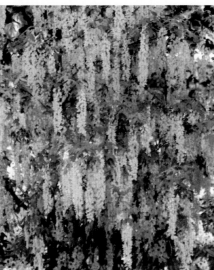

***Laburnum* x *watereri* cv. Vossii**

A hybrid Laburnum with showy racemes of golden coloured flowers.

LAFOENSIA

LYTHRACEAE

Lafoensia vandelliana

A small to medium evergreen tree from tropical America. It is grown in sub-tropical and tropical climates as an ornamental and for the production of yellow dye. This tree has large bunches of cream flowers and is propagated from seed.

LAGERSTROEMIA

LYTHRACEAE CREPE/CRAPE MYRTLE

Showy ornamental shrubs and trees native to Australia, Asia and the Pacific. They are grown in climates from temperate to tropical and a few will tolerate some frost. These plants benefit from regular pruning. Propagate from seed and cuttings.

Lagerstroemia archeriana

A small, free flowering tree with large heads of mauve, pink and white flowers.

LAGERSTROEMIA (cont)

Lagerstroemia indica cv. **Alba**
In summer, this cultivar has large heads of white flowers.

Lagerstroemia indica cv. **Newmanii**
This cultivar has large heads of flowers coloured pale pink.

Lagerstroemia indica cv. **Eavesii**
A cultivar with large heads of pale mauve flowers.

Lagerstroemia indica cv. **Pink**
Large heads of pink flowers bloom on this popular crepe myrtle.

Lagerstroemia loudonii
This upright, sparse, small tree has small heads of mauve flowers.

Lagerstroemia indica cv. **Heliotrope Beauty**
This cultivar has eye catching heliotrope coloured flowers.

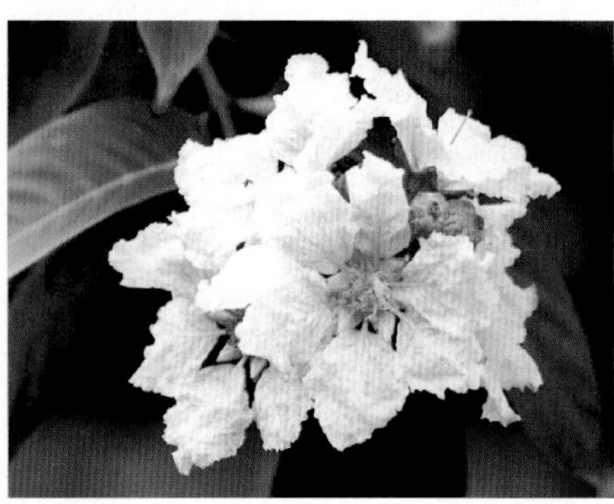

Lagerstroemia indica cv. **Mathewsii**
A small tree with showy heads of purple fading to pale mauve flowers.

Lagerstroemia indica cv. **Rubra**
A showy cultivar with large heads of rosy red coloured flowers.

LAGERSTROEMIA (cont)

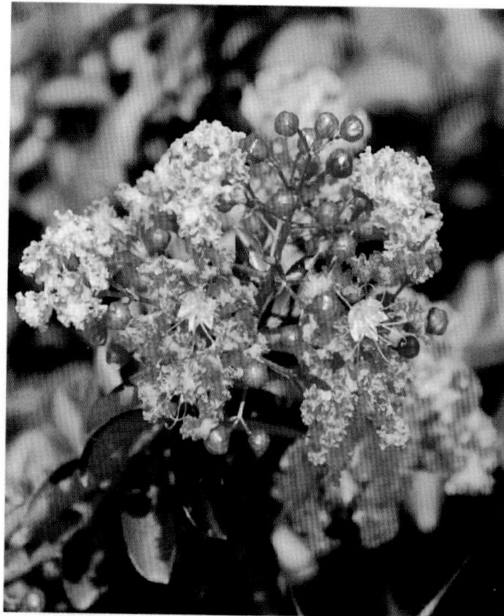

Lagerstroemia cv. **Pixie Pink**
A compact small shrub with large heads of pink flowers.

Lagerstroemia cv. **Pixie Red**
Pale red flowers bloom in large heads on this compact small shrub.

Lagerstroemia speciosa
PRIDE OF INDIA
syn. ***L. flos-reginae***
This upright small to medium tree gives an outstanding display of mauve flowers in large heads.

Lagerstroemia speciosa
cv. **Indian Rose**
On this upright small to medium tree, rose-pink flowers form in upright spikes.

Lagerstroemia tomentosa
Small and spreading, this tree has heads of white flowers.

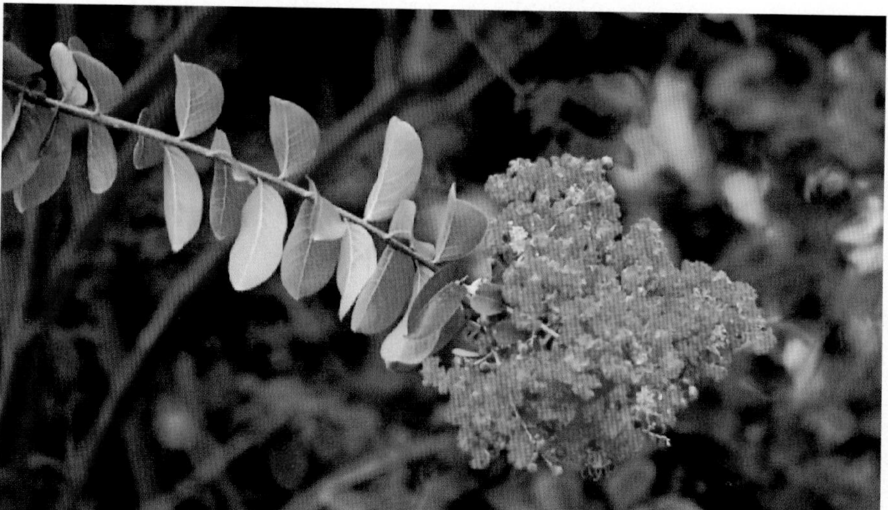

Lagerstroemia cv. **Pixie Rose**
This compact shrub has flower heads coloured rose-pink.

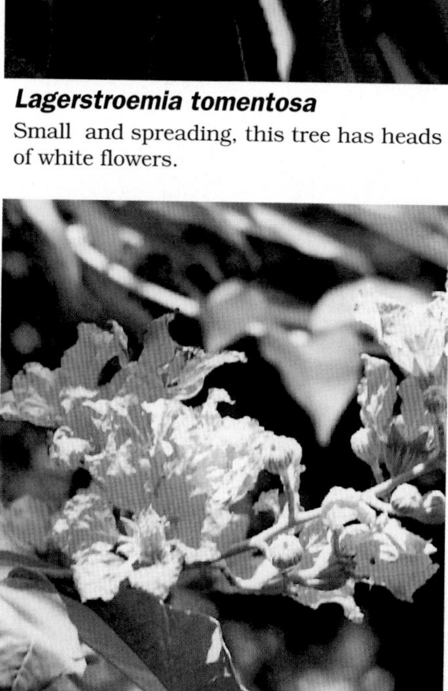

Lagerstroemia villosa
A small to medium bushy tree with long flower spikes of lilac-pink flowers.

LAGUNARIA

MALVACEAE

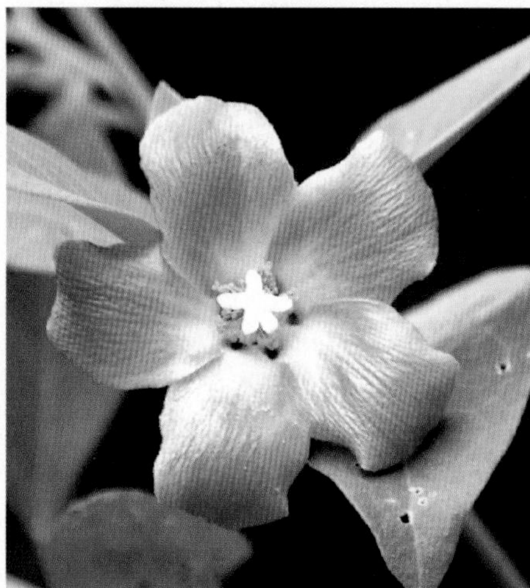

Lagunaria patersonii

LORD HOWE ISLAND HIBISCUS

A small to medium evergreen tree from Lord Howe Island. This tree is grown as an ornamental or a street tree for its showy rose-pink Hibiscus-like flowers. Fine hairs in the seed capsules can be irritating. In climates from cool temperate to sub-tropical, it grows in poor and sandy soils and is tolerant of salt spray. It is propagated from seed.

LAMBERTIA

PROTEACEAE

From Australia, these evergreen shrubs are grown as landscape plants in climates from cool temperate to sub-tropical. They are propagated from seed and tolerate poor soil.

Lambertia inermis

A small open shrub with lots of small heads of red flowers.

Lambertia multiflora

A free flowering shrub with heads of amber coloured flowers.

Lambertia formosa MOUNTAIN DEVIL

A prickly leaf shrub with flowers coloured pinky red. The plant flowers for many months and has unusual seed pods shaped like a devil's head.

LAMIUM

LAMIACEAE [LABIATAE]

Lamium maculatum

A sparse shrubby plant which is native to Europe. It has tall spikes of mauve flowers. Propagate from seed.

LANTANA

VERBENACEAE

Popular free flowering shrubs which are native to the tropics and grown as flowering ornamentals in climates from cool temperate to tropical, in a wide range of soils. Propagation of the cultivar Lantanas is from cuttings.

Lantana camara

A tall sparse shrub which has heads of pink and cream flowers. This plant can be a weed in many countries as the seed may be spread by birds and animals. The cultivars listed below do not have this problem as they rarely set viable seed.

Lantana camara cv. **Calypso**
A bushy free flowering shrub with flowers coloured pink and orange with some yellow.

Lantana camara cv. **Chelsea Gem**
Free flowering, this cultivar has orange-red flowers with some yellow.

Lantana camara cv. **Diadem**
A spreading shrub with pink and yellow coloured flowers.

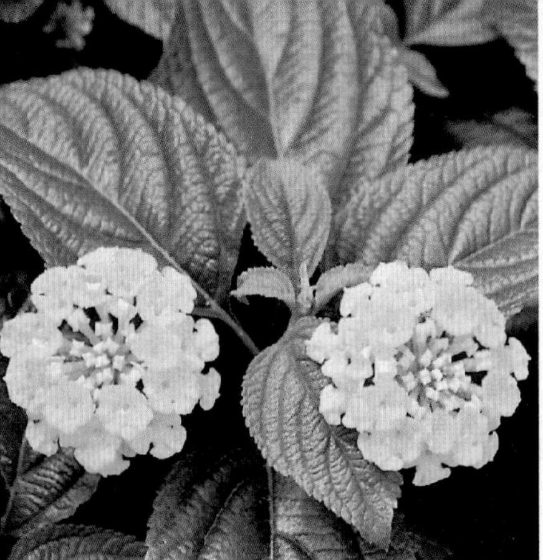

Lantana camara cv. **Drap d'Or**
This is a dwarf cultivar with bright yellow flowers.

Lantana camara cv. **Goliath**
Heavy flowering, this dwarf shrub has orange-red flowers.

Lantana camara cv. **Mutablis**
A spreading small shrub with bright pink flowers.

Lantana camara cv. **Nivea**
On this compact shrub the flowers are coloured cream and gold.

Lantana camara cv. **Snowflake**
A small spreading shrub with white flowers.

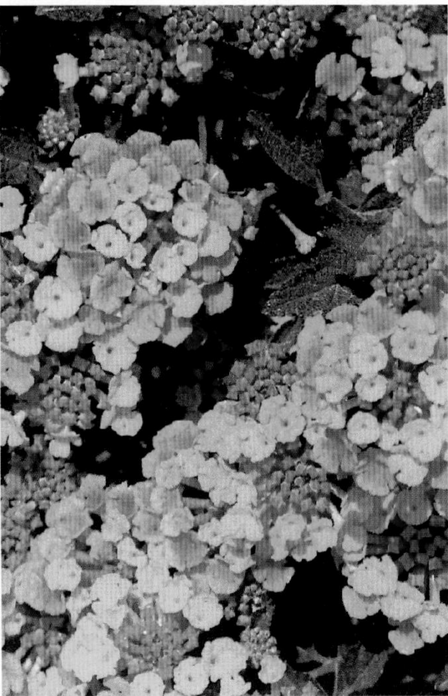

Lantana camara cv. **Spreading Sunset**
The flowers on this dense spreading shrub are gold and orange in colour.

LANTANA (cont)

Lantana camara cv. **Sundancer**
A compact small shrub with golden coloured flowers.

Lantana montevidensis
Mauve coloured flowers bloom on this low growing, spreading shrub.

Lantana montevidensis cv. **Variegata**
This spreading cultivar has grey and white variegated foliage and mauve flowers.

Lantana montevidensis cv. **White Lightning**
A spreading cultivar with white flowers.

LAPAGERIA

LILIACEAE

An evergreen woody climber which is native to Chile and tolerant of cool climates. Propagation is from seed and cuttings.

Lapageria rosea CHILEAN BELLFLOWER
A winter and spring flowering climber which has large, waxy, red bell shaped flowers.

Lapageria rosea var. ***albiflora***
A white flowered variety of the Chilean bellflower.

LAURUS

LAURACEAE

Laurus nobilis BAY TREE
A small, evergreen, slow growing tree native to the Mediterranean. It is widely grown in cool climates to produce bay leaves which are used in cooking. Propagate from seed and cuttings.

LAVANDULA LAVENDER

LAMIACEAE [LABIATAE]

Aromatic shrubs which are grown as ornamentals and commercially grown to produce essential oils. They are native to Europe and grow in climates from cool temperate to tropical. Propagate from seed and cuttings.

Lavandula angustifolia ENGLISH LAVENDER
This small grey leaf shrub has fragrant purple flowers.

Lavandula angustifolia
ssp. ***angustifolia***
cv. **Munstead (Compacta Nana)**
A low growing cultivar of this popular shrub.

Lavandula canariensis
CANARY ISLAND LAVENDER
This sparse shrub has fern-like leaves and lavender-blue flowers on erect spikes.

Lavandula dentata FRENCH LAVENDER
An aromatic grey leaf shrub with purple flowers.

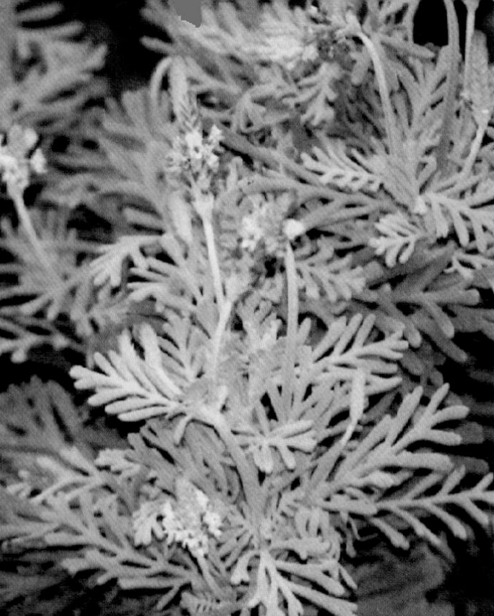

Lavandula pinnata
This small shrub has silver-grey fern-like leaves and lavender coloured flowers.

Lavandula stoechas
SPANISH LAVENDER
A perfumed grey leaf shrub with purple flowers.

Lavandula stoechas cv. **Alba**
A compact cultivar with white to soft mauve coloured flowers.

Lavandula stoechas
ssp. ***pedunculata***
Strong upright stems of purple flowers feature on this showy shrub.

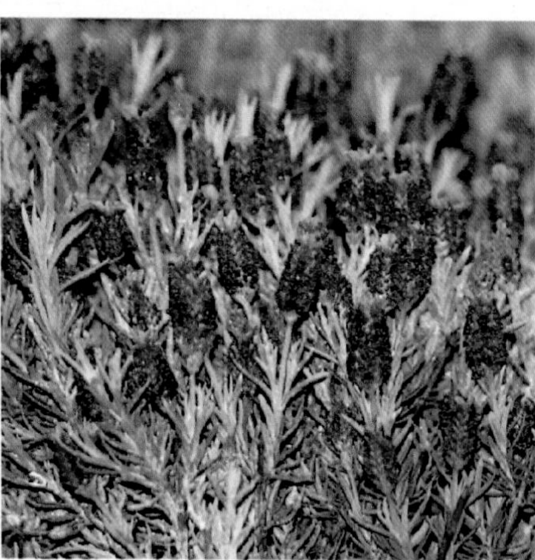

Lavandula stoechas cv. **Purple Fancy**
A cultivar with deep-purple flowers.

LAVATERA

MALVACEAE

Lavatera acerifolia
A medium shrub which is grown as a free flowering ornamental in climates from cool temperate to sub-tropical. It is propagated from seed and softwood cuttings.

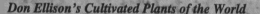

LAWSONIA

LYTHRACEAE

Lawsonia inermis HENNA

A small semi-evergreen tree, native to Asia, Africa and Australia. This plant prefers a warm climate and a well drained, slightly acid soil. It is grown as an ornamental for its showy heads of pink to salmon coloured flowers. Propagate from seed and tip cuttings under mist.

***Lawsonia inermis* cv. Alba**

A cultivar with white flowers.

LECHENAULTIA

GOODENIACEAE

Small, free flowering, showy shrubs native to Western Australia. These plants are grown as ornamentals in climates from cool temperate to sub-tropical. They require a well drained soil and are propagated from seed and cuttings.

Lechenaultia biloba

A small spreading shrub with clusters of showy blue flowers.

***Lechenaultia biloba* cv. White Flash**

This sparse growing cultivar has blue and white flowers.

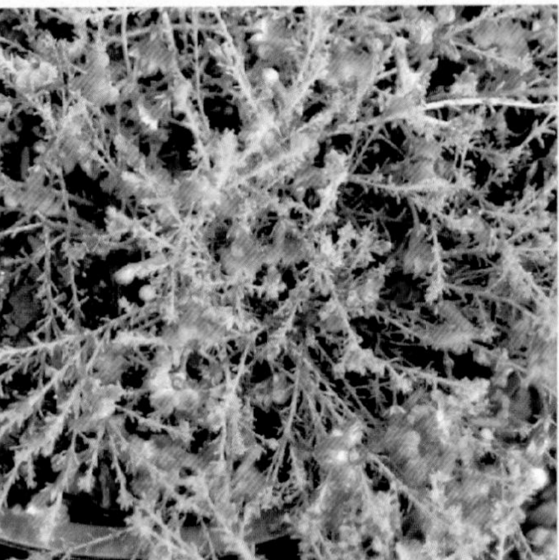

***Lechenaultia* cv. Candy Pink**

A spreading cultivar with rose-pink flowers.

Lechenaultia formosa

Orange-red flowers colour this spreading small plant.

Lechenaultia macrantha

This small plant has brownish pink and cream coloured flowers.

***Lechenaultia* cv. Scarlett O'Hara**

A low spreading plant with masses of small red flowers.

Lechenaultia striata

syn. ***L. helmsii***

A spreading small plant with flowers which can be pale blue, through pale yellow, to creamy white.

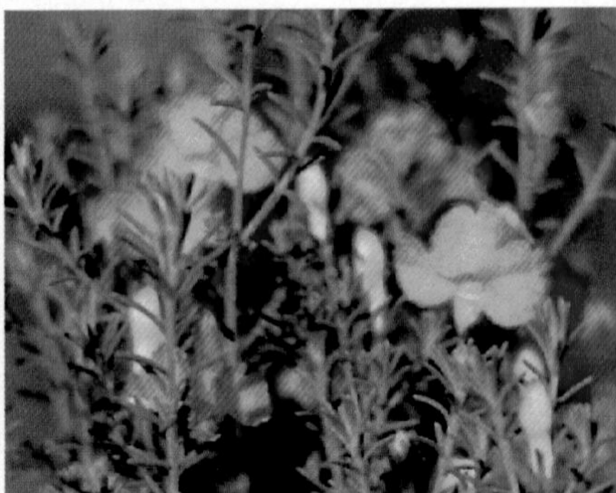

***Lechenaultia* cv. Tangerine**

An upright small plant with tangerine coloured flowers.

LECYTHIS

LECYTHIDACEAE

Lecythis ollaria MONKEY POT

Medium to large evergreen trees from tropical America. These trees need a tropical rainforest climate. They have showy mauve flowers followed by very large seed pods which give their common name. Propagate from seed.

LEEA

LEEACEAE

Evergreen shrubs and small trees native to the tropics of Asia, Africa and Australia. They are grown as showy ornamentals in sub-tropical and tropical climates, in good soil. Propagate from seed and cuttings.

Leea coccinea WEST INDIAN HOLLY

A dense shrub with large heads of bright red buds which open to pink flowers.

Leea indica BANDICOOT BERRY

An open crowned tall shrub with small white to pale pink flowers and large showy heads of fruit which are illustrated.

Lecythis ollaria

This illustration shows the large ornamental seed pods called Monkey pots.

LEIOPHYLLUM

ERICACEAE

Leiophyllum buxifolium SAND MYRTLE

A small spreading evergreen shrub which is native to North America. The shrub is grown as a free flowering ornamental for its clusters of small pinky white flowers. It grows in climates from cool to sub-tropical and is propagated from seed and cuttings.

LEONOTIS

LAMIACEAE [LABIATAE]

Leonotis leonurus LION'S-EAR

A medium aromatic upright shrub, native to South Africa. Leonotis are tolerant of poor soils in climates from temperate to tropical. Propagate from seed and cuttings. They have terminal spikes of orange coloured flowers.

Leonotis leonurus cv. **Alba**

A white flowered cultivar of this shrub.

LEPTOSPERMUM

TEA TREE

MYRTACEAE

Evergreen shrubs and small trees mostly native to Australia. They are hardy ornamentals but are also used for sand stabilisation and medicine. These plants have a wide climate range from cold temperate to tropical. Propagation is from seed and tip cuttings.

Leptospermum cv. **Cardwell**

A heavy flowering, lower growing form with white flowers in spring.

Leptospermum cv. **Copper Glow**

Developed by the Author, this popular cultivar has copper coloured leaves. It should only be grown from seed as when cutting-grown continually from the same plant it will revert back to green.

Leptospermum epacridoideum

FAIRY TEA TREE

A small open shrub with showy white to pale pink flowers.

Leptospermum laevigatum

COASTAL TEA TREE

From sandy areas by the sea, this tall shrub to small tree has white flowers.

Leptospermum cv. **Pink Cascade**

This low growing spreading shrub has masses of pink flowers in spring.

Leptospermum polygalifolium

syn. ***L flavescens***

TANTOON TEA TREE; WILD MAY

A tall variable shrub with masses of white flowers in spring.

Leptospermum cv. **Red Cascade**
In spring, this low growing spreading shrub is covered with red flowers.

Leptospermum rotundifolium
A sparse upright shrub with very large showy pink and white coloured flowers.

Leptospermum rotundifolium cv. **Alba**
A cultivar with large white flowers.

Leptospermum rotundifolium cv. **Pink Beauty**
This cultivar has large bright pink flowers.

Leptospermum scoparium MANUKA
Free flowering, this shrub is covered with pinky white flowers in spring.

Leptospermum scoparium cv. **Alba**
A dense shrub with double white flowers.

Leptospermum scoparium cv. **Ballerina**
This is a showy cultivar with double pink flowers.

Leptospermum scoparium cv. **Burgundy Queen**
A cultivar which has dark red double flowers.

Leptospermum scoparium cv. **Charmer**
Lavender-pink is the colour of the single flowers on this cultivar.

LEPTOSPURMUM (cont)

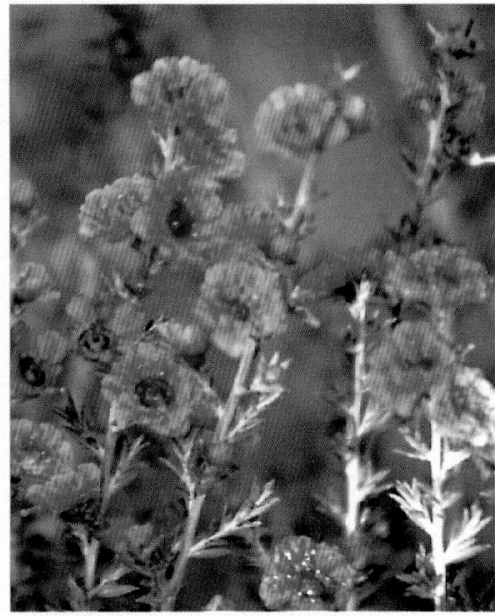

Leptospermum scoparium
cv. **Cherry Ripe**

This cultivar has attractive double light red flowers with occasional pink markings.

Leptospermum scoparium cv. **Lambethii**

A cultivar which has large single flowers of bright rose-pink mixed with paler pink flowers.

Leptospermum scoparium
cv. **Fascination**

Free flowering, this cultivar has double bright pink flowers.

Leptospermum scoparium
cv. **Nanum Roseum**

The single pale pink flowers bloom in profusion on this free flowering dwarf spreading shrub.

Leptospermum sericeum

Upright, this grey leaf shrub has showy pink flowers.

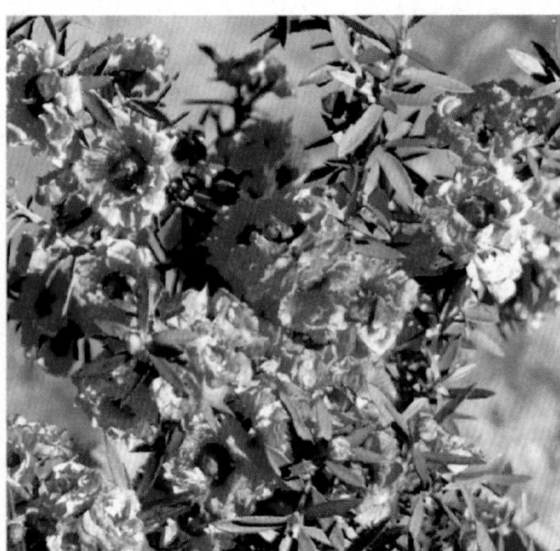

Leptospermum scoparium
cv. **Gaiety Girl**

A cultivar with double rose-pink flowers.

Leptospermum scoparium
cv. **Nicholsii Nana**

A cultivar which is very low growing and used as a ground cover. Flowers are crimson.

Leptospermum squarrosum

A compact shrub with large pale pink flowers along the branches.

LEUCADENDRON

PROTEACEAE

Native to South Africa, these shrubs and small trees are grown as ornamentals and for the cut flower trade. They prefer well drained, mostly sandy, soil in temperate climates. Propagate from seed and cuttings.

Leucadendron argenteum SILVER TREE

A very showy small tree which is grown for its striking silver foliage.

Leucadendron discolor - female

Upright and bushy, this shrub has showy cream flower bracts.

Leucadendron discolor - male

An upright bushy plant with cream flower bracts with a brown centre.

Leucadendron eucalyptifolium

Showy yellow flowers and bracts feature on this free branching upright shrub.

Leucadendron cv. **Harvest**

A showy cultivar with cream bracts and brown and yellow centres.

Leucadendron laureolum

An upright free branching shrub with green and yellow flower bracts.

Leucadendron laureolum cv. **Gem**

This cultivar has red and cream flower bracts.

Leucadendron laureolum cv. **Inca Gold**

An upright cultivar which has showy yellow bracts.

LEUCADENDRON (cont)

Leucadendron orientale
The showy flower bracts on this upright shrub are pink-red in colour.

***Leucadendron* cv. Safari Sunset**
Popular as a cut flower, this cultivar has red flower bracts.

***Leucadendron salignum* cv. Dragoneyes**
A cultivar which has flower bracts coloured cream and red.

Leucadendron salignum
Upright and sparse, this shrub has green and red flower bracts.

***Leucadendron salignum* cv. Red Devil**
This is a popular cultivar which has pinky red and cream coloured flower bracts.

***Leucadendron* cv. Silvan Red**
A popular cultivar which is grown for cut flowers. The flower bracts are coloured pink and red.

Leucadendron stelligerum
On this very sparse shrub the small flowers are coloured yellow with yellow bracts.

Leucadendron xanthoconus
A free branching shrub which has cream flower bracts and green centres.

LEUCAENA

Mimosaceae [Leguminosae]

Shrubs to small trees native to sub-tropical and temperate America. They are widely grown for soil stabilisation and as cattle feed especially in tropical and sub-tropical climates. Propagate from seed.

Leucaena leucocephala WHITE POPINAC

A tree widely used as cattle feed and for soil stabilisation. It has round cream flowers and masses of seed pods.

Leucaena trichodes

A shrub which is grown as an ornamental and for soil stabilisation.

LEUCOPHYLLUM

Scrophulariaceae

Leucophyllum frutescens ASH PLANT

An evergreen shrub which is native to North America. It has silver-blue leaves and upright spikes of mauve flowers in spring. This plant is an outstanding ornamental for temperate to tropical climates. Propagate from seed and cuttings.

LEUCOSPERMUM

Proteaceae

Shrubs and small trees native to Africa which are widely grown as ornamentals and for the cut flower trade. They prefer a well drained soil in a temperate climate. Propagate from seed and sometimes cuttings.

Leucospermum cordifolium

A spreading shrub with large heads of orange-red coloured, pincushion-like flowers.

Leucospermum erubescens

This sparse shrub has upright branches. The flowers are gold and orange in colour.

Leucospermum glabrum

An open crowned shrub with red and grey coloured flower heads.

LEUCOSPERMUM (cont)

Leucospermum grandiflorum

The flower heads on this upright shrub are golden yellow.

Leucospermum lineare

This shrub has large pincushion-like heads coloured red and cream, and thin leaves.

Leucospermum muirii

An open shrub with yellow pincushion-type flower heads. Insert shows bud.

Leucospermum patersonii

This is a sparse shrub with large apricot coloured flowers heads.

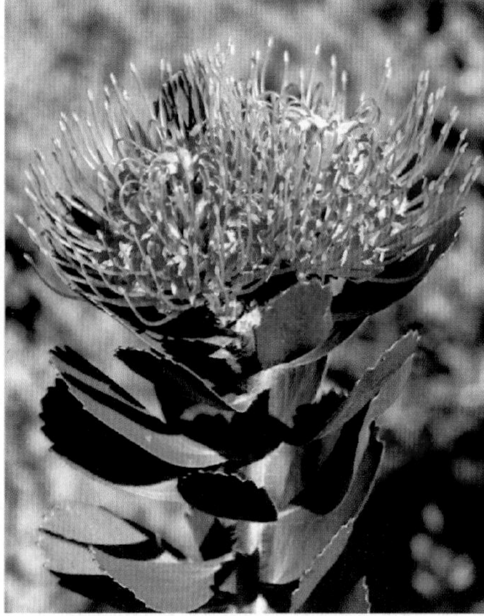

Leucospermum praecox

A coarse upright shrub with gold and red coloured flower heads.

Leucospermum reflexum

Bright red flower heads make this a popular plant for the cut flower trade.

***Leucospermum reflexum* cv. Lutea**

A cultivar with creamy yellow flower heads.

LEUCOTHOE

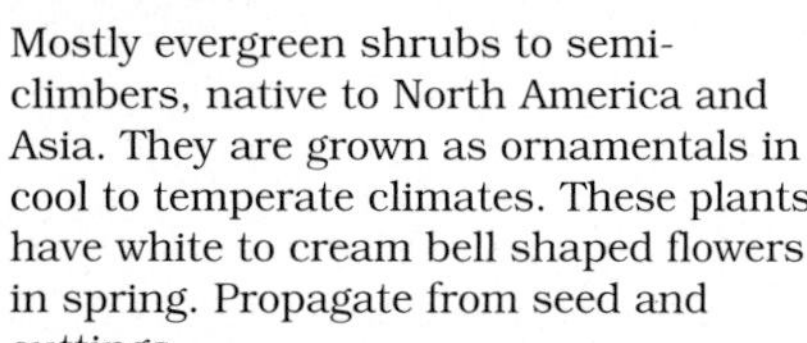

Ericaceae

Mostly evergreen shrubs to semi-climbers, native to North America and Asia. They are grown as ornamentals in cool to temperate climates. These plants have white to cream bell shaped flowers in spring. Propagate from seed and cuttings.

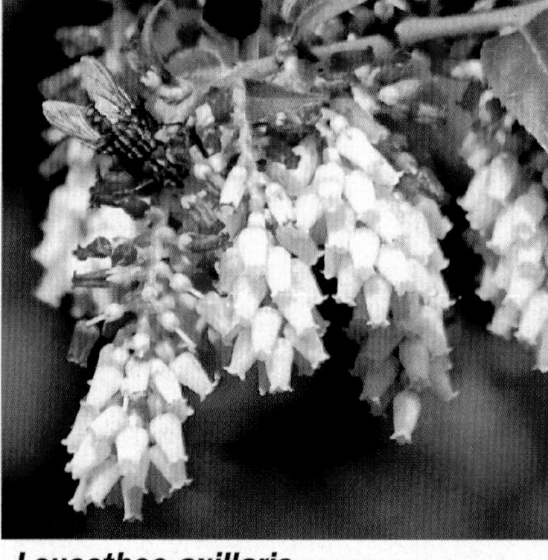

Leucothoe axillaris

A sparse evergreen shrub with large heads of pendulous, small, cream flowers in spring.

Leucothoe fontanesiana [2] DOG-HOBBLE

In spring, this sprawling evergreen shrub has racemes of small cream flowers.

LEUCOTHOE (cont)

***Leucothoe fontanesiana* cv. Rainbow**
A cultivar with multi-coloured leaves of pink, red, cream and green.

Leucothoe racemosa SWEET BELLS
This sprawling, semi-evergreen shrub has racemes of perfumed, small, cream flowers in spring.

Leucothoe walteri
A sparse shrub with bunches of small, pendulous, cream flowers in spring.

LIGUSTRUM PRIVET

OLEACEAE

Deciduous and evergreen shrubs and small trees which are native to Europe, Asia, Africa and Australia. Most are highly perfumed. Widely used for hedges, they will grow in poor soils but care should be taken with the more vigorous types as they can become weeds in some situations. Propagation is from seed and cuttings.

Ligustrum japonicum JAPANESE PRIVET
An upright evergreen shrub with large heads of perfumed white flowers.

Ligustrum obtusifolium
syn. ***L. ibota***
A deciduous bushy shrub with small, perfumed, white flowers in spring.

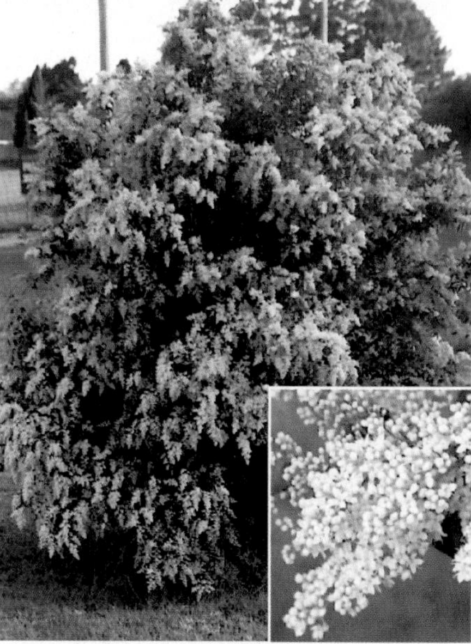

Ligustrum ovalifolium
This is a medium shrub with bunches of highly perfumed, small, white flowers.

***Ligustrum ovalifolium* cv. Aureum**
A cultivar with green and yellow variegated leaves.

***Ligustrum sinense* cv. Variegatum**
The leaves are green, edged with cream, on this small tree which has large bunches of small, perfumed flowers.

LIQUIDAMBAR

HAMAMELIDACEAE

Deciduous trees native to North America and Asia which are grown as ornamental feature trees. They are hardy trees and are tolerant of climates from cold to sub-tropical. Propagate from seed and by grafting.

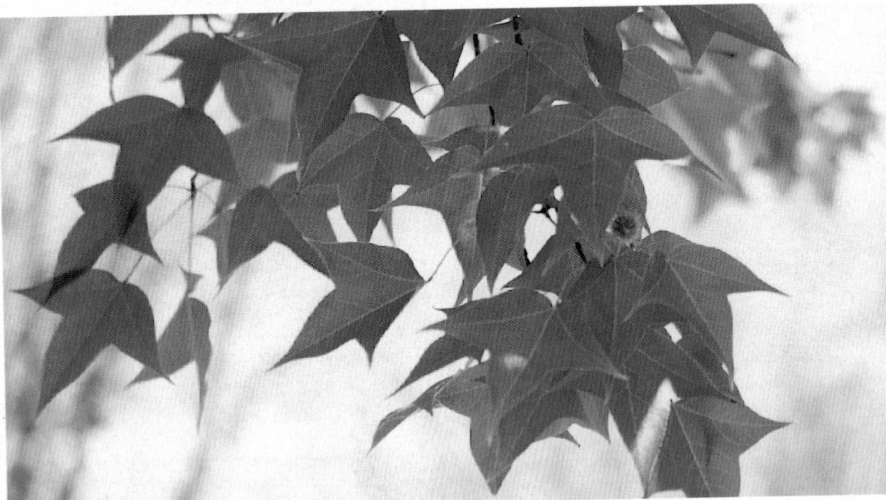

Liquidambar styraciflua SWEET GUM

A medium size tree grown for its colourful autumn foliage. The illustration shows the summer foliage.

Liquidambar styraciflua cv. **Canberra Gem**

The autumn foliage on this cultivar is highly coloured.

Liquidambar styraciflua cv. **Golden Treasure**

An outstanding cultivar with gold and green variegated foliage.

LIRIODENDRON

MAGNOLIACEAE

Liriodendron tulipifera TULIP TREE

A deciduous tall tree native to North America, it has showy tulip-like green flowers. Propagate from seed and cuttings, or by grafting.

Liriodendron tulipifera cv. **Aureo-marginatum**

A cultivar with green and yellow variegated leaves.

LOBELIA

CAMPANULACEAE

A diverse group of plants which are trees, shrubs, perennials and annuals and are found in climates from tropical to temperate. They are grown as flowering ornamentals and are propagated from seed and cuttings.

Lobelia cardinalis CARDINAL FLOWER
A shrubby upright plant with brownish bronze foliage and bright red flowers.

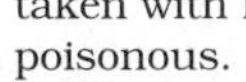

Lobelia chinensis
This is a bushy shrub with tubular red flowers.

Lobelia laxiflora
Bushy and free flowering, this shrub has red and yellow flowers.

LOMATIA

PROTEACEAE

Lomatia myricoides
A perfumed evergreen shrub from Australia. It has long heads of white flowers and is propagated from seed.

LONCHOCARPUS

FABACEAE [LEGUMINOSAE]

Deciduous and evergreen trees from tropical America, Africa and Australia. They are grown as showy ornamentals and to produce the insecticide Rotenone. Many Lonchocarpus may be found growing in swamps and poorly drained soils but others need a well drained soil. Propagate from seed but care should be taken with Lonchocarpus as some are poisonous.

Lonchocarpus capassa
This showy small tree has racemes of rosy mauve flowers.

Lonchocarpus bussei
A small tree with large bunches of mauve flowers.

Lonchocarpus punctatus
syn. ***L. violaceus***
A handsome tree with attractive racemes of flowers coloured mauve, violet and white.

LONICERA HONEYSUCKLE

CAPRIFOLIACEAE

Shrubs and climbers from the northern hemisphere, they may be deciduous or evergreen. Usually fast growing, and highly perfumed, honeysuckles grow in climates from cold temperate to tropical and are mostly very hardy. Propagate from seed and cuttings.

Lonicera* x *americana

A hybrid honeysuckle which has highly perfumed flowers coloured cream and rose-pink. This shrubby plant is a hybrid between *L. caprifolium* and *L. etrusca*.

***Lonicera* x *americana* cv. Rubra [Atrosanguinea]**

The fragrant flowers of this bushy cultivar are red and cream in colour.

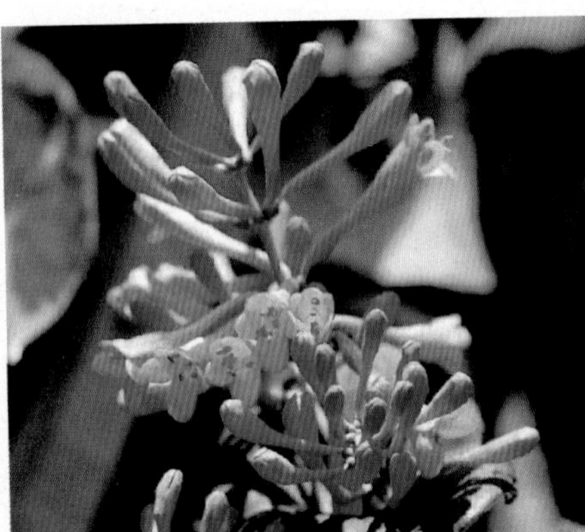

Lonicera* x *brownii

Cold hardy, this deciduous vine has bunches of perfumed yellow to orange-red flowers in spring and summer.

Lonicera caprifolium ITALIAN WOODBINE

A free flowering vine with perfumed pink and cream flowers.

Lonicera chrysantha

Deciduous, this tall shrub has golden flowers on upright stalks.

Lonicera discolor

A deciduous shrub which has bunches of red buds which open to perfumed pinky white flowers.

Lonicera etrusca

Showy bunches of yellowish fragrant flowers bloom on this sparse semi-evergreen shrub.

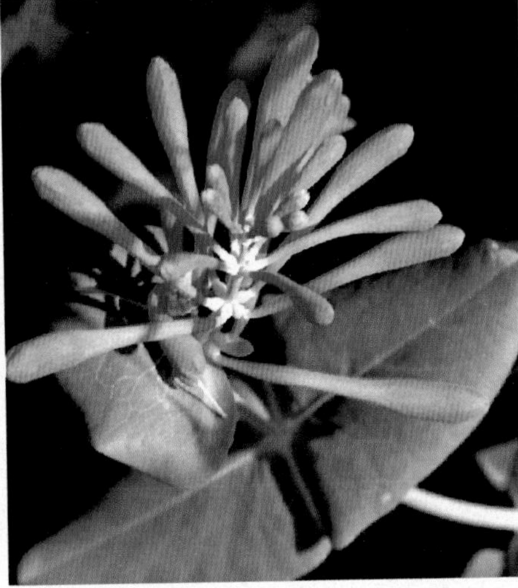

Lonicera* x *heckrottii

The colourful flowers of this hybrid shrub or semi-climber are red outside and yellow inside.

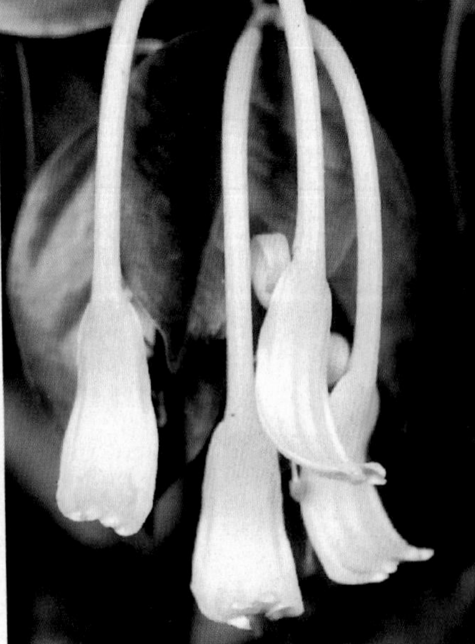

Lonicera hildebrandtiana

GIANT HONEYSUCKLE

This is a vigorous climber with heads of large yellow flowers.

LONICERA (cont)

Lonicera involucrata TWINBERRY
In spring this deciduous shrub has tubular red flowers.

Lonicera ledebourii
A deciduous shrub with tubular flowers coloured red and yellow.

Lonicera morrowii
Leggy and deciduous, this shrub has smallish leaves and clusters of small cream flowers in spring.

Lonicera japonica JAPANESE HONEYSUCKLE
A semi-climber with heads of perfumed cream flowers.

Lonicera maackii
This small deciduous tree has masses of small perfumed white flowers.

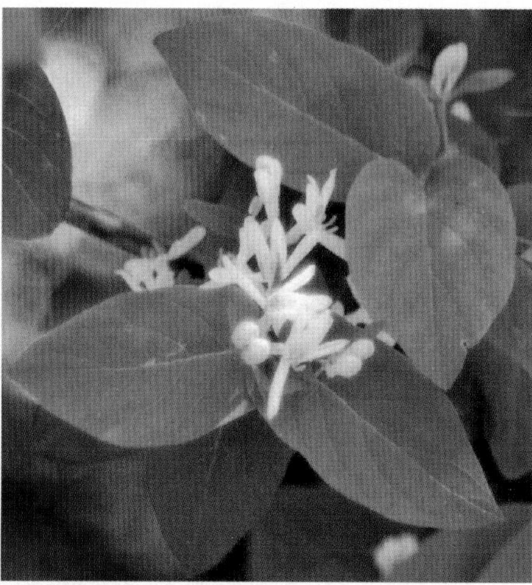

Lonicera* x *muendeniensis
A hybrid deciduous shrub with clusters of small white flowers.

***Lonicera japonica* cv. Halliana**
The white flowers of this evergreen cultivar turn yellow as they age.

Lonicera periclymenum WOODBINE
A climbing plant with heads of fragrant cream, white, yellow and some red flowers. There are many colour variations of this honeysuckle.

***Lonicera periclymenum* cv. Harlequin**

With cream and green variegated foliage, this cultivar has pink flower buds.

Lonicera pyrenaica

This erect shrub has cream coloured tubular flowers in spring.

Lonicera quinquelocularis

In spring, this tall deciduous shrub has clusters of fragrant cream flowers.

Lonicera sempervirens

CORAL HONEYSUCKLE

A vigorous evergreen climber which has bunches of red tubular flowers in spring.

***Lonicera tatarica* cv. Rosea**

The rose-pink buds of this cultivar open to paler pink flowers.

Lonicera tatarica

A deciduous shrub with small scarlet and yellow fragrant flowers.

***Lonicera tatarica* cv. Alba**

This cultivar has perfumed white flowers.

LOPHANTHERA

MALPIGHIACEAE

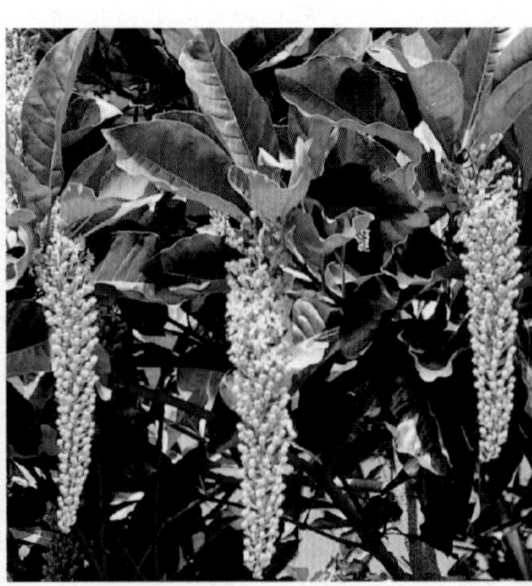

Lophanthera lactescens

One of the outstanding flowering trees of the world, this small to medium evergreen tree is native to tropical South America. It has long pendulous panicles of golden flowers, prefers a sub-tropical to tropical climate and is propagated from seed and semi-hard cuttings.

LOPHOSTEMON

Myrtaceae

Lophostemon confertus BRUSH BOX
syn. ***Tristania conferta***
This hardy evergreen Australian tree is grown as a street or park tree and used for timber. It has small white flowers. Propagate from seed or by budding, or grafting for cultivars.

Lophostemon confertus
cv. **Variegatus**
An outstanding cultivar with green and yellow variegated foliage.

Lophostemon confertus
cv. **Variegatus Crinkles**
This cultivar has twisted cream and green variegated leaves.

LOROPETALUM

Hamamelidaceae

Loropetalum chinense
A spreading evergreen shrub from Asia. It grows in climates from cool temperate to sub-tropical and has clusters of cream flowers. Propagate from seed.

LUCULIA

Rubiaceae

Flowering in the cooler months, these evergreen shrubs native to the Himalayas are grown as showy ornamentals. They need a well drained soil and prefer climates from cool temperate to warm temperate. Propagate from seed and cuttings.

Luculia grandifolia
This medium shrub has showy clusters of large white perfumed flowers.

Luculia pinceana
syn. ***L. gratissima***
Large heads of fragrant pink flowers form on this outstanding free flowering tall shrub.

***Luculia* Tsetensis**
Tall and upright, this shrub has large heads of white flowers.

LYSIDICE

Caesalpiniaceae [Leguminosae]

Lysidice rhodostegia
A fast growing, small, evergreen tree native to South East Asia. It is grown as a showy ornamental for large white flower bracts which change to mauve with age. The tree requires a warm climate with good soil. Propagate from seed and semi-hard cuttings under mist.

LYSIPHYLLUM

CAESALPINIACEAE [LEGUMINOSAE]

Small to medium trees which are native to Australia. They are free flowering and grown as ornamentals in climates from warm temperate to tropical. They will grow in poor soils and are propagated from seed.

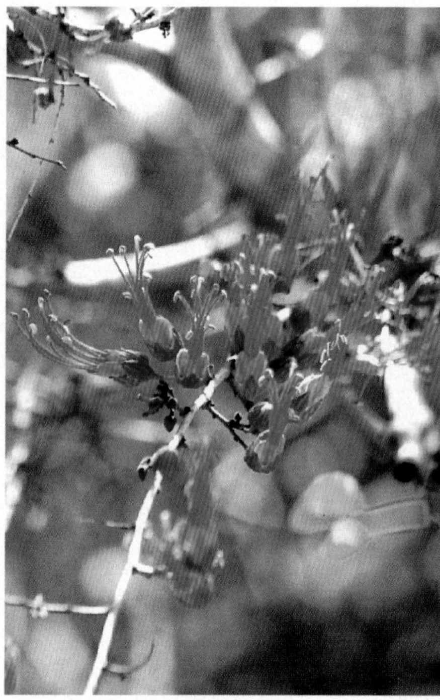

Lysiphyllum cunninghamii

A medium tree which has upright small clumps of red to maroon flowers.

Lysiphyllum hookeri MOUNTAIN EBONY

syn. ***Bauhinia hookeri***

A very showy small to medium tree with attractive flowers coloured white with red stamens.

MACADAMIA

PROTEACEAE

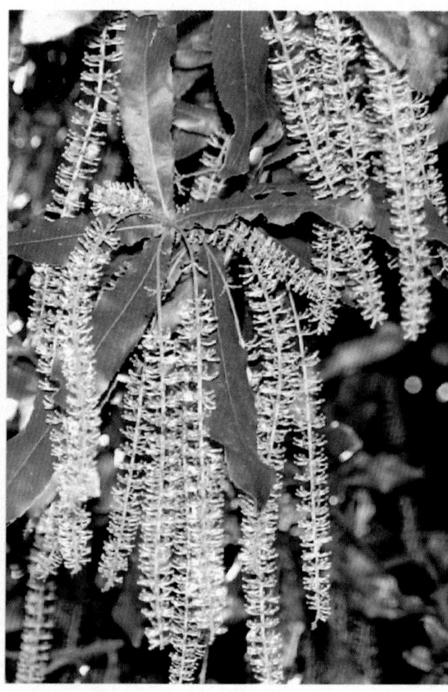

Macadamia integrifolia

MACADAMIA NUT

A medium size evergreen tree native to Australia. It is grown in warm temperate to tropical climates for the production of commercial nuts. The trees prefer a well drained rich soil. Flowers in racemes are creamish white when first open and change to reddish brown. Propagation is from seed or by grafting.

MACARANGA

EUPHORBIACEAE

Shrubs and small trees from Africa, Asia and Australia, which are grown as ornamentals. They prefer a rich soil in a sub-tropical or tropical climate. Propagate from seed or cuttings.

Macaranga grandifolia CORAL FLOWER

A small evergreen tree with clusters of red flowers which look like coral.

MACFADYENA

BIGNONIACEAE

Slender, evergreen climbers native to Central America and the Caribbean, they are grown in climates from temperate to tropical as very free flowering ornamentals. Propagate from seed.

Macfadyena uncata

This sparse vine has large yellow flowers in spring.

Macfadyena unguis-cati

CAT'S CLAW CREEPER

syn. ***Doxantha unguis-cati***

A free flowering climber with yellow, trumpet shaped flowers and attaching tendrils like cat's claws. It can become a pest in some situations.

MACKAYA

ACANTHACEAE

Mackaya bella

A dense, evergreen, tall shrub native to South Africa. It is grown as an ornamental for its showy heads of mauve flowers. The plant needs a climate from temperate to tropical. Propagate from seed and cuttings.

MAGNOLIA

MAGNOLIACEAE

Deciduous and evergreen shrubs and trees which are native to Asia and North and South America. They are widely grown throughout the world as outstanding flowering ornamentals. The deciduous forms are quite cold hardy whereas the evergreen Magnolias mostly prefer temperate to tropical climates. Propagation is from seed, which needs stratification if from a deciduous form, or from cuttings and by grafting.

Magnolia acuminata CUCUMBER TREE
A small to medium deciduous tree which has upright cup shaped flowers coloured cream and green.

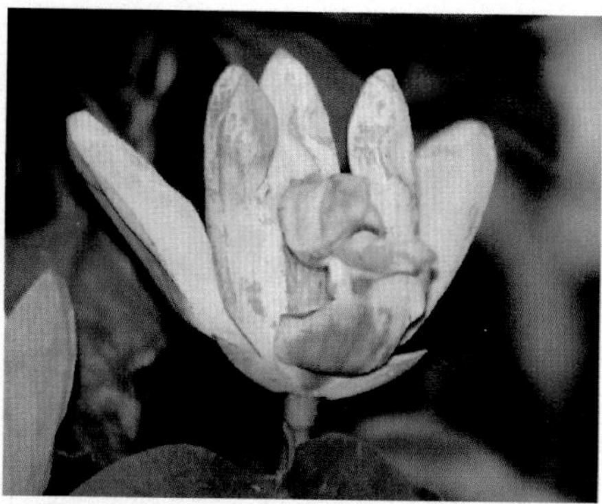

Magnolia acuminata var. ***subcordata***
syn. ***M. cordata***
With yellowish flowers, this variety is a compact small tree.

Magnolia x ***acuminata*** cv. **Elizabeth**
This hybrid between *M. acuminata* and *M. denudata* has large cream coloured flowers.

Magnolia campbellii ssp. ***campbellii***
A medium deciduous tree which has very large outstanding cup-type flowers coloured rose-pink on the outside and pinky white inside.

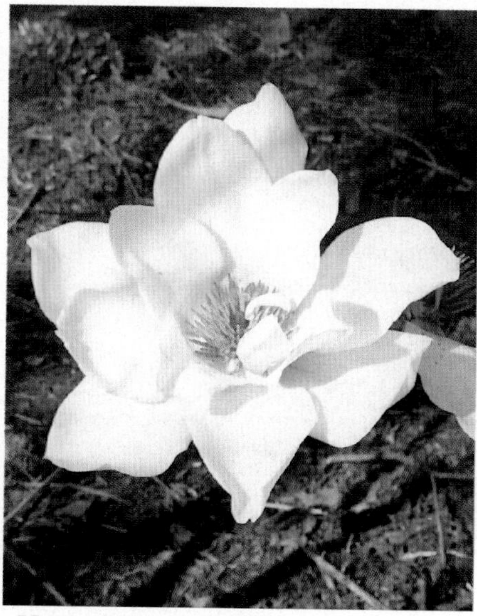

Magnolia campbellii ssp. ***campbellii*** var. ***alba***
On this cultivar, the white flowers are very large.

Magnolia campbellii ssp. ***campbellii*** cv. **Lennei**
A hybrid Magnolia with large flowers coloured purplish rose-pink and white.

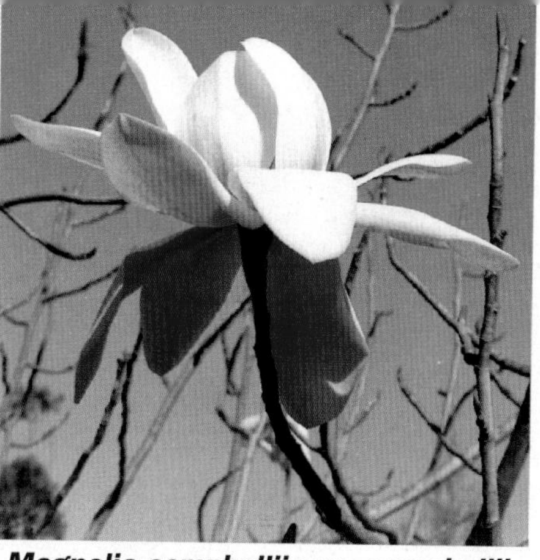

Magnolia campbellii ssp. ***campbellii*** cv. **Pale Pink**
This is an outstanding cultivar with pink flowers.

Magnolia x cv. **Caerhays Surprise**
With large pink flowers, this cultivar may be a hybrid of *M. sargentiana*.

Magnolia coco
syn. ***M. pumila***
A small to medium tropical evergreen tree with small white flowers.

MAGNOLIA (cont)

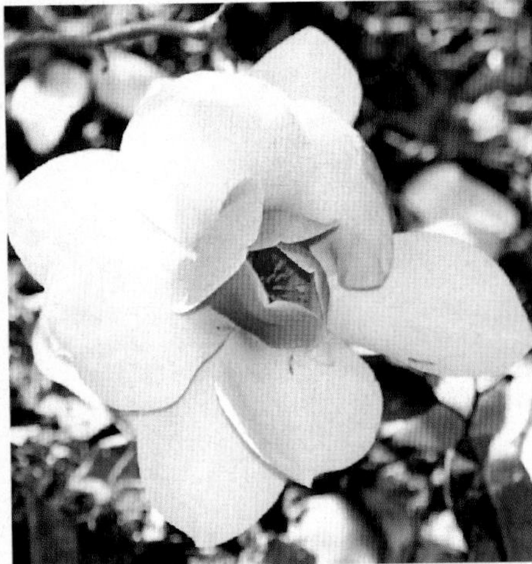

Magnolia cv. **Como**
The large cup shaped flowers of this small tree are pink and white in colour.

Magnolia denudata YULAN
Small and deciduous, this tree has large, showy, ivory coloured cup shaped flowers.

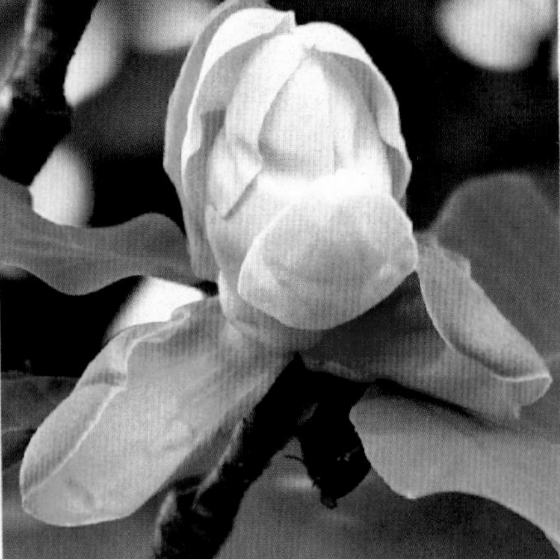

Magnolia hypoleuca
syn. ***M. obovata***
This medium spreading deciduous tree has large fragrant cup shaped flowers.

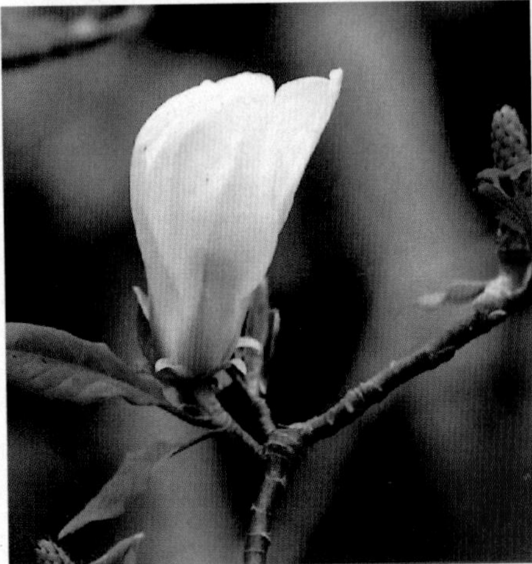

Magnolia cylindrica
On this small deciduous tree the upright white flowers have a touch of pink at the base of the petals.

Magnolia grandiflora LARGE FLOWERED MAGNOLIA
A medium, spreading, evergreen tree with large, white, cup shaped flowers.

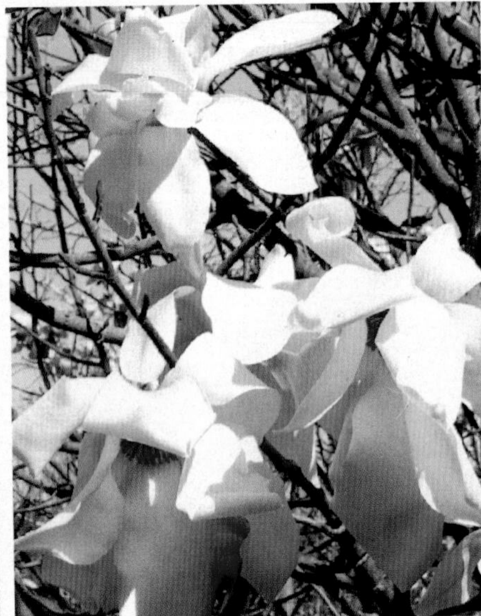

Magnolia dawsoniana
A small deciduous tree with fragrant nodding flowers coloured pale pink.

Magnolia cv. **Heaven Scent**
A hybrid of *M. liliiflora* cv. Nigra, this small deciduous tree has perfumed, pink and white flowers. One of the Gresham group.

Magnolia kobus
syn. ***M. thurberi***
On this small, deciduous, spreading tree the flowers are creamy white.

Magnolia kobus x ***M. stellata***
syn. ***M.*** x ***loebneri***
The flowers of this tall, deciduous shrub are white and star-like. This hybrid is now known as *M.* x *loebneri*.

Magnolia liliiflora MU-LAN
syn. ***M. quinquepeta***
A deciduous bushy shrub with purple-red to rose-pink goblet-like flowers.

Magnolia x ***liliiflora*** cv. **Ann**
Dark-mauve and white flowers feature on this compact hybrid shrub.

Magnolia x ***liliiflora*** cv. **Betty**
Tall and deciduous, this free flowering shrub has rosy wine coloured flowers.

Magnolia x ***liliiflora*** cv. **Centennial**
A hybrid cultivar with narrow mauve-pink to white petals.

Magnolia x ***liliiflora*** cv. **G. H. Kern**
A compact hybrid cultivar with pinky mauve and white flowers.

Magnolia x ***liliiflora*** cv. **Holland Red**
This showy cultivar has dark, reddish purple, goblet-like flowers.

Magnolia x ***liliiflora*** cv. **Jane**
A hybrid cultivar with bright rose-pink coloured flowers.

Magnolia x ***liliiflora*** cv. **Joy**
Long flowers coloured rosy claret bloom on this tall, deciduous shrub.

MAGNOLIA (cont)

***Magnolia* x *liliiflora* cv. Judy**
On this hybrid cultivar the flowers are pinkish.

***Magnolia* x *loebneri* cv. Leonard Messel**
Bushy and tall, this shrub to small tree has masses of showy pink flowers in spring.

***Magnolia* x *liliiflora* cv. Nigra**
Reddish purple goblet-like flowers are a feature of this cultivar.

***Magnolia* x *liliiflora* cv. Randy**
A hybrid cultivar with mauve-pink flowers.

***Magnolia* x *loebneri* cv. Merrill**
In spring, this cultivar has large white flowers.

***Magnolia* x *liliiflora* cv. Pinkie**
Late flowering, this tall deciduous shrub has rosy mauve coloured flowers.

***Magnolia* x *liliiflora* cv. Susan**
A compact hybrid cultivar with rose-pink flowers.

Magnolia officinalis
This small to medium deciduous tree has open, fragrant, cream flowers in spring.

Magnolia x ***raffillii*** cv. **Kew's Surprise**
Large rose-pink flowers bloom in profusion in spring on this small to medium tree.

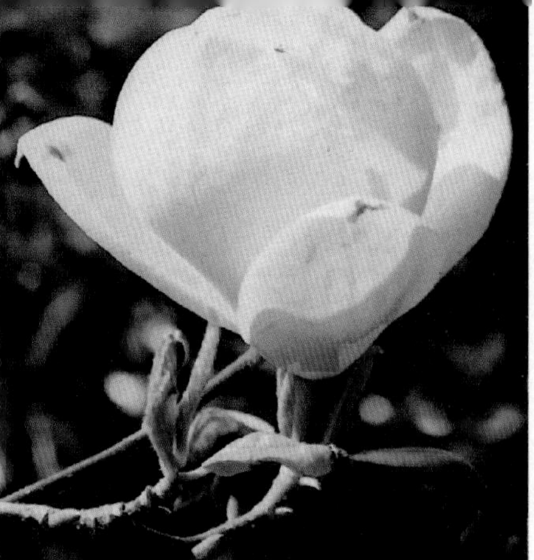

Magnolia cv. **Sayonara**
With creamy white flowers, this deciduous small tree is a hybrid between *M.* x *veitchii* and *M.* x *soulangeana* cv. Lennei Alba. One of the Gresham group.

Magnolia salicifolia ANISE MAGNOLIA
A deciduous tall shrub to small tree with medium size goblet shaped white flowers.

Magnolia sargentiana cv. **Caerhays Belle**
The large flowers of this free flowering, medium tree are coloured pale pink and carmine.

Magnolia sieboldii
A deciduous tall shrub with cup shaped pink flowers.

Magnolia x ***salicifolia*** cv. **Wada's Memory**
In spring, this small to medium, deciduous tree has upright white flowers. Believed to be a hybrid between *M. kobus* and *M. salicifolia.*

Magnolia sargentiana var. ***robusta***
Deciduous, this bushy, medium size tree has large, star shaped, pink and white flowers.

MAGNOLIA (cont)

Magnolia sieboldii ssp. ***sinensis***
syn. ***M. sinensis*** CHINESE MAGNOLIA
The cup-shaped flowers on this tall, broad, deciduous shrub are pinky white in colour.

Magnolia x ***soulangiana*** cv. **Alba Superba**
A showy cultivar with white cup shaped flowers with a touch of pink at the base of the petals.

Magnolia cv. **Slavin's Snowy**
Tall and open, this deciduous tree has long white flowers.

Magnolia x ***soulangiana*** cv. **Alexandrina**
This is a popular cultivar with rosy pink cup shaped flowers.

Magnolia x ***soulangiana*** cv. **Brozzonii**
A late flowering cultivar with large pink and white cup shaped flowers.

Magnolia x ***soulangiana***
CHINESE MAGNOLIA
A small deciduous tree which is a hybrid between *M. denudata* and *M. lilliflora*. It is very showy when covered with its upright, long, cup shaped flowers of rosy pink and white. Note *soulangiana* is commonly spelt *soulangeana*.

Magnolia x ***soulangiana*** cv. **Amabilis**
White flowers with touches of pink bloom on this slow growing, small, deciduous tree.

Magnolia x ***soulangiana*** cv. **Early Pink**
Early flowering, this cultivar has large purple-red cup shaped flowers.

Magnolia x ***soulangiana*** cv. **Lennei**
This is a late flowering cultivar with large purple-red cup shaped flowers.

Magnolia x ***soulangiana*** cv. **Lennei Alba**
On this cultivar the large cup shaped flowers are white with a touch of pink at the petal base.

Magnolia x ***soulangiana*** cv. **Norbertii**
The flowers of this slow growing cultivar are rosy pink and pale pink.

Magnolia x ***soulangiana*** cv. **Picture**
The flower petals of this deciduous small tree are white at the top, and wine at their base.

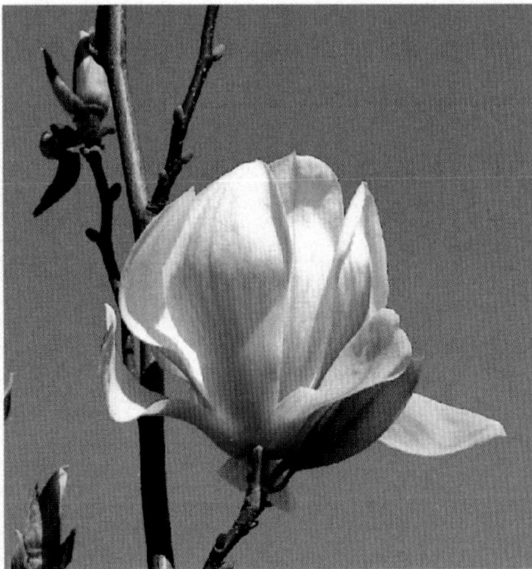

Magnolia x ***soulangiana*** cv. **Rosea**
A popular cultivar with large rose-pink and white flowers.

Magnolia x ***soulangiana*** cv. **Rustica Rubra**
Showy, this cultivar has burgundy coloured cup shaped flowers which are white inside.

Magnolia x ***soulangiana*** cv. **San Jose**
Free flowering, this cultivar has rosy pink cup shaped flowers.

Magnolia x ***soulangiana*** cv. **Triumphans**
The flowers of this cultivar are open-cup shaped and white.

Magnolia x ***soulangiana*** cv. **Vanhouttei**
An outstanding cultivar with burgundy coloured flowers.

MAGNOLIA (cont)

***Magnolia sprengeri* cv. Copeland Court**

The large flowers of this small to medium, deciduous tree are rose-pink to claret in colour.

***Magnolia sprengeri* cv. Diva**

This is a small deciduous tree with perfumed rosy pink and pale pink coloured flowers.

***Magnolia stellata* cv. Dawn**

The flowers of this cultivar have pale pink outer petals, the inner petals being almost white.

***Magnolia stellata* cv. King Rose**

On this cultivar the large flowers are pink and white in colour.

Magnolia stellata STAR MAGNOLIA

A bushy, deciduous, tall shrub to small tree with white star shaped flowers.

***Magnolia stellata* cv. Rosea**

A cultivar with white and rose-pink coloured flowers.

***Magnolia stellata* cv. Rosea Massey [Massey Rose]**

From U.S.A., this cultivar has pale pink to white coloured flowers.

***Magnolia stellata* cv. Waterlily**

A compact cultivar with pink buds opening to white flowers.

Magnolia* x *thompsoniana
This hybrid between *M. virginiana* and *M. tripetala* is a small tree with white cup shaped flowers.

***Magnolia* cv. Todd Gresham**
This hybrid between *M.* x *veitchii* and *M.* x *soulangiana* is a small deciduous tree with flowers of white and deep rose-pink. One of the Gresham group.

Magnolia tripetala 3
UMBRELLA MAGNOLIA
A deciduous small tree with a spreading crown and creamy white flowers.

Magnolia* x *veitchii
Deciduous, this small to medium tree is a hybrid between *M. campbellii* and *M denudata*. It has rose-pink and white flowers.

Magnolia virginiana SWEET BAY
A mostly evergreen small to medium tree which has ivory coloured cup shaped flowers.

X MAHOBERBERIS

BERBERIDACEAE

X *Mahoberberis neubertii*
A hybrid plant between a Mahonia and a Berberis. It is a hardy, evergreen shrub which prefers a mild climate. The plant has yellow flowers in spring and is propagated from cuttings.

Magnolia wilsonii
Tall and deciduous, this shrub to small tree has large white cup shaped, sometimes pendulous, flowers in spring.

m

MAHONIA

BERBERIDACEAE

Evergreen shrubs and small trees native to Asia and North and Central America. Most are cold hardy to -10 degrees Celcius and are grown for their showy flowers, their attractive fruit and decorative foliage. Mahonias prefer a well drained situation and respond well to fertiliser. Propagation is mostly from seed, also by division and grafting onto *Berberis thunbergii.*

Mahonia aquifolium OREGON GRAPE
syn. ***Berberis aquifolium***
An evergreen multi-branching shrub with golden yellow flowers in bunches followed by attractive bunches of grape-like fruit.

Mahonia aquifolium cv. **Apollo**
In late winter this cultivar has tight heads of golden yellow flowers.

Mahonia ehrenbergii
A small tree with cascading bunches of cream coloured flowers.

Mahonia bealei
This is an upright medium shrub with long leaves and pale yellow flowers in winter.

Mahonia eutriphylla
This medium shrub has prickly, holly-like leaves and yellow flowers.

Mahonia fortunei
A medium evergreen shrub with termina spikes of yellow flowers.

Mahonia japonica cv. **Hiemalis**
This is an open crowned cultivar which, in winter, has pale yellow flowers.

Mahonia lomariifolia
A tall evergreen shrub with clumps of erect spikes covered with yellow flowers.

Mahonia lomariifolia - fruit

The illustration shows the attractive bunches of fruit which hang like grapes.

Mahonia napaulensis

This is a medium shrub with terminal spikes of golden yellow flowers.

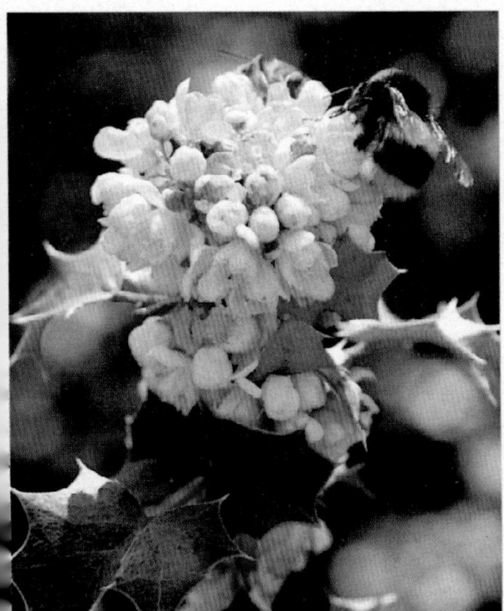

Mahonia trifolia

A small to medium shrub with holly-like leaves and heads of golden coloured flowers.

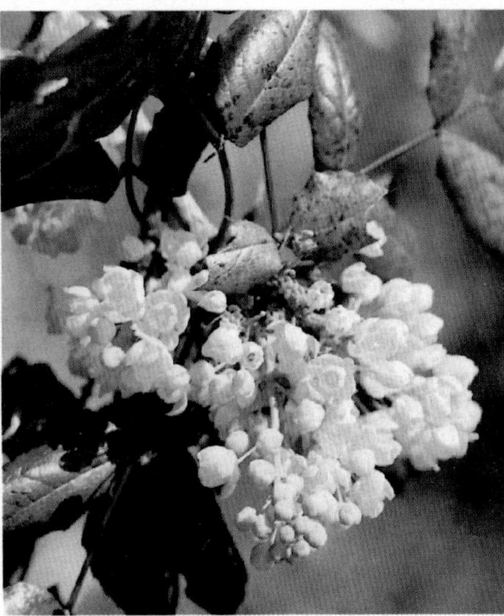

Mahonia* x *wagneri

From early spring to early summer, this small to medium hybrid shrub has clusters of yellow flowers. Foliage of these hybrids is variable.

***Mahonia* x *wagneri* cv. Moseri**

A showy cultivar grown for its attractive coloured foliage.

***Mahonia* x *wagneri* cv. Vicaryi**

This cultivar has large bunches of lemon-yellow flowers over several months. The foliage has red tinges in cold weather.

MALLOTUS

EUPHORBIACEAE

Mallotus japonicus

A deciduous small tree from Asia which is widely grown as an ornamental in cool to mild climates. It has spikes of pale yellow flowers. Propagate from seed and cuttings.

MALPIGHIA

Malpighiaceae

Evergreen shrubs from Central America and the Caribbean which are grown for their flowers and fruit in sub-tropical and tropical climates. Propagate from seed and cuttings.

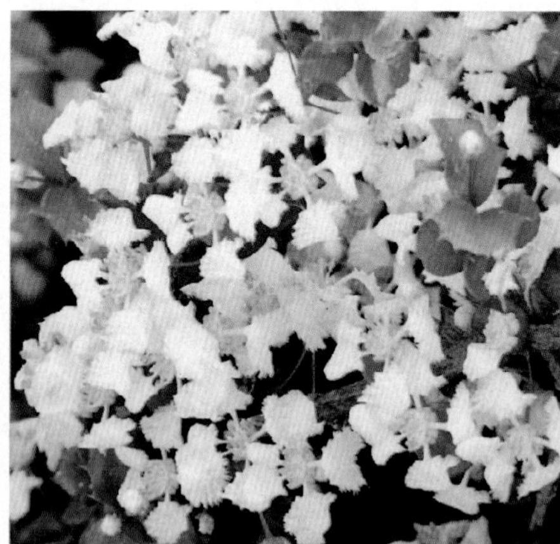

Malpighia coccigera MINIATURE HOLLY

A dense small shrub which is totally covered with showy pink flowers in spring.

Malpighia glabra BARBADOS CHERRY

This is an evergreen shrub with bright rose-pink flowers followed by edible red fruit which are high in Vitamin C.

Malpighia urens

An evergreen shrub with clusters of very pale pink flowers in spring.

MALUS APPLE

Rosaceae

Deciduous trees and shrubs native to Europe, Asia and North America. They are grown for their edible fruit and as spring flowering ornamentals. Apples are grown in climates from cold temperate to sub-tropical. Propagate from seed, with cultivars being budded or grafted.

***Malus* x *adstringens* cv. American Beauty**

Free flowering, the deep rose-pink flowers are followed by red fruit on this small, deciduous, hybrid tree.

***Malus* x *adstringens* cv. Hopa**

Clusters of rose-pink flowers in spring are followed by red fruit on this small, deciduous, hybrid tree.

***Malus* x *adstringens* cv. Niedzwetzkyana**

The flowers of this cultivar are deep rose-pink in colour.

Malus baccata

A deciduous tall shrub to small tree, with bunches of single white flowers in spring, followed by red fruit.

Malus baccata* var. *jackii

This variety has flowers coloured pink and white, followed by red fruit.

MALUS (cont)

Malus baccata var. ***mandshurica***

In spring this small tree is covered with white flowers. The small fruit are bright red.

Malus floribunda

A small tree with showy red buds followed by pink and white flowers in spring. The showy small fruit are coloured red.

Malus cv. **Henrietta Crosby**

Free flowering and deciduous, this small tree has masses of rosy red, single flowers in spring.

Malus cv. **Gorgeous**

A small tree with pink buds opening to white flowers. This tree has a heavy crop of small crimson fruit.

Malus hupehensis

This small tree has pale pink buds followed by white flowers. The small fruit are coloured yellow with a touch of pink.

Malus ioensis cv. **Plena**

Very popular, this crab apple has double pink flowers.

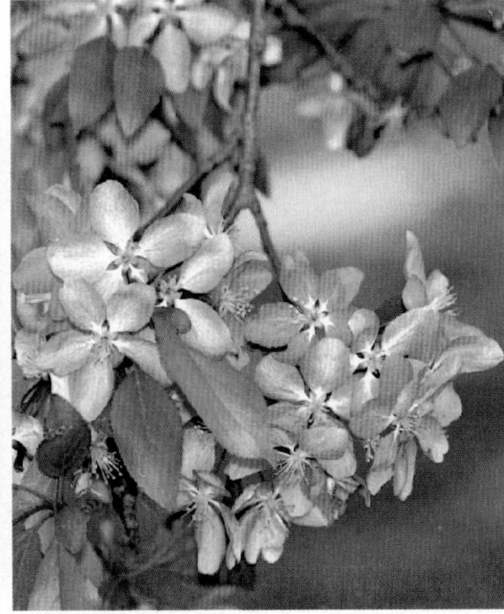

Malus cv. **Lake Irie**

In spring, this deciduous small tree has single, rose-pink flowers.

m

MALUS (cont)

Malus cv. **Laxton's Red**
This free flowering cultivar has deep rose-pink coloured flowers.

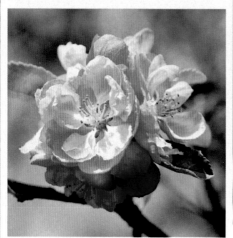

Malus x ***magdeburgensis***
The large, semi-double pink flowers of this small, deciduous tree are followed by fruit which are yellow, with red cheeks.

Malus x ***moerlandsii*** cv. **Liset**
Free flowering, this deciduous small tree has maroon coloured leaves and rosy red flowers in spring. The fruit are small, and deep red.

Malus x ***moerlandsii*** cv. **Profusion**
The rose-pink flowers of this showy cultivar cover the tree.

Malus prunifolia var. ***rinki***
In spring the rose-pink buds of this small deciduous tree open to almost white flowers. They are followed by yellowish, edible fruit.

Malus x ***purpurea***
A small hybrid tree with reddish new foliage and reddish purple flowers followed by purple-red small fruit.

Malus x ***purpurea*** cv. **Eleyi**
The pinky red flowers are followed by purple-red fruit on this popular cultivar.

Malus x ***purpurea*** cv. **Lemoinei**
A cultivar with brownish red new leaves and wine-red coloured flowers followed b purple fruit.

Malus x ***robusta***
Compact and deciduous, this tall shrub to small tree in spring has pale pink bud which open to white flowers. They are followed by oval, red fruit.

MALUS (cont)

Malus cv. **Royalty**
This cultivar has maroonish red flowers.

Malus sargentii
Pale pink buds open to white flowers which are followed by small red fruit on this tall shrub.

Malus spectabilis cv. **Riversii**
Yellow fruit follow the showy, pale pink, double flowers on this small tree.

Malus x ***sublobata***
The pink buds of this small, deciduous tree open to pink and white flowers, followed by yellow fruit.

Malus x ***zumi***
The rose-pink buds of this small, deciduous, conical shaped tree open to white and pink flowers, which are followed by red fruit.

Malus x ***schiedeckeri*** cv. **Hillieri**
A tall shrub with crimson-red buds opening to semi-double pink flowers.

Malus cv. **Wandin Glory**
A small tree with weeping foliage. It has white flowers followed by edible fruit.

MALVAVISCUS

MALVACEAE

Malvaviscus arboreus WAX MALLOW
A shrub from Central America which has pendulous red, partially unopened, Hibiscus-like flowers. This shrub needs a climate from warm temperate to tropical and is propagated from seed and cuttings.

Malvaviscus arboreus var. ***mexicanus***
A variety with pendulous flowers.

MALVAVISCUS (cont)

Malvaviscus arboreus cv. **Rosea**
On this cultivar the pendulous flowers are pink.

MANDEVILLA

APOCYNACEAE

A group of evergreen climbers and sometimes shrubs from tropical America. Although the name Mandevilla has been used for a long time there are still many nurserymen who continue to use the old name of Dipladenia, which has led to much confusion. These plants are very popular as free flowering outdoor plants in warm temperate to tropical climates and as indoor plants in cooler climates. They grow best in a rich soil with regular fertilising. Some are propagated from seed, but cuttings are used for the cultivars. It should be noted that some Mandevillas have plant variety rights registered, which prohibits general propagation of these PVR plants.

Mandevilla x ***amabilis***
cv. **Alice du Pont**
Of uncertain origin, this hybrid has bunches of large bright pink flowers over many months.

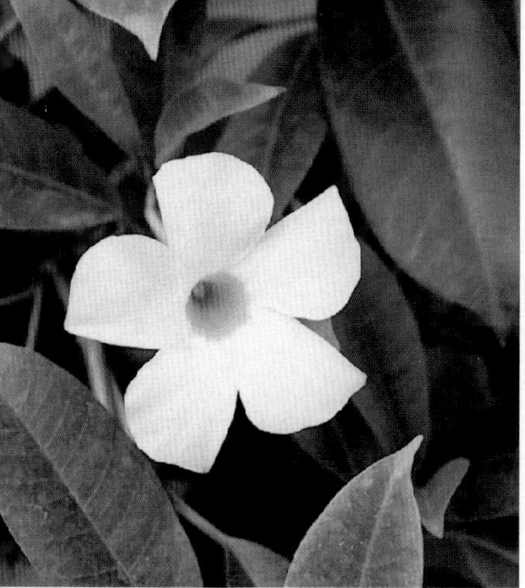

Mandevilla boliviensis
syn. ***Dipladenia boliviensis***
An evergreen climber with showy white flowers which have a golden centre.

Mandevilla boliviensis cv. **Swan Lake**
A cultivar which has been selected for its free flowering habit. Flowers are white.

Mandevilla laxa CHILEAN JASMINE
syn. ***M. suaveolens***
A free flowering evergreen climber which has white flowers. This climber is more cold tolerant than other Mandevillas.

Mandevilla laxa cv. **White Star**
The star shaped flowers of this cultivar are white.

Mandevilla sanderi
syn. ***Dipladenia sanderi***
Free flowering, this evergreen climber has masses of pink flowers over a long period.

Mandevilla sanderi cv. **My Fair Lady**
A cultivar which has cream flowers over many months.

MANDEVILLA (cont)

Mandevilla sanderi cv. **Red Riding Hood**
Flowering over a long period, this cultivar has pinkish red flowers.

Mandevilla sanderi cv. **Rosea**
A showy cultivar with rose-pink flowers over many months.

Mandevilla sanderi cv. **Scarlet Pimpernel**
Colourful and long flowering, this evergreen climber has scarlet coloured flowers.

Mandevilla sanderi cv. **Summer Snow**
A showy climber with pale pink flowers over many months.

MANETTIA

RUBIACEAE

Manettia luteo-rubra
BRAZILIAN FIRECRACKER
syn. ***M. bicolor***
Requiring a warm temperate to tropical climate, this modest climbing plant from South America has showy tubular red flowers with yellow ends. Propagate from softwood cuttings.

MANIHOT

EUPHORBIACEAE

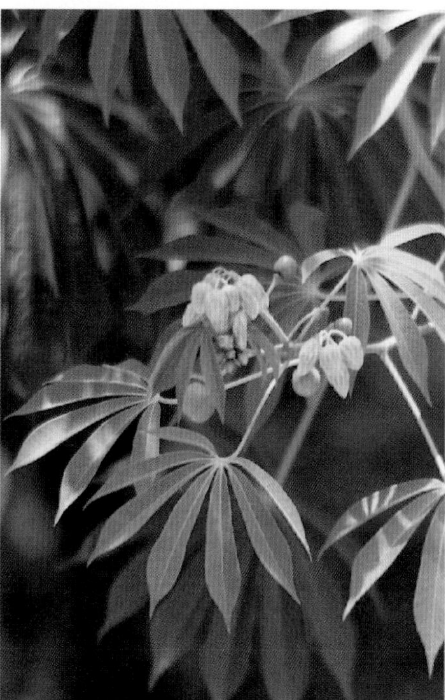

Manihot esculenta
CASSAVA; TAPIOCA PLANT
syn. ***M. utilissima***
This evergreen shrub from tropical America is grown as an ornamental plant, for food and to produce glue, alcohol and acetone. With cream flowers, it is propagated from seed and cuttings and by tuber division.

Manihot esculenta cv. **Variegata**
A showy cultivar which has green and yellow variegated leaves.

MANSOA

Bignoniaceae

Mansoa alliacea GARLIC VINE

syn. ***Pseudocalymma alliaceum***

The leaves of this evergreen climber from tropical America smell like garlic when crushed. With very large heads of dark-mauve to lilac trumpet flowers in summer, it needs a warm temperate to tropical climate with ample water. Propagate from seed and cuttings.

MARKHAMIA

Bignoniaceae

Evergreen shrubs to medium trees from Africa and Asia. They flower over a long period and have ribbon-like seed pods. Markhamias prefer climates from warm temperate to tropical and are propagated from seed.

Markhamia lutea

syn. ***M. hildebrandtii; M. platycalyx***

This is a small to medium tree with clusters of large golden yellow flowers which have brown stripes in the throat.

Markhamia stipulata

A tall shrub to small tree which has terminal clusters of large flowers coloured cream with a brownish red throat.

Markhamia zanzibarica

syn. ***M. acuminata***

A small upright tree which has clusters of flowers coloured brown and yellow.

MASCARENHASIA

Apocynaceae

Mascarenhasia arborescens

A small evergreen tree from Madagascar. It has clusters of perfumed white star shaped flowers over a long period. Propagate from seed and cuttings.

MEDICAGO

Fabaceae [Leguminosae]

Medicago arborea MOON TREFOIL

This medium, evergreen shrub with golden flowers and a deep root system is native to the Mediterranean area. It is used as an ornamental and for soil stabilization. Propagate from seed which requires scarification or hot water treatment.

MEDINILLA

MELASTOMATACEAE

Evergreen shrubs native to Africa, South East Asia and the Pacific, they are widely grown in sub-tropical and tropical areas as ornamentals for their showy heads of flowers. These shrubs are also grown in glass houses and conservatories in cooler climates. Propagation is from seed and cuttings.

Medinilla astronioides

A small shrub with clusters of pink buds which open into rose-pink flowers.

Medinilla magnifica

Lush and tropical, this large leaf shrub has large panicles of bright pink flowers.

Medinilla myriantha

Large panicles of bright pink flowers bloom on this small, compact, evergreen shrub.

Medinilla scortechinii

A compact shrub with panicles of pink flowers on orange stems.

Medinilla venosa

This open shrub has bunches of small pink flowers.

MEGASKEPASMA

ACANTHACEAE

Megaskepasma erythrochlamys

BRAZILIAN RED CLOAK

A free branching upright shrub which is native to South America. In climates from warm temperate to tropical, it is grown as an ornamental, for its large erect heads of red bracts and white flowers. This plant prefers a rich soil and is propagated from seed and cuttings.

MELALEUCA

MYRTACEAE

Melaleucas are commonly called paperbarks because of their flaky, paper-like bark. They are native to Australia and the Pacific and are grown as ornamentals, for the production of medicine and essential oils and for their bark which is used to line hanging baskets and in a form of art. Many prefer to grow in damp or swampy soils. Their climate range is from cold temperate to tropical. Propagation is from seed and cuttings.

Melaleuca alternifolia

A tall shrub to small tree which prefers damp heavy soils and a temperate to tropical climate. The leaves are used to produce medicinal tea-tree oil.

Melaleuca argentea

SILVER LEAF CADJEPUT

A tropical tree with shiny silver leaves and cream flowers. In ideal conditions in the wild, it can be a medium to large tree, but it is smaller in cultivation. If grown in temperate climates the leaves mostly lose their silver colour.

Melaleuca armillaris

BRACELET HONEY MYRTLE

Tolerant of some salt spray, this tall shrub to small tree has small leaves and ivory coloured flowers.

***Melaleuca armillaris* cv. Mauve**

A cultivar which has mauve bottlebrush-like flowers.

***Melaleuca bracteata* cv. Golden Gem**

A bushy tall shrub with golden foliage and cream coloured flowers.

Melaleuca calothamnoides

This is a free branching open crowned shrub which has bottlebrush-like flowers coloured green, cream and orange-red.

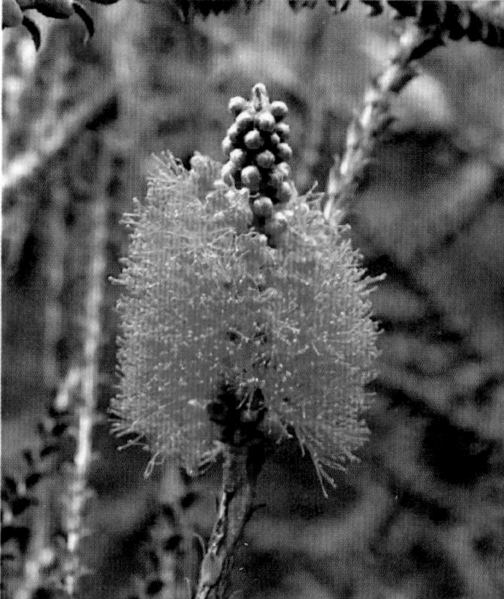

Melaleuca coccinea* ssp. *coccinea

GOLDFIELDS BOTTLEBRUSH

Suitable for dry climates, this medium shrub has small leaves and pinky red bottlebrush flowers.

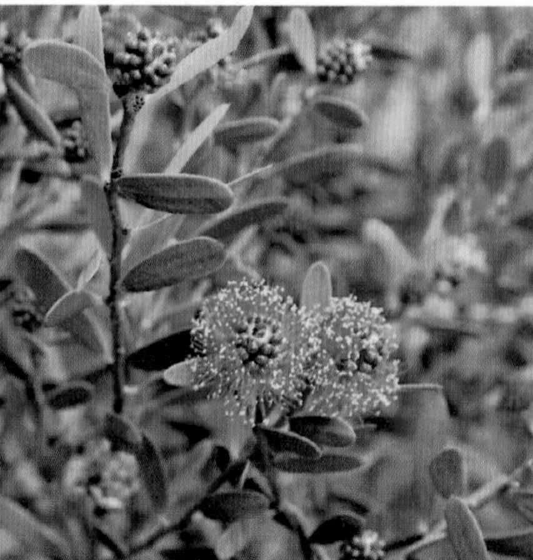

Melaleuca conothamnoides

A small shrub which has broad leaves and cerise coloured flowers. Suitable for dry climates.

Melaleuca dealbata

CLOUDY TEA TREE; HONEY TREE

Because it has a very high nectar yield, this small tropical tree with weeping foliage and cream flowers is an excellent tree for birds.

Melaleuca elliptica

GRANITE HONEY MYRTLE

Suitable for semi-arid climates, this is a medium open crowned erect shrub with red bottlebrush flowers.

Melaleuca filifolia* x *spathulata

This hybrid is a small shrub with cerise coloured flowers.

Melaleuca fulgens

SCARLET HONEY-MYRTLE

A small erect shrub with showy bottlebrush flowers coloured scarlet.

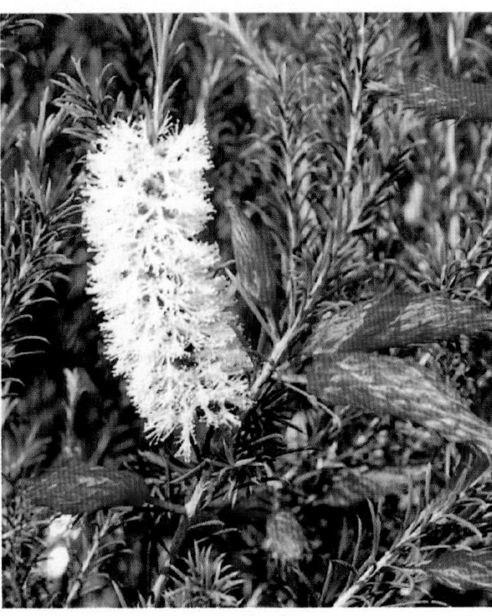

Melaleuca huegelii

CHENILLE HONEY MYRTLE

A tall shrub with reddish flower buds and cream flowers in spikes.

Melaleuca hypericifolia HILLOCK BUSH

The bottlebrush flowers of this tall rounded shrub are orange-red.

Melaleuca incana GREY HONEY MYRTLE

A medium shrub with greyish leaves and flowers coloured cream to yellow.

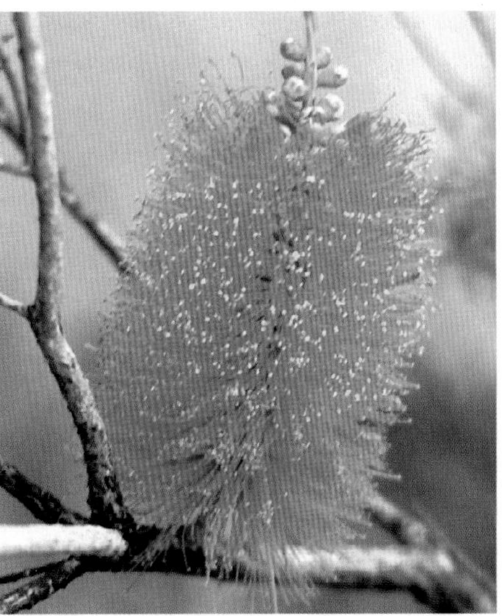

Melaleuca lateritia

ROBIN-REDBREAST BUSH

Sparse and upright, this shrub has showy orange-red bottlebrush flowers.

Melaleuca leiocarpa

A sparse shrub which has a pungent smell to the leaves. It has cream to yellow flowers. Suited to a dry climate.

MELALEUCA (cont)

Melaleuca leucadendra

WEEPING PAPERBARK

A medium to large tree which grows in damp situations and has masses of small cream coloured bottlebrush flowers.

Melaleuca leucadendra - fine leaf form

This form has leaves which are much narrower than other forms. Often spelt as *leucadendron* and *leucadendrum.*

Melaleuca linariifolia

FLAX LEAF PAPERBARK; SNOW-IN-SUMMER

A small upright tree with large heads of white coloured flowers.

***Melaleuca linariifolia* cv. Snowfire**

This small growing cultivar has cream coloured flowers.

Melaleuca megacephala

A small freely branching shrub with masses of small cream coloured flowers.

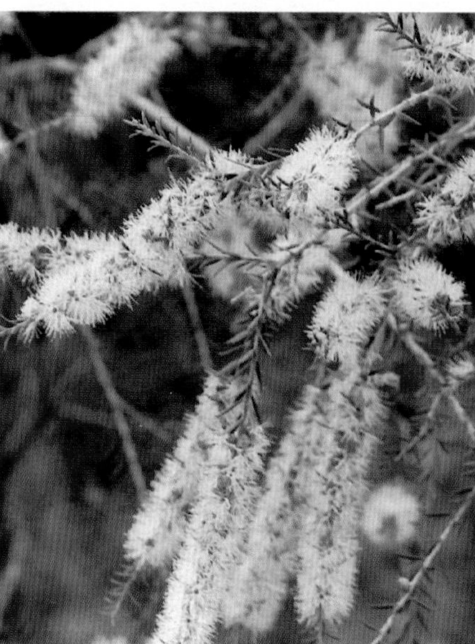

Melaleuca neglecta

This sparse shrub has long white coloured flower heads. Now referred to as *M. brevilfolia.*

Melaleuca nematophylla

Round, bright rose-pink flowers bloom on this small shrub. Now referred to as *M. filifolia.*

Melaleuca nodosa

A medium shrub which is covered with cream flowers in spring.

Melaleuca quinquenervia

BROAD LEAF PAPERBARK

Suitable for damp dituations, this medium tree has cream flower spikes.

Melaleuca radula
GRACEFUL HONEY MYRTLE
An open crowned shrub with pinky mauve flowers.

Melaleuca squamea
SWAMP HONEY MYRTLE
Sparse and upright, this shrub has masses of pinky lilac coloured flowers.

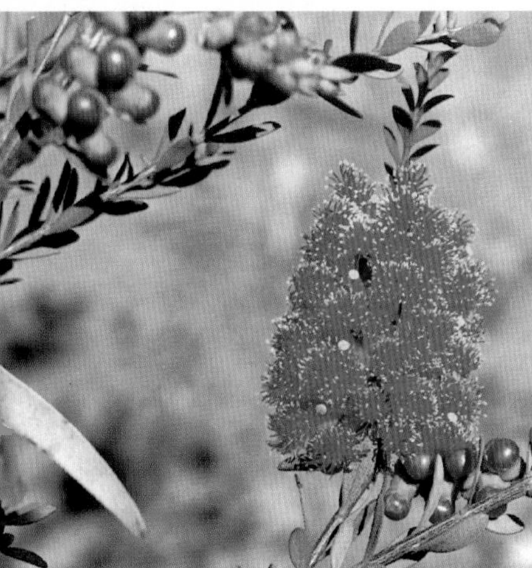

Melaleuca steedmanii
A sparse upright shrub. The showy bright red flower heads have distinct yellow anthers. Now referred to as *M. fulgens* ssp. *steedmanii.*

Melaleuca suberosa CORK BARK HONEY MYRTLE
Cerise coloured flowers along the branches feature on this sparse shrub.

Melaleuca tamariscina* ssp. *tamariscina
WEEPING PAPERBARK
A small tree which has large pendulous heads of cream flowers on pendulous branches.

***Melaleuca tamariscina* ssp. *tamariscina* cv. Rosea**
This very showy cultivar has pinky mauve coloured flowers.

Melaleuca thymifolia
The flowers of this small hardy shrub are mauve-violet.

***Melaleuca thymifolia* cv. Little Beauty**
A dwarf cultivar with violet coloured flowers.

MELALEUCA (cont)

Melaleuca thymifolia cv. **Nana**

This is a low growing spreading cultivar with mauve flowers.

Melaleuca thymifolia cv. **White Lace**

A cultivar which has white lace-like flowers.

Melaleuca thymifolia cv. **Pink Lace**

A cultivar which has pale pink lace-like flowers.

Melaleuca viridiflora cv. **Red Cloud**

A small tree with very large heads of red flowers which almost cover the tree.

Melaleuca thymifolia
cv. **Purple Splendour**

The flowers of this upright free flowering cultivar are purple in colour.

Melaleuca viridiflora var. ***rubiflora***

This small tree has clusters of bright red flowers and distinct yellow anthers.

Melaleuca wilsonii

WILSON'S HONEY MYRTLE

A spreading shrub with prickly leaves and cerise coloured flowers along the branches.

MELASTOMA

MELASTOMATACEAE

Evergreen shrubs and small trees which are native to Asia, Australia and tropical America. They prefer climates from temperate to tropical and flower over many months. These plants need plenty of water in hot weather. Propagate from seed and cuttings.

Melastoma affine

A medium evergreen Australian shrub which has large mauve coloured flowers over many months.

Melastoma candidum

The mauve flowers bloom over a long period on this bushy Asian shrub.

MELASTOMA (cont)

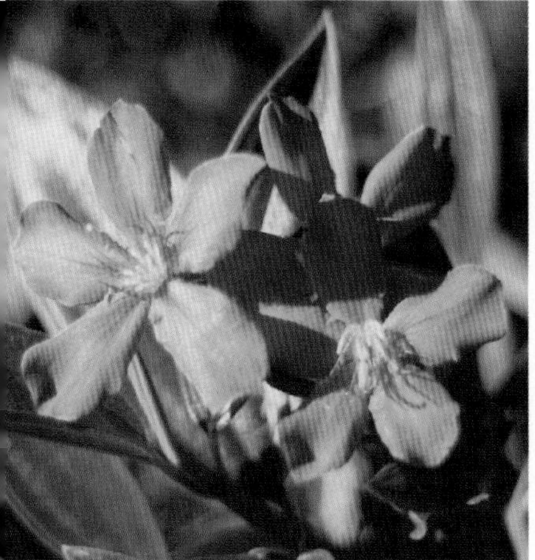

Melastoma denticulatum
A medium shrub with pale mauve flowers with petals which do not overlap.

Melastoma malabathricum
A medium shrub with pinky mauve coloured flowers over many months.

Melastoma sanguineum
Over many months, this medium, evergreen shrub has large, pinky purple flowers.

MELIA

MELIACEAE

Melia azedarach
CHINABERRY; WHITE CEDAR
A deciduous tree native to Australia, it is grown as an ornamental especially in dry climates and is used for both timber and medicine. Propagate from seed which is toxic.

MELIOSMA

SABIACEAE

Meliosma veitchiorum
A small to medium deciduous hardy tree which is native to China. It is grown as an ornamental in mild climates for its highly perfumed flowers. Propagate from seed or tip cuttings under mist.

MELLICOPE

RUTACEAE

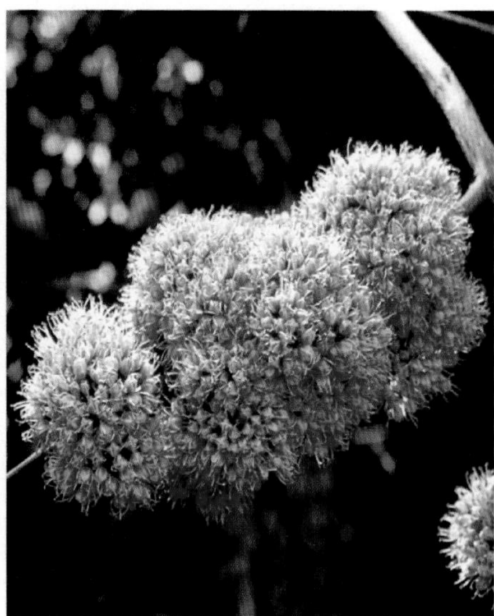

Mellicope elleryana CORKWOOD
syn. ***Euodia elleryana; Evodia elleryana***
An evergreen small to medium tree from Australia which is grown as an ornamental for its showy clusters of pink flowers.

MENZIESIA

ERICACEAE

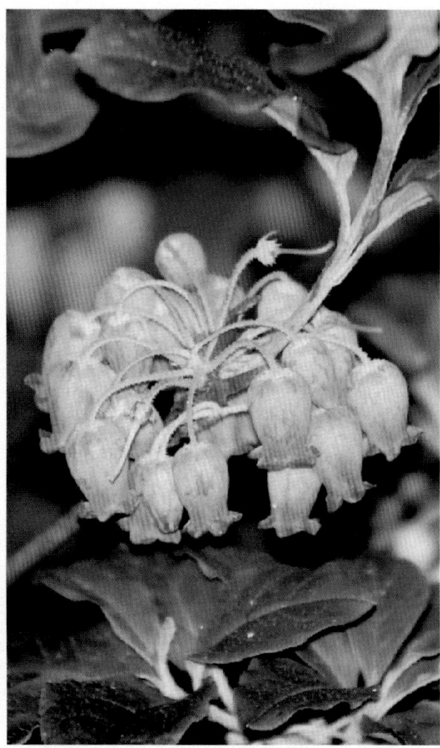

Menziesia ciliicalyx
This is a deciduous shrub native to Asia. In cool to mild climates it is grown as a showy ornamental for its rose coloured bunches of pendulous bell shaped flowers. Propagate from cuttings.

m

MERREMIA

Convolvulaceae

Merremia aurea SMALL WOOD ROSE

A rampant climber with large, heart shaped leaves and clusters of golden coloured flowers followed by decorative seed pods. This plant requires a warm climate and lots of water. Propagate from seed.

MESPILUS

Rosaceae

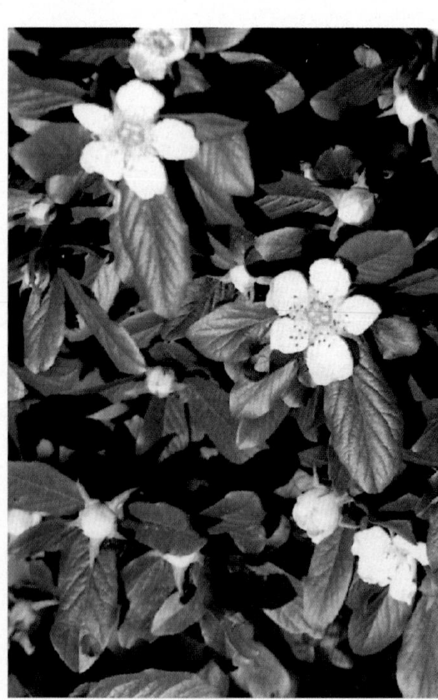

Mespilus germanica MEDLAR

Native to Europe and Asia, this deciduous tree has been grown for its edible fruit for more than 1000 years. It is widely grown as an ornamental in cool climates. It has showy white flowers and is propagated from seed and by budding or grafting.

Mespilus germanica cv. **Dutch**

A cultivar which has larger flowers and fruit.

Mespilus germanica cv. **Nottingham**

This cultivar is a more upright grower.

METROSIDEROS

Myrtaceae

Evergreen climbers, shrubs and small trees from Africa, South East Asia, Australia and New Zealand. They are grown as ornamentals for their colourful flowers. Many Metrosideros are tolerant of salt spray. These plants will grow in a wide range of soils, in climates from cool temperate to tropical. Propagation is from seed and cuttings.

Metrosideros carmineus

A climbing plant with heads of carmine coloured flowers.

Metrosideros excelsa

NEW ZEALAND CHRISTMAS TREE

A salt tolerant small tree which has large bunches of red flowers in summer.

Metrosideros excelsa cv. **Variegata**

A cultivar which has variegated leaves which are grey-green inside and cream on the edges.

Metrosideros queenslandica

A small rainforest tree which has golden coloured flowers. This tree needs dappled light.

Metrosideros cv. **Thomasii**
This is a hardy small tree with heads of red flowers.

MICHELIA

MAGNOLIACEAE

Evergreen trees, native to Asia, which grow in climates from cool temperate to tropical. They are free flowering, fragrant showy ornamentals which prefer open sunny situations. Propagate from seed and cuttings.

Michelia champaca
Over many months this small tree has fragrant, amber coloured flowers.

Michelia champaca cv. **Alba**
A form which has highly perfumed white flowers.

Michelia crassipes
Large perfumed flowers bloom along the branches of this small tree, which is suitable for cool climates.

Michelia doltsopa
Reasonably cold tolerant, this medium tree has large magnolia-like white flowers.

Michelia figo
PORT WINE MAGNOLIA; BANANA SHRUB
syn. ***M. fuscata***
A tall evergreen shrub with perfumed flowers which are whitish pink on the outside and port wine coloured inside.

Michelia yunnanensis
This open crowned small tree has large saucer shaped white perfumed flowers along the branches, and is suitable for cool climates.

MILLETTIA

FABACEAE [LEGUMINOSAE]

Shrubs, trees and climbers native to Africa, South East Asia, India, Madagascar and Australia. They are widely grown as ornamentals, in climates from temperate to tropical, for their showy flowers. Propagate from seed.

Millettia australis
A woody spring flowering climber which has long erect racemes of mauve to violet coloured flowers.

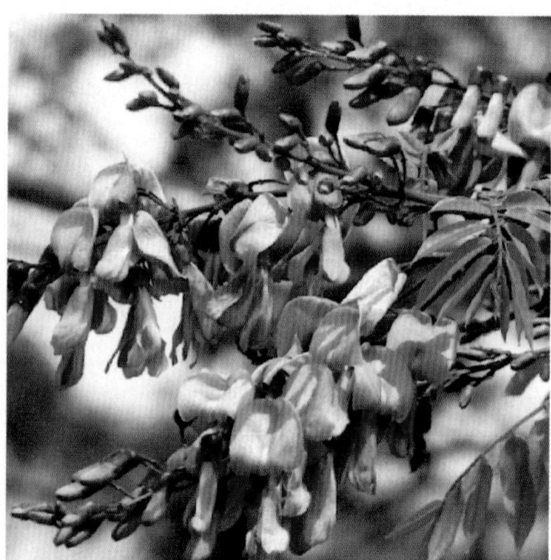

Millettia dura
Pendulous racemes of mauve to violet coloured flowers bloom on this small to medium size tree.

Millettia ferruginea
In spring, this small tree has large heads of rosy cerise coloured flowers.

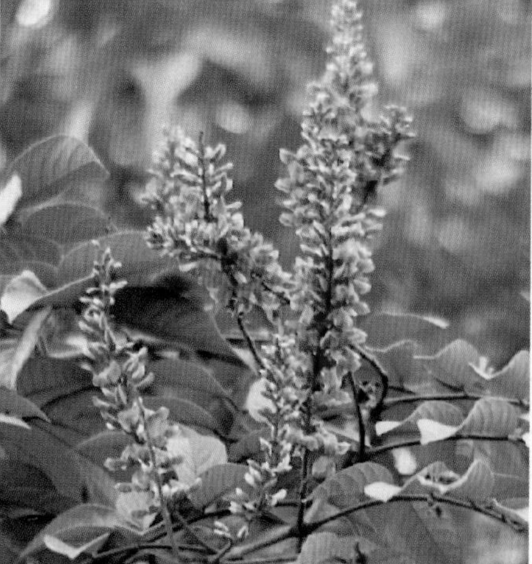

Millettia grandis
This small tree has erect spikes of violet coloured flowers.

Millettia megasperma NATIVE WISTERIA
There are large showy heads of lilac coloured flowers on this rainforest climber.

Millettia megasperma - seed pods
This illustration shows the large seed pods.

MIMUSOPS

SAPOTACEAE

Mimusops coriacea
A bushy tall shrub which is grown as an ornamental for its showy yellow fruit. It prefers a tropical or sub-tropical climate and is propagated from seed.

MINA [IPOMOEA]

CONVOLVULACEAE

Mina lobata
Native to tropical America, this climbing plant has bunches of red and cream coloured flowers. In cool climates it is grown as an annual. Propagate from seed. This genus is now referred to as Ipomoea.

MIRBELIA

FABACEAE [LEGUMINOSAE]

Mirbelia dilatata

A tall prickly leaf evergreen shrub from Western Australia which is grown as a showy flowering ornamental. It has large heads of pinky cerise flowers in spring. This plant grows in cool temperate to warm temperate climates and is grown from seed.

MITRARIA

GESNERIACEAE

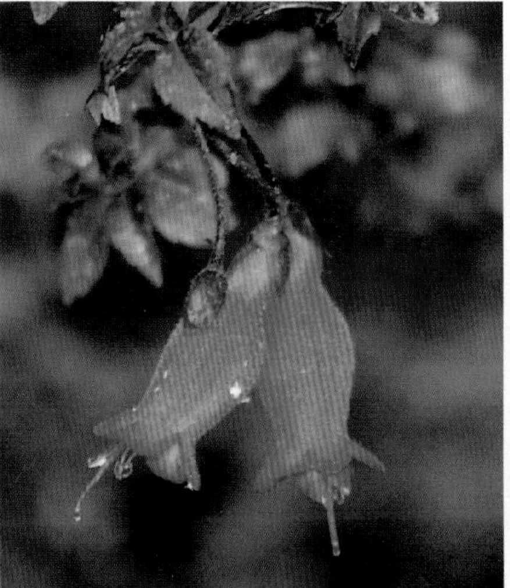

Mitraria coccinea

A semi-clumping evergreen shrub which is native to Chile. It is grown outdoors in warm climates and as an indoor plant in cooler climates. The plant prefers a moist rich soil. Flowers are tubular and orange-red in colour. Propagate from seed and cuttings.

MITRIOSTIGMA

RUBIACEAE

Mitriostigma axillare

Native to South Africa, this evergreen shrub has perfumed white flowers. It is grown as an ornamental in cool temperate to sub-tropical climates and requires an open site with well drained soil and ample water in hot weather. Propagate from seed or cuttings.

MONODORA

ANNONACEAE

Monodora myristica JAMAICA NUTMEG

A small evergreen tree native to central Africa. It is a tropical plant with unusually shaped highly perfumed cream and brown coloured flowers. Propagate from seed.

MONSTERA

ARACEAE

Evergreen, large leaf, climbing plants from tropical America which are grown as ornamentals and for fruit production. They are grown outdoors in climates from warm temperate to tropical and as indoor plants in cooler climates. Propagate from seed and cuttings.

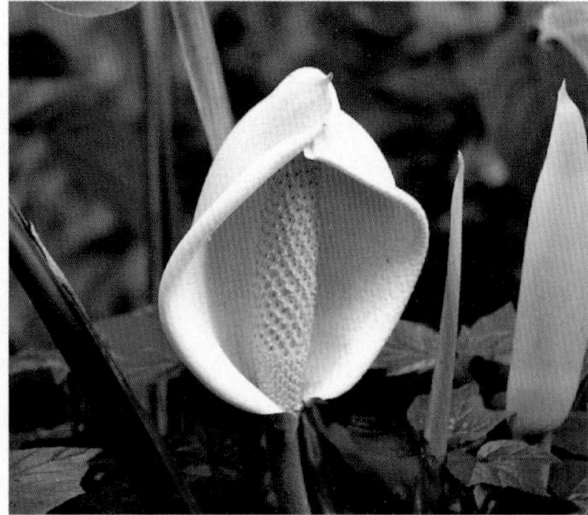

Monstera deliciosa FRUIT SALAD PLANT

A large, perforated leaf climber widely grown as an indoor plant. It has long edible fruit.

Monstera deliciosa cv. **Variegata**

A cultivar with green and white variegated foliage.

Monstera friedrichsthalii

Needing a warm situation, this is a climber with big perforations in the large leaves.

MONSTERA (cont)

Monstera obliqua SWISS CHEESE PLANT
A climbing plant with shiny leaves which are perforated.

MONTANOA

ASTERACEAE [COMPOSITAE]

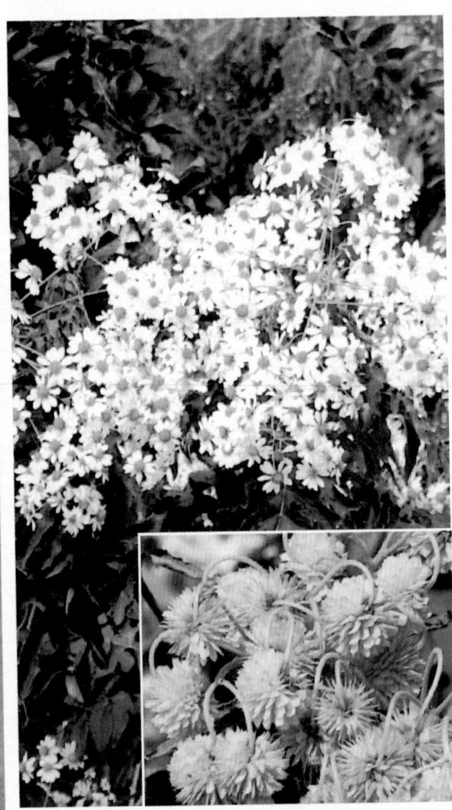

Montanoa bipinnatifida
A bushy shrub native to tropical America, it is grown for its large ornamental heads of white daisy flowers and showy white seed pods, in climates from warm temperate to tropical. Propagate from seed.

MORINDA

RUBIACEAE

Morinda citrifolia INDIAN MULBERRY
A tall bushy evergreen shrub which has bunches of white flowers followed by white fruit which is used in India and Asia in curries.

Morinda reticulata
From Australia, this tropical evergreen shrub has large cream flower bracts and bunches of cream flowers. It is grown as an ornamental in sub-tropical and tropical climates and is propagated from seed and cuttings.

MORINGA

MORINGACEAE

Moringa oleifera HORSERADISH TREE
syn. ***M. pterygosperma***
A deciduous small tree which is grown for its perfumed flowers, for its edible roots and for the oil produced from the seeds, which is used in perfumes. These trees have clusters of cream flowers followed by long seed pods. They require a warm climate and are propagated from seed.

MUCUNA

FABACEAE [LEGUMINOSAE]

Vigorous climbers and shrubs from the tropics which are grown for their showy flowers. They require a tropical climate and are propagated from seed.

Mucuna bennettii
This rambling climber has large long pendulous racemes of bright red flowers.

Mucuna novoguineensis
A free growing vigorous climber with showy large pendulous racemes of red flowers.

MUNDULEA

FABACEAE [LEGUMINOSAE]

Mundulea sericea CORK BUSH
A free flowering shrub from South Africa, it is grown as an ornamental for its showy heads of purple-violet flowers. It grows in climates from mild temperate to sub-tropical and is propagated from seed.

MURRAYA

RUTACEAE

Small trees and shrubs which are native to India, Asia and Australia. They are grown as ornamentals for their showy perfumed flowers and some for their edible leaves. These plants prefer a climate from temperate to tropical and are propagated from seed and cuttings.

Murraya koenigii CURRY LEAF
A small aromatic tree with bunches of cream flowers. The leaves are widely used to flavour curries.

Murraya paniculata ORANGE JESSAMINE
syn. ***M. exotica***
In spring and summer this tall evergreen shrub has masses of highly perfumed creamish white flowers.

MUSSAENDA

RUBIACEAE

Shrubs and twining plants, native to Africa, Madagascar and Asia, which are grown for their showy flower bracts. They grow in climates from temperate to tropical although most prefer the warmer temperatures. Propagate from seed and cuttings.

Mussaenda erythrophylla
A medium to tall bushy shrub with large red flower bracts and white flowers.

***Mussaenda erythrophylla* cv. Donna Luz** BANGKOK ROSE
This is a bushy tall shrub with large clusters of deep apricot coloured flower bracts.

***Mussaenda erythrophylla* cv. Fire Glow**
Spectacular in flower, this medium evergreen shrub has large clusters of bright red flower bracts.

***Mussaenda erythrophylla* cv. Flamingo**
This showy cultivar has large brightly coloured flower bracts of flamingo pink.

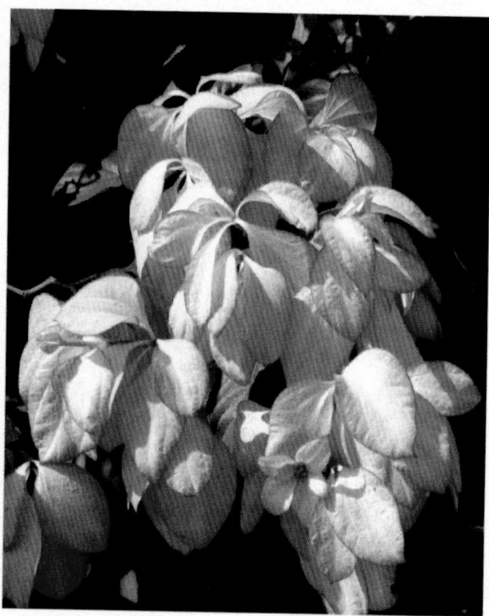

***Mussaenda erythrophylla* cv. Pink Dancer**
An outstanding bushy shrub with large heads of salmon-pink flower bracts.

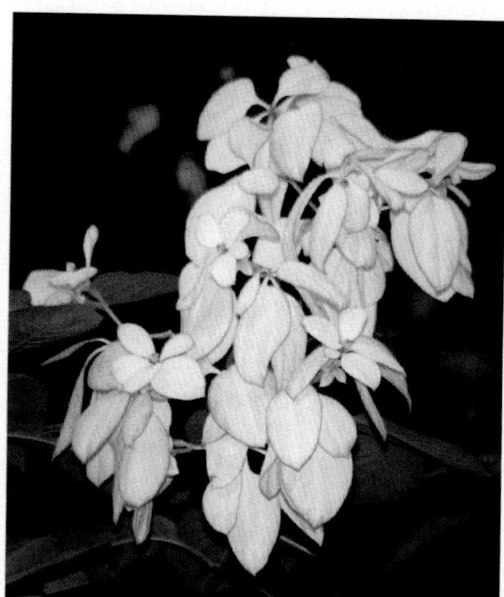

***Mussaenda erythrophylla* cv. Queen Sirikit**
The large showy heads of flower bracts are coloured pale pink on this bushy shrub.

MUSSAENDA (cont)

Mussaenda erythrophylla **cv. Rosea**
A bushy shrub with large heads of salmon-orange coloured flower bracts.

Mussaenda frondosa
Bushy and evergreen, this shrub has ivory coloured flower bracts and golden yellow flowers.

Mussaenda incana
A spreading evergreen shrub with ivory coloured flower bracts and yellow flowers.

Mussaenda philippica
Evergreen, this dense spreading shrub has large clumps of ivory coloured flower bracts and orange flowers.

Mussaenda philippica **cv. Aurorae**
This cultivar is a bushy evergreen shrub with large pendulous heads of white flower bracts.

Mussaenda **cv. Tropic Snow**
A spreading evergreen shrub with white flower bracts and yellow flowers.

MYOPORUM

MYOPORACEAE

Evergreen shrubs which are used as hedges and ornamental specimens and are native to Australia and Africa. They grow in cool temperate to tropical climates, in a wide range of soils. Propagate from seed and cuttings.

Myoporum insulare
This is an upright bushy shrub with small clusters of white flowers.

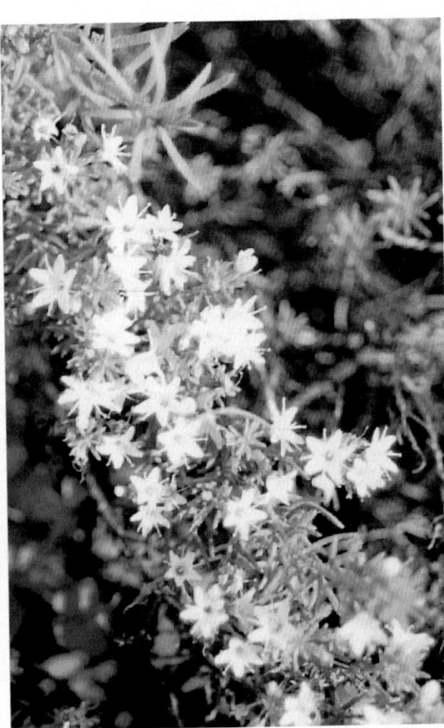

Myoporum parvifolium
A spreading ground cover shrub with white star shaped flowers which may cover the whole bush.

MYRISTICA

Myristicaceae

Evergreen trees native to Australia and South East Asia. They need a hot climate and adequate water and fertiliser. Propagate from seed and by grafting.

Myristica fragrans NUTMEG

A small evergreen tree which is used to produce commercial nutmeg and mace. It has small pale yellow flowers and cream seed pods.

Myristica insipida NATIVE NUTMEG

Endemic to Australia, this small evergreen tree has cream to yellow flowers and cream nutmeg fruit.

MYROXYLON

Fabaceae [Leguminosae]

Myroxylon balsamum BALSAM TREE

A small tree with a wide dense crown, which is native to South America. It needs a warm climate to produce its large seeds. The plant produces balsam which is used in medicine and perfume. Propagate from seed.

MYRTUS

Myrtaceae

Evergreen shrubs and small trees native to Africa, Europe, West Indies and North America. They are widely grown as ornamentals in cool temperate to tropical climates. Propagate from seed and cuttings.

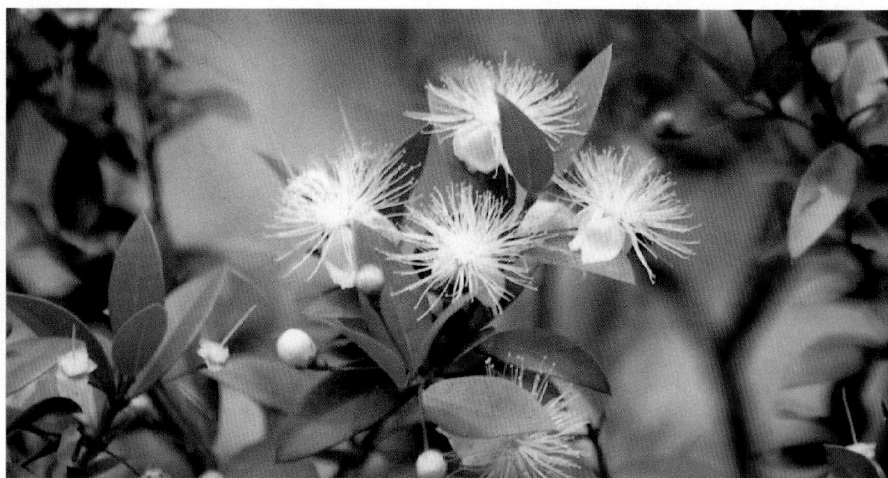

Myrtus communis GREEK MYRTLE; LOVE AND PEACE PLANT

A bushy shrub with delicate white flowers.

NANDINA

Berberidaceae

An evergreen shrub which has various cultivars and is native to India and Japan. Nandina is grown as an ornamental for its showy red coloured winter leaves and berries. It is tolerant of some frost which intensifies the leaf colour. Propagate by division or from cuttings and seed which needs to be soaked in water and kept just above freezing for 3 to 4 weeks before sowing.

Nandina domestica HEAVENLY BAMBOO

A clumping shrub which has clusters of small white flowers and bright red round fruit. The leaves colour red in winter.

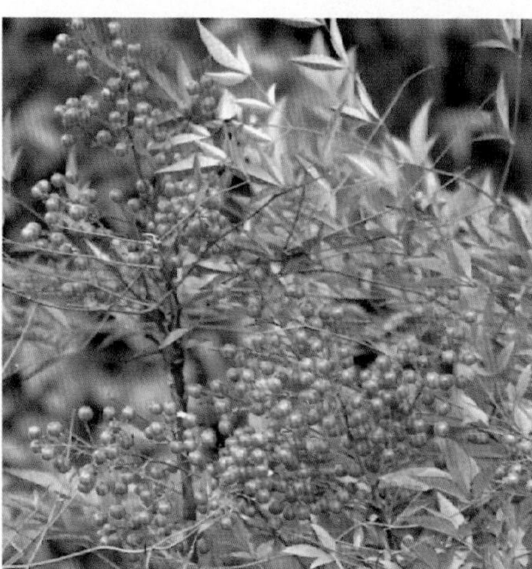

Nandina domestica - fruit

This illustration shows the colourful red fruit.

***Nandina domestica* cv. Harbour Dwarf**

A dwarf grower with bright red winter leaves.

NANDINA (cont)

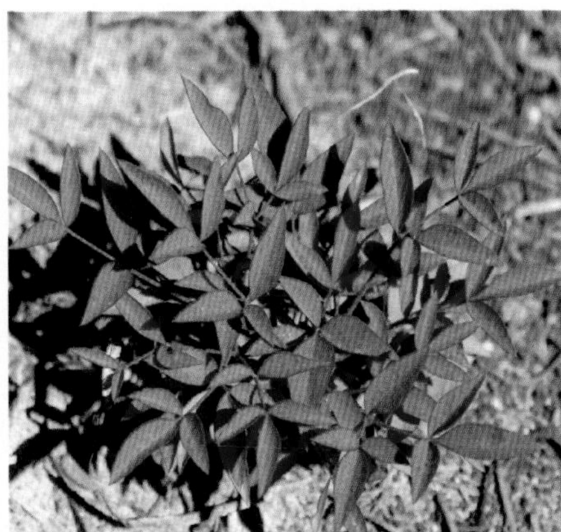

Nandina domestica cv. **Miniata**
In winter this small growing spreading Nandina has showy red leaves.

Nandina domestica cv. **Nana Purpurea**
A compact small plant which has red leaves most of the year which turn to purple-red in winter.

Nandina domestica
cv. **Pygmaea [Nana]**
This is a compact bushy plant which has red winter foliage.

NAUCLEA

RUBIACEAE [NAUCLEACEAE]

Nauclea orientalis LEICHHARDT TREE
A spreading tree which is native to Australia and South East Asia. It is an outstanding shade tree in parks and has showy round flowers, coloured cream. This tree requires a temperate to tropical climate and is propagated from seed.

NEMATANTHUS

GESNERIACEAE

Evergreen semi-climbing plants from South America which are widely grown as hanging basket plants. They are grown outdoors in temperate to tropical climates and indoors and glass houses in cooler climates. Propagate from seed and cuttings.

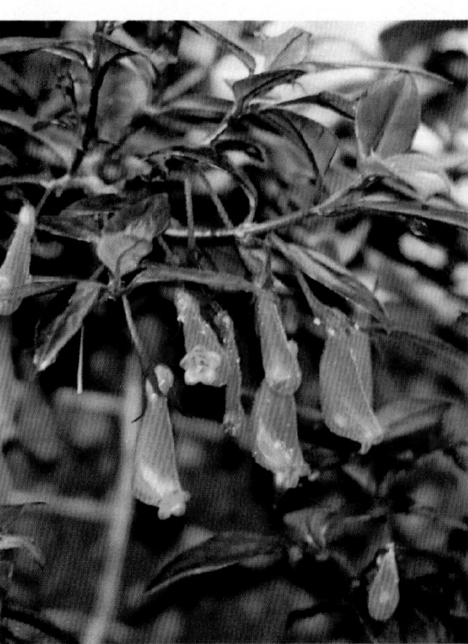

Nematanthus cv. **Black Magic**
The pendulous flowers on this cultivar are red, with yellow tips.

Nematanthus cv. **Castanet**
A semi-climbing evergreen plant with red and apricot coloured tubular flowers.

Nematanthus crassifolium
The tubular flowers of this spreading semi-climbing evergreen plant are red.

Nematanthus gregarius
A pendulous semi-climbing plant with shiny leaves and orange coloured flowers.

NEMATANTHUS (cont)

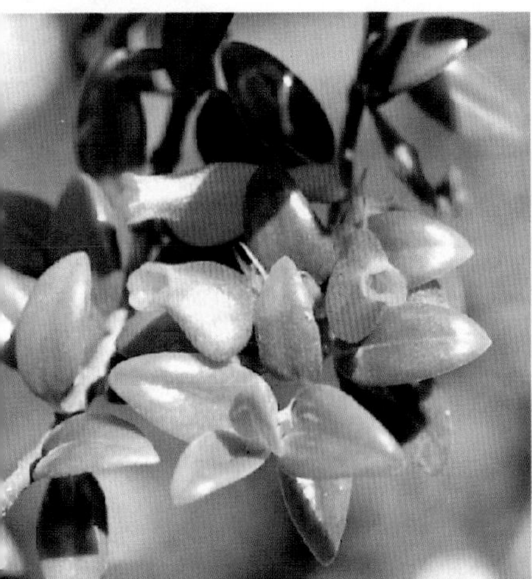

Nematanthus **cv. Minuette**
A semi-climbing pendulous spreading plant with red and yellow coloured flowers.

Nematanthus **cv. Tropicana**
This free flowering cultivar has orange and yellow striped flowers.

Nematanthus **cv. Moon Glow**
Bright pink and yellow flowers along the branches feature on this pendulous, semi-climbing plant.

Nematanthus **cv. Rubra**
This cultivar has dark red flowers along the branches.

Nematanthus **cv. Variegata**
This cultivar has golden yellow flowers and cream and grey-green variegated foliage.

NEOFABRICIA

MYRTACEAE

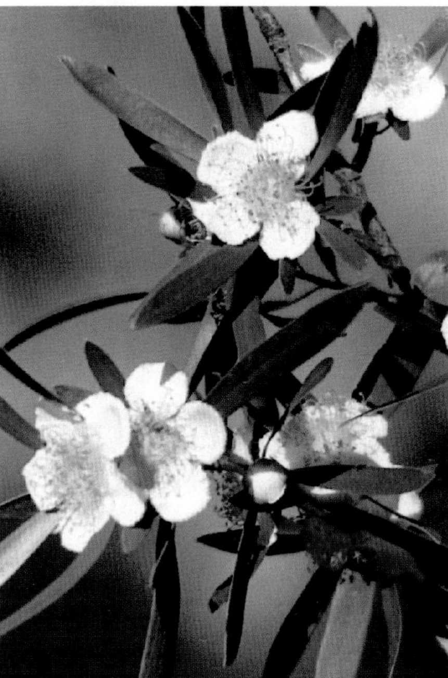

Neofabricia myrtifolia
syn. ***Leptospermum fabricia***
An upright Australian shrub which is grown as a flowering ornamental in climates from temperate to tropical. Flowers are clear yellow. It is grown from seed and cuttings.

NEONAUCLEA

RUBIACEAE

Neonauclea obtusa
A spreading medium evergreen tropical tree which has large flowers that look like yellow drumsticks. Propagate from seed.

NERIUM

OLEANDER

APOCYNACEAE

Native to the Mediterranean, these evergreen shrubs, although poisonous, are widely grown as flowering ornamentals in climates from cool temperate to tropical. They are mostly of medium size, but there are variations in height, from small to tall shrubs. Propagate from seed and cuttings. They need hard pruning after flowering.

Nerium oleander cv. **Doctor Golfin**
The flowers on this shrub are single and cerise-red, in large clusters.

Nerium oleander cv. **Mrs F. Roeding**
This cultivar has large bunches of semi-double salmon-pink flowers.

Nerium oleander cv. **Beryl Anderson**
A shrub with heads of double apricot-pink flowers which may vary in colour with age.

Nerium oleander cv. **Mademoiselle Dubois**
Late flowering, this cultivar has single white flowers.

Nerium oleander cv. **Petite Salmon**
A small bushy shrub with masses of single salmon-pink flowers.

Nerium oleander cv. **Charles Murcott**
This cultivar has large clusters of single pink flowers.

Nerium oleander cv. **Madoni Grandiflorum**
A medium evergreen shrub with large clusters of double white flowers.

Nerium oleander cv. **Pink Joy**
A bushy shrub with heads of single pink flowers.

NERIUM (cont)

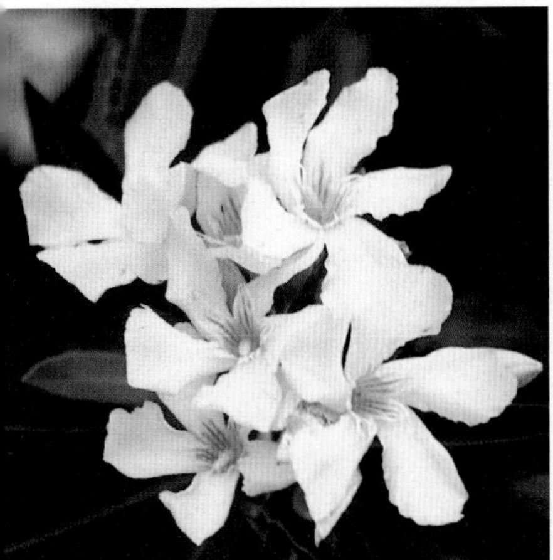

***Nerium oleander* cv. Souvenir d'August Roger**
Single, very pale pink flowers form in large heads on this bushy shrub.

***Nerium oleander* cv. Splendens**
A bushy shrub with large heads of double, bright pink flowers.

***Nerium oleander* cv. Splendens Variegata**
This bushy cultivar has showy green and yellow variegated leaves.

NESOCODON

CAMPANULACEAE

Nesocodon mauritianus
A small multi-branched evergreen shrub native to Mauritius. It has pale mauve bell shaped flowers and is grown as an ornamental in mild to sub-tropical climates. Propagate from seed and cuttings.

NEWBOULDIA

BIGNONIACEAE

Newbouldia laevis
A small to medium evergreen tree which is native to tropical Africa. It has large heads of pinkish flowers in spring. The tree is grown as an ornamental in sub-tropical and tropical climates. Propagate from seed.

***Newbouldia laevis* cv. Purple Fancy**
A cultivar which has pinky purple flowers in large tightly packed bunches.

NICOTIANA

SOLANACEAE

Nicotiana tabacum TOBACCO
A medium shrub which is native to tropical America, this plant is grown in warm climates to produce smoking tobacco. It has large leaves and flowers coloured green, cream or pink. Propagate from seed and grow as a biennial shrub.

n - o

NUXIA

Loganiaceae

Nuxia floribunda

A free flowering small tree native to South Africa. It has large showy heads of small cream flowers. This plant grows in climates from cool temperate to subtropical. Propagate from seed.

NUYTSIA

Loranthaceae

Nuytsia floribunda WESTERN AUSTRALIAN CHRISTMAS TREE

A small parasitic tree from Western Australia. It has very large heads of golden flowers in mid-summer. The plant prefers a temperate climate and needs to attach to grass or shrub roots. Propagate from seed.

OCHNA

Ochnaceae

Evergreen tropical shrubs which are grown as ornamentals for their flowers and showy seed pods. They will grow in a wide range of soils in climates from temperate to tropical. Propagate from seed.

Ochna kirkii BIRD'S EYE BUSH

A tall shrub with yellow flowers followed by black seeds, backed by red bracts.

Ochna serrulata MICKEY-MOUSE PLANT

A medium shrub with yellow flowers. The black seeds are backed with red bracts. This illustration shows these seeds.

Ochna thomasiana

A medium shrub with yellow cup type flowers. These are followed by black fruit.

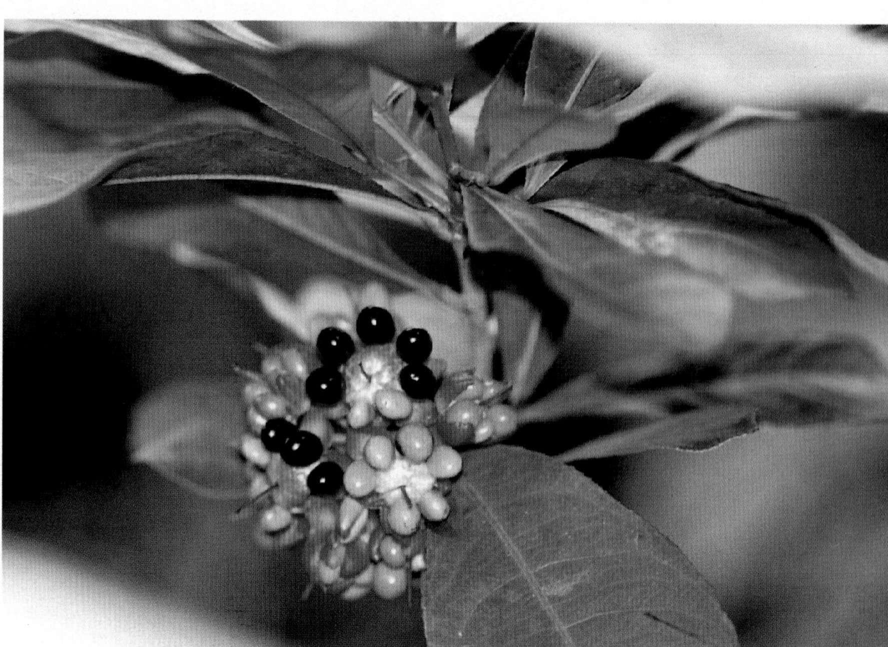

Ochna mossambicensis

This is a tall shrub with yellow flowers followed by black fruit with red calyces.

OCHROSIA

Apocynaceae

Ochrosia elliptica POKOSOLA

A small tree from Australia which is grown as an ornamental in sub-tropical to tropical climates for its yellow flowers and colourful, though toxic, red seeds. Propagate from seed. Illustration shows the colourful seeds.

ODONTADENIA

Apocynaceae

Odontadenia macrantha

An evergreen climber from tropical America. It has large heads of yellow to orange coloured flowers and needs a tropical climate. Propagate from seed or cuttings.

ODONTONEMA

Acanthaceae

Small to medium evergreen shrubs, native to tropical America. They are grown outdoors in sub-tropical and tropical climates as showy, flowering ornamentals, and in milder climates, as indoor plants. They benefit from pruning and fertilizing after flowering. Propagate from seed and cuttings.

Odontonema schomburgkianum

syn. ***Thyrsacanthus rutilans***

This is an open shrub with pendulous heads of red tubular flowers.

Odontonema strictum

A bushy evergreen shrub native to Central America. It is grown as a free flowering ornamental for its showy red flowers and needs a warm climate. The plant is often misnamed as *Justicia coccinea*. Propagate from seed, cuttings or by division.

OLEARIA

Asteraceae [Compositae]

Evergreen shrubs and small trees native to Australia and New Zealand. They have showy heads of daisy flowers and can be cold or warm climate plants. Olearias are propagated from seed and cuttings.

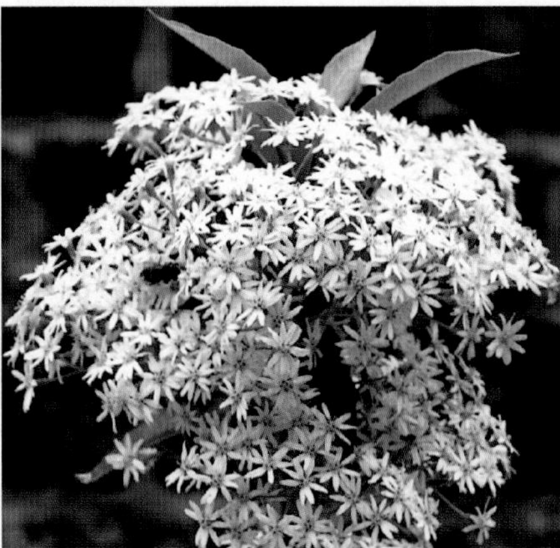

Olearia cheesemanii

A tall upright branching shrub with large heads of white flowers with yellow centres.

Olearia megalophylla

This is an open shrub with white daisy-type flowers with dark yellow centres.

Olearia phlogopappa

A medium shrub with aromatic foliage, it has large heads of white flowers with old gold centres.

OLEARIA (cont)

Olearia phlogopappa cv. **Coomber's Blue**
In spring this free flowering cultivar is covered with bluish flowers.

Olearia phlogopappa
cv. **Coomber's Pink**
This cultivar is covered with pink flowers in spring.

Olearia phlogopappa cv. **Rosea**
A cultivar which has pink flowers.

Olearia x ***scilloniensis***
In spring this bushy hybrid is covered with white flowers.

ONCOBA

FLACOURTIACEAE

Oncoba spinosa
A tall spiny evergreen shrub which is native to North Africa. It is grown in temperate to tropical climates for its showy large white flowers with yellow stamens. Propagate from seed and cuttings.

OPISTHIOLEPIS

PROTEACEAE

Opisthiolepis heterophylla
BLUSH SILKY OAK
A bushy evergreen small tree from Australia which is grown as an ornamental for its showy leaves and racemes of white flowers. It grows in climates from temperate to tropical. Propagate from seed.

ORTHOSIPHON

LAMIACEAE [LABIATAE]

Small free branching evergreen shrubs which are native to Australia and the Pacific. They are grown as ornamentals in climates from temperate to tropical. Propagate from seed and cuttings.

Orthosiphon aristatus
CAT'S MOUSTACHE
A small shrub which has upright spikes of small flowers with long anthers. The colour range of the flowers is from white to lilac.

ORTHOSIPHON (cont)

Orthosiphon stramineus
A small shrub which has erect spikes of white flowers which have long anthers. Often referred to as *O. aristatus*.

OSBECKIA

Melastomataceae

Evergreen shrubs which are native to many tropical countries and are grown for their bright coloured flowers. They will grow in climates from temperate to tropical and are propagated from seed and cuttings.

Osbeckia kewensis
A small spreading shrub with large showy flowers coloured cerise-violet.

Osbeckia rubicunda
This is an upright shrub with heads of large showy purple coloured flowers.

OSMANTHUS

Oleaceae

Evergreen shrubs and small trees which are native to Asia and grown for their perfume or colourful foliage. They grow in climates from cold temperate to sub-tropical and are propagated from seed or cuttings.

Osmanthus* x *burkwoodii
Preferring an alkaline soil, this small bushy shrub has very fragrant small white flowers.

Osmanthus fragrans FRAGRANT OLIVE
A small tree with bunches of very fragrant small flowers.

***Osmanthus heterophyllus* cv. Variegatus**
VARIEGATED HOLLY OLIVE
A small tree with cream and green variegated leaves and fragrant white flowers.

OSMOXYLON

ARALIACEAE

Small to medium bushy, evergreen, tropical shrubs, native to South East Asia. In cool to warm climates they are grown as indoor plants for their foliage, and are grown outdoors in tropical climates. They have small heads of whitish coloured flowers, and require plenty of water in hot weather, and annual fertilizing. Propagate from seed or cuttings.

Osmoxylon borneense

This small, tropical shrub is grown outdoors in sub-tropical to tropical climates, and as an indoor plant in milder climates. It has clusters of small white flowers.

Osmoxylon lineare

Widely grown as an indoor plant, this small, bushy shrub also is grown outdoors in tropical areas.

Osmoxylon lineare cv. **Miagos**

A showy cultivar with green and gold variegated foliage.

OSTEOMELES

ROSACEAE

Evergreen shrubs which are native to China and the Pacific and are grown for their delicate leaves and flowers. They will grow in climates from cold temperate to tropical. Propagate from seed and cuttings.

Osteomeles schwerinae

Fruit which are showy red, turning to blue-black, follow the clusters of cream flowers on this spreading bushy shrub. Often spelt *schweriniae.*

Osteomeles subrotunda

A small bushy shrub with small white flowers and showy blue-black fruit.

OSTEOSPERMUM

ASTERACEAE [COMPOSITAE]

Evergreen shrubs from Africa which are grown as ornamentals for their showy flowers. They grow in climates from cool temperate to tropical and are propagated from seed and cuttings. Osteospermums need lots of sunny weather for their flowers to be seen at their most outstanding.

Osteospermum fruticosum

A spreading dwarf shrub with colourful large daisy flowers coloured white, mauve and purple.

Osteospermum fruticosum
cv. **Burgundy Mound**

A cultivar which has cerise-violet coloured flowers.

Osteospermum cv. **Whirligig**

A hybrid cultivar with mauve daisy flowers with unusual twisted petals. This same plant is offered for sale under a wide range of names.

OTACANTHUS

SCROPHULARIACEAE

Otacanthus caeruleus

A free branching spreading small shrub native to Brazil. It has bluish mauve flowers with a white eye and is grown as a flowering ornamental in climates from warm temperate to tropical. Propagate from cuttings.

OWENIA

MELIACEAE

Owenia acidula EMU APPLE

A tall evergreen shrub from Australia, grown as an ornamental for its ferny foliage and showy round red fruit. It grows in climates from temperate to tropical and is propagated from seed. Illustration shows the colourful fruit.

OXYLOBIUM

FABACEAE [LEGUMINOSAE]

Oxylobium racemosum

A sparse evergreen Australian shrub which is grown in cool temperate to sub-tropical climates for its showy orange and red coloured flowers. Propagate from seed which needs hot water treatment.

PACHIRA

BOMBACACEAE

Small evergreen trees native to tropical America where they grow in wet or swamp soils. The plants are popular ornamentals especially in Japan where they are grown as bonsai plants. They grow in climates from warm temperate to tropical and are fast growing. Propagate from seed and cuttings.

Pachira aquatica WATER CHESTNUT

A small tree which tolerates wet soils. It has brush-type flowers which are yellow and red but may also be whitish in colour. Seed pods are large.

Pachira insignis WILD CHESTNUT

A small evergreen tree which has white flowers like a shaving brush. Flower colour may vary to cream or brownish red.

PACHYPODIUM

APOCYNACEAE

Succulent thorny shrubs, native to Africa and Madagascar, which are grown both for their flowers and their thorny appearance. They prefer a dry warm climate and a well drained soil. Propagate from seed or cuttings.

Pachypodium baronii

A very thorny shrub which has terminal clusters of showy pinky red flowers.

Pachypodium lamerei

This very thorny shrub has few branches and terminal bunches of white flowers.

PACHYSTACHYS

Acanthaceae

From tropical America, these evergreen shrubs are very free flowering and grow outdoors in climates from temperate to tropical. They are grown indoors or in glass houses in cooler climates. Propagation is mostly from cuttings.

Pachystachys coccinea

CARDINAL'S GUARD

An erect shrub which has long spikes of flowers in red bracts over a long period.

Pachystachys lutea GOLDEN CANDLES

A bushy shrub which has erect spikes of white flowers in gold bracts over many months.

PANDOREA

Bignoniaceae

Twining evergreen Australian vines which are grown for their showy flowers. They grow outdoors in climates from cool temperate to tropical and will tolerate some frost. These plants prefer a rich soil and full sun to flower at their best and will flower well in pots in glass houses in cool climates. Propagate from seed and cuttings.

Pandorea doratoxylon

INLAND WONGA VINE

A modest vine with large heads of flowers, cream on the outside and brown or purple inside. Often referred to as *P. pandorana* ssp doratoxylon.

Pandorea jasminoides

BOWER OF BEAUTY

Flowering over a long period, this is an evergreen climbing plant with large heads of pale pink flowers marked cerise inside.

***Pandorea jasminoides* cv. Alba**

A white flowered cultivar which flowers over several months.

***Pandorea jasminoides* cv. Red Eyes**

This cultivar has large bunches of off white flowers with red centres.

***Pandorea jasminoides* cv. Rosea**

The rose-pink flowers have purple-red centres on this cultivar.

PANDOREA (cont)

Pandorea jasminoides cv. **Variegata**
The variegated leaves of this showy cultivar are green and cream.

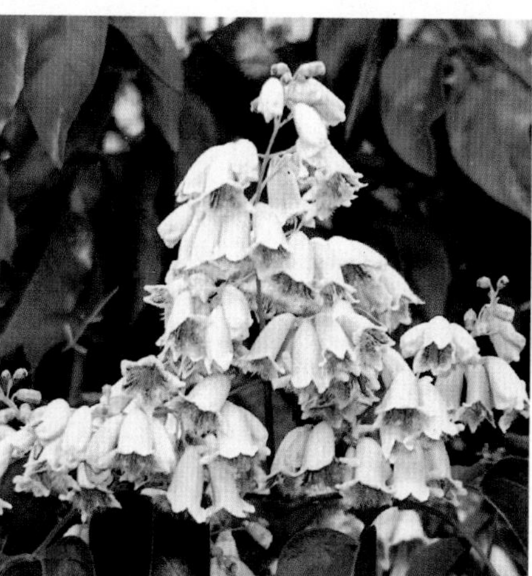

Pandorea pandorana

WONGA WONGA VINE

An evergreen vine with large flower heads of cream coloured flowers which are brown inside. Tolerant of some frosts.

Pandorea pandorana cv. **Alba**
A cultivar which has flowers that are white both inside and outside and have reddish stems.

Pandorea pandorana cv. **Snow Bells**
Spring flowering, this cultivar has large bunches of white flowers with yellow throats.

Pandorea pandorana cv. **Theodore**
A showy cultivar with large bunches of flowers coloured pale pink and cerise-purple.

PARKIA

MIMOSACEAE [LEGUMINOSAE]

Parkia javanica
A large spreading tropical tree which is native to Indonesia. It is grown as a park tree for shade. Parkia has flowers coloured yellow and white and round seed pods. Propagate from seed.

PARKINSONIA

CAESALPINIACEAE [LEGUMINOSAE]

Parkinsonia aculeata

JERUSALEM THORN

A small tree which has small spines, from tropical America. It is grown in warm climates for its large heads of fragrant golden yellow flowers. Propagate from seed.

PARMENTIERA

BIGNONIACEAE

Evergreen tall shrubs or small trees from tropical America which are grown as ornamentals for their flowers and unusual seed pods, some of which are edible. They will grow in sub-tropical and tropical climates and are propagated from seed.

Parmentiera cereifera CANDLE TREE
A small tree which has large white flowers followed by long candle-like seed pods which turn yellow.

Parmentiera edulis GUAJILOTE
The greenish white flowers of this small, spiny leaf tree are followed by large fruit which is edible.

p

PARTHENOCISSUS

VITACEAE

Deciduous woody climbers native to North America and Asia, which are grown for their colourful autumn leaves. They are quite cold tolerant and grow in climates as warm as sub-tropical. Propagate from seed and cuttings.

Parthenocissus henryana

Hardy and cold tolerant, this vine has green and silver leaves which turn red in autumn.

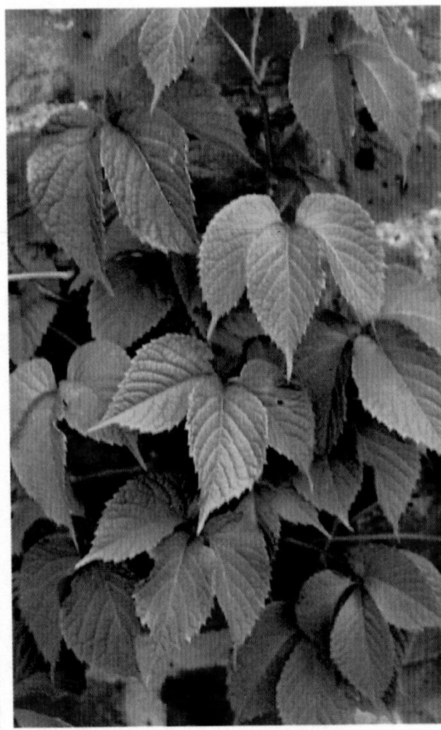

Parthenocissus himalayana

A vigorous climber which is cold tolerant. The green leaves turn brilliant red in autumn.

Parthenocissus quinquefolia

VIRGINIA CREEPER

In autumn this much branched spreading climber has brilliant red coloured leaves.

Parthenocissus tricuspidata

BOSTON IVY

This large woody climber has brightly coloured red leaves in autumn.

***Parthenocissus tricuspidata* cv. Veitchii**

A cultivar which has purple coloured new growth.

PASSIFLORA

PASSIONFLOWER

PASSIFLORACEAE

Grown for their showy flowers and some for their exotic fruit, these evergreen climbing plants are native to many countries. In climates from cool temperate to tropical they are grown outdoors, and in colder climates they are grown in glass houses and conservatories. They prefer a rich soil with plenty of humus and fertiliser and ample water in hot weather. Propagation is from seed or cuttings and by grafting.

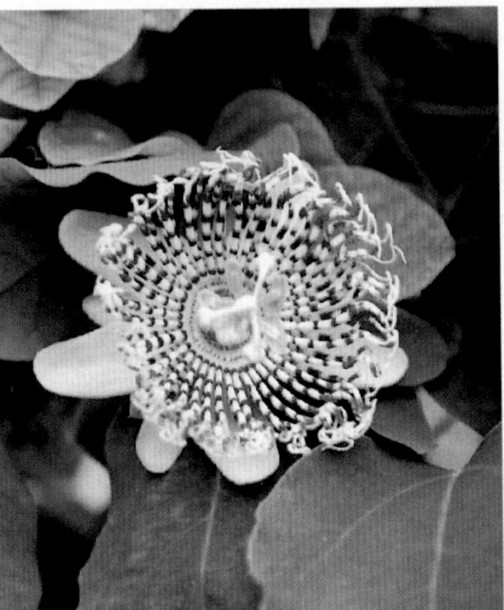

Passiflora actinia

The large flowers of this climber are coloured white and purple-blue, with white and green guard petals.

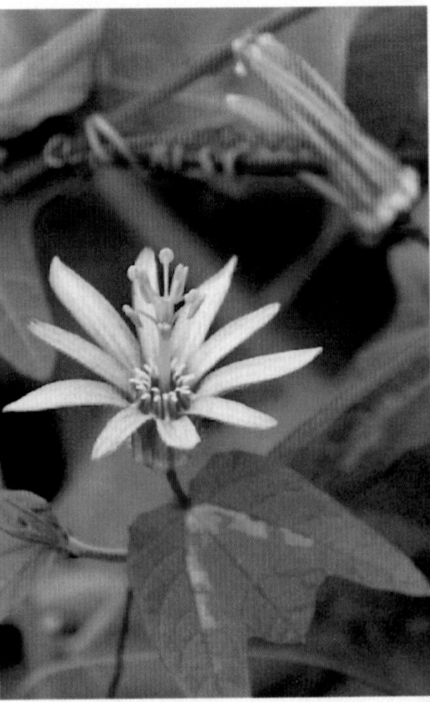

Passiflora adularia

A modest climber which is grown for its salmon-pink coloured flowers.

PASSIFLORA (cont)

Passiflora alata GRANADILLA

This vigorous climber has large showy flowers of cerise-maroon with blue markings. The large golden coloured fruit have the sweetest flavour of the edible passionfruit.

Passiflora aurantia

This slender vine has smallish salmon to orange flowers.

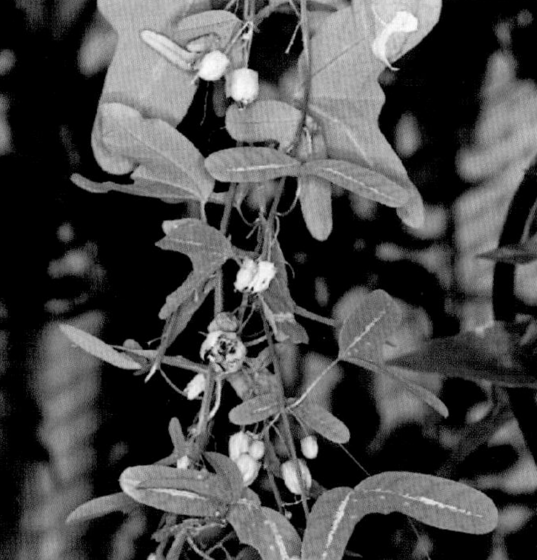

Passiflora allantophylla

Small yellow flowers and small leaves feature on this climber.

***Passiflora* cv. Amethyst**

A slender climber which has showy purple flowers. The petals reflex with age.

Passiflora belottii

A climber with large white and dark-mauve flowers.

Passiflora* x *allardii

A free flowering vine with large mauve-purple flowers.

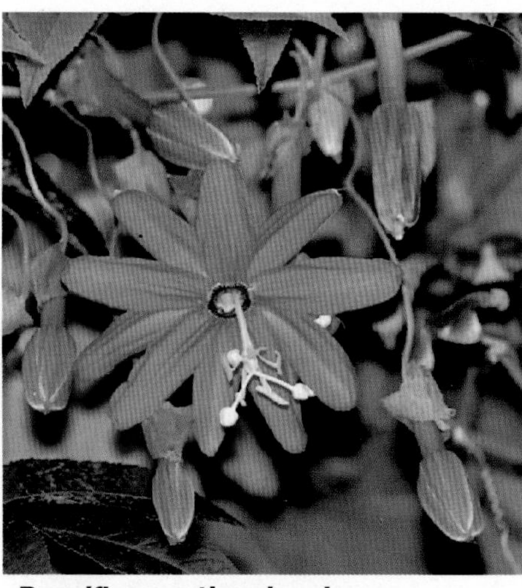

Passiflora antioquiensis LARGE BANANA PASSIONFRUIT

A slender vine which has bright pink flowers and yellow banana-looking edible fruit. Tolerant of light frosts.

Passiflora biflora

Mostly in pairs, the flowers of this slender climber are white, with yellow markings.

PASSIFLORA (cont)

Passiflora boenderii

This climber is grown for its showy green and yellow leaves.

Passiflora bryonioides

A twining vine with flowers coloured white and purple.

Passiflora caerulea

BLUE PASSION FLOWER

A widely grown slender vine which has blue and white coloured flowers and amber coloured non-edible fruit.

***Passiflora caerulea* cv. Constance Elliott**

A cultivar with white flowers.

***Passiflora caerulea* cv. Lynette**

The white flowers have green markings on this cultivar.

***Passiflora caerulea* cv. Merryon**

A cultivar which has flowers which are mostly white with a circle of purple.

***Passiflora caerulea* cv. Pierre Pomie**

Developed in France by M. Pomie, this free flowering cultivar has flowers of white, with a few mauve markings.

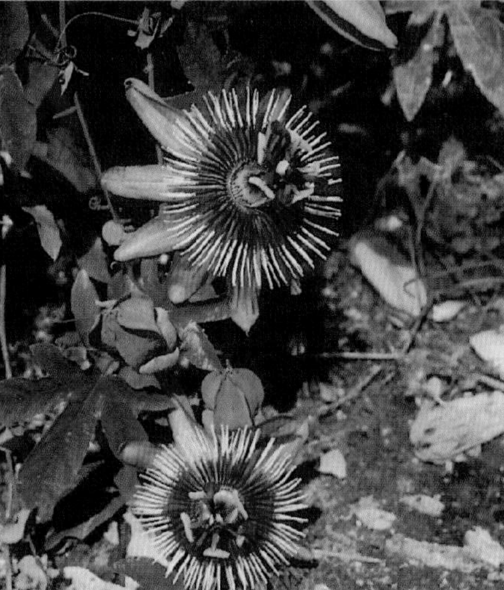

Passiflora caerulea* x *racemosa [6]

A hybrid passionfruit which has large flowers coloured purple, white and violet.

Passiflora capsularis

This is a modest climber which has white flowers and non-edible purple fruit.

PASSIFLORA (cont)

Passiflora cinnabarina
The flowers of this slender vine are coloured red and yellow.

Passiflora cirrhiflora 6
This rare vine has showy yellow flowers.

Passiflora citrina
A climber with medium sized yellow flowers.

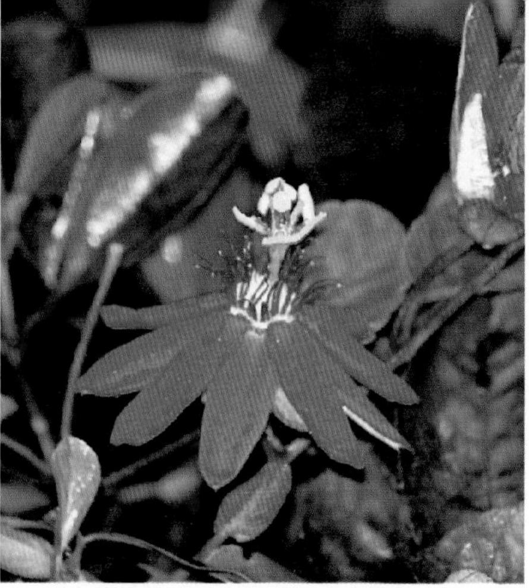

Passiflora coccinea
SCARLET PASSIONFLOWER
Very popular as an ornamental, this robust climber has bright red flowers with white centres.

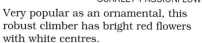

Passiflora coriacea
BAT-LEAF PASSION FLOWER
This climber has unusual large leaves shaped like bats wings and flowers coloured green with yellow and purple markings.

Passiflora edulis PURPLE GRANADILLA
Widely cultivated for its edible fruit, this vine has large white and purple coloured flowers.

Passiflora edulis
This illustration shows the edible fruit.

Passiflora edulis cv. **Golden Giant**
Very large yellow fruit are borne in winter on this cultivar.

Passiflora edulis cv. **Golden Giant**
This illustration shows the large juicy fruit.

PASSIFLORA (cont)

Passiflora edulis cv. **Panama Red**
The very large red fruit are borne in winter on this cultivar.

Passiflora cv. **Emperor Keiz Eugeni**
Free flowering, this climber has dark-mauve flowers.

Passiflora foetida LOVE-IN-A-MIST
A slender vine with whitish mauve flowers. Its small yellow fruit are covered with a net-like growth.

Passiflora foetida - fruit

Passiflora gracilis
Grown mostly as an annual, this slender vine has white flowers and bright red fruit.

Passiflora gracillima FROG'S LEGS
The attaching roots of this small climber look like frog's legs.

Passiflora helleri
The flowers of this sparse climber have twisted petals coloured white with a few purple markings.

Passiflora herbertiana
This is a slender climber which has creamy yellow, star shaped flowers.

Passiflora incarnata
In spring and summer this free flowering climber has showy large mauve flowers.

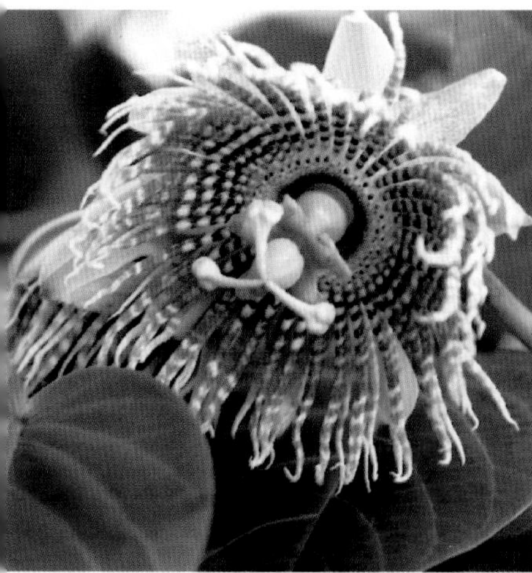

Passiflora laurifolia WATER LEMON

A tropical climber which has dark-blue coloured flowers and yellow to orange fruit which are edible. This plant is grown commercially.

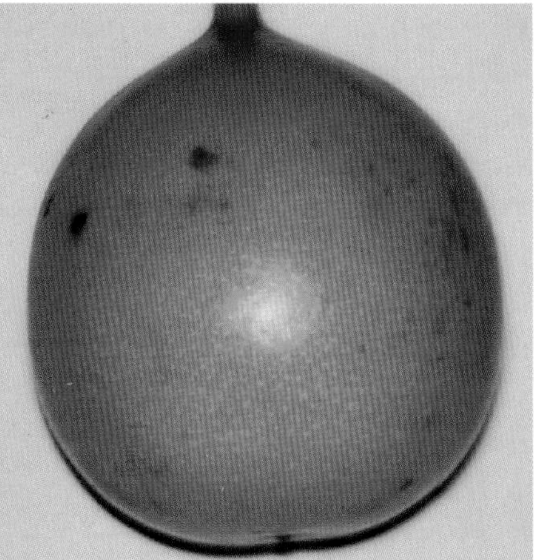

Passiflora ligularis SWEET GRANADILLA

Commercially grown, this widely cultivated tropical climber has white and blue coloured flowers and orange coloured fruit. Illustration shows ripe fruit.

Passiflora maliformis SWEET-CUP

A spreading vine with purple, white and brown coloured flowers and hard shelled edible fruit.

Passiflora manicata

RED PASSIONFLOWER

Free flowering, this vine has showy pinkish red flowers. Tolerant of light frosts.

Passiflora manicata cv. **Coral Glow**

A cultivar with showy bright pink flowers.

Passiflora manicata cv. **Coral Seas**

The flowers of this cultivar are coral pink.

Passiflora manicata* x *jamesonii 3

A hybrid passion flower which has colourful bright red flowers.

Passiflora menispermifolia 6

Very spectacular large flowers coloured purple, violet and white grow on this sparse vine.

Passiflora mollissima

BANANA PASSIONFRUIT

A slender climber which is commercially grown. It has bright pink flowers and yellow banana-like edible fruit. This passionfruit tolerates frosts of -4 degrees Celsius.

PASSIFLORA (cont)

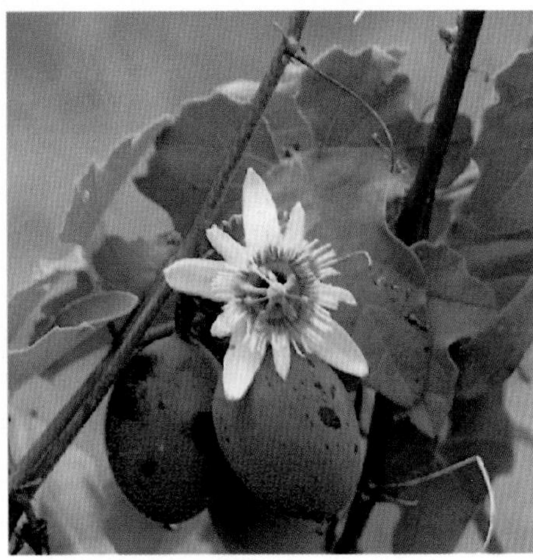

Passiflora morifolia
A sparse vine which has small white and purple coloured flowers and black fruit.

Passiflora organensis
This showy climber is grown for its multi-coloured leaves of pink, green and cream.

Passiflora perfoliata
The smallish flowers of this sparse climber are coloured dull red.

Passiflora platyloba
Hardy, this climber has blue, mauve and white flowers.

Passiflora cv. **Purple Haze**
The large flowers of this cultivar are purple and mauve, with white guard petals.

Passiflora quadrangularis
GIANT GRANADILLA
A vigorous vine with violet, maroon and white coloured flowers and giant football-sized edible fruit.

Passiflora quadrangularis
This illustration shows the large fruit.

Passiflora racemosa
CASCADING PASSION FLOWER
A warm climate climber which has cascading racemes of salmon to scarlet flowers.

Passiflora rubra
The small white flowers of this slender vine are followed by showy fruit coloured white and red.

Passiflora sanguinolenta
This bushy climber has masses of smallish pink flowers over many months.

Passiflora standleyi
This hardy vine has small to medium size mauve flowers.

Passiflora tatei
The upright flowers of this sparse climber are coloured rose-pink.

Passiflora seemannii
On this vigorous vine, yellow fruit follow the very attractive purple flowers which have white markings.

Passiflora subpeltata GRANADINA
A sparse vine which has white flowers and cream fruit.

Passiflora trifasciata
A showy climber grown for its colourful leaves of green and cream.

Passiflora serratifolia 6
A climber with large dark-mauve to violet coloured flowers.

***Passiflora* CV. Sunburst** 6
This hybrid is a slender climber with showy flowers coloured gold and orange.

Passiflora umbilicata 6
Tolerant of some frosts, this sparse vine has violet coloured flowers.

PASSIFLORA (cont)

Passiflora variolata
Over a long period, this climber has bright red flowers in profusion.

Passiflora violacea
Showy violet coloured flowers feature on this bushy climber.

Passiflora vitifolia
A bushy vine with bright red flowers which have white centres.

PAULOWNIA

SCROPHULARIACEAE

Fast growing, deciduous, medium size trees which are grown as flowering ornamentals and timber trees and are native to Asia. Tolerant of frosts once established, they will also grow in tropical climates. Propagation is from seed, root cuttings and semi-ripe wood cuttings.

Paulownia fortunei
This tree has large heads of foxglove-like flowers coloured pale mauve.

Paulownia kawakamii
This is a small tree with large heads of mauvish white foxglove-like flowers.

Paulownia tomentosa
Large heads of variable coloured flowers, mostly pinkish mauve with yellow throats, feature on this tree.

***Paulownia tomentosa* cv. Lilacina**
A cultivar which has showy heads of lilac coloured flowers.

PAVETTA

RUBIACEAE

Evergreen shrubs and small trees native to tropical and sub-tropical climates of many countries. They are grown for their showy flowers in climates from temperate to tropical. Propagate from seed and cuttings.

Pavetta australiensis* var. *australiensis
A small tree with large heads of white flowers.

PAVETTA (cont)

Pavetta lanceolata BRIDE'S BUSH

Perfumed small white flowers can totally cover this bushy rounded shrub in spring.

Pavetta natalensis NATAL BRIDE'S BUSH

A tall shrub with heads of small white flowers.

Pavetta opaca

A small tree with large heads of white flowers which have protruding white anthers.

PAVONIA

MALVACEAE

Sparse shrubs native to tropical America and Australia. They are grown as ornamentals in climates from temperate to tropical, and have Hibiscus-like flowers. Propagate from seed or softwood cuttings under mist.

Pavonia* x *gledhillii

An open crowned evergreen shrub with terminal red flowers.

Pavonia hastata

An open shrub with pale pink flowers which have maroon centres.

Pavonia makoyana

Terminal heads of rose-pink flowers bloom on this sparse shrub.

PEDILANTHUS

EUPHORBIACEAE

Succulent shrubs which are native to Central America and are grown outdoors in tropical and sub-tropical climates and indoors and glasshouses in cooler climates. They are hardy plants and are propagated from seeds, cuttings or by division.

Pedilanthus tithymaloides DEVIL'S BACKBONE

A free branching clumping shrub with green leaves and small red flowers.

Pedilanthus tithymaloides* ssp. *smallii

syn. ***P. smallii*** JACOB'S LADDER

Heart shaped leaves and small red flowers are the features of this small spreading shrub.

***Pedilanthus tithymaloides* ssp. *smallii* cv. Variegatus**

A multi-stem plant with white and green variegated leaves.

PEDILANTHUS (cont)

***Pedilanthus tithymaloides* cv. Variegatus**

This colourful cultivar has cream and green variegated foliage with touches of pink.

PELTOPHORUM

Caesalpiniaceae [Leguminosae]

Spreading open crowned free flowering trees which are native to Africa, South America and Asia. They are grown as street trees and feature park trees in sub-tropical and tropical climates. Propagate from seed.

Peltophorum africanum

YELLOW POINCIANA

Large spikes of yellow flowers grow on this medium spreading tree.

Peltophorum dubium

A medium spreading tree with open heads of yellow flowers.

Peltophorum pterocarpum

YELLOW FLAME; YELLOW FLAMBOYANT

Spreading and open crowned, this tree has large heads of golden yellow flowers.

PENTAPTERYGIUM

Ericaceae

Pentapterygium serpens

A small, evergreen, cold tolerant shrub with arching branches and bright red tubular flowers. Propagate from cuttings. This genus is now referred to as Agapetes.

PENTAS

Rubiaceae

Free branching small shrubs, native to Africa and the Middle East, which are grown as ornamentals in temperate to tropical climates. Small star shaped flowers grow in heads on these popular plants. Propagate from seed or tip cuttings.

***Pentas lanceolata* cv. Bright Pink**

STAR CLUSTER

A small bushy shrub with heads of bright rose-pink flowers.

***Pentas lanceolata* cv. Candy Stripe**

Bright pink flowers edged with pink make this a showy cultivar.

Pentas lanceolata **cv. Lavender Lady**
A cultivar which has lavender-mauve coloured flowers.

Pentas lanceolata **cv. Paradise**
A showy cultivar with flowers coloured bright pink, with white centres.

Pentas lanceolata **cv. Lilac Lady**
This cultivar has heads of dark lilac coloured flowers.

Pentas lanceolata **cv. Pink**
This cultivar has heads of pink coloured flowers.

Pentas lanceolata **cv. White Lady**
Heads of white coloured flowers are the feature of this cultivar.

Pentas lanceolata **cv. Pale Pink**
The flowers of this cultivar are pale pink.

Pentas lanceolata **cv. Royal Red**
A cultivar which has colourful heads of dark red flowers.

p

PERESKIA

CACTACEAE

Evergreen shrubs and climbers with spines and fleshy leaves and native to the Americas. They are grown for their showy flowers or colourful leaves in sub-tropical and tropical climates. Propagate from seed and cuttings.

Pereskia aculeata **cv. Godseffiana**

BARBADOS GOOSEBERRY

A very colourful semi-climber with gold and pink coloured leaves.

Pereskia grandifolia ROSE CACTUS

This spiny semi-climber or shrub has large pale pink flowers with prominent yellow stamens.

Pereskia sacharosa

A tall shrub which has large, cup shaped, bright pink flowers.

PERGULARIA

ASCLEPIADACEAE

Pergularia odoratissima

An evergreen tropical vine which has bunches of highly perfumed green star shaped flowers. Propagate from seed and cuttings.

PERISTROPHE

ACANTHACEAE

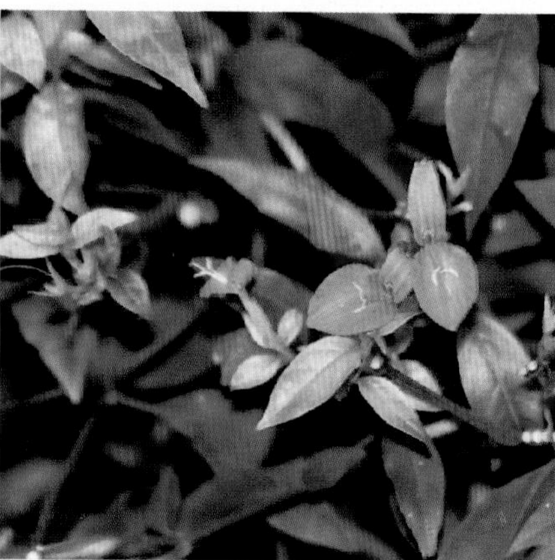

Peristrophe hyssopifolia

A spreading bushy small shrub which is native to Indonesia. It is grown as an ornamental in warm climates for its showy violet coloured flowers. Propagate from cuttings.

Peristrophe hyssopifolia **cv. Aureo-variegata**

MARBLE LEAF

A cultivar with yellow and green foliage.

PERSOONIA GEEBUNG

PROTEACEAE

Evergreen Australian shrubs which are grown as hardy ornamentals in cool temperate to sub-tropical climates. Propagate from seed.

Persoonia linearis

A thin leaf, open headed shrub with golden coloured flowers.

Persoonia pinifolia

An upright, open, medium shrub with terminal spikes of yellow flowers. The soft foliage of this shrub is widely used by florists.

PETREA

VERBENACEAE

Exotic tropical shrubs and semi-climbers native to the Americas and the Caribbean. They are widely cultivated in tropical and sub-tropical climates for their attractive star shaped flowers. Propagate from seed and cuttings.

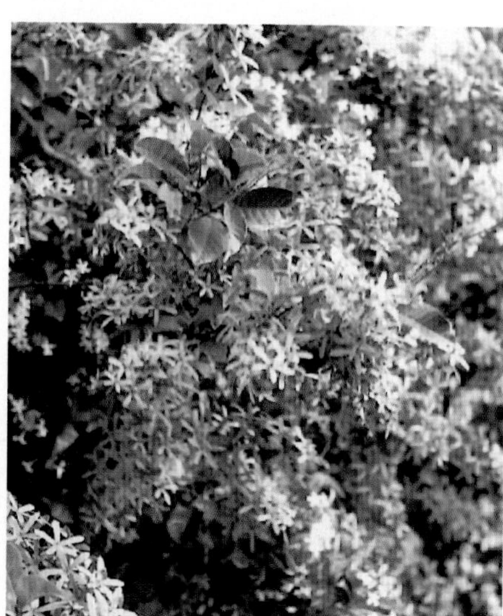

Petrea arborea BLUE PETREA

A sparse, semi-climbing, tall shrub which has large racemes of bluish lilac coloured flowers.

Petrea glandulosa WHITE PETREA

A climbing plant which has long pendulous racemes of large white flowers.

Petrea kohautiana FLEUR DE DIEU

In spring this showy climber has large sprays of mauve and violet coloured flowers.

Petrea volubilis PURPLE WREATH

A sparse climber with long racemes of violet to purple coloured flowers.

***Petrea volubilis* CV. Albiflora**

This is a white flowering cultivar of this showy climber.

PETROPHILE CONESTICKS

PROTEACEAE

Native to temperate Australia, these evergreen shrubs are grown as landscape plants. They are very hardy and are propagated from seeds.

Petrophile ericifolia

An open crowned shrub with small leaves and yellow flower heads.

PETROPHILE (cont)

Petrophile heterophylla

This open crowned medium shrub has long leaves and heads of cream coloured flowers.

PHALERIA

THYMELAEACEAE

Tall shrubs and small evergreen fragrant trees native to Australia and South East Asia. They are grown in warm temperate to tropical climates as feature trees. Propagate from seed.

Phaleria clerodendron

A small tree with bunches of very fragrant white flowers along the older branches and trunk.

Phaleria octandra

Red fruit follow the bunches of perfumed white flowers on this open crowned shrub.

PHEBALIUM

RUTACEAE

Evergreen woody shrubs which are native to Australia and New Zealand. They are grown as landscaping plants in a wide climate range and are propagated from seed and cuttings.

Phebalium squameum

A tall sparse shrub which has lots of white star shaped flowers in spring.

Phebalium squamulosum

An open branched shrub with bunches of star shaped flowers which may be white, cream or lemon in colour.

Phebalium stenophyllum

This is an erect shrub which has large heads of yellow star shaped flowers.

Phebalium whitei

Golden yellow flowers, which are larger than the flowers of the other Phebaliums, bloom on this erect woody shrub.

PHILADELPHUS

MOCK ORANGE

HYDRANGEACEAE [PHILADELPHACEAE]

Deciduous shrubs native to North America, Europe and Asia, they are widely grown as ornamentals in climates which range from very cold to sub-tropical. They are propagated from seeds and cuttings.

Philadelphus coronarius

A medium to tall shrub with fragrant white flowers in spring.

***Philadelphus coronarius* cv. Aureus**

The leaves are yellow on this cultivar.

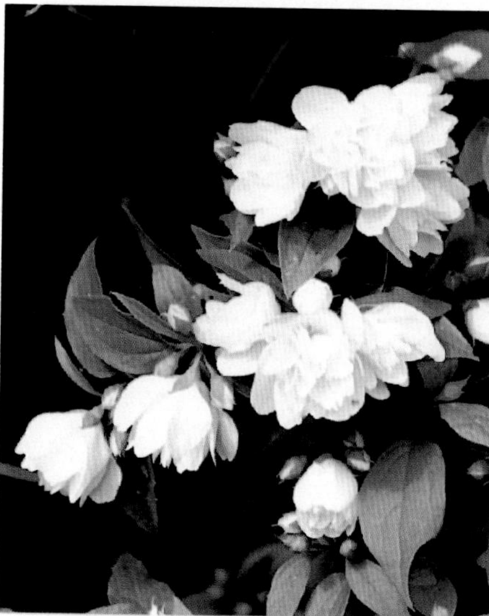

Philadelphus* x *lemoinei
cv. Manteau d'Hermine
A hybrid which is a free flowering medium shrub with white flowers.

Philadelphus pekinensis
A compact shrub with white flowers in spring.

Philadelphus* x *purpureo-maculatus
cv. Belle Etoile
This cultivar has large flowers with purple-cerise centres.

Philadelphus satsumanus
An upright shrub with white flowers which are square looking.

Philadelphus satsumanus
cv. Nikoensis
A cultivar which has cup shaped flowers and large yellow stamens.

Philadelphus subcanus
var. *magdalenae*
In late spring, this bushy medium to tall shrub has small bunches of large white flowers.

Philadelphus* x *virginalis 3
Of unknown origin, this hybrid has bunches of double white flowers in spring.

PHILODENDRON

ARACEAE

Evergreen shrubs and climbing plants with attractive leaves which are widely grown throughout the world as exotic indoor plants and are grown outdoors in sub-tropical and tropical climates. They are native to tropical America and prefer a good quality soil rich in humus, with regular applications of fertiliser. Propagation is from seed and cuttings.

***Philodendron* cv. Anderson's Red**
This hybrid Philodendron has large leaves which are red as they open then turn to a reddish olive-green in sunny positions.

PHILODENDRON (cont)

Philodendron angustisectum
syn. ***P. elegans***
A climbing plant with large deeply cut leaves.

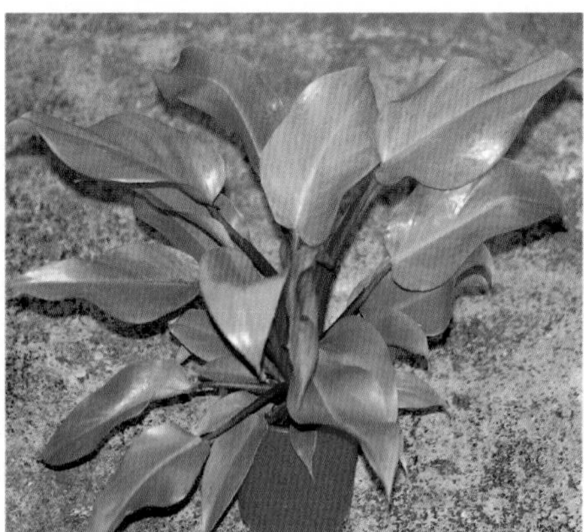

Philodendron cv. **Autumn**
The large leaves of this cultivar open pinkish red then turn to yellow and finally to green.

Philodendron cv. **Black Cardinal**
A vigorous climber which has large brownish burgundy coloured leaves.

Philodendron bipinnatifidum
A clumping plant with large deeply cut leaves. This plant is similar to *P. selloum* which has leaves not as deeply lobed.

Philodendron cannifolium
This is a prostrate plant which has long green leaves with fleshy stems.

Philodendron discolor
The leaves of this climbing plant are heart shaped, and coloured olive and brown.

Philodendron domesticum
SPADE-LEAF PHILODENDRON
syn. ***P. hastatum***
Widely used as an indoor plant, this is a hardy climber with large shiny green leaves.

PHILODENDRON (cont)

Philodendron **cv. Emerald Duke**
A hardy climbing plant with large shiny emerald green leaves.

Philodendron erubescens **cv. Red Wings**
The very large leaves of this hardy climber colour red in the shade and olive-green to red in the sun.

Philodendron **cv. Florida**
A climbing plant with deeply cut large green leaves.

Philodendron erubescens BLUSHING PHILODENDRON
The new reddish purple leaves turn brownish above and reddish on the underside on this climbing plant.

Philodendron fragrantissimum
The leaves on this bushy climber are large and furrowed.

Philodendron erubescens **cv. Burgundy**
Mostly grown indoors, this climbing plant has large burgundy coloured leaves.

Philodendron **cv. Evansii**
This hybrid between *P. selloum* and *P. speciosum* is a large leaf clumping plant.

Philodendron **cv. Goldilocks**
A showy climbing Philodendron with golden coloured leaves.

PHILODENDRON (cont)

***Philodendron imbe* cv. Variegatum**

The large leaves of this climber are variegated green and cream.

Philodendron leyvae

A bushy multi-heading Philodendron with lobed green leaves.

Philodendron melanochrysum

BLACK-GOLD PHILODENDRON

This climber has very large velvety leaves coloured blackish green.

***Philodendron* cv. Imperial Green**

A bushy climber with large green leaves.

***Philodendron* cv. Lynette**

The long leaves on this clumping plant are coloured greyish green.

Philodendron lacerum

This is a bushy climber with large deeply lobed leaves.

***Philodendron* cv. Magnificum**

A bushy climber with large dark green leaves and prominent whitish coloured veins.

Philodendron ornatum

syn. ***P. sodiroi***

A climber with large heart shaped leaves coloured green and grey.

PHILODENDRON (cont)

Philodendron cv. **Painted Lady**
The leaves on this climber are large and coloured green with yellow markings.

Philodendron pedatum
syn. ***P. laciniatum***
A climbing plant with large, lobed, green leaves.

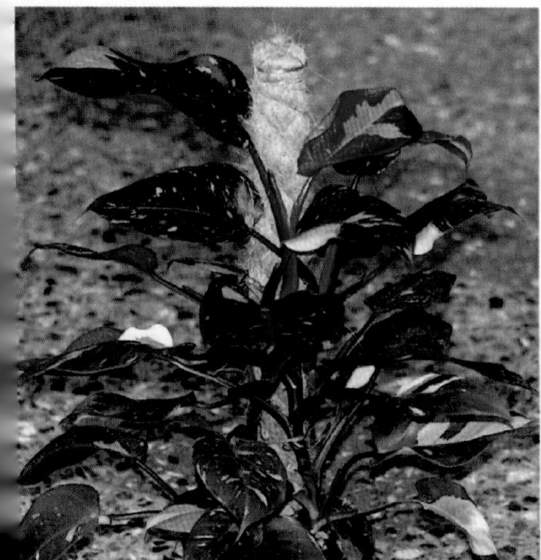

Philodendron cv. **Pink Princess**
A large leaf climber which has pink and brownish red coloured leaves.

Philodendron radiatum DUBIA PHILODENDRON
syn. ***P. dubium***
This is a bushy climbing plant with large deeply cut green leaves.

Philodendron cv. **Red Queen**
A hardy climbing plant with new leaves coloured red which then change to burgundy and finally to olive-green. The colour stays burgundy if grown in shade.

Philodendron sangiuneum
A climber with large green leaves which are coloured pinky apricot underneath.

Philodendron scandens ssp. ***oxycardium*** HEART LEAF PHILODENDRON
syn. ***P. oxycardium; P. cordatum***
A popular smaller leaf climbing Philodendron which is grown indoors world wide.

PHILODENDRON (cont)

Philodendron selloum
A large clumping plant with very large lobed leaves. A very widely grown Philodendron and often confused with *P. bipinnatifidum* which has leaves more deeply lobed.

***Philodendron* cv. Silver Cloud**
This showy, dense climbing plant has silver-grey coloured leaves.

Philodendron squamiferum
A hardy climber. Large deep cuts make five segments on the leaves.

Philodendron verrucosum
syn. ***P. triumphans***
A climbing plant with large heart shaped olive-green leaves with distinct greenish cream veins.

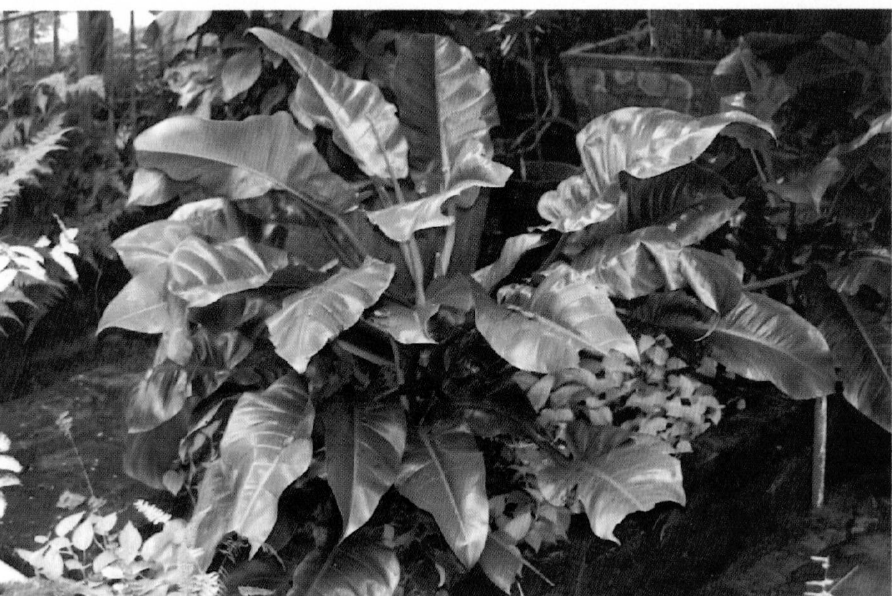

Philodendron wendlandii
The long large leaves are tinged with purple on this climber.

***Philodendron* cv. Xanadu**
A compact clumping plant with large deeply lobed leaves.

PHLOMIS

Lamiaceae [Labiatae]

Spreading shrubs native to the Mediterranean area, which are grown as ornamentals in cold temperate to sub-tropical climates. Some have highly aromatic foliage. They grow best in well drained soils. Propagate from seed or cuttings, or by division.

Phlomis fruticosa

A bushy shrub with greyish leaves and golden yellow flowers in spring.

Phlomis lycia

A spreading shrub with grey leaves and terminal heads of golden coloured flowers on erect stems.

PHOTINIA

Rosaceae

Native to Asia, these deciduous or evergreen shrubs and trees are grown as hedges and ornamentals in cool and cold climates to -15 degrees Celsius of frosts. They are propagated from seed and cuttings.

Photinia beauverdiana

A tall deciduous shrub with large heads of white flowers.

***Photinia* x *fraseri* cv. Robusta**

A medium growing tree with new red leaves and heads of white flowers.

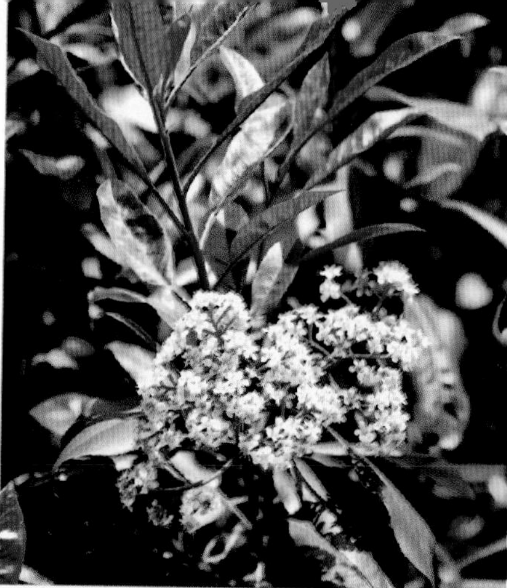

***Photinia* x *fraseri* cv. Rubens**

This tall, evergreen shrub has clusters of small creamy white flowers and red new growth.

Photinia glabra

An evergreen shrub which is a popular hedge plant. It has bright red new growth and heads of small white flowers.

PHYLICA

Rhamnaceae

Phylica plumosa CAPE MYRTLE

syn. ***P. pubescens***

From Africa, this medium, evergreen shrub has very hairy leaves and yellow flowers. It is grown as an ornamental in frost free, temperate climates. Propagate from seed and cuttings.

PHYLLANTHUS

EUPHORBIACEAE

Phyllanthus acidus GOOSEBERRY TREE

A small tree which is native to Asia. It is grown as an ornamental and for its fruit which is used in relishes. The tree prefers a rich soil and sunny aspect. Propagation is from seed.

PHYMATOCARPUS

MYRTACEAE

Phymatocarpus maxwellii

This small sparse shrub is endemic to Australia. It is grown in temperate climates as an ornamental for its showy round cerise coloured flowers. Propagation is from seed or cuttings.

PHYMOSIA

MALVACEAE

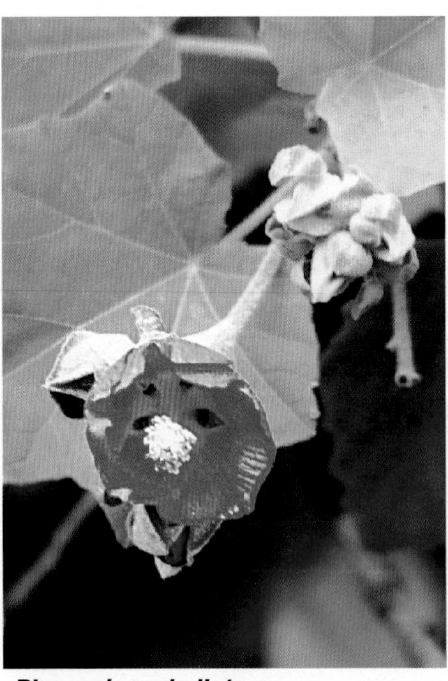

Phymosia umbellata

A dense small tree which is native to tropical America. In climates from temperate to tropical, it is grown as an ornamental for its bright pink Hibiscus-like flowers. Propagate from seed and cuttings.

PHYSOCARPUS

ROSACEAE

***Physocarpus opulifolius* cv. Dart's Gold** NINEBARK

Native to North America, this medium, deciduous shrub is grown as an ornamental for its colourful golden leaves, its unusual peeling bark and pink flowers. It is cold tolerant and is propagated from cuttings.

PHYTOLACCA

PHYTOLACCACEAE

Phytolacca dioica BELLA SOMBRA

A fast growing, spreading, evergreen, medium tree with a buttressed trunk. It is native to South America. Trees are either male or female and the flowers are creamy yellow, in raceme form. It prefers a temperate to tropical climate and is grown from seed.

PIERIS

ERICACEAE

Spring flowering evergreen shrubs, trees and vines which are native to Asia, Himalayas and North America. They are cold climate plants and some will tolerate temperatures to -25 degrees Celsius. These plants are popular ornamental specimens for their flowers and attractive foliage. Propagate from seed and cuttings. They prefer a semi-shaded situation with a moist, slightly acid soil.

Pieris floribunda FETTER BUSH

A small shrub which has cascading racemes of white bead-like flowers.

Pieris formosa

Tall and evergreen, this shrub has pendulous bunches of white, lily of the valley type flowers.

***Pieris formosa* cv. Wakehurst**

A bushy medium shrub which has showy racemes of white, urn shaped flowers in spring.

Pieris formosa* var. *forrestii

syn. ***P. forrestii***

A medium to tall shrub which has pendulous clusters of white, urn shaped flowers and crimson new growth.

Pieris japonica LILY OF THE VALLEY BUSH

This is a small to medium shrub with pendulous clusters of small, white, urn shaped flowers

***Pieris japonica* cv. Bert Chandler**

There are pendulous clusters of white flowers and new growth coloured cream, pink and red on this compact shrub.

***Pieris japonica* cv. Blush**

A cultivar which has long racemes of pale pink, urn shaped flowers in spring.

***Pieris japonica* cv. Chaconne**

This slow growing, medium shrub has pendulous bunches of creamy white flowers.

p

PIERIS (cont)

Pieris japonica **cv. Christmas Cheer**
A compact dwarf shrub with racemes of white flowers tipped with pink.

Pieris japonica **cv. Crimson Compact** [2]
The new growth is red on this compact bushy shrub which has pendulous racemes of white flowers on red stalks.

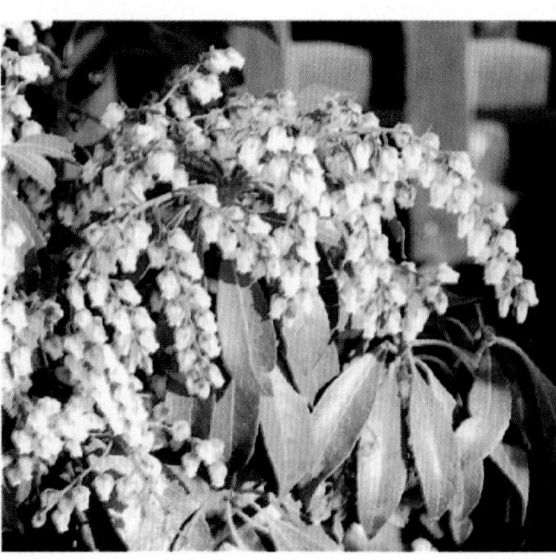

Pieris japonica **cv. Daisen**
A compact shrub with racemes of white and pink urn shaped flowers in spring.

Pieris japonica **cv. Debutante**
Small, white, bell shaped flowers form in clusters on this small to medium shrub.

Pieris japonica **cv. Dorothy Wyckhoff**
On this medium shrub the small white flowers are borne in pendulous racemes.

Pieris japonica **cv. Flaming Star**
This cultivar has pinky red new growth with older leaves being variegated cream and grey-green.

Pieris japonica **cv. Flamingo**
A bushy shrub with racemes of pink, urn shaped flowers in spring.

Pieris japonica **cv. Little Heath**
A compact low growing cultivar with cream and grey-green variegated leaves, the new growth being red.

Pieris japonica **cv. Mountain Fire**
This medium shrub has bright red new growth and open sprays of cream, urn shaped flowers.

Pieris japonica cv. **Nocturne**

Bushy and free flowering, this shrub has bunches of small, cream and white flowers.

Pieris japonica cv. **Pink Kiss**

This cultivar has upright bunches of small white flowers, with pink markings.

Pieris japonica cv. **Purity**

A bushy cultivar with masses of small, white flowers in pendulous bunches.

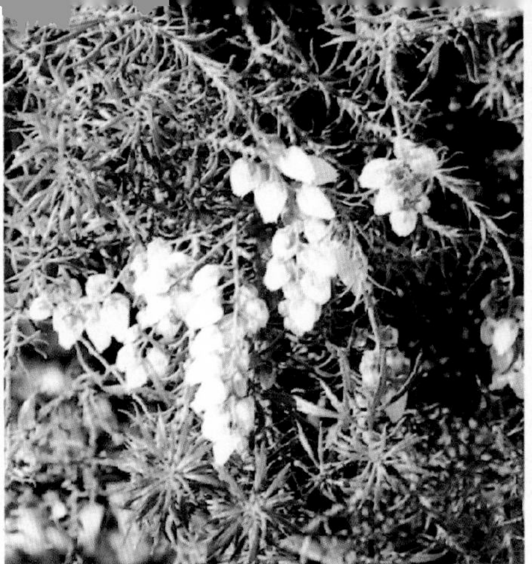

Pieris japonica cv. **Pygmaea**

There are fine leaves and small racemes of white, urn shaped flowers on this small spreading shrub.

Pieris japonica cv. **Spring Candy**

A compact cultivar with racemes of white, urn shaped flowers and crimson-red new growth.

Pieris japonica cv. **Valley Rose**

Long racemes of pink coloured urn shaped flowers and bright red new growth feature on this upright small shrub.

Pieris japonica cv. **Valley Valentine**

The sprays of pendulous bell shaped flowers on this showy cultivar are coloured bright pink, with white markings.

Pieris japonica cv. **Variegata**

This bushy cultivar has cream and green variegated leaves.

Pieris taiwanensis cv. **Variegata**

A compact medium shrub with green and white variegated leaves and clusters of white urn shaped flowers.

PIMELEA — RICE FLOWER

THYMELAEACEAE

Small to medium evergreen shrubs, native to Australia and New Zealand, which are grown as showy ornamentals. They grow in climates from cool temperate to tropical and require a well drained soil. Propagate from cuttings and seed which at times can be difficult to germinate.

Pimelea ferruginea PINK RICE FLOWER
A multi-branched shrub with showy heads of rose-pink flowers.

***Pimelea* cv. Pygmy White**
A compact bushy plant with heads of white flowers.

Pimelea rosea
This is a compact rounded plant with showy pink flower heads.

PIPER — PEPPER

PIPERACEAE

Shrubs and climbers which are native to many countries in climates from temperate to tropical. Some are grown as ornamentals and other are grown for commercial purposes. Propagation is from seed and cuttings.

Piper betle BETEL PEPPER
An evergreen climbing plant which is grown in South East Asia to be chewed as a flavouring with betel nuts.

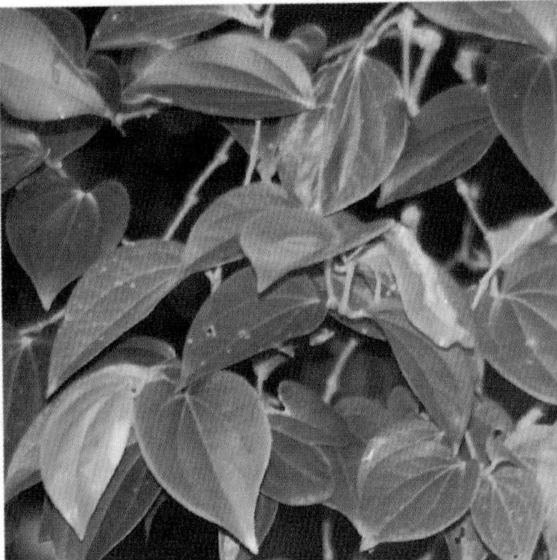

Piper nigrum COMMON PEPPER
A tropical vine which is grown to produce commercial black pepper.

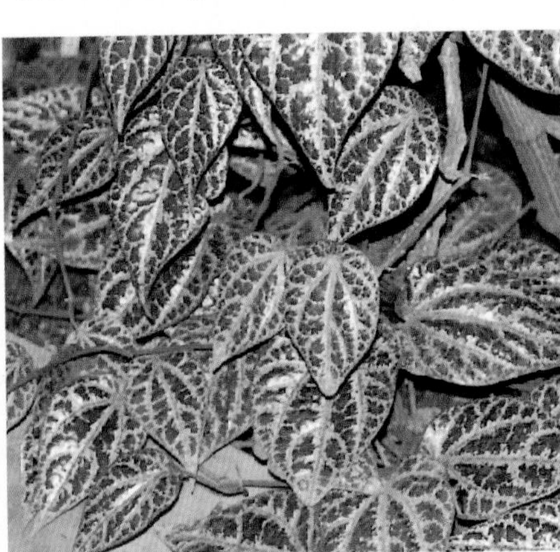

Piper crocatum
A climbing plant with heart shaped leaves coloured metallic green with pink and silver markings.

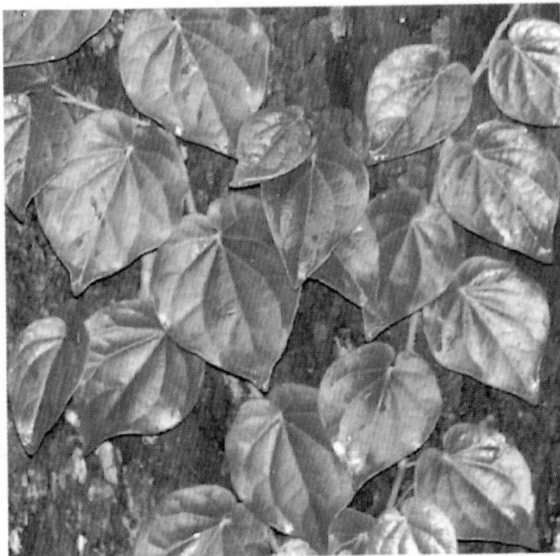

Piper novae-hollandiae GIANT PEPPER
A twining plant which normally grows on rocks and trees but is usually grown on bark totem poles as an indoor plant.

Piper magnificum LACQUERED PEPPER
An erect multi-stemmed plant with bronze-olive coloured large leaves which have a brownish underside.

Piper ornatum CELEBES PEPPER
A climber grown for its ornamental leaves which are coloured dark green with pink and silver markings.

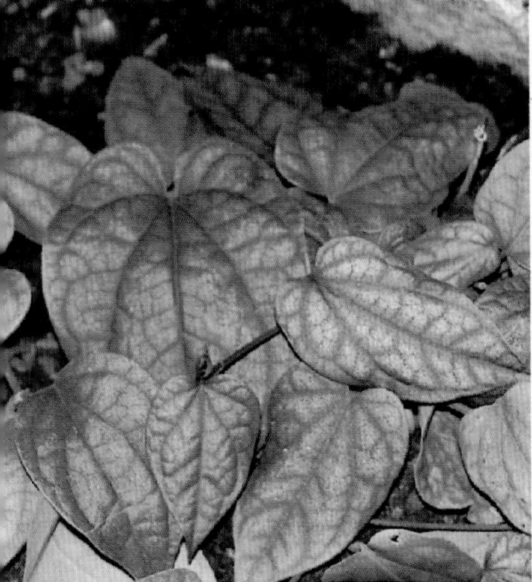

Piper sylvaticum

MOUNTAIN LONG PEPPER

A climbing plant with grey and silver heart shaped leaves.

Piptanthus tomentosus

This tall bushy shrub has hairy leaves and terminal heads of yellow coloured flowers.

PIPTANTHUS

FABACEAE [LEGUMINOSAE]

Tall shrubs which are native to the Himalayan area and are widely grown in cold temperate to temperate climates as ornamentals. They prefer a moderately fertile soil in full sun and benefit from annual pruning and fertilizer applications. Propagate from seed and cuttings.

Piptanthus nepalensis

A bushy tall shrub with terminal heads of golden coloured flowers. This is the most cold tolerant Piptanthus, from the Himalayan mountains.

PISONIA

NYCTAGINACEAE

Pisonia umbellifera cv. **Variegata**

PARA PARA

A small to medium evergreen tree with cream and green variegated leaves. It is native to Australia and New Zealand. The plant is grown outdoors in temperate to tropical climates and as an indoor plant in all climates. Propagate from cuttings.

PISTACIA

ANACARDIACEAE

Pistacia chinensis

A small evergreen tree which is native to Afghanistan. It is grown as a feature and street tree for its colourful autumn foliage. This tree consistently has showy foliage in warm temperate climates but is at its best in cooler climates where it withstands temperatures as low as -14 degrees Celsius. Propagate from seed.

p

PITHECOCTENIUM

BIGNONIACEAE

Pithecoctenium crucigerum
Native to tropical America, this is a slender evergreen climber. It has bunches of cream and yellow trumpet shaped flowers in spring. The plant will grow in climates from temperate to tropical and is propagated from seed and cuttings.

PITTOSPORUM

PITTOSPORACEAE

Aromatic evergreen shrubs and trees which are native to Australia, Africa, Asia and the Pacific. These plants are grown for their highly perfumed flowers, attractive seed pods and for their showy foliage. They are hardy plants and grow in climates which range from those having some frosts to warm tropical. Propagate from seed and cuttings.

Pittosporum eugenioides
cv. **Variegatum**
This cultivar is grown for its attractive variegated leaves which are coloured grey and cream.

Pittosporum moluccanum
A stately tall shrub with bunches of perfumed cream flowers and orange fruit. Suitable for semi-arid climates.

Pittosporum revolutum
BRISBANE LAUREL
An erect, open branched shrub which is grown for its very showy seed pod which, when open, exposes the bright orange-red seed. A plant covered with these open seed pods is very spectacular.

Pittosporum rhombifolium
QUEENSLAND PITTOSPORUM
A small tree which has bunches of perfumed cream flowers and showy heads of small bright orange seed pods which hold over many months.

Pittosporum tenuifolium
cv. **Abbotsbury Gold**
This cultivar has green and yellow variegated leaves.

Pittosporum tenuifolium
cv. **Garnettii**
A tall shrub grown for its colourful variegated leaves coloured grey and edged white.

Pittosporum tenuifolium
cv. **Gold Star**
The green and yellow variegated leaves of this cultivar darken with age to yellowish green and dark green.

PITTOSPORUM (cont)

***Pittosporum tenuifolium* cv. Irene Paterson**
This cultivar has variegated leaves coloured greenish grey with white markings.

***Pittosporum tenuifolium* cv. Sunburst**
An upright cultivar which has variegated leaves coloured green and cream.

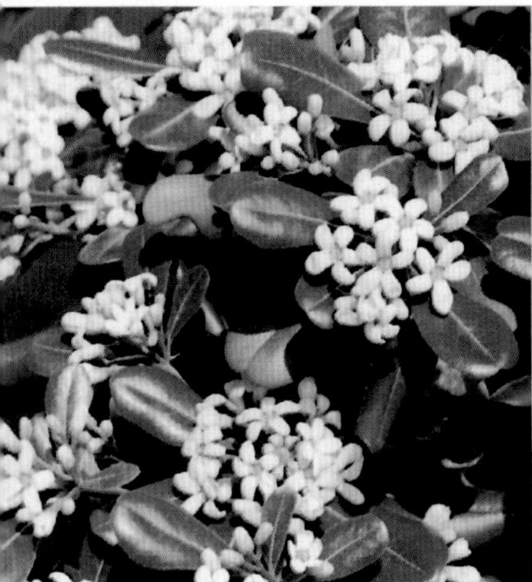

Pittosporum tobira JAPANESE PITTOSPORUM
This widely grown plant is a bushy tall shrub which has highly perfumed bunches of cream flowers.

***Pittosporum tobira* cv. Nana**
A very compact and bushy dwarf cultivar of this fragrant shrub.

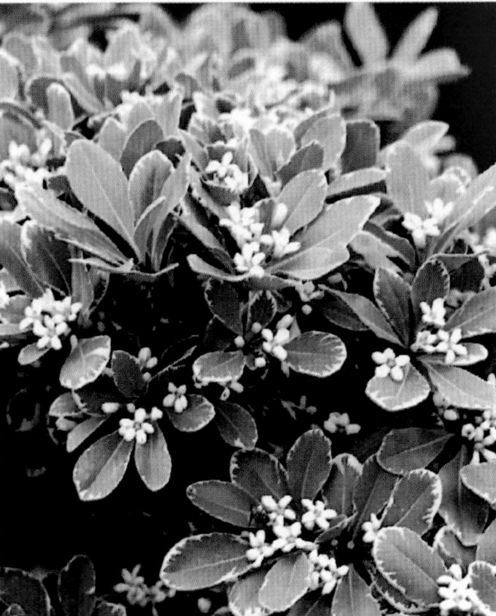

***Pittosporum tobira* cv. Variegata**
The variegated leaves of this compact shrub are coloured grey and tipped with cream.

Pittosporum undulatum VICTORIAN BOX
A small bushy tree with bunches of very fragrant, small flowers, followed by orange coloured berries.

***Pittosporum undulatum* cv. Variegatum**
A cultivar with variegated leaves coloured grey and cream.

PLECTRANTHUS

LAMIACEAE [LABIATAE]

Bushy evergreen plants and shrubs, native to Asia, Africa and Australia, which are grown as ornamentals for their flowers. They grow in climates from cold temperate to tropical and are propagated from seed and cuttings.

Plectranthus ecklonii
An upright bushy shrub with large heads of purple flowers.

Plectranthus saccatus
This bushy shrub has heads of violet coloured flowers.

PLECTRANTHUS (cont)

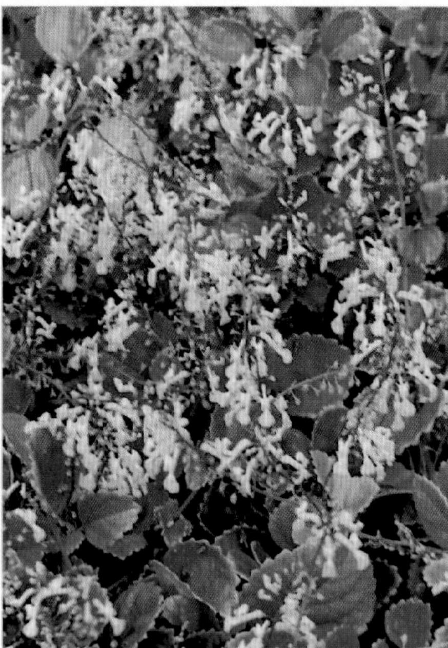

Plectranthus verticillatus
A ground cover plant with small spikes of cream flowers.

PLEIOGYNIUM

ANACARDIACEAE

Pleiogynium timorense
BURDEKIN PLUM
A medium spreading tree native to Australia. It is grown as a shade tree in parks and large gardens. The tree produces large, plum-like, edible (though rather sour) fruit and is grown in sub-tropical and tropical climates. Propagate from seed.

PLOIARIUM

THEACEAE

Ploiarium alternifolium SOMAH
Native to South East Asia, this shiny leaf, evergreen shrub has attractive pink, star shaped flowers over many months. It is grown in tropical and sub-tropical climates as an ornamental and for soil stabilization close to the coast. Propagate from seed.

PLUMBAGO

PLUMBAGINACEAE

Evergreen clumping shrubs and semi-climbers which are native to America, Africa, Asia and Australia, and are widely grown as showy ornamentals outdoors in temperate to tropical climates and as indoor plants in cooler climates. Propagate from seed or tip cuttings under mist.

Plumbago auriculata CAPE LEADWORT
syn. ***P. capensis***
A long stemmed shrub which has large heads of sky-blue flowers.

Plumbago auriculata cv. **Alba**
A cultivar which has heads of clear white flowers.

PLUMBAGO (cont)

Plumbago auriculata cv. **Royal Cape**
Large heads of light royal blue flowers make this a colourful cultivar.

Plumbago indica
syn. ***P. rosea***
A semi-climbing shrub which has heads of dark rose-pink flowers.

Plumbago scandens
A spreading shrub which has heads of white flowers and sticky seed pods.

PLUMERIA

FRANGIPANI

Apocynaceae

Deciduous and evergreen shrubs and small trees which have large heads of fragrant colourful flowers over many months. These flowers are widely used by florists in bouquets, corsages and garlands. Frangipani is native to tropical America and most grow in climates from temperate to tropical. Propagation is from fresh seed and from large cuttings. Immediately after taking the cutting, dip into soil or sand to stop the bleeding, then allow to dry in the shade for 2 to 4 weeks before planting.

Plumeria obtusa EVERGREEN FRANGIPANI
A small evergreen tree with large heads of perfumed white flowers which have yellow centres. This plant will only grow in a sub-tropical or tropical climate.

Plumeria obtusa var. ***sericifolia***
A variation which is smaller growing and has flowers with narrower petals.

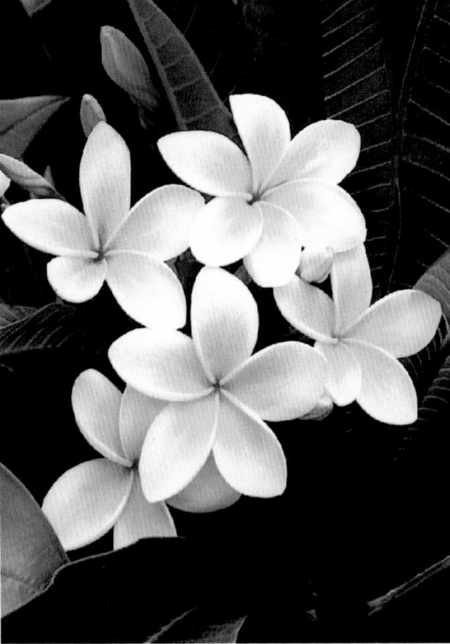

Plumeria rubra f. ***acutifolia*** FRANGIPANI
The most widely grown frangipani, with large fragrant flowers coloured white with a yellow centre. This plant may flower for up to 8 months of the year.

PLUMERIA (cont)

Plumeria rubra **cv. American Beauty**
A cultivar which has large open bunches of pinky red flowers.

Plumeria rubra **cv. Canary**
This highly fragrant cultivar has bunches of yellow and white flowers. The petals of this cultivar mostly stay incurved.

Plumeria rubra **cv. Fan Dancer**
This cultivar has large sparse heads of flowers coloured pink and gold with narrow reflexed petals.

Plumeria rubra **cv. Calypso**
Multi-coloured flowers of cerise, pink and yellow bloom on this cultivar.

Plumeria rubra **cv. Carmine Flush**
The flowers on this cultivar are coloured yellow and carmine. The petals are narrower than most cultivars.

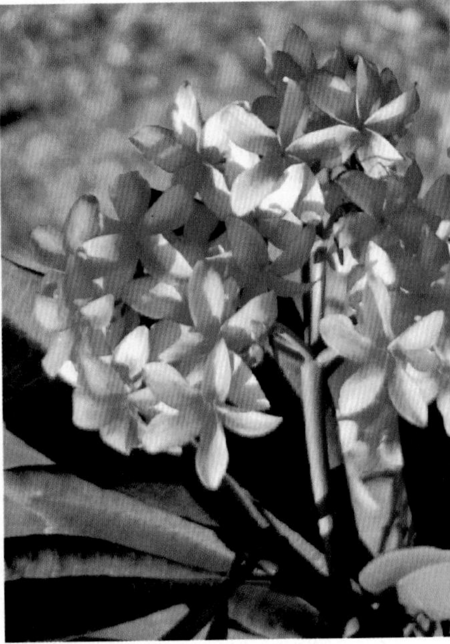

Plumeria rubra **cv. Flamingo**
A free flowering cultivar with large heads of bright pink flowers which have reflexed petals.

Plumeria rubra **cv. Can Can**
A showy cultivar with large bunches of flattish flowers coloured white, pink and gold.

Plumeria rubra **cv. Celadine**
A cultivar which has medium sized flower heads. The flowers are on longer than average stems and are mostly yellow with some white. The petals stay incurved.

Plumeria rubra **cv. Flore Pleno**
A very unusual cultivar which has double flowers coloured gold and white.

PLUMERIA (cont)

***Plumeria rubra* cv. Lady in Pink**
A cultivar which has tightly packed heads of flowers coloured bright pink with a small golden centre.

***Plumeria rubra* cv. Pink Pendula**
A cultivar which has very large pendulous heads of flowers coloured salmon-pink.

***Plumeria rubra* cv. Golden Kiss**
The flowers of this cultivar bloom in large heads, and are coloured golden yellow with touches of carmine.

***Plumeria rubra* cv. Maui Beauty**
This cultivar has upright heads of flowers coloured pink with a touch of gold in the centre. The petals are incurved.

***Plumeria rubra* cv. Pink Perfection**
This cultivar has large erect heads of flowers coloured pale pink with touches of rose-pink and yellow.

***Plumeria rubra* cv. June Bride**
A cultivar with medium heads of flowers coloured mostly white with some yellow. The flowers have incurved petals.

***Plumeria rubra* cv. Kauka Wilder**
This is a very colourful cultivar with medium size heads of flowers coloured cerise and gold.

***Plumeria rubra* cv. Pink Pearl**
A cultivar which has sparse heads of flowers which may droop. The flower colour is bright pink with centres being carmine and gold.

PLUMERIA (cont)

Plumeria rubra cv. **Pot of Gold**
A cultivar which has medium heads of large flowers coloured golden yellow.

Plumeria rubra cv. **Salmon Queen**
Very large heads of fragrant salmon pink flowers make this a spectacular frangipani.

Plumeria rubra cv. **Rainbow**
A very spectacular cultivar with large heads of flattish flowers coloured pink, apricot, yellow and gold.

Plumeria rubra cv. **Rosy Dawn**
The reflexed flowers of this cultivar bloom in large open heads and are coloured rose-pink, pale pink and gold.

Plumeria rubra cv. **Samoan Fluff**
A cultivar with very upright heads of flowers coloured white with yellow centres.

Plumeria rubra cv. **Red Pendula**
A cultivar which has large pendulous heads of pinkish red reflexed flowers on long stems.

Plumeria rubra cv. **Royal Red**
A cultivar which has large pendulous heads of crimson flowers on long stems.

Plumeria rubra cv. **Smokey**
The large flowers are coloured pink, orange and yellow with bluish smoky tonings on this cultivar.

PLUMERIA (cont)

***Plumeria rubra* cv. Sunset**
This cultivar has erect heads of flowers coloured yellow with cerise markings to the outer edges of the petals.

***Plumeria rubra* cv. Tellice Hagber**
A cultivar which has large heads of flowers coloured bright pink with gold centres.

Plumeria stenopetala
A compact shrub with large heads of flowers coloured white with a yellow centre. The petals of the flowers are narrow and reflexed.

Plumeria stenophylla
This compact shrub has large heads of white flowers with yellow centres. The narrow petals are incurved.

PODALYRIA

FABACEAE [LEGUMINOSAE]

Podalyria sericea
A medium growing shrub native to South Africa. It has heads of pinky mauve pea-type flowers in spring and grows in climates from cool temperate to sub-tropical. Propagate from seed and cuttings.

PODRANEA

BIGNONIACEAE

Free flowering evergreen climbers native to Africa. They grow in climates from temperate to sub-tropical. These climbers need plenty of water in hot weather and are propagated from seed and cuttings.

Podranea brycei QUEEN OF SHEBA
A vigorous climber with large heads of pinky carmine trumpet-type flowers in spring and summer.

Podranea ricasoliana
PINK TRUMPET VINE
A vigorous climber with large heads of pale pink trumpet-type flowers in spring and summer.

POLYALTHIA

ANNONACEAE

Evergreen shrubs and small trees native to tropical countries. They are grown as ornamentals for their unique shape or their showy flowers and fruit. These plants require a warm climate and a good soil. Propagate from seed.

Polyalthia longifolia var. ***pendula***

A very upright conical shaped small tree with large pendulous leaves.

Polyalthia obtusa

Tall and bushy, this shrub has perfumed creamy green flowers and showy clusters of red fruit which turn black.

POLYGALA

POLYGALACEAE

Mostly evergreen, these shrubs are found in many countries of the world. Only a few are grown as showy ornamentals.

Polygala x ***dalmaisiana***

A hybrid free flowering shrub which flowers during the summer months.

Polygala myrtifolia

A free branching evergreen shrub which is native to Africa. In cool temperate to sub-tropical climates, it is widely grown as an ornamental for its showy heads of purple pea-type flowers. Propagate from seed and cuttings.

POLYSCIAS

ARALIACEAE

Native to Asia, Australia and the Pacific, these ornamental shrubs and small trees are grown for their showy foliage. Most require tropical or sub-tropical climates but several will tolerate light frosts. They require plenty of water in hot weather and rich soil. Propagate from seed and cuttings. Some are widely grown as a low hedge outdoors and as indoor plants in cool climates.

Polyscias filicifolia FERN-LEAF-ARALIA

A dense multi-stemmed shrub with fern-like leaves which broaden as they age.

Polyscias filicifolia cv. **Aurea**

A cultivar which has finer fern-like leaves coloured gold.

POLYSCIAS (cont)

P

Polyscias guilfoylei
cv. **Alba Variegata**
On this multi-branching shrub the showy variegated leaves are coloured cream and green.

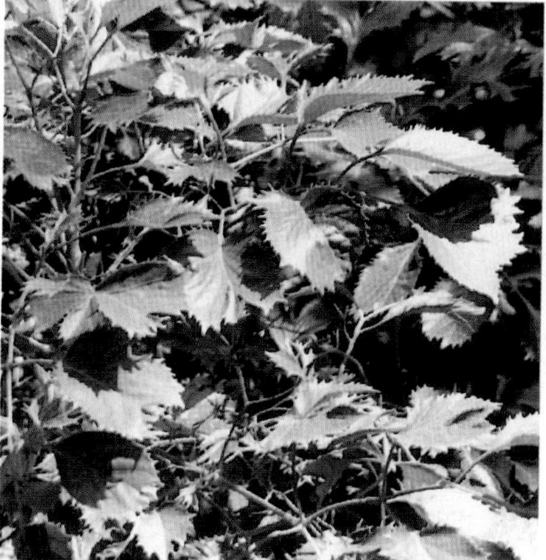

Polyscias guilfoylei cv. **Laciniata**
The leaves on this bushy cultivar are serrated.

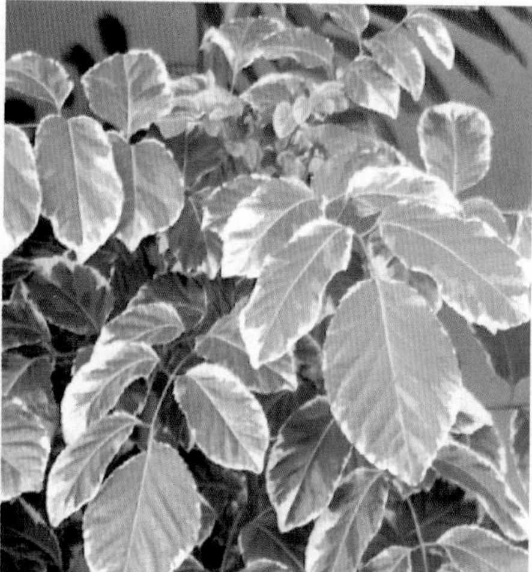

Polyscias guilfoylei cv. **Variegata**
A cultivar with large variegated leaves coloured grey and white.

Polyscias sambucifolia
This medium to tall shrub has fern-like leaves and cream flowers.

Polyscias scutellaria
A narrow multi-branching shrub with round green leaves.

Polyscias scutellaria cv. **Balfourii**
BALFOUR ARALIA
syn. ***P. balfouriana***
A narrow upright shrub with rough edged leaves.

Polyscias scutellaria
cv. **Crispata Aurea**
The partly twisted leaves of this upright shrub are coloured green and yellow.

Polyscias scutellaria cv. **Pennockii**
An upright cultivar with leaves coloured creamy yellow and green.

Polyscias scutellaria cv. **Variegata**
Variegated leaves coloured grey and white feature on this multi-branching shrub.

POMADERRIS

Rhamnaceae

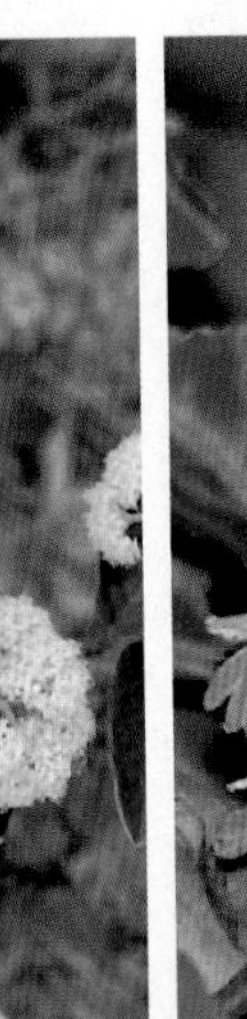

Pomaderris affinis

An Australian evergreen shrub, it is grown in cool temperate to sub-tropical climates as a showy ornamental for its golden coloured flowers. Propagate from seed and cuttings.

PONGAMIA

Fabaceae [Leguminosae]

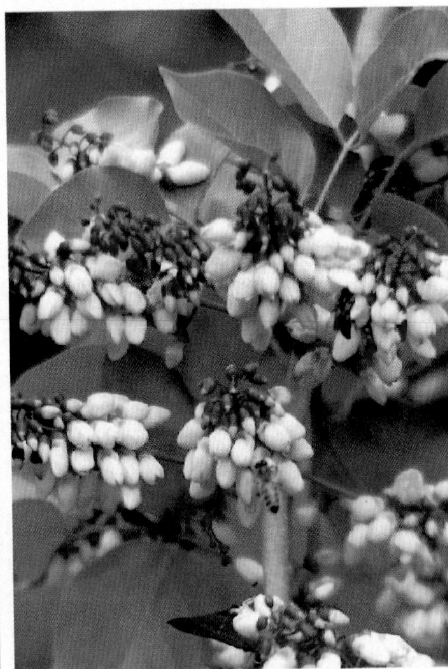

Pongamia pinnata INDIAN BEECH

A medium evergreen tree native to Australia, South East Asia and India. In sub-tropical and tropical climates it is widely planted as a feature or street tree for its large bunches of pale pink to mauve fragrant flowers. The crushed leaves are very aromatic. Propagate from seed.

PORPHYROCOMA

Acanthaceae

Porphyrocoma pohliana JADE MAGIC

A bushy small shrub which is native to Brazil. It has red and purple flower heads and is grown outdoors in climates from warm temperate to tropical and as an indoor plant in cooler climates. Propagate from seed and cuttings.

POTENTILLA

Rosaceae

Shrubs and herbs native to the northern hemisphere as far north as the Arctic region. They are very hardy and cold tolerant plants which prefer a slightly alkaline well drained soil in a sunny situation. These widely grown ornamental plants flower from mid-spring to late summer and benefit from regular fertilizing. The most widely grown is *P. fruticosa*, with many cultivars being available. These are propagated from cuttings.

***Potentilla fruticosa* cv. Beanii**

A cultivar which has white petals with a yellow centre. Petals do not overlap.

***Potentilla fruticosa* cv. Eastleigh Cream**

This cultivar has cream coloured flowers with yellow centres.

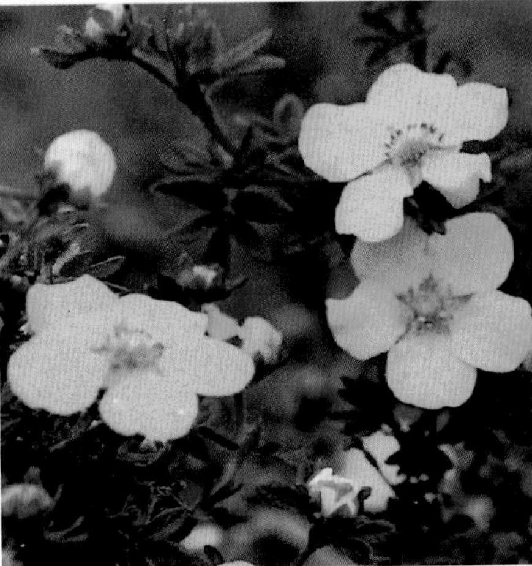

***Potentilla fruticosa* cv. Jackman's Giant**

Golden coloured flowers are the feature of this cultivar.

***Potentilla fruticosa* cv. Primrose Beauty**

A cultivar with primrose coloured flowers with overlapping petals.

POTENTILLA (cont)

Potentilla fruticosa cv. **Snowflake**
The white flowers of this cultivar have overlapping petals.

Potentilla fruticosa cv. **Tilford Cream**
A cultivar with cream flowers which have overlapping petals.

PREMNA

VERBENACEAE

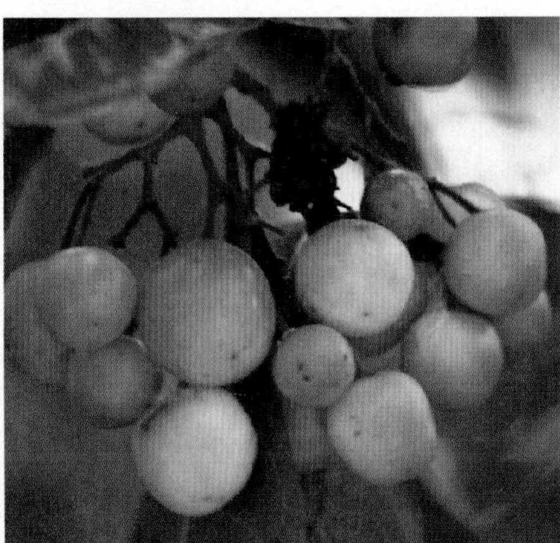

Premna lignum-vitae
YELLOW HOLLYWOOD
A medium evergreen tree with a spreading crown which is grown as a park tree and to produce commercial timber. It is native to Australia. The flowers are pinky purple and the highly coloured fruit are red with yellow markings. Propagate from seed.

PRESTONIA

APOCYNACEAE

Prestonia quinquangularis
syn. ***Echites rubrovenosa***
A sparse wiry climber which is native to tropical America. It requires a tropical climate outdoors or a heated glasshouse in cooler climates. The plant has olive-green to brownish leaves and small yellow flowers. Propagate from seed or cuttings, both of which require bottom heat.

PROSTANTHERA

AUSTRALIAN MINT BUSH

LAMIACEAE [LABIATAE]

Evergreen shrubs with aromatic foliage which are native to Australia. They are grown for their showy spring flowers in climates from cold temperate to sub-tropical. These plants need good drainage with plenty of water in hot weather. Propagation is from seed or cuttings.

Prostanthera cuneata cv. **Alba**
This white flowered cultivar is widely grown in cool climates.

Prostanthera incisa cv. **Rosea**
A bushy shrub which is covered with mauvish pink flowers in spring.

Prostanthera magnifica
This is an erect shrub with terminal spikes of mauve flowers in a purple calyx.

Prostanthera melissifolia
A medium shrub with round toothed leaves and purple flowers in profusion.

PROSTANTHERA (cont)

Prostanthera nivea
This open crowned shrub flowers profusely with pale mauve-blue flowers.

Prostanthera ovalifolia
A very free flowering shrub with masses of purple flowers in spring.

***Prostanthera ovalifolia* cv. Alba**
A cultivar of this free flowering shrub with white flowers.

Prostanthera rotundifolia
In spring this upright shrub is covered with mauve to purple flowers.

***Prostanthera rotundifolia* cv. Rosea**
This free flowering cultivar has rose-pink flowers.

PROTEA

PROTEACEAE

Native to Africa, these shrubs and small trees are grown as ornamentals and for cut flowers which are widely sought by florists all over the world. They mostly prefer a sandy well drained soil in climates from cool temperate to sub-tropical. Propagation is from seed and semi-hardwood cuttings.

Protea coronata
A bushy shrub with grey leaves and large flowers coloured greenish cream and white.

Protea cynaroides KING PROTEA
A sparse shrub with very large flowers with variable colours which may be red, pink, silver and white.

***Protea* cv. Duchess of Perth**
This cultivar has grey leaves and large red flower heads.

Protea eximia
syn. ***P. latifolia***
A grey leaf shrub with large pink and red flower heads.

PROTEA (cont)

Protea longifolia
This is a medium shrub with long leaves and pinky red flower heads.

Protea neriifolia OLEANDER LEAF PROTEA
A bushy shrub with large flower heads coloured pink to red.

Protea obtusifolia
The large flower heads on this bushy shrub are coloured pink to red.

***Protea* cv. Pinita**
A large flowering cultivar used for the cut flower trade. Flowers are pink inside and red outside.

***Protea* cv. Pink Ice**
An upright shrub with large flower heads coloured silvery pink.

Protea pudens
syn. ***P. minor***
Large flower heads coloured pinky red and white bloom on this low growing spreading shrub.

Protea repens - pink form
syn. ***P. mellifera***
A bushy shrub with long flower heads coloured pink and white.

Protea repens - red form
syn. ***P. mellifera***
A colour variation which has flower heads coloured red and white.

Protea repens - white form
syn. ***P. mellifera***
This colour variation has white flower heads with some yellow.

PROTEA (cont)

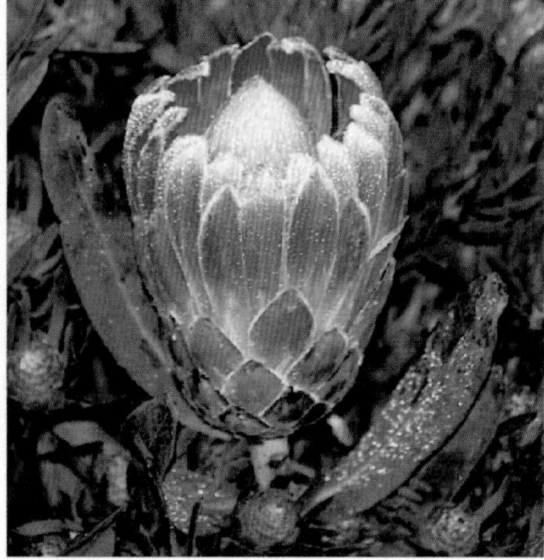

Protea cv. **Satin Pink**
Grown for cut flowers, this free flowering cultivar has large flowers which are pink dusted with pale pink.

Protea scolymocephala
A small spreading shrub with fully open flower heads coloured cream and white.

Protea stokoei
Large blunt flower heads coloured silvery rose-pink bloom on this grey leaf shrub.

Protea cv. **Sylvia**
A cultivar grown for cut flowers. The large flowers are bright red in colour.

PRUNUS

Rosaceae

Deciduous or occasionally evergreen shrubs and trees which are native to temperate climates of the Northern Hemisphere. They are grown in climates from very cold temperate to sub-tropical for their fruit and as flowering ornamentals. Species Prunus are grown from seed and some of these are used as rootstock for the cultivars which are grafted and budded. There are many variable names in Prunus especially the flowering cherries which are from indistinct parentage. Names may vary from country to country.

Prunus avium cv. **Plena** BIRD CHERRY
A small to medium tree with pendulous bunches of double white flowers in spring.

Prunus besseyi WESTERN SAND CHERRY
This bushy shrub has single white flowers with reddish black edible fruit.

Prunus x ***blireana***
A small tree which has outstanding purple foliage and double pink flowers.

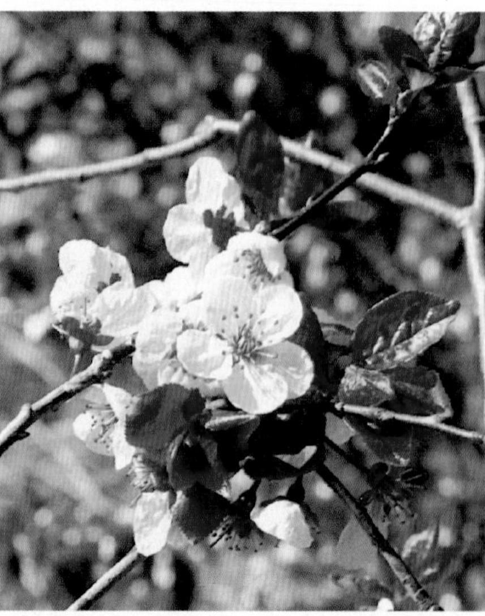

Prunus cerasifera cv. **Festeri**
Pink flowers and plum coloured foliage feature on this small tree.

PRUNUS (cont)

Prunus cerasifera cv. **Nigra**
A small tree with reddish purple leaves and pale pink flowers.

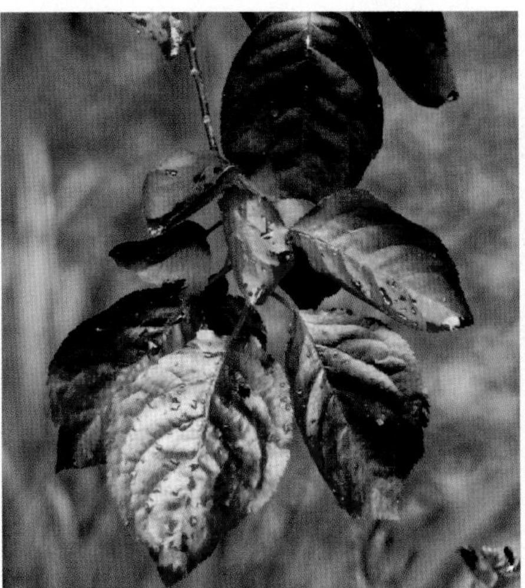

Prunus cerasifera cv. **Nigra** - leaves
This illustration shows the highly coloured leaves.

Prunus domestica cv. **Elvins**
FLOWERING PLUM
A medium to tall shrub which is covered with pink flowers in spring.

Prunus glandulosa
DWARF FLOWERING ALMOND
This small to medium shrub, in spring, has double pink flowers along the branches.

Prunus glandulosa cv. **Alba Plena**
A cultivar with double white flowers.

Prunus glandulosa cv. **Sinensis**
DWARF FLOWERING ALMOND
In early spring this sparse shrub has small double pink flowers.

Prunus incisa FUJI CHERRY
A tall shrub to small tree with pink and white coloured flowers in spring.

Prunus lusitanica PORTUGUESE LAUREL
An evergreen bushy tall shrub or small tree with long spikes of small white flowers.

Prunus mume cv. **Kyokkoh**
FLOWERING APRICOT
This is a small deciduous tree which has bright pink flowers in winter, before the new leaves appear.

PRUNUS (cont)

Prunus nipponica
JAPANESE ALPINE CHERRY
In spring this tall shrub to small tree has clusters of white to very pale pink flowers.

Prunus padus 2 BIRD CHERRY
A tall shrub to small tree with single white flowers in spring.

Prunus persica cv. **Alboplena**
FLOWERING PEACH
In spring, this upright small tree has bunches of double white flowers.

Prunus persica cv. **Lillian Burrows**
A small upright tree which is covered with double pink flowers in spring.

Prunus persica cv. **Rosea Nana**
Dwarf growing, this shrub has double rose-pink flowers in spring.

Prunus persica cv. **Rubro Plena**
A small tree which is covered with pinky red double flowers in spring.

Prunus persica cv. **Versicolor**
In spring, flowers of pink and cerise cover this small tree.

Prunus prostrata
Spreading over a large area, this low growing Prunus has single pink flowers in spring.

Prunus serrula BIRCH-BARK TREE
A small tree with shiny brown bark and small bunches of white flowers.

PRUNUS (cont)

Prunus serrulata

JAPANESE FLOWERING CHERRIES

The following cultivars are from the Sato-Zakura group of Prunus which are of uncertain parentage. Many experts believe they originated from *P. serrulata* and are generally known under this name.

Prunus serrulata cv. **Amanogawa** [7]
An upright small tree with double pink and white flowers in spring.

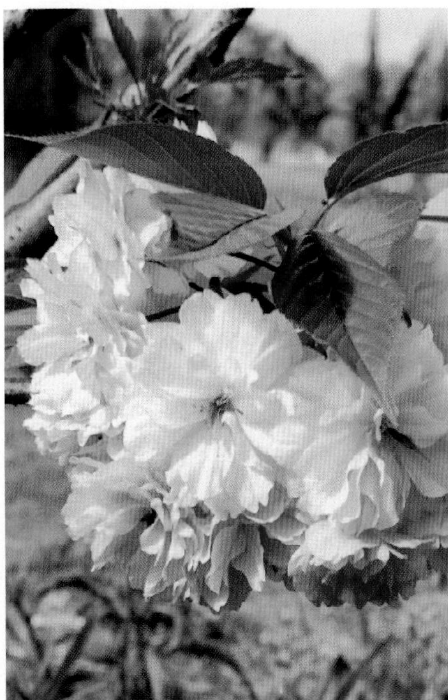

Prunus serrulata cv. **Deep Pink** [7]
This small tree has bronze coloured new foliage and rose-pink double flowers which fade as they age.

Prunus serrulata cv. **Fugenzo**
A small tree with heads of double pink flowers.

Prunus serrulata cv. **J.H. Veitch** [7]
In spring this small tree has heads of double pink flowers. Some authorities consider this as synonymous with *P. serrulata* cv. Fugenzo.

Prunus serrulata cv. **Kiku-Shidare [Zakura]** [7]
syn. ***P. serrulata*** cv. **Cheale's Weeping**
A small tree with pendulous branches and large bunches of double pink flowers.

Prunus serrulata cv. **New Red**
Reddish bronze new foliage and deep rose-pink double flowers feature on this small tree.

Prunus serrulata cv. **Ojochin**
An upright small tree with bronze coloured new foliage and pale pink double flowers.

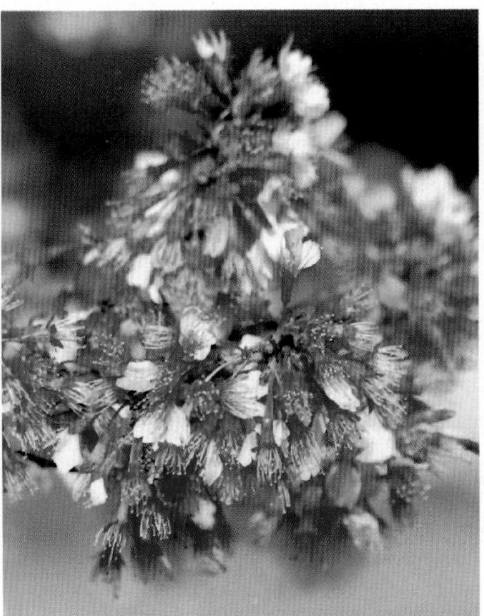

Prunus serrulata cv. **Okame**
On this tall shrub to small tree the flowers are pink to rose-pink.

PRUNUS (cont)

Prunus serrulata cv. **Okumiyako** 7
A wide crowned small tree which has rose-pink buds which open to double white flowers.

Prunus serrulata cv. **Pink Perfection**
Free flowering, this small tree has bunches of double pink flowers.

Prunus serrulata cv. **Sekiyama**
syn. **P. serrulata** cv. **Kanzan**
An upright small tree with bunches of double pink flowers.

Prunus serrulata cv. **Shiogama**
A cultivar with large heads of double, pale pink flowers which fade to white.

Prunus serrulata cv. **Shirotae**
syn. **P. serrulata** cv. **Mount Fuji**
This small treee has a spreading crown and bunches of semi-double to double white flowers.

Prunus serrulata cv. **Takasago**
A small tree with bunches of white to pale pink double flowers.

Prunus serrulata cv. **Tsukubane**
This cultivar has large heads of pink flowers which lighten in colour as they age.

Prunus serrulata cv. **Ukon** 7
Bunches of semi-double creamish green flowers bloom on this small tree which has a spreading crown.

Prunus subhirtella cv. **Pendula Rubra** 2
SPRING CHERRY
A small tree with a spreading crown and pendulous branches. The flower buds are ruby in colour and open to rose-pink. This tree is mostly grafted high above the ground to give a weeping effect.

PRUNUS (cont)

Prunus tenella DWARF RUSSIAN ALMOND
This small shrub with pink flowers needs a cold winter to promote a prolific flowering.

Prunus wrightii FLOWERING PLUM
A small tree with large single pink flowers in spring.

Prunus* x *yedoensis [7] TOKYO CHERRY
In spring this small upright broad tree has white flowers.

***Prunus* x *yedoensis* cv. Erecta** [7]
Very upright, this small tree has pink and white coloured flowers.

PSEUDAECHMANTHERA

ACANTHACEAE

Pseudaechmanthera glutinosa
A bushy free flowering shrub which grows in temperate to sub-tropical climates as an ornamental. It has terminal bunches of lilac-lavender flowers over a long period. Propagate from seed or cuttings.

PSEUDERANTHEMUM

ACANTHACEAE

Evergreen shrubs from many tropical countries. They are grown outdoors in climates from warm temperate to tropical for their attractive flowers and showy leaves. These plants prefer a soil rich in humus and regular fertiliser applications. Propagate from seed and cuttings.

Pseuderanthemum andersonii
An upright, free branching shrub with yellow new foliage and erect spikes of white flowers with cerise eyes.

***Pseuderanthemum* cv. Aurea**
The foliage on this bushy shrub is green and gold, flowers are white.

Pseuderanthemum cooperi
A small shrub with serrated leaves and white and mauve coloured flowers.

PSEUDERANTHEMUM (cont)

Pseuderanthemum kewense

CHOCOLATE PLANT

A bushy shrub with chocolate coloured leaves and bunches of white flowers.

Pseuderanthemum laxiflorum

This small bushy shrub has large bunches of rose-pink flowers.

***Pseuderanthemum laxiflorum* cv. Mini Purple**

A very dwarf shrub with heads of small purple flowers.

Pseuderanthemum reticulatum

Bushy and free branching, this shrub has heads of white flowers marked with carmine-cerise.

Pseuderanthemum seticalyx

A bushy shrub with very pale pink flowers with cerise eyes. Now called *Ruspolia seticalyx.*

***Pseuderanthemum* sp.**

This compact bushy shrub has serrated leaves and white flowers. Known in the nursery trade as *P. sinuatum.*

PSEUDOBOMBAX

BOMBACACEAE

Pseudobombax ellipticum

SHAVING-BRUSH TREE

syn. ***Bombax ellipticum***

An outstanding, medium size deciduous tree which has masses of large bright pink shaving brush-like flowers in spring, before the leaves appear. The new foliage is brownish purple and very colourful. This tree is highly regarded as one of the most outstanding flowering trees of the world. It is native to Central America, is propagated from seed and occasionally from cuttings and is grown in warm temperate to tropical climates.

Pseudobombax ellipticum

This illustration shows the brilliant shaving brush-type flower.

PSEUDOGYNOXYS

ASTERACEAE [COMPOSITAE]

Pseudogynoxys chenopodioides

MEXICAN FLAME VINE

syn. ***Senecio confusus***

A bushy climber with large showy heads of orange-red and yellow coloured flowers.

PSEUDOMORUS

Urticaceae

Pseudomorus brunoniana

Native to Norfolk Island, this medium to tall, dense, evergreen shrub has pendulous catkins of white flowers over several months. It is grown as an ornamental in climates from cool temperate to sub-tropical. Propagate from seed and cuttings.

PSEUDOPANAX

Araliaceae

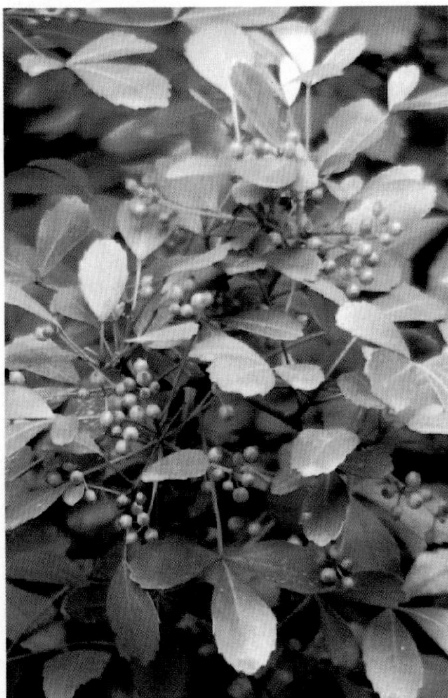

Pseudopanax lessonii HOUPARA

A small evergreen tree which is native to New Zealand. It is grown outdoors in climates from cold temperate to sub-tropical and is widely grown as an indoor plant. Propagate from seed and cuttings.

PSORALEA

Fabaceae [Leguminosae]

Psoralea pinnata BLUE PEA

An evergreen shrub with thin round leaves, which is native to South Africa. It has blue pea-type flowers and is grown in cold temperate to warm temperate climates. Propagate from seed.

PSYCHOTRIA

Rubiaceae

Psychotria capensis WILD COFFEE

A bushy shrub with green leathery leaves and terminal clusters of fragrant yellow flowers followed by black berries. It is native to South Africa and is grown as an ornamental. Propagate from seed.

PTEROCARPUS

Fabaceae [Leguminosae]

Evergreen tropical trees which are grown as ornamentals and used commercially for timber, dyes, kino and medical purposes. They are grown in sub-tropical and tropical climates and are propagated from seed.

Pterocarpus indicus PADAUK

A medium spreading tree with erect spikes of yellow flowers followed by large circular fruit. Produces a high quality timber.

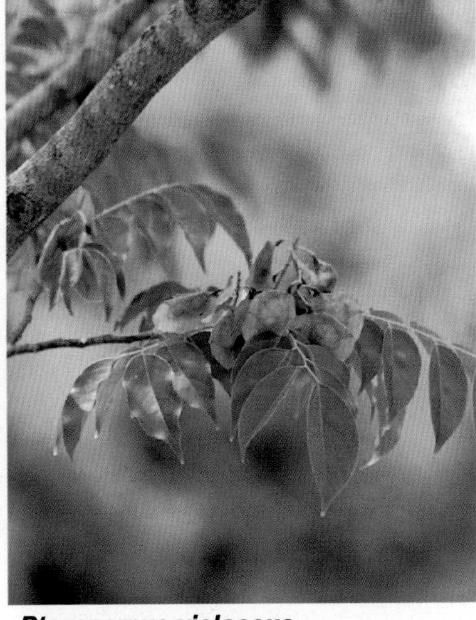

Pterocarpus violaceus

A medium tree with spikes of yellow flowers marked with violet, followed by flat round seeds which are illustrated.

PTEROSPERMUM

STERCULIACEAE

Evergreen shrubs and trees, native to India and South East Asia, which are grown as ornamentals for their showy flowers. They require a warm temperate to tropical climate and are propagated from seed.

Pterospermum acerifolium

A medium spreading tree with large maple-like leaves and large white flowers.

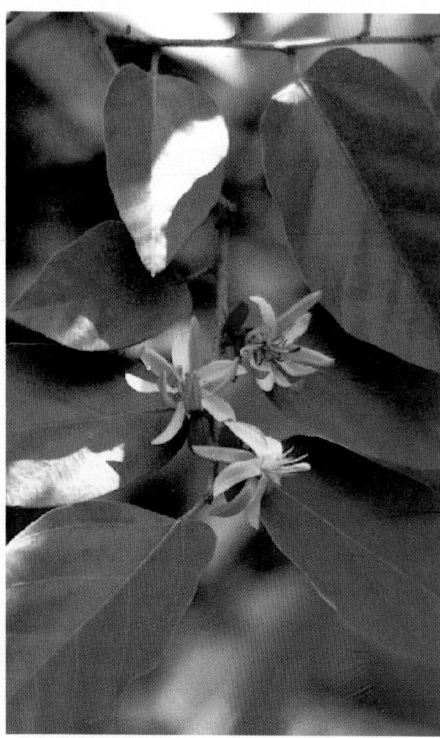

Pterospermum heterophyllum

A tall bushy shrub with clusters of small creamish white fragrant flowers.

PTYCHOSEMA

FABACEAE [LEGUMINOSAE]

Ptychosema sp.

A dense woody climber with erect spikes of yellow flowers. It grows in temperate to sub-tropical climates. Sometimes mistakenly referred to as *P. fassoglense*.

PULTENAEA

FABACEAE [LEGUMINOSAE]

Evergreen Australian shrubs which are grown in well drained soils, in climates from cold temperate to sub-tropical, as ornamentals. They are propagated from seed which needs hot water treatment or nicking.

Pultenaea daphnoides

An erect shrub with terminal heads of small amber coloured pea-type flowers.

Pultenaea elliptica

Terminal heads of orange and yellow coloured pea-type flowers bloom on this sparse shrub.

Pultenaea villosa

A small, fine leaf, spring flowering shrub. The gold pea-type flowers have an orange centre.

PUNICA

PUNICACEAE

Densely branched deciduous shrubs, native to Europe and Asia, which are grown as ornamentals or for their edible fruit. They are grown in climates from cold temperate to tropical and are propagated from seed and cuttings.

Punica granatum POMEGRANATE
A tall shrub which has red flowers and large edible fruit.

Punica granatum cv. **Flore Pleno**
syn. ***P. granatum*** cv. **Andrè le Roi**
A cultivar which has large double flowers coloured dark salmon and white.

Punica granatum cv. **Nana**
This dwarf growing cultivar has red flowers.

PYCNOSTACHYS

LAMIACEAE [LABIATAE]

Pycnostachys urticifolia
A much branched shrubby plant native to Africa. In climates from cold temperate to sub-tropical, it is grown as an ornamental for its heads of royal blue flowers. It is propagated from seed and cuttings.

PYROSTEGIA

BIGNONIACEAE

Pyrostegia venusta FLAME VINE
syn. ***Bignonia ignea; B. venusta***
An evergreen climber which is native to South America. It has large heads of bright orange flowers which cover the whole vine in early spring. The plant is widely grown throughout the world for its unforgettable show of colour and will grow in climates from temperate to tropical. Propagate from cuttings and suckers.

PYRUS

ROSACEAE

Deciduous trees native to south east Europe and Asia. They may be grown as ornamentals or for their fruit commonly called pears. They grow in climates from cold to warm temperate and are propagated from seed, cuttings or budding, or by grafting.

Pyrus nivalis SNOW PEAR
A flowering pear with bunches of white flowers.

Pyrus salicifolia WILLOW LEAF PEAR
A small deciduous tree with greyish leaves. The spring flowers are white with red stamens and may cover the whole tree.

QUASSIA

SIMAROUBACEAE

Quassia amara BITTERWOOD
A small evergreen tree native to tropical America, it is grown as an ornamental and for the production of a medicine called Quassia. The plant needs a warm climate and is propagated from seed.

q

QUERCUS

OAK

FAGACEAE

Deciduous and evergreen trees which are native to many countries and varying climates. They are used as ornamentals and to produce timber, dye, tannin and cork with seeds also being used as animal food. Many oak trees will tolerate cold climates and most are propagated from seeds which are called acorns. A few oaks are grafted.

Quercus bicolor SWAMP WHITE OAK

A medium spreading tree with large leaves and large acorns.

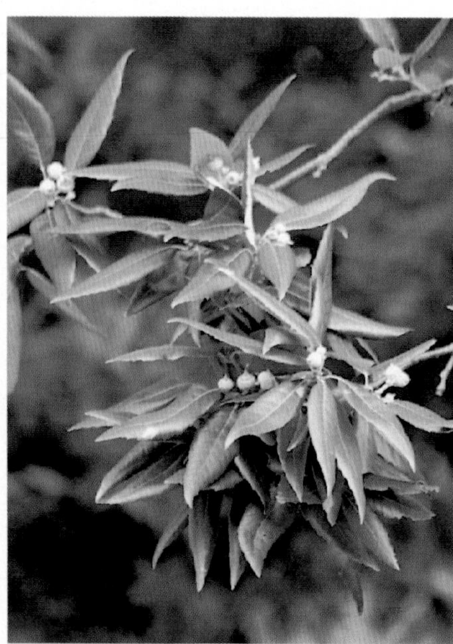

Quercus ilex EVERGREEN OAK

This broad crowned evergreen oak has small acorns.

Quercus palustris PIN OAK

A medium dense crowned tree with deeply lobed leaves and small round acorns.

***Quercus robur* cv. Atropurpurea**

The foliage of this cultivar is purple-brown.

***Quercus robur* cv. Concordia**

GOLDEN ENGLISH OAK

A broad crowned medium tree with yellow leaves and large acorns.

***Quercus rubra* cv. Aurea** RED OAK

This cultivar is a medium tree with a dense crown. It has golden leaves.

Quercus serratifolia

A medium tree with serrated leaves and large acorns.

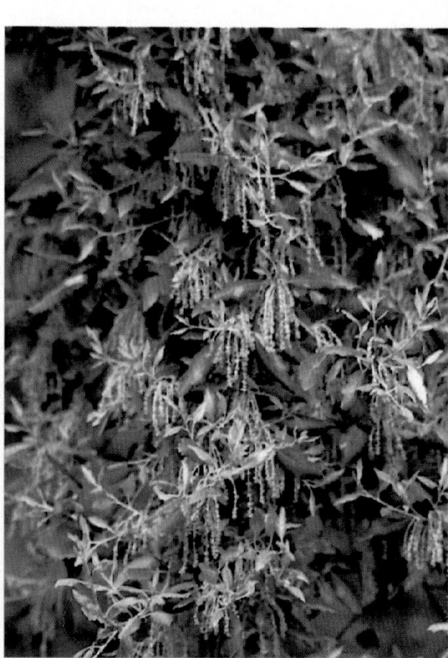

Quercus suber CORK OAK

A medium tree with large acorns and corky bark which is used to produce commercial cork.

QUERCUS (cont)

Quercus suber - bark

This illustration shows the corky bark.

QUISQUALIS

COMBRETACEAE

Climbers from tropical Africa and South East Asia. Two forms are widely grown as ornamentals in warm climates. They prefer a soil rich in humus to give their best colour. Propagate from seed and cuttings.

Quisqualis indica RANGOON CREEPER

A tough climber in warm climates. It has large heads of red or orange-red flowers over many months.

Quisqualis mussaendiflora

A colourful climber which has large flower heads made up of red bracts and small white flowers.

RADERMACHERA

BIGNONIACEAE

Evergreen trees native to Asia which are widely grown as outdoor and indoor ornamentals. Indoors they are grown in pots to control their size. Outdoors they prefer a climate from warm temperate to tropical and well drained soil. Propagate from seed and cuttings.

Radermachera frondosa

A small evergreen tree with perfumed white flowers which open in the daytime.

Radermachera sinica ASIAN BELL

This evergreen small tree has clusters of perfumed, white, bell shaped flowers which open at night.

Radermachera sinica cv. **Crystal Doll**

A new cultivar which has yellow and green variegated foliage.

RANDIA

RUBIACEAE

Tropical shrubs and trees which are mostly evergreen and are grown in warm climates as ornamentals, for their showy flowers. Propagate from seed and cuttings.

Randia fitzalanii

A small evergreen tree which has bunches of highly perfumed, white, star shaped flowers.

Randia formosa

An evergreen shrub with fragrant, white, star shaped flowers. Petals are partly reflexed.

r

RAUVOLFIA

Apocynaceae

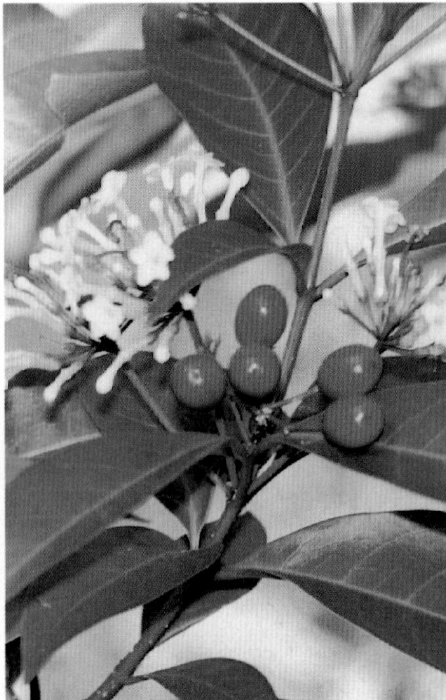

Rauvolfia verticillata
syn. ***R. chinensis***
Native to Asia, this evergreen shrub is grown in warm temperate to tropical climates as an ornamental and for the production of medicinal drugs. It is propagated from seed.

RAVENALA

Strelitziaceae

Ravenala madagascariensis
TRAVELLER'S PALM TREE
A palm-like tree which has broad leaves similar to the banana tree. It is native to Madagascar. The plant has blue and white flower clumps and is widely grown as an ornamental in sub-tropical and tropical climates. Propagate from seed.

RAVENIA

Rutaceae

Ravenia spectablis TORTUGO
A small evergreen shrub native to Cuba. It has showy flowers which may be red, violet or purple in colour. It is grown outdoors in warm climates and as an indoor plant in cooler climates. The plant prefers a rich moist soil. Propagate from seed and cuttings.

REEVESIA

Sterculiaceae

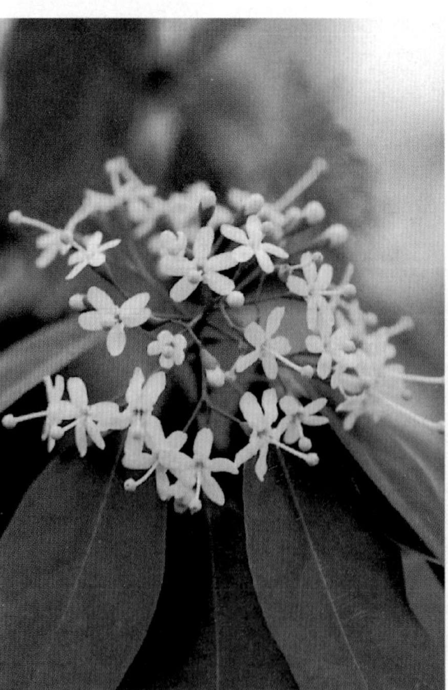

Reevesia thyrsoidea
An evergreen small tree, native to Asia. It is grown in warm climates as an ornamental for its perfumed heads of white flowers. Propagate from seed and cuttings.

REGELIA

Myrtaceae

Sparse evergreen shrubs from Australia which are grown as ornamentals in temperate to tropical climates. Propagate from seed.

Regelia punicea
A sparse shrub which has pendulous balls of red flowers.

Regelia velutina
An open upright shrub which is very hairy and has upright heads of red flowers with prominent yellow stamens.

REINWARDTIA

Linaceae

Reinwardtia indica YELLOW FLAX
syn. ***Linum trigynum; Reinwardtia trigyna***
Native to Asia, this bushy shrub has large yellow flowers and is grown in temperate to tropical climates as an ornamental. Propagate from softwood cuttings.

RHAPHIOLEPIS

ROSACEAE

Evergreen shrubs, native to Asia, which are widely grown as ornamentals for their showy flowers. They grow in climates from cool temperate to tropical and are propagated from seed and cuttings. Often spelt Raphiolepis.

Rhaphiolepis* x *delacourii
This hybrid between *R. indica* and *R. umbellata* is a bushy shrub and has heads of fragrant pink flowers in late spring.

***Rhaphiolepis* cv. Fergusonii**
A medium shrub which has heads of fragrant pale pink flowers in late spring.

***Rhaphiolepis* cv. Fergusonii Nana**
This cultivar is a very dwarf grower and has very fragrant flowers.

Rhaphiolepis indica INDIAN HAWTHORN
A medium shrub with large heads of perfumed white to pale pink flowers in spring.

***Rhaphiolepis indica* cv. Flamingo**
Compact, this shrub has large heads of fragrant bright pink flowers.

***Rhaphiolepis indica* cv. Rosea**
A medium shrub which has large heads of fragrant pink flowers.

***Rhaphiolepis indica* cv. Springtime**
This cultivar has bright pink flowers with white centres.

Rhaphiolepis umbellata
YEDDA HAWTHORN
syn. ***R. japonica***
A hardy shrub with perfumed white flowers. This plant is tolerant of some salt spray.

RHODAMNIA

MYRTACEAE

Rhodamnia rubescens
syn. ***R. trinervia***
A small evergreen tree native to Australia. It is grown as an ornamental for its delicate white flowers which have clusters of yellow stamens. This tree requires a climate from temperate to tropical and is propagated from seed and cuttings.

RHODOCHITON

SCROPHULARIACEAE

Rhodochiton atrosangunieum
syn. ***R. volubile*** PURPLE BELLS
A sparse climber native to Mexico which has pendulous dark purple flowers with a pink flower calyx. This plant prefers a mild climate and is grown from seed.

RHODODENDRON

ERICACEAE

Free flowering shrubs and trees from many countries throughout the world, in climates from cold to hot. They are widely grown for their showy heads of colourful flowers which are seen in a wide range of colours. Propagation is from seed and cuttings and by grafting.

***Rhododendron* cv. Abbey**
A bushy tall shrub with large heads of white flowers.

***Rhododendron* cv. Alice**
This bushy, tall, upright shrub has large heads of rose-pink flowers.

***Rhododendron* cv. Auguste van Geert**
A bushy tall shrub with large heads of carmine flowers.

Rhododendron augustinii
Heads of mauve-blue flowers feature on this compact shrub.

RHODODENDRON (cont)

Rhododendron cv. **Big Ben**
A tall bushy shrub with large heads of pink and white flowers.

Rhododendron cv. **Blue Diamond**
Small growing, this shrub has masses of lilac-blue flowers.

Rhododendron cv. **Blue Peter**
A medium shrub with large heads of flowers coloured mauve with a maroon centre.

Rhododendron calostrotum
This is a hardy, small, spreading shrub which has mauvish-pink flowers in spring.

Rhododendron campylogynum
A bushy spreading shrub with rosy violet coloured, bell shaped flowers in spring.

Rhododendron davidsonianum
Heads of pinky mauve flowers bloom on this tall shrub.

Rhododendron cv. **Desert Sun**
A tall shrub with large heads of flowers coloured deep rose-pink with yellow centres.

Rhododendron cv. **Earl of Athlone**
There are large heads of flowers coloured blood red on this medium shrub.

Rhododendron cv. **Fortune**
A tall shrub with large heads of cream coloured flowers.

RHODODENDRON (cont)

Rhododendron* x *fragrantissimum
A medium shrub with masses of fragrant white flowers.

***Rhododendron* cv. Jean Marie de Montague**
Large heads of red flowers bloom on this medium shrub.

***Rhododendron* cv. Kalimna**
A medium shrub with large heads of pink flowers.

***Rhododendron* cv. Frank Galsworthy**
This showy cultivar has large heads of dark red flowers with yellow markings.

***Rhododendron* cv. Joan Langdon**
A medium bushy shrub with heads of large cerise-red flowers.

Rhododendron kiusianum
In spring this spreading shrub is covered with rose-pink flowers.

***Rhododendron* cv. Freckles**
A medium shrub with large heads of pale pink flowers.

***Rhododendron johnstoneanum* cv. Double Diamond**
The flowers on this medium shrub are Gardenia like—double white with a touch of yellow in the centre.

***Rhododendron* cv. Lighthouse**
A medium shrub with large heads of scarlet-red flowers.

RHODODENDRON (cont)

r

Rhododendron lochiae
A tropical Rhododendron native to Australia, it is a small shrub with orange-red waxy looking flowers.

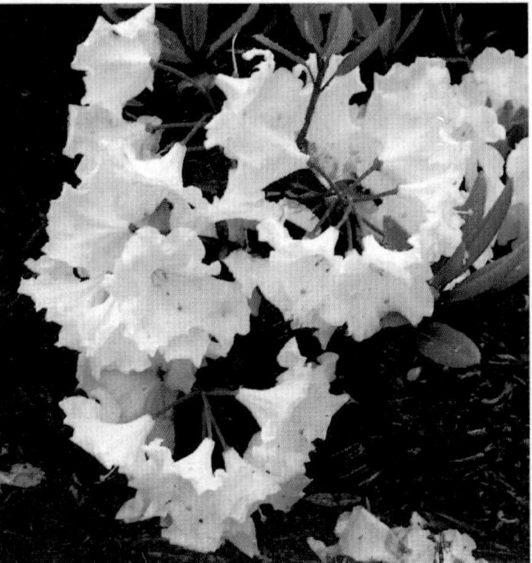

***Rhododendron* x *loderi* cv. King George**
A medium shrub with large bunches of flowers which open very pale pink and then change to white.

***Rhododendron* cv. Madam Cochet**
This is a medium shrub with large heads of violet coloured flowers which have pale mauve and gold markings.

***Rhododendron* cv. Margaret Mack**
Deep rose-pink flowers bloom in large heads on this medium shrub.

***Rhododendron* cv. Marion**
A medium shrub with heads of pale pink flowers with rose-pink markings.

***Rhododendron* cv. Max Sye** 2
There are large heads of flowers coloured red with a black centre on this medium shrub.

***Rhododendron* cv. Mrs G.W. Leak**
A medium shrub with large heads of pink flowers which have carmine centres.

***Rhododendron* cv. Nightwatch**
This is a small to medium shrub with large heads of dark red flowers with blackish purple centres.

Rhodendron nitens
A spreading low growing shrub with pinky violet coloured flowers in spring.

RHODODENDRON (cont)

Rhododendron nuttallii
A medium to tall shrub with heads of fragrant cream flowers.

***Rhododendron* cv. Professor Hugo de Vries**
A medium shrub with large heads of bright cyclamen-pink flowers.

***Rhododendron* cv. Saffron Queen**
A small shrub with heads of lemon-yellow flowers which have golden centres.

Rhododendron ponticum
Heads of deep lilac coloured flowers feature on this tall shrub to small tree.

***Rhododendron* cv. Rimfire**
This medium shrub has large heads of bright pinky red flowers.

***Rhododendron* cv. Sappho**
This is a medium shrub. The large heads of white flowers have deep maroon centres.

***Rhododendron* cv. President F.D. Roosevelt**
A medium shrub with green and gold variegated leaves and large heads of flowers which are pinkish white inside and have a broad red edge.

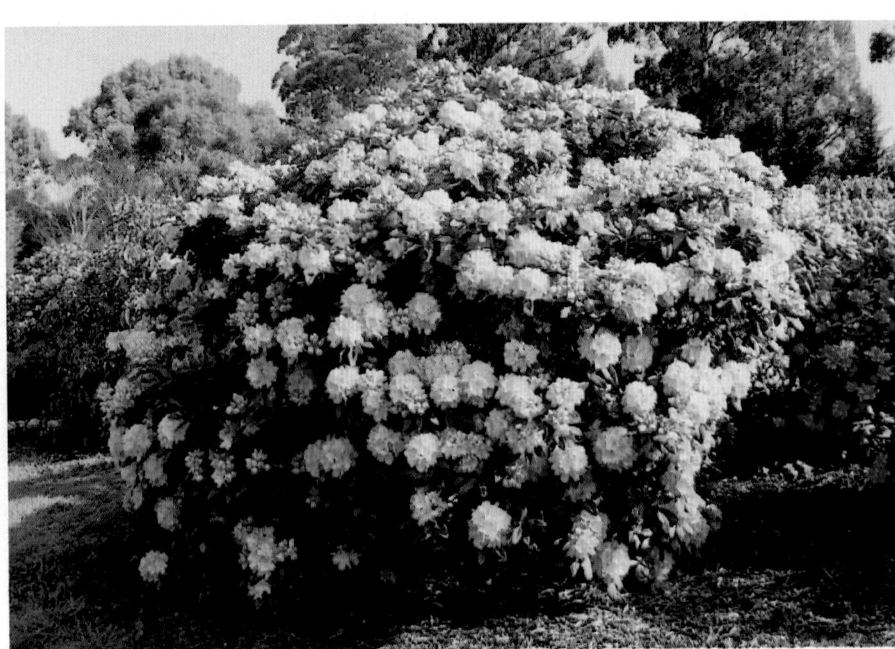

***Rhododendron* cv. Robyn**
A compact medium shrub with large heads of pink flowers.

RHODODENDRON (cont)

***Rhododendron* cv. Susette**
A medium shrub with large heads of lilac coloured flowers.

***Rhododendron* cv. Van Ness Sensation**
The flower heads on this medium shrub are of soft pink.

RHODODENDRON VIREYA

These shrub Rhododendrons are tropical in their natural habitat. Most grow in the mountains near the Equator where the climate may be quite mild. There has been considerable breeding of this plant in recent years and many very colourful cultivars have evolved. In cultivation they have adapted well and are grown successfully in climates from cool temperate to tropical and some will withstand a little frost. They flower most of the year and are now being grown with success in glass houses and conservatories in cold climates. Many growers are actively seeking a name change to Vireya rhododendron.

***Rhododendron (Vireya)* cv. Advocaat Cream**
A medium grower with large heads of partly ruffled cream flowers with yellow centres.

***Rhododendron (Vireya)* cv. Alisa Nicole**
A sparse grower with pendulous waxy red flowers.

***Rhododendron (Vireya)* cv. Archangel**
This is a medium shrub with heads of large flowers coloured cream.

Rhododendron veitchianum
A small shrub with masses of white flowers in small bunches.

***Rhododendron (Vireya)* cv. Arthur's Choice**
A medium grower with heads of large flowers coloured bright pinky salmon.

r

RHODODENDRON VIREYA (cont)

Rhododendron (Vireya) cv. **Australia II**
Heads of large pinky peach coloured flowers with partly ruffled petals feature on this medium shrub.

Rhododendron (Vireya) cv. **Birat Red**
A medium growing plant with heads of large salmon-red coloured flowers with partly reflexed petals.

Rhododendron (Vireya) cv. **Bob's Choice**
This is a bushy shrub with heads of pink coloured flowers and widely gapped partly ruffled petals.

Rhododendron (Vireya) cv. **Bold Janus**
Of medium size, this plant has large heads of golden yellow flowers.

Rhododendron (Vireya) cv. **Cherry Liqueur**
An upright shrub with heads of large flowers of light peach and pink.

Rhododendron (Vireya) cv. **Coral Flare**
A bushy shrub which has large flowers coloured bright candy pink.

Rhododendron (Vireya) cv. **Crinolette**
Small and sparse, this shrub has heads of medium sized flowers coloured pale pink with partly reflexed petals.

Rhododendron (Vireya) cv. **Clare Rouse**
This bushy cultivar has large flowers coloured orange and gold.

RHODODENDRON VIREYA (cont)

Rhododendron (Vireya) cv. **Cristo Rey**
A free flowering bushy shrub with heads of orange flowers which have yellow centres.

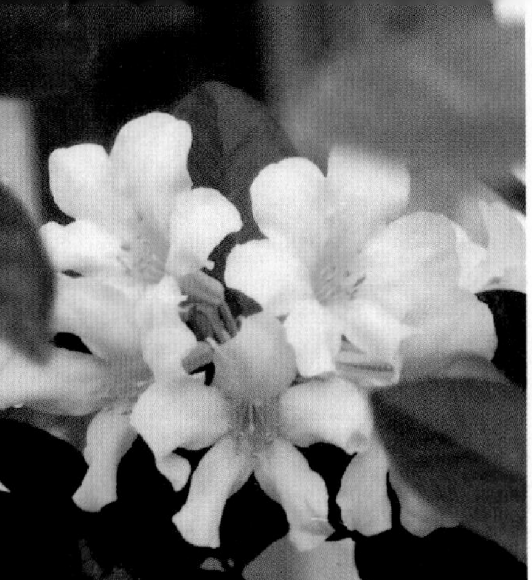

Rhododendron (Vireya) cv. **Elegant Bouquet**
Large cream coloured flowers which have yellow centres feature on this upright shrub.

Rhododendron (Vireya) cv. **Flaming Ball**
A bushy cultivar with large tight flower heads of bright orange flowers with touches of gold.

Rhododendron (Vireya) cv. **Don Stanton**
This is a sparse shrub with large tight heads of flowers coloured bright orange-red with gold markings.

Rhododendron (Vireya) cv. **Fire Plum**
A medium shrub with heads of bright pinky scarlet coloured flowers.

Rhododendron (Vireya) cv. **Gardenia**
This upright shrub has heads of large flowers coloured cream with yellow centres and partly reflexed petals.

Rhododendron (Vireya) cv. **Eastern Zanzibar**
An upright shrub with heads of large flowers coloured bright rose-pink and cream centres with partly ruffled petals.

Rhododendron (Vireya) cv. **Flamenco Dancer**
This sparse shrub has heads of amber coloured flowers which have widely gapped petals and are partly reflexed.

RHODODENDRON VIREYA (cont)

Rhododendron (Vireya) cv. **Golden Charm**
Medium sized apricot flowers with widely gapped petals are carried in large heads on this bushy shrub.

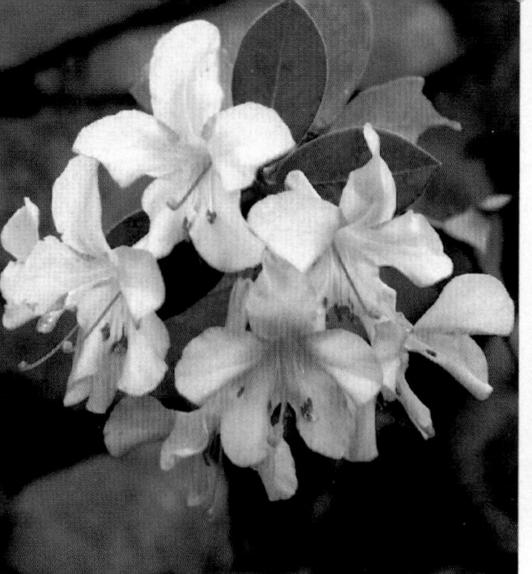

Rhododendron (Vireya) cv. **Highland Arabesque**
A sparse shrub with pendulous heads of large pink flowers.

Rhododendron (Vireya) cv. **Highland White Jade**
The heads of flowers on this upright shrub are coloured ivory-white.

Rhododendron (Vireya) cv. **Gwenevere**
There are large heads of cream flowers which have reflexed petals on this sparse shrub.

Rhododendron (Vireya) cv. **Highland Fair**
This sparse shrub has large tight heads of flowers coloured salmon-red.

Rhododendron (Vireya) cv. **Hot Tropic**
A bush cultivar which has heads of large flowers coloured gold with an orange overlay.

Rhododendron (Vireya) cv. **Hari's Choice**
An erect shrub with large heads of orange-red coloured flowers and partly reflexed petals.

Rhododendron (Vireya) cv. **Inferno**
This is an upright shrub which has heads of medium sized dark orange coloured flowers with partly ruffled petals.

RHODODENDRON VIREYA (cont)

Rhododendron (Vireya) cv. **Kisses**
Heads of pink flowers which have cream centres feature on this medium bushy shrub.

Rhododendron (Vireya) cv. **Little Ginger**
A sparse small shrub with heads of small to medium size flowers coloured orange.

Rhododendron (Vireya) cv. **Littlest Angel**
This is a sparse small shrub with heads of smallish waxy red flowers.

Rhododendron (Vireya) cv. **Krakatoa**
A bushy shrub with heads of amber coloured flowers which have reflexed and widely gapped petals.

Rhododendron (Vireya) cv. **Little Pinkie**
This sparse small shrub has large heads of small to medium size pink flowers.

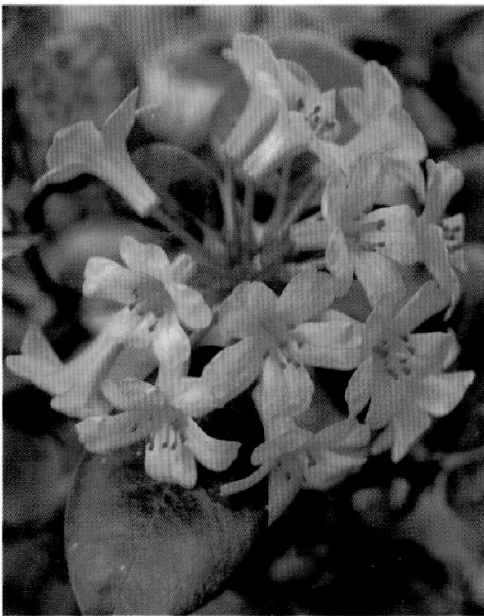

Rhododendron (Vireya) cv. **Lomac**
A bushy shrub with large heads of medium sized orange-red flowers.

Rhododendron (Vireya) cv. **Laetum**
The petals are widely gapped on the gold coloured flowers, borne in large heads, on this upright shrub.

Rhododendron (Vireya) cv. **Lorchris**
There are medium sized flowers coloured pink and rose-pink on this upright shrub.

RHODODENDRON VIREYA (cont)

Rhododendron (Vireya) cv. **Lovey**
An upright shrub with heads of large pink coloured flowers which have partly crinkled petals.

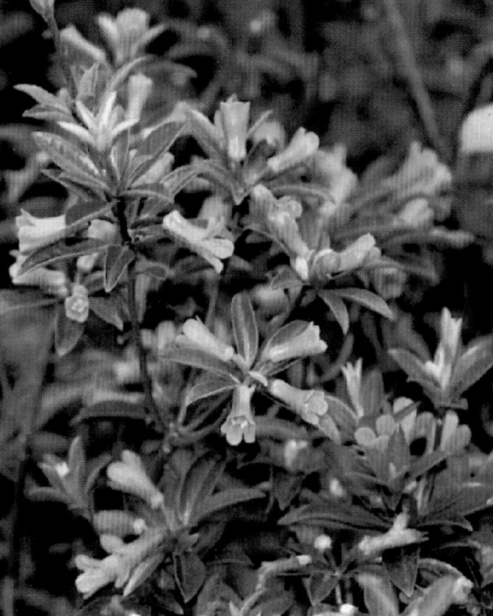

Rhododendron (Vireya) cv. **Penny Whistle**
A sparse small shrub with masses of small orange coloured flowers.

Rhododendron (Vireya) cv. **Pink Delight**
Medium sized heads of pinky red flowers bloom on this sparse shrub.

Rhododendron (Vireya) cv. **Paint Brush**
An upright grower, this shrub has heads of large flowers coloured apricot with flushings of pink.

Rhododendron (Vireya) cv. **Pink Cherub**
This upright shrub has heads of large flowers coloured rose-pink, pink and cream.

Rhododendron (Vireya) cv. **Pink Ray**
An upright shrub with heads of very pale pink flowers.

Rhododendron (Vireya) cv. **Pastenello**
Tight heads of large cream flowers with yellow centres feature on this upright shrub.

Rhododendron (Vireya) cv. **Pretty Cotton Candy**
A bushy shrub with heads of medium sized pink and cream coloured flowers which have reflexed petals.

RHODODENDRON VIREYA (cont)

Rhododendron (Vireya) **cv. Primrose Promise**

The primrose coloured flowers on this sparse shrub are of medium size, in pendulous heads.

Rhododendron (Vireya) **cv. Rosabelle**

A sparse shrub with heads of smallish flowers coloured light red.

Rhododendron (Vireya) **cv. Strawberry Parfait**

A bushy shrub with heads of large flowers coloured bright pinky red and cream inside. The petals are slightly ruffled.

Rhododendron (Vireya) **cv. Princess Alexandra**

A bushy shrub with large sparse heads of medium sized white flowers.

Rhododendron (Vireya) **cv. Rouse About**

Upright and sparse, this shrub has heads of flowers coloured gold with touches of orange.

Rhododendron (Vireya) **cv. Sunset Fantasy**

This bushy shrub has heads of large flowers coloured bright orange-red with yellow centres.

Rhododendron (Vireya) **cv. Raspberry Truffle**

This is an upright shrub with sparse heads of small to medium sized flowers coloured pinky red.

Rhododendron (Vireya) **cv. Simbu Sunset**

An upright shrub with heads of large flowers coloured gold in the centre and orange on the outside.

Rhododendron (Vireya) **cv. Sunset Gold 50**

An upright shrub which has large heads of flowers coloured orange and apricot, with yellow centres.

RHODODENDRON VIREYA (cont)

***Rhododendron (Vireya)* cv. Sweet Amanda**
Light cream coloured flowers which have yellow centres bloom in heads on this sparse shrub.

***Rhododendron (Vireya)* cv. Sweet Wendy**
An upright shrub with heads of flowers coloured yellow in the centre and cream, edged with pink on the outside.

***Rhododendron (Vireya)* cv. Tropic Summer**
This upright shrub has large heads of amber coloured flowers which have wide gaps between the petals.

***Rhododendron (Vireya)* cv. Tropic Tango**
Heads of medium sized flowers coloured light orange are the feature of this upright bushy shrub.

***Rhododendron (Vireya)* cv. Wattle Bird**
A sparse upright shrub with large heads of golden yellow flowers.

***Rhododendron (Vireya)* cv. White Rum**
This is a bushy shrub with heads of large white flowers.

***Rhododendron (Vireya)* cv. Zoelleri**
An upright shrub with tight heads of flowers coloured gold and orange.

RHODOMYRTUS

MYRTACEAE

Rhodomyrtus tomentosa
A small evergreen shrub which has showy bright rose-pink flowers and edible, aromatic, guava-like fruit. It is native to Asia and needs a warm climate. Propagate from seed.

RHODOTYPOS

ROSACEAE

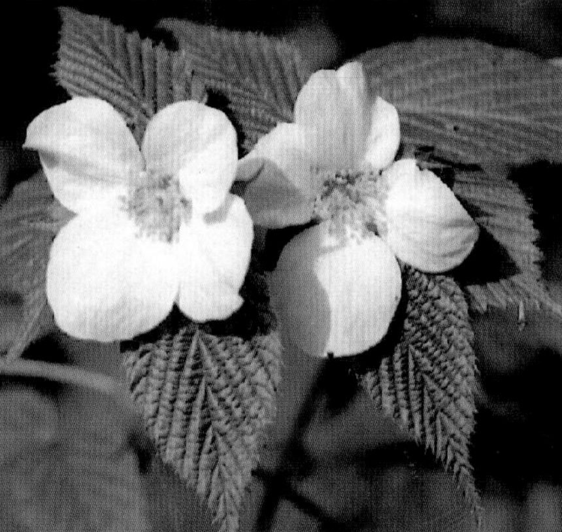

Rhodotypos scandens
A deciduous shrub native to China and Japan. It is widely grown in cool to cold climates for its showy white spring flowers. The plant is tolerant of a wide range of soils and is propagated from seed and cuttings.

RIBES

Grossulariaceae [Saxifragaceae]

Native to many countries, these deciduous shrubs are widely grown for their flowers, fruit or foliage. They benefit from annual pruning and fertilizing and prefer a cool to cold climate. Propagate from seed and cuttings.

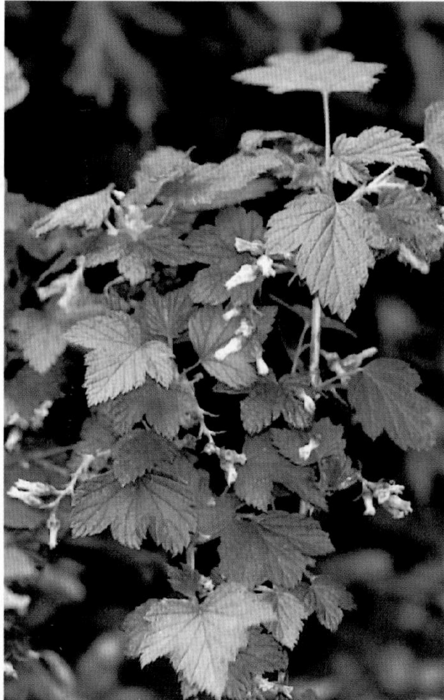

Ribes americanum

AMERICAN BLACK CURRANT

An open shrub with small whitish flowers followed by small black fruit.

Ribes laurifolium

In winter this bushy shrub has creamy white flowers.

Ribes odoratum

MISSOURI CURRANT; BUFFALO CURRANT

Black fruit follow the terminal clusters of fragrant yellow flowers on this medium shrub.

Ribes praecox cv. **Jonkeer van Tets**

This upright open shrub has racemes of cream flowers.

Ribes sanguineum WINTER CURRANT

This is a medium to tall shrub with pendulous heads of pink flowers in late winter.

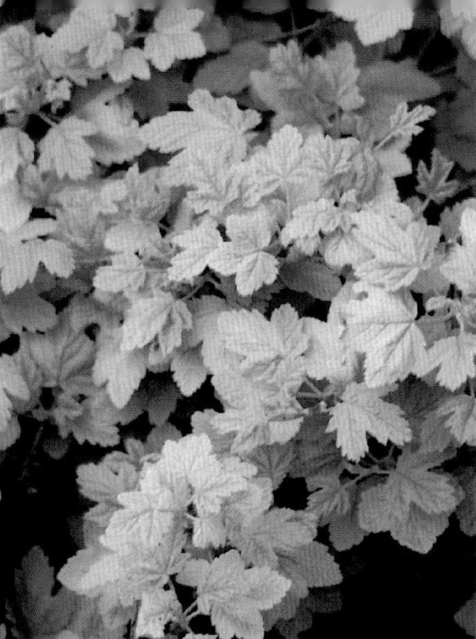

Ribes sanguineum cv. **Brocklebankii**

A cultivar which is grown for its showy yellow foliage.

Ribes sanguineum cv. **King Edward VII**

This is a cultivar with bunches of pink flowers.

Ribes speciosum

FUCHSIA-FLOWERED GOOSEBERRY

An open shrub with masses of red pendulous fuchsia-like flowers in spring.

r

RICHEA

Epacridaceae

Shrubby plants with strap-like leaves, native to Australia. They are grown as showy ornamentals in cool to temperate climates and prefer a rich, moist and slightly acid soil. Propagate from seed and cuttings.

Richea dracophylla
This open shrub has cone-like heads of white flowers.

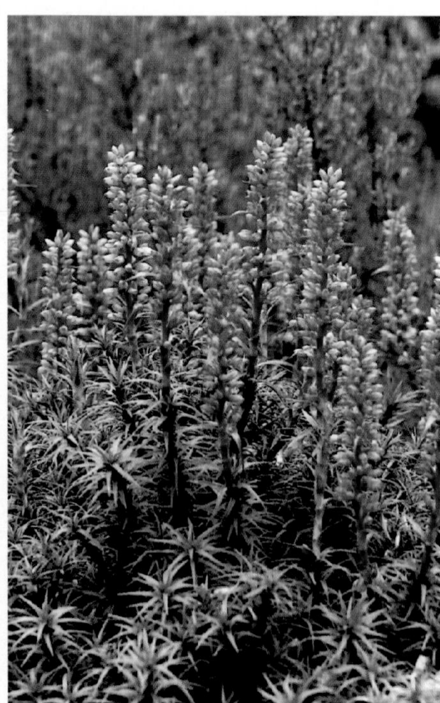

Richea scoparia
A widely grown, showy ornamental for cool to mild climates.

ROBINIA

Fabaceae [Leguminosae]

Deciduous trees and shrubs native to North America. They are widely grown as flowering ornamentals in climates from cold temperate to sub-tropical in a wide range of soils and are propagated by grafting and from seed which needs hot water treatment.

***Robinia* x *ambigua* cv. Decaisneana**
A showy small tree which has pendulous racemes of pink flowers in spring.

Robinia boyntonii
In spring this tall and thornless shrub has attractive bunches of rose-pink flowers.

Robinia fertilis
This small tree (closely allied to *R. hispida*) has rose-pink flowers in pendulous bunches. It has small hairs on the underside of the leaves.

Robinia hispida ROSE ACACIA
A tall shrub with racemes of pink flowers in profusion during spring.

Robinia kelseyi ALLEGHANY MOSS
A tall shrub with eye catching pendulous racemes of bright rose-pink flowers.

Robinia pseudoacacia BLACK LOCUST
Pendulous racemes of white flowers bloom in spring on this small to medium spreading tree.

ROBINIA (cont)

Robinia pseudoacacia cv. **Frisia**
An outstanding cultivar which has yellow leaves and pendulous racemes of white flowers.

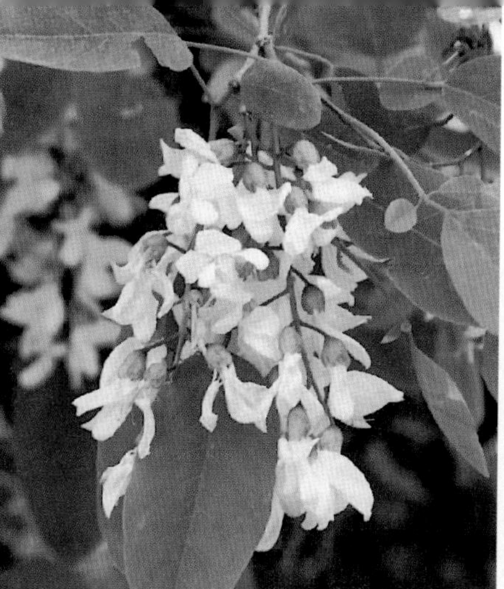

Robinia pseudoacacia cv. **Uniflora [Unifolia]**
This is a tall shrub which has pendulous racemes of white flowers in late spring.

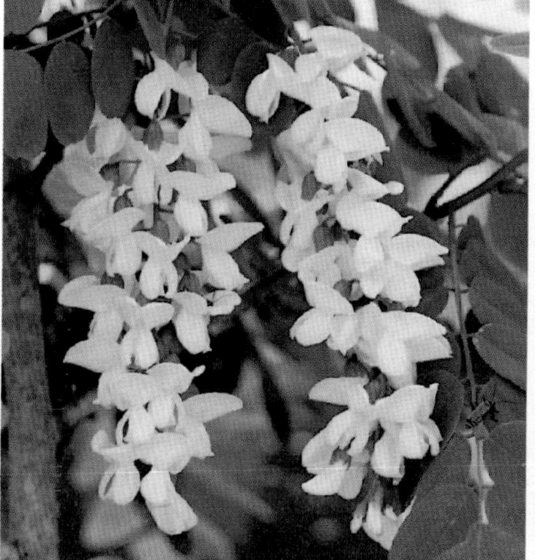

Robinia pseudoacacia cv. **Pyramidalis**
A small tree with sparse pendulous racemes of white flowers in late spring.

Robinia x ***slavinii*** cv. **Hillieri**
A free flowering hybrid cultivar which has bright mauve-pink flowers.

Robinia pseudoacacia cv. **Rosea**
The flowers on this cultivar are pale pink.

ROMNEYA

PAPAVERACEAE

Romneya coulteri 2 MATILIJA POPPY
A medium shrub native to Mexico and California. It is a free flowering ornamental which is grown for its large poppy-like flowers in late spring and summer. The plant requires good drainage and will tolerate frosts to -10 degrees Celsius. Propagate from seed.

RONDELETIA

RUBIACEAE

Grown as flowering ornamentals, these shrubs and trees are native to Central and South America and Polynesia. They grow in climates from cool temperate to tropical and are propagated from semi-hardwood cuttings.

Rondeletia amoema
A tall evergreen shrub which has large terminal bunches of pale pink flowers over several months in spring.

RONDELETIA (cont)

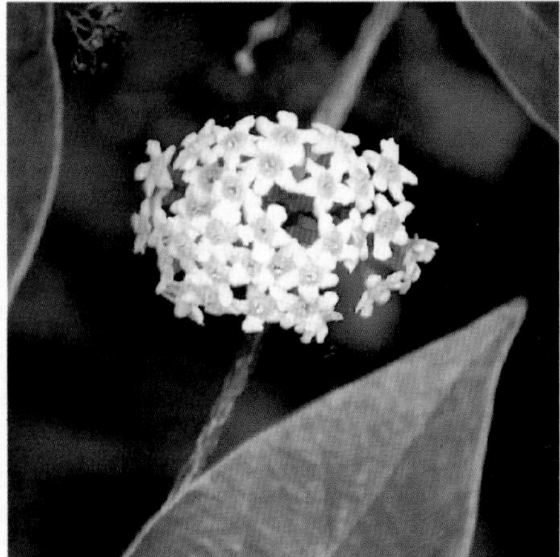

Rondeletia cordata
In summer this medium to tall shrub has heads of flowers coloured pink, with yellow throats.

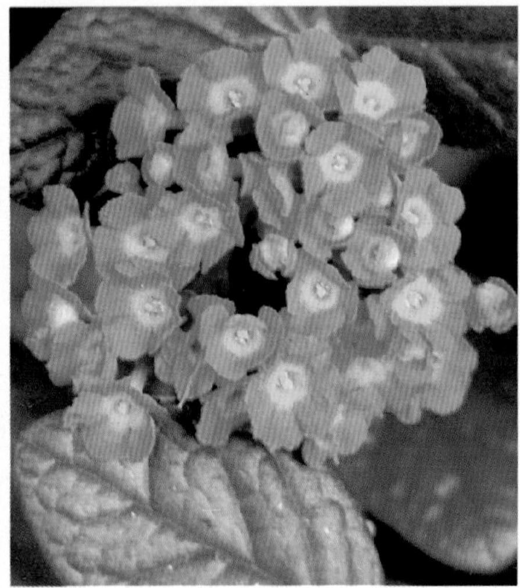

Rondeletia odorata
A sparse medium shrub which small terminal bunches of orange-red flowers in late spring and summer.

Rondeletia strigosa
Sparse and upright, this medium shrub has small terminal heads of pinky red flowers in spring.

ROSA

ROSACEAE

Deciduous and sometimes evergreen shrubs and climbers which are grown world wide as free flowering ornamentals and are among the most popular plants grown. They are native to many countries and their flowers come in a wide range of shapes and colours. Almost all roses have thorns along their branches. There are many thousands of different cultivars and species of roses being grown, some for their flowers and others for their perfume or growth habit. Many roses are quite tolerant of frosts to -12 degrees Celsius and some grow successfully in tropical climates. Roses are propagated in many ways. Seed propagation is used for some species and cold stratification will benefit germination. Other methods of propagation are from cuttings, by grafting and layering, with budding being the most widely used method. To grow roses successfully a spraying program for both insects and diseases is necessary, together with regular fertilising and winter pruning. Doing this will encourage the plant to bloom for more than six months of the year.

Rosa cv. **Adair Roche** [Floribunda]
A bushy small shrub with formal-type flowers coloured pale pink and rose-pink.

Rosa cv. **Anne Watkins** [Hybrid Tea]
A medium size shrub with large formal pink-rose flowers.

Rosa cv. **Alison Wheatcroft** [Floribunda]
A compact shrub with large bright red flowers.

Rosa cv. **Apricot Nectar** [Floribunda]
A compact shrub with formal-type buds opening to flowers coloured cream, apricot and amber.

ROSA (cont)

Rosa banksiae cv. **Lutea**

BANKSIA ROSE

A climbing rose which has very few prickles and has clusters of yellow flowers in spring.

Rosa cv. **Blue Moon** [Hybrid Tea]

A bushy shrub with large formal flowers coloured lavender-mauve.

Rosa cv. **Bridal Pink** [Floribunda]

A bushy small shrub with pink coloured flowers.

Rosa cv. **Century Two** [Hybrid Tea]

An upright shrub with pointed buds and fragrant bright pink flowers.

Rosa chinenis cv. **Cecil Brunner**

A tall shrub or semi-climber which has dainty pink, double, fragrant flowers in bunches.

Rosa cv. **Climbing Altissimo** [Floribunda]

A climbing rose with large, single, bright scarlet-red flowers.

Rosa cv. **Climbing Iceberg** [Floribunda]

A climbing rose with long bunches of smaller double white flowers.

Rosa cv. **Climbing Sparrieshoop** [Floribunda]

A climbing rose with upright bunches of flattish single blooms coloured pink.

Rosa x ***damascena*** var. ***semperflorens*** cv. **Quatre Saisons**

A small, very thorny shrub with double, bright pink flowers.

ROSA (cont)

Rosa cv. **Diamond Jubilee** [Hybrid Tea]

A bushy shrub with long lasting flowers coloured cream and buff.

Rosa cv. **Fèlicitè Parmentier**

A bushy rose with double, pale pink flowers.

Rosa cv. **Fragrant Cloud** [Hybrid Tea]

A bushy shrub with showy flowers coloured deep coral-red.

Rosa cv. **Friesia** [Floribunda]

A small compact shrub with yellow coloured flowers.

Rosa gallica cv. **Officinalis**

A bushy shrub with open semi-double flowers coloured cerise.

Rosa gallica cv. **Versicolor**

A bushy compact shrub with unusual flowers coloured pink and cerise.

Rosa cv. **Gold Rush** [Floribunda]

A free flowering small shrub with golden coloured flowers.

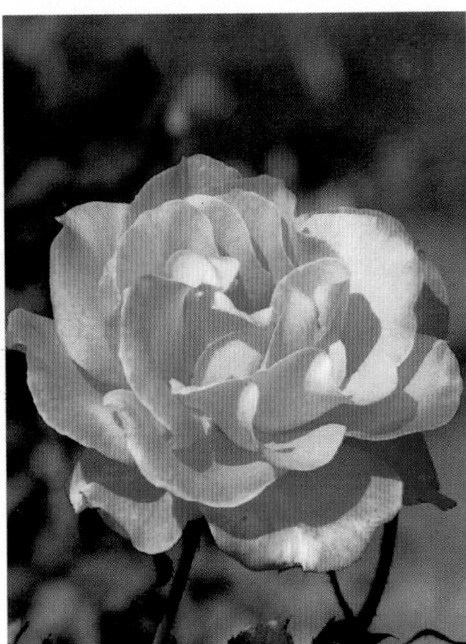

Rosa cv. **Granada** [Hybrid Tea]

A free flowering, early opening rose with red and yellow bi-coloured flowers.

Rosa cv. **Headline** [Hybrid Tea]

An upright shrub with large flowers which are coloured yellow with a touch of cerise.

Rosa cv. **Helen Traubel** [Hybrid Tea]
A free flowering upright plant which has good disease resistance and fragrant salmon-apricot coloured flowers.

Rosa cv. **Kentucky Derby** [Hybrid Tea]
A vigorous, disease resistant rose which has formal shaped fragrant flowers coloured burgundy-red.

Rosa cv. **La Ville de Bruxelles**
A bushy shrub with lots of very small thorns and bright pink flowers.

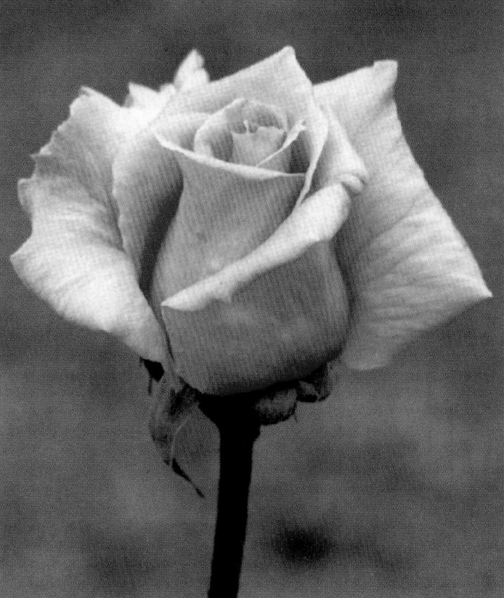

Rosa cv. **Lady Flo** [Hybrid Tea]
An upright shrub with formal perfumed blooms coloured bright pink and mid-pink.

Rosa cv. **Lady Rose** [Hybrid Tea]
A bushy medium rose with very showy flowers coloured bright salmon.

Rosa laevigata CHEROKEE ROSE
A vigorous climbing plant which has masses of single white flowers in spring.

Rosa cv. **Luna Yellow** [Miniature]
A compact small growing rose with yellow flowers.

Rosa cv. **Marilyn** [Miniature]
A dwarf growing rose with pink flowers.

Rosa cv. **Mount Shasta** [Hybrid Tea]
A disease resistant bushy rose with fragrant white flowers.

ROSA (cont)

Rosa cv. **Oklahoma** [Hybrid Tea]
A good cut flower, this vigorous rose has pointed buds and perfumed flowers of deep burgundy.

Rosa cv. **Olympiad** [Hybrid Tea]
A vigorous upright bush with showy scarlet-red flowers.

Rosa cv. **Peace** [Hybrid Tea]
syn. ***R.*** cv. **Mde A. Meilland**
A medium bush with very large fragrant flowers coloured yellow with pinkish red edges to the petals.

Rosa cv. **Portland Rose**
syn. ***R.*** cv. **Duchess of Portland**
A bushy shrub with large semi-double flowers coloured rosy red.

Rosa cv. **President Leopold Senghor** [Hybrid Tea]
An upright bush with long stems and large crimson blooms.

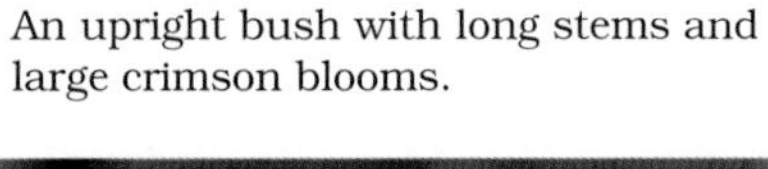

Rosa cv. **Pristine** [Hybrid Tea]
An upright shrub with long pointed buds and open flowers coloured white and soft pink.

Rosa cv. **Red Gold** [Floribunda]
A small bushy shrub with showy flowers coloured red and gold.

Rosa cv. **Regensberg** [Floribunda]
A free flowering, upright, bushy rose with semi-double flowers coloured bright rose-pink with white to pale pink markings.

Rosa rugosa
A bushy shrub with single, perfumed, bright pink flowers.

ROSA (cont)

Rosa rugosa var. ***alba***

A bushy rose with large, single, fragrant flowers.

Rosa rugosa
cv. **Frau Dagmar Hartopp**

A shrub which has fragrant single flowers coloured pale lilac-pink.

Rosa cv. **Rusticana** [Hybrid Tea]

A medium bushy shrub with large flowers coloured cream and pale apricot.

Rosa cv. **Tequila** [Miniature]

A dwarf growing rose with yellow flowers edged with red.

Rosa cv. **Violet Carson** [Floribunda]

A bushy shrub with formal rosebuds and flowers coloured apricot-pink.

Rosa cv. **Warm Wishes** [Hybrid Tea]

A cultivar with large orange flowers.

Rosa webbiana

An upright shrub with large, bright pink, single flowers.

ROSMARINUS

LAMIACEAE [LABIATAE]

Rosmarinus officinalis ROSEMARY

A dense, bushy, evergreen, aromatic shrub which is native to South Europe and North Africa and is grown as an ornamental for its aroma and pale blue flowers. The leaves are also used as a herb for cooking. Rosemary is grown in climates from cool temperate to tropical and is propagated from cuttings.

Rosmarinus officinalis
cv. **Rampant Roule**

This low growing cultivar bears its deep-lilac coloured flowers in profusion.

ROTHMANNIA

RUBIACEAE

Evergreen shrubs and small trees which have very fragrant blooms and are native to Africa. They are grown as ornamentals in frost free climates from mild temperate to sub-tropical. Propagation is mostly from seed, as cuttings which are occasionally grown do not seem to make vigorous plants.

Rothmannia capensis CANDLEWOOD
syn. ***Gardenia rothmannia***
A free flowering, tall shrub with fragrant flowers which are coloured cream with old gold and purple spots in the throat.

Rothmannia globosa
A free flowering tall shrub with clusters of perfumed, white, tubular flowers, cream inside.

Rothmannia longiflora
syn. ***Randia maculata***
A tall shrub. The large fragrant white flowers have purple stripes in the yellow throat. The petals are reflexed.

Rothmannia manganjae SCENTED BELLS
A tall shrub with large highly perfumed white flowers which have cerise coloured markings in the throat.

RUELLIA

ACANTHACEAE

From tropical America, Asia and Africa these evergreen shrubs are grown as ornamentals for their showy flowers. They require a climate from cold temperate to tropical and in the right situation will flower for many months. Propagate from seed and cuttings.

Ruellia colorata
A small, bushy, upright shrub with large heads of red bracts and central golden flowers.

Ruellia dipteracantha
This is a small, dense, spreading shrub which flowers over a long period. The showy lilac coloured flowers have prominent purple veins.

Ruellia elegans BRAZIL TORCH
syn. ***R. formosa; Arrhostoxylon elegans***
An upright small, bushy, many-stemmed shrub with terminal clusters of bright red flowers.

Ruellia graecizans
syn. ***R. amoena***
Bright red tubular flowers occur over many months on this sparse small shrub.

RUELLIA (cont)

Ruellia humilis
A bushy shrub with rosy violet flowers in spring and summer.

Ruellia macrantha
On this upright shrub the large bright rose-pink flowers have prominent veins.

Ruellia portellae
On this small freely branching shrub the leaves have a cream central stripe. Flowers are rose-pink and fade to pale mauve.

Ruellia rosea
This is a bushy shrub with cerise coloured flowers in spring.

Ruellia **sp.**
An open spreading shrub. Flower colour varies from blue to cerise. Known in the nursery trade as *R. squarrosa.*

Ruellia tuberosa
Free flowering, this small shrub has large mauve flowers which are deep purple inside.

Ruellia makoyana MONKEY PLANT
A dense spreading shrub which has green leaves marked with silver along the centres. The flowers are bright rosy purple in colour.

RUSCUS

LILIACEAE

Ruscus aculeatus BUTCHER'S BROOM
Native to Spain, this small, cold tolerant, evergreen shrub is grown in mild climates as an ornamental for its showy bright red winter berries, which are used by florists. It will tolerate poor soils and is propagated from seed and cuttings.

r

RUSPOLIA

Acanthaceae

Small evergreen shrubs native to Africa which are grown as free flowering ornamentals in climates from warm temperate to tropical. They require a humus rich soil to flower at their best. They are good glasshouse or conservatory plants in mild climates and are propagated from seed and cuttings.

Ruspolia hypocrateriformis

A small free branching shrub with heads of showy red flowers over many months.

Ruspolia seticalyx

This is a small upright shrub which has large heads of salmon-orange coloured flowers over many months.

RUSSELIA

Scrophulariaceae

Evergreen shrubs native to tropical America which are widely grown as landscape ornamentals outdoors in warm climates and as glasshouse or conservatory plants in cool climates. They will tolerate poor soils and are mostly propagated from cuttings.

Russelia equisetiformis FOUNTAIN BUSH syn. ***R. juncea***

A much branched small shrub which has a cascading form and thin round leaves. It has masses of pendulous, tubular, red flowers in spring and summer.

Russelia sarmentosa

An open upright shrub which has large heads of bright red tubular flowers over many months.

RUTTYA

Acanthaceae

Ruttya fruticosa

A bushy evergreen shrub which is native to South Africa. It has bunches of orange-red flowers with black markings over many months and is grown as an ornamental in climates from mild temperate to tropical. Propagate from seed or cuttings.

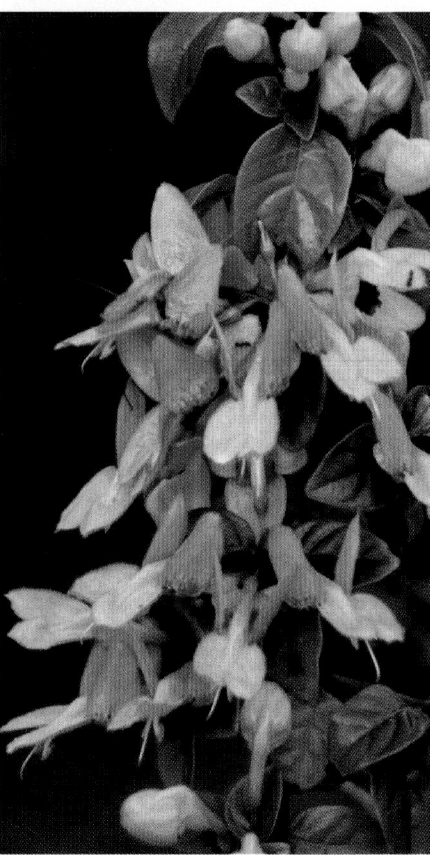

***Ruttya fruticosa* cv. Scholesei**

A showy cultivar which has old gold coloured flowers with black markings.

SALIX

Salicaceae

Deciduous trees and shrubs native to Europe which are grown as ornamentals and one form has timber used to make cricket bats. The branches are used by florists when the oval catkins are just opening. Propagation is from seed or cuttings.

Salix caprea PUSSY WILLOW

An upright small tree which is covered by showy catkins in spring.

Salix* x *gillotii

A prostrate grower, this shrub is very free flowering with upright, creamish flower spikes.

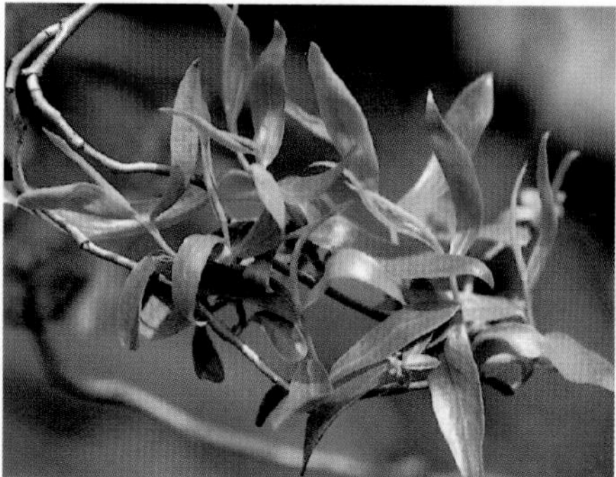

***Salix matsudana* cv. Tortuosa** TORTURED WILLOW

The twisted branches of this small tree, when cut and decorated with artificial leaves and flowers, form the base for artificial trees used in indoor decoration.

Salix myrsinites

Sparse and spreading, this small shrub has upright flower spikes coloured pinkish mauve.

***Salix nakamurana* cv. Yezoalpina**

This prostrate cultivar has upright, cream flower spikes.

SAMANEA

Mimosaceae [Leguminosae]

Samanea saman RAIN TREE

syn. ***Albizia saman; Pithecellobium saman***

A medium, short trunked, spreading tree from tropical America. It is widely grown in parks and large gardens in warm climates for its colourful pink shaving-brush type flowers. Propagate from seed.

SAMBUCUS

Caprifoliaceae

Sambucus nigra ELDERBERRY

A tall bushy shrub native to Europe, it is grown as an ornamental in climates from very cold temperate to sub-tropical. The plant has large heads of small white flowers. Propagate from seed and cuttings.

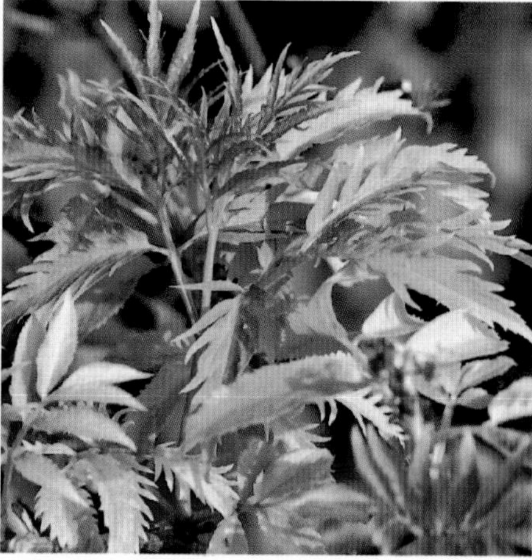

***Sambucus racemosa* cv. Plumosa Aurea**

A cultivar with golden foliage.

***Sambucus racemosa* cv. Sutherland Gold**

This ferny leaf shrub is grown for its showy golden foliage.

SANCHEZIA

Acanthaceae

Sanchezia speciosa

A bushy evergreen shrub with green and yellow leaves and erect spikes of golden coloured flowers. This shrub is grown outdoors in warm temperate to tropical climates and indoors in milder climates. It is native to South America. Propagate from cuttings.

SAPINDUS

Sapindaceae

Sapindus mukorossi CHINESE SOAPBERRY

A brittle, evergreen, small to medium tree native to Asia. It is grown as an ornamental for shade. The tree has heads of cream flowers and round fruit which are used as a soap substitute. Soapberry is cultivated in climates from temperate to tropical and propagated from seed.

SAPIUM

Euphorbiaceae

Sapium sebiferum CHINESE TALLOW TREE

This small tree is native to Asia and is widely grown in climates from cool temperate to sub-tropical for its highly coloured autumn leaves. Propagate from seed.

SARACA

Caesalpiniaceae [Leguminosae]

Small evergreen trees native to South East Asia which are grown as ornamentals for their showy flowers and fragrance. They need a sub-tropical to tropical climate and a soil rich in humus. Propagate from seed.

Saraca indica SORROWLESS TREE

A spreading small tree with large heads of orange-red flowers which are highly perfumed at night.

Saraca thaipingensis

This spreading small tree has very large heads of amber coloured night-fragrant flowers.

SARCOCOCCA

Buxaceae

Sarcococca hookeriana SWEET BOX

A medium, hardy, evergreen shrub which is native to China and the Himalayas. It is grown as an ornamental for its delicate fragrant pale pink to white flowers in winter. This plant prefers a slightly moist soil and a cool to mild climate. Propagate from seed and cuttings.

SARITAEA

Bignoniaceae

Saritaea magnifica
syn. ***Bignonia magnifica***
A very spectacular flowering, evergreen climber which has large heads of rosy purple coloured, trumpet-type flowers. It is native to South America. The plant needs a warm sub-tropical or tropical climate to be seen at its best, as well as a soil with lots of humus. When in flower it is regarded as one of the outstanding climbers of the world. Propagate from seed and cuttings under mist.

SAURAUIA

Actinidiaceae

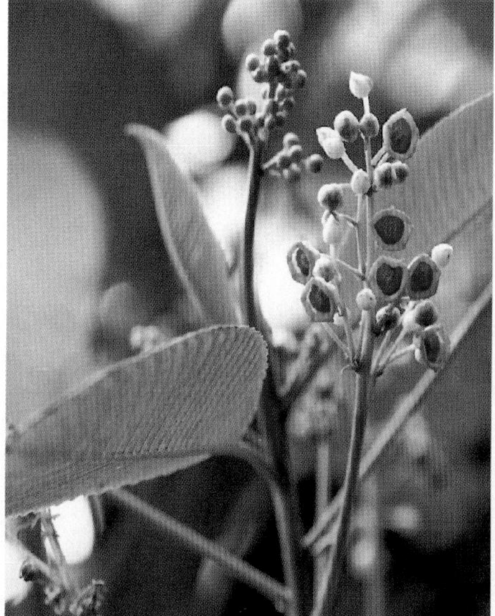

Saurauia napaulensis
In spring this sparse, evergreen shrub has bunches of small, bright pink, cup shaped flowers. It is grown as an ornamental in climates from cold temperate to warm temperate. Native to the Himalayan area, it is propagated from seed and cuttings.

SCHAUERIA

Acanthaceae

Schaueria flavicoma
syn. ***S. calicotricha***
Native to Brazil, this upright evergreen shrub is grown as an indoor plant in cool to temperate climates and outdoors in warm temperate to tropical climates. It is grown as an ornamental for its showy yellow heads of flowers. The plant prefers a rich moist soil. Propagate from seed and cuttings.

SCHEFFLERA

Araliaceae

Evergreen tropical and sub-tropical shrubs and small trees which are grown outdoors in temperate to tropical climates as landscaping plants and world wide as choice indoor plants. They have large terminal flower spikes followed by colourful seedy fruit along the spikes. Propagate from seed and cuttings.

Schefflera actinophylla UMBRELLA TREE
An erect small tree which has long horizontal flower heads of pinkish red flowers. It is grown outdoors as a street or feature tree and as a choice indoor plant.

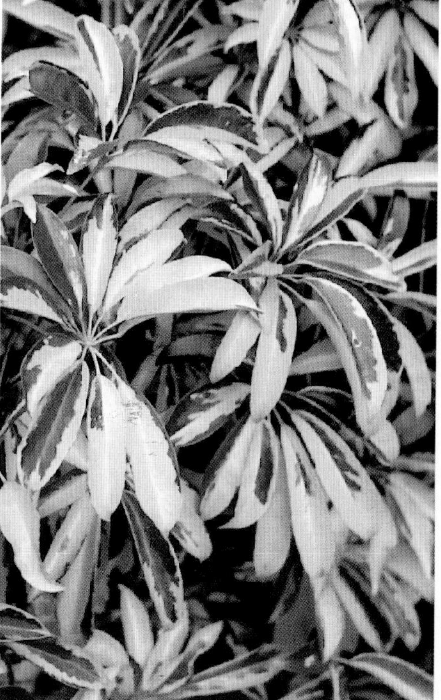

Schefflera actinophylla
cv. **Pot of Gold**
A cultivar with variegated leaves coloured gold and green.

SCHEFFLERA (cont)

Schefflera albido-bracteata cv. **Star Shine**

An attractive bushy shrub with palmate-type rippled grey-green leaves.

Schefflera arboricola

DWARF UMBRELLA TREE

Widely grown as an indoor plant, this is a compact bushy shrub which has pendulous spikes of golden coloured fruit.

Schefflera arboricola cv. **Cream and Green**

The variegated leaves of this cultivar are green and cream.

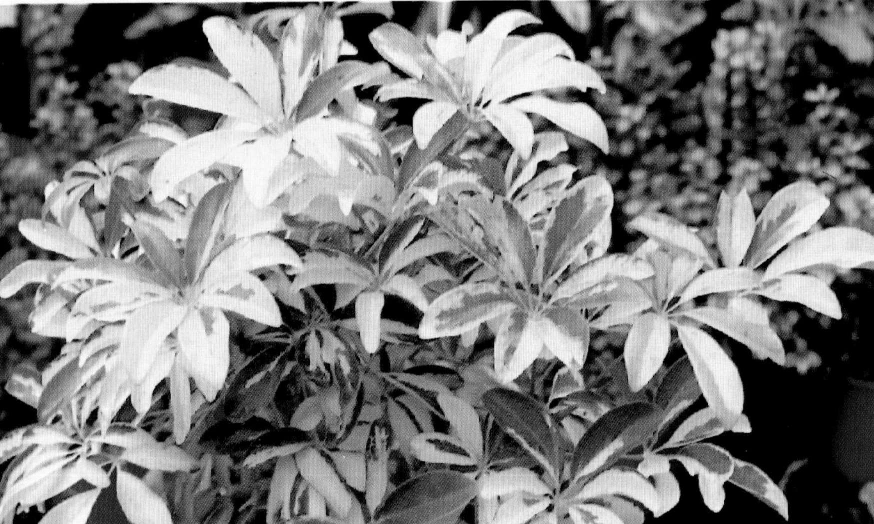

Schefflera arboricola cv. **Gold Rush**

This cultivar has bi-coloured leaves mostly gold and some green.

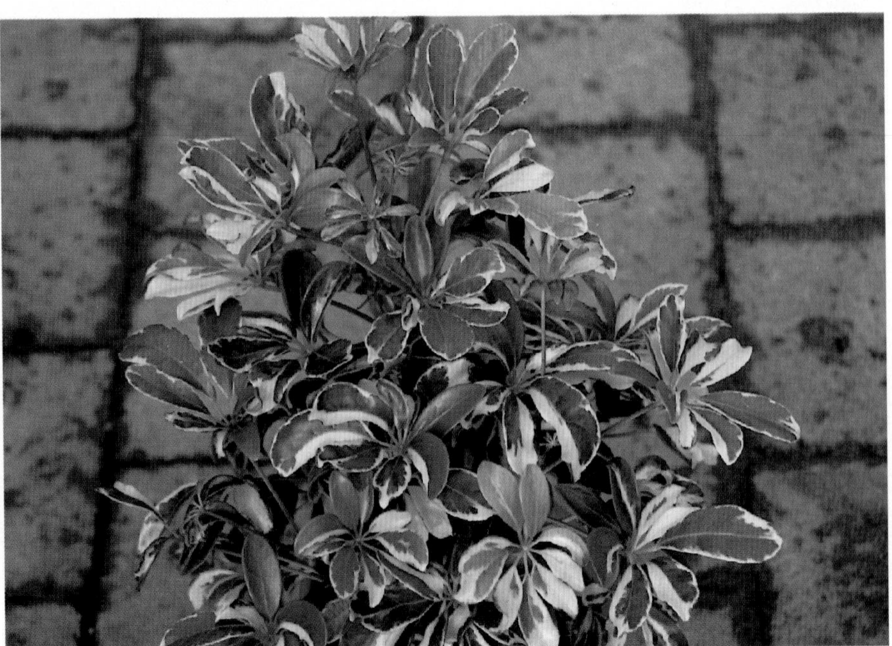

Schefflera arboricola cv. **Jacqueline**

A variegated leaf cultivar with green leaves and yellow markings mostly along the edges.

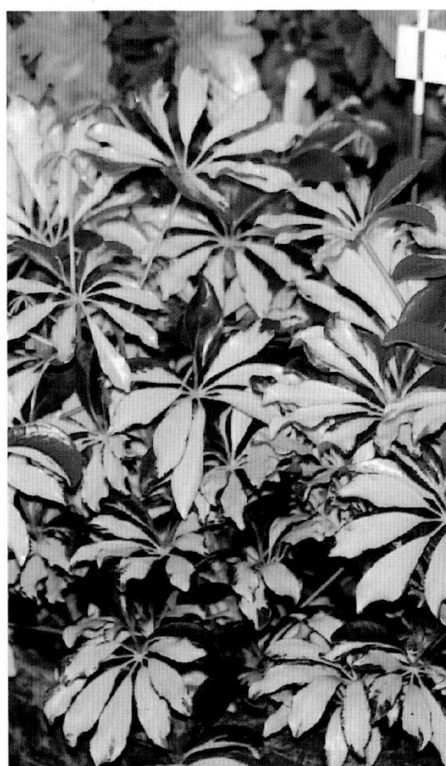

Schefflera arboricola cv. **Mrs de Smet**
A cultivar with white-cream leaves which have some green markings.

Schefflera arboricola cv. **Spotty**
This interesting upright growing cultivar has green leaves which are spotted and marked with yellow.

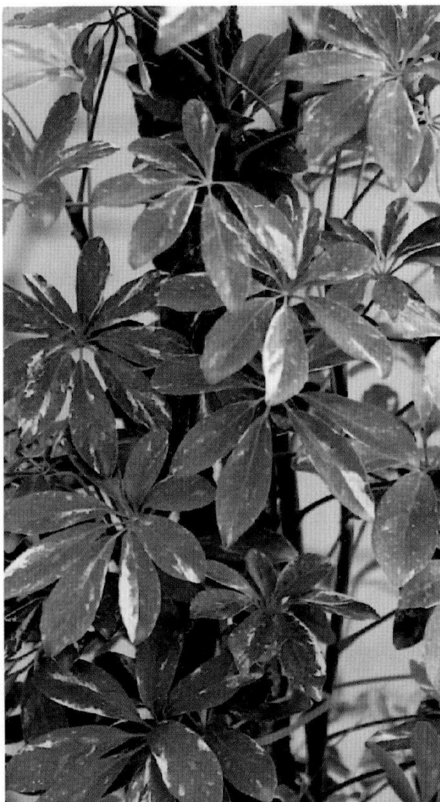

Schefflera arboricola cv. **Snowflake**
An upright open crowned cultivar which has green leaves dusted and marked with cream.

Schefflera arboricola cv. **Variegata**
The variegated leaves on this cultivar are coloured green with yellow inside on some of the leaves.

Schefflera elliptica GALAMAI-AMO
A bushy shrub to small tree with many thin upright branches and palmate-type leaves.

SCHEFFLERA (cont)

Schefflera insularum
A bushy compact shrub with large shiny palmate leaves.

***Schefflera* cv. Renate**
The ends of the palmate leaves are serrated on this bushy compact shrub.

***Schefflera* cv. Jakarta Jewel**
The leaves are pointed on this small compact spreading shrub.

***Schefflera* cv. Samoa Snow**
A small tree with palmate-type leaves coloured green with cream markings.

***Schefflera* cv. Oriental Magic**
An upright sparse shrub with open palmate leaves.

Schefflera pueckleri
This is a sparse crowned, erect, spreading small tree with open palmate leaves.

SCHEFFLERA (cont)

Schefflera setulosa

An erect small evergreen tree which has a brownish downy covering on the undersides of the leaves.

Schefflera venulosa STAR LEAF

A tall shrub with arching branches and palmate leaves. The flower buds are bright red and open white.

Schefflera versteegii

This is a tall shrub to small tree with large partly rippled palmate leaves.

Schefflera tomentosa

This dense small spreading tree has large palmate leaves.

SCHIMA

THEACEAE

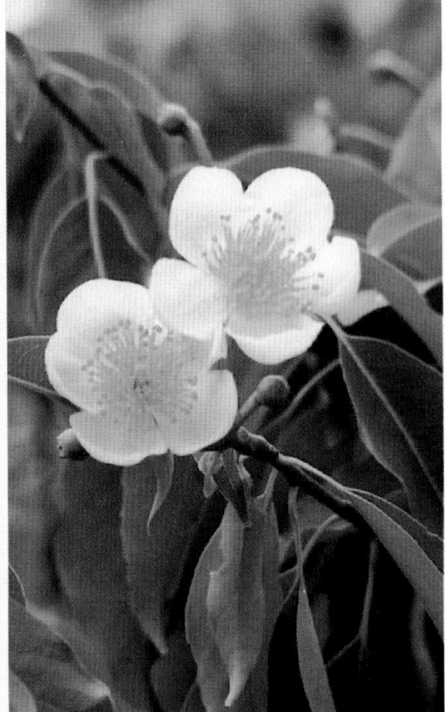

Schima wallichii

syn. ***S. argentea***

A small to medium bushy, evergreen tree which has large white flowers with prominent yellow stamens. It is native to South East Asia. Schima is grown as a landscape ornamental in temperate to tropical climates, and in cool climates it is grown in pots in glasshouses. Propagate from seed and cuttings.

S

SCHINUS

ANACARDIACEAE

Evergreen tall shrubs and small trees native to South America. They are ideal plants for dry temperate to tropical climates where they will grow in poor soils. Propagate from seed.

Schinus molle var. ***areira*** PEPPER TREE

A sparse, spreading, small aromatic tree which has ferny leaves and heads of small white flowers followed by round rose-pink berries.

Schinus terebinthifolia BRAZILIAN PEPPER TREE

A bushy tall shrub which has large bunches of small white flowers followed by bright red berries.

SCHISANDRA

SCHISANDRACEAE

Semi-climbing aromatic shrubs, native to East Asia and North America, which are grown for their showy flowers. They prefer a mild to cool climate and plenty of moisture in summer. Propagate from seed and cuttings.

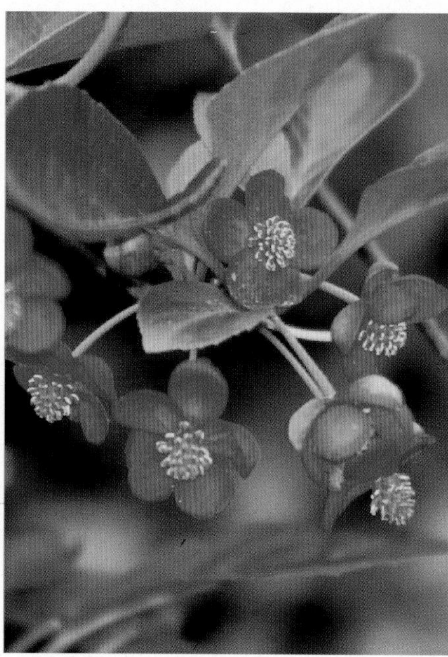

Schisandra grandiflora var. ***rubriflora***

A deciduous, semi-climbing, tall shrub which has showy bunches of red flowers in spring.

Schisandra sphenanthera

A deciduous semi-climbing shrub which has bunches of orange coloured spring flowers.

SCHIZOLOBIUM

CAESALPINIACEAE [LEGUMINOSAE]

Schizolobium parahybum TOWER TREE

A fast growing, tall, upright tree which has a broad canopy on top of a long straight trunk. The tree has large heads of bright yellow flowers and grows in climates from warm temperate to tropical. It is native to tropical America and is propagated from seed.

SCHOTIA

CAESALPINIACEAE [LEGUMINOSAE]

Shrubs and small trees which are native to South Africa and are grown as ornamentals for their showy flowers. They require a well drained soil and a climate from temperate to tropical. Propagate from seed.

Schotia brachypetala TREE FUCHSIA

A small spreading tree with large heads of upright, bright red flowers.

SCHOTIA (cont)

Schotia latifolia

ELEPHANT HEDGE BEAN TREE

A small spreading tree with large heads of pink and white coloured flowers.

SCHREBERA

OLEACEAE

Schrebera alata

An upright evergreen shrub native to Africa. It is grown as an ornamental in warm temperate to tropical climates for its fragrant flowers which are coloured white with maroon centres. Propagate from seed and cuttings.

SCINDAPSUS

ARACEAE

Scindapsus pictus

Native to Brazil, this showy climber is widely grown as an indoor plant for its showy heart shaped leaves coloured green and silver. It prefers a warm situation with rich soil. Propagate from cuttings.

SCUTELLARIA

LAMIACEAE [LABIATAE]

Scutellaria costaricana

SKULLCAP; DRAGONS TEARS

A small, upright, evergreen shrub native to Central America with large heads of flowers coloured bright red. It is grown as a showy flowering ornamental in sub-tropical and tropical climates in soils rich in humus. In cooler climates it is grown in glass houses and conservatories. Propagate from seed and cuttings.

SENECIO

ASTERACEAE [COMPOSITAE]

A very large group of flowering shrubs, climbers and herbs which are native to many countries of the world and grow in a wide range of climates and of soils. They are grown as ornamentals both outdoors and in conservatories. Propagate from seed and cuttings.

Senecio macroglossus NATAL IVY

A slender evergreen climber which has daisy-like flowers coloured light cream with yellow centres.

Senecio petasitis

CALIFORNIAN GERANIUM

This is a bushy, large leaf shrub with big heads of golden coloured flowers in spring.

SENECIO (cont)

Senecio scandens
A slender climber with small yellow daisy-type flowers.

Senecio tamoides PARLOUR IVY
This climber is bushy, with large heads of bright yellow flowers in spring.

SENNA

CAESALPINIACEAE [LEGUMINOSAE]

A group of mostly evergreen shrubs and trees native to many countries and many different climates. Many were previously called Cassia, especially those native to Australia. They are widely grown as colourful ornamentals and for medicinal purposes. Propagate from seed which benefits from soaking in lukewarm water for 1 to 2 hours prior to sowing. The varieties with very hard seed coats require hot water treatment.

Senna alata EMPRESS CANDLE PLANT
A medium, evergreen, bushy shrub with erect flower spikes of golden coloured flowers over many months.

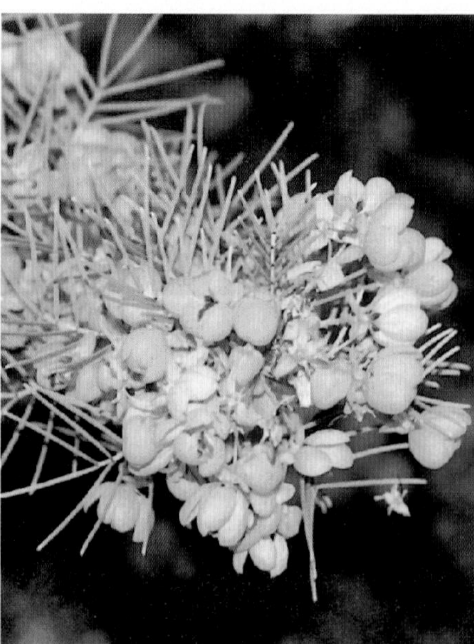

Senna artemisioides SILVER CASSIA
This small shrub has variable, fine, silverish leaves and yellow cup shaped flowers.

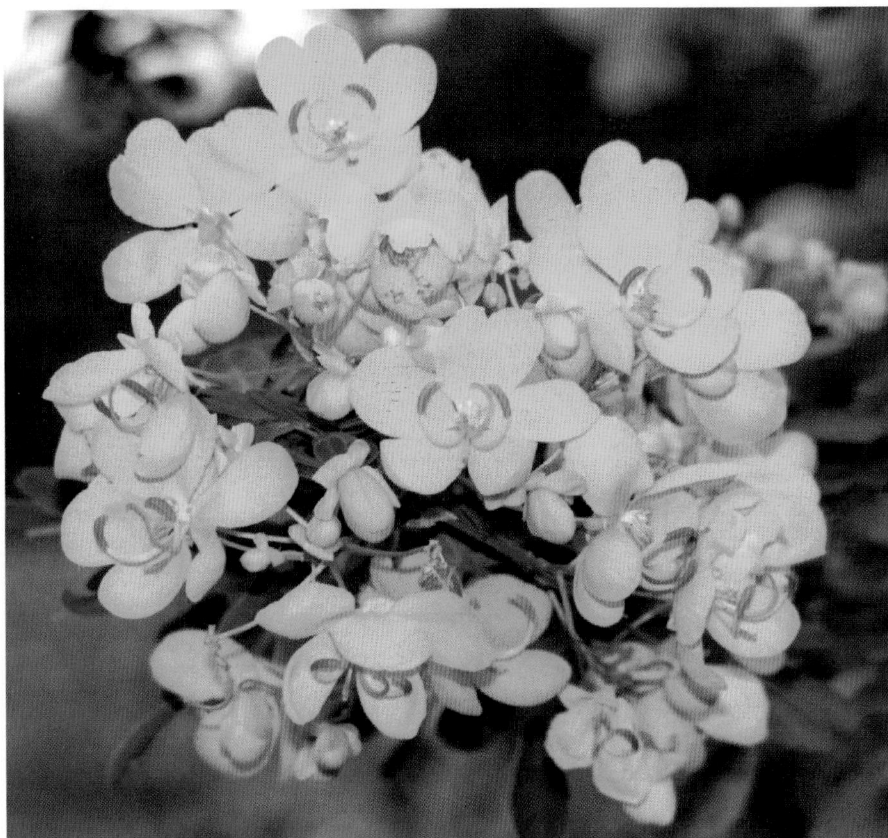

Senna candolleana GOLDEN CASSIA

Bushy and compact, this free flowering small to medium shrub has oval leaves and large bunches of golden yellow flowers in autumn and early winter. It may also flower in spring in some situations.

Senna* x *floribunda SHOWY CASSIA

syn. ***Cassia floribunda***

A free flowering, bushy, evergreen, medium size shrub with large heads of yellow flowers over many months in autumn. This shrub may also flower in spring. It has pointed leaves.

Senna didymobotrya POPCORN BUSH

Erect heads of bright yellow flowers bloom over many months on this bushy evergreen shrub.

Senna helmsii

syn. ***Cassia helmsii***

A small, bushy, arid climate shrub with silver leaves and heads of yellow flowers.

SENNA (cont)

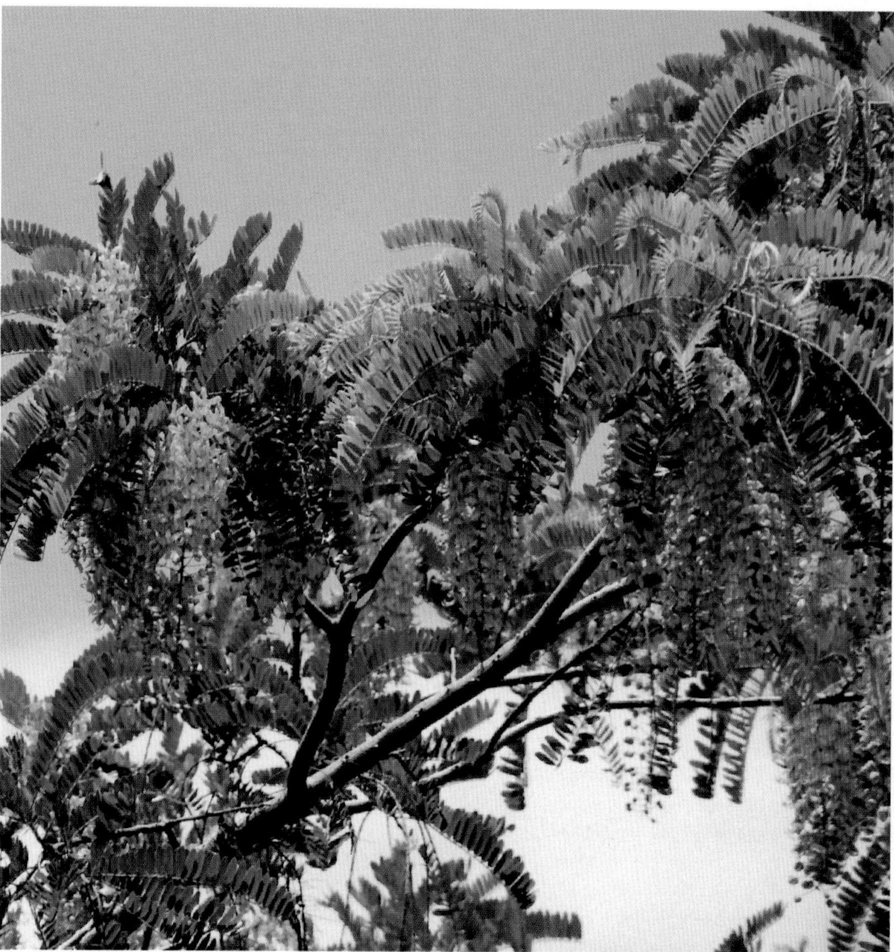

Senna macranthera **var.** ***micans*** CHAINS OF GOLD

A small to medium tree with cascading racemes of golden flowers.

Senna notabilis COCKROACH BUSH

syn. ***Cassia notabilis***

This compact bushy small shrub is covered in spring with yellow flowers. The seed pods that follow look like cockroaches—as illustrated.

Senna occidentalis COFFEE SENNA

syn. ***Cassia occidentalis***

A bushy upright shrub with clusters of yellow flowers. Used in medicine.

Senna multijuga

syn. ***Cassia multijuga***

A small to medium, evergreen, broad crowned tree with large heads of golden yellow buttercup-type flowers.

Senna nemophila

syn. ***Cassia eremophila***

Suitable for dry climates, this evergreen small shrub has variable silverish leaves and golden buttercup-type flowers.

Senna odorata

syn. ***Cassia odorata***

This is a small, variable, evergreen shrub with fine leaves and golden yellow buttercup-type flowers.

SENNA (cont)

Senna pallida
syn. ***Cassia biflora***
A medium, fine leaf shrub with arching branches and clusters of golden yellow flowers over many months.

Senna siamea KASSOD TREE
syn. ***Cassia siamea***
This evergreen small bushy crowned tree has clusters of pale yellow flowers over a long period.

Senna spectabilis SPECTACULAR CASSIA
syn. ***Cassia spectabilis; C. carnaval***
A small to medium bushy tree with large heads of bright yellow cup-type flowers.

Senna pleurocarpa
syn. ***Cassia pleurocarpa***
Upright and sparse, this shrub has terminal heads of yellow flowers. Suited to a dry climate.

Senna sturtii DESERT CASSIA
syn. ***Cassia sturtii***
Silver green leaves and yellow cup shaped flowers feature on this small, arid climate shrub.

Senna pumilio
syn. ***Cassia pumilio***
A dwarf spreading shrub with fine leaves and golden yellow flowers.

Senna singueana WILD CASSIA
syn. ***Cassia singueana***
A small bushy evergreen tree with heads of golden coloured buttercup-type flowers in spring.

SERISSA

Rubiaceae

A small evergreen shrub native to South East Asia. Grown as an outdoor ornamental in temperate to tropical climates, it is very hardy and flowers over a long period. Propagate from cuttings.

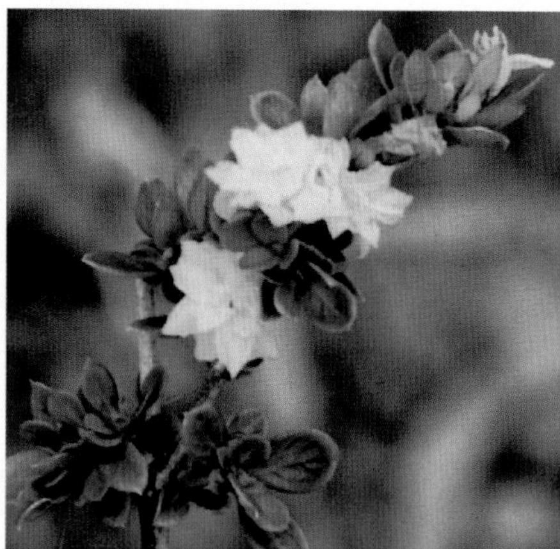

***Serissa foetida* cv. Flore Pleno**

A small sparse shrub with double white flowers along the branches.

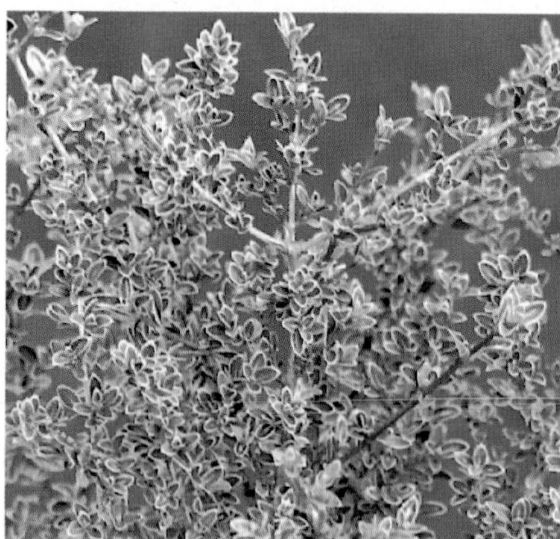

***Serissa foetida* cv. Snow Leaves**

This showy cultivar has green and pale cream coloured leaves.

***Serissa foetida* cv. Variegata**

A cultivar which has variegated leaves coloured green with a cream edge. This cultivar has much less cream on the leaves than the cultivar Snow Leaves.

SERRURIA

Proteaceae

Small shrubs, native to South Africa, which are grown as ornamentals and for cut flowers. They prefer a well drained soil and a temperate climate. Propagate from seed and cuttings.

Serruria florida BLUSHING BRIDE

A small evergreen shrub which has large heads of papery white flowers with touches of pink.

Serruria rosea

This is a small evergreen shrub with large showy heads of bright rose-pink papery flowers.

***Serruria* cv. Sugar and Spice**

A free flowering evergreen shrub with large heads of pink and white papery flowers.

SESBANIA

Fabaceae [Leguminosae]

Shrubs and trees which are tropical and sub-tropical. Sesbanias are native to Asia, Australia and tropical America. They are grown as flowering ornamentals in climates from temperate to tropical and are usually fast growing and used where a quick tree cover is needed. Propagate from seed.

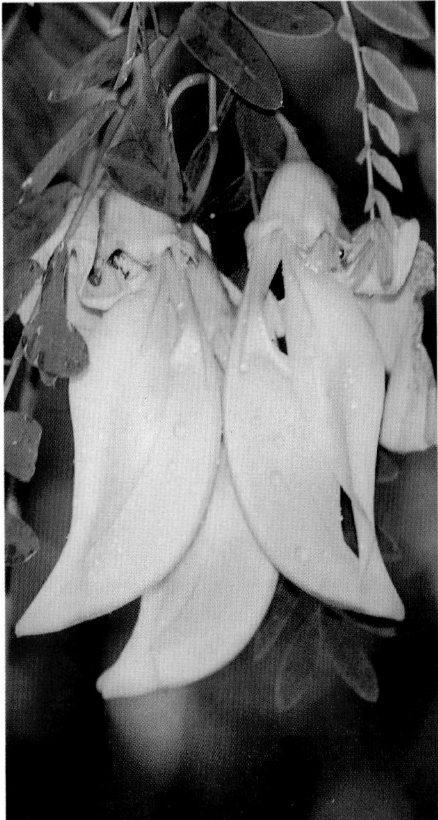

Sesbania formosa

An open crowned, small tree with heads of large, white, pea-type flowers.

***Sesbania grandiflora* cv. Alba**

WHITE WISTARIA TREE

This form has large pendulous white flowers and grows true to colour from seed.

Sesbania punicea

ORANGE WISTARIA SHRUB

syn. ***Daubentonia punicea***

This is a medium open shrub with pendulous racemes of bright orange flowers.

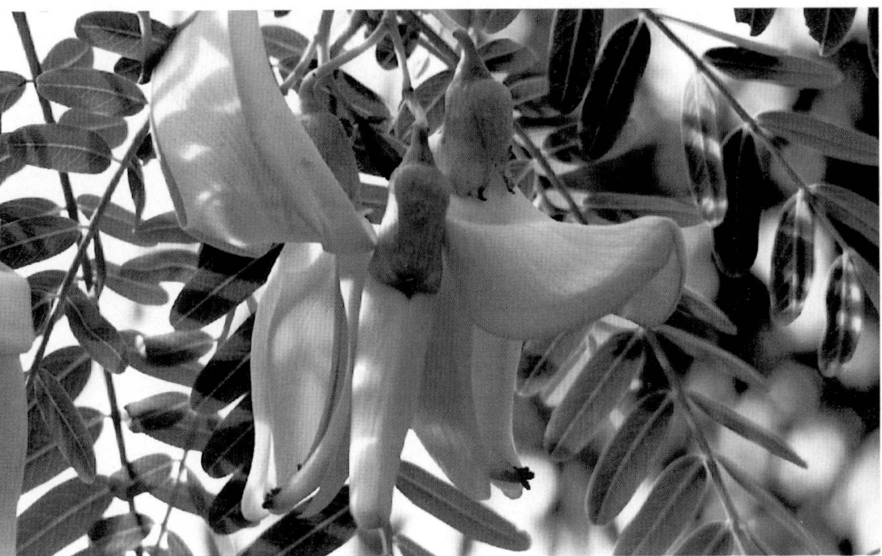

***Sesbania grandiflora* cv. Rosea**

A pale to mid-pink flowered cultivar of this tree which grows true to colour from seed.

Sesbania grandiflora

SCARLET WISTARIA TREE

A very upright, fast growing, evergreen small tree which has large pendulous parrots' beak-like flowers.

Sesbania tripetii

SCARLET WISTARIA SHRUB

syn. ***Daubentonia tripetii***

A medium open shrub with pendulous racemes of orange-scarlet coloured flowers.

S

SKIMMIA

RUTACEAE

Cold hardy, evergreen shrubs native to Asia. They have clusters of small white flowers followed by showy red berries and are widely grown in cold climates. Propagate from seed and cuttings.

Skimmia* x *confusa

This highly perfumed, bushy and spreading shrub has large terminal heads of cream flowers followed by sterile red fruit.

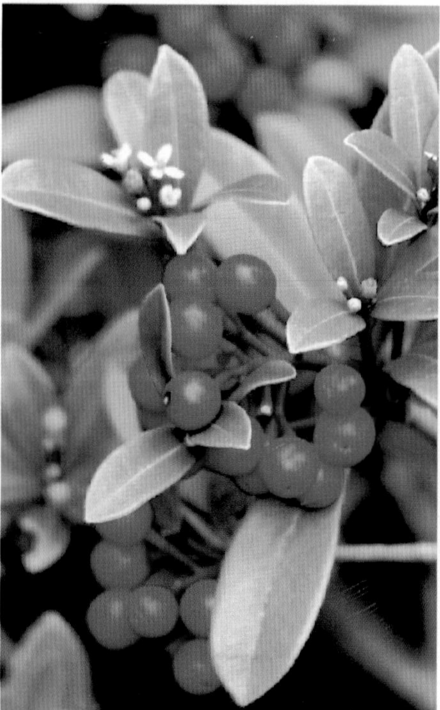

Skimmia japonica

A hardy shrub with small white flowers followed by bright red berries.

***Skimmia japonica* cv. Fructo Alba [Alba]**

A cultivar with white berries.

Skimmia japonica* ssp. *reevesiana

A shrub which has very large heads of bright red berries.

SLOANEA

ELAEOCARPUS

Sloanea australis* ssp. *australis

BLUSH ALDER

A small to medium evergreen tree native to Australia. It is grown outdoors in cool temperate to tropical climates for its heads of white daisy-like flowers which have yellow centres. Propagate from seed.

SOLANDRA

SOLANACEAE

Woody evergreen climbers or semi-climbers with large showy flowers, native to tropical America. They are grown as ornamentals in climates from temperate to tropical and will tolerate a wide range of soils. Propagate from cuttings.

Solandra grandiflora

An evergreen spreading semi-climber with large, creamy yellow, trumpet flowers.

***Solandra grandiflora* cv. Variegata**

An evergreen semi-climber with large grey-green and cream variegated leaves and very large, fragrant, cup shaped, amber coloured flowers.

Solandra maxima

A woody climber with large leaves and very large, cup-shaped, yellow flowers.

SOLANDRA (cont)

Solandra maxima cv. **Variegata**
An evergreen shrub with large green and cream variegated leaves and very large yellow flowers.

SOLANUM

Solanaceae

Shrubs, occasionally trees and climbers, from a wide range of countries and climates. Some are grown for their ornamental appearance while others, such as the common potato, are grown for their edible fruit or tubers. Some Solanums are poisonous. They are propagated from seeds, cuttings or tubers.

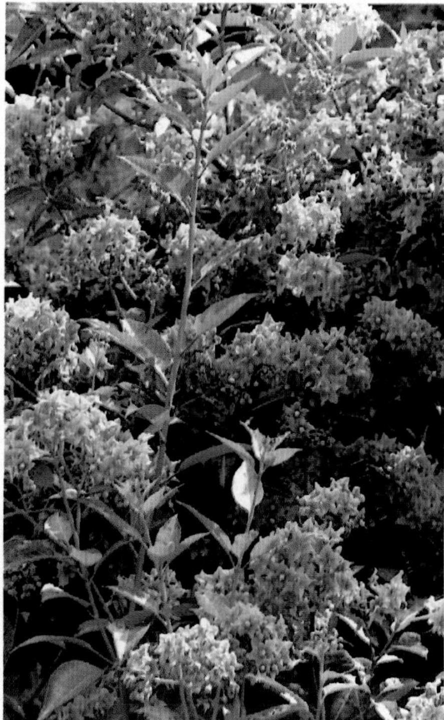

Solanum crispum
A semi-climbing shrub which has large heads of mauve flowers. It is ideal for cool climates.

Solanum ellipticum
From the arid climates of Australia, this bushy small shrub has grey leaves and blue flowers followed by round yellow fruit.

Solanum lasiophyllum
An erect rounded shrub with large grey leaves and dark blue flowers followed by oval yellow fruit.

Solanum mammosum NIPPLE FRUIT
This small shrub has violet coloured flowers and very unusual yellow fruit with nipple-like protrusions.

Solanum melongena cv. **Ovigerum**
GOLDEN EGGS
A bushy shrub which has blue flowers and fruit the size and shape of an egg. They are white at first then change to gold as they age.

Solanum orbiculatum
Small circular violet flowers bloom on this spreading, small leaf plant.

SOLANUM (cont)

Solanum quitoense NARANJILLA

A bushy shrub which has large decorative green leaves with purple-red veins. It has large, edible, orange coloured fruit.

Solanum wendlandii POTATO VINE

This woody vine has large heads of showy dark mauve flowers and round yellow fruit.

Solanum wrightii POTATO TREE

syn. ***S. macranthum***

A small spreading tree with bunches of large flowers which open purple, fade to mauve and then to white. It has round egg size fruit.

Solanum rantonnetii BLUE POTATO BUSH

A bushy, pendulous, branching shrub which is grown as an ornamental for its showy, circular, bluish purple flowers which cover the plant.

Solanum seaforthianum ST VINCENT LILAC

A sparse evergreen vine with showy heads of mauve flowers followed by bright red fruit.

SOLLYA

Pittosporaceae

Sollya heterophylla BLUEBELL CREEPER

An evergreen wiry vine which is native to Australia. When well grown, the plant is covered with bluebell-like flowers. It is tolerant of some frost and prefers a well drained soil. Propagate from seed and cuttings.

SOPHORA

FABACEAE [LEGUMINOSAE]

Evergreen and deciduous shrubs and trees native to many countries, growing in climates from cold temperate to tropical. They are widely grown as free flowering ornamentals in a wide range of soils. Propagate from seed and semi-mature cuttings.

Sophora macrocarpa
This tall evergreen shrub has small racemes of yellow flowers.

Sophora davidii
In spring this bushy, deciduous, cold climate shrub has large showy heads of pale blue flowers.

Sophora microphylla
A small evergreen tree with small leaves and pendulous bunches of golden yellow flowers in spring.

Sophora secundiflora MESCAL BEAN
Evergreen, this small to medium tree has upright bunches of violet-blue flowers.

Sophora glauca
syn. ***S. velutina***
A medium to tall evergreen shrub with pendulous racemes of flowers coloured white with touches of mauve.

Sophora tetraptera KOWHAI
syn. ***S. grandiflora***
A small to medium semi-deciduous tree with pendulous clusters of golden coloured flowers.

SOPHORA (cont)

Sophora tomentosa SILVERBUSH
Erect spikes of yellow flowers feature on this tall deciduous shrub.

Sorbus domestica
A small tree with heads of creamy white flowers followed by red fruit.

SORBUS

ROSACEAE

These deciduous trees and shrubs of the northern hemisphere are cold tolerant and are widely grown as ornamental plants for their flowers and colourful fruit. They are also widely used for soil stabilization. Sorbus should be propagated from seed which requires cold stratification.

Sorbus pohuashanensis
This small tree has large heads of cream coloured flowers followed by orange-red fruit.

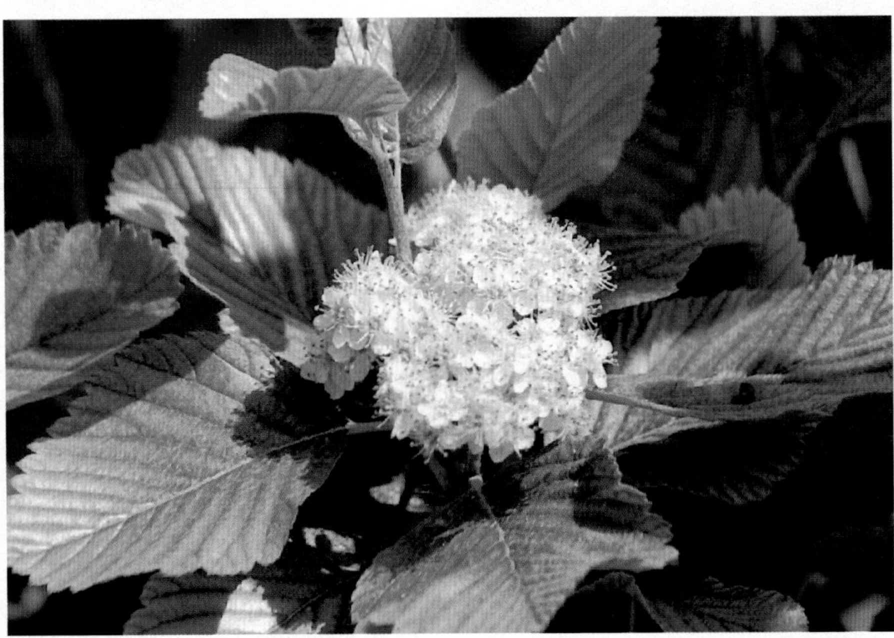

Sorbus aria WHITEBEAM
Orange-red fruit follow the large bunches of white flowers on this broad crowned small tree.

SPARMANNIA

TILIACEAE

Large leaf shrubs, native to Africa, which are grown outdoors in cool temperate to sub-tropical climates and grown in all climates as indoor plants. They are quite hardy in most soils and are propagated from seed and cuttings.

Sparmannia africana AFRICAN HEMP
A bushy, large leaf shrub. Flowering in large bunches, the small flowers have reflexed petals, and are white with yellow centres.

SPARMANNIA (cont)

***Sparmannia africana* cv. Flore Pleno**
A cultivar which has large bunches of double white flowers.

SPATHODEA

BIGNONIACEAE

Spathodea campanulata TULIP TREE
A small to medium, bushy, evergreen tree native to tropical Africa. It is a showy ornamental when grown in sub-tropical and tropical climates and has big heads of large, orange, tulip-like flowers over many months. Propagate from seed.

***Spathodea campanulata* cv. Aurea**
A cultivar with flowers coloured amber to old gold.

SPARTIUM

FABACEAE [LEGUMINOSAE]

Spartium junceum SPANISH BROOM
syn. ***Genista juncea***
An upright shrub with almost leafless stems which bear fragrant yellow pea-type flowers. It is native to Europe and is a hardy plant in climates from cold temperate to sub-tropical. Propagate from seed which needs hot water treatment.

SPIRAEA

Rosaceae

Deciduous shrubs, native to the northern hemisphere, which are grown as spring flowering ornamentals in climates from cold temperate to tropical, in a wide range of soils. Propagate from cuttings.

Spiraea alpina
Cold tolerant, this open, small shrub has round heads of white flowers in spring.

Spiraea bella
A bushy shrub with heads of pink flowers in spring.

Spiraea betulifolia
Heads of white flowers bloom on this bushy shrub in spring.

Spiraea cantoniensis REEVES SPIRAEA
A sparse upright shrub with large heads of fragrant, small, single, white flowers.

***Spiraea cantoniensis* cv. Lanceata**
WHITE MAY
This small shrub has arching branches and heads of small double white flowers.

SPIRAEA (cont)

Spiraea chamaedryfolia
Flowering in spring, this suckering shrub has heads of white flowers which have prominent stamens.

Spiraea* x *cinerea
In spring this small, bushy hybrid shrub has upright sprays of small, white flowers.

Spiraea gemmata
Free flowering, this sparse shrub has many heads of white flowers.

***Spiraea japonica* cv. Anthony Waterer** RED MAY
A small shrub which has odd yellow leaves and showy heads of small cerise coloured flowers.

***Spiraea japonica* cv. Candlelight**
This small, bushy shrub is grown for its colourful pale yellow leaves.

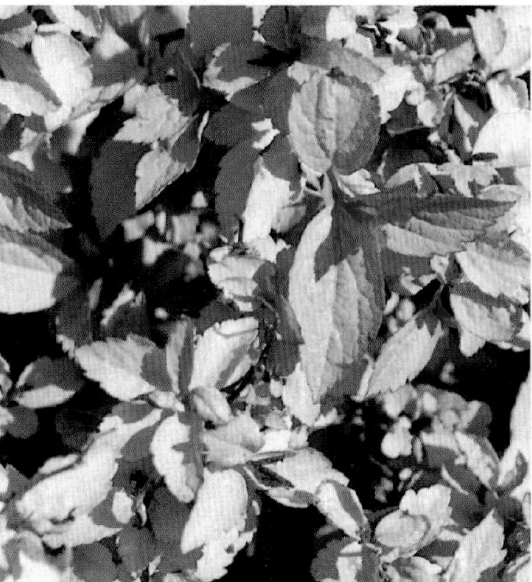

***Spiraea japonica* cv. Firelight**
The leaves of this bushy cultivar are coloured creamish green, with red and pink markings.

***Spiraea japonica* cv. Gold Mound**
This cultivar has lemon-yellow leaves.

SPIRAEA (cont)

Spiraea japonica cv. **Goldflame**
A compact bushy cultivar which has yellow leaves with red new growth.

Spiraea nipponica
This bushy medium shrub has flattish heads of small, white flowers.

Spiraea cv. **Pink Ice**
The new foliage is pink on this cultivar, which has heads of white flowers and variegated foliage of green and cream.

Spiraea miyabei
A small upright shrub with heads of white flowers which have prominent stamens.

Spiraea prunifolia BRIDAL WREATH
A sparse upright shrub which has dainty double white flowers on thin stems.

Spiraea pubescens
This small shrub has round heads of small white flowers, with mustard coloured centres.

SPIRAEA (cont)

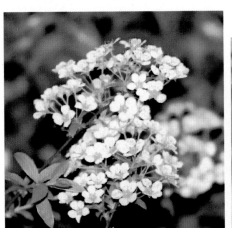

Spiraea thunbergii
In spring this fine leaf, twiggy shrub has terminal bunches of white flowers.

Spiraea trichocarpa
This is a small spreading shrub with dense heads of white flowers with creamy yellow centres.

Spiraea velutina
White flowers with prominent stamens bloom in roundish heads on this sparse shrub.

STACHYTARPHETA

VERBENACEAE

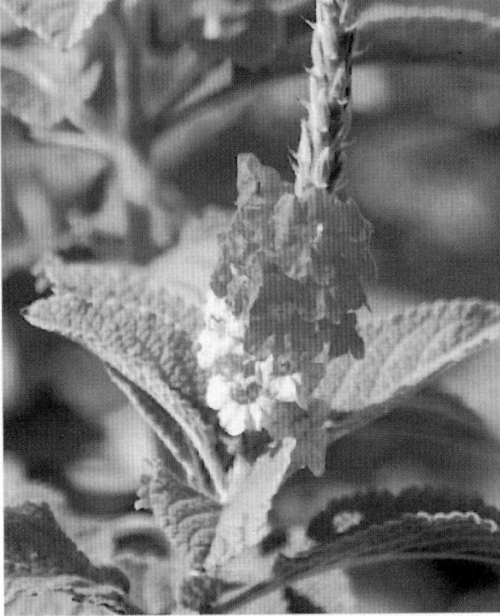

Stachytarpheta mutabilis
A sparse tall shrub native to tropical America, it is grown as an ornamental for its upright spikes of tightly packed small pink flowers. Over a six week period, the flowers open from the bottom to the top of the spike. It grows in a wide range of soils in climates from temperate to tropical. Propagate from seed and cuttings.

STACHYURUS

STACHYURACEAE

Stachyurus praecox
A deciduous shrub which is native to Japan. It is grown in cool climates as a free flowering ornamental for its pendulous racemes of small, yellow, bell shaped flowers. Propagate from seed and cuttings.

STAUNTONIA

LARDIZABALACEAE

Stauntonia hexaphylla
An evergreen twining vine native to Asia, this plant has highly fragrant clusters of white and purple coloured flowers. It prefers a cold temperate to warm temperate climate and is propagated from seed and cuttings.

STEMMADENIA

APOCYNACEAE

Stemmadenia litoralis
syn. ***S. galeottiana***
A tall evergreen shrub which is native to tropical America. In tropical to warm temperate climates it is grown as an ornamental for its fragrant, large, white flowers which are seen over many months. Propagate from seed and cuttings.

STENANTHEMUM

RHAMNACEAE

***Stenanthemum scortechinii* cv. White Mischief**

A small sparse shrub which is native to Australia and has small cotton wool-like flowers in profusion during spring. It is grown as an ornamental in climates from temperate to tropical and tolerates poor soils. Propagate from seed and cuttings.

STENOCARPUS

PROTEACEAE

Evergreen shrubs and small trees, native to Australia, which are grown, as ornamentals and street trees, for their unusual flowers. They are adaptable to climates from mild temperate to tropical and will grow in poor soils. Propagate from seed.

Stenocarpus salignus

A small to medium tree which has large bunches of twisted cream flowers in spring.

Stenocarpus sinuatus FIREWHEEL TREE

A small to medium upright tree with dense foliage. It has big clusters of large bright red flowers which resemble a wheel complete with spokes.

Stenocarpus sinuatus

Flowers fully open.

STEPHANOTIS

ASCLEPIADACEAE

Stephanotis floribunda

An evergreen twining vine which is native to Madagascar. It has very fragrant, white, trumpet shaped flowers. These flowers are widely used by florists in bouquets and corsages. The plant requires a temperate to tropical climate. Propagate from seed and cuttings.

STERCULIA

STERCULIACEAE

Deciduous or evergreen tropical trees native to many countries. They are grown as feature trees in parks and for street planting for their showy flowers and colourful seed pods. Some are used for timber production. They require a warm climate and are propagated from seed.

Sterculia foetida INDIAN ALMOND

A medium tree with a spreading crown. The large heads of orange-red flowers may almost cover the tree. The flowers have a strong odour.

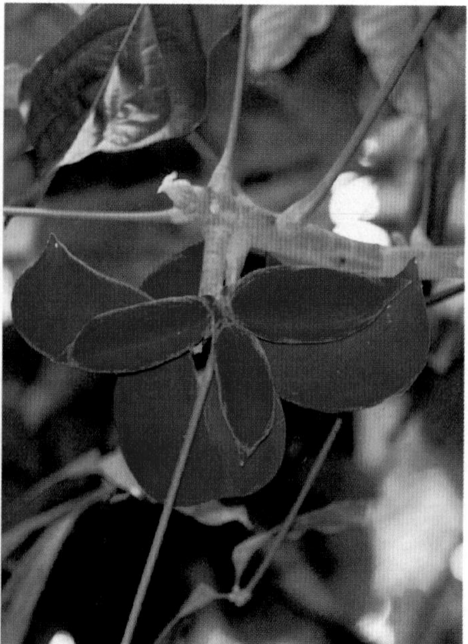

Sterculia mexicana

A small tree which is grown for its showy crimson coloured seed pods, which are illustrated.

STERCULIA (cont)

Sterculia quadrifida PEANUT TREE
This bushy crowned small tree has cream flowers followed by bright red colourful seed pods shaped like peanuts. The black seed is edible. Illustration shows the colourful seed pods.

Sterculia viscidula
A tall shrub to small tree which has showy bunches of red bell shaped flowers which are sticky to the touch.

STEREOSPERMUM

BIGNONIACEAE

Stereospermum kunthianum
PINK JACARANDA
A small open crowned deciduous tree native to Africa. It is grown in temperate to tropical climates for its large showy heads of pink jacaranda-like flowers. Propagate from seed.

STERIPHOMA

CAPPARACEAE [CAPPARIDACEAE]

Steriphoma paradoxum
An evergreen warm climate shrub which has showy orange and cream coloured flowers with long prominent stamens. It is grown outdoors in climates from warm temperate to tropical and indoors in other climates. Propagate from seed and cuttings.

STICTOCARDIA

CONVOLVULACEAE

Stictocardia campanulata
A slender stemmed vine with heart shaped leaves which is native to tropical Africa. Outdoors in temperate to tropical climates and in glass houses and conservatories in milder climates, it is grown for its large showy orange-red flowers. Propagate from seed and cuttings.

STIGMAPHYLLON

MALPIGHIACEAE

Evergreen slender vines which are native to tropical America and are grown outdoors in warm temperate to tropical climates and in glasshouses and conservatories in milder climates. Propagate from seed and cuttings.

Stigmaphyllon ciliatum GOLDEN VINE
A wandering slender vine which has large colourful heads of golden yellow flowers over many months in spring.

Stigmaphyllon littorale BUTTERFLY VINE
In spring this bushy twining vine has large heads of golden yellow flowers.

S

STREPTOSOLEN

Solanaceae

Streptosolen jamesonii FIREBUSH

syn. ***Browallia jamesonii***

A bushy evergreen shrub native to South America, it is grown as a spectacular flowering ornamental for its showy heads of bright orange with yellow flowers. Firebush grows outdoors in climates from mild temperate to tropical but is seen at its best in temperate climates free of frost. Propagate from tip cuttings.

Streptosolen jamesonii cv. **Ginger Meggs**

A cultivar with golden yellow flowers.

STROBILANTHES

Acanthaceae

Evergreen shrubs, native to tropical Asia, which are grown as flowering and colour leaf ornamentals in temperate to tropical climates. Propagate from cuttings.

Strobilanthes anisophyllus

syn. ***Goldfussia anisophylla***

A compact, bushy, small shrub with purple and olive-green leaves and mauve flowers.

Strobilanthes dyerianus PERSIAN SHIELD

syn. ***Perilepta dyeriana***

This upright small shrub is grown for its large highly coloured leaves of purple, mauve and green.

Strobilanthes gossypinus

A bushy shrub with large grey leaves and terminal spikes of mauve flowers.

STRONGYLODON

Fabaceae [Leguminosae]

Strongylodon macrobotrys JADE VINE

Native to the Philippines, this is a vigorous woody evergreen climber. It requires a wet tropical climate and has very large, long racemes of blue flowers over many months. Propagate from seed and cuttings.

STROPHANTHUS

Apocynaceae

Shrubs and semi-climbers native to tropical Africa and Asia, which are grown as flowering ornamentals. They are quite hardy, free flowering and grow outdoors in climates from temperate to tropical and in conservatories in milder climates. Propagate from seed and cuttings.

Strophanthus gratus

A spreading almost semi-climbing shrub with long branches and showy heads of pink flowers which have maroon centres.

STROPHANTHUS (cont)

Strophanthus preussii 4

A sparse semi-climbing shrub which has flowers coloured pale apricot-cream with amber and purple lines in the throat. It has very long tail-like parts cascading from the petals.

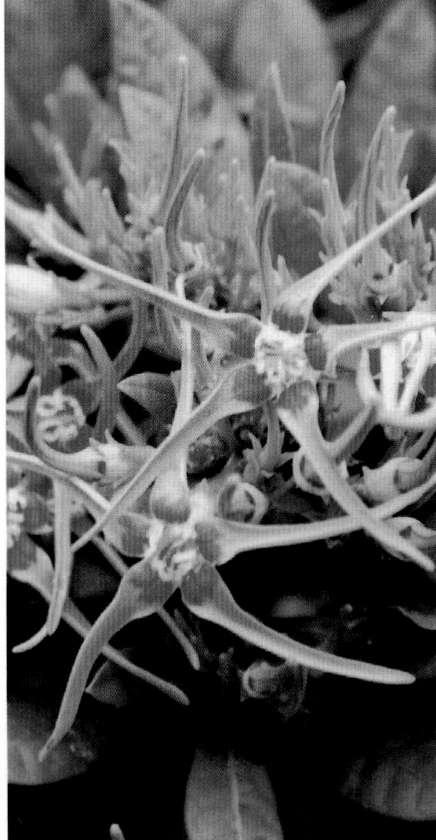

Strophanthus speciosus

syn. ***S. capensis***

A bushy spreading shrub with large heads of starfish-like flowers coloured apricot and red.

SUTHERLANDIA

FABACEAE [LEGUMINOSAE]

A small shrub with fine blue-grey foliage. Native to Africa, it is widely grown for its showy red flowers and unusual bladder-like seed pods. It prefers a warm dry situation and is grown as an indoor plant in cool climates. The plant responds to fertilizing and is propagated from seed.

Sutherlandia frutescens

A sparse upright shrub with bright red flowers in spring, followed by large inflated seed pods.

Sutherlandia montana

A bushy shrub with large heads of bright red flowers in spring. It has large bladder-like seed pods.

SWAINSONA

FABACEAE [LEGUMINOSAE]

Mostly evergreen shrubs native to Australia and New Zealand, they are grown as showy flowering ornamentals. *S. formosa* is one of the outstanding flowering plants of the world and to see large areas of land covered with these plants with their red and black flowers fully open is a sight to remember. Most Swainsonas are grown in hot and dry climates but are adaptable to glass house culture in cool climates. Propagate from seed and by grafting of some cultivars. Seed requires hot water treatment.

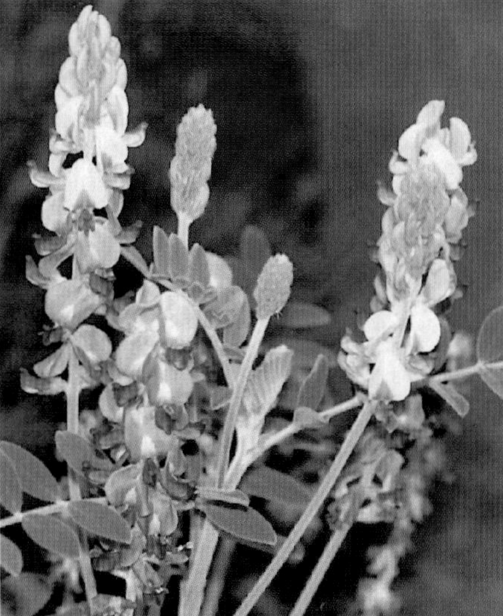

Swainsona canescens

An upright small shrub with erect spikes of bluish mauve coloured flowers.

Swainsona colutoides

This is a sparse spreading shrub with erect flower spikes of violet coloured pea-type flowers.

SWAINSONA (cont)

Swainsona formosa

STURT'S DESERT PEA

syn. ***Clianthus formosus***

A spreading or trailing plant with greyish leaves and large heads of red and black flowers on erect stems. This plant suits hot and dry situations and is an ideal hanging basket plant. The flowers are good for cut flowers. There has been much research carried out by the Flinders University in South Australia and the many new cultivars which follow have been developed there. It is probable that cultivar trade names will be used on these forms in the future.

Swainsona formosa cv. **Alba** 12

A cultivar which has bunches of clear white flowers.

Swainsona formosa

cv. **Clear Red Form** 12

This cultivar has dusky red coloured flowers.

Swainsona formosa

cv. **Crimson Form** 12

A cultivar which has crimson and black coloured flowers.

Swainsona formosa cv. **Marginata** 12

Flowers coloured red, white and black occur on this cultivar which has been around a long time.

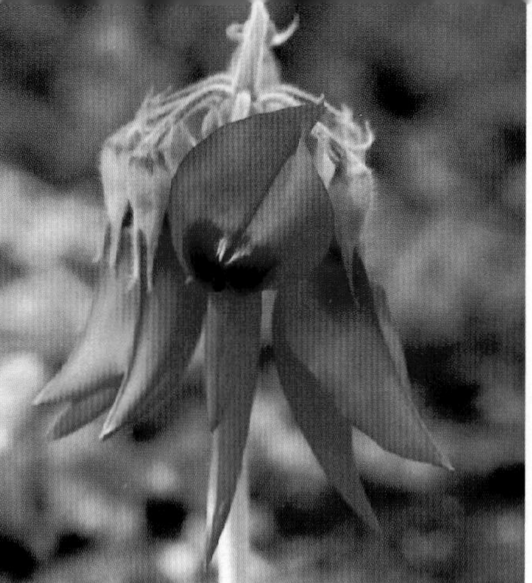

Swainsona formosa

cv. **Orange Form** 12

This cultivar has flowers which open as orange-red and then become more orange as they age.

Swainsona formosa

cv. **Pale Pink Form** 12

A cultivar which has pale pink flowers.

Swainsona formosa cv. **Pink Form** 12

A showy cultivar with flowers coloured pink and rose-pink.

SWAINSONA (cont)

Swainsona formosa CV. **Red Form** 12
A cultivar which has red flowers with small amounts of black in the centres.

Swainsona formosa
CV. **Red & Pink Form** 12
This cultivar has flowers of red and pink.

Swainsona galegifolia DARLING PEA
This small shrub has greyish leaves. Flower colour can vary from white, to yellow, to red, with pinky mauve being the most common colour.

Swainsona greyana
A free branching shrub with erect heads of cerise coloured flowers.

Swainsona CV. **Hermannsburg**
Erect stems hold the heads of purple flowers on this small spreading plant.

Swainsona stenodonta
This is a sparse shrub with erect spikes of maroon coloured flowers.

SWIETENIA

MELIACEAE

Swietenia mahagoni
WEST INDIAN MAHOGANY
A medium fast growing evergreen tree native to the Caribbean. It is grown in sub-tropical and tropical climates as a shade tree and to produce timber. This tree has bunches of small yellow flowers and is propagated from seed.

SYMPHORICARPOS

CAPRIFOLIACEAE

Symphoricarpos orbiculatus
CORALBERRY
A small, cold loving shrub with thin arching branches which is native to North America and China. It is grown as an ornamental, in cool and cold climates, for its colourful bunches of pink berries. Propagate from seed and cuttings.

SYNAPHEA

PROTEACEAE

Synaphea polymorpha
A small bushy shrub native to Australia, it requires a well drained soil in cool temperate to warm temperate climates and is grown as an ornamental for the bunches of golden coloured flowers it displays. Propagate from seed.

SYNGONIUM

ARACEAE

Grown for their decorative leaves, these climbers are grown mostly as potted plants indoors or in protected situations in warm temperate climates, and outdoors in subtropical and tropical areas. Propagate from cuttings or by division.

Syngonium hoffmannii
A hardy bushy climber with large leaves which have very prominent veins.

Syngonium podophyllum
A climbing evergreen plant from Central America which is grown world wide as an indoor plant and outdoors in warm temperate to tropical climates. Much breeding has been carried out with this plant to give a wide range of cultivars. *S. podophyllum* has arrowhead shaped leaves.

***Syngonium podophyllum* cv. Albolineatum**
A cultivar which has broader leaves with the leaf veins coloured creamy white.

***Syngonium podophyllum* cv. Frosty**
A broad leaf cultivar which has cream and green coloured leaves.

***Syngonium podophyllum* cv. Fantasy**
This cultivar has broad leaves with large white blotches on the green leaves.

***Syngonium podophyllum* cv. Jade Magic**
The arrowhead shaped leaves on this cultivar are coloured green and cream.

SYNGONIUM (cont)

Syngonium podophyllum cv. **Pixie**

The broad leaves of this bushy cultivar are coloured green with cream markings in the centre.

Syngonium podophyllum cv. **Spear Point**

This cultivar has narrow leaves coloured green and cream.

Syngonium podophyllum cv. **Silver Knight**

This bushy cultivar has broad silver-grey leaves.

Syngonium podophyllum cv. **Tiffany**

A bushy broad leaf cultivar which has new leaves coloured grey overlaid with pink.

Syngonium podophyllum cv. **White Butterfly**

A bushy cultivar with arrowhead shaped leaves that are creamy white with green splashes on the upper part, and pale green underneath.

Syngonium podophyllum cv. **Snooks**

A bushy cultivar with arrow shaped leaves coloured green with cream markings.

Syngonium podophyllum cv. **Ultra**

The leaves of this cultivar have an arrowhead shape and are coloured green overlaid with silver.

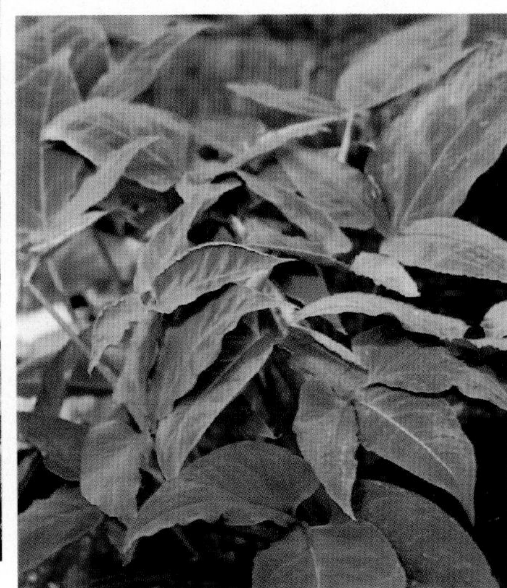

Syngonium wendlandii

A hardy climber with three bladed leaves, it is grown as an indoor plant.

SYRINGA

LILAC

Oleaceae

Deciduous shrubs and small trees native to Asia, especially the Himalayas, and parts of Europe. They are grown world wide in cold to mild climates for their attractive fragrant flowers in spring. There is a wide range of cultivars and hybrids grown as well as species forms. Many are grown from seed while the cultivars are grafted or budded using Ligustrum as one of the root stocks. Lilacs benefit from regular pruning and fertilising as well as a mulch in summer. Some cultivars and hybrids have indistinct origins.

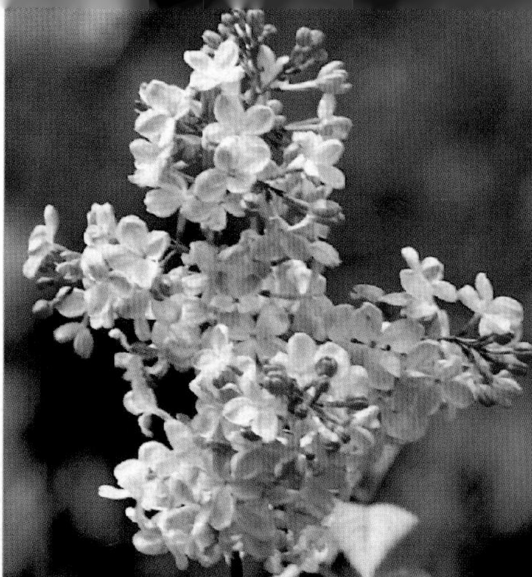

Syringa x ***hyacinthiflora*** cv. **Esther Staley**

This tall growing hybrid shrub has erect spikes of fragrant pink flowers.

Syringa emodi HIMALAYAN LILAC

This cold hardy, upright, tall shrub has large heads of pinky lilac coloured flowers in spring.

Syringa x ***hyacinthiflora*** cv. **Alice Eastwood**

A free flowering hybrid lilac. The fragrant mauve-pink double flowers form on erect spikes.

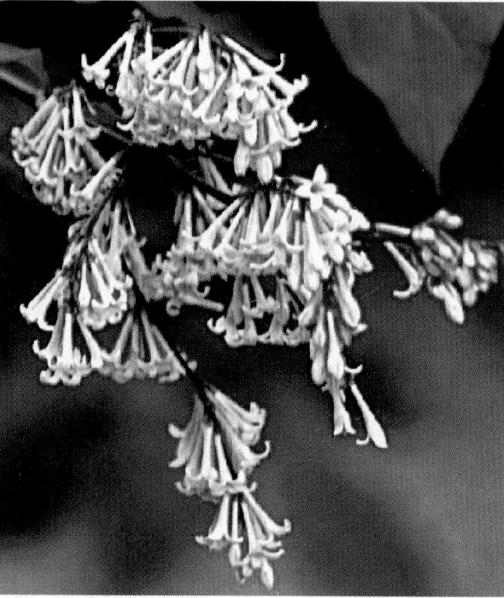

Syringa x ***josiflexa***

Very cold tolerant, this hybrid lilac has pendulous heads of mostly pink flowers.

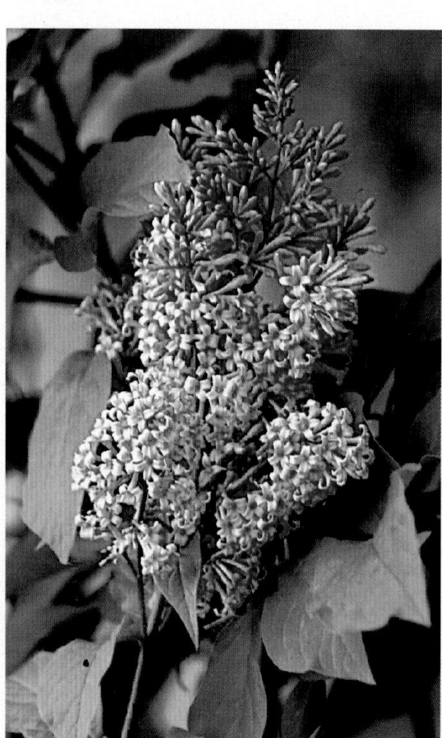

Syringa x ***henryi***

A hybrid tall shrub with large heads of rose-pink flowers in spring. Flower colour may vary from pale mauve to almost red in various soils.

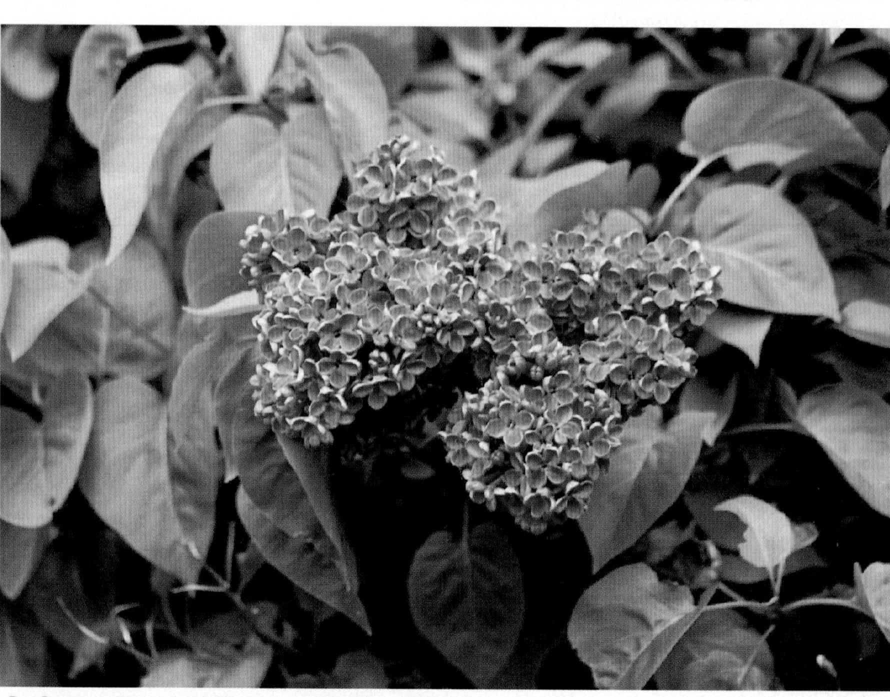

Syringa x ***hyacinthiflora*** cv. **Clarkes Giant**

A cultivar which has large heads of purple flowers.

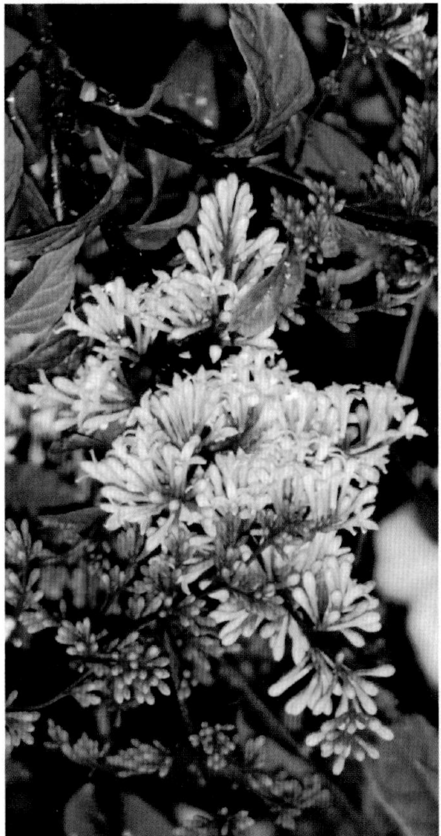

***Syringa* x *josiflexa* cv. Bellicent**
A cultivar which has dense heads of bright pink flowers.

Syringa josikaea HUNGARIAN LILAC
An open crowned tall shrub with large heads of rosy violet coloured flowers in spring.

Syringa meyeri
Sparse heads of fragrant lilac-pink flowers bloom on this small to medium shrub.

***Syringa meyeri* cv. Palibin**
A cultivar which has rosy lilac coloured flowers in tight bunches.

Syringa* x *persica PERSIAN LILAC
This is a densely branching shrub with a profusion of small upright spikes of single mauve-pink flowers.

SYRINGA (cont)

Syringa* x *prestoniae
A hybrid lilac with erect bunches of rosy lilac coloured flowers in spring.

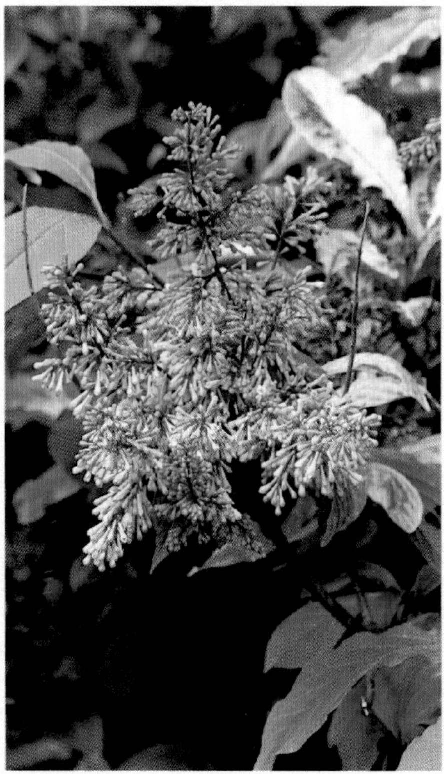

***Syringa* x *prestoniae* cv. Audrey**
Rose-pink flowers bloom in large bunches on this shrub.

Syringa reflexa
An upright shrub with pendulous heads of pink coloured flowers in spring.

Syringa tigerstedtii
An upright shrub with loose heads of pale pink flowers in spring.

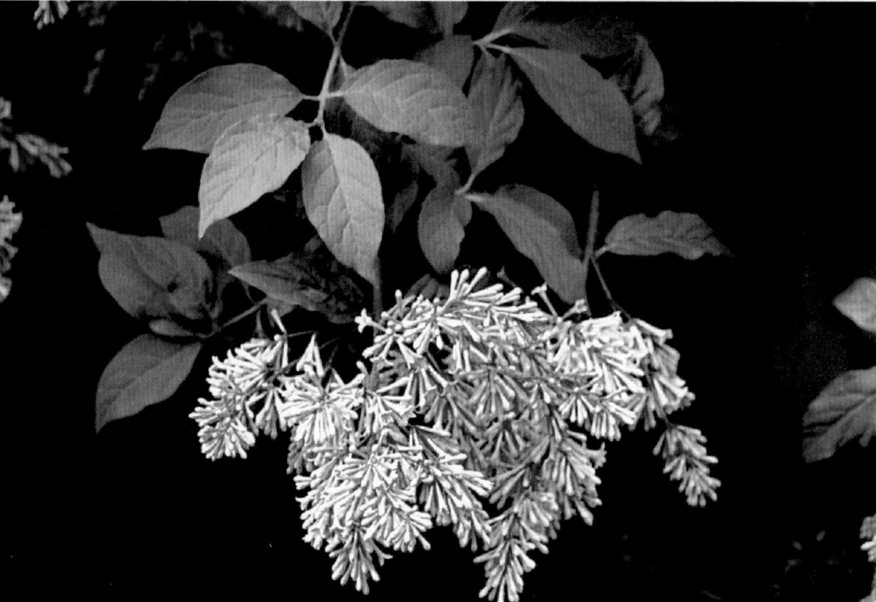

Syringa* x *swegiflexa
A hybrid shrub with large dense broad pendulous heads of rose-pink flowers in spring.

Syringa sweginzowii
This is a slender open crowned shrub with long sprays of pale pink flowers in spring.

Syringa villosa
An upright shrub with dense erect heads of rosy magenta coloured flowers in spring.

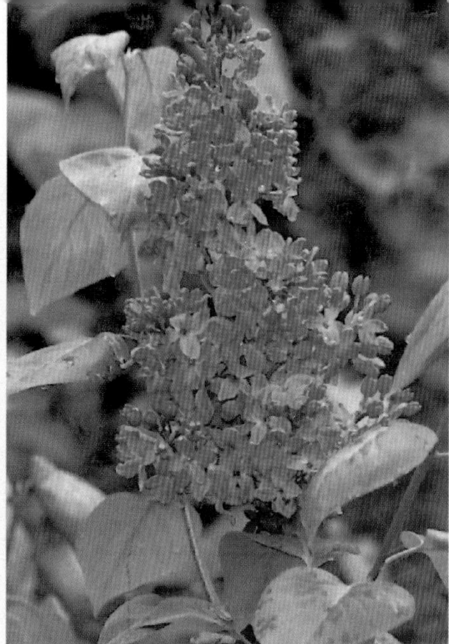

Syringa vulgaris cv. **Chris**
This cultivar has flowers coloured violet to purple.

Syringa vulgaris COMMON LILAC
Many of the outstanding cultivar lilacs derive from this plant, which is a bushy, upright, tall shrub with heads of lilac to pink flowers.

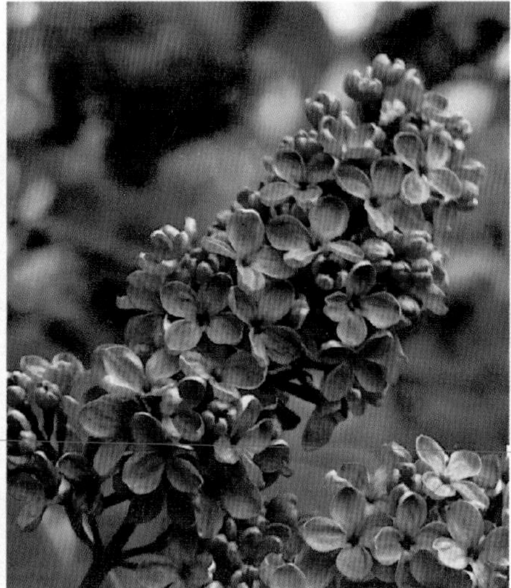

Syringa vulgaris cv. **Congo**
Upright and bushy, this cultivar has large flower heads of single, fragrant, dark violet flowers.

Syringa vulgaris cv. **Bright Centennial**
The flowers on this cultivar are reddish rosy pink.

Syringa vulgaris cv. **Capitaine Baltet**
A cultivar with large heads of lilac-pink coloured flowers in spring.

SYRINGA (cont)

Syringa vulgaris **cv. Fertile du Poitou**
An upright shrub with large spikes of single mauve-violet fragrant flowers.

Syringa vulgaris **cv. Firmament**
A heavy flowering cultivar with large heads of lilac coloured flowers.

Syringa vulgaris **cv. Holy Maid**
Upright heads of pale pink flowers occur on this cultivar.

Syringa vulgaris **cv. Hugo de Vries**
On this cultivar the large heads of flowers are coloured cerise-purple.

Syringa vulgaris **cv. Jacques Callot**
An upright tall shrub with spikes of mauve-lilac, fragrant, single flowers.

Syringa vulgaris
cv. Katherine Havemeyer [7]
A free flowering lilac with large heads of fragrant, double, mauve-violet coloured flowers.

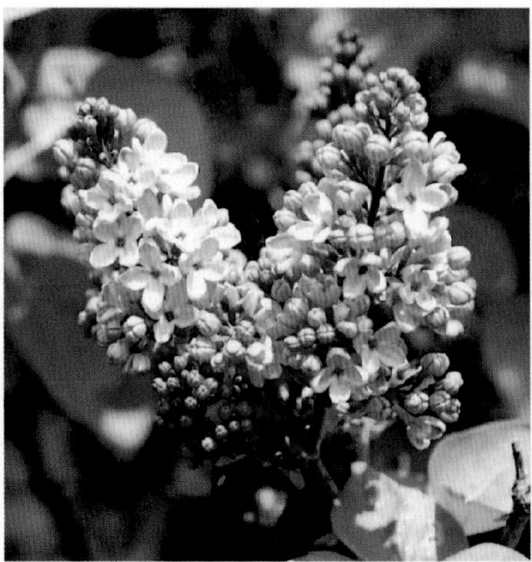

Syringa vulgaris
cv. Louis van Houtte
This cultivar has upright heads of lilac-lavender coloured flowers.

SYRINGA (cont)

***Syringa vulgaris* cv. Madame F. Morel**
The lilac-violet flowers on this cultivar bloom in heads.

***Syringa vulgaris* cv. Madame Lemoine**
This large shrub has large heads of fragrant double white flowers.

***Syringa vulgaris* cv. Miss Ellen Willmott**
An upright shrub with fragrant, double, pure white flowers on large heads.

***Syringa vulgaris* cv. Missimo** 7
An upright tall hybrid shrub with large erect heads of single fragrant violet coloured flowers.

***Syringa vulgaris* cv. Primrose** 7
This is a tall shrub with large heads of fragrant, single, primrose-yellow flowers.

***Syringa vulgaris* cv. Priscilla**
This cultivar has large heads of lilac coloured flowers.

***Syringa vulgaris* cv. Montaigne**
A free flowering, bushy, tall shrub with a profusion of fragrant pink flowers on upright spikes.

SYRINGA (cont)

Syringa vulgaris **cv. Sensation**
Upright and tall, this shrub has large heads of fragrant double flowers of violet edged with mauve.

Syringa vulgaris **cv. Vulcan**
A tall shrub with large spikes of purple coloured, single, fragrant flowers.

Syringa wolfii
This bushy medium shrub has heads of fragrant, pale mauve, single flowers.

Syringa yunnanensis
Small and free flowering, this shrub has heads of fragrant mauve-pink flowers in profusion.

SYZYGIUM

MYRTACEAE

Evergreen shrubs and trees native to many countries throughout the world. They are grown as ornamentals for their showy fruit or colourful flowers. Syzygiums are also grown for timber, essential oils, edible fruit and cloves. These plants are quite hardy but respond to fertiliser and good soil. Most require sub-tropical climates, but several species are tolerant of frosts in cool temperate climates. Propagate from seed and cuttings. Many Syzygiums were previously named Eugenia.

Syzygium australe CREEK SATINASH
syn. ***Eugenia australis; E. myrtifolia***
A small evergreen tree which has clusters of white flowers and large bunches of edible fruit. Tolerates light frosts.

Syzygium australe
This illustration shows the colourful purple fruit.

Syzygium corynanthum SOUR CHERRY
syn. ***Eugenia corynantha***
Bright red fruit follow the cream flowers on this small to medium broad crowned tree.

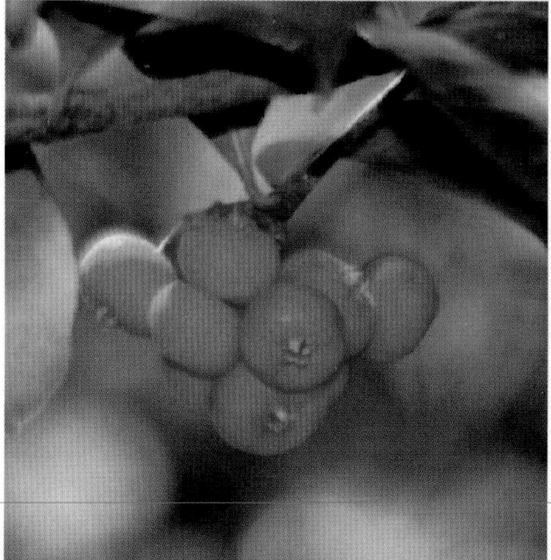

Syzygium fibrosum
This small tree has showy clusters of bright red fruit.

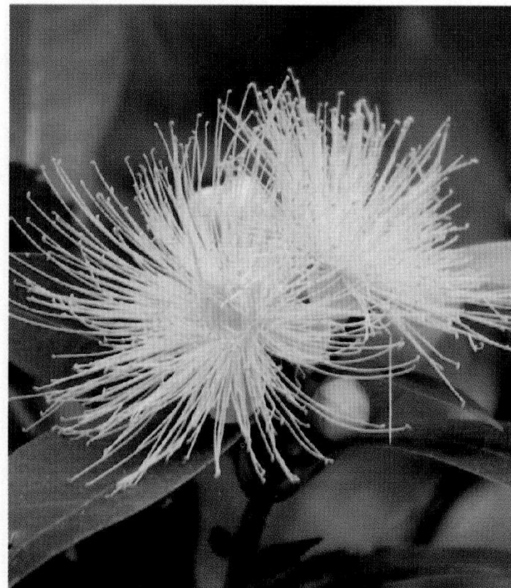

Syzygium jambos ROSE APPLE
A densely crowned small tree with large, fragrant, creamy yellow flowers followed by large, edible, yellowish coloured fruit which taste like rose water.

Syzygium luehmannii RIBERRY; SMALL LEAF LILLY PILLY
syn. ***Eugenia luehmannii***
A dense small tree with white flowers and very large clusters of small, red, edible fruit which are illustrated. It also has bright red-pink new growth.

Syzygium luehmannii - new growth

Syzygium malaccense MALAY APPLE
A spectacular small tree which has large cerise-purple coloured flowers followed by large, pinkish red, edible fruit. It requires a warm climate.

Syzygium malaccense - fruit
This illustration shows the large edible fruit which may be eaten raw, cooked or used to make wine.

Syzygium moorei COOLAMON
syn. ***Eugenia moorei***
A medium densely crowned tree with large heads of red flowers followed by clusters of large, round, edible, white fruit.

Syzygium oleosum BLUE LILLY PILLY
syn. ***Eugenia coolminiana; Syzygium coolminianum***
Often growing near the sea, this small tree has cream flowers followed by large bunches of round, purplish blue fruit.

S - T

SYZYGIUM (cont)

Syzygium paniculatum BRUSH CHERRY
syn. ***Eugenia paniculata***
A small bushy tree with white flowers followed by cerise coloured fruit.

Syzygium wilsonii ssp. ***wilsonii***
A medium bushy shrub with large pendulous pompom-like dark red flowers dusted with gold pollen, followed by clusters of small white fruit.

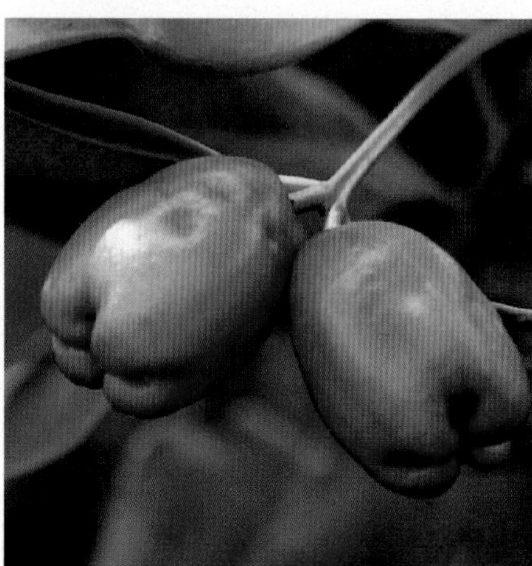

Syzygium papyraceum PAPERBARK SATINASH
A small bushy tree with brown papery bark. It has small mauve flowers followed by large, oblong, purple fruit.

Syzygium wilsonii ssp. ***wilsonii*** - fruit

TABEBUIA

BIGNONIACEAE

Evergreen or deciduous shrubs and trees from tropical America and the Caribbean. Some are regarded as being the most outstanding flowering trees in the world. There has been much natural hybridisation of those in cultivation and as a result there is considerable variation in many of the flowers and in some instances, indistinct positive identification. Tabebuias are grown as feature trees in very warm temperate to tropical climates for their outstanding flowers. Some are also grown for timber production. Propagate from fresh seed. The sizes indicated are when grown in gardens—they may be larger in the wild.

Syzygium samarangense JAVA APPLE
syn. ***Eugenia javanica***
White flowers are followed by large, bright red, pear shaped fruit on this small bushy tree.

Tabebuia argentea TREE OF GOLD
A small tree with thick leaves. The tree may be totally covered with large bunches of golden coloured, trumpet flowers in spring.

TABEBUIA (cont)

Tabebuia chrysantha

A small to medium open crowned tree with large heads of golden yellow flowers which all open together. Often confused with *T. chrysotricha*. The seed pods of this plant have few hairs and the flowers are a little darker.

Tabebuia chrysotricha

syn. ***Tecoma chrysotricha***

A sparse crowned small to medium tree with large heads of yellow flowers which may open over a period of a few weeks. The seed pods of this tree are quite hairy and this is the most noticeable way to identify this from *T. chrysantha*.

Tabebuia dubia ROBLE NEGRO

Densely crowned, this small tree has very leathery leaves and heads of pink coloured flowers.

Tabebuia guayacan

A medium tree with a large crown and tightly packed heads of golden yellow flowers.

Tabebuia hypoleuca

A densely crowned small tree with leathery leaves and small heads of bright rose-pink flowers in late spring.

Tabebuia impetiginosa

syn. ***T. avellanedae; T. ipe***

A small tree which may be leafless when in flower. The bright rose-pink to light purple flowers may totally cover the tree in spring.

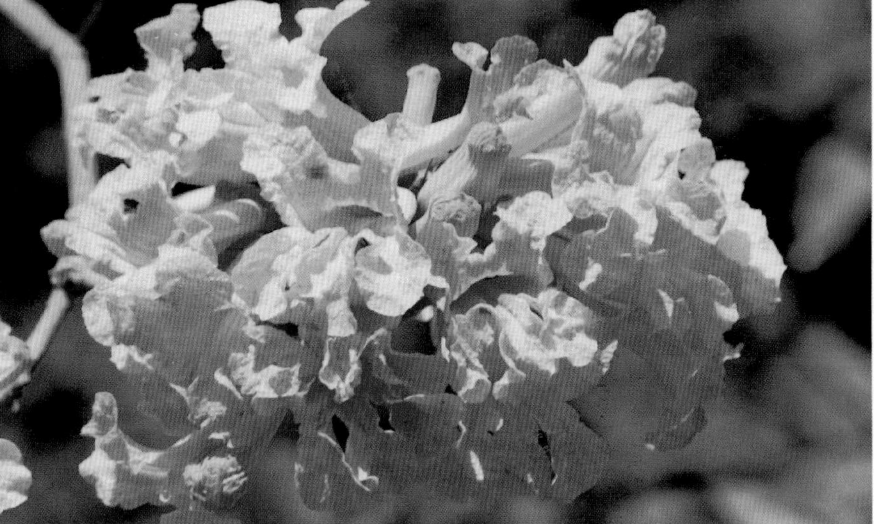

Tabebuia heterophylla PINK TRUMPET TREE

This small tree is usually leafless when it flowers in spring. Then, mostly, it is totally covered with almost round heads of bright pink trumpet flowers.

TABEBUIA (cont)

Tabebuia cv. **Miniata**

Large sparse heads of small pink flowers feature on this small evergreen tree.

Tabebuia riparia WHITEWOOD

syn. ***T. leucoxylon; Bignonia leucoxylon***

A tall shrub to small tree with bunches of very pale pink trumpet flowers which have yellow throats.

Tabebuia roseoalba

A small tree with large heads of pale pink trumpet flowers which have pale yellow throats. The colour may vary depending on the soil type.

Tabebuia pallida CUBAN PINK TRUMPET

A small tree with large heads of pale pink trumpet flowers which have yellow centres.

Tabebuia rosea PINK POUI

Leathery leaves and heads of mauve-pink trumpet flowers with yellow throats feature on this variable small to medium tree.

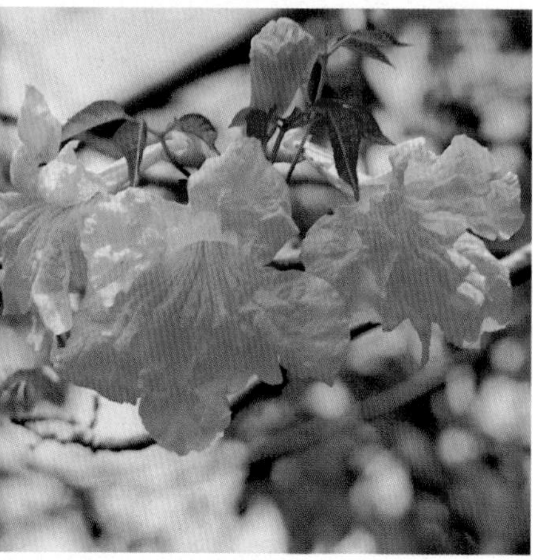

Tabebuia serratifolia YELLOW POUI

This tree is of medium size, with a dense spreading crown. It has heads of large golden yellow trumpet flowers.

Tabebuia palmeri PURPLE TRUMPET TREE

A small tree which may be leafless when in full bloom. It has large rounded heads of trumpet flowers coloured cerise to light purple. This tree is referred to as a synonym of *T. impetiginosa* which has lighter coloured flowers.

Tabebuia spectabilis

A small tree with large heads of golden yellow to orange-yellow trumpet flowers in spring.

Tabebuia cv. **St John**
An evergreen shrub with large trumpet shaped flowers coloured old rose.

TABERNAEMONTANA

APOCYNACEAE

Evergreen trees and shrubs with glossy leaves and milky sap, which are native to many tropical countries. In warm temperate to tropical climates they are grown outdoors for their fragrant blooms which may be seen over many months. Many are grown as glasshouse or conservatory plants in cooler climates. Propagate from seed and cuttings.

Tabernaemontana corymbosa
A free flowering, bushy, tall shrub to small tree with clusters of highly perfumed white flowers which have reflexed and partly twisted petals.

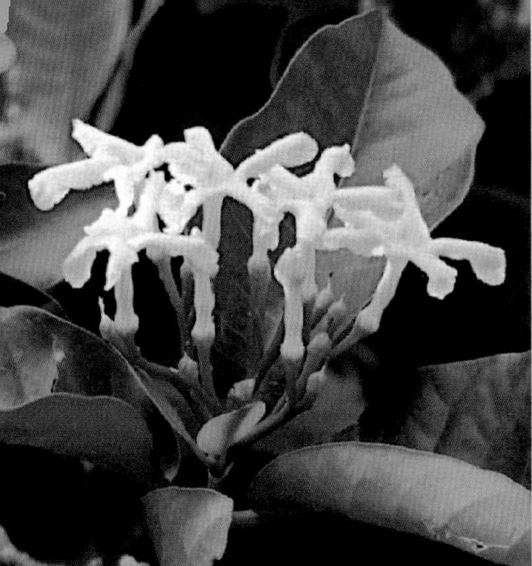

Tabernaemontana dichotoma
This is a small shrub with large white fragrant flowers in spring. The flowers have overlapping petals when they first open.

Tabernaemontana divaricata
PINWHEEL FLOWER
syn. ***T. coronaria; Ervatamia coronaria; E. divaricata***
A small shrub with fragrant white flowers which have reflexed partly twisted petals.

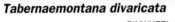

Tabernaemontana divaricata cv. **Flore Pleno**
A cultivar which has double white gardenia-like flowers.

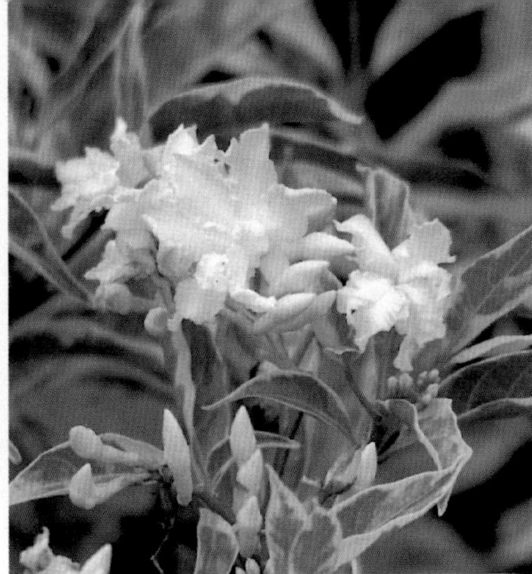

Tabernaemontana divaricata cv. **Plena Variegata**
This cultivar has double flowers and green and yellow variegated leaves.

Tabernaemontana divaricata cv. **Variegata**
A cultivar with green and yellow variegated leaves and fragrant single flowers.

Tabernaemontana pachysiphon
The fragrant trumpet flowers on this small tree are white with a yellow throat.

TABERNAEMONTANA (cont)

Tabernaemontana pandacaqui
A tall bushy shrub with large, fragrant, white, trumpet flowers.

Tabernaemontana ventricosa
Bushy and tall, this shrub has large heads of fragrant white flowers which have reflexed and partly twisted petals.

TAMARINDUS

CAESALPINIACEAE [LEGUMINOSAE]

Tamarindus indica TAMARIND
A small to medium, open crowned, evergreen tree introduced into Asia from tropical Africa. Ornamental, it produces edible bean-like fruit called Tamarinds, which are widely eaten throughout Asia. It has clusters of showy orange and white coloured flowers. The tree requires a tropical or sub-tropical climate and a well drained soil. Propagate from seed.

Tamarindus indica - seed pods

TAMARIX

TAMARICACEAE

Tall shrubs and small trees with thin conifer-like foliage. They are native to Europe and Asia and are widely grown as ornamentals for their colourful flowers, especially in dry situations. Some varieties may become weeds in semi-desert situations such as the Middle East and Australia. The two types shown here are good garden specimens. Propagate from seed and cuttings.

Tamarix gallica MANNA PLANT
A cold and dry-tolerant small tree with fine foliage and masses of pink flowers which cover the tree in spring.

Tamarix pentandra FLOWERING CYPRESS
A fine leaf tree which has very large pendulous heads of bright pink flowers in spring.

TECOMA

BIGNONIACEAE

Evergreen shrubs and small trees which are native to tropical and sub-tropical America and are grown as ornamentals for their showy flowers. They grow in a wide range of soils in climates from temperate to tropical. Propagate from seed.

Tecoma alata
syn. ***Stenolobium alatum***
A bushy evergreen shrub with large heads of orange and yellow trumpet flowers. This plant is at times mistakenly called *Tecoma* x *smithii* which has very little orange on the flowers and leaves which are quite different.

Tecoma castanifolia
syn. ***T. gaudichaudi***
This is a sparse, evergreen, tall shrub with large upright heads of golden coloured trumpet flowers.

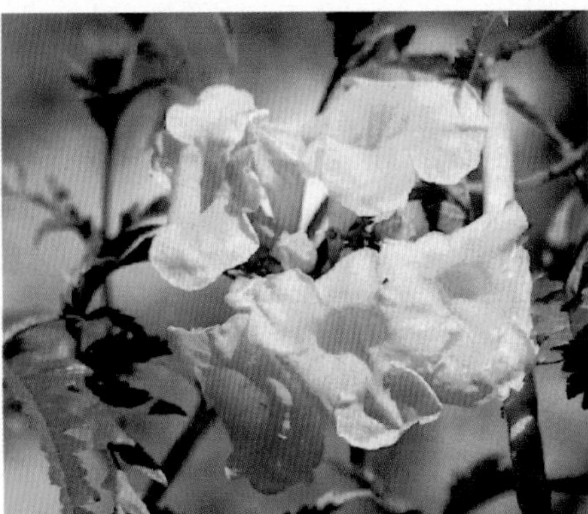

Tecoma filicifolia
Yellow flowers and thin serrated leaves feature on this evergreen shrub.

Tecoma garrocha
syn. ***Stenolobium garrocha***
A medium shrub with pendulous heads of orange coloured trumpet flowers.

Tecoma* x *smithii
A hybrid tall shrub which has large heads of yellow trumpet flowers which have touches of orange.

Tecoma stans YELLOW BELLS
A small tree which has very large heads of bright yellow trumpet flowers over a long period.

TECOMANTHE

BIGNONIACEAE

Evergreen climbers native to Australia, New Zealand, New Guinea and Malaysia. They are free flowering with large heads of flowers. These climbers require a temperate to tropical climate and a soil rich in humus. They are grown in cooler climates in conservatories and glass houses. Propagate from seed and cuttings.

***Tecomanthe* cv. Cape York**
A bushy climber with large heads of cerise coloured flowers in spring.

TECOMANTHE (cont)

Tecomanthe dendrophila
A wandering woody climber which, if left unpruned, may reach the top of tall trees. It has very large heads of pinkish red flowers with white tips and throat.

Tecomanthe hillii
FRASER ISLAND CLIMBER
This is a small bushy climber which has large showy heads of bright pink flowers with pale pink throats.

***Tecomanthe* cv. Roaring Meg Creek**
A bushy climber with large heads of tubular flowers coloured pink and rose-pink.

Tecomanthe speciosa
The most cold tolerant Tecomanthe, this is a bushy climber with pale yellow trumpet-type flowers.

Tecomanthe venusta
A woody climber which has large, rosy red coloured flowers with pale pink throats. Now referred to as synonymous with *T. dendrophila*.

TECOMARIA

BIGNONIACEAE

Tecomaria capensis* ssp. *capensis
CAPE HONEYSUCKLE
syn. ***Tecoma capensis***
A bushy, erect, tall shrub which has large bunches of orange-red tubular flowers. It is native to Africa. This shrub is widely grown as a hardy hedge in climates from mild temperate to tropical. Propagate from seed and cuttings.

***Tecomaria capensis* ssp. *capensis* cv. Aurea**
A cultivar with yellow flowers.

***Tecomaria capensis* ssp. *capensis* cv. Harmony Gold**
This cultivar has apricot coloured flowers.

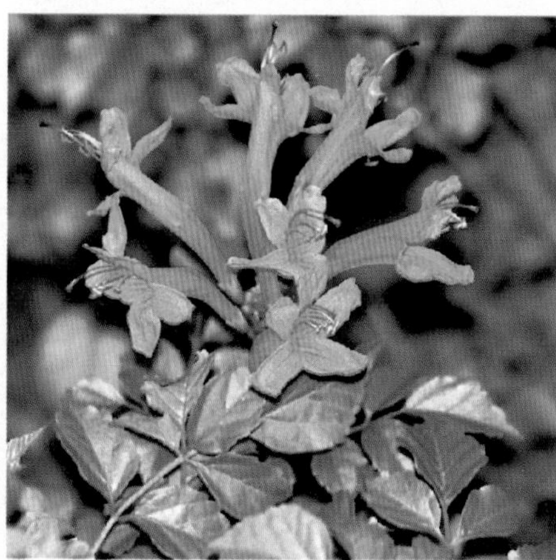

***Tecomaria capensis* ssp. *capensis* cv. Orange Glow**
The flower colour of this cultivar is orange.

TECOMELLA

BIGNONIACEAE

Tecomella undulata HONEY TREE
A small tree native to India and Arabia. It is free flowering and likes a warm climate and a well drained soil. The large yellow flowers supply much nectar, which gives the tree its common name. Propagate from seed.

TECTONA

VERBENACEAE

Tectona grandis TEAK

Native to South East Asia, this is a tall, deciduous, fast growing tree which produces the timber called Teak. It is grown as an ornamental park tree in tropical and sub-tropical climates for its large heads of small bluish flowers, and as a shade tree. Propagate from seed.

TELANTHOPHORA

ASTERACEAE [COMPOSITAE]

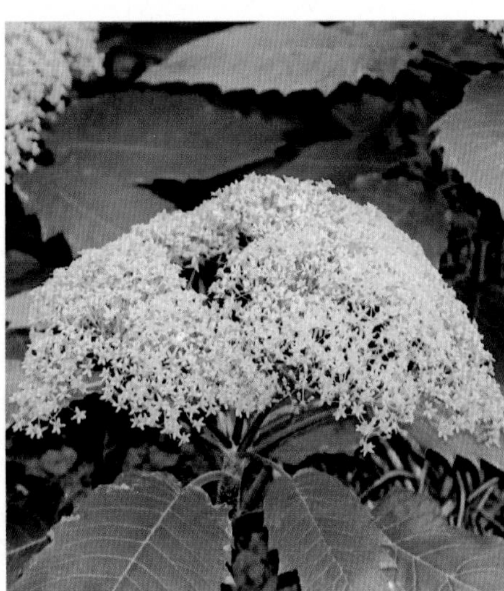

Telanthophora grandifolia

syn. ***Senecio grandifolius***

Evergreen, this medium to tall evergreen shrub has large leaves and very large heads of yellow flowers.

TELOPEA WARATAH

PROTEACEAE

Free flowering evergreen shrubs and small trees, native to Australia, which are grown as ornamentals and for the production of cut flowers. They require a well drained soil in climates from cold temperate to warm temperate. It is advisable to prune lightly after flowering and when fertilising use a fertiliser without phosphorous. Propagate from seed and cuttings.

Telopea mongaensis MONGA WARATAH

A small evergreen tree which will tolerate frosts up to -10 degrees Celsius when established. It has large bright red flowers which are long lasting when used as cut flowers. This tree benefits from pruning after flowering.

Telopea oreades GIPPSLAND WARATAH

A small tree. The large red flower heads are used as cut flowers. It is tolerant of frosts of up to -10 degrees Celsius when established.

Telopea speciosissima WARATAH

This is a sparse shrub with long strong stems and large bright red flower heads which are very choice cut flowers. Tolerant of light frosts. Floral emblem of New South Wales, Australia.

Telopea speciosissima CV. **Alba** 12

A rare white flowered cultivar.

Telopea speciosissima CV. **White Eyes**

This cultivar has red flowers with white markings.

TELOPEA (cont)

Telopea truncata
A small evergreen tree which is tolerant of some cold, it has bright red flowers in spring.

TEMPLETONIA

FABACEAE [LEGUMINOSAE]

Templetonia retusa COCKIES TONGUE
A small evergreen shrub native to Australia. It is grown in temperate climates as an ornamental for its showy orange-red flowers. Propagate from seed.

TEPHROSIA

FABACEAE [LEGUMINOSAE]

Tephrosia grandiflora
This small African shrub has rose-pink pea shaped flowers in spring to early summer. It is grown as an ornamental in cool temperate to tropical climates, but may become naturalised easily in warmer areas. Propagate from seed which requires hot water treatment.

TERMINALIA

COMBRETACEAE

Tropical trees which mostly grow near the sea in many countries. They are grown as ornamentals and to produce dyes, oils, tannin and edible nuts. Terminalias grow in sandy well drained soils in sub-tropical and tropical climates. Some have colourful leaves and others have showy flowers. Propagate from seed.

Terminalia arenicola
A small evergreen tree which has spikes of cream flowers. The leaves change colour as the purplish fruit ripen.

Terminalia brassii
The creamy white flowers bloom in large heads on this small to medium tree.

Terminalia catappa
An open crowned semi-deciduous tree which is salt tolerant. It has white flowers followed by large fruit which have edible kernels. The leaves turn bright red before they fall.

Terminalia muelleri
A small bushy tree with long spikes of white flowers and masses of small fruit.

TERMINALIA (cont)

Terminalia myriocarpa
An upright medium evergreen tree with large cascading bunches of rose-pink flowers in racemes.

Terminalia sericea
A small evergreen tree with spikes of creamish yellow flowers and brownish red flat seed pods, illustrated.

TERNSTROEMIA

THEACEAE

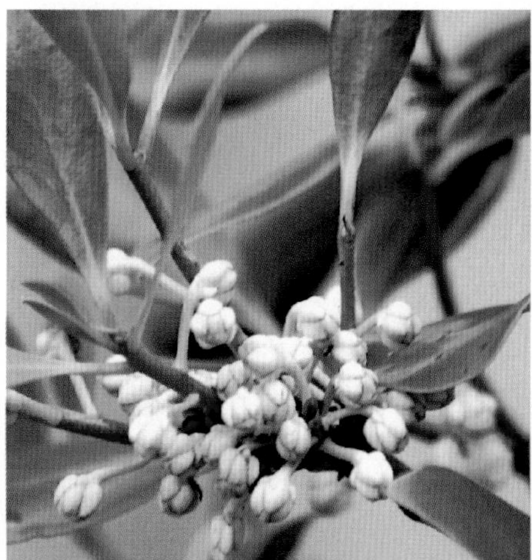

Ternstroemia japonica
An evergreen small tree native to Japan. It is grown in cool temperate to sub-tropical climates as an ornamental for its delicately perfumed white flowers. Propagate from seed.

TETRADENIA [IBOZA]

LAMIACEAE [LABIATAE]

Tetradenia riparia MOSCHOSMA
syn. ***Iboza riparia***
A tall African shrub which is grown as an ornamental for its very showy pale mauve flowers and for its aromatic leaves. Moschosmas grow best in climates from mild temperate to sub-tropical. Propagation is mostly from softwood cuttings.

TETRATHECA

TREMANDRACEAE

***Tetratheca ciliata* cv. Alba**
A cultivar with pure white flowers.

Tetratheca thymifolia
A small evergreen shrub native to Australia. It has pendulous, bright pink, small flowers and is grown in cool temperate to sub-tropical climates as a spring flowering ornamental. Propagate from seed.

t

THEOBROMA

Sterculiaceae

Theobroma cacao COCOA

A small evergreen tree from tropical America, it has pink and yellow coloured flowers on the trunk and large branches, followed by orange-brown coloured fruit. The seed from this fruit is used to produce commercial cocoa and chocolate. This tree requires a tropical climate and is propagated from seed.

THESPESIA

Malvaceae

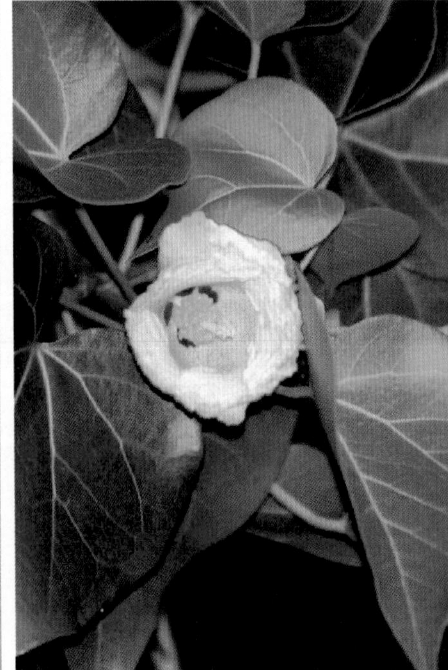

Thespesia populnea PORTIA TREE

Evergreen, this is a small to medium tree which is native to pan-tropical sea shores. It is grown as an ornamental in tropical and sub-tropical climates where sea spray is present. It has yellow Hibiscus-like flowers. Propagate from seed.

THEVETIA

Apocynaceae

These evergreen shrubs and small trees with milky sap are native to tropical America and the Caribbean. They are grown as ornamentals in temperate to tropical climates in a wide range of soils. Parts of the plant are poisonous. Propagate from seed.

Thevetia peruviana YELLOW OLEANDER
syn. ***T. neriifolia***
A tall shrub to small tree with bright yellow pendulous bell shaped flowers over many months.

Thevetia peruviana - orange form
A cultivar which has pendulous orange bell shaped flowers.

Thevetia thevetioides
This is a tall shrub to small tree which has heads of large, golden yellow, bell shaped flowers.

THUNBERGIA

ACANTHACEAE

Shrubs and climbing plants, native to Africa, Asia and Madagascar, which are grown in temperate to tropical climates as outdoor ornamentals. They are grown in glass houses and conservatories in cooler climates. Some Thunbergias are grown outdoors as annuals in cold climates and may become weeds in tropical climates away from their native habitat. Widely used to cover fences and grow over pergolas, they are propagated from seed and cuttings.

Thunbergia alata BLACK-EYED SUSAN

A twining vine which has orange coloured flowers with black centres. It is grown indoors as a hanging basket plant and outdoors as an annual in cool climates, and as a permanent vine in warm climates.

***Thunbergia alata* cv. Alba**

A cultivar which has white flowers with black centres.

***Thunbergia alata* cv. Moonglow**

This cultivar has apricot coloured flowers.

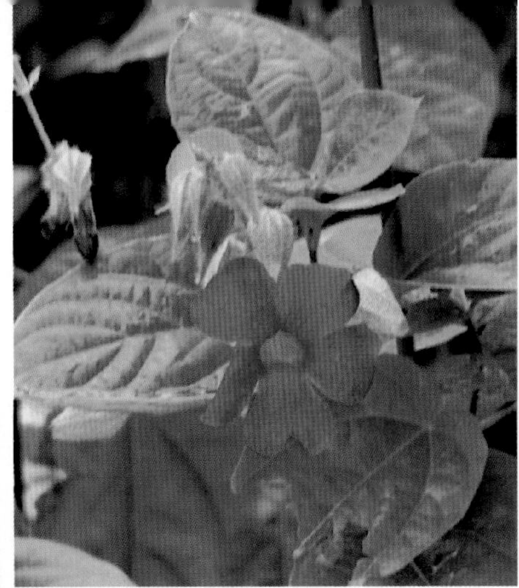

Thunbergia battiscombei

A bushy semi-climber which has royal blue coloured flowers with yellow centres.

Thunbergia erecta KING'S MANTLE

An erect shrub with trumpet type flowers coloured bluish purple with yellow throats. It flowers for many months of the year.

***Thunbergia erecta* cv. Alba**

A cultivar which has white flowers with yellow throats.

THUNBERGIA (cont)

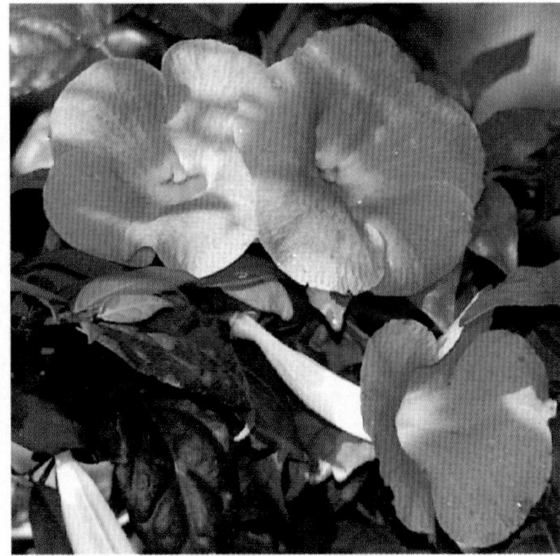

Thunbergia erecta cv. **Blue Moon**
Larger bluish mauve coloured flowers bloom on this cultivar.

Thunbergia grandiflora cv. **Alba**
A cultivar which has white flowers with yellow throats.

Thunbergia fragrans ANGEL WINGS
A twining climber with large clear white flowers over a long flowering period.

Thunbergia grandiflora cv. **Variegata**
This is a free flowering cultivar with green and cream variegated foliage and mauvish blue flowers.

Thunbergia grandiflora BLUE TRUMPET VINE; CLOCK VINE; BLUE SKY FLOWER
Vigorous and free flowering, this vine has long pendulous racemes of mauvish blue flowers. It may become a weed in some situations.

Thunbergia gregorii
syn. ***T. gibsonii***
Often grown as an outdoor annual in cold climates, this twining climber has gold to orange coloured flowers.

Thunbergia laurifolia

Large lilac coloured flowers bloom on this vigorous tropical to sub-tropical climber.

Thunbergia togoensis

A semi-climbing shrub with hairy buds and dark blue flowers with yellow centres.

Thunbergia mysorensis

A specular evergreen climber which is seen at its best when growing over a pergola where the long pendulous racemes of brown and yellow flowers hang down. The flowers open from the top of the raceme first and take weeks to open all the way down.

TIBOUCHINA GLORY BUSH

MELASTOMATACEAE

Shrubs and small trees native to South America, mainly in Brazil, which are grown as spectacular flowering ornamentals in temperate to tropical climates. They are fast growing, soft wooded plants and to see one of the free flowering types in full bloom is a sight to behold. Tibouchinas require plenty of water in hot weather. Propagate from seed and cuttings.

Tibouchina granulosa

PURPLE SPRAY BUSH

A tall shrub with large erect heads of purple flowers in autumn.

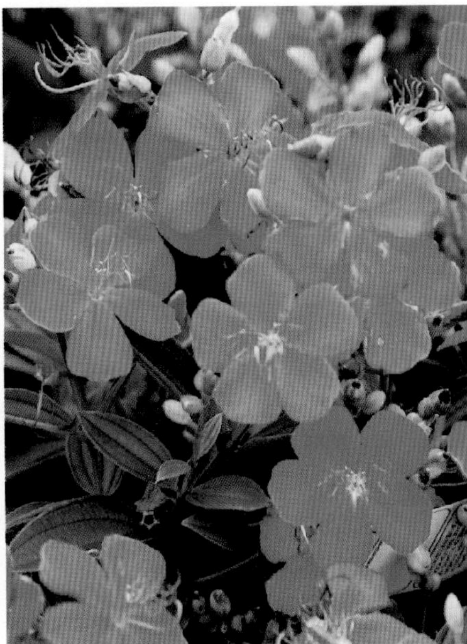

Tibouchina granulosa cv. **Jules**

syn. ***Lasiandra*** cv. ***Jules***

This is a small bushy shrub with bunches of purple flowers in summer and autumn.

TIBOUCHINA (cont)

Tibouchina granulosa **cv. Kathleen**

PINK SPRAY BUSH

In autumn this cultivar has large erect heads of rose-pink coloured flowers.

Tibouchina heteromalla

A medium shrub with large erect heads of purple flowers.

Tibouchina holosericea

A bushy multi-stemmed shrub with erect spikes of whitish pink flowers.

Tibouchina laxa **cv. Noeline**

A tall shrub to small tree with large bunches of multi-coloured flowers which open white then change to pink and mauve.

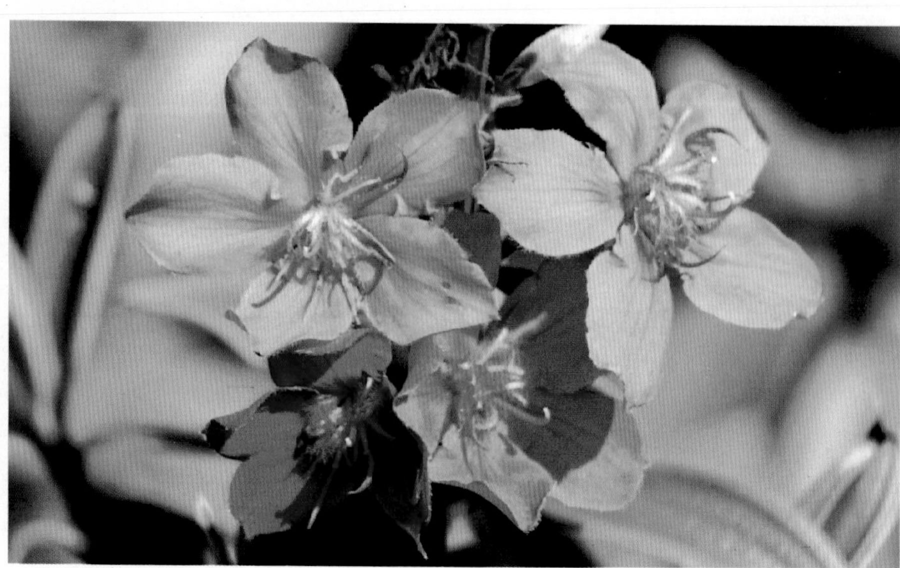

Tibouchina lepidota

A small bushy tree with large mauve-purple flowers in erect heads.

TIBOUCHINA (cont)

Tibouchina lepidota cv. **Alstonville**

Spectacular and free flowering, this small tree has large purple flowers in bunches which cover the whole tree in autumn. One of the outstanding flowering trees of the world.

Tibouchina lepidota
cv. **Alstonville Variegata**

A showy cultivar with purple flowers and green and cream variegated foliage.

Tibouchina macrantha

In autumn this bushy shrub has large purple flowers.

Tibouchina urvilleana 3

A much branched tall shrub with large purple flowers over many months.

Tibouchina multiflora

A free branching shrub with upright spikes of purple flowers with white centres.

Tibouchina sp.

This bushy shrub has large pinky mauve flowers singularly or in bunches. Sometimes known in the nursery trade as *T.* cv. Rosea.

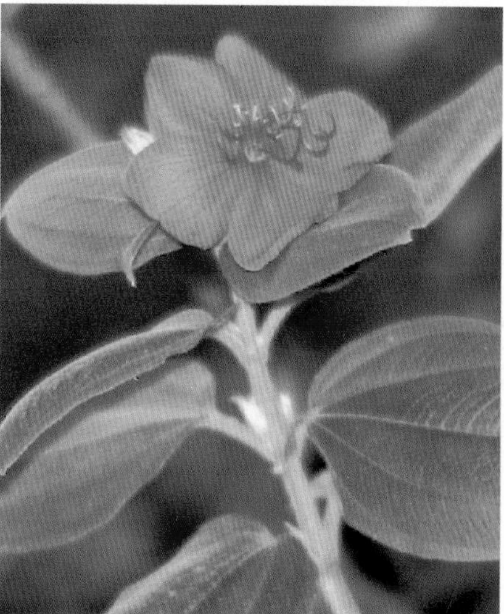

Tibouchina viminea

Tolerant of light frosts, this upright shrub has large violet-purple flowers, mostly singular.

t

TIPUANA

Fabaceae [Leguminosae]

Tipuana tipu PRIDE OF BOLIVIA

A fast growing, semi-deciduous, medium spreading tree native to South America, it is widely grown in tropical and sub-tropical climates as a shade, park or street tree. It tolerates poor soils and has cascading bunches of old gold coloured flowers in spring. Propagate from seed.

TOECHIMA

Sapindaceae

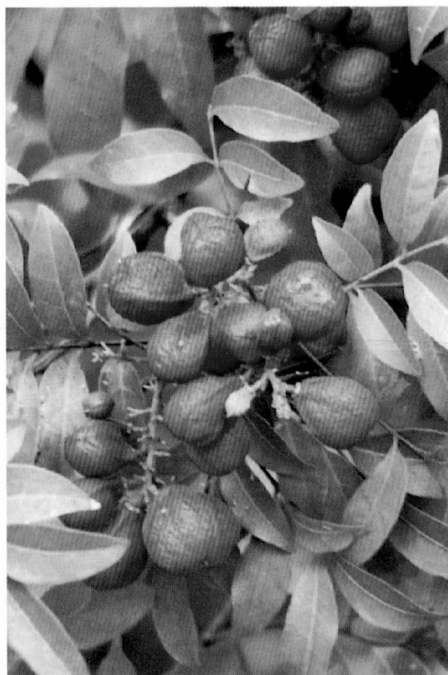

Toechima dasyrrhache

BLUNT LEAVED STEELWOOD

An evergreen tall shrub to small tree which is native to Australia. It is grown as an ornamental for the colourful red fruit which follow its white flowers. Toechima grows in temperate and sub-tropical climates and is propagated from fresh seed.

TOONA

Meliaceae

Toona australis RED CEDAR

syn. ***Cedrela australis; C. toona; C. toona*** var. ***australis***

This large deciduous tree, native to Asia and Australia, is grown as an ornamental and for production of very valuable high quality red cedar timber. It has small fragrant white flowers. The new leaves, which are brownish red, are illustrated. Red cedar grows in temperate to tropical climates. The growing tips may be attacked by grubs of the cedar moth which will stunt the growth of the tree. Propagate from seed and cuttings.

Toona sinensis

This deciduous medium tree is grown in cool climates for its outstanding spring display of new foliage which is bright pink to red. Propagate from seeds and cuttings.

TRACHELOSPERMUM

Apocynaceae

Evergreen climbers from India to China and Japan, they are grown both as climbers and ground covers and have highy perfumed flowers which some people may find overpowering. They are free flowering in the spring and are widely grown. Propagate from cuttings.

Trachelospermum asiaticum

A sparse climber with large bunches of fragrant cream flowers in spring.

Trachelospermum jasminoides

STAR JASMINE

syn. ***Rhynchospermum jasminoides***

A free flowering climber with clusters of small, white, very fragrant, star shaped flowers in spring.

Trachelospermum jasminoides cv. **Variegatum**

A cultivar with variegated leaves of green and white, with pink new growth.

TRIPLARIS

Polygonaceae

Evergreen shrubs and trees native to South America which, in tropical and sub-tropical climates, are grown as ornamentals for their very colourful display. They prefer a moist soil high in humus to give the best flowering. There are male and female trees and they are propagated from seeds.

Triplaris americana 10 ANT TREE

A small to medium tree with the female tree having large bunches of orange-red flowers.

Triplaris caracassana

On this small to medium tree the large bunches of red flowers on the female trees change to crimson as they age.

Triplaris surinamensis LONG JOHN

A very spectacular small to medium tree which has large bunches of red flowers in racemes on the female trees. This is regarded as one of the most outstanding flowering trees in the world. Referred to by many authorities as synonymous with *T. americana* and *T. weigeltiana* despite the different flower colour.

Triplaris surinamensis - male

This illustration shows the male flower spikes.

TRISTANIOPSIS

Myrtaceae

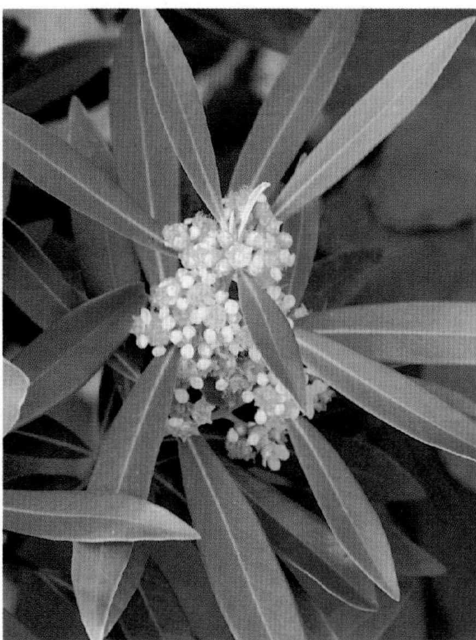

Tristaniopsis laurina WATER GUM

syn. ***Tristania laurina***

A small to medium size evergreen tree which is native to Australia. It mostly grows along river and creek banks and is cultivated in climates from cold temperate to sub-tropical as an ornamental or a street tree. Water gum has bunches of small bright yellow flowers and shiny leathery leaves. Propagate from seed.

TRISTELLATEIA

Malpighiaceae

Tristellateia australasiae

A twining evergreen climber which is native to Asia and the Pacific, it is used to cover fences and pergolas in tropical and sub-tropical climates. It has erect bunches of small yellow flowers and is propagated from seed and cuttings.

TROCHODENDRON

TROCHODENDRACEAE

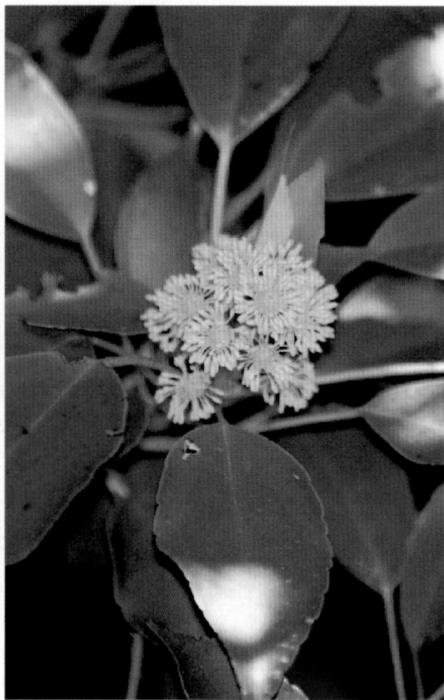

Trochodendron aralioides WHEEL TREE

A small to medium, evergreen, shiny leaf tree which has bunches of creamy yellow flowers. It is native to Asia and grows in climates from cold temperate to tropical where it is used as a shade or ornamental tree. Propagate from seed and cuttings.

TROPAEOLUM

TROPAEOLACEAE

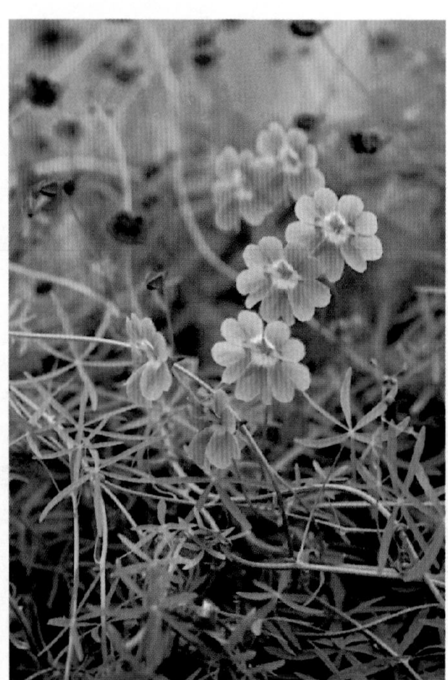

Tropaeolum azureum

This wiry climber has showy dark-mauve flowers.

Tropaeolum tricolorum FLAME FLOWER

A dense climber native to South America, it is widely grown in cool to mild climates for its showy covering of bright red flowers. It prefers a rich moist soil. Propagate from seed and cuttings.

TURNERA

TURNERACEAE

Turnera ulmifolia

A small shrub with dark green leaves which is native to South America. It is grown as an ornamental for its large yellow flowers. Although the flowers are short lived, it does flower over a long period. The plant prefers a moist situation in full sun and is propagated from seed and cuttings.

TURRAEA

MELIACEAE

Turraea floribunda HONEYSUCKLE TREE

Native to South Africa, this deciduous shrub is grown as an ornamental in temperate to sub-tropical climates for its reflexed and fragrant cream flowers. Propagate from seed and cuttings.

TURRAEA (cont)

Turraea obtusifolia

A medium size South African shrub with white flowers over a long period in spring.

TWEEDIA

ASCLEPIADACEAE

Tweedia coerulea

syn. ***Oxypetalum coeruleum***

A small evergreen shrub native to South America. It is grown widely in temperate to tropical climates as a permanent small shrub and as an annual plant in cold climates. The plant has bright blue, star shaped flowers for many months. Propagate from seed. Genus is now referred to as Oxypetalum.

ULMUS

ULMACEAE

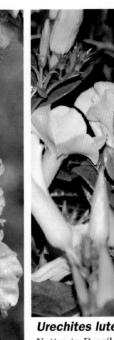

Ulmus glabra WYCH ELM

A medium deciduous tree native to Europe and Asia Minor which is widely grown in cold and mild climates. It has large clusters of small flowers followed by circular green seed pods. Propagate from seed.

URECHITES

APOCYNACEAE

Urechites lutea YELLOW MANDEVILLA

Native to Brazil, this is a free flowering, hardy, evergreen climber which has masses of yellow flowers in summer. It requires a rich soil and a climate from warm temperate to tropical when grown outdoors. It is propagated from cuttings under mist, and from seed. Often referred to in nursery trade as *Mandevilla* cv. Sun Dial.

UVARIA

ANNONACEAE

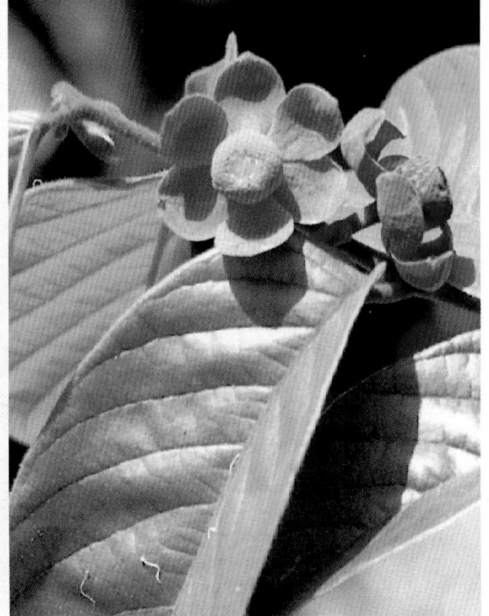

Uvaria microcarpa

A bushy tall shrub which is native to Asia. It is grown in warm temperate climates as an ornamental for its brick red flowers and for its edible fruit. Propagate from seed.

VACCINIUM

ERICACEAE

Small deciduous or evergreen shrubs native to the cool and cold climates of the northern hemisphere. They are grown for their showy flowers or edible fruit, and are propagated from seed or cuttings.

Vaccinium consanguineum

A small shrub with pendulous pale pink flowers in spring.

Vaccinium mortinia

syn. ***V. floribundum***

A small spreading shrub with showy bunches of pink and white flowers in spring.

Vaccinium corymbosum BLUEBERRY

The clusters of white flowers on this hardy shrub are followed by edible fruit called blueberries.

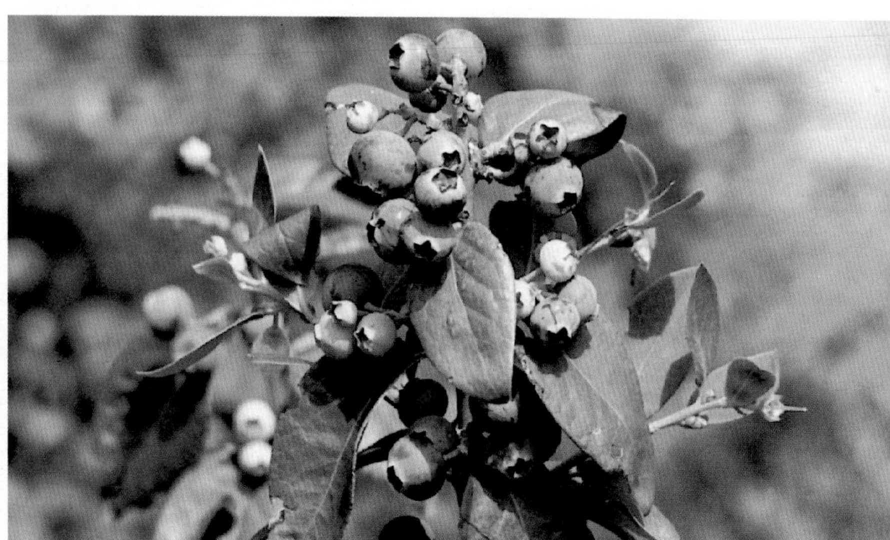

Vaccinium corymbosum - ripe fruit

Vaccinium ovatum

EVERGREEN HUCKLEBERRY

This is an erect bushy shrub with bunches of pendulous flowers coloured pink and white.

VANILLA

Orchidaceae

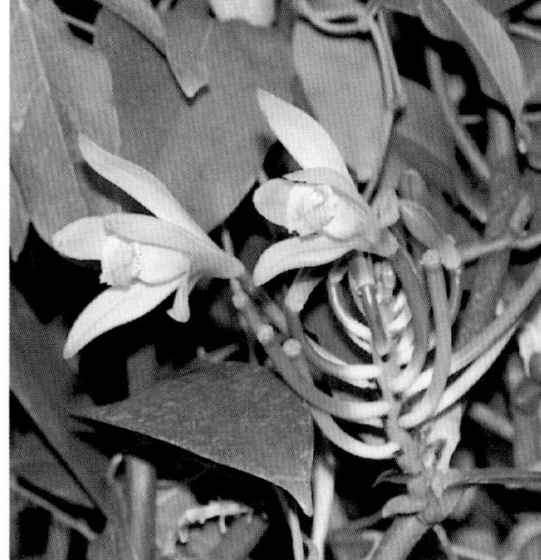

Vanilla planifolia VANILLA

This climbing plant is native to tropical America. It has cream orchid flowers followed by pods which are used to produce commercial vanilla. This plant needs a tropical climate and is propagated from seed and cuttings.

VERTICORDIA

FEATHER FLOWERS

Myrtaceae

Native to Western Australia, these evergreen shrubs have light feathery flowers and are grown as ornamentals in well drained soils. They are widely used as cut flowers and are propagated from cuttings or seed which may benefit from smoke treatment before sowing. Feather flowers grow in climates from mild temperate to tropical depending on the species.

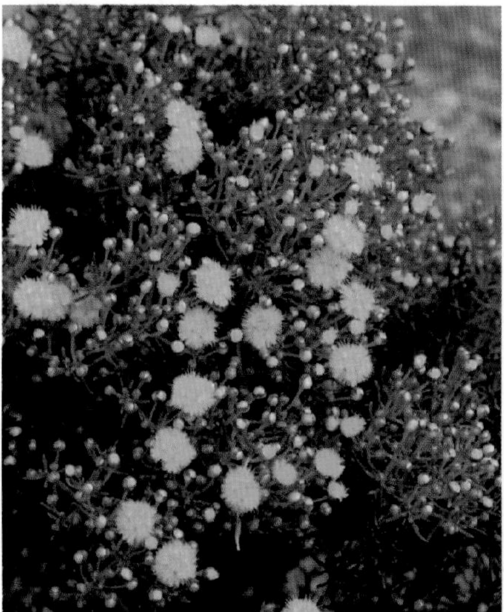

Verticordia chrysantha

A free branching small shrub which is covered with bright yellow flowers in spring. Suitable for temperate climates.

Verticordia drummondii

In spring this sparse shrub with pendulous branches has clusters of old rose coloured flowers.

Verticordia grandiflora CLAW FEATHER FLOWER

A small upright shrub with large heads of bright yellow flowers in spring.

Verticordia grandis

This is an upright sparse shrub with greyish leaves and terminal heads of bright red flowers in spring.

VERTICORDIA (cont)

Verticordia helichrysantha
A scrambling shrub with creamy yellow flowers in spring.

Verticordia plumosa
An upright branching shrub with terminal heads of rose-pink flowers in spring.

VIBURNUM

CAPRIFOLIACEAE

Shrubs and small trees which are deciduous or evergreen and native to Europe, America and Asia. They are widely grown throughout the world as fragrant flowering ornamentals and are usually cultivated in very cold temperate to warm temperate climates. Propagate from seed and cuttings. Many Viburnums have large and small flowers on each head. The large flowers are usually sterile.

Viburnum buddleifolium
This open, semi-evergreen shrub has large heads of pink buds which open to small white flowers.

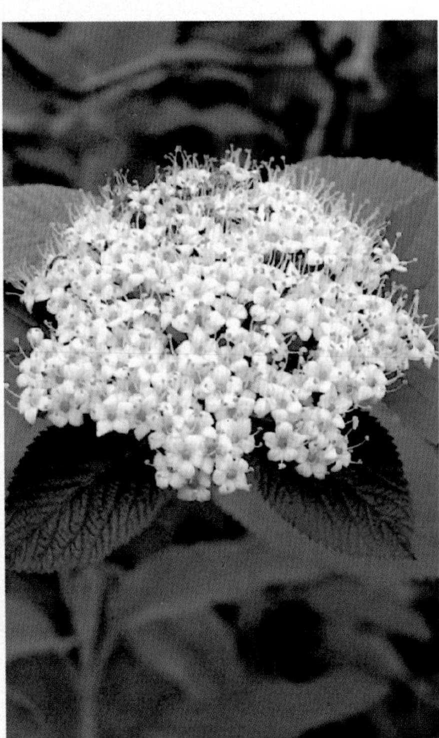

Viburnum burejaeticum
A tall, cold tolerant, deciduous shrub with large flattish heads of fragrant white flowers followed by blue-black fruit.

Viburnum* x *burkwoodii
A semi-evergreen hybrid shrub with large heads of small flowers which open pink and fade to white.

VIBURNUM (cont)

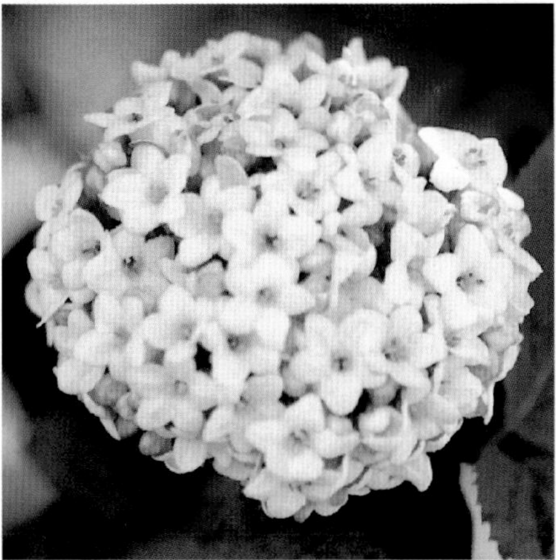

Viburnum* x *carlcephalum
Round heads of pink buds open to small white flowers on this medium, deciduous shrub.

Viburnum carlesii
An upright deciduous shrub with globular heads of small fragrant flowers coloured white and rose-pink. The fruit are blue-black.

***Viburnum carlesii* cv. Charis**
The flowers of this sparse cultivar open rose-pink and then fade to white.

Viburnum davidii
This bushy evergreen shrub has large heads of small, white flowers tinged with pink.

Viburnum dentatum
A tall deciduous shrub with large irregular heads of small white flowers followed by bluish black fruit.

Viburnum dilatatum
This is a medium to tall deciduous shrub with flattish open heads of small white flowers followed by scarlet coloured fruit.

VIBURNUM (cont)

Viburnum dilatatum - fruit

Viburnum hupehense
Deciduous, this shrub has large heads of small white flowers in spring.

Viburnum japonicum
A bushy evergreen shrub with sparse flower heads of small white flowers and red fruit.

Viburnum japonicum cv. **Variegatum**
A cultivar with variegated leaves coloured cream and green with red fruit.

Viburnum x ***juddii***
This bushy shrub has flattish heads of white flowers.

Viburnum lentago SHEEPBERRY
A vigorous tall shrub with heads of cream coloured flowers followed by blue-black berries.

Viburnum macrocephalum
In spring this semi-evergreen tall shrub has large rounded heads of white flowers.

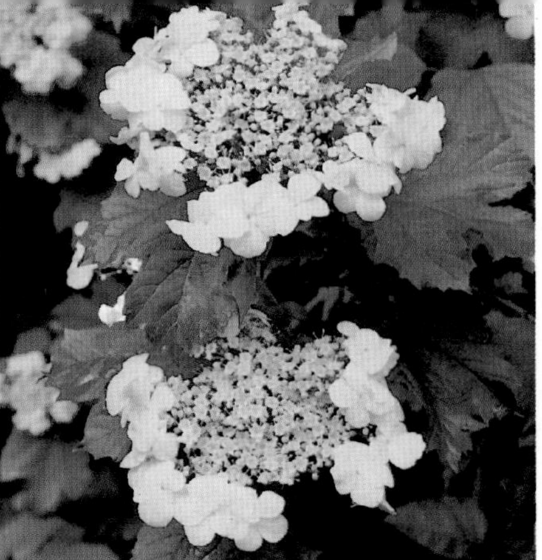

Viburnum opulus
cv. **Notcutt's Variety**
A deciduous tall shrub with heads of white flowers in spring.

Viburnum opulus
cv. **Sterile** GUELDER ROSE
This tall shrub has large round balls of white flowers in spring.

Viburnum odoratissimum
A tall evergreen shrub with white flowers and bright red fruit which are illustrated.

Viburnum opulus
A bushy deciduous shrub. The white flowers which bloom in large heads can be either sterile or fertile.

VIBURNUM (cont)

Viburnum plicatum
A medium deciduous shrub with flat heads of large and small white flowers.

***Viburnum plicatum* cv. Pink Beauty**
Heads of large and small white flowers, edged with pink as they age, feature on this medium deciduous shrub.

***Viburnum plicatum* cv. Grandiflorum**
On this medium deciduous shrub the white flowers bloom in round heads.

Viburnum prunifolium BLACK HAW
A tall deciduous shrub with flat heads of small white flowers and coloured autumn leaves. The roots are used in medicine. The fruit are blue-black.

***Viburnum plicatum* cv. Lanarth**
A medium, spreading, deciduous shrub with large heads of small and large white flowers.

***Viburnum plicatum* cv. Mariesii**
This is a low growing spreading deciduous shrub with large flat heads of large and small white flowers.

***Viburnum sargentii* cv. Onondaga**
A bushy shrub with large flat heads of flowers. The flowers are white and the flower buds are red.

VIBURNUM (cont)

Viburnum sp.
A deciduous shrub with flat heads of large white flowers. Often referred to as *V. sub mollis.*

Viburnum tinus LAURUSTINUS
This is a tall evergreen shrub which has heads of pink buds which open to white flowers.

Viburnum tinus cv. **Variegatum**
A cultivar with cream and green variegated leaves.

VIGNA

FABACEAE [LEGUMINOSAE]

Vigna marina DUNE BEAN
A twining evergreen vine which is native to Australia and the Pacific. It grows in sandy dune areas near the sea and can be cultivated in mild temperate to tropical climates where it is used to stabilise sand dunes. The plant has yellow pea-type flowers and edible roots. Propagate from seed.

VIRGILIA

FABACEAE [LEGUMINOSAE]

Native to South Africa, these fast growing evergreen small trees are grown when a quick cover or screen by an ornamental tree is needed. They tolerate poor soils and will survive in frosts as low as -4 degrees Celsius when established. These trees will grow in climates from cold temperate to sub-tropical. Propagate from seed which needs to be soaked in warm water for up to 4 hours prior to sowing.

Virgilia divaricata KEURBOOM
A compact crowned fast growing small tree with very large heads of fragrant cerise coloured flowers over several months in spring. Smaller than *V. oroboides.*

Virgilia oroboides
syn. ***V. capensis***
In late spring this open crowned, fast growing, small tree has very large heads of fragrant pea type flowers coloured rose-pink.

VITEX

VERBENACEAE

Shrubs and trees, native to many countries of the world, in climates from temperate to tropical. They are hardy plants and are widely grown as feature ornamental street trees and hedges. Many are very aromatic. Propagate from seed and cuttings.

Vitex agnus-castus CHASTE TREE
An aromatic upright tall shrub or small tree which has long erect spikes of mauve flowers.

VITEX (cont)

Vitex carvalhi

This hardy, small, evergreen tree has an open crown and dark mauve coloured flowers in spring.

Vitex trifolia cv. **Purpurea**

The leaves of this cultivar are olive-green on top and purple on the underneath. It has lavender-mauve flowers and is widely grown as a street tree.

Vitex lucens PURURI

Native to New Zealand, this medium tree has sparse bunches of violet coloured flowers in spring. Tolerant of some frost.

Vitex trifolia cv. **Variegata**

Green and cream variegated leaves and lavender-mauve flowers feature on this cultivar.

Vitex trifolia

A wide crowned bushy shrub which is widely grown as a hedge. It has spikes of small lavender-mauve flowers.

WARSZEWICZIA

RUBIACEAE

Warszewiczia coccinea

A tall shrub to small tree native to Central and South America. It is grown in tropical and sub-tropical climates as a flowering ornamental for its long flower heads made up of rosy red calyx lobes and yellow flowers. Propagate from seed and cuttings.

WEIGELA

Caprifoliaceae

These deciduous shrubs which are native to Asia are widely grown in climates from cold temperate to sub-tropical. They are free flowering ornamentals and almost 200 cultivars have been grown throughout the world. Propagate from seed or cuttings.

Weigela coraeensis
In spring this stiff upright shrub has pale pink flowers.

Weigela floribunda
Free flowering, this sparse medium shrub has bell shaped carmine-red flowers.

***Weigela florida* cv. Alba Rosea**
This cultivar has pale pink funnel shaped flowers.

Weigela florida
A medium shrub with large bunches of pink funnel shaped flowers in spring.

Weigela decora
An upright free branching shrub with cream coloured flowers which turn red with age.

***Weigela florida* cv. Alba**
A free flowering cultivar with white funnel shaped flowers.

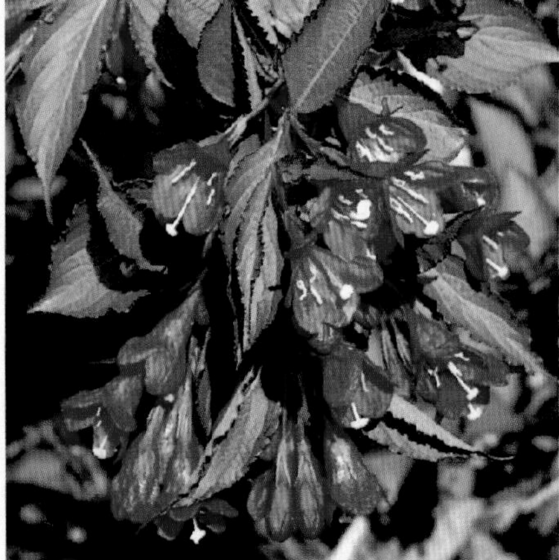

***Weigela florida* cv. Eva Rathke**
The funnel shaped flowers on this cultivar are coloured crimson.

WEIGELA (cont)

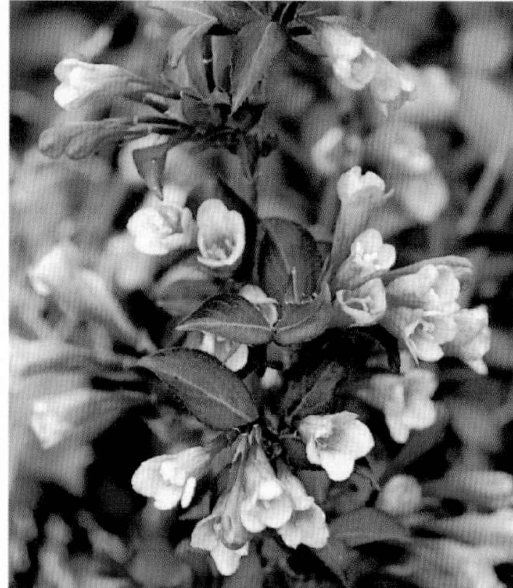

Weigela florida cv. **Foliis Purpureus**
A cultivar which has rose-pink flowers and leaves tinted with purple.

Weigela florida cv. **Variegata**
This cultivar has rose-pink funnel-type flowers and green and cream variegated foliage.

Weigela florida cv. **Red Prince**
The ruby red flowers are slow to open on this cultivar.

Weigela florida cv. **Vanhouttei**
An upright cultivar with flowers coloured carmine and pink.

Weigela florida cv. **Victoria**
A free flowering cultivar with rose-pink coloured flowers.

Weigela hortensis
Masses of smallish pink flowers bloom on this medium shrub.

WEIGELA (cont)

Weigela japonica
A medium to tall shrub with masses of pink and pale pink flowers in spring.

Weigela **cv. Kosterana Variegata**
This cultivar has cream and green variegated foliage. The flowers are pink and pale pink.

Weigela japonica **cv. Isolina**
A cultivar with carmine coloured flowers which are twisted.

Weigela **cv. Looymansii Aurea**
A bushy shrub with yellowish leaves and masses of pink flowers.

Weigela japonica **cv. Sinica**
The white flowers turn pink as they age on this free flowering cultivar.

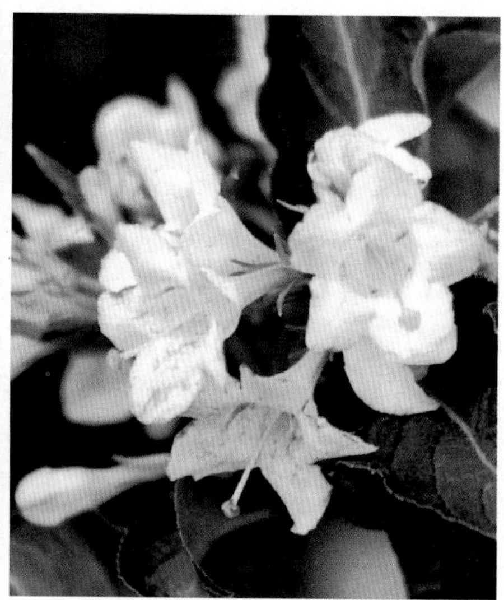

Weigela maximowiczii
In spring this erect sparse shrub has greenish yellow, fading to white, flowers.

WEIGELA (cont)

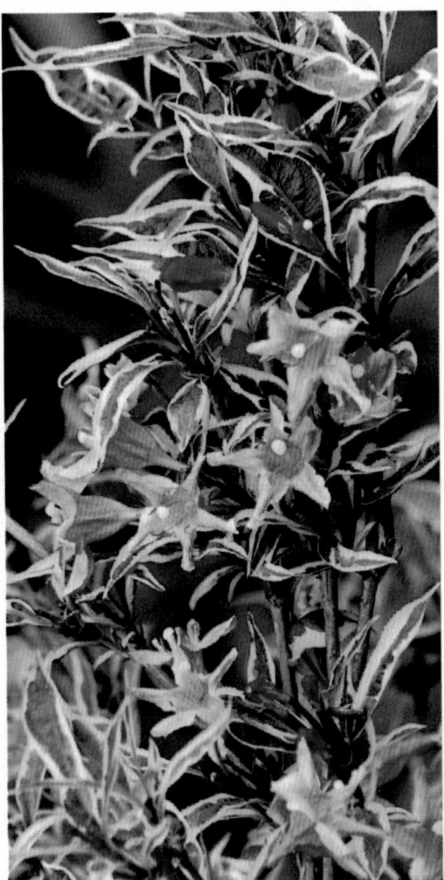

Weigela middendorffiana
A bushy shrub with cream tubular flowers which are yellow in the throat.

Weigela praecox cv. Variegata
A free branching shrub with pink star shaped flowers. It has cream and green variegated foliage.

WESTRINGIA

Lamiaceae [Labiatae]

Evergreen Australian shrubs which are widely grown in situations which may receive salt spray. They are cultivated in climates from cool temperate to sub-tropical and are propagated from seed and cuttings.

Westringia dampieri
A compact shrub with bunches of small white flowers most of the year.

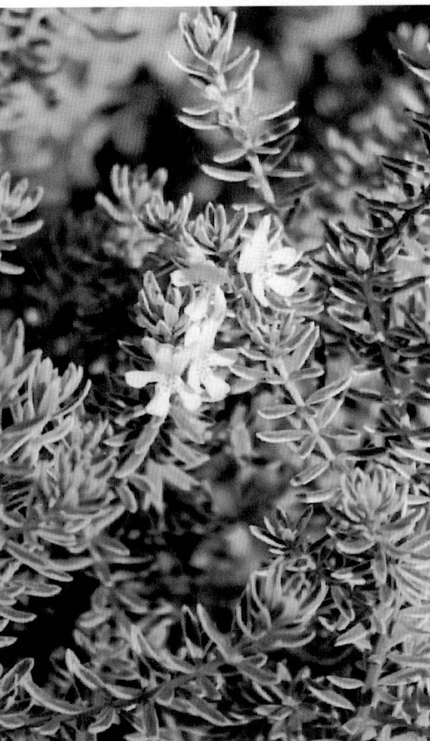

Westringia fruticosa cv. Variegata
A cultivar with variegated foliage coloured grey-green and edged in cream.

Westringia fruticosa COAST ROSEMARY
syn. ***W. rosmariniformis***
This is a rounded shrub with pale bluish white flowers. It is very tolerant of salt spray.

Westringia glabra
The flowers on this upright evergreen shrub are pale mauve.

WESTRINGIA (cont)

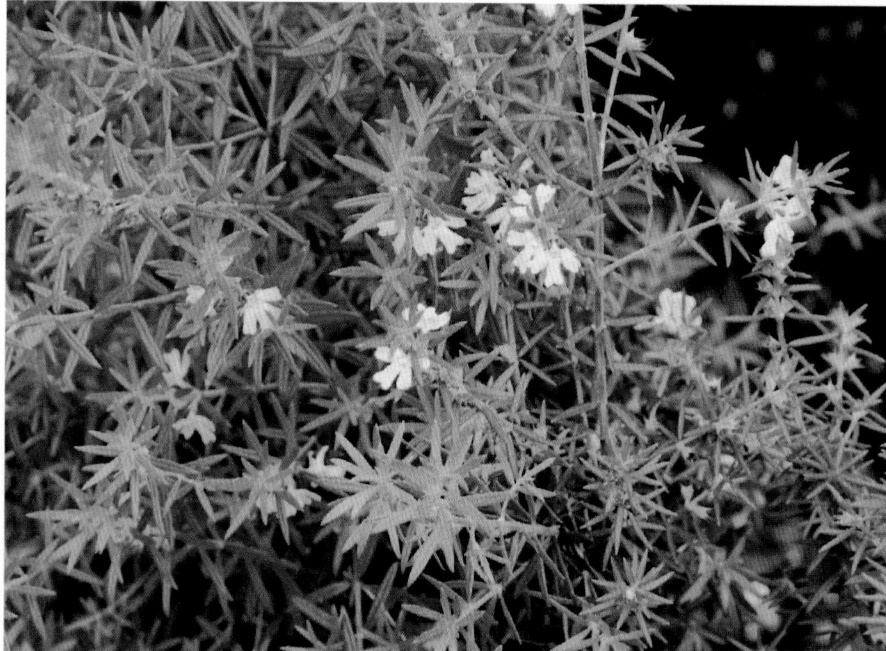

Westringia cv. **Wynyabbie Gem**
A hybrid Westringia which has pale mauve flowers most of the year.

WIGANDIA

Hydrophyllaceae

Shrubs and small trees, native to tropical America, which are grown as ornamentals in temperate to tropical climates. Propagate from seed and cuttings.

Wigandia caracasana
A sparse upright shrub with terminal heads of mauvish pink flowers.

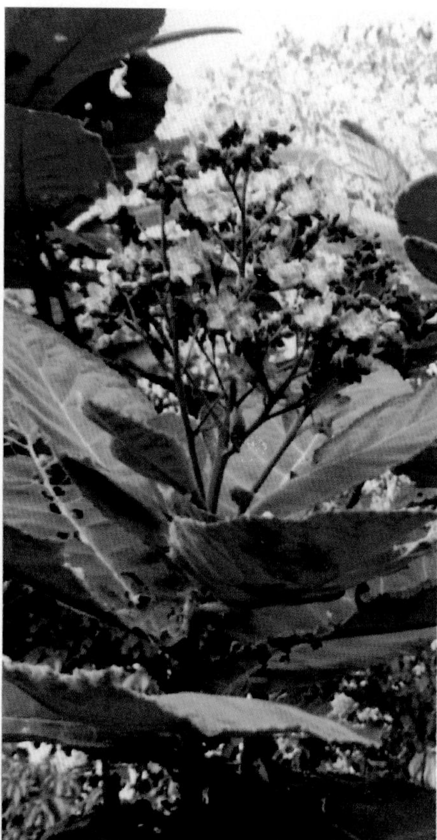

Wigandia urens 3
A tall large leaf shrub which has erect heads of purple flowers. It is native to Peru. This plant is grown as a showy flowering ornamental in warm temperate to tropical climates and requires a soil rich in humus. Propagate from seed.

WHITFIELDIA

Acanthaceae

Whitfieldia elongata WHITE CANDLES
An upright evergreen shrub with large erect heads of white flowers. It is grown as an ornamental in temperate to tropical climates and is native to Africa. The plant requires a soil rich in humus to flower at its best. Propagate from seed and cuttings.

WHITFORDIODENDRON

Fabaceae [Leguminosae]

Whitfordiodendron atropurpureum
syn. ***Millettia atropurpurea***
A medium evergreen tree native to Asia. The tree has upright heads of orange to purple flowers and requires a tropical climate. Propagate from seed.

WISTERIA

FABACEAE [LEGUMINOSAE]

Woody deciduous climbers native to Asia and North America, they are widely grown as free flowering, showy, spring ornamentals. They require a climate from cold temperate to sub-tropical and are tolerant of some frost to -20 degrees C. Many are grown as weeping standards or to cover fences and pergolas. Propagate from seed and cuttings.

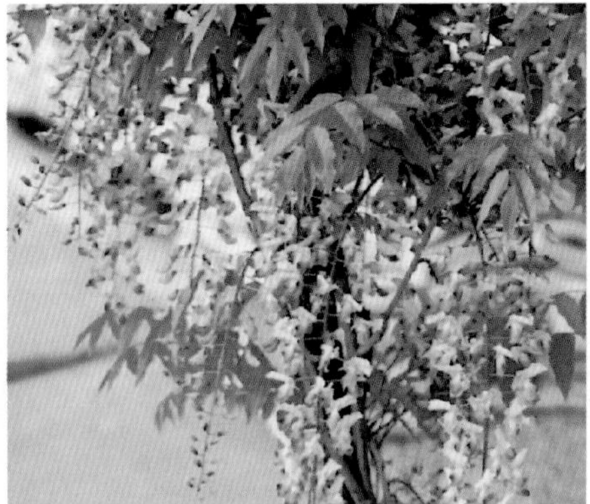

Wisteria floribunda JAPANESE WISTERIA
A free flowering climber which has pendulous racemes of bluish mauve flowers in spring.

Wisteria floribunda cv. **Alba**
A white flowered cultivar which, in spring, has cascading stems of flowers.

Wisteria floribunda cv. **Issai**
Lavender coloured racemes of flowers occur on this cultivar.

Wisteria floribunda cv. **Longissima Alba**
This very free flowering cultivar has very long pendulous racemes of white flowers.

Wisteria frutescens
A spring flowering climber which has pendulous racemes of violet coloured flowers.

Wisteria frutescens cv. **Magnifica**
Free flowering, this cultivar has long racemes of lilac coloured flowers.

Wisteria floribunda cv. **Carnea**
This cultivar has cascading racemes of flowers coloured pale mauve-pink.

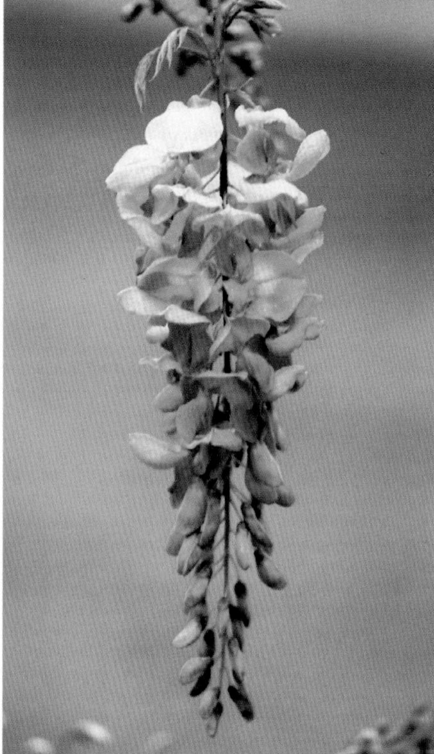

Wisteria sinensis CHINESE WISTERIA
A spring flowering climber which has long cascading racemes of violet-blue flowers.

Wisteria sinensis cv. **Alba**
A cultivar with long racemes of white flowers.

Wisteria sinensis cv. **Alba Rosea**
Flowering in spring, this cultivar has cascading racemes of white flowers which have touches of pink.

Wisteria sinensis cv. **Black Dragon**
A cultivar with racemes of double blue-mauve flowers.

Wisteria sinensis cv. **Plena**
This cultivar has long cascading racemes of double lilac coloured flowers in spring.

Wisteria venusta
A spring flowering climber with long racemes of white coloured flowers.

XANTHOCERAS

SAPINDACEAE

Xanthoceras sorbifolium
A tali, erect, deciduous shrub which is native to China. In cool climates the shrub is grown as an ornamental for its showy bunches of small pink flowers.
It benefits from annual pruning and is propagated from seed, cuttings or suckers.

XANTHORRHOEA

XANTHORRHOEACEAE [LILIACEAE]

Xanthorrhoea australis GRASS TREE
A thin leaf shrub endemic to Australia. It is grown as a landscape plant in climates from cool temperate to sub-tropical and has tall thin flower spikes which remain on the plant for many months. Propagate from seed.

XANTHOSTEMON

MYRTACEAE

Native to Australia, these small evergreen trees are grown as showy flowering ornamentals in tropical and sub-tropical climates. They prefer a soil rich in humus and plenty of water in hot weather. Propagate from seed or cuttings.

Xanthostemon chrysanthus GOLDEN PENDA
A bushy tree which has large heads of golden coloured flowers in winter.

Xanthostemon oppositifolius
A small sub-tropical tree with cream flowers in autumn. A good landscape plant.

Xanthostemon paradoxus
This bushy tree has grey leaves and old gold coloured flowers in autumn.

YUCCA

AGAVACEAE

Evergreen shrubs which have long leaves, mostly with tip thorns, and are native to North America. They are grown as landscape plants for their tall flower spikes. Flowers are bell shaped. These plants prefer a well drained soil in climates from cool temperate to sub-tropical. Propagate from seed or by division.

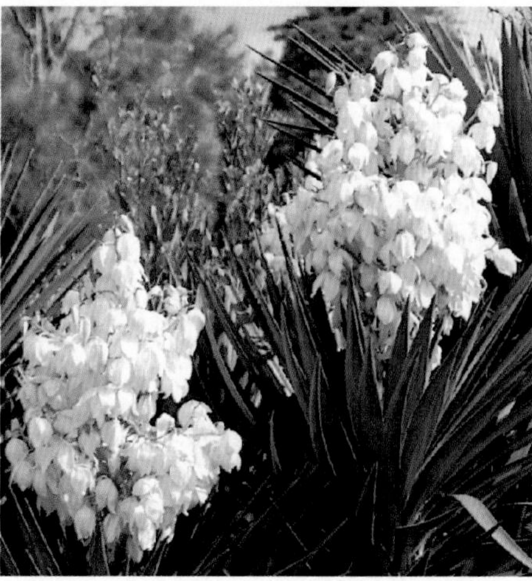

Yucca aloifolia SPANISH BAYONET
A bushy upright shrub with very large dense heads of ivory coloured flowers.

***Yucca aloifolia* cv. Marginata**
The green leaves are edged with yellow on this cultivar.

Yucca elephantipes SPINELESS YUCCA
syn. ***Y. gigantea***
Very large dense heads of ivory flowers feature on this tall shrub or small tree.

Yucca filifera
syn. ***Y. flaccida***
This spreading multi-headed shrub has tall spikes of cream coloured flowers.

Yucca gloriosa
This upright shrub has large heads of cream coloured flowers with reddish markings. The leaves are pointed.

Yucca gloriosa cv. **Variegata**
A bushy shrub with pointed leaves which are variegated cream and green. The flowers on the tall spikes occur in large heads and are ivory coloured.

Yucca recurvifolia
A bushy shrub with large heads of pink and white, or white only, flowers.

Yucca schidigera
This bushy shrub has very large heads of tightly packed flowers coloured white with touches of purple.

Yucca cv. **Golden Sword**
This cultivar has yellow and green striped leaves. Cream flowers bloom on tall spikes.

YUCCA (cont)

Yucca schottii
A bushy upright shrub with large heads of ivory coloured flowers.

Yucca torreyi
A bushy clumping shrub with large heads of ivory to cream flowers.

Yucca valida
This is a tall bushy clumping shrub that has large heads of ivory coloured flowers.

ZAUSCHNERIA [EPILOBIUM]

ONAGRACEAE

Zauschneria cana CALIFORNIA FUCHSIA
A small bushy shrub native to California, it has greyish leaves and bunches of tubular red flowers. This plant grows in cool temperate to sub-tropical climates in a dry situation. Propagate from seed and cuttings. Now referred to as *Epilobium canum*.

ZELKOVA

ULMACEAE

Zelkova serrata JAPANESE ZELKOVA
A deciduous medium tree from Japan which is grown as a coloured leaf ornamental and for timber. Zelkova needs a cold climate and is propagated from seed, root cuttings and by grafting.

ZIERIA

RUTACEAE

Zieria cytisoides
A medium bushy shrub which is native to Australia. It is grown in climates from cold temperate to sub-tropical as an ornamental for its masses of pale pinkish white flowers. This shrub needs a well drained soil and is propagated from seed and cuttings.

A

Genus — **ABELIA**
Family — **CAPRIFOLIACEAE**
Abelia chinensis—GLOSSY ABELIA
Species — **Common Name**

D

E

H

I

J

K

L

M

P

S

T

Index - Common Names

A

B

C

D

E

F

G

H

I

J

K

L

M

T

U

V

W

Y

Z

Index - Synonyms

A

B

C

D

E

Glossary

Anther	The part of the stamen bearing the pollen
Bract	A leaf like part of a plant found close to the flower. Often brightly coloured and much larger than the flower
Calyx	A group of sepals at the base of a flower which protect the petals prior to the flower opening
Catkin	A pendulous spike of flowers
Exserted	Extending beyond the surrounding parts
Lignotuber	A woody swelling at the base of the trunk, containing growth buds
Mutation	A gene change usually on one branch of a plant which may cause a variation to flower or foliage. Subsequent propagation from this portion of the plant will have the new characteristics. See illustration of *Euphorbia pulcherima* cv. Alba, p242. Plants may sometimes be made to mutate by using the chemical colchicine
Palmate	Divided like a hand—usually 5 or 7 lobes
Pinnate	Leaflets on either side of a central stalk
Raceme	A spike of flowers which may be upright or pendulous
Reflexed	Edges turned downwards
Sepal	Individual sections of a calyx which are usually green but may be highly coloured
Stamen	Comprising the filament and anther, which form the pollen producing male part of the flower
Stratify	A treatment to break seed dormancy by chilling at freezing or up to 2° above freezing for 4 to 8 weeks
Style	Part of the female organ of the plant, connecting the pollen receptor to the ovary

Suggested Reading

Bailey	Hortus
Bricknell	Gardeners Encyclopaedia of Plants and Flowers
Brooker & Kleinig	Eucalypts Vols 1, 2 and 3
Elliott & Jones	Encyclopaedia of Australian Plants
Galle	Azaleas
George	Banksia Book
Graf	Hortica
Graf	Tropica
Harrison	Climbers
Holliday	Melaleucas
Jones	Ornamental Rainforest Plants
Jones & Gray	Climbing Plants in Australia
Krempin	Know Your Indoor House Plants
Lloyd	Clematis
Macaboy	Camellias
Macaboy	What Flower is That?
Macaboy	What Shrub is That?
Macaboy	What Tree is That?
McMakin	Flowering Plants of Thailand
Menninger	Flowering Trees of the World
Menninger	Flowering Vines of the World
Olde & Marriott	Grevilleas Vols 1,2 and 3
Simmons	Acacias Vols 1 and 2
Wrigley & Fagg	Banksias, Waratahs and Grevilleas

Addenda and Errata

In a book of this magnitude, it is inevitable some discrepancies will emerge in the first edition. Some are noted below, but the publisher welcomes correspondence on any modifications or suggested improvements for incorporation in future editions to further enhance the worth of this publication to those interested in identifying and growing the plants illustrated.

Pultenaea villosa and *Strophanthus speciosus* are depicted sideways.

Lagunaria pattersonii is also called the Norfolk Island Hibiscus.

The following plants have been depicted out of alphabetical order. *Acer pseudoplatanus* cv. purpureum, *Adenium obesum* cv. Rhonda, *Asparagus densiflorus* cv. Compacta, *Azalea* x Knap Hill cv. Homebush, *Callistemon rigidus, Callistemon* cv. Taree Pink, *Cordyline terminalis* cv. Rose Queen, *Cuphea micropetala, Dracaena deremensis* cv. Souvenir de Schriever, *Dracaena marginata* cv. Carmine Tricolour, *Gardenia augusta* cv. Florida, *Grevillea* cv. Red Hooks, *Hedera helix* cv. Goldheart, *Helicteres, Heliotropium.*